성문 종합영어

宋成文

성문출판사

머 리 말

누구나 자기 책을 세상에 내놓을 때 으레 하는 이야기가, 이 한 권이면 모든 것을 마스터하고 각종 시험의 어려운 관문을 통과할 수 있다는 것이다. 시중에 범람하는 많은 책들이 저마다 이런 화려한 머리말을 담고 속삭이며 혹은 떠들며 학생들을 부르니, 그들이 현기증을 느끼는 것도 당연하다.

학생들이 자주 찾아와서 어느 영어학습서를 읽으면 좋겠느냐고 조언을 구한다. 그럴 때마다, 선뜻 자신 있게 권할 책이 쉬 머리에 떠오르지 않는다. 답답한 심정이다. 이 답답한 마음이 저자로 하여금 이 책을 쓰게 한 동기가 되었다. 「학생들에게 "영어의 바른 길"을 제시하자!」 오직 이 한 마음으로 이 책을 집필했다. 가뜩이나 범람하는 책들 속에 하잘것없는 것을 또 하나 보태어 학생들의 방향의식을 혼란시킨다면 이 얼마나 큰 죄악이겠는가!

이 한 권으로 영어를 쉽게 마스터하고 어려운 시험에 무난히 합격한다고 감히 단언하고 싶지 않다. 그것은 책도 좋아야 하지만, 그 책을 읽는 독자의 학습태도도 건전해야 하기 때문이다. 양서를 택해 그 책의 내용과 특징을 파악하고 그것을 충분히 이해하며, 꾸준히 학습해 나간다면, 성공하지 못하는 것이 오히려 이상스러울 것이다.

이 책은 모두 20 단원으로 구성되어 있다. 각 단원마다 기본문법설명, 문법 · 작문, 단문독해, 장문독해, 실력체크 (Ⅰ) · (Ⅱ), 어휘 · 발음, 숙어의 7부로 이루어진다. 이 책 한 권으로 영어의 모두를 체계적으로 학습할 수 있게끔 한 종합영어학습서이다. 특히, 이번 개정판에서는 TOEIC · TOEFL을 준비하는 독자들을 위해 가급적 TOEIC · TOEFL 관련 내용을 많이 실었다. 부디 영어의 바른 길[正道]을 따라 꾸준히 공부하여 영어실력에 획기적인 향상이 있기를 바란다.

끝으로 이 책의 개정판을 내는데 많은 도움을 준 최학준, 장병모 두 분에게 심심한 사의를 표한다.

저 자 씀

Diligence is the mother of good luck, and God gives all things to industry. Then plough deep while sluggards sleep, and you shall have corn to sell and to keep.

— Benjamin Franklin —

근면은 행운의 어머니이며, 신은 근면한 자에게 모든 것을 주신다. 그러므로, 나태한 자가 잠을 자는 동안 깊이 밭갈이 하라. 그러면 팔고 또 저장할 수 있는 곡식을 얻으리라.

— 벤자민 프랭클린 —

차 례

제 1 장 동사의 종류(Verb)

제 2 장 동사의 시제(Tense)

제 3 장 부정사(Infinitive)

제 4 장 동명사(Gerund)

제 5 장 분사(Participle)

제 11 장 관사(Article)

제 12 장 대명사(Pronoun) I

제 13 장 대명사(Pronoun) II

제 14 장 형용사(Adjective) I

제 15 장 형용사(Adjective) II

제 16 장 부 사(Adverb)

제 17 장 일치와 화법(Agreement & Narration)

제 18 장 전치사(Preposition)

제 19 장 접속사(Conjunction)

제 20 장 도치 · 강조 · 생략 · 공통관계 · 삽입 · 동격 (Inversion, Ellipsis, etc.)

장문독해 차례

1. 동 사 의 종 류(Verb)

기본 문법 설명

A. 문형과 동사의 종류	(1) In big cities, pollution **worsens** every year. (2) The destruction of the ozone layer **is** now a worldwide problem. (3) Human beings alone **speak** languages made up of words. (4) Who **gave** you such a nice picture? (5) We all **considered** him a reliable man. * The ship **made** for its home port. She will **make** a good lawyer. The accountant **makes** $100,000 a year. The tailor will **make** you a new suit. Overeating **made** her ill.
B. 주의해야 할 동사의 용법	(1) ⓐ He **sent** me the package by airmail. ⇨ He **sent** the package **to** me by airmail. ⓑ He **bought** his wife a mink coat. ⇨ He **bought** a mink coat **for** his wife. (2) The car slowed down as it **approached** the corner. Economists **discussed** ways of ending the recession. (3) He **graduated from** law school in 1996. I **sympathize with** the plight of the homeless. (4) That will **save** me a lot of trouble. (5) Could you **explain** the rules of the game **to** me? The murderer **confessed** his crime **to** the police. (6) The attorney **decided** *to prosecute* him for perjury. (7) I don't **mind** *waiting* a few more days. (8) The travel agency **furnished** me **with** the information for the trip. ⇨ The travel agency **furnished** the information for the trip **to** me. (9) I **dreamed** a curious *dream*.

A. 문형과 동사의 종류

목적어를 가지는 동사를 **타동사**라 하고, 가지지 않는 동사를 **자동사**라 한다. 그리고, 보어의 유무에 따라 각각 **불완전동사, 완전동사**로 구별된다.

(1) **S+V** (완전자동사)
(대도시에서는 오염이 해마다 악화되고 있다.)
(2) **S+V+C** (불완전자동사)
(오존층의 파괴는 지금 세계적인 문제이다.)
(3) **S+V+O** (완전타동사)
(인간만이 낱말로 구성된 언어를 말한다.)
(4) **S+V+O+O** (완전타동사[수여동사])
(누가 너에게 그런 좋은 그림을 주었느냐?)
(5) **S+V+O+C** (불완전타동사)
(우리 모두는 그를 믿을 수 있는사람으로 생각했다.)

* make가 그 용법에 따라 자동사, 타동사가 되는 예 :
(그 배는 모항을 향해 갔다.) … 완전자동사
(그 여자는 훌륭한 변호사가 될 것이다.) … 불완전자동사
(그 회계사는 일년에 십만 달러를 번다.) … 완전타동사
(그 재단사는 너에게 새 옷을 만들어 줄 것이다.) … 완전타동사[수여동사]
(과식해서 그녀는 탈이 났다.) … 불완전타동사

☞ These potatoes *peel* easily. (자동사)
He *peeled* a banana. (타동사)

B. 주의해야 할 동사의 용법

(1) 수여동사와 전치사

4형식 문장에서 간접목적어와 직접목적어의 순서를 바꾸면 간접목적어 앞에 전치사가 와서 3형식 문장으로 바뀐다. 전치사는 대개 to나 for가 온다.

ⓐ **to**가 오는 경우 : send, give, lend, pay, offer, show, tell, write 등.
ⓑ **for**가 오는 경우 : buy, make, get, choose, find, play, cook 등.

(2) 자동사로 혼동하기 쉬운 타동사

approach, discuss, marry, attend, address, inhabit, mention, reach, enter등.
(그 차는 모퉁이에 접근하자 속력을 줄였다.)
(경제학자들은 불경기를 끝낼 방법들에 대해 토의했다.)

(3) 타동사로 혼동하기 쉬운 자동사

graduate from, sympathize with, experiment with, add to, complain about, allude to, reply to, operate on, refer to 등.
(그는 1996년에 법과 대학원을 졸업했다.)
(나는 집없는 사람들의 어려운 처지를 동정한다.)

(4) 두개의 직접목적어를 갖는 완전타동사

save, envy, cost 등은 두개의 직접 목적어를 취하는 동사로, 두 목적어의 순서를 전치사를 사용하여 바꿀 수 없다.
(그것은 나의 수고를 많이 덜어줄 것이다.)
I *envy* you your good fortune.
(나는 너의 행운이 부럽다.)

(5) 수여동사로 착각하기 쉬운 완전타동사

explain, confess, suggest, propose, introduce, announce, describe 등은 간접목적어를 취하는 수여동사가 아니므로 '~에게'는 **to**를 이용해 나타낸다.
(그 게임의 규칙들을 나에게 설명해 주시겠습니까?)
(그 살인자는 경찰에 자기범죄를 자백했다.)

(6) 부정사를 목적어로 취하는 동사

decide, wish, hope, care, choose, determine, pretend, refuse 등.
(그 검사는 그를 위증죄로 기소하기로 결정했다.)

(7) 동명사를 목적어로 취하는 동사

mind, enjoy, give up, avoid, finish, escape, admit, deny, consider, practice, risk, miss, postpone, resist, excuse, put off 등.
(나는 며칠 더 기다려도 상관없다.)

(8) 공급동사

furnish [provide, supply] A with B = furnish B to A = A에게 B를 제공하다
present A with B =A에게 B를 선물하다
endow A with B = A에게 B를 기부하다
(그 여행사는 나에게 여행 정보를 제공해 주었다.)

(9) 동족목적어

They fought a fierce *battle*.
He died a miserable *death*.
She smiled her *brightest* (*smile*).

C. 불완전 동사와 보어	(1) 주격보어 ⓐ He was too honest a **merchant**. He became **poor**. ⓑ He remained **single** all his life. She turned **pale** at the news. ⓒ The child came home **crying** bitterly. The city lies utterly **destroyed**. ⓓ He has lived a **bachelor** for a long time. (2) 목적격보어 ⓐ The jury found the defendant **innocent**. They elected him **chairman**. ⓑ He kept me **waiting** long. I felt myself **touched** on the shoulder. ⓒ I never heard him **speak** badly of others. I'll have him **come** early tomorrow morning. ⓓ She told me **to come** here. (3) 보어의 형식 ⓐ He's just **a** cunning **impostor**. The scenery was unbelievably **beautiful**. ⓑ By the time he arrived the meeting was **over**. ⓒ He ran himself **out of breath**. ⓓ We all expect him **to come**. ⓔ He appeared **satisfied** with the result. She stood **leaning** against the wall. ⓕ The fact is **that I know nothing about it**. His own efforts have made him **what he is**.
D. 합성타동사	(1) Everybody **laughed at** him. P.S. **stands for** "postscript." (2) Gambling **brought about** his ruin. They **carried out** their plan at last. (3) We are **looking forward to** your coming. I cannot **put up with** his insolence. (4) She **took care of** the baby. He **took part in** the rally.

C. 불완전동사와 보어

(1) **주격보어**

ⓐ (그는 너무 정직한 상인이었다.)
(그는 가난해졌다.)
He=merchant ; He=poor의 관계이며, 주어의 동작·상태를 나타낸다. 이와같이 주어의 설명이 되는 말을 주격보어라 한다.

ⓑ (그는 한평생 독신으로 남았다.)
(그녀는 그 소식에 얼굴이 창백해졌다.)
Please keep *quiet*.
Velvet feels *smooth*.
You look *tired*.
Your dream may come *true*.
(네 꿈이 실현될지도 모른다.)
The food has run *short*.
(식량이 부족해졌다.)
Her cheeks went *red*.
The report proved *false*.
This medicine tastes *bitter*.

ⓒ (그 아이는 몹시 울며 집에 왔다.)
(그 도시는 완전히 파괴되었다.)
She stood *waiting* for the bus.
He left *unnoticed*.
(그는 눈에 띄지 않게 떠났다.)

ⓓ (그는 오랫동안 독신으로 살아왔다.)
He died a *beggar*. (그는 거지로 죽었다.)
He went an *enemy* and came back a *friend*.
(그는 갈 때는 적이었으나 돌아올 때는 친구였다.)

(2) **목적격보어**

목적어의 동작·상태를 나타내며, 목적어를 설명하는 것을 목적격보어라 한다.

ⓐ (배심원단은 그 피고가 무죄라는 것을 알았다.)
(그들은 그를 의장으로 선출했다.)
The sight struck me *dumb*.
She cried herself *blind*.
He worked himself *ill*.
Anxiety kept him *awake* all night long.
He shaved his face *smooth*.
They called him a *liar*.

ⓑ (그는 나를 오래 기다리게 했다.)
(내 어깨를 누가 만지는 것을 느꼈다.)
She felt her heart *beating* wildly.
(그녀는 가슴이 몹시 뛰는 것을 느꼈다.)
I heard my name *called* behind me.
(내 이름을 뒤에서 부르는게 들렸다.)

ⓒ (나는그가 남의 흉을 보는 것을 들어본적이 없다.)
(나는 내일 아침 일찍 그를 오게하겠다.)
I observed her *shed* tears.
(나는 그녀가 눈물을 흘리고 있는 걸 알아챘다.)
Make the horse *jump* a barrier.
(그 말에게 장애물을 뛰어넘게 해라.)
I will let you *know* what was decided.
(나는 네에게 결정된 바를 알려주겠다.)

ⓓ (그녀가 나를 여기에 오라고했다.)
The captain commanded his men *to attack*. (대장은 부하들에게 공격하라고 명령했다.)
Our teacher allowed me *to be* absent.
(우리 선생님이 내가 결석하는 것을 허락해 주셨다.)

(3) **보어의 형식**

보어는 명사, 형용사 외에 부사, 구, 부정사, 분사, 절이 되기도 한다.

ⓐ 명사, 형용사가 보어 ⓑ 부사가 보어
ⓒ구가 보어 ⓓ부정사가 보어
ⓔ분사가 보어 ⓕ절이 보어

D. 합성타동사 (군동사)

(1) 자동사+전치사=타동사
break into (침입하다)
take after (~를 닮다)

(2) 동사+부사=타동사
bring up (양육하다)
put off (연기하다)

(3) 동사+부사+전치사=타동사
look up to (존경하다)
look down on (얕잡아보다, 깔보다)

(4) 동사+목적어+전치사=타동사
find fault with (흠잡다)
make light of (경시하다)

문 법 · 작 문

A. 이탤릭체인 동사의 종류를 말하여라.

(1) Much *remains* for us to do.
(2) The bank will *remain* open while renovations are carried out.
(3) Never in her life had she *felt* so happy.
(4) She *felt* her face flush at the sight of him.
(5) The bread doesn't *bake* well in this oven.
(6) He's a competent officer, but I doubt he'll *make* a general.
(7) Her dress *caught* on a nail passing by.
(8) They *shouted* themselves hoarse.
(9) This bloodstain won't *wash* out no matter how hard I try.
(10) He *lay* buried under the snow.
(11) The seminar *turned* out a great success.
(12) The school *turned* out some good scholars.
(13) She *fell* an easy prey to his power of seduction.
(14) Do you *feel* at home in your new office?
(15) His rudeness *rendered* me speechless.
(16) They found the place a prosperous village, and *left* it a ruin.
(17) They *beat* him black and blue because he had stolen their money.
(18) To meet the standard of being a basketball player, you are required to *stand* 6 feet tall.
(19) He *twisted* the sack shut.
(20) They *flung* the door wide open to greet their friends.

B. Correct the errors:

(1) When he arrived at home, the evening was far advanced.
(2) The operation on his broken spine was proved to be a complete success.
(3) Mr. Smith left from New York a few days ago.
(4) He planned to build his own house, and was learning to lie bricks.
(5) I am afraid I did two mistakes in dictation.
(6) This hotel reminds me the one we stayed in last year.
(7) He is belonged to an elite club which is very hard to get into.
(8) The war was resulted from the economic rivalries of the two nations.
(9) Henry asked us not to mention about his fiasco in the test.
(10) As far as I concern, the steps you suggest leave nothing to be desired.
(11) He presented at the meeting in spite of his illness.
(12) These plans look well on paper, but we can't be sure they will work.

C. 다음의 공란에 전치사가 필요하면 써 넣어라.

(1) Don't count (　　) your chickens before they are hatched.
(2) We're counting (　　) winning this contract.
(3) He apologized (　　) her for stepping on her foot.
(4) She is in prison awaiting (　　) trial.
(5) Dr. Smith operated (　　) the patient.
(6) The governor greeted (　　) the mayor with a big hug.
(7) Jane decided (　　) the green gown.
(8) Do you believe (　　) resurrection or reincarnation?
(9) You have to attend (　　) the meeting and attend (　　) what is being said.
(10) The government entered (　　) a genuine dialogue with the terrorists.
(11) He resembles (　　) his father in appearance, but not in character.
(12) This new office machine dispenses (　　) the need for a secretary.
(13) I presented him (　　) a native painting as a souvenir.
(14) This book comprises (　　) twenty chapters.
(15) The lawyer inquired (　　) the client if he would sue the company.
(16) Who are you going to marry (　　)?
(17) I'll accompany (　　) Sue and accompany (　　) her on the piano while she plays the violin.

D. Translate the following into English:

(1) 어젯밤에는 바람이 몹시 불어서 나는 잠을 잘 잘 수 없었다.

____

(2) 내가 어렸을 때 일어난 그 일은 아직도 내 기억에 생생하다.

____

(3) 아버님은 예순이시다. 그러나, 연세에 비해 매우 젊어 보이신다.

____

(4) 그 소식을 듣고 그는 깊은 한숨을 쉬었다.

____

(5) 그 책을 다 읽은 뒤에 나에게 빌려 주시오.

____

(6) 자식의 죽음으로 인해 그 여자는 거의 미쳤다.

____

(7) 그 여자는 매일 저녁 어머니가 설거지하시는 것을 돕는다.

____

'What I Did Yesterday'라는 제목으로 70어 내외의 글을 지어라.

● 단 문 독 해 ●

I watched **the boxing match** on TV last night.
Every morning he gives her **piano lessons**.

1. I want **to make** the future better than the past. I don't want it contaminated by the mistakes and errors with which history is filled. We should all be concerned about the future because that is where we will spend the remainder of our lives.

notes :
*contaminate 오염시키다
*error 잘못
*be filled with ~ = ~로 가득 차다
*be concerned about ~ = ~에 대해 근심하다
*remainder 나머지

▶▶According to the above paragraph, which of the following is appropriate to describe the writer's attitude?

① historical and objective
② philosophical and pensive
③ future-oriented and optimistic
④ past-oriented and emotional
⑤ pessimistic and sarcastic

▶▶영작하시오.
우리의 역사를 채우고 있는 그런 과오를 우리는 다시 되풀이 해서는 안된다.

2. A young man wrote to me the other day lamenting his ignorance and requesting me to tell him **what books to read** and **what to do** in order to become learned and wise. I sent him a civil answer and the advice that occurred to me.

notes :
*lament 슬퍼하다
*ignorance 무지, 무식
*learned [lə́:rnid] 학식있는
*civil 공손한
*occur to~ = ~에게 생각나다 (=strike)

▶▶According to the above paragraph, which of the following is **not** correct?

① The young man was aware of his own ignorance.
② The young man asked the writer to recommend him some useful books.
③ The young man asked for advice on books to become learned and wise.
④ The writer accepted the young man's advice and decided to act on it.
⑤ The writer was considerate enough to reply to the young man's letter.

▶▶영작하시오.
막 돌아서려고 할 때 좋은 생각이 떠올랐다.

3. When a young man has thoroughly comprehended **the fact** that he knows nothing, and that he is of but little value, the next thing for him to learn is that the world cares nothing for him — that he must take care of himself.

notes :
*comprehend 이해하다
*but = only
*care nothing for ~ = ~을 전혀 돌보지 않다

▶▶The writer holds the opinion that a young man should be (　　) and (　　).

[modest, shy, impudent, carefree, careless, self-reliant]

▶▶영작하시오.

인생에서 맨 먼저 알아야 할 것은 자신밖에 아무도 의지할 사람이 없다는 사실이다.

4. Science is the attempt to discover, by means of observation, and reasoning based upon it, first, particular facts about the world, and then laws connecting facts with one another and in fortunate cases making **it** possible **to foretell** future occurrences.

notes :
*reasoning 추리
*based upon = ~에 입각한
*foretell 예언하다
*occurrence 발생

▶▶Science is the (　　) to discover particular facts about the world and laws connecting those facts (　　) observation and reasoning based upon it.

[method, endeavor, motive, from, about, through]

▶▶영작하시오.

그 공장은 일꾼없이도 임무를 수행할 수 있는 새로운 기계를 설치했다.

5. ⓐ My father is an eminently sensible man. If ⓑ I reflect on my childhood, I see **how admirable his treatment of me has always been**. I fancy I must have been at one time rather hard to manage. Yet he neither let me have my own way nor angered me by his opposition.

notes :
*sensible 분별 있는
*have one's own way = 제멋대로 하다, 마음대로 하다

▶▶Which of the following is most suitable to describe the underlined ⓐ and ⓑ?

① obstinate — stubborn
② hot-blooded — rational
③ cool-headed — cautious
④ sensitive — imaginative
⑤ reasonable — mischievous

▶▶영작하시오.

그는 항상 자기 멋대로 하려고 든다.

The scenery of the island is **breathtaking**.
In the old days people believed some diseases **incurable**.
He returned home **a millionaire**.

6. Education is a continuous process which cannot be confined within the college classroom. Textbook and instructor will **remain indispensable** to education, but increasingly today there is an emphasis on the type of intellectual development that comes from the experience of living together with others of one's own generation.

notes :
*process 과정
*emphasis 강조, 중점
*intellectual development = 지적인 발전

▶▶Which does **not** correspond with the above paragraph?
① Education should be considered as lifelong learning.
② The textbook has been and will be a requisite for education.
③ The teacher will remain a crucial factor in education.
④ These days extracurricular activities tend to be regarded as very important.
⑤ Teaching social skills is now very important in life.

▶▶영작하시오.
그 집사(butler)는 한평생 주인에게 충실했다.

7. It is reported that a weightless man has succeeded in walking on nothing, and returning to the capsule that he calls home. This cosmic achievement **makes** race hatreds or petty nationalisms **trivial**. If men may one day walk together in space, what does it matter whether the skin beneath the space-suit is pink, black or brown?

notes :
*weightless man =astronaut, cosmonaut 우주비행사
*one day는 과거, 미래공용

▶▶Which is most suitable for the writer's main argument?
① Human beings must be educated to meet the demands of the space age.
② Even in the past, racism was considered trivial.
③ Applications for astronauts should be granted regardless of the applicants' skin color.
④ Racial discrimination and nationalism should not be an issue in this age of cosmic achievement.
⑤ The cosmic accomplishment brightens our hope of space travel.

▶▶영작하시오.
그녀가 미인이든 아니든 무슨 상관이 있느냐?

8. Though I have read so much, I am a bad reader. I read slowly and I am a poor skipper. I **find** it **difficult** to **leave** a book, however bad and however much it bores me, **unfinished**. I could count on my fingers the number of books that I have not read from cover to cover.

notes :
*skipper (책을) 띄엄띄엄 읽는 사람
*bore 싫증나게 하다
*He left the work unfinished.
*could는 가정법

▶▶ The writer reads books (   ) and always reads them (   ).
[poorly, lightly, widely, at, from, through]

▶▶ 영작하시오.
너는 그것을 만지지 않고 내버려 두어야 한다.

9. I heartily believe that it is you that can make our nation **what it should be among free nations in the world**, just as it was our forefathers that made it **what it is**.

notes :
*heartily 진심으로
*that it is에서 문장 끝까지가 believe의 목적어
*forefathers 조상

▶▶ The (   ) of our nation depends on us, just as it depended on our (   ) for what it is now.
[freedom, result, future, ancestors, foremen, descendants]

▶▶ 영작하시오.
오늘 내가 이렇게 된 것은 숙부님 덕이다.

10. He did not go to college **a gentleman**, but neither did he return **one**; he went to college **an ass**, and returned **a prig**; to his original folly was added a vast quantity of conceit.

notes :
*one = a gentleman
*ass 바보
*prig 학자인 체하는 사람
*conceit 자부심
*a vast quantity of conceit는 주어
*요즘은 *as* a gentleman의 형태가 더 보편적

▶▶ Which of the following is most appropriate to describe the writer's attitude to the above-mentioned man?
① concerned and dismayed
② cynical and contemptuous
③ embarrassed and frustrated
④ negative and suspicious
⑤ sympathetic and anguished

▶▶ 영작하시오.
10년 만에 그는 전혀 딴 사람이 되어 돌아왔다.

● 장 문 독 해 ●

Warming-up

We **found** a wild boar **caught** in a trap.
We have a code of ethics (that) we **live by**.
Defeated in battle, the enemy surrendered.
Don't **take it for granted that** you'll marry her.
If he is rich, he is not happy.

1 A new civilization is emerging in our lives, and blind men everywhere are trying to suppress it. The agricultural revolution of about 10,000 years ago started what we can describe as the First Wave of historic change. The industrial revolution of about 300 years ago launched today's dying Second Wave civilization. Today we find ourselves caught up in the explosive Third Wave of change. We shouldn't be surprised to find that every rule we have lived by is changing. It always happens when one epoch gives way to another.
Second Wave civilization adjusted daily life to the throb of machines. Raised in this civilization, the parents take it for granted that everyone must arrive and work at the same time, that rush-hour traffic is unavoidable, that mealtimes must be fixed, and that children must be trained in punctuality. They cannot understand why their children seem so casual about keeping appointments and why, if the nine-to-five job was good enough for them, it should suddenly be regarded as intolerable by their children.
The reason is that the Third Wave, as it sweeps in, carries with it a completely different sense of time. If the Second Wave tied life to the tempo of the machine, the Third Wave challenges this mechanical adjustment, alters our most basic social rhythms, and, in so doing, frees us from the machine.

Alvin Toffler: *The Third Wave*

Notes

civilization 문명 / emerge 나타나다 / suppress 은폐하다 / agricultural 농업의 / industrial 산업의; *industrious* 근면한 / launch 출발시키다 / explosive 폭발적인 / every rule (that) we have lived by / adjust A to B=A를 B에 적응시키다 / throb 고동, 맥박 / punctuality 시간엄수 / casual 느슨한 / if=though / the nine-to-five job 9시에서 5시까지 일하는 것/ sweep in ~로 휩쓸려 들어오다 / alter 바꾸다, 변화시키다

Question

1. 밑줄친 부분과 뜻이 같도록 빈칸에 적절한 말을 골라 쓰시오.

why their children seem so relaxed and (　　　) about keeping their appointments

[careless, careful, cautious, diligent, good]

2. 본문에서 설명된 각 시대의 특징이 되도록 빈칸을 채우시오.

ⓐ the First Wave	: the (a　　　) revolution
ⓑ the Second Wave	: the industrial revolution, the (m　　　) age
ⓒ the Third Wave	: human (f　　　) from machinery

3. Which does **not** correspond with the Second Wave?
   ① We are so accustomed to the Second Wave that we are not yet fully prepared to meet a new civilization.
   ② The Second Wave began with the emergence of the industrial revolution hundreds of years ago.
   ③ Human society has run according to the principles of machinery.
   ④ Older people take it for granted that every rule they have lived by is changing and are fully prepared to meet the coming new age.
   ⑤ Everyone has been taught in school to think highly of his or her punctuality.

4. Which does **not** correspond with the Third Wave?
   ① One of the most remarkable changes caused by the Third Wave is that the sense of time is altered.
   ② Oncoming changes caused by the arrival of the Third Wave should be considered natural and unavoidable.
   ③ Despite the advent of the Third Wave the established ways of doing things will continue for a considerable time.
   ④ Older people don't know what to do or how to deal with younger people in the midst of the whirl caused by the Third Wave.
   ⑤ All rules which used to regulate human beings are being changed for the betterment of our living conditions.

Production

(1) 그가 그런 일을 하고 있는 것을 알게 되면 너는 놀랄 것이다.
(2) 그 다음날 아침 눈떠보니 우리는 원주민들에게 둘러싸여 있었다.
(3) 그는 으레 자기가 대표로 선출될 것이라고 여기는 것 같다.

● 장 문 독 해 ●

Warming-up

To some life is pleasure; **to others suffering**.
It **would** be wrong to tell a lie to your parents.
It may be that he has done it by accident.
She was **not wholly** satisfied.
His sudden death **led** me **to** think over the meaning of life.

2 Man has existed for about a million years, and scientific technique for, at most, 200 years. Seeing what it has already accomplished, it would be very rash to place any limits upon what it may accomplish in the future. But scientific knowledge is an intoxicating draught, and ⓐit may be one which the human race is unable to sustain. It may be that, like the men who built the Tower of Babel in the hope of reaching up to heaven, so the men who pursue the secrets of the atom will be punished for their impiety by providing by accident the means of exterminating the human species, and perhaps all life on this planet. From some points of view, such a consummation might not be wholly regrettable, but ⓑthese points of view can hardly be ours. Perhaps somewhere else, in some distant nebula, some unimportant star has an unimportant planet on which there are rational beings. Perhaps in another million years their instruments will tell them of ⓒour fate, and lead ⓓthem to agree on an agenda for a conference of foreign ministers. If so, man will not have lived in vain.

Bertrand Russell: *The Limits of Human Power*

Notes

rash 성급한 / intoxicating 취하게 하는 / draught 한 모금(=draft) / sustain ~을 견디다 / It may be that=Perhaps / impiety 불경(不敬) / exterminate 전멸시키다 / consummation 결말 / regrettable 유감스러운 / nebula 성운(星雲) / rational beings 이성적 생물 / instrument 기구 / lead A to B(동사) A를 B하도록 이끌다 / agenda 협의 사항 / in vain 헛되이

Question

1. 본문의 밑줄 친 ⓐ, ⓓ가 가리키는 것이 알맞게 짝지어진 것은?
① scientific technology — our foreign ministers
② existence of man — human beings
③ the Tower of Babel — aliens' ministers
④ scientific knowledge — rational beings
⑤ human race — aliens' instruments

2. 본문의 밑줄친 ⓑthese points of view 의 내용을 다음과 같이 쓸 때, 빈칸에 알맞은 말을 쓰시오.

opinions that the annihilation of human beings caused by (n) (w) is not absolutely regrettable

3. 밑줄 친 ⓒ의 구체적 내용을 15자 내외의 우리말로 쓰시오.

4. Which of the following does **not** correspond with the passage?
① Seeing what we have already attained in 200 years of science, it is hard to say how far science will progress and what it will do.
② To place any limits on what future scientific techniques will accomplish would be too hasty.
③ Through mentioning the Tower of Babel, the writer suggests that human beings will be punished for the creation and usage of nuclear weapons.
④ The writer has definite evidences of the existence of intelligent life on other planets.
⑤ Perhaps human beings cannot expect to endure all the problems arising from the never-ending advancement of scientific technology.

5. Which of the following is most suitable to describe the tone of the writer expressed in the last sentence?
① realistic ② emotional ③ pathetic
④ humorous ⑤ sarcastic

Production

(1) 그는 한 밑천 잡을 희망으로 미국으로 건너갔다.
(2) 생명체가 존재하는 어떤 별들이 있을는지 모른다.
(3) 그가 성실하여, 나는 그의 제안에 동의하게 되었다.
(4) 당신의 삶이 자식에게 교훈이 될 수 있다면 아마 당신은 헛되이 살지는 않았을 것이다.

실력체크 I

1 다음 글의 제목을 골라라.

Of all the institutions that have come down to us from the past, none is in the present day so disorganized and derailed as the family. Affection of parents for children and of children for parents is capable of being one of the greatest sources of happiness, but in fact at the present day the relations of parents and children are, in nine cases out of ten, a source of unhappiness to both parties, and in ninety-nine cases out of a hundred a source of unhappiness to at least one of the two parties. This failure of the family to provide the fundamental satisfactions which in principle it is capable of yielding is one of the most deep-seated causes of the discontent which is prevalent in our age.

① Duty to Parents
② The Disorganization of the Family
③ Affection for Parents
④ Love for the Family
⑤ The Society and the Family

notes :
institution 제도 / derail 탈선하다 / in nine cases out of ten 십중팔구 / both parties 부모와 자식 양쪽 / yield 생산하다 / deep-seated 뿌리깊이 박힌 / prevalent 널리 퍼진

2 다음 글의 교훈이 되도록 아래 주어진 글의 공란에 4단어의 영어를 써라.

A fly settled one day on a pot of honey, and finding it very much to his taste, began to eat it along the edge. Little by little, however, he soon crept farther away from the edge, and into the pot, until at last he found himself stuck fast. His legs and wings had become so sticky with the honey that he could not use them. Just then a moth flew by, and seeing him struggling there, said, "Oh, you foolish fly! Were you so greedy as to be caught like that? Your appetite was too much for you." The poor fly had nothing to say. But by and by, when evening came, he saw the moth flying round and round the lamp, each time a little closer to the flame, until at last he flew straight into it, and was burned to death. "What!" said the fly, "are you foolish, too? You laughed at me for being too fond of honey; yet all your wisdom did not keep you from playing with fire."

＊It is easier to see the faults of _____ _____ _____ _____.

notes :
fly 파리 / fly (날다)-flew-flown / little by little 조금씩, 점점 / stick-stuck-stuck / sticky 끈적끈적한, 달라붙는 / moth 나방 / so ~ as to = so ~that / appetite 식욕 / by and by = soon

3 다음 글을 읽고 아래 물음에 답하여라.

> The disastrous feature of our civilization is that it is far more developed materially than spiritually. ⓐIts balance is disturbed. Through the discoveries which now place the forces of Nature at our disposal in such an unprecedented way, the relations to each other of individuals, of social groups, and of States have undergone a revolutionary change. Our knowledge and our power have been enriched and increased to an extent that no one would have thought possible. We have ⓑthereby been enabled to make the conditions of human existence incomparably more favorable in numerous respects, but in our enthusiasm over our progress in knowledge and power we have arrived at ⓒa defective conception of civilization itself. We value too highly its material achievements, and no longer keep in mind as vividly as is necessary the importance of the spiritual element in life.

notes :
disastrous 비참한, 재해의 / materially 물질적으로 / unprecedented 선례가 없는 / incomparably 비교할 수 없을 만큼 / numerous 다수의 / defective 결함있는, 불완전한

(1) 밑줄 친 ⓐ, ⓑ, ⓒ를 구체적으로 설명하여라.
(2) 이 글의 표제가 될 부분을 본문 속에서 골라라.

4 다음 글의 핵심을 가장 잘 요약한 것을 골라라.

> Man is but a reed, the most feeble thing in nature; but he is a thinking reed. The entire universe does not need to arm itself to crush him. A vapor, a drop of water suffices to kill him. But, if the universe were to crush him, man would still be more noble than that which killed him, because he knows that he dies and the advantage which the universe has over him; the universe knows nothing of this. All our dignity consists, then, in thought. By it we must elevate ourselves and not by space and time which we cannot fill. Let us endeavor, then, to think well; this is the principle of morality.

notes :
reed 갈대 / feeble 연약한 / suffice 충분하다 / elevate 높이다, 향상시키다 / morality 도덕

① Man is nothing but a reed.
② Man knows his mortality.
③ Nature is superior to man.
④ Man is great because of his thinking ability.
⑤ Man can never fill time and space.

실 력 체 크 II

A. Choose a suitable word:

(1) You'll begin to feel sleepy as the drug (enters, enters into) the bloodstream.

(2) The storm is supposed to (reach, reach at) Atlanta by noon.

(3) The senator (addressed, addressed to) the audience in French.

(4) The police met local people to (discuss, discuss about) recent racist attacks.

(5) Wild boars (inhabit, inhabit in) this forest.

(6) Please (explain, explain to) me what this means.

(7) He (wrote, painted, drew) my face on the blackboard.

(8) Did they (announce, announce about) their engagement last night?

(9) When he (approached, approached to) his destination, he felt relieved.

(10) You can (substitute, replace) margarine for butter in the recipe.

(11) Please (bring, take) that package to me.

(12) May I (use, borrow) your telephone?

(13) Do you own this house, or do you (borrow, hire, rent) it?

(14) The post office was (stolen, robbed) last night.

(15) Mary (studies, learns) at the university.

(16) I don't think they will (accept, receive) our invitation.

(17) We (watched, saw) the soccer game on television.

(18) Please (answer, reply) to my e-mail as soon as possible.

(19) He (wore, put on) a new coat and went out.

B. 틀린 것을 고쳐 써라.

(1) John introduced Bill and Sue each other.

(2) He announced us the winner of the competition.

(3) Buying the new model will save time and money from you.

(4) The cement barrier protects traffic from passing.

(5) It did not take long before new troubles arose.

(6) I sympathized John when he lost his job.

(7) She graduated the University of Michigan in 2001.

Answer: A. (1) enters (2) reach (3) addressed (4) discuss (5) inhabit (6) explain to (7) drew (8) announce (9) approached (10) substitute (11) bring (12) use (13) rent (14) robbed (15) studies (16) accept (17) watched (18) reply (19) put on

B. (1) to each other (2) announced the winner of the competition to us (3) save you time and money (4) protects → prevents (5) did not take → was not (6) sympathized with (7) graduated from

C. A군의 문장과 같은 문형을 B군에서 각각 두 개씩 골라라.

(A군) (ㄱ) Please excuse my being so late.
(ㄴ) The government set prisoners free.
(ㄷ) Did his family live on his salary?
(ㄹ) I remain yours truly.
(ㅁ) Has he paid you and your friends the money?

(B군) (1) He looks every inch a gentleman.
(2) We think it most dangerous your climbing the mountain alone.
(3) Many people died in the aftermath of the radioactive leakage.
(4) He claims he has nothing to do with the matter.
(5) I left my father quite well last year.
(6) Does my singing in the room above disturb you?
(7) There's no doubt that he will come.
(8) Please send me by express the articles mentioned in my list.
(9) Things will come right.
(10) I will make you a new suit.

D. 지시대로 다음 문장을 다시 써라.

(1) He thinks himself a great poet. (밑줄 친 부분을 절로)
(2) We found the lost child hiding in the cave. (밑줄 친 부분을 절로)
(3) My sister was young when she died. (2형식의 단문으로)
(4) This fish smells, and it is nasty. (2형식의 단문으로)
(5) The doctor ordered him to take a month's rest. (밑줄 친 부분을 절로)
(6) My father wished me to become a doctor. (밑줄 친 부분을 절로)
(7) He patted me on the back in a friendly way. (give를 써서 4형식으로)
(8) Impatiently, he opened the letter by tearing it. (5형식으로)
(9) They resemble each other closely. (There is의 구문으로)
(10) I feel I must tell him the truth. (my duty를 써서 5형식으로)
(11) They must apologize to us for the situation going from bad to worse. (owe를 써서 4형식의 문장으로)

Answer: C. (ㄱ) - (4), (6) (ㄴ) - (2), (5) (ㄷ) - (3), (7) (ㄹ) - (1), (9) (ㅁ) - (8), (10)
D. (1) that he is a great poet (2) that the lost child was hiding in the cave (3) My sister died young. (4) This fish smells nasty. (5) that he (should) take a month's rest (6) that I would become a doctor (7) He gave me a friendly pat on the back. (8) Impatiently he tore the letter open. (9) There is a close resemblance between them. (10) I feel it my duty to tell him the truth. (11) They owe us an apology for the situation going from bad to worse.

어 휘 · 발 음

A. 다음 빈 자리에 적당한 말을 골라 넣어라.

(1) He has long been engaged in the ______ profession.
① literary ② literate ③ literal ④ liberal

(2) The monarchy is seen as an ______ in present-day society.
① anarchy ② anachronism ③ archeology ④ architecture

(3) No one will question his ______ as a great conductor.
① statue ② stature ③ status ④ statute

(4) He accepted the ______ of his family and friends.
① consul ② council ③ counsel ④ console

B. 밑줄 친 단어의 반의어를 공란에 써 넣어라.

(1) There was a vacant seat beside him.
"Sir, is this seat ______ ?" I said.

(2) They must have violated fire regulations.
Fire regulations should be ______ .

(3) The agreement, not having been signed, was void.
The ticket is ______ for off-peak travel only.

(4) A study of a skylark is not necessarily zoological.
The lilies of the field have a value for us beyond their ______ one.

(5) The terminal cancer patient begged a painless suicide.
The two brothers have been charged with an attempted ______.

C. 우리말의 뜻이 되는 것을 골라라.

(1) 불을 피우다 : (make, raise, cause, catch) a fire
(2) 위험을 무릅쓰다 : (break, put, commit, run) a risk
(3) 열매를 맺다 : (bind, bear, carry, set) fruit
(4) 눈물을 흘리다 : (flow, make, shed, fall) tears
(5) 의사의 진찰을 받다 : (ask, inquire, consult, suffer) a doctor
(6) 자전거를 타다 : (drive, ride, get, rush) a bicycle
(7) 팔짱을 끼다 : (fold, join, hold, fasten) one's arms
(8) 숨을 죽이다 : (set, kill, hold, take) one's breath
(9) 발 조심하다 : (see, look, watch, hold) one's step
(10) 천천히 하다 : (hold, slow, get, take) one's time

Answer: A. (1) ① (2) ② (3) ③ (4) ③ B. (1) occupied[taken] (2) observed (3) valid (4) botanical (5) murder C. (1) make (2) run (3) bear (4) shed (5) consult (6) ride (7) fold (8) hold (9) watch (10) take

D. 다음 문장들의 괄호 안에 공통으로 들어갈 단어를 쓰시오.

(1) (a) With your lack of experience, I don't think you (   ) a chance of winning.

(b) We made the rules last year and they still (   ).

(c) The defeated troop made a last (   ) at the bridge.

(2) (a) The young man (   ) a hasty glance at the girl in blue jeans.

(b) This time the actress was (   ) for the part of Lady Macbeth.

(c) The doctor put his left leg into a plaster (   ).

E. 주어진 문장의 밑줄 친 부분과 같은 의미로 쓰인 것을 고르시오.

(1) Hundreds of people were <u>rendered</u> homeless by the earthquake.

① The man has <u>rendered</u> me a great deal of service.

② Poetry can never adequately be <u>rendered</u> into another language.

③ The surprise party <u>rendered</u> Susan speechless.

④ The performance hardly <u>rendered</u> the playwright's conception.

(2) He <u>pressed</u> his guests to stay a little longer.

① She <u>pressed</u> the juice from the grapes.

② The family was always <u>pressed</u> for money.

③ The speaker <u>pressed</u> his point, returning to it again and again.

④ The girl <u>pressed</u> her father for a raise in allowance.

F. 다음 각 문장의 괄호 안에 들어갈 적당한 단어를 고르시오.

(1) This theater (   ) nearly 3,000 people.

① holds ② includes ③ keeps ④ occupies

(2) My father is very observant; nothing (   ) his notice.

① avoids ② escapes ③ helps ④ keeps

(3) Nothing could (   ) me to do such a thing.

① indicate ② involve ③ induce ④ insist

G. 다음을, 액센트의 위치에 주의하여 그 뜻을 적어라.

(1) désert	( )	(2) mínute	( )	(3) dígest	( )
desért	( )	minúte	( )	digést	( )
(4) próduce	( )	(5) fréquent	( )	(6) cónverse	( )
prodúce	( )	frequént	( )	convérse	( )

Answer: D. (1) stand (2) cast E. (1) ③ (2) ④ F. (1) ① (2) ② (3) ③
G. (1) 사막 ; 버리다[도망하다] (2) 분(分) ; 상세한 (3) 요약 ; 소화하다
(4) 농산물 ; 생산하다 (5) 빈번한 ; 자주 드나들다 (6) 반대의 ; 담화하다

숙 어

(1) **a close call** (=a narrow escape from danger *or* death) 위기일발, 구사일생
☞ The speeding taxi nearly hit her; that was *a close call*.

(2) **abide by** (=keep, be faithful to, obey) 지키다, 따르다
☞ I have to *abide by* the contract I've signed.

(3) **abound in(*or* with)** (=be plentiful in, be rich in) ~이 풍부하다
☞ This coastline *abounds in* (or *with*) rare plants.

(4) **account for** (=explain) 설명하다
☞ How can you *account for* what happened today?

(5) **add up** (=calculate the total of ; make sense)
합계를 내다 ; (주로 부정문에서) 이치[조리]에 맞다
☞ *Add up* all the money I owe you.
His statements in this case don't *add up*.

(6) **add up to** (=amount to, total) 합계 ~이 되다
☞ His total debts will soon *add up to* over $90,000.

(7) **after hours** (=after usual business time) 일과후에, 폐점후에
☞ I want you to clean food spills off the table *after hours*.

(8) **all at once** (=suddenly, all of a sudden, on a sudden) 갑자기
☞ *All at once*, the boat hit a rock and capsized.

(9) **all but** (=almost) 거의
☞ The party was *all but* over when we arrived.

(10) **all in all** (=considering everything) 대체로
☞ *All in all* his condition has improved since he underwent the surgery.

(11) **allow for** (=consider, take~into account) ~을 고려하다
☞ You must *allow for* his youth and inexperience.

(12) **answer for** (=be responsible for) 책임지다
☞ They have to *answer for* the President's safety.

⒀ **anything but** (=never) 결코 ~아닌 **nothing but** (=only) 단지
☞ I'll eat *anything but* dog meat. He is *nothing but* a cheat.

⒁ **apart[aside] from** (=except for, in addition to) ~은 별도로, ~이외에도
☞ *Apart from* the question of expense, the project is impracticable.
The government has plenty of problems to deal with, *apart from* inflation.

⒂ **around the clock** (=all day and all night) 밤낮으로 쉬지않고
☞ We worked *around the clock* to keep the agreed date with the buyer.

⒃ **as a rule** (=usually, on the whole) 통상, 대체로
☞ *As a rule* vegetable oils are better for health than animal fats.

⒄ **as of** (=starting from, as from) ~부터 (시작하여)
☞ Our fax number is changing *as of* April 5.

⒅ **as the crow flies** (=in a straight line) 직선거리로
☞ It's just 2 miles from here to town *as the crow flies*.

⒆ **ask for it[trouble]** (=behave in a way that is sure to result in trouble) (스스로) 화를 자초하다
☞ Drinking alcohol before driving is really *asking for it*.

⒇ **ask one out** (=invite one on a date) 누구에게 데이트 신청하다
☞ I'd like to *ask* her *out*, but I'm worried she'd say no.

Exercise

▶▶ 주어진 단어들을 포함한 글을 지어라. 필요하면 어형을 변화시켜라.

1. members / team / abound / courage
2. sickness / account / absence
3. stay / work / hours / finish
4. all / once / hear / noise
5. I / answer / honesty
6. aside / joking / mean / by
7. work / clock / finish / job
8. as / rule / men / tuxedos / parties
9. house / mile / lake / crow
10. asking / trouble / driving / that

2. 동사의 시제(Tense)

기본 문법 설명

A. 현재시제

(1) He **is** an expert in child psychology.
She **has** a fair complexion.
The monument **commemorates** war heroes.
He **kisses** her and **hurries** for a bus.

(2) ⓐ I **like** fish better than meat.
ⓑ My family **keeps** early hours.
ⓒ Light **travels** at a velocity of 186,000 miles per second.
ⓓ The plane **leaves** for Hongkong tomorrow morning.
ⓔ Give me a call if you **need** any help.
ⓕ Caesar **crosses** the Rubicon and **enters** Italy.
ⓖ Dryden **says** that none but the brave deserve(s) the fair.

B. 과거시제

(1) The car **stopped** at the traffic light.
My grandmother **wove** rugs from old pieces of cloth.

(2) ⓐ World War II **broke** out in 1939.
ⓑ She often **took** her dog for a walk after dinner.
We **used to** go swimming in the lake before it became polluted.
I **would** visit her every day except when it rained.
ⓒ The thieves **got** away before the police arrived.

C. 미래시제

(1) ⓐ I **will** have to walk home if I miss the last bus.
ⓑ You **will** be sorry later if you quit school now.
ⓒ He **will** be glad to hear that the dispute has been settled.

(2) ⓐ **Will** I be able to read and write Spanish soon?
ⓑ **Will** you be home this afternoon?
ⓒ When **will** she be back?

D. 진행형

(1) ⓐ Father **is watching** a soccer game on TV now.
ⓑ Father **was watching** a soccer game on TV when I entered the room.
ⓒ Father **will be watching** a soccer game on TV when I go to bed.

A. 현재시제

(1) **형식**

현재 시제의 형식은 be, have 동사를 제외한 일반동사는 3인칭 단수에 -s, -es를 붙이는 것 외에는 모두 원형과 같다.

☞ 어미가 [s, z, ʃ, ʒ, tʃ, dʒ]의 음으로 끝나면 -es를 붙인다.
kisses, buzzes, washes

☞ 어미가 o이면 -es를 붙이고, 어미가 y이고 그 앞이 자음이면 y를 i로 고쳐 -es를 붙인다. goes, echoes, does [dʌz], hurry ⇨ hurries 그러나 buy ⇨ buys

(그는 아동심리학의 전문가이다.)
(그녀는 얼굴이 희다.)
(그 기념비는 전쟁영웅들을 기념한다.)
(그는 그녀에게 키스하고 버스를 타기 위해 서두른다.)

(2) **현재 시제의 용법**

ⓐ 현재의 사실
(나는 고기보다 생선을 더 좋아한다.)

ⓑ 현재의 습관
(우리집은 일찍 자고 일찍 일어난다.)

ⓒ 불변의 진리
(빛은 초당 186,000 마일의 속도로 나아간다.)

ⓓ 미래의 대용
(그 비행기는 내일 아침 홍콩을 향해 출발한다.)

☞ **왕래 발착 동사**, 즉 come, arrive, depart, go, leave, meet, start, return, sail, ride 등은 미래를 나타내는 부사, 부사구와 같이 쓰여 미래를 나타낼 때가 많다.

ⓔ 시간과 조건을 나타내는 부사절에서 현재는 미래를 나타낸다.
(어떤 도움이든 필요하면 내게 전화해라.)
When he *comes* here, I will tell him about it.

☞ 명사절에서는 미래형을 쓴다.
I don't know if he *will* come.

ⓕ 역사적 사실
(Caesar가 루비콘 강을 건너 이탈리아로 들어간다.)…과거의 일을 눈앞에 생생하게 표현하는 수사적 용법이다.

ⓖ 옛 사람, 옛 책에 쓰인 말을 인용할 때 현재형을 쓰면 생생한 표현이 된다.
(용감한 자만이 미인을 얻을 자격이 있다고 Dryden은 말한다.)

B. 과거시제

(1) **규칙활용** …어미에 -ed를 붙인다.

stop ⇨ stopped (단모음+자음)
try ⇨ tried (자음+y)

☞ 2음절의 동사가 「단모음+단자음」으로 끝나고 액센트가 뒤 음절에 오면 자음을 중복하고 -ed를 붙인다.
omít ⇨ omitted, prefér ⇨ preferred, occúr ⇨ occurred
그러나 vísited, óffered, límited

☞ picnic ⇨ picnicked, mimic ⇨ mimicked

(그 차는 교통신호에 따라 섰다.)

불규칙활용 (☞ p.36, 37 불규칙동사변화표)
…어미에 -ed를 붙이지 않는 다른 형태
(할머니는 헌 천조각으로 깔개를 짰다.)

(2) **과거 시제의 용법**

ⓐ 과거의 사실·동작·상태
He *relinquished* all rights to the property.

ⓑ 과거의 습관적 동작
(그녀는 종종 저녁식사 후 산책을 위해 그녀의 개를 데리고 나갔다.)
또한 used to, would를 이용해 과거의 습관을 나타낼 수 있다.
(우리는 그 호수가 오염되기 전에는 그곳에 수영하러 다니곤 했다.)
(난 비가 올 때를 제외하고는 매일 그녀를 찾아 가곤했다.)

ⓒ 과거형이 과거완료를 대용
접속사 before가 시간의 순서를 나타내기 때문에 대용이 가능함.
I went out after I *finished* the work.

C. 미래시제(단순미래)

(1) **평서문**	(2) **의문문**
I will ~.	Will I ~?
You will ~.	Will you ~?
He will ~.	Will he ~?

***의지미래**: 조동사 will, shall 참조(p.132 D)

I will ~.	Shall I ~?
You shall ~.	Will you ~?
He shall ~.	Shall he ~?

D. 진행형

(1) ⓐ 현재진행형	I am doing it
ⓑ 과거진행형	I was doing it
ⓒ 미래진행형	I will be doing it

(내가 잠자리에 들때 아버지는 TV로 축구경기를 보고 계실 것이다.)

	(2) ⓐ Mary **is** always **complaining** about something. ⓑ We **are having** supper at nine this week. ⓒ Where **are** you **spending** your next summer vacation? ⓓ I **was seeing** a friend of mine off when you saw me at the airport.
	(3) ⓐ The ice **is going to** crack. ⓑ His new film **is going to** be a great success. ⓒ My mother **is going to** buy some groceries.
E. 현재완료	(1) ⓐ **Haven't** you **had** a checkup yet? ⓑ He **has stopped** smoking and drinking. (2) ⓐ **Have** you ever **climbed** Mt. Halla? ⓑ I **have been** to Honolulu. (3) ⓐ I **have lost** my wallet. ⓑ He **has gone** to the airport. (4) ⓐ He **has been dead** for seven years. ⓑ It **has been raining** since the day before yesterday. (5) ⓐ I will pay him as soon as he **has finished** the work. ⓑ He is the greatest philosopher that **has** ever **lived**.
F. 과거완료	(1) ⓐ I **bought** a cellular phone, but I **lost** it the next day. ⓑ I lost the cellular phone which I **had bought** the day before. (2) ⓐ When we got to the hall, the concert **had** already **started**. ⓑ I recognized Mrs. Brown at once, for I **had seen** her several times before. ⓒ He **had gone** fishing when I visited him. ⓓ She was then thirty years old and **had been married** five years. It **had been raining** for three days when I reached the island. (3) ⓐ No sooner **had** they **seen** a policeman coming than they ran away. ⓑ Hardly **had** the plane **taken** off when the wind began to blow hard. ⓒ We **had hoped** that we would be able to call on you.

(2) 진행형은 순간적인 동작의 계속의 뜻 외에 습관, 반복을 의미할 수 있다.
ⓐ 성질, 습관
ⓑ 일시적 동작의 반복
ⓒ 미래를 나타낸다.
ⓓ **지각, 감정, 소유, 상태**를 나타내는 동사 (know, love, see, have, resemble 등)는 진행형을 못 쓴다.
I *know* him. He *loves* me.
☞ 그러나, 일시적인 동작과 동사의 뜻이 바뀔 때는 쓸 수 있다.
He is *having*[eating] his breakfast.
He is *seeing* the sights of Seoul.

(3) **be going to의 용법**
ⓐ (얼음이 막 깨지려고 한다.)
ⓑ (그의 새 영화는 아마 대성공이 될 것이다.)
ⓒ (어머니는 몇몇 식료품을 살 예정이시다.)

E. 현재완료

「**have+과거분사**」의 형태이며, 현재에 있어서의 동작의 **완료**, 현재까지의 **경험**, 과거 동작이 현재에 미치는 **결과**, 현재까지의 동작·상태의 **계속**을 나타낸다.

☞ 현재완료는 명백히 과거를 나타내는 어구와는 같이 쓰이지 않는다.
{I have finished it *yesterday*. (×)
{I finished it yesterday. (○)
{*When* have you seen her? (×)
{When did you see her? (○)

☞ just는 현재완료, just now는 과거와 함께 쓰지만 구어체에서는 혼용된다.
I finished it *just now*.
I have *just* finished it.

☞ yet은 의문문, 부정문 }에 쓴다.
already는 긍정문
Has he seen it *yet*?
No, he has*n't* seen it *yet*.
He has seen it *already*.
그러나, already가 의문문에 사용될 때는 놀람을 나타낸다.
Has he seen it *already*?

(1) **완료** : 막 ~하였다
(2) **경험** : (이전에) ~한 적이 있다
ⓐ (한라산에 오른 적이 있느냐?)
ⓑ (나는 호놀룰루에 가본 적이 있다.)
☞ I *have been to* the station.
(나는 정거장에 갔다 왔다.)

(3) **결과** : ~해 버렸다 (그 결과 지금은 ~하다)
ⓐ (나는 지갑을 잃어버렸다.)
그 결과 지금 지갑이 없다는 뜻.
ⓑ (그는 공항에 갔다.)
그래서 지금 여기에 없다는 뜻.

(4) **계속** : 현재까지의 동작·상태의 계속
ⓐ 과거부터 현재까지의 상태의 계속
= It is[has been] seven years since he died.
= Seven years have passed since he died.
= He died seven years ago.
ⓑ 과거부터 현재까지의 동작의 계속
…현재완료진행형

(5) ⓐ 때나 조건을 나타내는 부사절에서 미래완료의 대용으로 현재완료를 쓸 수 있다. 그러나 구어에서는 (특히 미식영어) 잘 쓰지 않는다. 대개 현재형으로 쓰는 수가 많다.
= I will pay him as soon as he *finishes* the work.
ⓑ that has ever lived는 the greatest를 강조한다.

F. 과거완료

(1) ⓐ 동작이 일어난 순서대로 쓴 글이다.
ⓑ 「산 행동」은 「잃어버린 행동」보다 먼저 일어났으므로 과거완료로 했다.

(2) 과거완료는 과거의 어떤 때를 기준하여 그 때까지의 **완료, 경험, 결과, 계속**을 나타낸다.
ⓐ 완료 ⓑ 경험 ⓒ 결과
ⓓ 계속
(그녀는 그때 30세였으며 결혼한지 5년이었었다.)
(내가 그 섬에 도착했을 때 3일간 비가 계속 내리고 있었다.)…과거완료진행형

(3) ⓐ = As soon as they saw a policeman coming, they ran away.
ⓑ (비행기가 이륙하자마자 바람이 몹시 불기 시작했다.)
☞ as soon as 는 통상 과거로 쓴다.
no sooner ~ than, } 은 과거완료를 쓰며, 주어의 도치에 주의하여라.
hardly[scarcely] ~when
ⓒ (방문하고 싶었습니다만 그러지 못했습니다.) … had hoped는 이루지 못한 희망을 나타낸다.
☞ expect, intend, want, desire 등 소망의 뜻이 있는 동사가 과거완료로 쓰이면 이루지 못한 사실을 나타냄.

G. 미래완료	(1) You **will have arrived** in Rome by this time tomorrow. (2) He **will have seen** much of the world by that time. (3) She **will have been** in hospital for a month by next Sunday. It **will have been raining** for a week by tomorrow.

▶ 불규칙 동사의 변화 ◀

A. 원형·과거형·과거분사형이 동일한 것 (**A — A — A형**)

burst, cast, cost, cut, hit, hurt, let, put, read, set, shed, shut, split, spread, thrust 등.

B. 과거형·과거분사형이 동일한 것 (**A — B — B형**)

bring	brought	brought
buy	bought	bought
fight	fought	fought
sell	sold	sold
bleed	bled	bled
feed	fed	fed
build	built	built
lay	laid	laid
pay	paid	paid
keep	kept	kept
catch	caught	caught
teach	taught	taught
wind	wound	wound
speed	sped	sped
lead	led	led
spend	spent	spent
hear	heard	heard
sleep	slept	slept
weep	wept	wept
hold	held	held
leave	left	left
lose	lost	lost
mean	meant	meant
shine	shone[shined]	shone[shined]
win	won	won

G. 미래완료

「will+have+과거분사」의 형태이며, 통상 미래의 어떤 때를 나타내는 어구를 동반하는데, 그 때까지의 완료·경험·계속 등을 나타낸다.

(1) (너는 내일 이맘때까지는 로마에 도착해 있을 것이다.) … 완료
(2) (그때까지면 그는 세상 물정을 많이 알게 되었을 것이다.) … 경험
(3) (그여자는 다음 일요일이면 한달 간 입원해 있는 셈이 된다.) … 계속
(비가 내일까지 오면 한주일 동안 오는 셈이 될 것이다.) … 미래완료진행형

▶ 불규칙 동사의 변화 ◀

C. 서로 다른 것 (**A — B — C형**)

begin	began	begun
drink	drank	drunk
rise	rose	risen
write	wrote	written
choose	chose	chosen
bite	bit	bitten
blow	blew	blown
shave	shaved	shaven
show	showed	shown
swim	swam	swum
sing	sang	sung
drive	drove	driven
strive	strove	striven
freeze	froze	frozen
weave	wove	woven
hide	hid	hidden
tear	tore	torn
fly	flew	flown
shake	shook	shaken
sow	sowed	sown
swell	swelled	swollen
tread	trod	trodden
wear	wore	worn

D. 원형과 과거분사형이 동일한 것 (**A — B — A형**)

come	came	come
run	ran	run

※ lie lied lied ; lie lay lain ; lay laid laid
fall fell fallen ; fell felled felled
wind wound wound ; wound wounded wounded
saw sawed sawn ; sow sowed sown ; sew sewed sewn

문 법 · 작 문

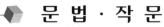

A. 다음 동사의 과거형·과거분사형과 현재분사형을 적어라.

(1) begin (2) occur (3) cry
(4) lie (5) mimic (6) choose

B. 괄호 안의 동사를 적당한 형으로 고쳐라.

(1) He was ill, so he (lie) in bed all day.
(2) I'll put off my departure if it (snow) tomorrow.
(3) Mary wants to know if you (go) to the store with her.
(4) "What you (do) all this while?" "Oh, nothing particular."
(5) He's promised to call me as soon as he (get) home from work.
(6) Turkey (be) a republic since 1923.
(7) There (be) many changes around here since I was a child.
(8) I (know) him for many years before he (become) a minister.
(9) I hardly (walk) a mile when it began to rain.
(10) I (climb) Mt. Dobong three times, if I climb it again.

C. 괄호 안에서 용법이 맞는 것을 골라라.

(1) "Where are all the glasses?" "They (will be, are being) washed at the moment."
(2) Look out, or you (shall, will) be run over.
(3) "(Shall, Will) he be able to cope with the work?" "Yes, he will."
(4) He said that the Korean War (had broken, broke) out in 1950.
(5) I (hear, am hearing) someone moving about in the next room.
(6) The rumor that all the crew were saved (proves, has proved) to be true.
(7) He has (gone, been) to New York. He is not here.
(8) He said he would (raise, rise) my salary if I worked harder.

D. 다음 각 문장에서 틀린 동사의 용법을 바로 잡아라.

(1) When has the trouble started?
(2) I've received an urgent message from her an hour ago.
(3) It has passed many years since he came here.
(4) I wonder when he comes back.
(5) The road was muddy, as it rained the previous day.
(6) By the time you arrive here I will start.
(7) Father is usually going to his office by bus.
(8) He has been waiting for an hour, and so did I.

(9) After the earthquake the city was resembling a battlefield.
(10) He has and will always be faithful to his wife.
(11) I lived with other people in a shared house for the past ten years.
(12) I lost the watch he gave me.
(13) Jack was sick for a week when he was sent to hospital.
(14) Prices rose ten times as high as ten years ago.
(15) The prisoner was sentenced to be hung.
(16) It must be born in mind that there is no royal road to learning.
(17) I have gone to the airport to see a friend off.
(18) I have visited New York, but he didn't.
(19) All has gone well up to that time.
(20) He has died these ten years.
(21) It will not be long before our firm will break even.
(22) Our school is standing on a hill and commands a fine view.
(23) The trees are falling their leaves.

E. Translate the following into English:

(1) 내가 준비할 때까지 잠깐 기다리시오.

____

(2) 여가가 있으면 저의 집에 와 주시겠습니까?

____

(3) 기차로 가면 정오까지는 거기에 도착할 것이다.

____

(4) 그는 지금 시내 구경을 하고 있다.

____

(5) 지금까지 어디 있었느냐? 너를 사방에서 찾고 있었다.

____

(6) 나는 그가 남을 칭찬하는 것을 들어 본 적이 없다.

____

(7) 그가 잠이 깼을 때, 그의 가족은 벌써 아침식사를 마친 뒤였다.

____

(8) 그를 전에 만나본 적이 있었으므로 나는 곧 그를 알아보았다.

____

(9) 그가 올해 다시 입학 시험을 치면 세 번 치는 셈이 된다.

____

'Our School'이라는 제목으로 90어 내외의 글을 지어라.

● 단 문 독 해 ●

기본시제 · 완료시제

1. Much will be done if we do but **try**. No one knows what one can do **till one has tried**; and few try their best **until they have been forced** to. "If only I could do such and such," sighs the despondent youth. But nothing gets done if one only **wishes**.

notes :
*do but try에서 do는 강조용법
*but = only
*sigh 한숨쉬다
*despondent 낙심한

▶▶Which is most related to the above paragraph?
① Sour grapes. ② Every cloud has a silver lining.
③ Know yourself. ④ Nothing ventured, nothing gained.
⑤ Speak of the devil.

▶▶영작하시오.
무슨 일이든지 전력을 다해야 한다.

2. From the beginning of time the tide **has ebbed and flowed**. From the beginning of time light has followed darkness, spring winter, life death. The Earth and all in the boundless universe **move** with the ease of a bird in flight and the rhythm of its song.

notes :
*tide 조수
*ebb (조수가) 빠지다
*flow (조수가) 밀려 들다
*spring (has followed) winter
*boundless 끝없는
*of its song에서 its = a bird's

▶▶Which is the main idea of the above paragraph?
① The ebb and flow
② Life and death
③ The change of season
④ The mechanism of the universe
⑤ The alternation of light and darkness

▶▶영작하시오.
그는 인생의 영고 성쇠를 경험했다.

3. My heart was sad for her sake, and though I **had ceased** to love her, I **found** no consolation. A painful sense of emptiness had replaced the bitter anguish of before; and it was perhaps even harder to bear. Love **may go** and memory yet **remain**, memory may go and relief even then may not come.

▶▶Which of the following does **not** correspond with the writer?

① Nothing could relieve him of his sadness caused by her.

② The sense of emptiness was perhaps more unbearable than the distress previously brought about by her.

③ His sadness didn't abate even after he fell out of love with her.

④ He could not give up his love for her though he thought he had ceased to love her.

⑤ Love may go but the memory lingers on and relief is slow in coming.

▶▶영작하시오.

한 결혼한 여자에 대한 그의 짝사랑은 그에게 견딜 수 없는 고통을 주었다.

notes :
*for her sake에서 sake는 이유를 뜻함
*consolation 위안
*anguish 고뇌
*even harder에서 even은 비교급을 강조
*relief 안도감

4. There was once a beggar who **had tried** many ways to get money. At last he thought he would pretend to be dumb. Now one day a gentleman who **had known** the beggar by sight **passed** by. He went up to the beggar and asked him suddenly: "How long have you been dumb?" The beggar was taken by surprise and quite forgot that he was 'dumb.' He answered quickly: "Oh, ever since I was born, sir."

▶▶Which best describes the tone of the above paragraph?

① informative ② sentimental ③ sarcastic
④ humorous ⑤ instructive

▶▶영작하시오.

나는 그 사람의 얼굴만 알고 있다.

notes :
*try many ways = 여러가지 방법을 써보다
*pretend to = ~인체 하다
*Now 그런데
*know ~ by sight = ~의 얼굴을 알고 있다
*ever since = ~한 이후로 죽

5. I once met a woman who, having been left with a fortune, said that she would never feel free till she **had gotten** rid of her property. Possessions, she maintained, made one a slave, and one became their servant and not their master.

▶▶Which does **not** correspond with the above paragraph?

① It seems that the woman inherited a large sum of money.

② The woman was very delighted to inherit a lot of money.

③ She was not as comfortable as she used to be after a fortune was handed down to her.

④ She thought that possessions only led to the restriction of one's freedom.

⑤ She did not want to be a slave to money.

▶▶영작하시오.

그는 돈문제로 그 차를 처분해야 했다.

notes :
*(화법을 바꾸면) said, "I will never feel free till I have gotten rid of my property."

We do **not** know the value of health **until** we lose it.
It will **not** be long **before** you get well.
I had **not** waited long **before** he came.

6. Worn out by anguish and exertion, I sank into a death-like slumber; and it was **not until** the following morning when the sun rose that I came to my senses.

notes :
*worn out = 지친
*exertion 노고
*slumber 잠
*come to one's senses = 제정신이 들다

▶▶The writer (　　) full possession of his senses (　　) when the sun rose the following morning.
[regained, recouped, received, often, after, only]

▶▶영작하시오.
의장이 나타나고 나서야 회의가 시작되었다.

7. It was **not** long **before** we again met by chance. We came face to face at a street corner in my neighborhood, and I was struck by a change in him.

notes :
*by chance = 우연히
*be struck by ~ = ~에 놀라다

▶▶When the writer (　　) across him soon again at a street corner in his neighborhood, he was surprised to find him a completely (　　) man.
[come, saw, came, crazy, calm, changed]

▶▶영작하시오.
머지않아 우리의 소원 대로 한국은 통일 될 것이다.

8. A silence fell suddenly between us which I somehow expected to be unbroken. But it **had not fallen** for more than a few seconds **when**, in the utter stillness, I distinctly heard rapid steps coming nearer and nearer along the street.

notes :
*A silence fell = 침묵이 흘렀다
*it had not fallen에서 it = the silence
*stillness 조용함
*distinctly 분명히

▶▶Which is most appropriate to describe the mood of the above passage?
① peaceful and calm
② noisy and disturbing
③ quiet and tense
④ scary and gruesome
⑤ compelling and thrilling

▶▶영작하시오.
꽤 걸어가고 나서야 나는 지갑이 도난당한 것을 알았다.

9. I had been taught in my home across the sea that thrift was one of the fundamentals in a successful life. My family had come from a land (the Netherlands) noted for its thrift; but we **had been** in the United States only a few days **before** the realization came home strongly to my father that they had brought their children to a land of waste.

notes :
*thrift 절약, 검소
*fundamentals 기본
*be noted for ~ = ~로 유명하다
*only a few = 불과 얼마 안되는
*come home to ~ = ~의 가슴에 뼈저리게 와 닿다

▶▶Which of the following is incorrect?

① The above paragraph seems to be a part of the writer's life story.

② The phrase 'across the sea' means 'across the Atlantic'.

③ The homeland of the writer was renowned for its frugal way of living.

④ The writer is thankful to his father for bringing him to the land of affluence.

⑤ The writer was in his childhood when his family immigrated to America, the land of opportunity.

▶▶영작하시오.

업계에서 그는 기업인수합병(M&A)에 대한 공격적인 추진력으로 유명하다.

I ran and ran, **until** I reached the station.

10. The more carefully nature has been studied, the more widely has order been found to prevail, while what seemed disorder has proved to be nothing more than complexity; **until**, at present, no one is as foolish as to believe that anything happens by chance, or that there are any real accidents which have no cause.

notes :
*order 질서
*prove = turn out
*nothing more than = only
*by chance 우연히

▶▶Which does **not** correspond with the above paragraph?

① On examination an apparent disorder may turn out to be a complicated order.

② Where there's smoke, there's fire.

③ All happenings in nature are subject to the law of cause and effect.

④ The writer accepts that some events happen accidentally.

⑤ These days everybody knows better than to believe that many things happen by accident without any cause.

▶▶영작하시오.

아무도 그런 거짓말을 믿을만큼 그렇게 어리석지는 않다.

● 장 문 독 해 ●

Warming-up

He comes from **God knows where**.
Spring came and flowers began to bloom, and with them **my heart**.
Spring changed to summer, **summer to** autumn, **autumn to** winter with its cold dreary days.
It wasn't **simply that** he didn't like it, it was **more that** he felt he was incapable of doing it.

1 The ditches were dry most of the year, but when they weren't dry, they were roaring. As the snows melted in the hills the ditches began to roar and from somewhere, God knows where, arrived frogs and turtles, water snakes and fish. In the spring of the year the water hurried, ⓐ and with it the heart, but as the fields changed from green to brown, the blossoms to fruit, the shy warmth to arrogant heat, the ditches slowed down and the heart grew lazy. The first water from the hills was cold, swift and frightening. ⓑ It was too cold and busy to invite the naked body of a boy. Alone, or in a group, a boy would stand on the bank of a ditch and watch the water for many minutes, and then, terribly challenged, fling off his clothes, make a running dive, come up gasping, and swim across to the other side. If the boy was the first of a group to dive, the others would soon follow, in order not to walk home in shame. It wasn't simply that the water was cold. It was more that it had no time for boys. ⓒ The springtime water was unfriendly as anything could be.

William Saroyan: *My Name Is Aram*

Notes

frogs ~ fish는 주어 / God knows where = Nobody knows where / the heart (hurried) / arrogant 교만한 / would는 과거의 습관 / terribly challenged = as he was terribly challenged / gasping 숨을 헐떡이는 / fling off 벗어 던지다 / as anything could be 무엇에도 못지 않게끔

Question

1. 본문의 ⓐ의 구체적 내용을 우리말로 쓰시오.

2. 본문의 밑줄친 ⓑ를 다음과 같이 바꾸어 쓸 때, 빈칸에 가장 적절한 단어를 골라 쓰시오.

It was so cold and (   ) that a boy couldn't (   ) in it.

[deep, swift, snowy, stand, cross, swim]

3. Which does the underlined sentence ⓒ imply?
   ① Spring came and brought many hibernating animals to children swimming in the water.
   ② Due to a heap of things which had to be done in spring, most children had no time to swim in the water.
   ③ As the springtime water was most unfriendly to the boys, they didn't welcome spring but eagerly waited for summer to come.
   ④ The ditches were too narrow and shallow for the boys to swim in.
   ⑤ The cold and rapid flows in the ditches scared the boys and made them hesitate to dive in the ditches.

4. Which does **not** correspond with the passage?
   ① The springtime water roaring in the ditches originated from the snow covering the hills.
   ② Spring came filling the ditches with fresh water, alive with many creatures.
   ③ As it grew hotter and the flows in the ditches slowed down, the boys would swim and catch fish in them.
   ④ The reason why the boys hesitated to jump into the stream was that the water was extremely cold and the flow of water too swift.
   ⑤ The boys considered those who wouldn't dive into the cold ditches as cowards.

Production

(1) 강물은 소년들이 헤엄치기에는 너무나 차가웠다.
(2) 첫 기차 시간에 늦지 않으려고 나는 일찍 일어났다.
(3) 그는 제일 먼저 출근하고, 제일 늦게 퇴근했다.

● 장 문 독 해 ●

Warming-up

He is **no more** fit to be a priest **than** I am.
Life is, **at best**, a sea of trouble.
The man, **in short**, is not to be trusted.
I was writing of something **that** I did not know about.
He is poor — so much **so** that he can hardly make ends meet.
How is **it** in the market?

2 My plan was clear, concise, and reasonable, I think. For many years I have traveled in many parts of the world. In America I live in New York, or dip into Chicago or San Francisco. But New York is no more America than Paris is France or London is England. Thus I discovered that I did not know my own country. I, an American writer writing about America, was working from memory, and ⓐ the memory is at best a faulty, warpy reservoir. I had not heard the speech of America, smelled the grass and trees and sewage, seen its hills and water, its color and quality of light. I knew the changes only from books and newspapers. But more than this, I had not felt the country for twenty-five years. In short, I was writing of something that I did not know about, and it seems to me that in a so-called writer ⓑ this is criminal. My memories were distorted by twenty-five intervening years. So it was that I determined to look again, to try to rediscover this big country.

***John Steinbeck:** Travels with Charley*

Notes

dip into ~을 살짝 들여다 보다; 잠깐 들르다 / at best 잘 해야 / warpy 비뚤어진 / reservoir 저수지 / sewage 하수 오물 / in short 간단히 말해, 요컨대 / criminal 범죄의 / distort 왜곡시키다 / intervening 사이에 끼인 / So it was that ~ = 사정은 이상과 같은 것이어서 ~

Question

1. 본문의 밑줄친 부분 ⓐ를 다음과 같이 바꾸어 쓸 때, 빈칸에 가장 적절한 단어끼리 짝지어진 것은?

the memory is at best a(n) (   ), (   ) accumulation of knowledge

① flawed — credible ② accurate — momentous
③ inadequate — disinterested ④ imperfect — distorted
⑤ deficient — significant

2. 밑줄친 ⓑthis의 구체적 내용을 30자 내외의 우리말로 쓰시오.

3. Which does **not** correspond with the passage?
① Though New York is a typical city, it can't represent every characteristic of America.
② The writer feels that writing something only by relying on his faulty memory can be regarded as a criminal act.
③ The writer thinks highly of direct experience rather than established knowledge.
④ Because one's memory is accumulated throughout one's life, it is an important reliable source from which one can derive necessary materials for writing.
⑤ The writer decided to rediscover America because he realized that if he wanted to write about it he had to experience all of it by himself instead of wholly relying on his memory.

4. Which is **not** suitable to describe the writer of the passage?
① He regrets having lived isolated from the real America for twenty-five years.
② He was not confident in the accuracy of his memory.
③ He realized that books and newspapers were very helpful to his writing.
④ He was eager to rediscover all aspects of his country.
⑤ He was conscious of his lack of knowledge about his nation.

Production

(1) 네가 미치지 않은 것처럼 나도 미치지 않았다.
(2) 간단히 말해, 인간은 태어나서 고생하다 죽는다.
(3) 당신은 이 문제에 별로 관심이 없는 것처럼 내게는 보인다.
(4) 여름 휴가를 어디에서 보낼 것인지, 마음이 섰습니까?

실력체크 I

1 다음 글을 읽고 아래 물음에 답하시오.

notes :
struggle 애쓰다, 고투하다 / a flat tire 펑크난 타이어 / interpret 해석하다 / extremely 지극히 / "Can't you see I have (got a flat tire), you dumb ox?" / dumb 벙어리의, 바보의 / in a short while 얼마 안 가 / similar 비슷한 / intelligent 지적인, 총명한 / intelligible 이해할 수 있는 / surface 표면적인

> Let us suppose that we are on the roadside struggling with a flat tire. A not-very-bright-looking but friendly youth comes up and asks, "Got a flat tire?" If we insist on interpreting his words literally, we will regard this as an extremely silly question and our answer may be, "Can't you see I have, you dumb ox?" If we pay no attention to ⓐ what the words say, however, and understand ⓑ his meaning, we will return his gesture of friendly interest by showing equal friendliness, and in a short while he may be helping us to change the tire. In a similar way, many situations in life demand that we pay no attention to what the words say, since the meaning may often be a great deal more intelligent and intelligible than the surface sense of the words themselves.

(1) ⓐ와 같은 뜻을 나타내는 부분을 본문 속에서 골라라.

(2) ⓑ의 내용을 구체적으로 다른 영어로 써라.

2 다음 글을 읽고 아래 질문에 답하여라.

notes :
particular 특정한 / environment 환경 / reflect 반영하다 / distinctive feature 현저한 특징 / emphasis 강조 / the masses 대중 / intellectuals 지식인 / informed 지식이 있는 / electorate 선거민 / kindergarten 유치원 / regardless of ~에 상관없이

> The American educational system, like that of any other country, has grown up to meet the needs of the particular environment in which it developed, and it reflects the history of the country. Thus it differs somewhat from the systems of other countries. Perhaps its most distinctive feature is its emphasis on the education of the masses rather than on the education of the intellectuals. The philosophy of the American educational system is that a democracy depends on a fully informed electorate, and that therefore each citizen should receive the best education that it is possible for him to receive. As a result, in America most children in the same community attend school together from kindergarten through high school regardless of differences in their intellectual ability or in family background.

(1) 미국 교육의 가장 두드러진 특징은 무엇인가?

(2) 미국 교육의 특징이 나타나는 예를 들어라.

3 필자는 밑줄 친 부분에서 서술하고 있는 내용을, 아버지에 대해서는 구체적으로 어떻게 말하고 있는가?

> She was a largish woman, a bit taller than Father, with hair a good deal fairer than his and had a tendency to wear black dresses. But except on Sundays I never remember her without an apron. It would be an exaggeration, but not a very big one, to say that I never remember her when she wasn't cooking. <u>When you look back over a long period you seem to see human beings always fixed in some special place and some characteristic attitude. It seems to you that they were always doing exactly the same thing</u>. Well, just as when I think of Father I remember him always behind the counter, his hair covered with flour, adding up figures with a stump of pencil which he moistens between his lips, and just as I remember Uncle Ezekiel, with his ghostly white whiskers, straightening himself out and slapping his leather apron, so when I think of Mother I remember her at the kitchen table, with her forearms covered with flour, rolling out a lump of dough.

notes :
fair = blond 금발의 / tendency 경향 / exaggeration 과장 / attitude 태도 / figure 숫자 / stump 연필 몽당이 / moisten 적시다 / whiskers 구레나룻 / straighten 똑바로 하다 / forearm 팔뚝 / dough 가루반죽 / lump 덩어리

4 다음 글의 제목으로 적당한 것을 골라라.

> Fear and its companion pain are two of the most useful things that men and animals possess, if they are properly used. If fire did not hurt when it burnt, children would play with it until their hands were burnt away. Similarly, if pain existed but fear did not, a child would burn itself again and again, because fear would not warn it to keep away from the fire that had burnt it before. A really fearless soldier — and some do exist — is not a good soldier, because he is soon killed; and a dead soldier is of no use to his army. Fear and pain are therefore two guards without which men and animals might soon die out.

notes :
possess 소유하다 / similarly 마찬가지로 / exist 존재하다 (existence 존재) / keep away 멀리하다 / of no use = useless / die out 사멸하다

① Children and Fear
② A Fearless Soldier and a Dead Soldier
③ The Evil of Fear and Pain
④ The Value of Fear and Pain
⑤ A Fearless Soldier Is Brave

실 력 체 크 Ⅱ

A. 적당한 단어로 공란을 메워라.

(1) The great fire _____ many people homeless in the city.

(2) Efforts were _____ to remedy the state of affairs.

(3) They seem to quarrel _____ the clock.

(4) He will come _____ for a large fortune when his uncle dies.

(5) The concert came _____ well as planned.

B. 다음 대화의 내용을 직접화법이 들어가지 않는 영문(60~70어)으로 다시 써라.

▶ Dialogue on an Airplane Flight from New York to Seoul.

Mr. Brown : This is my fourth trip to Seoul. How about you?

Mr. Baker : I travel to Korea frequently for my business.

Mr. Brown : You sound like a New Yorker. Do you live in New York?

Mr. Baker : Yes, I do. I'm a native New Yorker. I live in the Chelsea district of Manhattan.

Mr. Brown : Oh, really? I live in Chelsea, too. But New York is a funny place. I don't know my next-door neighbor.

Mr. Baker : I live on West Twenty-first Street.

Mr. Brown : I do, too. I live on West Twenty-first Street, too.

Mr. Baker : I live at number 12.

Mr. Brown : I live at number 14. You're my neighbor, My name's Brown.

Mr. Baker : My name's Baker. How do you do?

Mr. Brown : How do you do? Pleased to meet you.

C. 다음 대답이 나올 의문문을 만들되, ( ) 안에 있는 낱말들을 써라.

(1) ___(find out)___? By my long observation and experiment.

(2) ___(expect, go)___? I expect John to go there.

(3) ___(pick up)___? In my dictionary.

(4) ___(Europe, America)___? By way of America.

Answer: A. (1) left (2) made (3) around (4) in (5) off

B. In an airplane from New York to Seoul, Mr. Brown and Mr. Baker met. At first, they thought they were complete strangers to each other. But in the course of their conversation, they came to realize they were next-door neighbors in Chelsea, New York. From this dialogue we understand that New York is a very funny place where people do not know even their immediate neighbor.

C. (1) How did you find out the fact? (2) Who do you expect to go there? (3) Where did you pick up the word? (4) Are you going there by way of Europe or America?

D. (　　　) 안에서 알맞은 것을 골라라.

(1) I (appreciate, thank, welcome) your gift very much.
(2) Would you please (afford, spare, permit) me a few moments?
(3) I am sorry for the trouble I've (caused, inflicted, set) you.
(4) You are (spoken, wanted, talked) on the telephone.
(5) I think I'll (commit, appoint, leave) everything to your discretion.
(6) We're (regarded, imagined, supposed) to attend the meeting tomorrow.
(7) I'm expecting him (at any moment, just now, on the spot).
(8) Excuse me for asking you at such short (time, notice, advance).
(9) Be sure to make (an agreement, a promise, an appointment) before you call on him.

E. 두 사람의 대화가 완성되도록 공란을 적당한 낱말로 채워라.

(1) A: There's only one piece of cake ______.
B: May I have it, please?
A: You divide it with your sister.
B: ______ shall I divide it?
A: You can cut it any way you want, but _____ Mary have a first choice.
(2) A: Can I borrow your vacuum cleaner? Mine's out of order again.
B: Be my ______.
(3) A: This is a secret. Never tell anyone, especially Sue.
She has a big ______.
B: Really?
(4) A: You paid 100 dollars for that necktie? That's highway ______!
B: You're right. Come to think of it, I got ripped ______.

F. 다음 글의 이탤릭체 단어를 괄호속의 단어로 대치하여 다시 쓰시오.

(1) The President *gave* them large privileges in return for their services. (bestow)
(2) I was *addressed* by a lady on the street. (speak)
(3) Nature *gave* him literary talent. (endow)
(4) The philosopher *gave* them all his knowledge. (impart)
(5) He *attained* his success through industry. (owe)

Answer: D. (1) appreciate (2) spare (3) caused (4) wanted (5) leave (6) supposed (7) at any moment (8) notice (9) an appointment
E. (1) left, How, let (2) guest (3) mouth (4) robbery, off
F. (1) bestowed large privileges on them (2) spoken to (3) endowed him with (4) imparted all his knowledge to them (5) owed his success to industry

어 휘 · 발 음

A. 공란의 단어를 완성하여라.

(1) It's a matter of life and *d*______.

(2) Everything that happens has cause and *e*______.

(3) The ebb and the *f*______ of the tides result from the attraction of the moon.

(4) Most plants don't *s*______ become big, but they grow gradually.

(5) He replied in the negative, but she in the *a*______.

(6) After I've done something foolish or wrong, I always *r*______ it.

(7) The lecture hall was crowded, although *a*______ was not compulsory.

(8) In order to cut well, a knife must be *s*______.

(9) The smooth stretch of grass in front of a house is called a *l*______.

B. 공란에 다음 단어의 올바른 어형을 써 넣어라. (단, 1회만 쓸 것)

smile, sneer, grin, cheer, giggle, chuckle

(1) She ______ graciously as she passed through the ______ crowds.

(2) The winner ______ broadly at his girlfriend after the game.

(3) The arrogant celebrity ______ at the man who asked for an autograph.

(4) The schoolchildren ______ when the headmaster tripped over his gown as he was mounting the school platform.

(5) The reader, obviously finding the book very amusing, sat quietly ______ to himself.

C. 괄호 속의 단어를 적당한 어형으로 고쳐라.

(1) There is a (sense) difference between red and pink.

(2) The eye is (sense) to light.

(3) There is no jewel (compare) to diamond.

(4) In order to (broad) his knowledge, he went to America.

(5) An (impress) person is easily impressed by an impressive scene.

(6) He is the most (imagine) architect I have ever met.

(7) I wish to employ a (rely) man to help me with my work.

(8) A good command of English is (essence) to the position.

Answer: A. (1) death (2) effect (3) flow (4) suddenly (5) affirmative (6) regret (7) attendance (8) sharpened (9) lawn
B. (1) smiled, cheering (2) grinned (3) sneered (4) giggled (5) chuckling
C. (1) sensible (2) sensitive (3) comparable (4) broaden (5) impressionable (6) imaginative (7) reliable (8) essential

발음에 주의할 단어

ache	[eik]
allow	[əláu]
ancient	[éinʃənt]
arrow	[ǽrou]
beard	[biərd]
blood	[blʌd]
bomber	[bάmər]
bosom	[búzəm]
bough	[bau]
bowl	[boul]
breath	[breθ]
breathe	[briːð]
brooch	[broutʃ, bruːtʃ]
brow	[brau]
bury	[béri]
career	[kəríər]
castle	[kǽsl]
ceiling	[síːliŋ]
cleanse	[klenz]
colonel	[kə́ːnl]
comb	[koum]
comfort	[kʌ́mfərt]
corps	[kɔ́ər, kɔ́ərz]
cough	[kɔːf]
cousin	[kʌ́zn]
crow	[krou]
debt	[det]
decease	[disíːs]
depot	[dépou]
dessert	[dizə́ːrt]
disease	[dizíːz]
draught	[drǽft]
drought	[draut]
drown	[draun]
exhibit	[igzíbit]
fatigue	[fətíːg]
flood	[flʌd]
flour	[fláuər]
food	[fuːd]
foot	[fut]
fowl	[faul]
gauge	[geidʒ]
globe	[gloub]
glove	[glʌv]
heart	[hɑːrt]
height	[hait]
heir	[ɛər]
houses	[háuziz]
indict	[indáit]
iron	[áiərn]
island	[áilənd]
leisure	[léʒər]
leopard	[lépərd]
loose	[luːs]
lose	[luːz]
meadow	[médou]
meant	[ment]
measure	[méʒər]
mustache	[məstǽ(ː)ʃ]
naked	[néikid]
oven	[ʌ́vn]
owl	[aul]
pear	[pɛər]
pleasure	[pléʒər]
plough	[plau]
pour	[pɔːr]
prove	[pruːv]
quay	[kiː]
receipt	[risíːt]
route	[ruːt]
said	[sed]
says	[sez]
seize	[siːz]
sew	[sou]
shepherd	[ʃépərd]
smooth	[smuːð]
soup	[suːp]
sour	[sáuər]
southern	[sʌ́ðərn]
steak	[steik]
stomach	[stʌ́mək]
subtle	[sʌ́tl]
sweat	[swet]
sword	[sɔːrd]
Thames	[temz]
thorough	[θʌ́rə]
tomb	[tuːm]
tongue	[tʌŋ]
tough	[tʌf]
tour	[tuər]
vague	[veig]
victual	[vítl]
walk	[wɔːk]
warm	[wɔːrm]
weapon	[wépən]
wicked	[wíkid]
women	[wímin]
wood	[wud]
work	[wəːrk]
worm	[wəːrm]
worthy	[wə́ːrði]
wound	[wuːnd]

숙 어

(1) **at least** (=not less than ; at any rate) 적어도 ; 어쨌든
☞ It will cost *at least* ten dollars.
The hotel was noisy and dirty, but *at least* it was cheap.

(2) **at length** (=at last ; in detail) 드디어 ; 상세하게
☞ *At length* he came back. They spoke *at length* about the situation.

(3) **at odds with** (=on bad terms with) ~와 불화관계인
☞ They're constantly *at odds with* each other.

(4) **at random** (=without aim) 함부로, 닥치는 대로
☞ The gunman walked into the crowded hall and fired *at random*.

(5) **at one's wits' (wit's) end** (=not knowing what to say *or* do) 어찌할 바를 몰라
☞ Her son keeps getting into trouble, and she is *at her wits' end* about what to do.

(6) **at the mercy of** (=wholly in the power of) ~에 좌우되어
☞ The hostage's life was *at the mercy of* the cruel terrorists.

(7) **attend to** (=take care of, see to) 처리하다
☞ One secretary *attends to* all of the paperwork in my office.

(8) **attribute … to ~** (=ascribe … to ~) …을 ~의 탓으로 돌리다
☞ He *attributed* his success *to* his talent and hard work.

(9) **be absorbed in** (=be engrossed[immersed] in) ~에 열중하다
☞ I *was absorbed in* a computer game and didn't hear you call.

(10) **be anxious about** (=be uneasy about) 근심하다
be anxious to+동사=be anxious for+명사 (=be eager for) 갈망하다
☞ People *are* naturally *anxious about* their health.
I'*m anxious to* be a lawyer. We'*re* all *anxious for* peace.

(11) **be apt to** (=be liable to, be likely to) ~하기 쉽다, ~할 것 같다
☞ These shoes *are apt to* slip on wet ground.

(12) **be bound to+동사** (=be certain to) 반드시 ~하다
be bound for+명사 (=be going in a certain direction) ~으로 향하다
☞ He lacks competitive spirit, so he *is bound to* lose.
Their first meeting was on a plane which *was bound for* Moscow.

(13) **be capable of** (=be able to) ~할 능력이 있다
☞ Do you think he *is capable of* lifting 200 pounds?

(14) **be due to+명사** (=be caused by) ~에 기인하다
be due to+동사 (=be expected to) ~할 예정이다
due to (=owing to) ~ 때문에
☞ The accident *was due to* his careless driving.
The President *is due to* make a speech on television this evening.
He had no choice but to quit his job *due to* bad health.

(15) **be forced to** (=be obliged to, be compelled to) ~하지 않을 수 없다
☞ We *were* all *forced to* comply with his request.

(16) **be in charge of** (=be responsible for) ~을 책임지다
☞ Officer John Cooper will *be in charge of* this investigation.

(17) **be in the way** (=cause inconvenience) ~에 방해되다
☞ I can't get past; that suitcase *is in the way*.

(18) **be worse off** (=be poor) 궁핍하다
be well off (=be rich) 유복하다
☞ He seems to *be worse off* these days.
He used to be as poor as could be, but he *is well off* now.

Exercise

▶▶ 주어진 단어들을 포함한 글을 지어라. 필요하면 어형을 변화시켜라.

1. describe / village / length
2. boat / mercy / waves
3. attend / problem / myself
4. attribute / success / luck
5. soon / absorbed / book
6. he / anxious / safety
7. apt / wasteful / time
8. bound / pass / test
9. success / due / hard
10. help / simply / in / way

3. 부 정 사(Infinitive)

기본 문법 설명

A. 부정사의 종류	(1) **To obey** the law is everyone's duty. (2) He is not a man **to break** his promise. (3) We stopped **to take** a rest. (4) **To tell the truth**, I don't like your conduct.
B. 명사적 부정사	(1) **To put** solar energy to use is still expensive. (=**It** is still expensive **to put** solar energy to use.) (2) My New Year's resolution is **to quit** smoking. (3) ⓐ We want **to go** to Europe for a vacation. ⓑ I've found **it** difficult **to believe** him. (4) The question is **how to carry** out the plan.
C. 형용사적 부정사	(1) He was the first man **to reach** the South Pole. (2) There are many sights **to see** here. (3) I have no house **to live in**. (4) He designated the place where we *were* **to meet**.
D. 부사적 부정사	(1) They're selling it **to raise** money for crippled children. (2) One morning he awoke **to find** himself famous. (3) She was hurt **to find** that no one admired her performance. (4) They must be crazy **to let** the child drive their car. (5) I would be happy **to date** that beautiful girl. (6) ⓐ My boss is *slow* **to make** up his mind. ⓑ You are old *enough* **to support** yourself.
E. 독립부정사	**To do him justice**, he's a fairly thorough teacher. I've known him for years; he's my friend, **so to speak**.

A. 부정사의 종류

(1) 명사적 용법 [주어로 쓰였음]
(2) 형용사적 용법 [명사를 수식했음]
(3) 부사적 용법 [동사를 수식했음]
(4) 독립부정사 [문장 전체를 수식했음]

B. 명사적 부정사

(1) **주어**의 역할
주어로서 부정사가 문두에 오는 일은 드물며, 그 대신 형식주어 **It**을 쓴다.
(태양열을 이용하는 것은 아직도 비싸다.)
(2) **보어**의 역할
(3) **목적어**의 역할
ⓐ to go는 want의 목적어이다.
ⓑ it는 가목적어, to believe가 진목적어
(4) **「의문사+to부정사」=명사구**
I don't know *what to do.*
I don't know *where to go.*
I don't know *when to do* it.
I don't know *who(m) to go* with.

C. 형용사적 부정사

(1) (그는 남극에 도착한 최초의 인간이었다.)
수식당하는 명사가 부정사의 의미상의 주어가 될 경우
(2) (여기는 구경할 만한 곳이 많다.)
수식당하는 명사가 부정사의 의미상의 목적어가 될 경우
(3) **부정사와 관계대명사**
(나는 살 집이 없다.)
「전치사+관계대명사+to부정사」에서 관계대명사가 빠지면, 전치사는 뒤에 온다.
I have no house in which to live.
(= I have no house to live in.)
Give me a chair to sit on.
(= Give me a chair on which to sit.)
(4) **「Be+to」의 용법 (주격보어)**
(그는 우리들이 만나기로 되어있는 장소를 지정했다.)
① **예정** : 「~하기로 되어 있다」
We *are to* arrive there at five.
② **의무** : 「~하여야 한다」
You *are to* finish it by six.
③ **운명** : 「~할 운명이다」
He *was* never *to* see his home again.
④ **가능** : 「~할 수 있다」
No one *was to* be seen on the street.
(= No one *could* be seen on the street.)
⑤ **의도** : 「~하려면」 (= intend to)
If you *are to* succeed, you must work hard.(성공하려면 열심히 일해야 한다.)

D. 부사적 부정사

(1) **목적** : 「~하기 위하여」
to raise money = in order [so as] to raise money
(2) **결과** : 「~해서 …하다」
(어느 날 아침 눈을 떠 보니, 그는 자기가 유명해진 것을 알았다.)
He grew up *to be* a great poet.
He went to Africa *never to return.*
The frog tried several times, *only to fail.*
He got up *so early as to* be on time for the first plane. (so ~ as to = so ~ that)
(3) **원인** : 「~하니」 (감정의 원인)
He was pleased *to hear* it.
I am sorry *to give* you so much trouble.
(4) **이유·판단의 근거** :
「~을 보니」, 「~을 하다니」
He was foolish *to agree* to the proposal.
(5) **조건** : 「만일 ~이면」
= I would be happy *if I could date* that beautiful girl.
You'll do well *to speak* more slowly.
(6) **형용사·부사 수식**
He is hard *to please.*
(그는 비위맞추기가 힘들다.)

E. 독립부정사

to do one justice = 공정히 말해
so to speak = 말하자면
to begin with = 우선
strange to say = 이상한 이야기지만
to make a long story short = 간단히 말해
to be sure = 확실히
to make matters worse = 설상가상으로
not to speak of ~ = ~은 말할 것도 없이
to be frank (with you) = 솔직히 말해서

F. 보어부정사	(1) ⓐ *She* seems **to feel** nauseous from the boat ride. ⓑ *He* happened **to be** out that day. (2) ⓐ He told *me* **not to do** so. ⓑ I believe *him* **to be** a winner in the next election.
G. 완료부정사	(1) ⓐ He seems **to yearn** for his lost popularity. ⓑ He seems **to have yearned** for his lost popularity. (2) ⓐ I intended **to come** earlier. ⓑ I intended **to have come** earlier.
H. 부정사의 의미상 주어	(1) ⓐ I expect **to travel** a lot this year. ⓑ I expect *him* **to travel** a lot this year. (2) ⓐ It is impossible **for you to solve** the question. I count **on you to help** me with this work. ⓑ It is time **for you to go** to bed. ⓒ I work hard **for my family to live** in comfort. (3) It is not easy **to speak** several languages fluently. (4) It was a bit *careless* **of her to break** two glasses.
I. 원형부정사	(1) At eight o'clock Jane *heard* him **go** out. (2) What *makes* you **think** so? (3) We *cannot but* **feel** disgusted with his rudeness. (4) He *did nothing but* **laugh** without saying a word. (5) You *had better* **consult** a doctor.
J. 기 타	(1) This problem is **too** important for me alone **to handle**. (2) This book is easy **enough** for me **to read**. (3) I was told **not to trust** what I read in the newspapers. (4) You may go if you want **to**. (5) **To think** that such a little boy should have done it! (6) You are **to blame** for it.

F. 보어부정사

(1) **주격보어** : 주어가 부정사의 의미상 주어가 된다. (2형식)

ⓐ = It seems that *she* feels ~.

ⓑ = It happened that *he* was out ~.

[happen to = 우연히 ~하다]

(2) **목적격보어** : 부정사의 의미상 주어는 목적어가 된다. (5형식)

ⓐ = He told me (that) *I* should not do so.

ⓑ = I believe that *he* will be ~.

<*cf.*> *He* promised me *to do* so. (4형식)

He asked *me to do* so. (5형식)

G. 완료부정사

(1) ⓐ **단순부정사**일 때 : 부정사의 시제는 본동사와 동일 시제 또는 나중 시제이다.

= It *seems* that he yearns for his lost popularity.

He is sure *to succeed*.

= I'm sure that he *will* succeed.

ⓑ **완료부정사**일 때 : 부정사의 시제는 본동사보다 앞선다.

= It seems that he *yearned* (혹은 *has yearned*) ~.

* He seemed to yearn for his lost popularity.

= It *seemed* that he *yearned* ~.

* He seemed to have yearned for his lost popularity.

= It *seemed* that he *had yearned* ~.

(2) (난 더 일찍 오려고 했다.)

(난 더 일찍 오려고 했으나 못 왔다.)

wished, hoped, intended, expected, was, were 등의 다음에 완료부정사가 오면 이루지 못한 사실을 나타낸다.

소망의 동사가 포함된 과거완료 다음에 단순부정사를 써도 이루지 못한 사실을 나타낼 수 있다.

I *had intended* **to come** here earlier.

H. 부정사의 의미상 주어

부정사의 의미상 주어는 문장 중의 한 말이 겸용할 경우와, 특히 명시할 경우, 그리고 생략될 경우가 있다.

(1) ⓐ 의미상 주어가 문장의 **주어**와 일치

= I expect that I will travel a lot this year.

ⓑ 의미상 주어가 **목적어**와 일치

= I expect that he will travel a lot this year.

(2) 「**for+목적격+to 부정사**」로 to 부정사의 의미상 주어를 나타낸다. * 동사, 형용사가 관용구로서 for 아닌 다른 전치사를 수반할 때 의미상 주어를 유도하기 위해 「for+목적격」의 for를 쓸 필요는 없다.

I rely *on you to be* discreet.

I am not ashamed *of myself to talk so*.

(3) 부정사의 의미상 주어가 「**일반인**」일 때는 명시하지 않는다.

(4) 「**of+목적어+부정사**」로 부정사의 의미상 주어를 나타낸다. 이 문형에는 careful, careless, good, foolish, honest, kind, nice, silly, rude 등의 사람의 성질을 나타내는 형용사가 쓰인다.

I. 원형부정사

(1) 지각동사 뒤에는 원형부정사가 온다.

(2) 사역동사 뒤에는 원형부정사가 온다.

= Why do you think so?

Please help me (*to*) *do* it.

(3) cannot but 원형 = ~하지 않을 수 없다

(4) do nothing but 원형 = ~하기만 한다

(5) had better 원형 = ~해야 한다

J. 기타

(1) **too ~ to**

= This problem is so important *that* I alone *can't* handle **it**.

(2) **enough to**

= This book is so easy *that* I *can* read **it**.

(3) **부정사의 부정** : 부정어(not, never)를 부정사 앞에 놓는다.

You had better *not be* idle.

(4) **대부정사**(代不定詞) : 부정사의 반복을 피하기 위해 **to**만 쓰는 것.

= ~ if you want to (*go*). go의 생략

(5) **감탄문을 만드는 부정사**

(6) **부정사의 태**(態) : 부정사 중에는 능동형으로 수동태의 의미를 나타내는 것이 있다.

= You are *to be blamed* for it.

문 법 · 작 문

A. 틀린 것을 고쳐라.

(1) The actress let the reporters to ask her questions.
(2) I'd better not to waste any more of your time.
(3) He's not enough mature to be given so much responsibility.
(4) I was made enter the room by myself.
(5) I must have someone to carry the box for me.
(6) I cannot but to feel sorry for his failure.
(7) Company rules forbade us smoke in the factory.
(8) Are all of us necessary to be present at the meeting this afternoon?
(9) She did nothing but to cry all day long.
(10) Let it be not done.
(11) Could I get you do me a small favor?
(12) I've found advantageous to combine my business trip with my vacation.
(13) He is reported to be killed in the war.
(14) I expect seeing him on Monday.
(15) I did not know to whom ask the questions of.
(16) She allowed herself to kiss by him.
(17) He always enjoys to read a detective story.
(18) You should have known better than believe such a foolish thing.

B. 다음 각 항의 문장의 뜻의 차이를 말하여라.

(1) She did not try to smile.
She tried not to smile.
(2) She has no one to talk to in the city.
She has no one to talk to her in the city.
(3) Do you have anything to write?
Do you have anything to write with?
Do you have anything to write on?
(4) There is nothing to see.
There is nothing to be seen.
(5) I hoped to see him again.
I hoped to have seen him again.

C. 다음 (1)~(6)의 부정사의 용법과 같은 용법을 ⓐ~ⓔ에서 골라라.

ⓐ To err is human, to forgive divine.

ⓑ The boy grew up to be a great musician.

ⓒ You have no need to go there.

ⓓ To be frank, John, you're not suitable for the job.

ⓔ He must be foolish to behave like that.

(1) He is not a man to do things by halves.

(2) He left his home, never to return.

(3) What a good scholar he must be to write such a splendid book!

(4) I know what it is to be in debt.

(5) To make matters worse, it grew dark.

(6) The noise grew and grew to fill the whole building.

D. 공란에 적당한 말을 써 넣어라.

(1) "Would you like to have dinner with me tonight?"
"I'd like (　　　), but I'm sorry I have a previous engagement."

(2) This situation is (　　　) tough for her alone to cope with.

(3) He was the first (　　　) come and the last (　　　) leave the office.

(4) The hot weather is partly (　　　) blame for the water shortage.

(5) I'm sorry not to (　　　) answered your letter sooner.

E. 공란을 메워, 위 문장과 뜻이 같아지게 하여라.

(1) In the first place, you must call on her at her house.
To begin (　　　), you must call on her at her house.

(2) You were foolish to agree to his proposal.
It was foolish (　　　) (　　　) to agree to his proposal.

(3) It seems comfortable to sleep in this bed.
This bed seems comfortable (　　　) sleep (　　　).

(4) It is likely that our team will win the soccer game.
Our team is (　　　) (　　　) win the soccer game.

(5) I stepped aside so that the fat lady could pass.
I stepped aside (　　　) the fat lady (　　　) pass.

(6) He is not too old to learn.
He is (　　　) so old that he can (　　　) learn.

F. 다음 각 문장을 부정사를 사용해서 단문(單文)으로 바꾸어라.

(1) It seems that she was beautiful in her day.
(2) Do you promise that you'll never repeat what I've just said?
(3) I expected that you would be promoted to the new position.
(4) I hoped that I would finish the work by six, but I could not do so.
(5) It is natural that you should get angry.
(6) It is believed that he is living a comfortable life.
(7) I firmly believed that he had been innocent of the crime.
(8) I hurried to the station lest I should be late for the train.
(9) It is desirable that the examination results be made public by then.
(10) I regret that I must inform you of this sad news.
(11) The state-of-the-art equipment was so expensive that we couldn't buy it.
(12) He left Korea and never returned.
(13) He tried, but only failed.
(14) Actors are usually the kind of people who love being the center of attention.
(15) She had no money that she could send to her son.
(16) They were surprised when they saw such beautiful scenery.
(17) Tom, it's time you should wash up and go to bed.
(18) She had no friend with whom she could talk about the matter.
(19) I worked hard but could not carry out my plan.
(20) I would be glad if I had the chance to meet her face-to-face.
(21) To my astonishment, I found him bankrupt.
(22) The colonel ordered that all his officers should attend the parade.
(23) It happened that I sat beside her in the theater.

G. 다음 각 문장을 복문(複文)으로 고쳐 써라.

(1) Do you wish me to make a complaint about it?
(2) He believes me to have been in the wrong.
(3) I got to the station too late to catch the train.
(4) He is tall enough to touch the ceiling.
(5) His bravery was such as to startle the world.
(6) What is the first thing to be done?
(7) The commander ordered the deserter to be shot.
(8) We're sure to see you again before your departure.

H. 괄호 안의 동사의 형태를 바로 잡아라.

(1) Can you manage (finish) packing those parcels by yourself?

(2) It would be better (persuade) him (work) rather than to force him.

(3) It's a pity you failed to see the film. You ought to (see) it; it was so wonderful.

(4) He felt himself (lift) up.

(5) The rain caused the weeds (grow) fast.

(6) She likes to have the house (look) clean and tidy.

(7) I never hear her (praise), and there are few (love) her.

(8) You must take it upon yourself (get) through with the work.

(9) (Think) my own brother has betrayed me!

(10) We'll have the house (paint) green.

(11) Nothing was to (see) but water.

I. Translate the following into English:

(1) 동석하지 않은 사람을 험담하는 것은 매우 나쁜 버릇이다.

(2) 이 지역에는 방문할 곳이 많다.

(3) 이렇게 외로운 곳에 당신을 오래 기다리게 하여 미안합니다.

(4) 김 박사가 오늘 저녁 8시에 라디오를 통해서 강연하기로 되어 있다.

(5) 가치없는 책을 많이 읽느니보다 몇 권의 좋은 책을 주의깊게 읽어야 한다.

(6) 건강을 유지하기 위해, 매일 적어도 한 시간씩 걷도록 당신에게 권합니다.

(7) 잃어버린 것으로 포기했던 책을 찾아서 매우 기뻤다.

(8) 어떤 일을 잘 하기 위해서는, 네가 하는 일에 진실로 흥미를 가져야 한다.

(9) 영어는 사실상 세계어다. 영어를 읽고 쓰고 이야기할 수 있는 것이 우리에게 필요하다.

(10) 나는 그에게 당신 신을 닦도록 하겠습니다.

'Friendship'이라는 제목으로 80어 내외의 글을 지어라.

● 단 문 독 해 ●

To know oneself is difficult.
I have nothing **to do**.
He left his home **never to return**.
Strange to say, the door opened by itself.

1. No one will dispute the fact that kindness is a fine virtue. **To say** a person is kind is to say that he is gentle, considerate, and charitable. He puts the comfort of others before his own convenience. In looking back over the people we have known and loved, we can all remember certain men and women who were outstanding for their kindness.

notes :
*dispute=argue against
*charitable 자비로운
*In looking back ~ = When we look back ~

▶▶Which of the following can describe the underlined word, He?
① an egotist ② an altruist
③ an optimist ④ a pessimist
⑤ a self-centered man

▶▶영작하시오.
학창 시절을 회상해 볼 때 나는 좀 난폭하고 고집이 세었던 것 같다.

2. It is perhaps true to say that memory is the faculty of poetry, because imagination itself is an exercise of memory. There is nothing we imagine which we do not already know. And our ability **to imagine** is our ability **to remember** what we have already once experienced and **to apply** it to some different situation.

notes :
* which we do not already know에서 which의 선행사는 nothing
* apply A to B = A를 B에 적용하다

▶▶윗글의 내용에 맞지 않는 것을 골라라.
① Poetry is also a product of memory.
② Imagination itself is a product of memory.
③ Imagination is the ability to create something new from nothing at all.
④ Memory is the source of all human imagination.
⑤ Imagination is the ability to apply our memories to a new situation.

▶▶영작하시오.
당신이 원하는 것으로서 당신이 갖고 있지 않은 것이 있습니까?

3. Life, **to be** deep and strong, must be touched and tempered by sadness, as sunlight is sweetest when softened by shadows; as music, **to be** melodious, must have a minor chord in it.

notes :
*temper 섞다
*when (it is) softened
*melodious 선율적인
*minor chord 단조음

▶▶According to the above paragraph, which is **not** correct?
① A tune can be enhanced by the addition of a minor chord.
② Life becomes enriched through overcoming adversities.
③ A carefree man can enjoy a happy life.
④ Life with no grief is likely to be shallow and weak.
⑤ A man trained in sorrow can realize the profundity of life.

▶▶영작하시오.
첫 기차 시간에 닿기 위하여 나는 일찍 일어났다.

4. Have you never rushed dripping from the bath, or chewing from the table, or dazed from the bed, **only to be told** that you are a wrong number?

notes :
*table 식탁
*dazed는 주격보어
*a wrong number 잘못 걸린 전화 번호

▶▶Which of the following is **not** appropriate to describe the emotion of the underlined word, you?
① vexed ② annoyed
③ elated ④ irritated
⑤ bothered

▶▶영작하시오.
그는 90세까지 살았다.

5. Nothing is more pleasant for the members of a household than to gather in front of a roaring fire, entertained by the delights of the company, **not to mention** the special food and drink.

notes :
*not to mention = not to speak of = to say nothing of = let alone ~은 말할 것도 없이

▶▶윗글의 내용에 맞도록 공란을 채워라.
There is no place like (   ). [here, happiness, home]

▶▶영작하시오.
그는 영어는 말할 것도 없이 불어도 잘 한다.

He is **too** honest **to** tell a lie.
He is rich **enough to** buy a Rolls-Royce.

6. We have only a few more decades to live on this earth, and we lose many valuable hours thinking over small things that will soon be forgotten by us and by everybody. No, let us devote our life to worthwhile actions, feelings and thoughts. For life is **too** short **to** be little.

notes :
*devote A to B = B에 A를 바치다[헌신하다]
*worthwhile 가치있는, 보람있는

▶▶Our life is too short and valuable to spend worrying about ( ) things.
[mindful, trivial, simple]

▶▶영작하시오.
인생은 너무 짧아 모든 일에 다 흥미를 느낄 수는 없으니, 하나의 목표에 우리의 시간을 모두 바치자.

7.Trifles light as air are to the jealous proofs as strong as holy writ. A handkerchief of his wife's seen in Cassio's hand, was motive **enough** to the deluded Othello **to** pass sentence of death upon them both, without once inquiring how Cassio came by it.

notes :
*trifles 사소한 일
*the jealous = jealous people
*holy writ = the Bible
*come by=obtain

▶▶Driven by ( ), Othello put his wife and Cassio to death.
[jealousy, rage, hatred]

▶▶영작하시오.
그 사람은 그 죄로 인해 사형 선고를 받았다.

He allowed **me to do** so.

8. Although both love and knowledge are necessary, love is in a sense more fundamental, since it will lead **intelligent people to seek** knowledge, in order to find out how to benefit those whom they love.

notes :
*intelligent 총명한 ; *intelligible* 이해할 수 있는
*benefit 은혜를 주다

▶▶윗글의 내용과 일치하도록 주어진 문장의 빈 칸에 가장 알맞은 것은?
In a sense love is the ( ) source of knowledge.
① additional ② secondary ③ unchangeable
④ primary ⑤ permanent

▶▶영작하시오.
그는 가난해서 학업을 중단하지 않을 수 없었다.

We **are to** meet here at six this evening.
You **are to** finish it by five.
Not a soul **is to** be seen on the street.
He **was** never **to** see his home again.
If you **are to** succeed, you must work hard.

9. In a few days our vacation will begin; ⓐeverybody is joyous and animated at the prospect, because everybody **is to** go home. ⓑI know that I **am to** stay here during the five days that the holidays last, and that I will be very alone during that time.

notes :
*animated 활기에 찬, 생기있는
*at the prospect = 그 기대에

▶▶Which of the following is most suitable to describe the emotion of the underlined ⓐ and ⓑ?

ⓐ	ⓑ	ⓐ	ⓑ
① enthusiastic	vigorous	② pleased	disgusted
③ lonesome	jealous	④ delighted	energetic
⑤ cheerful	lonely		

▶▶영작하시오.
그들이 그 시합에 이길 가망이 있느냐?

10. Europeans are not concerned, like Americans, with the question of how a third world war **is to** be won, but only with the question of how it **is to** be avoided.

notes :
*is to be won = can be won
*is to be avoided = can be avoided

▶▶Europeans are only interested in how to (　　　) a third world war, not how to (　　　) it.
[pursuit, save, prevent, win, lose, favor]

▶▶영작하시오.
그는 이 사건에 관계가 없다.

11. Besides our primary obligation to God, we **are to** love our country, and **to** honor its ruler as representing it. We **are to** love the brotherhood, that is to say, our fellow Christians. And we **are to** honor all men.

notes :
*are to = should(의무)
*brotherhood 형제, 여기서는 '기독교 신자'

▶▶First of all we have to (　　　) God and we must hold all human brothers (　　　) to us.
[treasure, worship, like, close, near, dear]

▶▶영작하시오.
그는 그로부터 3시간 후, 즉 11시경 귀가했다.

12. The intellectual and social movement which **was to** dispel the darkness of the Middle Ages and prepare the way for those who would ultimately deliver reason from her prison, began in Italy in the thirteenth century.

notes :
*was to dispel에서 was to는 '운명'
*her는 reason을 의인화해 여성으로 취급

▶▶윗글의 her prison 에 상응하는 어구를 본문에서 찾아 쓰시오.

▶▶영작하시오.
그 부자(父子)는 두 번 다시 만나지 못할 운명이었다.

13. Music is a universal language understood by all peoples. This common saying is quite true, but we must not forget that some experience of music is necessary if a person **is to** understand it.

notes :
*a universal language = 만국어

▶▶본문의 밑줄 친 부분과 대체하기에 가장 알맞은 것은?
① is able to understand it
② is expected to understand it
③ is obliged to understand it
④ is destined to understand it
⑤ intends to understand it

▶▶영작하시오.
9시 전에 거기에 닿으려거든 서둘러야 할 것이다.

I **heard** her **sing**.
I **made** him **go** there.

14. I would **have** every student **know**, and the sooner the better, that there can be no thorough appreciation of the literature or culture of any country ancient or modern without an exact knowledge of the language.

notes :
*would = wish to
*know that ~로 계속 됨
*appreciation 이해

▶▶The writer of the above passage emphasizes that the full understanding of the literature or culture of any country comes only after acquiring its (   ).
[literature, culture, language]

▶▶영작하시오.
어머니는 나에게 세탁물을 빨랫줄에 널라고 하셨다.

15. She flung the door wide open for him, silently **watched** him **go** out, and not until she heard the front door close behind him did she make a move at all. But then she threw herself down upon the sofa and burst into tears.

notes :
*fling a door open = 문을 확 열어젖히다
*not until ~ did she … 부정어구로 인해 도치

▶▶What situation does the above paragraph describe?
① a scene where a male meets a female
② a scene where a pair of lovers break up
③ a scene where a girl joyfully welcomes a boy
④ a scene where a man sees off his girlfriend
⑤ a scene where a man promises to meet a girl again

▶▶영작하시오.
그는 문을 쾅 닫고 말 한 마디 없이 가 버렸다.

It is easy **for** you **to do** so.

16. Civilization is a product of adversity. The great civilizations of all time seem to have arisen where nature made production possible only a part of the year, and thus made it necessary **for man to work** and save up for the time when he could not produce. Man does not naturally like to work steadily, and if nature enables him to avoid it, he usually seems content to loaf rather than labor and progress.

notes :
*adversity 역경
*steadily 끊임없이
*loaf 게으르게 시간을 보내다(놀고 지내다)

▶▶According to the above paragraph, which of the following is correct?
① Without adversity, man's productivity would increase.
② Human civilization was accomplished through the struggle against adversity.
③ The writer blames environmental adversity for the decrease of produce.
④ Great civilizations are not to be found in naturally less-favored lands.
⑤ Man is by nature lazy and cannot be expected to keep up a high level of civilization.

▶▶영작하시오.
비행기 덕분에 우리는 2, 3일에 세계를 일주할 수 있다.

My only wish is **to live** in peace.

17. Though to be read is not motive which impels the author to write, his motive is other, once he has written his desire is **to be read**, and in order to achieve that he must do his best to make what he writes readable.

notes :
*impel 재촉하다 (= urge)
* once ~ = 일단 ~하면

▶▶다음 중 윗글의 내용과 일치하지 않는 것은?

① Every author does not write in order to be read by many readers.

② To be read by many readers is not every author's original motive of writing.

③ Once he has written, an author wants his writings to be read by as many readers as possible.

④ Every author should try to do his utmost to make his writings readable.

⑤ Every author writes in order to make his works best-selling books.

▶▶영작하시오.

일단 무엇인가 계획을 세웠으면, 그것을 성취하기 위해 최선을 다해야 한다.

He seems **to work** hard.
He seems **to have worked** hard.
I **intended to have gone** there.

18. There was no one in sight but a girl of about twelve, with her eyes covered with a bandage, who was being led carefully between the flowerbeds by a little boy. She stopped, and evidently asked who it was that had come in, and he **seemed to be** describing me to her.

notes :
*flowerbed 화단
*who it was that had ~에서 it was that이 의문사 who를 강조함

▶▶Which of the following does **not** correspond with this passage?

① The above-mentioned female must have hurt her eyes.

② I was on intimate terms with the girl.

③ There are three characters in the story.

④ The girl felt my presence, though she couldn't see me.

⑤ The boy beside the bandaged girl explained my appearance to her.

▶▶영작하시오.

그는 두목의 감시를 받고 있다.

19. A great many things which in times of lesser knowledge we imagined to be superstitious or useless, prove today on examination **to have been** of immense value to mankind. Probably no superstition ever existed which did not have some social value; and the most seemingly disgusting or cruel sometimes turn out **to have been** the most precious.

notes :
*superstitious 미신적인
*immense 엄청난
*disgusting 구역질 나는

▶▶Which does **not** correspond with the above paragraph?

① Many superstitious things were thought to be worthless in the past.

② There may not be a superstition that has no value to us.

③ The author's attitude to the value of superstition is positive.

④ Only a few superstitions proved invaluable through some investigations.

⑤ Some superstitions we thought to be highly absurd proved to have been very useful to us.

▶▶영작하시오.

그 소문은 알고 보니 거짓이었다.

20. Sometimes, looking back, one is appalled at one's errors, one seems **to have wasted** so much time in idle byways, and often **to have mistaken** the road so completely that whole years appear wasted.

notes :
*be appalled at ~ = ~에 소름이 끼치다
*byway 옆길
*mistake the road = 길을 잘못 들다

▶▶We are quite shocked to find that we have wasted so much time (   ) off the right path of life.

[thinking, wasting, wandering]

▶▶영작하시오.

우리는 그 무서운 학살현장을 보고 소름이 끼쳤다.

21. I **intended to have left** the party before midnight but had to stay rather late. Because if I had left early, it could have ruined the exciting atmosphere.

notes :
*ruin 망치다
*atmosphere 분위기

▶▶I had to remain at the party till (   ) midnight lest I should (   ) the merry mood of the party.

[after, over, at, cause, spoil, see]

▶▶영작하시오.

우리는 모든 것이 잘 되면 내년에 호주에 갈 작정이다.

● 장 문 독 해 ●

Warming-up

He went back **satisfied** with my explanation.
We **could** still win — the game isn't over yet.
We stood **face to face with** death.
Almost **unnoticed**, he stole away from us.
He **proved himself** a good teacher.
Every moment may be **put to** some **use**.

1 It seems the curse of modern man continually to confront new possibilities of self-destruction. He emerged from World War Ⅱ armed with nuclear power to obliterate all human life. His population has since grown at a rate that could threaten disaster on a global scale. And now he has come face to face with <u>a new man-made peril</u>, the poisoning of his natural environment with noxious doses of chemicals, garbage, fumes, noise, sewage, heat, ugliness and urban overcrowding. Nearly unnoticed, the scourge of pollution has already spread so far that a few scientists say only a drastic cure can prevent devastation as thorough as that of nuclear holocaust. Every nation, large and small, is confronted with environmental hazards. And thus conservation of the environment seems to be the chief task of our century. Man has had his Age of Exploration, and proved himself a master at discovering the riches of his planet. He has moved on to an Age of Exploitation, and demonstrated great skill in putting those riches to use. Now the time is long overdue for an Age of Conservation to begin. The battle against pollution must begin now or it will be too late.

***Newsweek**: The Ravaged Environment*

Notes

obliterate 말살하다 / noxious 해로운 / dose 분량 / chemicals 화학물 / garbage 쓰레기 / fumes 연기 / sewage 하수, 오물 / scourge 천벌, 재앙 / pollution 오염 / devastation 황폐 / holocaust 대파괴 / exploitation 개발, 이용 / overdue 기한이 넘은, 때늦은 / ravage 황폐케 하다

Question

1. Which is **not** related to the underlined phrase?
   ① nuclear power ② environmental hazards
   ③ noxious doses of chemicals ④ the scourge of pollution
   ⑤ limited resources

2. 다음은 본문에서 언급한 각 시대와 그 시대의 특징을 말한 것이다. 각 공란에 알맞은 말을 쓰시오.
   (1) the Age of (　　) : discovery of resources of the earth
   (2) the Age of (　　) : utilization of resources of the earth
   (3) the Age of Conservation : preservation of the (　　) of the earth

3. According to the passage, which of the following is **not** correct?
   ① Growing rates of population may cause global calamity.
   ② The main cause of the poisoned earth is human acts.
   ③ Perhaps conservation of the environment will be our main task throughout this century.
   ④ A large percentage of pollution was caused by nuclear weapons.
   ⑤ We should take urgent measures to avoid the desolation of the Earth.

4. What does this passage mainly discuss?
   ① Modern urban problems caused by overcrowding.
   ② The urgency of taking steps to settle the pollution problem.
   ③ The destructive power of nuclear weapons.
   ④ The evil effect caused by the devastation of our surroundings.
   ⑤ The transitional period from the Age of Exploitation to the Age of Conservation.

Production

(1) 폭도들이 삼삼오오(in twos and threes) 곤봉, 화염병 (a Molotov cocktail), 심지어 소총으로 무장하고 모여들었다.
(2) 그는 자기가 그 어려운 일에 적임자임을 입증했다.
(3) 지금이야말로 우리들 모두가 조국을 위해 일어서서 일할 때다.

● 장 문 독 해 ●

Warming-up

Unless you read between the lines, you will **get** nothing **out of** any book.

I want to persuade **you to** do as you are told to.

In the course of his remarks, he made the following statement.

There are two ways **in which** we can help him.

Traveling has **done** me a lot of **good**.

2 You know you have "to read between the lines" to get the most out of anything. I want to persuade you to do something equally important in the course of your reading. I want to persuade you to "write between the lines." Unless you do, you are not likely to do ⓐthe most efficient kind of reading. There are two ways in which one can own a book. The first is the property right you establish by paying for it, just as you pay for clothes and furniture. But this act of purchase is only the prelude to possession. Full ownership comes only when you have made it a part of yourself, and the best way to make yourself a part of it is by writing in it. An illustration may make the point clear. You buy a beefsteak and transfer it from the butcher's refrigerator to your own. But you do not own the beefsteak in the most important sense until ⓑyou consume it and get it into your blood stream. I am arguing that books, too, must be absorbed in your blood stream to do you any good.

***Mortimer J. Adler**: How to Mark a Book*

Notes

read between the lines 행간의 숨은 뜻을 읽다 / in the course of ~하는 도중에 / be likely to ~할 것 같다 / efficient 효과적인 / own 소유하다 / property right 소유권 / establish 확립하다 / purchase 매입 / prelude 서곡 ; *postlude* 후주곡 / illustration 실례 / transfer 옮기다 / consume 소화하다, 소비하다 / blood stream 혈관 / argue 주장하다 / do good 이익이 되다

Question

1. 본문의 내용에 맞도록 다음 문장의 빈칸을 주어진 철자로 시작하는 적당한 말로 골라 채우시오.

To read between the lines is to find (   ) meanings.

[hidden, real, true]

2. Choose two answers that correspond with the underlined phrase, ⓐthe most efficient kind of reading.
   ① to purchase a book
   ② to understand what the author really means
   ③ to claim the property right of a book
   ④ to write your own book
   ⑤ to write what you think in a blank space

3. Which of the following does the underlined phrase, ⓑyou consume it and get it into your blood stream, imply?
   ① to possess a book
   ② to purchase a book
   ③ to get the property right of a book
   ④ to make a book a part of yourself
   ⑤ to memorize what you read thoroughly

4. 다음 중 본문에 대한 설명으로 가장 알맞은 것은?
   ① 일반적인 상식과 상반되는 내용을 대치시켜 설명하였다.
   ② 책을 이해하는 과정을 역순으로 설명했다.
   ③ 일상 생활의 친근한 예를 비유로 들어 특정한 주제를 설명하였다.
   ④ 자신의 주장을 표면적으로 드러내지 않고 있다.
   ⑤ 독서보다 쓰기의 중요성을 강조하고 있다.

Production

(1) 나는 그에게서 아무것도 얻어낼 수 없었다.
(2) 보다 열심히 일하지 않으면 너는 아마 성공하지 못할 것이다.
(3) 이 약은 너에게 효험이 있을 것이다.
(4) 그는 그 소설 읽는 데 열중했다.
(5) 완전한 소유는 책을 자신의 일부로 했을 때에만 온다.

실 력 체 크 Ⅰ

1 다음은 영국의 물리학자가 미국의 과학계를 시찰하고 난 후 쓴 감상문이다.

What the American scientist has, above all, is energy and activity. He is not a shy and unsociable person hidden in his own laboratory. Not infrequently you will find him flying across the continent, giving lectures 1,000 miles from home, or meeting hundreds of others at a conference. There are always people coming and going, ceaselessly discussing the latest experiment or theory, arguing in front of a projector or over cups of coffee. There is a thick web of communication so that everyone knows what everyone else is doing, and every bit of scientific knowledge spreads rapidly from one laboratory to another. Of course, all this is extremely valuable, and some people, original, quick-witted, fluent in thought and word, thrive in this atmosphere. Yet I think it has its dangers. Scientific work is not easy, and a really deep idea is unlikely to come in the hour or so that one will spend talking with a particular person on a particular topic. An atmosphere of intellectual bustle is not favorable to quiet concentration, to unhurried experiments, to brooding over a single problem. There is always the temptation <u>to jump on the latest band wagon</u>, instead of making a thorough study of a narrow field. And I am afraid originality seems sometimes to be emphasized too much in America, and is often not easily distinguishable from superficial brilliance.

notes :
atmosphere 분위기 / in the hour or so 한 시간 가량 안에 / topic 화제, 주제 / bustle 법석, 부산함 / brood over ~을 곰곰이 생각하다 / originality 독창성 / superficial 피상적인 / brilliance 화려함

(1) 밑줄 친 부분의 내용을 설명하여라.
(2) 작자는 미국에 있어서의 독창성에 대해 어떻게 생각하고 있는가?
(3) 작자의 주장을 가장 잘 나타내는 문장 하나를 골라라.

2 공란에 들어갈 말을 골라라.

A well-known publisher told me the other day that he was recently asked to equip a library in a new house in North London, and the instruction he received was to provide books that would fit the shelves which had been fixed. It was not the (1)_______ of the books that mattered, but the (2)_______.

notes :
well-known 유명한 / equip (장비를) 갖추다 / shelf 서가(書架) / matter = be important

① size ② contents ③ appearance ④ shelves ⑤ library

3 다음 글을 읽고 밑의 물음에 답하여라.

The world is full of people—appallingly full; it has never been so full before, and they are all tumbling over each other. Most of these people one doesn't know and some of them one doesn't like; doesn't like the color of their skins, say, or the shapes of their noses, or the way they blow them or don't blow them, or the way they talk, or their smell, or their clothes, or their fondness for jazz or their dislike of jazz, and so on.

Well, what is one to do? There are two solutions. One of them is the Nazi solution. If you do not like people, kill them, banish them, segregate them, and then strut up and down proclaiming that you are the salt of the earth. The other way is much less thrilling, but it is on the whole the way of the democracies, and I prefer it. If you don't like people, put up with them as well as you can. Don't try to love them: you cannot, you will only strain yourself. But try to tolerate them. On the basis of that tolerance a civilized future may be built. Certainly I can see no other foundation except on the basis of tolerance.

notes:
appallingly 무지무지하게 / tumble 엎어지다 / banish 추방하다 / ségregate 분리하다 / strut 뽐내며 걷다 / the salt of the earth 세상의 소금[성서], 이 세상의 가장 중요한 존재 / put up with = endure, tolerate / strain oneself 무리[과로]를 하다

(1) 작자는 왜 밑줄 친 부분과 같은 말을 하고 있는가?

(2) 앞으로의 문명은 무엇에 의해 존속해 나갈 수 있다고 작자는 말하는가?

4 다음 글의 밑줄친 부분의 구체적인 내용을 100자 내외의 우리말로 써라.

South Korea's warring generations disagree on just about everything having to do with lifestyle and money. Necessity forced the elders to be frugal and cautious. Their main life goal was to amass enough won to buy a house and educate their children. As a result, about half of all South Koreans under 40 attended college, an experience that's made them smarter, more employable—and significantly less Confucian. They're avid consumers, great fans of foreign fashion and travel lovers, all vices in their parents' eyes. Worse, the kids often play on credit. To them, how to spend money is as important as how to make it, and the priorities they set—buying cars before they own homes, say—sometimes shock their parents.

—Newsweek—

notes:
warring 서로 싸우는 / necessity 필요, 곤궁 / frugal 절약하는 / cautious 주의 깊은 / amass 축적하다, 모으다 / employable 고용할 수 있는 / Confucian 유교적인, 공자의 (*cf.*) Confucius 공자 / avid 탐욕스런, 열광적인

실력체크 II

A. 괄호 안에서 문맥에 맞는 단어를 골라라.

(1) She is (adept, adapt) at playing the guitar.
(2) He is sincere and quite without (affectation, affection).
(3) She looked up at him with large (childlike, childish) eyes.
(4) This hat (complements, compliments) the dress better than that one.
(5) Our homes and offices need a (continuous, continual) supply of electricity.
(6) They write letters demanding (human, humane) treatment of prisoners.
(7) After this latest affair he hardly seems (credulous, credible) as a politician.
(8) Upon his (disease, decease) the house will pass to his wife.
(9) She covered her head in (deference, difference) to Muslim custom.
(10) Such waste of money is to be (deprecated, depreciated) at a time like this.
(11) Driving on that icy road is (paramount, tantamount) to suicide.
(12) The population of Los Angeles is an (aggregate, aggravate) of people from nearly all the world's countries.
(13) He showed his (humanism, humanity) by helping his neighbor.

B. 두 문장의 뜻이 같아지도록 공란의 단어를 완성하여라.

(1) Our team has always won against yours.
Our team has always b_____ yours.
(2) They took no notice of our warning.
They i_____ our warning.
(3) I am afraid that she may not keep her promise.
I d_____ that she will keep her promise.
(4) She said that she had done so.
She d_____ that she had not done so.
(5) The man would not take the money.
The man r_____ to take the money.

Answer: A. (1) adept (2) affectation (3) childlike (4) complements (5) continuous (6) humane (7) credible (8) decease (9) deference (10) deprecated (11) tantamount (12) aggregate (13) humanity
B. (1) beaten (2) ignored (3) doubt (4) denied (5) refused

C. 공란을 메워 두 문장의 뜻이 같아지도록 하여라.

(1) I tried to persuade him, but offended him after all.
I tried to persuade him _____ _____ offend him.

(2) I am not in any way responsible.
I am in no way _____ blame.

(3) As I'm not a fast runner, I can't keep up with you.
I can't run fast _____ _____ keep up with you.

(4) He was so foolish that he missed the point.
He was too foolish _____ _____ miss the point.

(5) Have you decided a place for your new house?
Have you decided _____ _____ build your new house?

(6) We could not see anybody in the house.
Nobody _____ _____ be seen in the house.

(7) I will not go, if I have to go alone.
I would rather _____ _____ than go alone.

(8) I had no difficulty in finding his office.
It was quite _____ _____ me _____ find his office.

(9) His new proposal is worth considering.
It is _____ _____ consider his new proposal.

(10) It is very dangerous for children to play with lighters.
Lighters are very dangerous _____ children _____ play _____.

(11) He is too wise to be fooled by such a fake.
He knows _____ _____ to be fooled by such a fake.

(12) He realized the value of his health only after he lost it.
It was not _____ he lost his health _____ he realized its value.

(13) It is quite a surprise to see you here.
You are the _____ man I expected to see here.

(14) Let's keep this matter secret from others.
Let's keep this matter _____ ourselves.

(15) Everyone admits that he has done his best.
No one _____ that he has done his best.

Answer: C. (1) only to (2) to (3) enough to (4) not to
(5) where to (6) was to (7) not go (8) easy for, to
(9) worthwhile to (10) for, to, with (11) better than (12) until, that
(13) last (14) to (15) denies

어 휘 · 발 음

A. 주어진 단어의 올바른 어형을 공란에 써라.

conquest, fair, fluent, triumph, hesitant, choose

(1) Right temporarily defeated is stronger than evil ______.
(2) The dictator had plans to ______ the whole world.
(3) This exam is designed to test your ______ in English.
(4) Faith is necessary to victory. If you ______ in striking at the ball, it is ten to one that you miss it.
(5) The film was ______ good, but not brilliant.
(6) If the product doesn't work, you are given the ______ of a refund or a replacement.

B. Substitute a word for the bold-faced part:
(1) He **left out** the third question in the examination.
(2) The enemy **gave in** without further resistance.
(3) You must **take into account** the fact that he was ill.
(4) They will **try out** the machine tomorrow.
(5) How did such a strange thing **come about**?
(6) We were all **taken in** by his sweet talking.
(7) The revolution **came to pass** after years of plotting.
(8) It was **little short of** a miracle.
(9) Some friends **dropped in on** us last evening.
(10) His carelessness **brought about** the accident.

C. 접두사 in-을 붙여 반의어를 만들 수 있는 단어를 두 개 골라라.

(1) honesty (2) natural (3) possible
(4) advantageous (5) close (6) ability
(7) common (8) familiar (9) worthy
(10) fortune (11) ordinary (12) famous

Answer: A. (1) triumphant (2) conquer (3) fluency (4) hesitate (5) fairly (6) choice
B. (1) omitted (2) surrendered (3) consider (4) test (5) happen (6) deceived
(7) occurred (8) almost (9) visited (10) caused
C. (6), (12)

D. 문맥에 가장 적합한 단어를 아래에서 골라 빈칸에 채워라. (필요하면 어형을 변화시키되 한번씩만 사용할 것)

(1) a. The only ______ she received was a scratch on her arm.
b. After a long illness, he suffered from a ______ of strength.
c. Whoever breaks a window may have to pay for the ______.

① damage	② injury	③ loss

(2) a. The sky became darker; it was ______ we were going to have rain.
b. The stars are ______ on a cloudy night.
c. There was a ______ chill in the air.

① visible	② noticeable	③ evident

(3) a. We hadn't thought of the incident until she ______ it.
b. Lots of people have ______ on my new plan.
c. The boy's father ______ he would not let him go swimming again.

① declare	② mention	③ comment

E. 다음 각 문장이 완성되도록 적당한 단어를 선택하시오.

(1) He got 5% of the profits in ______ for having thought of the original idea.
① acceptance ② response ③ acknowledgement ④ reward

(2) That old gentleman is still in full ______ of his health.
① rapture ② enjoyment ③ happiness ④ joy

(3) Throughout the journey the stranger ______ us with stories of his many adventures in Africa.
① depressed ② conscripted ③ traversed ④ enthralled

F. 다음 글을 글 끝에 주어진 수 만큼 끊어 읽어라.

(1) Trifles light as air are to the jealous proofs as strong as holy writ. [2]

(2) Some books are to be tasted, others to be swallowed, and a few to be chewed and digested. [4]

Answer: D. (1) a. injury b. loss c. damage (2) a. evident b. invisible c. noticeable
(3) a. mentioned b. commented c. declared E. (1) ④ (2) ② (3) ④
F. (1) Trifles light as air are / to the jealous / proofs as strong as holy writ.
(2) Some books are to be tasted, / others / to be swallowed, / and a few / to be ~.

숙 어

(1) **be inclined to** (=be disposed to ; tend to) ~하고 싶어하다 ; ~하는 경향이 있다

☞ I'*m inclined to* agree with what you were saying in the meeting.
I'*m inclined to* get tired easily.

(2) **be up to** (=do something bad ; depend on) (나쁜 일을) 꾸미다 ; ~에 달려 있다

☞ When he's quiet like this, I know he'*s up to* something.
It'*s up to* you whether to go or not.

(3) **beat around the bush** (=approach indirectly) 말을 빙빙 돌리다

☞ I wish you'd stop *beating around the bush* and tell me what you really want.

(4) **beat up** (=strike repeatedly) (상습적으로) 때리다

☞ She told the police that her husband had *beaten* her *up*.

(5) **behind the times** (=old-fashioned) 시대에 뒤떨어진

☞ Her ideas about raising children are *behind the times*.

(6) **believe it or not** (=something is very surprising but true) 믿지 않겠지만

☞ I asked my boss for a month's holiday and, *believe it or not*, he agreed!

(7) **beside oneself** (=very upset *or* excited) (흥분·노여움 등으로) 제 정신이 아닌

☞ He was *beside himself* with rage when he saw the mess.

(8) **between you and me** (=in confidence, between ourselves) 우리끼리 얘긴데

☞ *Between you and me*, I think she's pregnant.

(9) **break away** (=escape from someone *or* something) 달아나다, 벗어나다

☞ Two policemen were holding him, but he managed to *break away*.

(10) **break into** (=enter by force) 침입하다

☞ He was arrested on suspicion of *breaking into* a house and committing a burglary.

(11) **break out** (=occur suddenly) 갑자기 발생하다

☞ A fire *broke out* on the top floor of the building.

(12) **break up** (=disperse, scatter ; split up) 해산시키다 ; 헤어지다

☞ The police *broke up* the demonstration. We *broke up* in March.

(13) **bring about** (=cause to happen) 발생시키다, 야기하다

☞ This crisis has been *brought about* by the stupidity of our politicians.

(14) **bring home to** (=cause one to realize) ~을 절실히 느끼게 하다

☞ Her death *brought home to* me the sorrow of life.

(15) **bring up** (=raise, rear) 키우다, 양육하다

☞ *Bringing up* children is both difficult and rewarding.

(16) **burst into+명사, burst out ~ing** (=begin suddenly) 갑자기 ~하다

☞ When she saw him, she *burst into* tears.
I *burst out* laughing when I saw his funny outfit.

(17) **by all means** (=in every possible way) 어떤 일이 있어도

☞ I plan to make use of this opportunity *by all means*.

(18) **by degrees** (=gradually) 점차로

☞ The economy seems to be improving *by degrees*.

(19) **by leaps and bounds** (=very rapidly and greatly) 급속도로

☞ His business has grown *by leaps and bounds*.

(20) **by turns** (=in rotation, one after the other, alternately) 교대로

☞ On the drive to Chicago, the three men took the wheel *by turns*.

(21) **by virtue of** (=because of, as a result of) ~때문에, ~의 결과로

☞ He succeeded *by virtue of* his tenacity rather than his talent.

Exercise

▶▶ 주어진 단어들을 포함한 글을 지어라. 필요하면 어형을 변화시켜라.

1. wonder / rascal / up
2. stop / beat / get / point
3. prisoner / break / guard
4. thief / break / through / window
5. fire / break / factory
6. understand / break / boyfriend
7. several / rain / bring / flood
8. degrees / friendship / love
9. tend / sick / turns
10. exempt / military / virtue

4. 동 명 사(Gerund)

기본 문법 설명

A. 동명사의 명사적 성질	(1) **Smoking** cigarettes can cause heart disease. (2) It is **throwing** your money away. (3) I've enjoyed **talking** to you. (4) Thank you for **answering** so promptly. (5) Tickets for a **sleeping** car are double the price.
B. 동명사의 완료형과 수동형	(1) ⓐ I am sure of his **being** a man of ability. ⓑ I am sure of his **having been** a man of ability in his youth. (2) ⓐ I don't like **being asked** to make a speech. ⓑ I never heard of such a thing **having been done**.
C. 동명사의 의미상 주어	(1) **Asking** questions is not a shame. (2) I object to **marrying** her. (3) I object to **his** [**him**] **marrying** her. (4) I object to my **son marrying** her.
D. 동명사와 부정사의 비교	(1) Prices continue **rising**. = Prices continue **to rise**. (2) ⓐ She remembers **seeing** him before. ⓑ Please remember **to give** my best regards to your wife. (3) ⓐ I **finished correcting** my composition. ⓑ They **hope to visit** us next year.
E. 동명사의 관용적 용법	(1) There is **no accounting** for his prolonged absence. (2) It is **no use** your **arguing** with him. (3) I **could not help pitying** him. (4) This is the tree **of my own planting**. (5) **On seeing** the cop, the thief took to his heels. (6) **It goes without saying that** ships can't rival aircraft for speed. (7) Our flower bed **needs weeding**.

A. 동명사의 명사적 성질

동명사는 동사와 명사의 역할을 한다.
☞ 현재분사는 동사와 형용사의 역할

(1) Smoking이 목적어를 취하는 점에서는 동사적 성격이 있으며, Smoking cigarettes 전체가 주어인 점에서 명사적 성격이 있다.
(2) throwing은 보어
(3) talking은 enjoyed의 목적어
(4) 동명사 answering은 전치사 for의 목적어이며 (명사적 성격), 그리고 부사 so promptly에 의해 수식 (동사적 성격)되고 있다.
(5) a sléeping car (침대차 ; 동명사)
= a car *for* sleeping
a sléeping báby (현재분사)
= a baby who is sleeping

B. 동명사의 완료형과 수동형

(1) ⓐ (나는 그가 유능한 사람임을 확신한다.)
··· 시제는 본동사와 일치
= I *am* sure that he *is* a man of ability.
ⓑ (나는 그가 젊었을 때는 유능한 사람이었다고 확신한다.)
동명사의 완료형 : 시제가 본동사보다 하나 앞선다.
= I *am* sure that he *was* a man of ability in his youth.
(2) ⓐ (나는 연설 부탁을 받는 것을 싫어한다.)
··· being asked 는 수동태
We are afraid of *being misunderstood.*
ⓑ (나는 그런 일이 이루어졌다고는 들어보지 못했다.)
= I never heard that such a thing *had been done.*

C. 동명사의 의미상 주어

(1) asking의 의미상 주어는 일반인.
(2) marrying의 주어는 문장의 주어 I이다. 그래서 marrying 앞의 my[me]를 생략했다.
(3) marrying의 의미상 주어 he와 이 글의 주어 I 가 다르므로 his[him]을 붙였다.
(4) marrying의 주어는 my son이다. 동명사의 의미상의 주어가 대명사인 경우는 소유격(his), 목적격(him) 어느 쪽도 무방하지만 명사인 경우는 대부분 목적격(my son)이 사용 된다.

D. 동명사와 부정사의 비교

(1) 의미상 차이 없이 동명사, 부정사 양쪽을 다 목적어로 취할 수 있는 동사
(2) 목적어를 동명사로 썼을 때와 부정사로 썼을 때 의미가 달라지는 경우
ⓐ (그녀는 그를 전에 본 기억이 난다.)
ⓑ (잊지말고 내 안부를 당신 아내에게 전해 주세요.)
☞ I stopped *smoking*. [3형식]
(담배 피우는 것을 끊었다.)
I stopped *to smoke*. [1형식]
(담배를 피우기 위해 섰다.)
(3) 어떤 동사는 목적어로서 동명사만을 혹은 부정사만을 취한다.
ⓐ 동명사만을 목적어로 취하는 동사
mind, enjoy, give up, avoid, finish, escape, admit, consider, deny, permit, postpone, practice 등은 동명사를 취한다.
ⓑ 부정사만을 목적어로 취하는 동사
wish, hope, care, choose, expect, refuse, decide, mean, plan 등은 부정사를 취한다.

E. 동명사의 관용적 용법

(1) There is no ~ing = It is impossible to ~
(2) It [There] is no use ~ing
= It is of no use to ~
(3) cannot help ~ing
= cannot (choose) but + 원형
(4) of one's own ~ing = 과거분사+by oneself
(5) on ~ing = as soon as
(6) It goes without saying that ~.
= It is needless to say that ~.
(7) need ~ing = need to be+과거분사
* feel like ~ing = feel inclined to ~
* make a point of ~ing
= make it a rule to ~
* be worth ~ing
= It is worthwhile to 원형
* be on the verge of ~ing
= be about to 원형
* come near (to) ~ing
= nearly escape ~ing
* be far from ~ing = be never ~
* What do you say to ~ing? = Let's ~.

문 법 · 작 문

A. 괄호 안에서 맞는 것을 골라라.

(1) Have you finished (to send, sending, sent) e-mails?

(2) All the employees were busy (to do, doing) their various tasks.

(3) Would you mind me (to sit, sitting) by you?

(4) You must stop (thinking, to think) before you act.

(5) Please remember (to call, calling) on me again.

(6) You'll soon get used to (drive, driving) your new car.

(7) I look forward to (receive, receiving) your reply as soon as possible.

(8) Somehow I feel like (to cancel, canceling) the contract.

(9) (At, In, On) finding the news true, she began to cry.

(10) This pencil needs (sharpening, to sharpen).

B. 각 문장의 틀린 부분을 고쳐라.

(1) He insisted to go for a drive in this stormy weather.

(2) His disability prevents him to walk.

(3) Unless you two stop to fight, I'll call the police.

(4) She pretended being interested, but I could see she wasn't.

(5) I remember to scream for hours when I was a baby.

(6) Are you sure of he will investigate it fairly?

(7) No one has ever succeeded to explain this phenomenon.

(8) It is no good to try to bribe the policeman.

(9) She came near to drown in the lake.

(10) I don't care running the risk.

(11) She devoted herself to look after him.

(12) You will have to speak a little louder. He is hard to hear.

(13) He is above to do such a mean thing.

(14) I never see you without think of my brother.

(15) He regrets being not able to help me.

C. 다음의 ~ing로 끝나는 말은 분사(P)인가, 동명사(G)인가?

(1) a sleeping baby

(2) a dining car

(3) a sleeping bag

(4) a magnifying glass

(5) a neighboring village

(6) a swimming suit

D. 다음 각 항의 문장의 뜻의 차이를 말하여라.

(1) ⓐ I hate lying. ⓑ I hate to lie.

(2) ⓐ I like swimming. ⓑ I like to swim now.

(3) ⓐ She went on saying. ⓑ She went on to say.
(4) ⓐ Try to do so. ⓑ Try doing so.
(5) ⓐ He is sure of success. ⓑ He is sure to succeed.

E. 공란을 적당한 단어로 채워라.
(1) This picture is (   ) her own painting.
(2) The witness denied (   ) seen the accused.
(3) In this newspaper only the TV listings and the sports page are (   ) reading.
(4) I have no doubt (   ) his succeeding.
(5) I cannot (   ) laughing at your silly idea.
(6) The glass is very fragile; it needs (   ) with care.

F. 나머지 부분을 완성하여 두 문장의 뜻이 같게 하여라.
(1) I make it a rule to read the Bible every day.
I make a point of ________________________ .
(2) The company was about to declare bankruptcy.
The company was on the verge of __________ .
(3) He was caught while he was stealing.
He was caught in the act of _______________ .
(4) Needless to say, the patient needs an immediate blood transfusion.
It goes without _________________________ .

G. 괄호 속의 동사를 맞게 고쳐라.
(1) Please excuse my (be) late.
(2) You should practice (play) the piano regularly.
(3) We've had to postpone (go) to France for two weeks.
(4) I repent (have followed) his advice.
(5) Finally we decided not (invest) much money in the project.
(6) You'd better avoid (go) shopping on Saturdays.
(7) He went over to America with the view of (study) physics.

H. 다음 각 문장을 동명사를 사용하여 단문으로 바꾸어 써라.
(1) I'm so proud that my son's been chosen for the national team.
(2) He was not ashamed that he had cheated on his wife.
(3) He still insists that he did nothing wrong.
(4) We have no doubt that he is sick in bed.

(5) As soon as her car arrived, the crowd started cheering.
(6) He was nervous because he had not spoken in public before.
(7) I don't like you to lie in bed till late on Sunday morning.
(8) He not only holds an important office, but often writes good novels.
(9) Is this also a picture that you have drawn by yourself?
(10) Whenever I meet him, I think of his dead father.
(11) She repented that she had spanked her child and promised never to do it again.
(12) I remember that you promised me to do so.
(13) He denied that he had told a lie.
(14) He always complains that his boss is useless and he has too much work.
(15) That he has such poor health is against him.
(16) It is impossible to deny that this has been a difficult year for him.
(17) Though he was very learned, he lacked common sense.
(18) There is every reason why you should be displeased.
(19) Will you be so kind as to help me carry this suitcase?
(20) I didn't go myself, but sent my representative.
(21) I cannot but think that he is still alive.
(22) His mother scolded him because he broke her favorite vase.
(23) Let's take a walk for a while after dinner, shall we?
(24) When we learn a foreign language, it is necessary to advance step by step.
(25) Be polite when you speak to others.
(26) I've always regretted that I didn't study harder at school.

I. 다음 각 문장을 복문으로 바꾸어 써라.
(1) I forgot the doctor advising me not to eat salty foods.
(2) She is proud of having won the first prize in the beauty contest.
(3) He started early with the intention of getting a good seat.
(4) I'm convinced of her telling the truth.
(5) Do you mind my opening the window?
(6) All the lights go out on the clock striking ten.
(7) I don't think it fair your speaking ill of him.
(8) Is there any possibility of his succeeding in raising enough funds?

J. 괄호 속의 동사의 올바른 어형을 써서 뜻이 통하게 하여라.
(1) So far from poverty (be) a misfortune, it may, by vigorous self-help, (convert) into a blessing.

(2) Animals do all they have to do without (teach).
(3) A book which is worth (read) at all is likely to (read) more than once.
(4) His composition was far from (satisfy) his teacher.
(5) She got a little money by (let) others (paint) pictures of her.
(6) A man who picks up and reads any book that he happens to come across, is in great danger of (become) weary of reading or (poison) by it.
(7) (Go) by plane I do not consider as traveling at all; it is merely (send) to a place, and very little different from becoming a parcel.
(8) Man is sometimes more generous when he has little money than when he has plenty; perhaps to prevent his (think) to have but little.

K. Translate the following into English:

(1) 그는 한 마디 말도 없이 그 곳을 떠났다.

(2) 사람이 돈 쓰는 법을 모르면 돈을 저축해도 소용이 없다.

(3) 영어로 편지 쓰는 것은 영작문의 좋은 연습이다.

(4) 어젯밤 나는 TV를 끄지 않고 잠들어 버렸다.

(5) 21세기 말까지 과학이 어느 정도 발달할지 알 수가 없다.

(6) 나는 그가 거짓말을 했다고 생각하지 않을 수 없다.

(7) 실수하는 것을 너무 두려워 말고, 대담하게 말하도록 하여라.

(8) 여행에서 돌아오자 나는 아버님이 중병을 앓고 계시는 것을 알았다.

(9) 이렇게 좋은 날씨에 집안에 박혀 있을 수는 없다.

(10) 그는 숙제하는 것을 게을리 한다고 꾸중을 들었다.

(11) 비 때문에 어제 우리는 드라이브를 할 수 없었다.

'Spring'이라는 제목으로 50어 내외의 글을 지어라.

● 단 문 독 해 ●

She is proud of her son **being** intelligent.

1. There is no evidence of prehistoric man **having made** war, for all his stone implements seem to have been designed for **hunting**, for **digging,** or for **scraping** animal hides and we can be pretty sure that even if he did, any wars between groups in the hunting stage of human life would have been both rare and mild.

notes :
*make war = 전쟁을 걸다
*implement 도구
*hide (동물의) 가죽

▶▶According to the above paragraph, the instruments of prehistoric men were devised for (   ), not for battle.
[strategy, killing, survival]

▶▶영작하시오.
그가 유죄라는 증거는 없다.

There is no know**ing** what may happen.
It is no use cry**ing** over spilt milk.
On leav**ing** school, he went into business.
Luck is **of our own** mak**ing**.
I **cannot help** laugh**ing** at his foolish idea.
It goes without saying that knowledge is power.
The book **is worth** read**ing** intensively.

2. She thought her family should all retire to the country for the summer, that the children might have the benefit of the mountain air, for <u>**there was no** living in the city</u> in this sultry season.

notes :
*retire (조용한 장소 따위에) 가다
*(so) that … may ~ = …가 ~하기 위해
*sultry 무더운

▶▶문맥상 밑줄 친 'there was no living in the city' 와 바꾸어 쓸 수 있는 문장은?
① no one lived in the city
② it was impossible to live in the city
③ nobody was to be seen in the city
④ there was not a soul living in the city
⑤ the whole city looked vacant

▶▶영작하시오.
나는 가족이 편히 살도록 열심히 일한다.

3. The discipline should not be excessive — we do not want prohibition for prohibition's sake; and it must not be capricious — **it is no use** forbidd**ing** a thing one day and allow**ing** it the next.

notes :
*discipline 규율
*excessive 과도한, 지나친
*for 명사's sake = ~을 위해
*capricious 변덕스러운

▶▶ The writer maintains that the discipline should be (　　).
① variable　② changeable　③ flexible
④ consistent　⑤ timely

▶▶ 영작하시오.
네가 그것을 부정하려고 해도 소용없다.

4. Owing to Mary's face being buried in her hands, she did not notice a form which came quietly on to the porch, and **on** see**ing** her, first moved as if to retreat, then paused and regarded her. Mary did not raise her head for some time, and when she looked around her face was wet and her eyes drowned and dim. "Mr. Smith," she said, "how long have you been here?"

notes :
*notice 알아차리다, 인지하다
*form 사람의 모습
*as if (it were) to retreat
*regard 주시하다
*dim 몽롱한

▶▶ 본문의 내용으로 미루어 보아 다음 빈칸에 들어갈 가장 적절한 말은?
It seems that Mary has been (　　).
① sleeping　② reading　③ cooking
④ weeping　⑤ retreating

▶▶ 영작하시오.
한국에 오신 지 얼마나 됩니까?

5. To save embarrassment to people still living I have given to the people who play a part in this story names **of my own** mak**ing**, and I have in other ways taken pains to make sure that no one should recognize them.

notes :
*save 덜어주다
*embarrassment 곤혹
*pains = efforts

▶▶ The writer didn't use the (　　) names of living people in his novel (　　) they should be recognized by readers.
[fictional, fictitious, real, lest, so]

▶▶ 영작하시오.
이것은 그가 직접 그린 그림이다.

6. **No** one **can help** influenc**ing** others, however little he may wish to do so or how little he may be conscious of what he is doing. None can be neutral; if he is not doing good, he will in some sense be doing harm.

notes :
*be conscious of ~ = ~을 의식하다
*however[no matter how] little he may 양보의 부사절
*neutral 중립의

▶▶Which of the following is the writer's ultimate argument?
① We may affect others in spite of ourselves.
② Human beings unavoidably have influence on one another.
③ Some of us are doing harm to others unconsciously.
④ We have to make efforts to benefit others by our good deeds.
⑤ We can't remain neutral all through our life.

▶▶영작하시오.
우리는 남에게 영향을 주고 또 영향을 받지 않을 수 없다.

7. **It goes without saying that** when we read the lives of great men we cannot but be struck by the manner in which all kinds of experiences that might in themselves seem to be random, or even disastrous are made use of in the long run.

notes :
*lives of great men = 위인들의 전기
*random 무계획적인
*disastrous 비참한
*in the long run = 결국

▶▶We can't help being impressed by the way great men utilize (   ) as a steppingstone to (   ).
[power, success, failure, adversity, method]

▶▶영작하시오.
그 여자는 언제나 여가를 선용한다.

8. The great inventions of Thomas A. Edison were the fruit of long and painstaking effort. "Genius is one percent inspiration and ninety-nine percent perspiration," was the way he explained his success. He also said: "I never did anything **worth doing** by accident, nor did any of my inventions come by accident; they came by work."

notes :
*painstaking 고된
*inspiration 영감
*perspiration 땀 (= sweat)

▶▶Edison attributed his success to his (   ) rather than to his (   ).
[accident, fortune, perspiration, luck, inspiration]

▶▶영작하시오.
많은 책이 출판되지만, 읽을 가치가 있는 것은 별로 없다.

I object to **being treated** like this.
They **never** meet **without** quarrel**ing**.
The work is **far from** (be**ing**) satisfactory.

9. She had never enjoyed the game more thoroughly. The thing that mattered was the game itself rather than winning it. Even **being beaten** did not matter.

notes :
*more thoroughly (than she was enjoying it then)
*mattered = was important

▶▶(   ), she did her best in competitions.
[One way or another, Win or lose, Good or bad]

▶▶영작하시오.
처벌 받을까 두려워 그는 도망쳤다.

10. The English people think that there are no other men like themselves, and no other world but England; they **scarcely** see a handsome foreigner **but** they say that he looks like an Englishman; and they **cannot** set any delicious food before a foreigner **without** ask**ing** if such a thing is made in his country.

notes :
*no other world but 에서 but = except
*scarcely A but B = A하면 반드시 B한다 = cannot A without B(ing)

▶▶According to the above passage, which of the following is most suitable to describe the English people?
① considerate ② impolite ③ self-centered
④ ruthless ⑤ self-contained

▶▶영작하시오.
그 사람 외에는 누구나 다 그것을 알고 있는 것 같다.

11. We live in the kind of world in which there is no possibility of order without concern for the right of others, which means that there must always be restraints, which means that simple freedom, **far from** be**ing** a natural right, is obviously irrational.

notes :
*natural right = 타고난 권리
*obviously 분명히
*irrational 불합리한

▶▶We should (   ) others' rights and (   ) our excessive freedom to maintain our society.
[respect, reduce, see, eliminate, restrain, refrain]

▶▶영작하시오.
그가 또 실패했는데, 그로 해서 그 여자는 화가 났다.

● 장 문 독 해 ●

Warming-up

I think it is easy **for** you **to** do the work.
I have seen him **beat** his students.
I felt myself **watched** and my heart **beating**.
There stood a sign **that read** "Keep out."
I found **it** difficult **to work** the new machine.

1 I guess it is easy for those who have never felt the stinging darts of segregation to say "wait".
But when you have seen vicious mobs lynch your mother and father at will and drown your sisters and brothers at whim; when you have seen hate-filled policemen curse, kick, brutalize and even kill your black brothers and sisters; when you suddenly <u>feel your tongue twisted and your speech stammering</u> as you seek to explain to your six-year-old daughter why she can't go to the public amusement park that has just been advertised on television, and see tears welling up in her little eyes when she is told that "Funtown" is closed to colored children, and see the depressing clouds of inferiority begin to form in her little mental sky, and see her begin to distort her little personality by unconsciously developing a bitterness toward white people; when you are humiliated day in and day out by nagging signs that read "white" and "colored"; when you are harried by day and haunted by night by the fact that you are a Negro, living constantly at tiptoe stance; when you are forever fighting a degenerating sense of "nobodyness" — then you will understand why we find it difficult to wait.

***Martin Luther King**: Why we can't wait*

Note

stinging darts of segregation 인종 차별의 날카로운 화살 ; *integration* 인종 무차별 / vicious mobs 악의에 찬 군중 / lynch 사형(私刑)을 가하다 / at will 멋대로 / at whim 변덕으로 / twist 꼬부라지다 / stammer 말을 더듬다 / depressing 침울한 / inferiority 열등 의식 / distort 비틀어지게하다 / bitterness 원한 / humiliate 굴욕을 주다 / nagging 성가신 / harry 괴롭히다 (=harass) / stance 자세 / degenerate 타락하다

Question

1. Choose an appropriate word for the blank to replace the underlined phrase, <u>feel your tongue twisted and your speech stammering</u>.

are at a (   ) for words

[lost, loss, failure]

2. Which of the following is most suitable to describe the author's emotion?
   ① miserable and regretful
   ② scared and unmanly
   ③ bashful and sorrowful
   ④ skeptical and cynical
   ⑤ tiresome and bothersome

3. Which of the following does **not** correspond with the above-mentioned 'we'?
   ① We have felt the stinging darts of racial discrimination.
   ② We have been abused by ruthless policemen.
   ③ We have resigned from public offices against our will.
   ④ We've seen our children suffering from an inferiority complex.
   ⑤ We've been refused into places for whites.

4. 다음 중 본문의 전개 방식으로 알맞은 것은?
   ① 비교와 대조의 방법을 써서 글을 서술하고 있다.
   ② 낙천적이고 즐거운 어투로 글을 서술하고 있다.
   ③ 역사적인 사건에 대해 여러 각도로 설명하고 있다.
   ④ 각각 상반된 주장을 나열한 뒤 그에 대해 적절한 예를 들어 설명하고 있다.
   ⑤ 일상생활의 구체적 예를 들어 주장을 뒷받침하고 있다.

Production

(1) 나는 그날 아침처럼 그렇게 화려하게 태양이 솟는 것을 본 적이 없다.
(2) 그 노인은 우리를 웃기곤 하는 이야기를 해 주곤 했다.
(3) 그는 언덕에 서서 철새들이 하늘 높이 북쪽으로 날아가고 있는 것을 보았다.
(migratory birds)

● 장 문 독 해 ●

Warming-up

The first thing **to do** is to depend upon yourself.
A good son is always **anxious to** please his parents.
After rain comes sunshine; after winter, **spring**; after sorrow, **joy**.
Of all the mountains in the world, Mt. Everest is the highest.
If he doesn't work hard, he **is sure to** fail, and he will have only himself **to blame**.

2 The most important thing to learn in life, is how to live. There is nothing men are so anxious to keep as life, and nothing they take so little pains to keep well. This is no simple matter. "Life," said Hippocrates, at the commencement of his medical Aphorisms, "life is short, art is long, opportunity fleeting, experiment uncertain, and judgment difficult." ⓐHappiness and success in life do not depend on our circumstances, but on ourselves. More men have ruined themselves than have ever been destroyed by others: more houses and cities have perished at the hands of man, than storms and earthquakes have ever destroyed. There are two sorts of ruin; one is the work of time, the other of men. Of all ruins, the ruin of Man is the saddest, and a Man's worst enemy, as Seneca said, is the one in the breast. ⓑProvidence does not create evil, but gives liberty, and if we misuse it we are sure to suffer, but will have only ourselves to blame.

***Lord Avebury**: The Use of Life*

Note

take pains 수고하다 / Hippocrates (460-377 B.C.) a famous Greek physician, surnamed "the Father of Medicine" / commencement 시작 / aphorism 금언(金言), 격언 / opportunity 기회 / fleet 도망치다, 사라지다 / experiment 실험 / circumstances 환경 / destroy 파괴하다 / perish 죽다, 사라지다 / the other (is the work) of men / Seneca (died 65 A.D.) a Roman philosopher and dramatist / breast 가슴 / Providence 신(神) / create 창조하다

Question

1. 본문의 첫부분 'The most important ~ and Judgment difficult.' 의 내용과 일치하도록 다음 빈 곳에 가장 알맞은 말은?

   Man is very eager to keep his life, but he does not make efforts to live a (   ) life.

   ① long ② worthy ③ simple
   ④ painful ⑤ comfortable

2. 다음 두 문장이 각각 본문의 ⓐ와 ⓑ의 요점이 되도록 적절한 단어를 골라 쓰시오.

   ⓐ Man is the (   ) of his own fate.

   ⓑ Not God but man is (   ) for all the evil on earth.

   [mate, master, doer, responsible, response, maker]

3. According to this passage, which of the following is **not** correct?

   ① Life is more important than anything, though it is short.
   ② The destruction human beings have caused is more serious than that caused by natural disasters.
   ③ Sometimes our circumstances have more influence on success in life than our efforts do.
   ④ Man's ultimate enemy lies inside him, not outside him.
   ⑤ God gave human beings the liberty to choose between good and evil.

4. 본문의 내용에 따라, 두 빈칸에 적절한 말이 가장 잘 짝지어진 것은?

   Our life is too precious and short to waste. Therefore we should devote ourselves to making our world better by doing good (   ) and avoiding (   ).

   ① judgment — misjudgment ② deeds — misdeeds
   ③ beginning — ending ④ start — conclusion
   ⑤ calculation — miscalculation

Production

(1) 그 때 나는 그를 몹시 만나고 싶었지만, 뜻하지 않은 긴급한 일 때문에 그를 방문할 수 없었다.
(2) 너의 성공 여부는, 네가 가지고 있는 것을 어떻게 이용하느냐에 달려 있다.
(3) 우리 반의 모든 학생들 중에서 그가 가장 총명하고 부지런하다.
(4) 방 밖으로 나갈 때는 꼭 문을 닫도록 해라.

실 력 체 크 Ⅰ

1 다음 글을 읽고 밑의 물음에 답하여라.

Once in England he no longer delayed, but made straight for his native village. He had left it on foot, and had walked nearly forty miles to the nearest railway; but now a new line carried him to the village itself. From a junction on the main line, the train took a winding course among the hills, stopping at every station and sometimes waiting for a considerable time to allow cattle or goods to be loaded. Olivero—in England he had been named Oliver—still retained the black cloak and wide-brimmed hat in which he had left South America, and he was therefore a conspicuous figure among the country farmers and their wives who, from time to time, shared the carriage with him. He remained silent and reserved in his corner, gazing out at the countryside and noticing the signs of change which thirty years had inevitably produced. Late in the afternoon he found himself in familiar country: the outline of the hills, the slopes filled with trees, the church towers and an isolated house or two were recognized with an unexpected influx of emotion but the towns, with their stations and accompanying sheds, were seen from a strange aspect. He was relieved to find that his own station was some distance from the village: he was not prepared to plunge too suddenly into the heart of his past.

notes:
delay 지체하다 / junction 접선역 / winding 구불구불한 / considerable 상당한 / conspicuous 눈에 띄는 / carriage 객차 / inevitably 불가피하게 / slope 언덕 / isolated 고립된 / influx of emotion 격한 감정 / shed 차고, 헛간 / aspect 면, 각도

(1) Choose the best title for the above passage:
① A Fair Day ② Olivero's Native Village ③ Homecoming
④ Changes in the Countryside ⑤ Sightseeing

(2) 윗 글을 읽고, Olivero 씨에 대해 아는 바를 간단히 적어라.

2 다음 글의 밑줄친 부분을 구체적으로 설명하여라.

Hero-worship is a dangerous vice, and one of the minor merits of a democracy is that it does not encourage it, or produce that unmanageable type of citizen known as the Great Man. It produces instead different kinds of small men—<u>a much finer achievement</u>. But people who cannot get interested in the variety of life, and cannot make up their own minds, get discontented over this, and they long for a hero to bow down before and to follow blindly.

notes:
hero-worship 영웅숭배 / merit 장점 / achievement 성취, 업적 / variety 다양성 / discontented 불만족한, 불만스러운 / blindly 맹목적으로

3 다음 글의 (1), (2)에 들어갈 것을 ①~⑤에서 골라라.

> What is a wise man? What is wisdom? What does it mean to act wisely? Being wise does not necessarily mean learning a lot of facts or getting a lot of knowledge from books. A wise man understands human nature, relationships among humans, and the complex situations in which humans become involved. Through his own experience and understanding he knows how humans are likely to act and react in a given set of circumstances, and so he makes his own decisions and controls his own acts so that they will have the best possible results, both for himself and for others. Thus a wise man is defined not by what he __(1)__ but by what he __(2)__.

notes :
not necessarily 부분부정 / relationship 관계 / human = human being 인간 / complex 복잡한 / involve 관련시키다 / circumstances 환경 / define 정의하다

① does　② learns　③ knows　④ has　⑤ likes

4 다음 글을 읽고 아래 물음에 답하여라.

> How long will it take to build a computer complex enough to duplicate the human brain? Perhaps not as long as some think. Long before we approach a computer as complex as our brain, we will perhaps build a computer that is at least complex enough to design another computer more complex than itself. (a)<u>This more complex computer could design one still more complex and so on and so on and so on.</u> In other words, once we pass (b)<u>a certain critical point</u>, the computers take over and there is a 'complexity explosion'. In a very short time thereafter computers may exist that not only duplicate the human brain—but far surpass it. Then what? Well, (c)<u>mankind is not doing a very good job of running the earth right now.</u> Maybe, when the time comes, we ought to step gracefully aside and hand over the job to someone who can do it better. And if we don't step aside, (d)<u>perhaps super-computers will simply move in and push us aside.</u>

notes :
duplicate 복제하다 / in other words = 바꾸어 말하면 / critical 결정적인, 중대한 / take over = 대신하다 / explosion 폭발적 증가 / surpass 능가하다 / step aside 옆으로 비키다

(1) (a), (c)를 우리말로 옮기시오.
(2) 글 중 (b) a certain critical point는 구체적으로 무엇인지 25자 내외의 우리말로 써라.
(3) (d)의 내용을 구체적으로 설명하여라.

실력체크 II

A. Fill in each blank with a suitable word:

(1) I cannot look at this photo without ______ reminded of my brother.

(2) It was a difficult business ______ everything ready in time.

(3) A brief correspondence led to her ______ engaged as a teacher.

(4) I dislike ______ someone look over my shoulder to read my newspaper.

(5) Little did I dream ______ seeing you here.

B. Choose a right one:

(1) Are you going to keep me (to wait, waiting) all day?

(2) As I grow older, I find myself (to get, getting) more and more interested in Korean history.

(3) She considered (to go, going) abroad for graduate work.

(4) I am anxiously waiting for that day (to arrive, arriving).

(5) I appreciate him (to give, giving) me some legal advice.

C. 괄호 안의 동사를 옳은 형으로 고쳐라.

Dear Emily,

I have been very busy for the last three or four weeks, so please forgive me for not (① *answer*) your letter sooner. I have had (② *prepare*) for my examinations. I worked very hard, (③ *sit*) up till late almost every night. I even gave up (④ *play*) tennis after school. Now the examinations (⑤ *be*) over and I can enjoy some free hours before the spring term (⑥ *start*).

Yesterday, I went to a big bookstore and found the book you wanted, so I had it (⑦ *ship*) to you direct from the store. I hope you don't mind (⑧ *wait*) for a month or so. I am sure you will enjoy (⑨ *read*) it. I am looking forward to (⑩ *hear*) from you.

Yours sincerely,

Tom

Answer: A. (1) being (2) getting (3) being (4) having (5) of
B. (1) waiting (2) getting (3) going (4) to arrive (5) giving
C. ① having answered ② to prepare ③ sitting ④ playing ⑤ are ⑥ starts ⑦ shipped ⑧ waiting ⑨ reading ⑩ hearing

D. 위의 문장과 같은 뜻이 되도록 공란을 채워라.

(1) You have guessed wrong.
Your guess is (   ) of the mark.

(2) That is not intelligible at all.
That makes absolutely no (   ).

(3) It is unlikely that he has already heard the news.
The (   ) are that he has not heard the news yet.

(4) I would give anything to have a look at the picture.
How I (   ) I could have a look at the picture!

(5) According to tradition the mountain arose in a single night.
Tradition (   ) it that the mountain arose in a single night.

E. 각 문장의 밑줄 친 ①~④중에서 문법상 틀린 곳을 찾아 고치시오.

(1) The duties of the secretary ①are ②to take the minutes, ③mailing the correspondence, and ④calling the members before meetings.

(2) ①Recent studies ②have shown that ③many think that ④having not a college education is a great handicap.

(3) ①The idea that the computer ②will someday match or exceed the intellectual abilities of human beings ③have been put forward repeatedly ④ever since the computer was invented.

(4) If you devoted ①half as much time and energy to solving problems ②as you do ③to worry about them, ④you wouldn't have any worries.

(5) ①The most Americans were killed in World War II than ②in any other war ③since the country was ④founded.

(6) When he was young, he ①longed to write great novels like those of Tolstoy ②who ③would win ④him fame.

Answer: D. (1) wide (2) sense (3) chances (4) wish (5) has
E. (1) ② to take→taking (2) ④ having not→not having (3) ③ have been→has been
(4) ③ to worry→to worrying (5) ① The most→More (6) ② who→which

어 휘 · 발 음

A. 공란에 다음 단어의 올바른 어형을 써넣어 뜻을 완성하라.

fail, succeed, agree, marry, argument

Happiness in ___(1)___ depends not on whether couples argue, but on what they argue about. A polite ___(2)___ over money is often an indication of ___(3)___ , while verbal battle over what kind of flowers to plant next to roses is a sure sign of ___(4)___ .

B. 다음 글의 공란은 모두 「~이 된다(become)」란 뜻이 있는 동사가 필요하다. become 외의 동사를 옳은 어형으로 공란에 집어넣되, 같은 것을 두 번 써서는 안 된다. (단 turn은 두 번 써도 된다.)

(1) The days are (　　) longer and longer.
(2) Galileo (　　) blind in his old age.
(3) In autumn the leaves of trees, such as maples, (　　) red.
(4) The last wound he received (　　) fatal.
(5) If you don't take better care of yourself, you will (　　) ill.
(6) That dream of yours may (　　) true some day.
(7) The report, though many people believed it, (　　) out false.
(8) I believe your son will (　　) a good doctor.
(9) At the time the oil was (　　) short in that country.
(10) Gradually, as you (　　) older, you will realize the truth of what I am now saying.

C. 밑줄 친 부분을 한 단어로 나타내어라.

(1) The train arrived <u>exactly on time</u>.
(2) The design was <u>in the form of a circle</u>.
(3) Tom was <u>inclined to pick a quarrel</u>.
(4) Although the food was good, I had no <u>inclination to eat</u>.
(5) Although the two vessels collided with a sharp impact, the damage was found, on inspection, to be <u>of little or no significance</u>.

Answer: A. (1) marriage (2) disagreement (3) failure (4) success B. (1) getting (2) went (3) turn (4) proved (5) fall (6) come (7) turned (8) make (9) running (10) grow C. (1) punctually (2) circular (3) quarrelsome (4) appetite (5) negligible

D. 다음 ( )에 가장 적당한 말을 고르시오.

(1) Kiwifruit's sweet, succulent flesh dotted with tiny ( ) seeds can be used in salads and desserts.

① invisible ② audible ③ edible ④ tangible

(2) "The future of our country is inseparably ( ) to modernization," the President told the nationally televised news conference.

① linked ② compared ③ due ④ likened

(3) Poland's more than 70,000 war invalids are ( ) official cards granting them first priority to purchase the most coveted major items, including furniture and appliances.

① received ② issued ③ delivered ④ bestowed

(4) A CIA spokesman refused to comment on any details of the reports but said that "there are no Americans ( ) in Nicaragua or its waters."

① included ② excluded ③ involved ④ revolved

(5) The discoveries of science often are a ( ); on the one hand they give us valuable pesticides that enable the farmer to grow more abundant crops, but on the other hand they injure wildlife and upset the balance of nature.

① mixed blessing ② blessing in disguise

③ cloud with a silver lining ④ golden opportunity

E. 주어진 문장의 밑줄 친 부분과 같은 의미로 쓰인 것을 고르시오.

(1) The red lines on the map <u>represent</u> railways.

① He <u>represented</u> himself to others as a wealthy man.

② He is going to <u>represent</u> Hamlet in that play.

③ My goal is to <u>represent</u> my country at the Olympics.

④ In this painting the cat <u>represents</u> evil and the bird, good.

(2) You need an <u>even</u> surface to work on.

① The parson preached in an <u>even</u> tone of voice.

② The table has an <u>even</u> finish, with no bumps.

③ My child doesn't know an <u>even</u> number from an odd number yet.

④ The chances of success or failure are <u>even</u>.

Answer: D. (1) ③ (2) ① (3) ② (4) ③ (5) ① E. (1) ④ (2) ②

숙 어

(1) **call for** (=demand, require) 요구하다
☞ It's the sort of work that *calls for* a high level of concentration.

(2) **call off** (=cancel) 취소하다
☞ The union threatened a strike but *called* it *off* at the last minute.

(3) **care for** (=like) 《의문문,부정문에서》 좋아하다 ; (=look after, nurse) 돌보다
☞ I don't really *care for* coffee. Would you *care for* another drink?
Who will *care for* the children if their mother dies?

(4) **carry on** (=manage) 경영하다
☞ Despite the recession, he is *carrying on* his business on a large scale.

(5) **catch sight of** (=get a glimpse of) ~을 얼핏 보다 (↔ **lose sight of**)
☞ I *caught sight of* my former teacher while I was shopping today, but she turned a corner and I *lost sight of* her.

(6) **cheer up** (=become happier ; make one happier) 기운나다; 기운을 내게 하다
☞ *Cheer up*! The news isn't too bad. My friends tried to *cheer* me *up*.

(7) **come across** (=find unexpectedly) 우연히 발견하다
☞ In cleaning out the attic, I *came across* a few remembrances of my grandmother's.

(8) **come by** (=obtain) 얻다, 획득하다
☞ A good job like that is very hard to *come by* these days.

(9) **come down with** (=become ill with) 병에 걸리다
☞ At the age of four she *came down with* acute pneumonia.

(10) **come to** (=become conscious) (의식을) 회복하다
☞ As the anesthetic wore off, the patient *came to*.

(11) **come true** (=really happen, become real) 실현되다, 실제로 일어나다
☞ All of his warnings *came true* when the stock market crashed.

(12) **come up with** (=think of) ~을 생각해 내다
☞ He *came up with* a new idea for increasing sales.

⒀ **be concerned about** (=be anxious about) ~을 걱정하다
be concerned with (=have interest in) ~에 관심이 있다
☞ I'*m concerned about* his health. I'*m* not *concerned with* it.

⒁ **cope with** (=manage successfully) 대처하다
☞ His counseling has helped me *cope with* my difficulties.

⒂ **count for nothing[little]** (=be of no[little] importance) (거의) 중요하지 않다
☞ Knowledge without common sense *counts for nothing*[*little*].

⒃ **count in** (=include) 끼워주다
☞ If you're all going to the party, *count* me *in*.

⒄ **count on** (=rely on) 믿다, 기대하다
☞ You can *count on* her to do a good job.

⒅ **cut a fine figure** (=make a fine appearance) 이채를 띠다, 두각을 나타내다
☞ With her beauty she *cut a fine figure* among them.

⒆ **cut in** (=interrupt) 방해하다, 끼어들다
☞ I was talking to him when she *cut in* on our conversation.

⒇ **deal[trade] in** (=buy and sell things) 판매하다, 장사하다
deal with (=treat) 다루다, 취급하다
☞ The police said he was *dealing*[*trading*] *in* stolen goods.
The manager tried to *deal* politely *with* the angry customers.

㉑ **depend on** (=rely on) ~에 달려 있다 ; 의지하다
☞ It *depends on* your experience. I have no one but you to *depend on*.

Exercise

▶▶ 주어진 단어들을 포함한 글을 지어라. 필요하면 어형을 변화시켜라.

1. situation / call / action
2. take / ballet / cheer
3. come / books / attic
4. family / come / with / flu
5. throw / water / face / come
6. hope / lawyer / come
7. cope / all / work
8. count / weather / fine
9. how / deal / problem
10. all / family / depend

5. 분　　사(Participle)

기본 문법 설명

A. 분사의 형용사적 용법	ⓐ **a sleeping** baby an **exciting** story ⓑ **fallen** leaves a **broken** window ⓒ Who is that girl **wearing** an exotic hat? Do you happen to know a stumpy man **called** Ben? You'd better take the train **leaving** at two. ⓓ Of those **invited** only a few came to the party. She acted like one **overwhelmed**.
B. 보어로서의 분사	ⓐ He kept **walking** in the same direction. The door remained **locked** for a long time. He sat at his desk **surrounded** by books and papers. ⓑ I saw him **snatching** the handbag and **running**. I felt myself **watched** in the dark. I *hád* my car *repaired.*　　I *got* my car *stólen.* I *had him repair* my car.　　I *got him to repair* my car.
C. 분사구문	ⓐ **Walking** along the street, I ran into an old friend. **Left** alone, she felt dead tired. ⓑ Not **knowing** what to do, he asked me for help. **Tired**, I went to bed earlier than usual. ⓒ **Turning** right, you'll find the post office on your right. Some books, **read** carelessly, will do more harm than good. ⓓ **Admitting** what you say, I still think you're wrong. **Born** from the same parents, they bear no resemblance to each other. ⓔ **Walking** on tiptoe, I approached the window. **Singing** and **dancing** together, we had a good time. The train starts at six, **arriving** there at ten.

A. 분사의 형용사적 용법
분사는 형용사처럼 직접 명사에 부가하여 수식어로서 사용된다.
☞ 현재분사 — 능동적인 의미
과거분사 — 수동적인 의미
ⓐ a sleeping baby
= a baby who is sleeping
an exciting story
= a story which excites people
ⓑ fallen leaves (낙엽) — 완료의 의미
= leaves which have fallen
a broken window — 수동의 의미
= a window which is broken
ⓒ 분사가 보어, 목적어 혹은 부사적 수식어구를 동반할 때는 보통 명사의 뒤에 놓인다.
(이국적인 모자를 쓰고 있는 저 젊은 여자는 누구니?) … 목적어를 동반
(혹시 Ben이라는 땅딸막한 남자를 아세요?) … 보어를 동반
(2시에 떠나는 기차를 타야한다.)
… 부사구를 동반
ⓓ 분사가 대명사를 수식할 때는 단독일 때에도 뒤에 놓인다. 따라서 invited가 대명사 those의 뒤에 왔다.
(초대받은 사람들 중에서 불과 몇 사람만 파티에 왔다.) (그녀는 마치 압도당한 사람처럼 행동했다.)
… overwhelmed는 one을 수식

B. 보어로서의 분사
분사도 형용사처럼 보어로서 주어 혹은 목적어를 서술적으로 수식한다.
ⓐ **주격보어**로서
(그는 같은 방향으로 계속 걸었다.)
… walking은 주격보어
(그 문은 오랫동안 잠겨져 있었다.)
… locked는 주격보어
(그는 책과 서류에 둘러싸여 자기 책상에 앉아 있었다.)
… surrounded는 (유사) 주격보어
ⓑ **목적격보어**로서
(나는 그가 핸드백을 들치기해 달아나는 것을 보았다.)
snatching과 running은 목적격 보어
(나는 어둠속에서 감시당하고 있는듯한 느낌이 들었다.)
… watched는 목적격 보어
have (*or* get) + 목적어 + 과거분사
(차를 수리시켰다) (차를 도난당했다)
* have + 사람 + 원형부정사
= get + 사람 + to 부정사
(나는 그에게 내 차를 수리시켰다.)

C. 분사구문
분사가 유도하는 구가 주문을 부사적으로 수식할 때, 그 분사구(分詞句)를 분사구문 (Participial Construction)이라 한다.
ⓐ **시간**
Walking along the street,
= While I was walking along ~ ,
Left alone, = When she was left alone,
ⓑ **이유**
Not knowing what to do,
= As he didn't know what to do,
(Being) tired, = As I was tired
ⓒ **조건**
Turning right, = If you turn right,
read carelessly,
= if they are read carelessly,
(어떤 책들은 부주의하게 읽히면 이익보다는 해가 된다.)
ⓓ **양보**
Admitting what you say,
= Though I admit what you say,
Born from~,
= Though they were born from ~,
(같은 부모에게서 태어났지만, 그들은 서로 닮은 데가 없다.)
ⓔ **부대상황** (동시상황)
원래 주격보어로서, 주절의 동작이 행해질 때의 주어의 상황을 나타냄
(발끝으로 살살 걸어, 나는 창가에 다가갔다.) … walking on tiptoe와 approach는 동시에 일어난 일이다.
= I walked on tiptoe and approached the window.
(함께 노래하며 춤추며 우리는 재미있게 놀았다.)
= *As we sang* and *danced* ~.
= … at six, *and arrives* there ~.

D. 분사구문의 시제	ⓐ **Having received** no answer from him, I faxed him again. ⓑ **While swimming** in the river, he drowned.
E. 독립 분사구문	ⓐ **The sun having set**, we gave up looking for them. ⓑ **It being** fine, we set out on a picnic. ⓒ We'll start tomorrow, **weather permitting**. ⓓ He was reading a book, **his wife knitting** beside him.
F. 무인칭 독립 분사구문	**Strictly speaking**, he is an amateur, not a professional. **Judging from** his accent, he must be a German.
G. ~ing as it does의 형	**Standing as it does** on the hill, the villa commands a fine view.
H. 문두에 나오는 주격보어	**Impatient** from the heat, he left town for the country. **A man of social instincts**, he had many acquaintances.
I. 부대상황	It was a misty morning, **with** little wind **blowing**. The hostage sat on the chair, **with** his eyes **bandaged**.

● 영어의 비유적 표현의 중요성 ●

The child had to stand in the corner. (벌섰다)
They snapped their fingers at him. (경멸했다)
He tipped his hat to me. (가볍게 인사했다)
He walked under a ladder and failed the examination.
(사다리 밑을 걸으면 재수가 없다는 속담이 있다)
The passengers prayed that the thread of life might hold.
(the thread of life는 수명)
Time left his footprints on her brow. (주름살이 생겼다)
He is not as black as he is painted.
(남들이 말하듯 그렇게 악인은 아니다)
His heart trouble reared its unwelcome head again.
(뱀이 머리를 드는 비유, 즉 반갑지 못한 일이 일어나는 것)

D. 분사구문의 시제

ⓐ 분사구문이 나타내는 시간은 주절의 술부동사의 시제와 일치하지만, 그보다 앞선 시제를 나타낼 때는 「**having+과거분사**」를 쓴다.
Having received~,
= As I had received~,
Not having seen him for a long time, I did not recognize him at first.
(=As I *had not seen* him~)

ⓑ 분사구문의 뜻이 때·이유·조건 등 어느 것인지 혼동을 방지하기 위해, 해당 접속사를 분사구문의 앞에 부가할 경우가 있다.
Swimming in the river,를 As he swam in the river,로 잘못 해석하지 않도록 While swimming in the river로 하여 뜻을 명백히 하였다.

E. 독립분사구문

분사구문에는 의미상 주어가 있다. 이것이 주문의 주어와 같을 때는 나타낼 필요가 없지만, 다를 때는 분사의 앞에 분사의 주어를 첨가해 나타내 주어야 한다.

ⓐ 때
The sun having set,
= Because the sun had set,
Night *coming* on, we left for home.

ⓑ 이유
It being fine, = As it was fine,
My knife *slipping*, I cut myself severely.

ⓒ 조건
weather permitting
= if (the) weather permits
Other things *being* equal, I would prefer this one.

ⓓ 부대상황
= He was reading a book, and his wife was knitting beside him.
(그는 책을 읽고 있었고, 그의 부인은 남편 옆에서 뜨개질을 하고 있었다.)
… 남편이 책을 읽는 것과 부인이 뜨개질하는 것은 동시에 일어나는 일이다.

☞ (x) Having read the book, it was thrown away.
(o) Having read the book, I threw it away.

F. 무인칭독립분사구문

독립분사구문은 의미상 주어가 필요하지만, 그것이 막연한 일반인을 나타낼 때는 생략할 수 있다.
Strictly speaking, (엄격히 말해)
= If we speak strictly,
Judging from~, (~으로 판단하건대)
= If we judge from ~,
Generally speaking, (일반적으로 말해)
= If we speak generally,
Taking all things into consideration,
(만사를 고려하면)

G. ~ing as it does의 형

(저렇게 언덕 위에 서 있으므로 그 별장은 전망이 좋다.)
… as it does는 분사구문의 뜻을 강조하기 위해 덧붙인 것이다. as는 양태를 나타내는 접속사, it는 여기서 the villa, does는 stands의 대동사이다.

H. 문두에 나오는 주격보어

Being을 보충하면 이유를 나타내는 분사구문이 된다.
= Being impatient from~,
(더위를 참을 수 없어서, 그는 도시를 떠나 시골로 내려갔다.)
= Being a man of~,
(사교성이 풍부한 사람이었으므로, 그는 아는 사람이 많았다.)

I. 부대상황

「**with+목적어+분사**」: 부대상황을 나타내는 독립분사구문에 with가 붙을 때도 있다. 이 때 목적어와 분사는 주어·술어의 관계가 성립되어야하며 이 관계가 능동이면 현재분사, 수동이면 과거분사가 된다.
with little wind blowing
= and little wind *was blowing*
(바람이 거의 불지 않는 안개 낀 아침이었다.)
with his eyes bandaged
= and his eyes *were bandaged*
(인질은 눈에 붕대가 감긴 채 의자에 앉아있었다.)

문 법 · 작 문

A. 맞는 단어를 골라라.

(1) A (drowning, drowned) man will catch at a straw.
(2) The news soon became widely (knowing, known).
(3) The children kept (pestered, pestering) me to take them to the zoo.
(4) Was there anything that made you (embarrassed, embarrassing)?
(5) It was a really (exciting, excited) game, and the spectators grew more and more (excited, exciting).
(6) I'm sorry to have kept you (waiting, waited) so long.
(7) He came home in high spirits (satisfying, satisfied) with the result.
(8) I smelled the woman (wearing, worn) some spicy perfume.
(9) A (rolled, rolling) stone gathers no moss.
(10) Things (done, doing) by halves are never done right.
(11) He ran along with his shirt (hanging, hung) and his jacket (tearing, torn).
(12) We can buy a paper (containing, contained) the news of the world for a dime.

B. 이탤릭체 부분을 바꾸어, 다음 각 문장을 단문으로 고쳐라.

(1) Apple-trees *which are covered* with ripe apples are a beautiful sight.
(2) The girl *who is picking* the petals off the daisy is my sister.
(3) I was surprised to see *that a pine tree was growing* on the wall of the huge rock.
(4) She was *so tender-hearted that she could not bear* his plight.
(5) Do you remember the song *which the children sang*?

C. 공란을 적당한 단어로 메워라.

(1) There is a lot of time (　　) for the 9:30 train.
(2) (　　) from an airplane, all the houses looked just like toys.
(3) With this work (　　), we went home.
(4) (　　) all things into consideration, he must be a lucky guy.
(5) There (　　) no bus service, we had to walk all the way to the village.
(6) (　　) all his money stolen, he felt miserable.
(7) Do to others as you would be (　　) by.
(8) Silk is of immense value, forming as it (　　) the staple export of the country.
(9) The policeman came too late and found the thief (　　) and the room in disorder.
(10) His advice (　　) good, we had no choice but to follow it.
(11) (　　) that he had the best intentions, his conduct was productive of mischief.

D. 다음 문장 안의 틀린 부분을 고쳐라.

(1) I want it deliver by this coming Friday.
(2) He stood leaned against the wall.
(3) I can rest assuring that he's doing everything possible to solve it.
(4) The news set my heart throbbed.
(5) Having read the book, it was sold.
(6) Shall I get your trunk carry by a porter?
(7) Another thing that he did was to have a history of England wrote.
(8) They are pleasant that the import restrictions are being relaxed.
(9) The poison, using in a small quantity, will prove to be a medicine.
(10) The dog, training carefully, will become a faithful servant.
(11) His house, situating on a hill, commands a splendid view.
(12) Comparing with their national power, ours pales.
(13) I'm sure I can make myself understand in English.
(14) Wearing nothing but a light sweater, the cold wind drove me indoors.
(15) She busied herself to prepare for the interview.
(16) The teacher, having not heard the bell, kept on teaching.
(17) Writing in haste, the book has many faults.
(18) I have been to the photographer's to take my picture.
(19) He seemed well reading in French literature.
(20) He went out, with his dog followed behind.
(21) With night came on, we hurried home.
(22) The window has been kept closing all day.
(23) He felt himself being gently touched on the shoulder, and looking around his father stood before him.
(24) My telling him the truth, he's positive he'll keep it under his hat.
(25) The article being made of iron, it will not break.
(26) I was blown off my hat by the wind.
(27) Have you ever seen towns destroying by bombing?
(28) After months of drilling, we found oil gushed out from a well.
(29) You must make yourself respecting in the business world.
(30) The seizing rebel leaders included three women.
(31) Those expecting failed to turn up.
(32) The package, having wrongly addressed, reached him late.

E. 다음 각 문장을 분사구문이 든 문장으로 바꾸어 써라.

(1) He was very tired from working, and so he sat down to take a break.
(2) I had finished my daily task of inputting the sales figures and I had nothing more to do.
(3) As it had rained heavily the previous night, part of the road subsided.
(4) As there was nothing left to do, he was allowed to go home.
(5) As I did not know what to say, I remained silent.
(6) A ball flew into the room, and broke the vase on the desk.
(7) The car broke down on the way. The trip took longer than we'd expected.
(8) Since they had no keys, no entrance was possible.
(9) When the traveler was overtaken by night among the mountains, he did not know which road to follow.
(10) A foreign travel, if it is properly conducted, will serve to broaden our horizons.
(11) I sat reading a novel, while my wife was drying her hair by me.
(12) They were enjoying skiing on the steep slope, and the sun was shining brightly overhead.
(13) The woman has always been idle and dishonest, and so I must dismiss her.
(14) If you get across the river by the sightseeing boat, you'll arrive at the famous spa.
(15) It is difficult to hire an efficient man, because the salary is small.
(16) The cry brought her to the window.
(17) I ran all the way to the station, and arrived there breathless.
(18) He sat down to rest a little. He had had a long and tiring walk.

F. 다음 각 문장의 분사구문을 절(節)로 바꾸어 써라.

(1) Having made an obvious mistake, he still refused to admit it.
(2) Jaywalking on the street, he was run over by a taxi.
(3) United, we stand; divided, we fall.
(4) The game over, the crowd dispersed.
(5) Born in better times, he would have been a great ruler.
(6) The boy, having been praised, worked the harder.
(7) Admitting what you say, I can hardly approve of your proposal.
(8) Taken by surprise by the burglar, he was severely wounded.
(9) With the work finished, she looked happy.

G. 괄호 속의 동사의 바른 어형을 적어라.

(1) She was sitting with her arms (cross), staring at him.

(2) Mary heard herself (mention) as the most (accomplish) girl in the neighborhood.

(3) Such a violation of discipline, if (pass) unnoticed, will have a very injurious effect on the students.

(4) The love of money has (call) the root of all evil. But the fact is that most of us spend our lives (work) for money, (worry) over it, and some of us even kill and die for it.

(5) I have somewhere seen it (observe) that we should make the same use of a book that the bee does of a flower.

(6) (Wear) out by his struggle with the storm, Crusoe fell asleep, and when he awoke, he found himself on a desert island, with nothing to (see) but the (wreck) ship and some trees and bushes.

H. Translate the following into English;

(1) 버스는 너무 만원이어서 나는 쭉 서 있어야만 했다.

(2) 어제는 일요일이며, 날씨도 좋고, 또 특별히 할 일도 없어서, 낚시를 갔다.

(3) 그 여자의 집 가까이 갔을 때 나는 그 여자가 피아노 치는 소리를 들었다.

(4) 나는 머리를 깎으러 방금 이발소에 갔다왔다.

(5) 그는 약 한 시간이 지나면 돌아오겠다고 말하면서 나갔다.

(6) 일반적으로 말해, 우리 한국사람들은 외국어를 말할 때 좀 지나치게 겁을 낸다.

(7) 그 전투에서 부상당한 병사들이 병원으로 후송되었다.

(8) 쉬운 영어로 씌어져 있으므로, 이 책은 초보자에게 알맞다.

(9) 그의 집에 그렇게 가까이 살지만, 나는 좀처럼 그를 만나지 못한다.

(10) 해가 졌으므로 우리는 서둘러 집으로 향했다.

'Autumn'이라는 제목으로 70어 내외의 글을 지어라.

● 단 문 독 해 ●

Barking dogs seldom bite.
English is a language **spoken** all over the world.
The children came **running** to her.
Suddenly I heard my name **called** behind me.

1. Then I also think of the full-grown gourds, which can be seen on the **thatched** roofs of the country houses, the red peppers **drying** on mats along the road and the delicious apples, pears, persimmons and grapes to be found in abundance in shops both large and small. Then there is the irresistible scent of chestnuts being roasted over charcoal fires on carts along the street.

notes :
*gourd 조롱박
*thatched roof = 초가지붕
*persimmon 감
*scent 냄새
*charcoal fire = 숯불

▶▶윗글에서 연상되는 가장 적절한 말은?
① elegant ② delicate ③ dreary
④ plentiful ⑤ gorgeous

▶▶영작하시오.
그가 죽었다는 내용의 이메일을 나는 그녀로부터 받았다.

2. A sad-faced man came into my flower shop early one morning. I was ready to take his order for a funeral piece, but this time I guessed wrong. He wanted a basket of flowers **sent** to his wife for their wedding anniversary. "And what day will that be?" I asked. Glumly he replied, "Yesterday."

notes :
*a funeral piece = 조화
*glumly 우울하게, 슬프게

▶▶윗글의 내용에 맞는 것을 하나 골라라.
① The man was by nature gloomy.
② The man was a henpecked husband.
③ The man's wife awoke him early in the morning to buy flowers.
④ The florist offered his condolences to the sad-faced man.
⑤ It seems that the man's wife gave him a hard time for forgetting their wedding anniversary.

▶▶영작하시오.
나는 그 꽃가게에서 결혼 5주년 기념 꽃바구니를 아내에게 보냈다.

Walking along the street, I met a friend of mine.
Lost in thought, he did not notice me.
Admitting what you say, I still don't believe it.
Turning right, you will find the post office.
Walking on tiptoe, I approached the window.

3. **Having invented** machinery, man has become enslaved by it, as he was long ago enslaved by the gods created by his imagination. It is machinery which has allowed women and children to enter the factory and which at the same time has disorganized the family and the home.

notes :
*machinery (집합적) 기계류
*become enslaved = 노예가 되다
*disorganize (조직을) 해체시키다

▶▶What's the writer's attitude toward machinery?
① positive ② indifferent ③ critical
④ neutral ⑤ optimistic

▶▶영작하시오.
내가 그녀를 처음 만난 것은 어느 맑은 가을날이었다.

4. Our senses, by an effect almost mechanical, are passive to the impression of outward objects, whether agreeable or offensive, but the mind, **possessed** of a self-directing power, may turn its attention to whatever it thinks is proper.

notes :
*mechanical 기계적인
*passive 수동적인
*self-directing 자기 통제의

▶▶While our senses are passive, our mind is (   ).
[negative, active, inert, idle]

▶▶영작하시오.
선생님께 칭찬을 받았으므로 그녀는 매우 기뻤다.

5. **Being** stupid and **having** no imagination, animals often behave far more sensibly than men. Efficiently and by instinct they do the right, appropriate thing at the right moment — eat when they are hungry, look for water when they feel thirsty, rest or play when they have leisure.

notes :
*sensibly 지각[분별력]있게
*efficiently 효과적으로
*appropriate 적절한

▶▶Animals live (   ), but they often behave far more (   ) than men.
[instinctively, sensitively, pensively, sensibly]

▶▶영작하시오.
네 말을 인정은 하지만 너의 제안에 찬성할 수는 없다.

6. **Uncontrolled,** the forces of nature may be dangerous and destructive, but once **mastered**, they can be bent to man's will and desire. Today, for instance, electricity is man's humble servant, performing a thousand tasks with tremendous efficiency.

notes :
*Uncontrolled = If they are uncontrolled
*once mastered = once they are mastered <once 접 일단 ~하면>
*tremendous 엄청난
*efficiency 능력, 능률

▶▶윗글의 내용에 일치하도록 다음 빈칸에 들어갈 말이 가장 잘 짝지어진 것은?

( ), the forces of nature can be of benefit to the well-being of human beings. Otherwise, they can cause ( ).

① Uncontrolled — tremendous destruction
② Uncontrolled — mass destruction
③ Controlled — natural disasters
④ Mastered — man-made catastrophe
⑤ Controlled — environmental disruption

▶▶영작하시오.

마침내 그들은 내 뜻을 따랐다.

7. In short, we all go through life **wearing** glasses colored by our own tastes, our own calling, and our own prejudices, **measuring** our neighbors by our own standards, **summing** them up according to our own private arithmetic. We see subjectively, not objectively; what we are capable of seeing, not what there is to be seen.

notes :
*go through life = 인생을 살아가다
*calling 직업
*standard 기준
*sum up = 판단하다; 요약하다
*arithmetic 계산[셈]

▶▶According to the above passage, which is most suitable for the blank?

In conclusion, human beings are ( ).

① prejudiced but generous
② biased and egotistical
③ self-centered but objective
④ altruistic but subjective
⑤ intolerant but beneficent

▶▶영작하시오.

그는 장래를 생각하면서 자지 않고 오랜 동안 누워 있었다.

It being fine, we went for a walk.
Generally speaking, the Koreans are diligent.
With an eye **bandaged**, I could not write properly.

8. The first star to come out in the evening is called the Evening Star, but, **strictly speaking**, it is not a star at all; it is a planet. Planets are different from the stars. They do not give off any light of their own but shine by reflecting the sunlight that falls on them. There are nine of these planets traveling around the sun, **the earth being** one of them.

notes :
*planet 혹성, 행성
*give off = 발산하다
*the earth being = and the earth is

▶▶According to the above paragraph, which of the following is incorrect?

① It would be more reasonable to call the first star in the evening the Evening Planet, instead of the Evening Star.
② There are nine planets in the solar system.
③ Stars can not only emit their own light but reflect the sunlight.
④ The earth is a kind of planet belonging to the solar system.
⑤ Venus looks bright thanks to the sunlight.

▶▶영작하시오.

그의 어조로 판단하건대 그는 영국인임에 틀림없다.

9. **With** their minds **fixed** on the future, Americans found themselves surrounded with ample land and resources and troubled by a shortage of labor and skill. They set much value on technical knowledge and inventiveness which would unlock the riches of the country and open the door to a glorious future.

notes :
*ample 광대한
*shortage 부족
*set much value on ~ = ~을 높이 평가하다

▶▶Why did Americans think highly of technical knowledge and inventiveness?

Because they realized that their industries were (   ) of skilled technical man-power, though they were (   ) with abundant natural resources.

[low, long, short, blessed, dissatisfied, burdened]

▶▶영작하시오.

그는 두손을 호주머니에 넣은채 땅을 물끄러미 보면서 소나무에 기대어 있었다.

장 문 독 해

Warming-up

Some men feel themselves born **out of place**.

He lived his whole life **an alien** and remained **aloof** from society.

We must have something that we may **attach ourselves to**.

He finally **hit upon** a place to which he strongly felt himself attracted.

The name Harry Potter **is familiar to** many readers.

1 I have an idea that ⓐsome men are born out of their due place. Accident has cast them among certain surroundings, but ⓑthey always have a nostalgia for a home they don't know. They are strangers in their birthplace, and the leafy lanes they have known from childhood or the populous streets in which they have played, remain but a place of passage. They may spend their whole lives aliens among their kindred and remain aloof among the only scenes they have ever known. Perhaps it is this sense of strangeness that sends men far and wide in the search for something permanent to which they may attach themselves. Perhaps some deep-rooted atavism urges the wanderer back to lands which his ancestors left in the dim beginnings of history. Sometimes a man hits upon a place to which he mysteriously feels that he belongs. Here is the home he sought, and he will settle among scenes that he has never seen before, among men he has never known, as though they were familiar to him from his birth. Here at last he finds rest.

***W. Somerset Maugham**: The Moon and Sixpence*

Note

surroundings 환경 / leafy 잎이 무성한 / lanes 오솔길 / populous 사람이 많은 / but=only / kindred 친척(들) / permanent 영원한 / attach oneself to ~에 애착을 느끼다 / deep-rooted 뿌리 깊이 박힌 / atavism 격세유전 (=throwback) / urge 재촉하다 / wanderer 방랑자 / ancestor 선조 / hit upon ~을 우연히 만나다 / belong to ~에 속하다

Question

1. 밑줄 친 ⓐ와 같은 뜻이 되도록 한 단어를 골라 채우시오.
   some men are born in the (   ) place
   [weird, wrong, right]

2. Why do the underlined ⓑthey feel strange in their birthplace? Choose an **unsuitable** answer.
   ① Because of their sense of strangeness caused by atavism.
   ② Because their birthplace is not their due place.
   ③ Because they are not well-acquainted with their birthplace.
   ④ Because of their sense of belonging somewhere else.
   ⑤ Because they feel homesick for a place they don't know.

3. Which of the following does **not** correspond with the 'people' mentioned in the passage?
   ① They don't feel comfortable and remain aloof from others in their hometown.
   ② Once in a while a man finds a place where he feels as if it were his own home.
   ③ Their strange disposition is perhaps caused by a throwback to another time.
   ④ Their forefathers had similar characteristics.
   ⑤ They live as if they were aliens among their peers all their lives.

4. What does the author mainly discuss?
   ① a destructive instinct
   ② a fighting instinct
   ③ a homing instinct
   ④ a desire for possession
   ⑤ an instinct for self-conservation

Production

(1) 그는 그녀를 전혀 모르는 체했다.
(2) 결국 그가 목숨을 바친 그 위험한 일을 맡도록 재촉한 것은 바로 그의 책임감이었다.
(3) 자기도 모르는 고향에 대해 향수를 느끼며, 한평생을 방황하면서 남모를 무엇을 찾아 헤매는 사람들이 있다.

● 장 문 독 해 ●

Warming-up

I spent a whole winter in the country, **kept** indoors much of the time.

If we are not rich, we have good friends.

They had no lamps to read books **by**.

That dream of yours may come true someday.

His desire for peace **echoes** through all his poems.

2 If you have lived a whole winter in the country, far from shops and cinemas, kept indoors much of the time, trudging to school through rain and mud and cold, you know what a marvelous relief it is when spring comes. Imagine how much more relief <u>it</u> must have been to primitive man. He had no shops or cinemas anyway: he didn't even have books to read in the long winter evenings: and if he had had books, there were no lamps to read them by. He was often terribly cold. He worried whether the food he had stored would last him through the winter. Worst of all, he was never absolutely sure that summer would return at all. So the first day of spring came as a miracle to him. Now he could be warm again: now he could go out into his fields and didn't need to be afraid of starving. That passionate desire of his for the end of winter, that feeling of wonderful relief when the weather at last began to turn warm, echoes through poetry right up to our own day. It is in our blood, so to speak, and that is why so much fine poetry has all through ages been written about spring.

***C. D. Lewis**: Poetry for You*

Note

keep indoors 방 안에 박혀 있다 / trudge 터벅터벅 걷다 / mud 진흙 / relief 위안; 구원, 구제 / primitive man 원시인(原始人) / miracle 기적 / passionate 정열적인 / echo 메아리치다 / so to speak 말하자면

Question

1. 본문 5행의 밑줄친 it가 가리키는 내용을 우리말로 간단히 쓰시오.

2. 아래 질문에 대한 답이 되도록, 빈칸에 들어갈 가장 적절한 것은?

Why does the author mention a primitive man's life?

Because he wants us to know that our thirst for the coming of spring is (   ).

① strong ② instinctive ③ unquenchable
④ unbearable ⑤ everlasting

3. According to the passage, which of the following is **not** correct?
① People living in the country suffer from the inconvenience of winter life.
② Primitive man looked forward to spring because of his precarious life in rigorous winter.
③ Winter was a bitter and monotonous season for primitive man.
④ There were more poems about spring than those about winter.
⑤ The coming of spring seemed to be a miracle to primitive man.

4. Which of the following is most suitable for the main idea of this passage?
① The inconvenience of living in the country in winter
② Spring is a wondrous season
③ Contemporary poetry about winter and spring
④ How anxiously primitive man waited for spring
⑤ Why there are so many good poems about spring

Production

(1) 중국인으로 나를 잘못 알고 중국어로 나에게 말을 걸어왔다.
(2) 그는 그 책을 살 돈이 없었다.
(3) 그 계획의 성공은 당신이 협조하느냐에 달려 있다.
(4) 무엇보다 나쁜 것은 그는 돈도 없었고 건강도 좋지 못했다.

실력체크 I

1 Read the following passage and answer as directed:

> Dining one evening with his friends, young Dr. Aidid, a lonely Hindu widower with three children, was interrupted by a call to the hospital where he served under the arrogant Dr. Callendar. Aidid regretfully left his friends and arrived by cab at the hospital, only to find that Dr. Callendar had departed without leaving him a message. (ㄱ)<u>To add insult to injury</u>, just as Aidid was about to leave, his cab was abruptly occupied by two English women who did not even bother to thank him.
> Upset at this typical treatment at the hands of the English, (ㄴ)<u>Aidid dropped into a Hindu temple for a moment of peace</u>. Seeing an English woman there, he shouted at her, assuming she had not removed her shoes. But the English woman, Mrs. Moore, was sensitive to Hindu custom, and had entered the temple barefooted. (ㄷ)<u>This</u> pleased Dr. Aidid so much that he started a conversation with Mrs. Moore who had recently arrived in India and wanted to see as much of it as possible. Dr. Aidid was pleased to find that (ㄹ)<u>Mrs. Moore shared his low opinion of Dr. Callendar</u>.

notes :
add insult to injury 피해를 주고 또 모욕하다 / not bother ~조차도 하지 않다 / upset at ~에 기분이 상한 / barefooted 맨발로

(1) 밑줄 친 (ㄱ)의 insult와 injury의 내용을 구체적으로 설명하여라.
(2) 밑줄 친 (ㄴ), (ㄹ)을 해석하여라.
(3) 밑줄 친 (ㄷ)의 This의 내용을 구체적으로 설명하여라.

2 다음 글을 읽고 아래 물음에 답하여라.

> Both of them fell desperately in love with Isabel, but Bateman saw quickly that she had eyes only for Edward and devoted to (1)<u>his friend</u>, he resigned himself to the role of a trusting friend. He passed bitter moments, but he could not deny that Edward was worthy of (2)<u>his good fortune</u>, and anxious that nothing should impair the friendship he so greatly valued, he took care never to disclose his own feelings. In six months (3)<u>the young couple</u> were engaged.

notes :
desperately 필사적으로 / devoted to=as he was devoted to / resign oneself to (~에) 순응하다 / anxious that=as he was anxious that / engage 약혼시키다

(1) his friend는 누구를 말하는가?
(2) his good fortune은 구체적으로 무슨 뜻인가?
(3) the young couple은 누구를 가리키는가?

3 다음 글을 읽고 아래 질문에 답하여라.

> In various ways schools are separated from the rest of the life of the community, and therefore there is the ever-present danger that education may become artificial and remote from the real things of everyday life. When the purpose of a school is merely book-knowledge, the cleavage between school and life does not matter so much. In certain conditions (ㄱ)a form of education which had little to do with the business of life could last for centuries, as it did in China, where public officials were required to pass a test in archery long after firearms had become the established means of warfare. Today, however, when the school undertakes the responsibility of preparing its students for the life outside its walls, the separation of the school from life, and the unreality of the subjects studied, are matters of grave concern. (ㄴ)It becomes necessary to bring the world into the school and the school into the world.

notes :
community 공동사회 / ever-present 언제나 존재하는 / cleavage = gap / archery 궁술 / firearms 화기 / undertake(책임 등을) 맡다 / matters of grave concern 중대한 관심사

(1) 학교와 사회가 분리되면 어떤 위험이 있는가?
(2) 오랜 기간 변화되지 않았던 교육 형태의 실례를 들어라.
(3) 밑줄 친 (ㄱ)을 우리말로 번역하여라.
(4) 밑줄 친 (ㄴ)이 주장하는 교육의 목적은 무엇인가?

4 다음 글을 읽고 아래 물음에 답하여라.

> The moment we arrived I was formally introduced to the most unruly dog that guests had ever suffered under. This notorious dog, who was called Wessex, had, I am sure, the longest biting list of any domestic pet. His proud master lost no time in telling us that the postman, who had been bitten three times, now refused to deliver any more letters at the door. Wessex's thick and unbrushed mass of hair made it impossible to guess to which, if any, breed he was supposed to belong, and I did not think it would be civil to ask.

notes :
notorious 악명높은 / pet 애완 동물 / lose no time in ~ing 곧 ~하다 / to which 의 to는 belong에 걸린다 / if any 도대체 있다면 / breed 종류, 혈통 / civil 공손한

(1) 밑줄 친 부분을 해석하여라.
(2) 필자가 실례라고 생각하고 묻지 않은 질문은 어떤 질문인가?

실력체크 II

A. Fill in each blank with a suitable word:

(1) The good ______ by these measures is greater than the harm.

(2) Thickly ______ with snow, it appeared bright on a fine winter day.

(3) A conflict ______ been avoided, and agreement reached, I felt relieved.

(4) I got my long trousers ______ and my short skirt ______ by my tailor.

(5) The surroundings not ______ familiar to me, I couldn't find the place.

(6) ______ to, he turned back.

(7) ______ up in a better family, he would not have gone wrong.

(8) We often hear it ______ that they are men of action.

B. 괄호 안에서 문맥에 맞는 단어를 골라라.

(1) She is (eminent, imminent) in the field of linguistics.

(2) A trucker dumped toxic waste in a lake in (fragrant, flagrant) violation of the law.

(3) He was (graceful, gracious) enough to invite us to his home.

(4) The French Revolution was of great (historic, historical) importance.

(5) We should try and make (judicious, judicial) use of the resources available to us.

(6) The daughter has a (likelihood, likeness) to her mother.

(7) He thinks that she is not a (literal, literary) writer.

(8) The work was well paid but (seasonable, seasonal).

C. 주어진 부분으로 시작하여 다음을 영작하시오.

(1) 환경보존문제는 여전히 21세기의 중심 문제가 될 것이다.

How to ______________________________.

(2) 어느 정도 이상의 문명이 정말로 인류에게 유익한가는 의심스럽다.

It ______________________________.

(3) 믿는 친구한테 배반당하는 것처럼 실망스러운 일은 없다.

Nothing is ______________________________.

Answer: A. (1) done (2) covered (3) having (4) shortened, lengthened (5) being (6) Spoken (7) Brought (8) said B. (1) eminent (2) flagrant (3) gracious (4) historical (5) judicious (6) likeness (7) literary (8) seasonal C. (1) preserve the environment will still be the main problem of the 21st century. (2) is doubtful whether a civilization beyond a certain degree will really be useful to mankind. (3) more disappointing than being betrayed by a friend we trust.

D. 윗 글과 뜻이 같아지도록 밑줄 친 부분을 완성하여라. (괄호 속의 말을 사용하여라)

(1) If you follow this road, you will get to the station. (take)
This road ________________.

(2) How did you come to this conclusion? (led)
What ________________?

(3) Nobody can speak so eloquently as he. (speaker)
He ________________.

(4) I was not equal to the problem. (beyond)
The problem ________________.

(5) I could not have succeeded if you had not helped me. (indispensable)
Your ________________.

E. Correct the errors in the following:

(1) Leaving to himself, he was at a loss what to do.
(2) She says her husband is hard pleasing.
(3) She was very neat, dressing in spotless white from shoes to hat.
(4) They are countries which obey to the rules of international law.
(5) She suggested me that we should meet at the station at ten.
(6) My brother in Seoul immigrated to America last year.
(7) You have to eat this medicine twice a day.
(8) He counted it, all things considering, the happiest part of his life.
(9) His story was so disappointed that I went out of the room unnoticed.

F. 두 문장이 같은 뜻이 되게 공란을 메워라.

(1) Many persons went to see the launching of the ship.
Many persons went to see the ship ________.

(2) He was standing alone, folding his arms.
He was standing alone, ________ his arms ________.

(3) Your shirt needs mending.
You must ________ your shirt ________.

Answer: D. (1) will take you to the station (2) led you to this conclusion (3) is the most eloquent speaker of all (4) was beyond me (5) help was indispensable to my success E. (1) Leaving→Left (2) pleasing→to please (3) dressing→dressed (4) obey to→obey (5)suggested→suggested to (6) immigrated→emigrated (7) eat→take (8) considering→considered (9) disappointed→disappointing F. (1) launched (2) with, folded (3) have [get], mended

어휘 · 발음

A. 다음 빈칸에 들어갈 가장 적당한 말을 고르시오.

(1) When the teacher noticed the student's furtive glances at his next classmate's paper, he concluded the student was ______ on the test.
① cunning ② deceiving ③ taking in ④ cheating

(2) We were certain that the disaster was ______ .
① impeccable ② inherent ③ innumerable ④ imminent

(3) The old man in his walk and talk, his recollections of childhood days, his lapses of memory, indicated that he was ______ .
① adolescent ② oblivious ③ senile ④ sentimental

(4) The long ______ volcano has recently shown signs of life.
① active ② live ③ dormant ④ brisk

(5) In order to photograph ______ animals, elaborate flashlight equipment is necessary.
① domestic ② wild ③ nocturnal ④ live

(6) A chain of accidental circumstances brought about these ______ results.
① greedy ② covetous ③ unexpected ④ insatiable

(7) After several ______ attempts to send the satellite into space, the spacecraft was finally launched successfully.
① painstaking ② occasional ③ random ④ excellent

B. 주어진 단어와 뜻이 같도록, 빈칸에 주어진 철자로 시작되는 단어를 쓰시오.

(1) The country is struggling to r______ its birth rate. (decrease)

(2) P______ is born from narrow-mindedness. (bias)

(3) A dove is often used as an e______ of peace. (symbol)

(4) He was as t______ in the use of time as in spending money. (frugal)

(5) P______ the problem before making a final decision. (consider)

Answer: A. (1) ④ (2) ④ (3) ③ (4) ③ (5) ③ (6) ③ (7) ①
B. (1) reduce (2) Prejudice (3) emblem (4) thrifty (5) Ponder

중 요 반 의 어

abolish	establish	import	export
absolute	relative	internal	external
abstract	concrete	lass	lad
active	passive	loose	tight
add	subtract	lyric	epic
amateur	professional	maximum	minimum
ancestor	descendant	mental	physical
ascend	descend	natural	artificial
chaos	order	negative	positive
comic	tragic	nominal	substantial
complex	simple	normal	abnormal
conquer	surrender	objective	subjective
conservative	progressive	obscure	obvious
consume	produce	Occident	Orient
creditor	debtor	odd	even
defense	offense	optimist	pessimist
deficient	sufficient	particular	general
deflation	inflation	permanent	temporary
demand	supply	permit	prohibit
destroy	construct	plenty	scarcity
domestic	foreign, wild	practice	theory
dynamic	reserved	precede	follow
emigration	immigration	private	public
epilogue	prologue	prose	verse
exit	entrance	quality	quantity
expert	layman	rear	front
extreme	moderate	reward	punishment
fault	merit	rough	smooth
female	male	rural	urban
fertile	sterile, barren	shorten	lengthen
gather	scatter	sober	drunken
guest	host	tame	wild
guilty	innocent	tiny	huge
horizontal	vertical	vice	virtue

숙 어

(1) **distinguish A from B** (=distinguish between A and B) A와 B를 구별하다
☞ I sometimes have difficulty *distinguishing* Spanish *from* Portuguese.

(2) **distinguish oneself** (=make oneself noticeable) 두각을 나타내다
☞ She has already *distinguished herself* as an athlete.

(3) **do away with** (=get rid of, abolish) 제거[폐지]하다
☞ These ridiculous regulations should have been *done away with* years ago.

(4) **do justice to = do one justice** (=treat one fairly) 공정히 평가하다
☞ His remarks *do justice to* the author.
She's a boring teacher, but to *do her justice*, a very thorough teacher.

(5) **do[manage] without** (=continue to live or do something without having a particular thing) ~없이 지내다
☞ He always says he couldn't *do[manage] without* his cellular phone.

(6) **draw on** (=make use of) ~을 이용하다
☞ The chairman was good at *drawing on* the members' expertise.

(7) **drop in** (=visit unexpectedly) (예고없이) 들르다, 방문하다
☞ Let's *drop in* on him while we're in the neighborhood.
Please, *drop in* at my office anytime this week.

(8) **dwell on** (=think a lot about) 곰곰히 생각하다
☞ He tends to *dwell* too much *on* unimportant issues.

(9) **end in** (=result in) 결과 ~이 되다, 결국 ~으로 끝나다
☞ The conversation *ended in* an argument.

(10) **engaged in** (=busy with) ~하느라 바쁜, ~에 종사하고 있는
☞ These days I'm *engaged in* writing a new computer program.

(11) **exert oneself** (=make an effort) 노력하다
☞ She *exerted herself* all year to earn good marks in mathematics.

(12) **fall back on** (=depend on in case of need) ~에 의지하다
☞ When she lost her job, she *fell back on* piano playing for money.

(13) **fall in with** (=become involved with) ~와 어울리다
☞ In high school, he *fell in with* the wrong crowd and ended up in jail.

(14) **fall short of** (=fail to reach) ~에 못 미치다, 미달하다
☞ His jump *fell* three inches *short of* the world record.

(15) **familiar with+사물 or 사람** (=having a good knowledge of) ~을 잘 아는
familiar to+사람 (=well known to) ~에게 잘 알려져 있는
☞ We are *familiar with* this proverb. I'm *familiar with* his mother.
What the speaker told us tonight was all *familiar to* us.

(16) **far from** (=not at all ; instead of) 결코 ~이 아닌 ; ~하기는 커녕
☞ I am *far from* blaming him. *Far from* being angry, he's delighted.

(17) **feel for** (=have sympathy for ; grope for) ~을 동정하다 ; ~을 더듬어 찾다
☞ I really *feel for* his bereaved family.
She *felt* in her bag *for* a lipstick.

(18) **feel like ~ing** (=be inclined to) ~하고 싶다[싶은 기분이다]
☞ Somehow I *feel like canceling* the contract.

(19) **find fault with** (=criticize) ~을 비난하다, 흠을 잡다, 트집잡다
☞ I've never *found fault with* anything you've ever done.

(20) **fix up** (=repair) 고치다
☞ The garage man *fixed up* the old car and sold it at a profit of $500.

Exercise

▶▶ 주어진 단어들을 포함한 글을 지어라. 필요하면 어형을 변화시켜라.

1. do / with / tax
2. I / without / car
3. drop / time / week
4. boss / engaged / work
5. exert / help / people
6. case / fail / something / fall
7. trip / short / expectations
8. far / happy / results / election
9. feel / bag / pen
10. She / fault / way /dress

6. 조 동 사(Auxiliary Verb)

기본 문법 설명

A. **MAY** **MIGHT**	(1) ⓐ You **may** use this lawn mower only if you bring it back soon. ⓑ I **may**[**might**] **go** bowling this afternoon. ⓒ I **may**[**might**] **have made** some minor mistakes. ⓓ I expect you **may** enter a university if you try. ⓔ He said it **might** rain. (⇦ He said, "It may rain.") (2) ⓐ **May** all your dreams come true! ⓑ He works very hard **so** (**that**) his family **may** live in comfort. ⓒ He **may** be a bright boy, **but** he is quite selfish. ⓓ He **may well** be proud of being a self-made man. You **may**[**might**] **as well** go there right away. You **may**[**might**] **as well** throw your money into a ditch **as** spend it on gambling. ⓔ You **might** visit the Metropolitan Museum when you go to New York.
B. **CAN** **COULD**	(1) ⓐ **Can** Mary ski really well? Yes, she **can**. / No, she **can't**. She **can** speak Spanish fluently as well as English. ⓑ **Can** I have some more salad? If you get through with your homework, you **can** go out and play. ⓒ Boys, you **cannot** play baseball in the garden. ⓓ The politician's excuse for the scandal **cannot** be true. ⓔ He **cannot have confessed** his crime so obediently. ⓕ She said she **could** not run fast. (⇦ She said, "I cannot run fast.") ⓖ **Could** you show me the way to the nearest bus stop?

A. MAY, MIGHT

(1) **일반적 용법**

ⓐ 허가 : 「~해도 좋다」
(금방 돌려만 준다면 이 잔디 깎는 기계를 사용해도 좋다.) … 여기서 may는 can으로 바꿔 쓸 수 있다.

ⓑ 현재의 추측 : 「~일지도 모른다」
(난 오늘 오후 볼링치러 갈지도 모른다.)

ⓒ 과거의 추측 : 「~였을지도 모른다」
(난 몇몇 사소한 실수를 했을지도 모른다.)

ⓓ 가능 : may = can
(나는 네가 노력하면 대학에 들어갈 수 있다고 본다.)

ⓔ 시제의 일치
(비가 올지도 모른다고 그는 말했다.)

(2) **특수 용법**

ⓐ 기원문 : 「~하기를!」, 「~하소서!」
(당신의 모든 꿈이 이루어지길!)
May he live long! (부디 그의 장수를!)
May you both be happy!
(두분 부디 행복하소서!)

ⓑ 목적 : **so (that) ~ may**
= in order that ~ may
「~하기 위하여[하도록]」
(그는 가족이 편히 살 수 있도록 매우 열심히 일한다.)

ⓒ 양보 : **may ~ but**
「비록 ~이라 해도」, 「과연 ~이지만」
(그는 비록 머리는 좋은 소년이지만, 매우 이기적이다.)

ⓓ 당연 : **may well**
= have (a) good reason to
(그가 자수성가한 사람이라는 것을 자랑스럽게 여기는 것은 당연하다.)
may[might] as well
= have no strong reason not to
「~하는 편이 좋다[낫다]」
(너는 당장 거기에 가는 것이 낫다.)
may[might] as well … as ~
「~할 바에는 …하는 편이 낫다[좋다]」
(너는 도박에 돈을 쓸 바에는 그 돈을 시궁창에 버리는 편이 낫다.)

ⓔ **might** : 「~하는 것이 좋다」는 정중한 제안의 뜻을 갖는다.
(뉴욕에 가시면 메트로폴리탄 박물관을 방문하는 것이 좋습니다.)

B. CAN, COULD

ⓐ 능력·가능 : 「~할 수 있다」

ⓑ 허가 : 「~해도 좋다」
(숙제를 끝내면 나가 놀아도 좋다.)

ⓒ 금지 : 「~해서는 안 된다」
(얘들아, 정원에서 야구를 해서는 안 된다.)

ⓓ 강한 부정 추측 : 「~일 리가 없다」
(스캔들에 대한 그 정치가의 변명은 사실일 리가 없다.)
Can the report be true? … 강한 의심
(그 보도는 과연 사실일까?)

ⓔ 「**cannot have 과거분사**」
= 「~이었을 리가 없다」
… 과거의 부정 추측
(그가 그렇게 순순히 범죄사실을 자백했을 리가 없다.)

ⓕ 시제의 일치
(빨리 뛸 수 없다고 그녀는 말했다.)

ⓖ 공손한 말씨
(가까운 버스 정류장으로 가는 길을 가르쳐 주시겠습니까?)
… Could는 Can 보다 정중한 말씨

▶ 단 문 해 석 ◀

(1) Something *may have happened* to him.
(2) He *may well* get angry.
(3) I thought I *may*[*might*] *as well* inform him of my plan.
(4) Mary asked if she *might* be excused from the test.
(5) I *told* him that he *could not* be sick.
(6) Who *could* have sent me this letter?
(7) He is *as* happy *as can* be.
(8) You *cannot* praise him *too* much.
(9) I *cannot* see him *without* thinking of his father.
(10) You *may*[*might*] *as well* reason with the wolf *as* try to persuade him.

C. **MUST** **HAVE TO** **HAD TO**	(1) ⓐ We **must** abolish these absurd regulations. ⓑ The spoiled boy **must** always have his own way. ⓒ We all **must** die sometime. ⓓ You **must not** park your car there without permission. ⓔ You **must** be tired after such a long journey. ⓕ They **must have forgotten** about the meeting. (2) ⓐ You **don't have to** knock. Just come in. ⓑ I **had to** queue for a long time. ⓒ I **will have to** phone him later. ⓓ He said he **must** [**had to**] look after the child.
D. **WILL** **SHALL**	(1) ⓐ No matter what happens, I **will** do as I please. ⓑ If you won't tell her the truth, I **will**. ⓒ She says she **will** leave here. (2) ⓐ You **shall** have higher wages, if you work hard. ⓑ No person **shall** enter this library without my permission. (3) ⓐ **Shall** I close the door?—Yes, please. ⓑ **Will** you call on her first thing tomorrow morning? ⓒ **Shall** we go to the party together? When **shall** he visit you? *Let* him come any time. (4) ⓐ Boys **will** be boys. ⓑ The door **won't** shut. ⓒ He **will** listen to music alone in his room for hours. ⓓ This **will** be your luggage, I suppose. ⓔ Freedom of speech **shall** not be violated. ⓕ Nation **shall** rise against nation.
E. **DO**	(1) **Do** come and see me again. (2) I do not borrow, nor **do** I lend; that's my principle. (3) If she doesn't deserve to be happy, who **does**?

C. MUST, HAVE TO, HAD TO

⑴ **must의 용법**

ⓐ 필요·의무 :「~하여야 한다」
(우리는 이 불합리한 규정들을 폐지해야 한다.)

ⓑ 주장 (그 버릇없는 소년은 언제나 자기 고집대로 해야 한다.)

ⓒ 필연·불가피 :「반드시 ~한다」
(우리는 모두 언젠가는 반드시 죽는다.)

ⓓ 금지 (must not = mustn't)
(허락없이 그곳에 차를 주차시켜서는 안된다.)

ⓔ 추측 :「~임에 틀림없다」
(그렇게 긴 여행을 했으니 피곤함에 틀림없다.)

ⓕ 과거의 추측 :「~했음에 틀림없다」
(그들은 그 모임에 대해 잊어 버렸음에 틀림없다.)

⑵ **have to, had to의 용법**

ⓐ { have to = must
don't have to = don't need to }
(노크할 필요 없습니다. 그냥 들어오세요.)

☞ You *must* be very tired, because you've walked as long as five hours. (5시간이나 걸었으므로 너는 아주 피곤할 것 임에 틀림없다.)
— must 대신 have to를 사용할 수 없다. must는 추측 (~임에 틀림없다)에도 쓰이지만, have to는 필요·의무에만 쓰이고 원칙적으로 추측에는 쓰이지 않는다.

ⓑ had to는 must의 과거형이다.
(난 오랫동안 줄을 서야했다.)

ⓒ will have to는 must의 미래시제
(난 나중에 그에게 전화해야 한다.)

ⓓ 간접화법에서 must의 과거는 had to 또는 그대로 must를 쓴다.
(자기가 그 어린애를 돌봐야 한다고 그는 말했다.)

D. WILL, SHALL

⑴ 주어의 의지를 나타내는 will
이 때의 will은 [wíl]하고 강하게 발음한다.

ⓐ (무슨 일이 있어도, 나는 내가 하고 싶은 대로 하겠다.)

ⓑ (네가 그녀에게 진실을 말하지 않는다면 내가 말하겠다.)

ⓒ (그녀는 자기가 이곳을 떠날 것이라고 말한다.)
= She says, "**I will** leave here."

⑵ 말하는 사람의 의지를 나타내는 shall

ⓐ = I will give you higher wages, if you work hard.

ⓑ = I will not let any person enter this library without my permission.

⑶ 상대방의 의지를 묻는 shall, will

ⓐ (문을 닫을까요? — 네, 그러세요.)
Shall I call a taxi for you?
Yes, please. *or* No, thank you.

ⓑ (내일 아침 제일 먼저 그녀를 방문하시 겠습니까?)
Will you pass me the salt, please?
Will you have another cup of tea?

ⓒ (우리 함께 파티에 갈까요?)
(언제 그에게 당신을 방문하게 할까요? 언제든 오게 하시오.)

⑷ will, shall의 특수 용법

ⓐ 습성·경향

ⓑ 거부 :「아무리 해도 ~하지 않다」

ⓒ 습관 :「곧잘 ~한다」

ⓓ 추측 : (아마 이것이 당신의 짐이겠죠.)
You *will* have heard the rumor.
(너는 그 소문을 들었을 것이다.)

ⓔ 법률·규칙 :
(언론의 자유를 침해해서는 안된다.)

ⓕ 예언 :
(나라가 나라를 대항해 일어날지니라.)

E. DO

⑴ 강조의 조동사 : (꼭 다시 와 주세요.)

⑵ 어순 도치 : (나는 빌리지도 않고 빌려주지도 않는다; 그것이 나의 원칙이다.)

⑶ 대동사 : (그녀가 행복해질 자격이 없다면 누가 있겠느냐?)

F. **WOULD** **SHOULD** **OUGHT TO**	(1) ⓐ However hard I tried, he **would** not take the money. ⓑ He **would** often go swimming in the river, while he was in the country. ⓒ He **would** have been about twenty when he crossed the Pacific alone on a yacht. ⓓ He who **would** catch fish, must not mind getting wet. (2) ⓐ You **should** stop swearing in front of your children. ⓑ You **should have been** more careful. ⓒ It's necessary that you **should** tell her before she books the tickets. ⓓ She insisted that I (**should**) stay longer for dinner. ⓔ How **should** I know if she's married or not? ⓕ They **should** be there by now, I think. (3) ⓐ They **ought to** apologize to him for that. ⓑ If he left home at seven, he **ought to** arrive about now. ⓒ I told him that he **ought to** look for her. ⓓ You **ought to have come** a little earlier.
G. **NEED** **DARE**	(1) ⓐ **Need** he work so hard? He **needs** to work hard. ⓑ He **needn't** become involved in this dispute at all. ⓒ He **need not have hurried** if he had gotten up a little earlier. As he had enough time, he **did not need** to hurry. (2) ⓐ I **dare** not bother him while he's writing. ⓑ How **dare** you say such a thing to my face? ⓒ He **dares** to insult me in spite of everything I've done for him.
H. **USED TO**	(1) I **used to** ride my bike to my school. (2) It **used to** be thought that the earth was flat. There **used to** be a theater around here. (3) **Did** he **use to** call on you every Sunday? He **did not use to** (*used not to*) call on me every Sunday. (4) I'**m** not yet **used to** handl**ing** the new equipment.

F. WOULD, SHOULD, OUGHT TO

(1) **would의 용법**

would는 will의 과거형이므로 will의 용법에 상응한다.

ⓐ 과거의 거부
(내가 아무리 애써도 그는 한사코 그 돈을 받으려고 하지 않았다.)

ⓑ 과거의 습관
(시골에 있을 때 그는 그 강으로 자주 수영하러 가곤 했다.)

ⓒ 과거의 추측
(그가 요트를 타고 혼자 태평양을 횡단했을 때는 20세 쯤이었을 것이다.)

ⓓ would = wish to
(고기를 잡고자 하는 사람은 물에 젖는 것을 꺼려해서는 안된다.)

(2) **should의 용법**

ⓐ 의무·당연 :「~해야 한다」
(아이들 앞에서 욕설은 말아야 한다.)

ⓑ 과거에 하지 않은 일을 비평한다.
「~했어야만 했는데」
(너는 좀더 조심했어야 했는데.)

ⓒ It is 다음에 necessary, important, proper, natural, right, well, good, wrong, rational 등이 오면 종속절에 should를 쓸 수 있다.
—이 때 should는 해석하지 않는다.
(그녀가 표를 예약하기 전에 네가 그녀에게 말할 필요가 있다.)

ⓓ insist, suggest, propose, demand, order, desire, wish, request 등의 동사 다음에 계속되는 that절 내에 should가 관용적으로 쓰인다. 그러나 특히 미식 영어에서는, 이 should를 빼고 원형을 많이 쓴다.
(그녀는 내가 만찬에 좀더 오래 머물러 달라고 졸랐다.)

ⓔ 수사의문문이다. 평서문으로 쓰면 「I don't know at all if she's ~.」이다.
(그녀가 미혼인지 기혼인지 내가 어떻게 알겠는가?)

ⓕ 예상 혹은 기대를 나타낸다.
= It is likely that they are there by now. (아마 지금쯤은 그들은 거기에 있을 것이다.)

(3) **ought to의 용법**

should와 거의 같은 뜻으로 쓰인다.

ⓐ「~해야 한다」: (그것에 대해 그들은 그에게 사과해야 한다.)

ⓑ「당연히 ~일 것이다」: (7시에 집을 떠났으면, 그는 지금쯤은 당연히 도착해야 할 것이다.)

ⓒ must의 뜻 (과거) : (그 여자를 찾아야 한다고 나는 그에게 말했다.)

ⓓ「~했어야만 했는데」
ought to[should] have come

G. NEED, DARE

need, dare는 의문문·부정문에서 조동사, 긍정문에서는 본동사의 역할을 한다. 그러나 need는 현대영어에서는 점차 본동사로만 사용하는 경향이 있다.

(1) ⓐ = Does he *need* to work ~?

ⓑ = He doesn't *need* to become ~.

ⓒ (조금만 더 일찍 일어났더라면 그는 서두를 필요가 없었다.)
(충분한 시간이 있었기 때문에 그는 서두를 필요가 없었다.)

(2) ⓐ (글을 쓰는 동안은 나는 감히 그를 성가시게 할 수 없다.)
= I don't *dare* to bother him ~.

ⓑ (내 면전에서 감히 어떻게 그런 말을 하느냐?)
= How do you *dare* to say ~?

ⓒ (그를 위해 모든 것을 해줬음에도 불구하고 그는 감히 나를 모욕한다.)

H. USED TO

(1) 과거의 습관
(나는 한때 자전거로 학교에 다니곤 했다.)

(2) 과거의 사실·상태
(전에는 지구가 평평하다고들 생각했었다.)
(전에는 이 근처에 극장이 하나 있었다.)

(3) used to의 의문문·부정문
Did he use to ~ ?
(일요일마다 당신을 방문하곤 했습니까?)
did not use to ~ = used not to ~

(4) used to 원형 = 과거의 습관
be[get] used to (동)명사
= ~에 익숙하다[해지다]

문 법 · 작 문

A. Fill in each blank with a suitable word:

(1) In short the rumor _____ be false; I simply can't believe it.
(2) It _____ have rained during the night, for the road is wet.
(3) He _____ have said so, for he knew nothing about it.
(4) We didn't _____ to wait long. A bus came almost at once.
(5) We _____ be too careful of our health.
(6) He _____ to have reached Seoul by now.
(7) Let's face up to our responsibilities, _____ we?
(8) This winter hasn't been so cold, _____ it?
(9) Have another cup of tea, _____ you?
(10) How _____ you talk to me like that!
(11) This _____ to be the best restaurant in town.
(12) You _____ as well expect the river to flow backward as expect to move me.
(13) It was a grand sight; you _____ have seen it.
(14) Little _____ I dream that I left my home, never to return.
(15) I proposed a motion that the chairman _____ resign.
(16) Who _____ come in but the very man we were talking of?
(17) _____ his soul rest in peace!
(18) _____ it be true that he committed suicide?
(19) It is high time that the boy _____ be sent to school.
(20) Who are you that you _____ speak like this?
(21) We're not sure when, but we do know that accidents _____ happen.

B. Rewrite the following sentences as directed:

(1) The statement may be true. (부정문)
(2) He must have been ignorant of the fact. (부정문)
(3) What you said must be true. (부정문)
(4) Passengers now may carry more than one piece of hand baggage onto the aircraft. (부정문)
(5) Can I reach Mr. Brown at home? (미래 시제)
(6) You must support your family. (과거 시제)
(7) Will it be necessary for John to come here? (John을 주어로)
(8) I am sure her sickness is a mere cold. (Her sickness를 주어로)
(9) It is possible that he has succeeded. (He를 주어로)

C. Correct the errors in the following sentences:

(1) He says the government shall do all it can to root out corruption.
(2) John used to live in London, and so were his parents.
(3) He has to be sick, for he looks very pale.
(4) The services that he has done for the public can be praised too highly.
(5) He worked very hard in order that he will get a promotion.
(6) When a boy, he should often go swimming in the river.
(7) I sincerely hope you to succeed in losing weight.
(8) I prayed to God that he should come back safe.
(9) Who can tell what shall become of the world?
(10) If you should be happy, try to be a little optimistic.
(11) He was so obstinate that he should not listen to my advice.
(12) I could rather live alone than live with such a drunkard.
(13) Eventually you'll get used to deal with difficult customers.

D. Translate the following sentences into English:

(1) 너는 외출해도 좋지만, 어둡기 전에 돌아와야 한다.

____

(2) 그가 위인이라는 것은 부인할 수 없다.

____

(3) 그가 그런 바보짓을 했을 리가 없다.

____

(4) 나는 그에게 담배를 끊으라고 계속해서 충고를 했으나, 내 말을 들으려고 하지 않았다.

____

(5) 어렸을 때 나는 여기 해변가에서 놀곤 했다.

____

(6) 회의에 늦지 않으려고 그는 일찍 일어났다.

____

(7) 어제 어머님이 편찮으셔서, 그는 집에 있어야 했다.

____

(8) 자기의 자유뿐만 아니라 남의 자유도 존중해야 한다.

____

'Health'라는 제목으로 70어 내외의 글을 지어라.

● 단 문 독 해 ●

Children **will** be noisy.
The door **will** not open.
He **will** often sit up all night.
You **shall** have this watch.
Freedom of speech **shall** not be violated.
Seek, and you **shall** find.

1. A child that always receives sympathy **will** continue to cry over little troubles; the ordinary self-control of the average adult is achieved only through knowledge that no sympathy will be won by making a loud complaint.

notes :
*sympathy will continue에서 will은 현재의 습관
*no sympathy will be 의 will은 단순미래
*complaint 불평

▶▶(1) 본문의 밑줄친 부분을 다음과 같이 쓸 때 빈칸에 적절한 한 단어를 쓰시오.

only when he (k　　) that

(2) We should not indulge a child in whatever he wishes to do (　　) he should grow up a (　　) person who can do nothing without a helping hand.
[unless, lest, if, dependent, desirous, diligent]

▶▶영작하시오.

그녀는 자기의 불행에 대해 울고 있었다.

2. God was sorry that Adam and Eve had disobeyed him. Sin and fear had spoiled the fellowship between them. God said to Eve, "Because you listened to the Tempter's voice and disobeyed me, you **shall** have pain and trouble all the days of your life."

notes :
*spoil 해치다, 망치다
*fellowship 친교(親交)
*the Tempter = Satan
*life 생애

▶▶Adam and Eve were (　　) by Satan into disobeying God and they were (　　) to live painfully all through their lives.
[tainted, told, tempted, doomed, demanded, warned]

▶▶영작하시오.

오랫동안 소식을 올리지 못해 죄송합니다.

3. Man does not live by bread alone, but neither does he live by taking thought alone. I love to think, and talk and feel, but cannot forget that I have hands which clamor to be put to use, arms which **will** not hang idle.

notes :
*Man (관사없이) 사람, 인간
*take thought = 숙고하다
*clamor 시끄럽게 굴다
*will not hang idle 에서 will not은 의인화된 주어의 '거부'를 나타낸다

▶▶Because a man is composed of both (　　　　　), it is necessary for him to make the best use of both of them.
[mind and body, flesh and blood, thought and action]

▶▶영작하시오.
저 컴퓨터는 놀고만 있다. 우리는 그것을 잘 이용해야 한다.

He **cannot have gone** far yet.
She **must have been** a beauty in her day.
He **may have done** it.

4. Looking back, I infer that there **must have been** something in me a little superior to the common run of youths, otherwise the above-mentioned men, so much older than me and higher in academic position, would never have allowed me to associate with them.

notes :
*the common run of youths = 보통 젊은이들
*otherwise 그렇지 않았다면
*than me는 than I로 함이 원칙이나, 일상대화에서는 이것도 허용된다. 이 글은 Charles Darwin의 자서전에서 뽑은 것이다.

▶▶Which of the following does **not** correspond with the above paragraph?
① The writer believes that he was far above the ordinary young men in intelligence.
② Because there was something exceptional in him, the writer could keep company with his seniors in age and learning.
③ The writer's outstanding ability enabled him to socialize with the eminent scholars.
④ It seems that the writer was kind of arrogant and didn't behave well in the society of his contemporaries.
⑤ The writer complacently recollects his young days spent in high academic circles.

▶▶영작하시오.
그에게는 무엇인가 우리들보다 좀 뛰어난 면이 있었다.

5. The history of mankind is the history of man's activity, and so long as human nature and man's material conditions are what they are, so long **must** economic and industrial factors have a potent influence in our political and social life.

notes :
*so long as = while
*what they are = 오늘의 그들
*potent 강력한

▶▶The economy and industry which (　　　) from man's activity are sure to strongly (　　　) our political and social life.
[resultant, result, went, affect, effect, inform]

▶▶영작하시오.
여기에 계시고 싶은 대로 계십시오.

6. You **may have heard** of that lovely land called Italy, the land of golden sunshine and warm, soft air. There the skies are almost always blue — such a wonderfully deep blue, that Italy is often called "The Land of Blue Skies."

notes :
*문어, 시 등에서 skies (복수형)를 쓰는데, 이는 heavens, hopes, fears, wishes 등의 경우와 같이 강의복수형(Intensive Plural)이다

▶▶The above paragraph describes the natural (　　　) of Italy.
[bounty, skies, beauty]

▶▶영작하시오.
그를 어디선가 전에 만난 것 같긴한데 기억이 안난다.

He **may well** be proud of his son.
You **may as well** go at once.
You **may as well** not know a thing **as** know it imperfectly.

7. Language is a living thing. A word is like a plant or an animal. It comes into existence, it grows, changes its form, matures and falls into decay. Thus the science of language is as interesting and fascinating as Botany or Zoology, and the linguist who studies printed pages **may well** be compared to the naturalist who hunts the field for his specimens.

notes :
*come into existence [being] = 생기다
*mature 성숙해지다
*fall into decay = 쇠퇴하다
*fascinating 매혹적인
*botany 식물학
*compare A to B = A를 B에 비유하다
*specimen 표본

▶▶Language is to a linguist what a plant is to a (　　),
or what an animal is to a (　　).
[forest, scientist, botanist, zoo keeper, zoo, zoologist]

▶▶영작하시오.
네가 그 소문이 사실이라고 생각하는 것도 무리가 아니다.

8. I have been asked to speak on the question of how to make the best of life, but **may as well** confess at once that I know nothing about it. I cannot think that I have made the best of my own life, nor is it likely that I will make much better of what may or may not remain to me.

notes :
*make the best of = 최대한 이용하다, 선용하다
*confess 고백하다
*nor is it likely에서 nor = and also ~ not
*make much better of = 훨씬 더 ~를 잘 이용하다

▶▶Which of the following is most suitable to describe the writer of the above paragraph?
① self-confident and arrogant
② conceited and selfish
③ reckless and foolish
④ indiscreet and impudent
⑤ unpretentious and humble

▶▶영작하시오.
대기 오염에 관해 연설해 달라고 그는 부탁을 받았다.

9. Economic laws can no more be evaded than can gravitation. We **might as well** attempt to reverse the motion of the earth on its axis **as** attempt to reverse the industrial progress and send men back into the age of homespun.

notes :
*A whale is *no more* a fish *than* a horse is.
*axis 지축
*homespun 수직물(手織物)

▶▶윗글의 내용과 일치하도록 다음 문장의 괄호안에 알맞은 말을 고르시오.
We must accept that economic laws are (　　) phenomena just as natural laws.
① flexible　　② adjustable
③ unavoidable　　④ uncertain
⑤ manageable

▶▶영작하시오.
그에게 돈을 빌려 줄 바에는 차라리 던져 내버리는 게 낫다.

We **should** obey our parents.
You **should have been** more careful.
It is **strange** that he **should have failed**.
Who should come in **but** our teacher himself!

10. A man **should** never be ashamed to admit he has been in the wrong, which is but saying in other words that he is wiser today than he was yesterday.

notes :
*admit 자백하다
*which의 선행사는 to admit ~ wrong
*but = only

▶▶윗글의 내용에 부합하도록 주어진 문장의 빈칸에 알맞는 말을 고르시오.
The wise man is always ready to (　　　) his faults.
① deny　② confess　③ refuse
④ announce　⑤ control

▶▶영작하시오.
그는 자기가 그것을 했다고 자백했다.

11. It is one of the most tragic facts in the recent development of science that the conquest of the air, which on all grounds **should have worked** towards the unification of the world and the harmony of mankind, has actually become our most threatening danger.

notes :
*~, which = ~, although it
*on all grounds = 모든 면에서 보아
*unification 통일

▶▶Which of the following does the writer criticize?
① The reckless development of science
② The serious problem of air pollution
③ The misuse of aircraft
④ The integration of the world
⑤ The threat caused by scientific technology

▶▶영작하시오.
그는 건강상의 이유로 사직하고자 한다.

12. I was gazing at the swans floating on the lake with happy thoughts in my mind, when **who should** touch me on the elbow **but** the little girl whom I had mentioned!

notes :
*gaze at = 응시하다
*swan 백조
*float 떠다니다
*mention 언급하다

▶▶다음이 윗글의 밑줄친 부분과 뜻이 같도록 할 때, 괄호 안에서 알맞은 것은?
and then to my surprise I was touched on the elbow by none other (then, than, that) the little girl I had mentioned.

▶▶영작하시오.
매일 그녀는 앉아서 먼 산을 바라보곤 했다.

13. I know that a fairly good income is very **important**; but it is still more important that a man **should** follow the vocation for which he is best fitted, whether it happens to be well paid or not.

notes :
*fairly 꽤, 매우
*vocation 직업
*follow the vocation =직업에 종사하다
*be fitted for = ~에 적합하다

▶▶윗글의 내용과 일치하도록 다음 빈칸에 가장 적절한 것은?

In choosing an occupation, (　　　　　).

① what is important is not fitness, but a good income
② a good income is more important than one's aptitude
③ what is important is not so much a good income as fitness
④ a good income is no less important than fitness
⑤ a good income is as important as fitness

▶▶영작하시오.

어제 나는 버스 안에서 우연히 옛 친구를 만났다.

He **would** go, say what I might.
He who **would** catch fish, must not mind getting wet.
He **would** sit for hours without saying a word.
I **would rather** die **than** live in dishonor.

14. Those Americans whom I most honor, and who were the founders of their country, never accepted money for their service. Washington **would** accept no salary as commander-in-chief for seven years, nor as president for eight years.

notes :
*honor 존경하다
*founders 설립자들
*commander-in-chief 총사령관
*nor as president에서 nor = and ~ not

▶▶윗글을 읽고 다음 빈칸에 가장 알맞은 것을 고르시오.

The writer admires Washington (　　　　　).

① because of Washington's social status
② just because Washington founded his country
③ because he was moved by Washington's self-sacrifice
④ because Washington donated much money for the foundation of his country
⑤ because Washington served as commander-in-chief and president of his country for so long.

▶▶영작하시오.

그는 나의 충고에 귀를 기울이려고 하지 않았다.

15. ① In gazing at a mountain range from a distance, the peaks seem to rise clear against the sky. ② There seem to be no obstacles to hinder him who **would** climb to the top. ③ What seemed so simple at a distance grows infinitely complex as you draw nearer. ④ So is it with life. ⑤

notes :
*a mountain range = 산맥
*obstacle 장애물
*hinder 방해하다
*complex 복잡한

▶▶윗글의 문맥으로 보아 아래 주어진 문장이 들어가기에 가장 적절한 곳은?

But as you draw near, everything changes.

▶▶영작하시오.

나무들이 아침 하늘에 시꺼멓게 보였다.

16. With every passing day his health improved. "Ah," he **would** exclaim to me, "island life has charms not to be found everywhere! Half the ills of mankind might be shaken off without doctor or medicine by mere residence in this lovely portion of the world."

notes :
*might는 가정법
*by 이하가 조건절의 대용(if we merely resided)

▶▶윗글의 내용에 부합하도록 주어진 문장의 빈칸에 알맞은 말을 고르시오.

In this paragraph, the man believes island life is much more (　　) to his health than doctors or medicine.

① adequate　② benevolent　③ appropriate
④ useful　⑤ beneficial

▶▶영작하시오.

하루하루 지남에 따라 내가 이 나라에서 해야할 임무가 점점 끝나가고 있다는 것을 나는 알게 되었다.

17. With all my faults I have a warm heart; and poor as I am, I **would rather** deny myself the necessities of life **than** do an ungenerous thing.

notes :
*with all = for all, in spite of
*necessities of life = 생활 필수품

▶▶Which is most suitable to describe the writer?

① clever and intellectual
② witty and humorous
③ cruel and cold-blooded
④ generous and warm-hearted
⑤ pessimistic and selfish

▶▶영작하시오.

비록 부자이지만 그는 불행하다.

notes :
*calling 직업
*do without = ~없이 지내다 (=manage without)
*the first = 전자, the second= 후자
*the one = milk
*the other = news
*refreshment 청량제
*would rather ~than = would sooner ~ than = would as soon ~ as
*the first being for = as the first is for
*mental (refreshment)

18. The milkman has a rival in early calling, and that rival is the newspaper boy. Both milk and news are required for breakfast and the London businessman **would as soon** do without the one **as** the other, the first being for his bodily refreshment and the second for his mental.

▶▶According to the above paragraph, London businessmen would rather do without (   ).
[news than milk, milk than news]

▶▶영작하시오.
(1) 담배 없이 지내기가 매우 어렵다는 것을 나는 알았다.
(2) 나는 혼잡한 버스로 가기보다 차라리 걸어가겠다.

He **used to** take a walk early in the morning.
I **am** not **used to** be**ing** treated like this.

19. Her anger never lasted long, and, having humbly confessed her fault, she sincerely repented and tried to do better. Her sisters **used to** say that they rather liked to get Jo into a fury, because she was such an angel afterwards.

notes :
*confess one's fault = ~의 잘못을 인정했다
*repent 뉘우치다
*fury 분노

▶▶Which of the following does **not** correspond with the above paragraph?
① She never hesitated to recognize her faults.
② She used to be more considerate after she was furious.
③ She seemed to be a person who easily got angry, but soon repented having gotten mad.
④ Her sisters didn't mind her getting angry because they knew she became an angelic woman afterwards.
⑤ She seldom got angry and tried to be more angelic.

▶▶영작하시오.
저는 차라리 당신이 그 일을 그만두었으면 싶은데요.

20. The air of that island was so genial and balmy that we could have slept quite well without any shelter; but we **were** so little **used** to sleep**ing** in the open air, that we did not quite relish the idea of lying down without any covering over us.

notes :
*genial = mild
*balmy 향기로운
*relish = enjoy
*covering = shelter, roof

▶▶Although the air of that island was warm and pleasant, we still wanted to sleep under a (　　) as we weren't (　　) to sleeping in the open air.

[ceiling, attic, roof, accustomed, adjusted, comforted]

▶▶영작하시오.

당신의 도움이 없었다면, 나는 그것을 할 수 없었을 것이다.

Man eats **lest** he **should** die.
Man eats **so that** he **may** live.
Man eats **for fear that** he **should** die.
I work hard **so as to** succeed.

21. Modern man, enclosed by four walls and chained to an indoor job, realizes that he is shortening his days. He needs exercise, and he knows it; but when he asks for guidance he receives so much conflicting advice that he is afraid to accept any of it **lest** he **should** make bad matters worse.

notes :
*enclose 둘러싸다
*chain 속박하다
*his days에서 days는 수명
*conflicting 모순되는

▶▶According to the above paragraph, which of the following is incorrect?

① Modern man is forced to live under too stressful an environment.

② Modern man imperatively needs exercise to improve his health which is impaired by his working conditions.

③ Given too much confusing advice on exercise, modern man is at a loss which to choose.

④ It is better for modern man to devise his own method of doing exercise, ignoring others' conflicting advice.

⑤ Modern man, kept indoors doing monotonous work all day long, is in danger of becoming unhealthy.

▶▶영작하시오.

그가 보지 않도록 그것을 감추어라.

22. We should always put aside something, **so that**, in the event of our being unable to work due to unemployment, sickness, or old age, we **may** not starve nor be compelled to ask charity from others.

notes :
*put aside = save
*in the event of = ~할 경우 (= in case of)
*unemployment 실업

▶▶윗글의 내용과 일맥 상통하도록 다음 빈칸에 가장 적절한 것은?

We should always save some money for a (　　) day.

① sunny　② cloudy　③ stormy
④ rainy　⑤ snowy

▶▶영작하시오.

노년에 남에게 의존하지 않기 위해 무엇인가 저축해야 한다.

23. He was looking at the dog, afraid to approach him, **for fear** the animal **should** show his teeth, were it only from habit; and equally afraid to run away, lest he should be thought a coward.

notes :
*approach ~에 접근하다
*equally 동시에
*coward 겁쟁이

▶▶When we are placed in a situation like the above, we say we are between the (　　) and the deep blue sea or a rock and a (　　) place.

[devil, dog, coward, strange, hard, dangerous]

▶▶영작하시오.

누가 들을까봐 그는 목소리를 낮추었다.

24. The lower animals must have their bodily structure modified **in order to** survive under greatly changed conditions. They must be rendered stronger, or acquire more effective teeth or claws, for defense against new enemies; or, they must be reduced in size, **so as to** escape detection and danger.

notes :
*I *had* my watch *stolen* on the bus.
*rendered = made
*claws 발톱
*detection 탐지

▶▶윗글의 내용과 일치하도록 아래 문장의 괄호안에 알맞은 말을 고르시오.

The above paragraph has to do with the (　　) of the fittest in a changing environment.

① struggle　② strife　③ survival
④ strength　⑤ strain

▶▶영작하시오.

너는 그 충치를 빨리 뽑아야 한다.

● 장 문 독 해 ●

Warming-up

We can**not** be **too** careful of our health.
He is young, **it is true**, **but** he is wise.
I thank you for **taking the trouble to** reply.
This sweet wine **is intended to** be drunk after a meal.
The letter is **being** written by him.
It's yours **for the asking**.

1 ⓐ We cannot know too much about the language we speak every day of our lives. Most of us, it is true, can get along fairly well without knowing very much about our language and without ever taking the trouble to open a volume of The Oxford English Dictionary. But knowledge is power. The power of rightly chosen words is very great, whether those words are intended to inform, to entertain, or to move. English is rapidly becoming a cosmopolitan means of communication and it is now being studied by numerous well-trained investigators on both sides of the Atlantic. It is highly exhilarating to contemplate the progress made in the study of English up to now. ⓑ That assertion, too often repeated, that Englishmen are not really interested in their own language, is no longer valid. At last we English are showing an awakened interest in our mother tongue as something living and changing. This we see in many differing spheres: in national and local government, in business and journalism, in film and radio, in school and university. Let us all join freely in ⓒ the quest and let us share gladly in that intellectual joy of language studies which is ours for the seeking every day of our lives.

Simeon Potter: *Our Language*

Notes

get along 살아가다 / take the trouble to 일부러 수고하여 ~하다 / move 감동시키다 / cosmopolitan 세계적인 / exhilarating 기분좋게 하는 / contemplate (곰곰이) 생각하다 / assertion 주장 / valid 타당한 / awakened 각성된 / sphere 분야 / local government 지방자치기관 / quest 탐구 / for the seeking=if only we seek for it

Question

1. 본문의 밑줄친 부분 ⓐ와 같은 뜻이 되도록 다음 빈칸에 적절한 한 단어를 골라 쓰시오.

It is (   ) to know too much about the language we speak

[important, inappropriate, impossible]

2. 본문의 밑줄친 ⓑThat assertion 이 가리키는 구체적 내용을 우리말로 쓰시오.

3. What does the underlined word ⓒthe quest imply?
   ① the quest for an international language
   ② the quest for how to choose right words
   ③ the quest for learning more about our mother tongue
   ④ the quest for a means of communication
   ⑤ the quest for a method to investigate the mother tongue

4. According to the passage, which of the following is **not** correct?
   ① It is untrue that we English are not interested in our own language.
   ② If we are to make our daily communication more effective, we should choose the correct words to use.
   ③ Englishmen have shown a growing interest in their own language in many different fields.
   ④ Much progress has been made in the study of English up to the present day.
   ⑤ We may get along well without the exact knowledge of our mother tongue, but we cannot expect to make a great success in life.

Production

(1) 책을 선택하는 데 있어서 아무리 주의해도 지나치지 않다.
(2) 낙엽으로 덮인 정원은 쓸쓸한 광경이었다.
(3) 그 소년은 사실 총명은 하나 매사에 경솔하다.

● 장 문 독 해 ●

Warming-up

The defeated do not always remain defeated.
Their conversation **ended in** a quarrel.
He has saved himself **in the act of** losing his property.
The rule does not **apply to** the case.
We **owe** our prosperity **to** his great leadership.

2 It is remarkable that in so many great wars it has been the defeated who have won. The people who were left worst at the end of the war were generally the people who were left best at the end of the whole business. For instance, the Crusades ended in the defeat of Christians. But they did not end in the decline of the Christians: ⓐ they ended in the decline of the Saracens. ⓑ That huge prophetic wave of Muslim power which had hung in the very heavens above the towns of Christendom, that wave was broken, and never came on again. The Crusaders had saved Paris in the act of losing Jerusalem. The same applies to that epic of Republican war in the eighteenth century to which we Liberals owe our political creed. The French Revolution ended in defeat: the kings came back across a carpet of the dead at Waterloo. The Revolution had lost its last battle; but it had gained ⓒ its first object. It had cut a chasm. The world has never been the same since. No one after that has ever been able to treat the poor merely as a pavement.

G. K. Chesterton: *The Giant*

Notes

the Crusades 십자군전쟁(여러차례 원정했기 때문에 복수), 성전(聖戰) / end in ~으로 끝나다 / defeat 패배 / decline 쇠퇴 / Saracen (십자군에 대항한) 회교도 / huge 거대한 / prophetic 예언의 / Muslim power 회교도 세력 / Christendom 기독교국 / Crusader 십자군 전사 / apply to ~에 적용되다 / epic 서사시; *lyric* 서정시 / Republican war 공화국 전쟁 / Liberal 영국의 자유당 당원 / creed 신조 / revolution 혁명 / carpet 융단, 양탄자 / chasm 갈라진 틈 / pavement 보도, 인도

Question

1. 본문의 밑줄친 ⓐthey 가 가리키는 것을 찾아 쓰시오.

2. What does the underlined phrase ⓑ That huge prophetic wave of Muslim power imply?
   ① The prophecy meaning the decline of the Saracens
   ② The prophetic power of Christians
   ③ The sign implying failure in the Crusades
   ④ The saving of the Saracens from the Crusaders
   ⑤ The approaching power of Muslims against Christians

3. 본문의 밑줄친 ⓒ의 내용을 구체적으로 쓰시오.

4. According to the passage, which of the following is incorrect?
   ① Throughout history, the winners have actually been the losers in so many great wars.
   ② The Christians lost the Crusades.
   ③ The Crusades caused the prosperity of the Saracens.
   ④ The French Revolution had lost its last battle against the kings.
   ⑤ After the French Revolution the aristocracy could not wield its almighty power over the poor as before.

5. 본문의 전개방식으로 가장 알맞은 것은?
   ① 두 가지 대비되는 사실을 대조하며 서술했다.
   ② 주제문을 제시한 뒤 구체적 예를 들어 설명했다.
   ③ 다양한 주제를 여러 문장으로 서술하였다.
   ④ 먼저 적절한 예를 제시한 뒤 주제를 서술하였다.
   ⑤ 관계없는 역사적 사실을 단순 나열하였다.

Production

(1) 죽은 사람들과 죽어 가는 사람들이 그 싸움터에 흩어져 있었다.
(2) 제가 아직 살아 있는 것은 당신 덕택입니다.
(3) 이 규칙은 모든 경우에 적용된다.
(4) 나를 어린애로 취급하지 말아라.

실력체크 I

1 다음 글을 읽고 아래 물음에 답하여라.

The population crisis is here now, and it is the destruction of present and future civilizations. The world has two choices. Either we drastically alter our concepts of marriage and child bearing and the customs attached to them, to where we have but two children per family, or the wealthy will continue to devour the poor at an ever increasing rate. At the same time, the environment will steadily grow worse, thus being able to support fewer and fewer people. Why is there a crisis and what has brought it about? The principal reason for the current overpopulation of people in the world is that through man's intellect, science and technology, we have achieved a low death rate. The control of untimely death by scientifically applied humanitarianism has created a self-supported monster. Babies now have a greater chance of living long enough to produce children in turn — hence a population explosion. Not long ago, from 250 to 300 out of every 1,000 babies born died in infancy; now from four-fifths to nine-tenths of the babies who used to die survive. If we are going to have a low death rate culture — and, of course, we all want our babies to live — then we must also adopt a low birth rate culture. If babies of the future are to live, there must be fewer of them. No matter how much food there is, it is obvious that the birth rate cannot continue to exceed the death rate.

notes :
drastically 철저하게 / alter 바꾸다, 변경하다 / bearing 출산 / devour (동물·사람이) 게걸스럽게 먹다 / untimely 때 아닌 / humanitarianism 인도주의, 박애주의 / self-supported 스스로 살아 나가는 / infancy 유아기, 유년 / adopt 채택[채용]하다 / birth rate 출산율

(1) 윗 글의 제목을 본문에서 찾아 영어로 써라.
(2) 윗 글의 밑줄 친 부분이 의미하는 바를 구체적으로 설명하여라.
(3) 윗 글의 요지를 40자 이내의 우리말로 써라.

2 아래 밑줄 친 this difference of mental attitude를 구체적으로 설명하여라.

Is man the center and the lord of all animals? Or is he but one among a million existences which make up the living universe? There is nothing which divides the East and the West so fundamentally as this difference of mental attitude: the difference in the idea of man's true place in the universe and his relation to the world about him. If the former is the Western idea of man, the latter is essentially that of the East.

notes :
but = only / existence 존재(물) / make up 구성하다, 이루다 (= compose) / fundamentally 근본적으로

3 (B)의 단문은 (A)의 내용을 요약한 것이다. (1)~(5)의 공란에 들어갈 말을 보기에서 골라라. 필요하면 어형을 변화시켜라.

(A) What is freedom? Does freedom mean doing exactly as we please? No, that would soon encroach on the freedom of others. We may, for example, choose our own television or radio entertainment without fearing that a knock on the door will herald armed guards come to drag us off to prison for watching a forbidden program. This freedom of choice, however, does not give us the right to turn the volume of our set so loud that we disturb the neighbors—especially after midnight. We are free to assemble in large groups for football and baseball games, but we aren't free to hit a spectator in front of us over the head with a bottle when we disagree with him.

notes :
encroach 침해하다 / herald = proclaim the approach of / drag 끌고가다 / set = television or radio set / spectator 구경꾼

(B) Laws (1) our (2) so that the freedom of each citizen is (3). As long as our (4) do not (5) others, we are free to act, speak, and worship as we please.

▶▶보기 neighbor, please, action, freedom, protect, limit, forbidden, hurt, responsibility

4 다음 글을 읽고 밑의 물음에 답하여라.

Where do the pollutants come from? There are two main sources—sewage and industrial waste. As more detergent is used in the home, so more of it is finally discharged with the sewage into our rivers, lakes and seas. Detergents harm water birds by dissolving the natural fatty substances which keep their feathers waterproof. Sewage itself, if it is not properly treated, pollutes the water and prevents all forms of life in rivers and the sea from receiving the oxygen they need. Industrial waste is even more harmful since it contains, among other things, compounds of copper, lead, and nickel, all of which are highly poisonous to many forms of aquatic life.
So, if we want to stop this pollution the answer is simple: sewage and industrial waste must be purified. It may already be too late to save some rivers and lakes but others can still be saved if the correct action is taken at once.

notes :
pollutants 오염물질 / sewage 하수 / industrial waste 산업폐기물 / detergent 세제 / discharge 배출하다 / dissolve 분해시키다 / fatty substances 지방분 / compounds 화합물 / pollute 오염시키다 / oxygen 산소 / purify 정화하다

(1) 환경오염의 두가지 원인을 우리말로 적어라.
(2) 윗 글의 제목이 될 부분을 본문에서 찾아 써라.

실 력 체 크 Ⅱ

A. 다음 ⓐ, ⓑ가 동일한 의미가 되도록 (   ) 안에 주어진 단어들을 적당한 순서로 배열하여 ⓑ의 _____ 을 채워라.

(1) ⓐ They anticipated that there would be some trouble in that family.
ⓑ They _____ in that family.
(some, happen, saw, to, was, trouble, likely, that)

(2) ⓐ We are often tempted to despise the less talented.
ⓑ We _____ the less talented.
(feel, liable, for, contempt, to, are)

(3) ⓐ I cannot consent to your proposal until my scruples are removed.
ⓑ Your proposal cannot have my approval until _____.
(wrong, is, it, nothing, prove, there, that, you, with)

(4) ⓐ I congratulated myself on my narrow escape from the fire.
ⓑ I considered _____ the fire.
(escaped, myself, fortunate, barely, on, of, out, having)

(5) ⓐ Although he failed in that matter, we must make allowances for his youth.
ⓑ Although he failed in that matter, we must remember _____.
(severe, be, and, he, not, young, is, that, too)

B. 위의 문장과 같은 뜻이 되도록 공란을 메워라.

(1) I wonder if he has taken a wrong bus.
He _____ _____ taken a wrong bus.

(2) It is almost certain that he has forgotten the promise.
He _____ _____ forgotten the promise.

(3) How can you be so bold as to travel with no money?
How _____ you travel with no money!

(4) It is not right that you laughed at his mistakes.
You _____ not _____ laughed at his mistakes.

(5) I would choose death before disgrace.
I _____ _____ die than disgrace myself.

Answer: A. (1) saw that some trouble was likely to happen (2) are liable to feel contempt for (3) you prove that there is nothing wrong with it (4) myself fortunate on having barely escaped out of (5) that he is young and not be too severe
B. (1) may, have (2) must, have (3) dare (4) should, have (5) would rather

C. 공란을 적당한 단어로 메워라.

(1) Please sleep ______ my proposal and let me know your decision.
(2) Is your house insured ______ fire?
(3) As likely as ______, he has forgotten all about it.
(4) I'm afraid you can't see the forest ______ the trees.
(5) The house needs to be done ______.
(6) Let's drink ______ our reunion.
(7) His ability is open to question, but his honesty is ______ question.
(8) He never goes back ______ his promise.
(9) We took ______ each other instantaneously.
(10) The sight of the ruins brought ______ to me the meaning of war.

D. 지시대로 다음 문장를 바꿔 써라.

(1) We will be able to reach the hotel before dark. (밑줄 친 곳을 절로)
(2) He retired early on account of ill health. (밑줄 친 곳을 절로)
(3) Swimming, he said, is a sport that requires endurance and perfect timing. (that을 in which로 바꿔서)
(4) Many people away from home for the first time find it difficult to overcome homesickness. (find it difficult를 find difficulty로)
(5) Since it is raining, I would rather take a cab than go on foot. (would rather를 prefer로 바꿔서)

E. 영어의 속담 "A stitch in time saves nine."을 50어 내외의 영문으로 설명하여라.

F. 50어 이내의 영문으로 자기 소개를 하여라.

G. 다음 낱말의 정의를 영어로 내리되, 10단어 이상으로 써라.

(1) A library is a ______________________________.
(2) A dentist is a ______________________________.
(3) The Internet is a ______________________________.

Answer: C. (1) on (2) against (3) not (4) for (5) up (6) to (7) beyond (8) on (9) to (10) home D. (1) before it gets dark (2) because he was in ill health (3) in which endurance and perfect timing are required (4) find difficulty in overcoming homesickness (5) I prefer taking a cab to going on foot. E. If we take a stitch in time, it will save nine stitches that we might have to take later on. In the same way, it is important to take a necessary step just in time or before it is too late. This kind of caution will save us a lot of trouble. F. My name is Hong Gil-dong. I live in Masan City with my parents and two sisters. One of my sisters is a graduate student and the other is an accountant. My hobbies are reading, mountain-climbing, and cycling. It's my dream to go to the United States after graduating from college. G. (1) place where a collection of books is kept for reading (2) person who deals with the prevention and treatment of teeth diseases (3) huge computer network of electronic mail and information

어 휘 · 발 음

A. 오른쪽에 주어진 밑줄 친 단어와 결합하여 왼쪽에 쓰여진 의미가 될 수 있는 접두사를 골라라.

> 보기 to work together　　operate 답 ⓒ
> ⓐ micro-　ⓑ bi-　ⓒ co-　ⓓ post-　ⓔ un-

(1) to sail around　　navigate
ⓐ bi-　ⓑ circum-　ⓒ dis-　ⓓ re-　ⓔ trans-

(2) occurring two times a year　　annual
ⓐ dis-　ⓑ contra-　ⓒ co-　ⓓ bi-　ⓔ auto-

(3) to see before others　　view
ⓐ micro-　ⓑ mis-　ⓒ post-　ⓓ pre-　ⓔ re-

(4) across the continent　　continental
ⓐ inter-　ⓑ micro-　ⓒ trans-　ⓓ un-　ⓔ circum-

(5) a story of one's own life written by oneself　　biography
ⓐ auto-　ⓑ bi-　ⓒ circum-　ⓓ post-　ⓔ super-

(6) to come together again　　unite
ⓐ pre-　ⓑ re-　ⓒ sub-　ⓓ super-　ⓔ trans-

(7) to take away confidence　　courage
ⓐ en-　ⓑ inter-　ⓒ re-　ⓓ un-　ⓔ dis-

(8) to get a wrong meaning　　understand
ⓐ un-　ⓑ trans-　ⓒ re-　ⓓ pre-　ⓔ mis-

(9) not worried　　concerned
ⓐ dis-　ⓑ mis-　ⓒ un-　ⓓ over-　ⓔ sub-

B. 각 문장에 쓰인 'free'의 뜻을 ⓐ~ⓘ에서 골라라.

(1) Do you have any rooms free?
(2) The accused left the court a free man.
(3) He is free with his money.
(4) He left one end of a rope free.
(5) You are free to go or stay as you please.

ⓐ liberated	ⓑ unprejudiced	ⓒ at liberty
ⓓ unconstrained	ⓔ loose	ⓕ licentious
ⓖ generous	ⓗ vacant	ⓘ without payment

Answer: A. (1) ⓑ (2) ⓓ (3) ⓓ (4) ⓒ (5) ⓐ (6) ⓑ (7) ⓔ (8) ⓔ (9) ⓒ
B. (1) ⓗ (2) ⓐ (3) ⓖ (4) ⓔ (5) ⓒ

엑센트에 주의할 단어

ábsolute
accéssory
ádmirable
ágriculture
altérnative
áncestor
árchitect
artifícial
átmosphere
authórity
barómeter
biógraphy
canál
certíficate
círcumstance
characterístic
cómfortable
cómmerce
cómparable
cónsequence
contémporary
contríbute
demócracy
démocrat
démonstrate
diámeter
díplomat
distríbute
económical
ecónomy
electrícity
energétic
enthusiástic
éssence
Européan
famíliar
geómetry
habítual
harmónious
hýpocrite
ígnorant
indivídual
índustry
indústrial
ínfamous
ínfinite
ínfluence
ínstrument
íntellect
intelléctual
ínteresting
intérpret
ínterval
lámentable
mathemátics
méchanism
mélancholy
miráculous
míschievous
mómentary
monótonous
nécessary
necéssity
neverthelé́ss
occúr
opportúnity
ópposite
órigin
oríginal
originálity
Pacífic
partícular
peculiárity
phótograph
photógraphy
picturésque
polítícian
propagánda
prefér
préferable
psychólogy
psychológical
récognize
recommend
represént
representátive
ridículous
responsibílity
sátisfy
scientífic
simultáneous
signíficant
súbstitute
superfícial
techníque
thermómeter
triúmphant
últimate
úniverse

숙 어

(1) **fix A up with B** (=arrange for A to have B ; introduce B to A)
A에게 B를 마련해[알선해] 주다 ; A에게 B를 소개시켜 주다
☞ I know someone who's able to *fix* you *up with* a good job.
I have a nice girl I'd like to *fix* you *up with*.

(2) **flatter oneself that** (=be pleased with one's belief that)
혼자 속으로 믿고 좋아하다
☞ He *flatters himself that* he'll be able to get her in the long run.

(3) **follow suit** (=do as someone else has done)
남이 하는대로 하다, 선례를 따르다
☞ Once one bank raises its interest rate, all the others will *follow suit*.

(4) **fool around** (=waste time doing nothing) 빈둥거리다
☞ Instead of studying, he spends all his spare time *fooling around*.

(5) **for a song** (=for very little money, cheaply) 헐값으로, 염가로
☞ Because the shop's closing down, most of the stock is going *for a song*.

(6) **for all I know** (=perhaps) 아마
☞ All his family may be living somewhere in North America *for all I know*.

(7) **for better or for worse** (=under good or bad circumstances) 좋든 싫든간에
☞ Will you promise to stay with me *for better or for worse*?

(8) **for fear of** (=because of anxiety about) ~을 두려워하여
☞ I dare not go there *for fear of* him seeing me.

(9) **for free** (=without charge, free of charge) 무료로
☞ You can't expect the doctor to treat you *for free*.

(10) **for good** (=for ever) 영원히, 아주
☞ We thought she'd come for a visit, but it seems she's staying *for good*.

(11) **for good measure** (=as something extra, in addition) 덤으로, 추가로
☞ After I'd weighed the pears, I put in another one *for good measure*.

⑿ **for nothing** (=without payment ; in vain ; without reason)
공짜로 ; 헛되이 ; 이유 없이

☞ When we bought the house we got all the furniture as well *for nothing*.
All my efforts were *for nothing*. They quarrelled *for nothing*.

⒀ **for once** (=this once) 한 번만[이번만]

☞ Can't you be nice to each other (just) *for once*?

⒁ **for one thing** (=in the first place) 우선, 첫째는

☞ *For one thing* I am busy; for another I don't have any money.

⒂ **for one's[dear] life** (=desperately) 필사적으로

☞ He hung on to the ledge *for his life*.

⒃ **for short** (=for brevity's sake) 줄여서, 생략하여

☞ The World Trade Organization is called WTO *for short*.

⒄ **for the most part** (=mostly, on the whole) 대부분, 대개

☞ Korean TV sets are, *for the most part*, of excellent quality.

⒅ **for the sake of** (=for the benefit of) ~을 위하여

☞ We have to stop fighting *for the sake of* family unity.

⒆ **for lack of** (=for want of) ~이 부족하여

☞ The project failed *for lack of* financial backing.

⒇ **for the time being** (=for the moment, for the present) 당분간

☞ *For the time being* I'm tied up, but I'll get to it first thing next month.

(21) **forget it** (=overlook it) (칭찬·사죄 등에 대해) 괜찮아요, 됐어요

☞ "Thanks so much for helping me." "*Forget it*, it was nothing."

Exercise

▶▶ 주어진 단어들을 포함한 글을 지어라. 필요하면 어형을 변화시켜라.

1. flatter / speaker / class
2. raise / glass / follow
3. boy / fool / park
4. lock / door / fear / thief
5. meals / provide / free
6. cling / branch / life
7. David / Dave / short
8. inhabitant / part / diligent
9. save / sake / family
10. plant / die / lack

7. 태 (Voice)

기본 문법 설명

A. 태의 종류와 전환

(1) ⓐ All the members of the club **respect** him.

ⓑ He **is respected** by all the members of the club.

(2) ⓐ Kidnappers **abduct** children.

⇨ Children **are abducted** by kidnappers.

ⓑ Kidnappers **abducted** the child.

⇨ The child **was abducted** by kidnappers.

ⓒ Kidnappers **will abduct** the child.

⇨ The child **will be abducted** by kidnappers.

ⓓ Kidnappers **has abducted** the child.

⇨ The child **has been abducted** by kidnappers.

ⓔ Kidnappers **had abducted** the child.

⇨ The child **had been abducted** by kidnappers.

ⓕ Kidnappers **will have abducted** the child.

⇨ The child **will have been abducted** by kidnappers.

ⓖ Kidnappers **are abducting** the child.

⇨ The child **is being abducted** by kidnappers.

ⓗ Kidnappers **can abduct** the child.

⇨ The child **can be abducted** by kidnappers.

B. 주의할 수동태

(1) The boss promised **us higher wages**.

⇨ ⓐ **We** were promised higher wages by the boss.

⇨ ⓑ **Higher wages** were promised to us by the boss.

(2) His bravery in the war made **him** a hero.

⇨ **He** was made a hero by his bravery in the war.

(3) Her sudden death made **him change** his mind.

⇨ **He** was made **to change** his mind by her sudden death.

(4) **Who** invented that alibi to avoid punishment?

⇨ **By whom** was that alibi invented to avoid punishment?

A. 태의 종류와 전환

(1) **능동태와 수동태**

동작의 관점의 차이에 의해 생기는 동사의 표현 형식을 태(態)라고 한다.

- **능동태** : 동작을 하는 쪽에 중점을 둠
- **수동태** : 동작을 받는 쪽에 중점을 둠

「능동태 ⇨ 수동태」

- 주어 … 능동태의 목적어가 됨
- 동사 … 「be+과거분사」
- by~ … 능동태의 주어가 by 뒤에 와서 부사구를 이룸

He wrote this letter. [능동태]
S V O

This letter was written by him. [수동태]
S V 부사구

ⓐ (그 클럽의 모든 회원들이 그를 존경한다.) … 능동태

ⓑ (그는 그 클럽의 모든 회원들에 의해 존경 받는다.) … 수동태

☞ 목적어가 있는 문장이 모두 수동태로 바뀌지는 않는다. have(=possess), resemble, lack, become 등은 수동태가 안 되는 동사들이다.

(2) **수동태의 시제**

ⓐ 현재 (are abducted)
ⓑ 과거 (was abducted)
ⓒ 미래 (will be abducted)
ⓓ 현재완료 (has been abducted)
ⓔ 과거완료 (had been abducted)
ⓕ 미래완료 (will have been abducted)
ⓖ 진행형 (is being abducted)
(be+being+과거분사)
ⓗ 조동사 (조동사+be+과거분사)

B. 주의할 수동태

(1) **4형식의 수동태**

4형식의 문장은 대개 간접목적어를 주어로 하든지, 직접목적어를 주어로 하여 두 개의 수동태가 가능하다.

ⓐ 간접목적어를 주어로 했다.
ⓑ 직접목적어를 주어로 했다.

☞ 간접목적어가 보류목적어로 될 때는 그 앞에 **to, for, of** 등을 놓는다.

A letter was sent *to* me by him.
A watch was bought *for* me by him.
Some questions were asked *of* me by him.

☞ 4형식 문장이 반드시 두 개의 수동태가 되는 것은 아니다.

4형식의 make, write, sell, send, sing, pass 등의 동사는 수동태가 하나뿐이다.

I *wrote* him a letter.
⇨ A letter was written to him by me.
She *sang* me a song.
⇨ A song was sung for[to] me by her.

(2) **5형식의 수동태**

5형식의 문장을 수동태로 고쳐 쓰면 2형식의 문장이 된다.

☞ 일반인을 나타내는 we, you, one, they, people, someone, somebody 등은 수동태에서는 보통 생략된다.

We must wear seat belts.
= Seat belts must be worn (by us).

(3) **보어가 원형부정사인 수동태**

술부동사가 지각동사 또는 사역동사일 경우, 원형부정사는 수동태에서는 「**to 부정사**」가 된다. 그러나 현대영어에서는 지각동사일 경우는 to 부정사보다는 현재분사를 쓰는 것이 더 보편적이다.

We heard him *sing*.
⇨ He was heard *to sing*[*singing*].
We made her *do* the work.
⇨ She was made *to do* the work.

(4) **의문문의 수동태**

Who ⇨ By whom이 되며, 그 위치는 문두에 둔다.

When did you finish it?
⇨ When *was* it *finished* (by you)?
What language do they speak in Brazil?
⇨What language *is spoken* in Brazil?

	(5) **We** generally **assume** that money is everything. ⇨ **It is** generally **assumed** that money is everything. ⇨ Money **is** generally **assumed to** be everything. (6) Everybody **laughed at** my jokes. ⇨ My jokes **were laughed at** by everybody. (7) **Submit** the report at once. ⇨ **Let** the report **be submitted** at once. **Don't** delay your departure. ⇨ **Don't let** your departure **be** delayed. ⇨ **Let** your departure **not be** delayed. (8) ⓐ Nothing I do satisfies my wife. ⇨ My wife is satisfied **with** nothing I do. ⓑ Everybody knows the words of this song. ⇨ The words of this song is known **to** everybody. ⓒ His sudden death astonished me. ⇨ I was astonished **at** his sudden death. ⓓ The women didn't seem to interest him. ⇨ He didn't seem to be interested **in** the women.
C. 수동태의 용법과 종류	(1) ⓐ He **was killed** in the Vietnam War. ⓑ Spanish **is spoken** in Mexico, too. ⓒ Some things **have been said** here tonight that should not **have been spoken**. ⓓ The child **was run over** by a car. ⓔ He made a speech and **was asked** many questions at the end. ⓕ On the way home, I **was caught** in the rain. (2) ⓐ Our house **is painted** every year. ⓑ Our house **is painted** green. (3) ⓐ This latest-model computer **sells** very well. ⓑ I **was** greatly **astounded** at the sight. ⓒ I **had** my hat **blown** off by the wind. ⓓ The meal is now **cooking**. ⓔ They were not **to blame** for the accident.

(5) **목적어가 명사절인 경우의 수동태**
가주어 It을 내세우든지, that절 속의 주어를 수동태의 주어로 한다.
Everyone *expects* that she will marry him.
⇨ It *is expected* that she will marry him.
⇨ She *is expected* to marry him.

(6) **군동사의 수동태**
군동사는 수동태에서 한 단위로 취급된다.
She *looked down on* him.
⇨He was *looked down on* by her.
They *speak well of* him.
⇨He is *well spoken of*.

(7) **명령문의 수동태**
「Let+목적어+be+과거분사」의 형태를 사용한다.
☞ 명령문의 부정은 두 가지가 있다.
「Don't let+목적어+be+과거분사」
「Let+목적어+not+be+과거분사」

(8) **동작의 행위를 나타내는 전치사**
능동문의 주어는 수동태에서 대개 전치사구로 나타나는데 그 때의 대표적인 전치사는 by이지만, 동사에 따라 다른 전치사가 오는 경우가 있다.
ⓐ (내 아내는 내가 하는 일은 무엇이든 불만이다.)
The sky was covered *with* dark clouds.
ⓑ (이 노래의 가사는 모든 사람에게 알려져 있다.)
A man is known *by* the company he keeps. (사람은 그가 사귀는 친구에 의해 알 수 있다.)
ⓒ 기쁨, 슬픔, 놀람 따위의 감정을 나타내는 동사는 보통 수동태로 나타내며, 여기 수반하는 전치사는 대개 at, with 등이다.
I am pleased *with* my students.
I was surprised *at* his conduct.
ⓓ (그는 그 여자들에게 흥미가 있는 것 같지 않았다.)
I was tired *from* the work.
I was tired *of* my quiet life.
The street is crowded *with* a lot of people.

C. 수동태의 용법과 종류

(1) **수동태가 많이 쓰이는 경우**
ⓐ 능동태의 주어가 분명하지 않을 때
ⓑ 능동태의 주어가 막연한 일반인을 나타낼 때
ⓒ 행위자를 나타내지 않는 것이 좋다고 생각될 때
(말하지 말았어야 할 것을 오늘 밤 여기서 몇 가지 말했다.)
ⓓ 능동태의 주어보다는 수동태의 주어에 더 관심이 있을 때
ⓔ 앞 문장과의 연결상으로
(그는 연설을 했다. 그리고, 그 연설 끝에 많은 질문을 받았다.)
ⓕ 수동의 의미가 거의 없이 자동사로 느껴지는 경우

(2) **동작수동태와 상태수동태**
ⓐ = We paint our house every year.
(우리 집은 매년 페인트칠을 한다.) … 동작
ⓑ = We have painted our house green.
(우리 집은 녹색 페인트 칠이 되어 있다.) … 상태
The doors are shut at seven every evening. … 동작
The doors are shut now. … 상태

(3) **주의할 수동태**
ⓐ (이 최신형 컴퓨터는 매우 잘 팔린다.)
… 형식은 능동이나 뜻은 수동이다.
Ripe oranges *peel* easily.
ⓑ (나는 그 광경을 보고 매우 놀랐다.)
… 형식은 수동이나 뜻은 능동이다. 특히 감정을 나타내는 말에 많다.
ⓒ 「have[get]+목적어+과거분사」
… 을 ~당하다, …을 ~시키다
I had my watch stólen. (당하다)
I hád my watch mended. (시키다)
ⓓ = The meal is now being cooked.
The movie is now playing.
= The movie is now being played.
ⓔ = They were not to be blamed for the accident.
a house to rent : 셋집
water to drink : 음료수

문 법 · 작 문

A. Fill in each blank with a suitable word:

(1) The quote 'The tree is known _____ its fruit' can be found in the Bible.

(2) The news that he'll resign soon is known _____ everybody.

(3) We were very surprised _____ the result of the election.

(4) I am not fully satisfied _____ the standard of your work.

(5) How much of the Earth's surface is covered _____ water?

(6) She is married _____ an American who's here as a diplomat.

(7) The milk produced _____ cows, goats and sheep is drunk _____ humans or made _____ butter and cheese.

(8) You're soaked! Did you get caught _____ the shower?

B. 괄호 속의 동사의 올바른 어형을 정하여라.

(1) The United Nations Charter (sign) in 1945.

(2) It (believe) that the current political situation is critical.

(3) Animals instinctively know how to live without (teach).

(4) Criticism is not fault-finding, it is a balanced opinion. No statement must (make) without a reason.

(5) It was reported that a bloody knife (find) close to the (murder) man.

(6) Great English poets (bury) in Westminster Abbey when they die.

(7) The king had the precious stones (bring) before him.

(8) To love and to (love) is the greatest happiness on earth.

(9) The cruel practice that people kill an adulteress by throwing stones at her has long (do) away with.

C. 다음 각 문장의 태(Voice)를 바꾸어라.

(1) We will send her a lovely suit.

(2) Your money could be put to good use instead of being left idle in the bank.

(3) We saw two little boys wallowing in the mud.

(4) Sign the paper and mail it at once.

(5) The mayor is giving an opening address in the city hall.

(6) Somebody must have taken it away.

(7) Who do you think will win the gold medal?

(8) Don't keep it a secret that he stole the money.

(9) Is salt sold by the pound?

(10) They say that the lilac originally came from the north of Persia.

(11) My secretary will take good care of your travel arrangements.

(12) No one ever took me for an Italian before.

(13) One might have heard a pin drop.
(14) No one has ever solved the problem.
(15) Let these facts be regarded as of special importance.
(16) Her father let her stay out late just that once.
(17) People used to think that the sun went around the earth.
(18) Scholars have always looked up to him as a great benefactor of learning.
(19) Nobody took any notice of what she had said.
(20) The stuck-up new manager is ill spoken of by the people.
(21) What cannot be cured must be endured.
(22) What makes you say such a rude thing?
(23) Your composition is well written.
(24) No questions were asked of us.
(25) Naturally they expect you to interest yourself in the job they have offered you.

D. Translate the following into English:

(1) 오늘 아침 나의 집 근처에서 개 한 마리가 트럭에 치었다.

(2) 네가 그런 바보 짓을 하면 너는 비웃음을 받을 것이다.

(3) 어둠 속에서 갑자기 낯선 사람이 나에게 말을 걸어 왔을 때 나는 매우 놀랐다.

(4) 태풍 주디에 의한 호우 때문에 전 시가지가 물에 잠겼다.

(5) 그는 현재의 지위에 매우 만족하고 있는 것 같다.

(6) 비록 젊지만 그는 유능하며, 그를 매우 소중히 여기고 있다고 한다.

(7) 어제 나는 학교에서 집으로 돌아오는 길에 소나기를 만나 흠뻑 젖었다.

(8) 새로 오신 그 선생님은 인격자이므로 학생들의 평판이 좋다.

(9) 사람의 가치는 그의 사회적 지위에 의해서가 아니라, 그의 인격에 의해 평가되어야 한다.

'Abraham Lincoln'이라는 제목으로 70어 내외의 글을 지어라.

● 단 문 독 해 ●

I was **told** that it could not **be done** that way.
The house is **being built** by Jack.
Let it **be done** by him.

1. By and by I **was told** by someone that birds could not **be caught** by putting salt on their tails, that I **was being made a fool of**, and this was a great shock to me, since I **had been taught** to believe that it was wicked to tell a lie. Now for the first time in my life I discovered that there were lies and lies, or untruths that were not lies.

notes :
*by and by 얼마 안 있어
*make a fool of ~ = ~을 놀리다
*wicked 사악한
*for the first time = 처음으로

▶▶윗글의 내용과 일치하도록 다음 빈칸에 적절한 것을 고르시오.
The above paragraph describes how the writer grew out of his childish (　　) and awoke to the (　　) of life.
① disappointment　② behavior　③ innocence
④ realities　⑤ tragedy

▶▶영작하시오.
나이를 먹음에 따라 거짓말에도 가지가지가 있다는 것을 알게 될 것이다.

2. **Let** wealth **be regarded** by some society of the future as a mere means to the proper ends of human life, and whether it is rich or poor on the whole, its wealth **will be** fairly **distributed**, and that society in pursuit of those ends will be happy and healthy.

notes :
*Let some society of the future regard wealth as a mere means ~
*end 목적

▶▶Which is the main idea of the above paragraph?
① One day in the future, society should use its wealth as a means to achieve a higher standard of living.
② The large fortune of the wealthy should be distributed among the poor to make a fair society.
③ Future society should realize that only the proper use of its wealth could make it happy and healthy.
④ Our future happiness depends on whether our society is rich or poor.
⑤ Our future well-being is dependent on the increasing number of wealthy people in our society.

▶▶영작하시오.
우리 모두는 행복을 추구하고 있다.

3. The picnic-park **was reached** at last. Lunch boxes **were** quickly **opened** and the contents were not long in disappearing. Those mothers who felt sure in the morning that too much lunch **was being packed** up, should have been there to see what happened to those sandwiches and cakes. Every bit of food **was eaten**, and it was quite likely that if as much more **had been brought**, it would have gone the same way.

notes :
*contents 내용, 알맹이
*as much = 같은 양
*too much lunch was being packed up, = they were packing up too much lunch,

▶▶Which does **not** correspond with the above paragraph?

① The above paragraph describes the scene of the children devouring lunch with relish in the park.

② The mothers felt a little bit worried that they might have packed too much lunch for their children.

③ Even though the children had eaten all the food, the writer believed, they could have eaten just as much again.

④ The mothers who had packed the lunches could not believe their eyes when they saw the children eat up their lunches instantly.

⑤ The writer wished that the mothers had been with their children to see them eat lunch so heartily.

▶▶영작하시오.

다시는 그 여자를 만날 수 없을 것 같다.

4. People in high positions **are** of course more **thought of** and **talked about**, and have their virtues more praised, than those whose lives **are passed** in humble everyday work, but every sensible man knows how necessary that humble everyday work is, and how important it is to us that it **should be done** well.

notes :
*lives는 life의 복수
*마지막 it = that humble everyday work

▶▶Which of the following is the most suitable title for the above paragraph?

① The necessity of hard work

② The necessity of important people

③ The importance of humble everyday work

④ The inconspicuous life of humble folk

⑤ The superiority of well-known people

▶▶영작하시오.

그 일을 즉시 시작하는 것이 우리에게 얼마나 중요한지 알아야 한다.

He **is thought** to be rich.
It is **said** that he is honest.
Great care should **be taken of** it.

5. A man was run over by a car in High Street yesterday. The car was driven by Mr. White. An ambulance was called, and the man was taken to the nearest hospital. The injured man has not been identified yet. He was dressed in a brown coat and grey pants. His age is estimated to be about thirty-five. Anyone who may know this man **is asked** to telephone the police.

notes :
*identify 신원을 확인하다
*estimate 추정하다

▶▶Which is the type of writing of the above paragraph?
① An editorial ② An advertisement ③ An essay
④ An article ⑤ A comment

▶▶영작하시오.
그 여자는 하얀 옷을 입고 있었으며, 나이에 비해 젊어 보였다.

6. Wellington **is said** to have chosen his officers by their noses and chins. The standard for them in noses must have been rather high, to judge by the portraits of the Duke, but no doubt he made allowances. Anyhow, by this method he got the men he wanted.

notes :
*officer 부하장교
*chin 턱
*to judge by = if we judge by
*no doubt = 틀림없이
*allowances 참작, 고려

▶▶윗글의 내용과 부합하도록 다음 빈칸에 가장 적절한 것은?
Judging from the above paragraph, it seems that Wellington was a very (   ) man.
① eccentric ② bland ③ generous
④ shrewd ⑤ meticulous

▶▶영작하시오.
그의 젊음을 우리는 참작해야 한다.

7. And about noon word came through that Bones's slave ship **had been sighted** near the island. **Great care** must **be taken**, the message said, because the slave ship was in all readiness to sail at a moment's notice. All the sailors **were warned** to keep very quiet, so that the navy ship could sneak up on the slaver unawares.

notes :
*word 기별, 소식
*come through = 도달되다
*be sighted = 발견되다
*in all readiness to ~ = ~할 만반의 준비를 갖추고
*at a moment's notice = 당장에, 즉시
*sneak up on ~ = ~에 몰래 다가가다

▶▶Which best describes the mood of the above paragraph?

① loose and relaxed ② calm and placid
③ grotesque and weird ④ tense and thrilling
⑤ gloomy and sad

▶▶영작하시오.

그가 올 수 없다는 통지가 왔다.

I had [**got**] my watch stolen.
I had [**got**] my watch repaired.

8. Instead of **having** everything **done** for him, the child should be allowed to do things by himself; instead of **having** all his decisions **made** for him, he should be given an opportunity to make his own decisions and encouraged to think for himself.

notes :
*instead of ~ing = ~하는 대신에
*be allowed to ~ = ~하도록 놔두다
*opportunity 기회

▶▶Which of the following is most suitable for the main topic of the above paragraph?

① Children should be reared to have their own way.
② Education should be focused on improving our children's sociability.
③ Children should be given every opportunity to think and decide by themselves.
④ Children should be encouraged to cooperate with each other.
⑤ Children should be taught to respect seniors and to be thankful to others who help them.

▶▶영작하시오.

그 장군은 모든 일을 자기 부하들이 해주는데 익숙해 있다.

9. While there are judges who will decide fairly, and courts in which every man can **get** justice **done** to him, the country is safe from all the danger and discontent which always spring up where there is no justice.

notes :
*while = ~하는 한
*court 법정
*get justice done to him = 자기에게 정의가 베풀어지도록 하다
*spring up = 생겨나다

▶▶Without a(n) (   ) and impartial legal system, our society would be put in (   ), rife with dissatisfaction and unrest.

[fair, unjust, biased, doom, danger, risk]

▶▶영작하시오.

그 집은 바람에 지붕이 날아갔다.

● 장 문 독 해 ●

Warming-up

Political freedom, **as** we enjoy it, came out of a long struggle through many centuries.

The situation **requires** that prompt action should be taken to meet it.

I have done so in **the firm belief that** I am right.

The scenery was **too** beautiful **for** words; we were struck speechless by it.

The vase was **so** badly broken **as to** be irreparable.

1 Liberty is built on peace and can have no other foundation. War and disorder are its two great enemies. Our free government, as we enjoy it, is the substitution of law for force, of argument for physical strife. It is an achievement of many centuries; it rests on the belief that free discussion is the likeliest way of doing justice and reaching sensible conclusions about policy. But ⓐit has rules of its own which must be obeyed. It requires tolerance and mutual forbearance. It requires that minorities should submit for the time being, when they are outvoted in Parliament; and be content to work for a future in which ⓑthey will have made their views prevail by reason and argument. If any of these assumptions fail, ⓒif our feelings become literally too strong for words, if minorities will not submit and fly from words to blows, or majorities so abuse their power as to drive minorities to physical resistance, then it is all up with liberty.

J. A. Spender: *Freedom*

Note

foundation 기초 / disorder 무질서 / free government 자유주의 정치 / enjoy 향유하다 / substitution 대리, 대용 ; súbstitute A for B / argument 의논, 토론 / physical strife 육체적 투쟁 / achievement 업적 / rest on ~에 달려 있다 / likely = suitable / sensible 현명한 / conclusion 결론 / tolerance 아량 / mutual forbearance 상호 자제 / minority 소수 ; majority 다수 / submit 굴복하다 / for the time being = for the present 당분간 / outvote 투표로 이기다 / Parliament 국회 / prevail 우세하다 / assumptions 가정(假定), 전제(前提) / literally 문자 그대로 / blows 구타 / abuse 남용하다 / resistance 저항 / be all up 만사가 끝나다 It *is all up* with him. = He is ruined.

Question

1. 본문의 밑줄친 ⓐit와 ⓑthey가 가리키는 말이 올바르게 짝지어진 것은?

ⓐ	ⓑ
① liberty	— sensible conclusions
② free government	— rules
③ free discussion	— majorities
④ liberty	— minorities
⑤ free government	— minorities

2. 밑줄친 ⓒ와 같은 뜻이 되도록 적절한 말을 골라 쓰시오.

if our feelings become ( ),

[uncontrollable, inflamed, impassioned]

3. According to this passage, which of the following does **not** correspond with the essential factors of free government?

① law ② argument
③ free discussion ④ mutual forbearance
⑤ physical resistance

4. According to the passage, which of the following is **not** correct?

① We can derive justice from free discussion.
② Tolerance and mutual forbearance are necessary to keep free government.
③ Minorities are required to submit to majorities when they are lost in the vote.
④ The physical strife of the outvoted minorities is a necessary evil in a democracy.
⑤ It is not desirable for majorities to abuse their power.

Production

(1) 버터 대신에 마아가린을 쓸 수 있다. (substitute A for B)
(2) 모든 지식은 경험에 의존한다.
(3) 나는 당분간 이 호텔에 숙박하려고 한다.
(4) 그녀의 논평은 너무 유치해서 고려할 가치가 없을 정도였다.

● 장 문 독 해 ●

Warming-up

The servant who, gently **treated**, is ungrateful, **treated** ungently, will be revengeful.

They reduced their other expenditures to **such** a point **that** they lived an almost beggarly life.

It is not an illusory dream, but a dream **attainable** in our own time.

2 In the future days, which we seek to make secure, we look forward to a world founded upon four essential human freedoms. The first is freedom of speech and expression—everywhere in the world.

The second is freedom of every person to worship God in his own way—everywhere in the world.

The third is freedom from want—which, translated into world terms, means economic understandings which will secure to every nation a healthy peace time life for its inhabitants—everywhere in the world.

The fourth is freedom from fear—which, translated into world terms, means a world-wide reduction of armaments to such a point and in such a thorough fashion that no nation will be in a position to commit an act of physical aggression against any neighbor—anywhere in the world.

That is no vision of a distant millennium. It is a definite basis for a kind of world attainable in our own time and generation. That kind of world is the very antithesis of the so-called new order of tyranny which the dictators seek to create with the crash of a bomb.

***Franklin D. Roosevelt:** "Four Freedoms" Speech*

Note

founded on ~에 입각한 / speech and expression 언론과 표현 / in one's own way 자기 나름으로 / inhábitant 주민 / world terms 세계적인 의미 / reduction of armaments 군비 축소 / fashion = way / aggression 침략 / millénnium 천년의 기간 / antíthesis 정반대 / so-called 소위, 이른바 / order 질서 / tyranny 폭정 / dictator 독재자

Question

1. Which of the following is the main idea of this passage?
   ① a vision of a distant millennium
   ② a world attainable in our own time
   ③ four fundamental human freedoms
   ④ recovery from poverty and everlasting prosperity
   ⑤ prevention of war through reduction of armaments

2. Which of the following is **not** the purpose of this passage?
   ① to persuade ② to explain ③ to inform
   ④ to announce ⑤ to determine

3. Which can replace the underlined word, want?
   ① desire ② surplus ③ wish ④ lack ⑤ affluence

4. Mark the following sentences T(true) or F(false) according to the passage.
   ① We should seek to make our future days safe and sound.
   ② Dictators seek to create a new order of the world by means of war.
   ③ Freedom from want is the last thing we should try to seek.
   ④ We can attain an ideal new world in our own time if we try.
   ⑤ Freedom of speech and expression is one of the essential human rights.
   ⑥ We expect with pleasure an ideal new world of peace and prosperity.
   ⑦ We should try to achieve a global reduction of armaments.
   ⑧ We should try to seek freedom of religion all over the world.
   ⑨ We should try to attain economic prosperity solely for our own country.
   ⑩ No nation should be so armed as to invade other countries.

Production

(1) 우리는 두 달 동안 여기저기 여행했다. 그래서, 이제는 모두 빨리 집으로 돌아가기를 고대한다.
(2) 어떤 책들은 부주의하게 읽으면 이익보다 오히려 해를 끼친다.
(3) 이 책은 매우 쉬운 영어로 씌어져 있으므로 초보자도 이해할 수 있다.

실 력 체 크 I

1 다음 글을 읽고 아래 물음에 간결하게 답하여라.

For centuries, a common belief was that people are born to be what they are. Other theories existed, but the widespread explanation for individual differences was that differences in heredity accounted for them. Some people, it was said, were born naturally good and some were born bad. Also inborn, it was believed, were such traits as truthfulness, honesty, conscientiousness, and industry, as well as such traits as bad temper, laziness, and untidiness. People talked of born saints, born criminals, born leaders, and born cowards.

Then the pendulum swung the other way. Experience began to be a deciding factor. Identical twins were studied and were found to have different personalities if reared in different homes where the experiences would not be similar. When placed in homes with capable loving parents, infants with poor heredity often grew up into competent, well-adjusted adults.

It is now evident that neither heredity alone nor experience alone accounts for individual differences. Heredity appears to be the stronger influence in some respects, experience in others. But usually both contribute to the uniqueness of each individual.

The detailed patterns of physical structure are known to be inherited—color of eyes, shape of nose, height, and bone size, for example. Aptitudes and potential intelligence are also believed to be strongly influenced by heredity. Other behavior tendencies may prove to be inborn—certain types of preferences and personal needs, for example. Such tendencies, however, along with aptitudes and intelligence, will be much more dependent on experience for the precise way in which they develop than are the physical traits.

notes :
what they are 있는 그대로, 지금의 그들 / heredity 유전 / account for ~의 중요한 원인이 되다 / inborn 선천적인 / traits 특성, 특질 / conscientiousness 양심, 성실성 / temper 기질 / untidiness 단정하지 못함 / pendulum 시계의 추 (the swing of the pendulum (세론, 인심의) 추세) / identical twin 일란성 쌍둥이 / well-adjusted 환경에 잘 조정된 / adults 어른 / contribute to ~의 원인의 하나가 되다 / uniqueness 독특성 / aptitude 적성, 소질 / potential 발전의 가능성이 있는 (a potential genius 천재의 소질이 있는 사람) / behavior tendency 행동 취향 / preference 좋아하는 것 / along with ~과 더불어

(1) '개인차가 생기는 원인'에 대해 최초에는 어떤 설명이 일반적이었는가?

(2) 밑줄 친 the pendulum swung the other way라는 비유에 의해 필자는 무엇을 말하려고 하는가?

(3) 현재는 어떻게 생각되고 있는가?

(4) 적성과 지능, 개인적인 기호 혹은 요구 등에 대해 어떻게 진술하고 있는가?

2 다음 글을 읽고 아래 질문에 답하여라.

A patrol car appears in the driver's rearview mirror, and the flashing light goes on. The driver anxiously stops his car, and the policeman asks to see his license. It is just a routine check; the driver has not been going too fast or doing anything noticeably wrong. Then the officer glimpses the bag of marihuana......

Such spot checks by policemen are common practice. Last week, by a vote of 8 to 1, the U. S. Supreme Court decided that they are unconstitutional. No longer will a policeman be able to stop a car at random to look at a driver's license unless he has some objective reason to suspect that the law has been broken. The case before the court involved a driver who was arrested on charges of possession of marihuana after his car was stopped during a 'routine' license check. The police officer was not looking for marihuana. "I saw the car in the area and was not busy at the moment, so I decided to stop it," he explained. The state argued that random checks contributed to highway safety by taking unlicensed drivers and unregistered cars off the road. The court disagreed. Expressing the opinion of the majority, Justice Byron White said that the safety factor was 'of little significance at best,' and that it was not enough to exceed the 'Fourth Amendment's prohibition against unreasonable searches and seizures. The decision means that the police will no longer be able to use such questionable reasons as the length of a driver's hair or the color of his skin to stop a car. In the court's view, wrote White, random checks by policemen are 'a disturbing show of authority'; people have as much reason to expect privacy from government intrusion in their cars, he added, as they do in their homes.

notes :
flashing light 섬광등 / go on (전등이) 켜지다 / noticeably 눈에 띄게 / glimpse 얼핏 보다 / spot check 즉석 검문 / common practice 흔한 관례 / unconstitutional 위헌의 / at random 함부로, 되는대로 / on charges of ~ = ~의 혐의로 / of little significance 그다지 중요하지 않은 / the Fourth Amendment 헌법 제 4조 수정안 / prohibition 금지(령) / seizure 압류, 몰수 / authority 권한, 직권 / intrusion 침입, 강요

(1) 윗 글의 내용에 부합하는 것을 하나 고르시오.

① 윗 글의 운전자는 마리화나 중독 혐의로 경찰의 수시검문을 받았다.

② 미국 연방대심원은 객관적인 이유에 근거한 경찰의 노상 검문은 합법적이라고 평결하였다.

③ 경찰이 범죄자 색출을 위해 풍기문란 행위 같은 사소한 이유로 운행 중인 차를 세우는 것은 때로 필요하다.

④ 교통안전은 불심검문으로 인한 운전자의 불쾌감보다 우선한다.

⑤ 국민은 자신의 집에서처럼 자기의 차 안에서도 사생활을 보호받을 권리가 있다.

(2) 윗 글의 경찰의 주장과 미국 연방 대법원의 평결 내용을 간단히 적어라.

실 력 체 크 II

A. 다음 문장에서 틀린 것을 바로 잡아라.

(1) His only fault is what he has no faults.
(2) I think there is no necessity of both of our going there.
(3) I'm looking for a room — as a cheap room as I can get.
(4) It is famous that a bear will not touch a dead body.
(5) I employed a woman whose past I knew nothing.
(6) When I came to my senses, I found me alone with her.
(7) This room has not been slept for years.
(8) The burglar must have entered from the front door.

B. [A]의 각 문장과 같은 취지의 문장을 [B]에서 골라라.

[A] (1) A fox is not taken twice in the same snare.
(2) Look before you leap.
(3) We never miss the water till we are dry.
(4) Years know more than books.
(5) Repentance comes too late.
(6) God helps those who help themselves.

[B] ⓐ Beauty is in the eye of the beholder.
ⓑ Don't make a mountain out of a molehill.
ⓒ The older I grow, the more I learn.
ⓓ It is no use crying over spilt milk.
ⓔ Success will come through one's own independence.
ⓕ Think today and speak tomorrow.
ⓖ Don't count your chickens until they are hatched.
ⓗ A good thing lost is a good thing valued.
ⓘ Good luck does not always repeat itself.
ⓙ Where there is a will, there is a way.

C. 다음을 영어로 옮겨라.

(1) 여기가 어디냐? (2) 서두르지 마라.
(3) 이 자리에 누가 있습니까? (4) 어서 사양말고 드세요.

Answer: A. (1) what→that (2) our→us (3) as a cheap→as cheap a (4) famous→well-known (5) nothing→nothing of (6) me→myself (7) slept→slept in (8) from→through
B. (1) ⓘ (2) ⓕ (3) ⓗ (4) ⓒ (5) ⓓ (6) ⓔ
C. (1) Where are we now? (2) Take it easy. (3) Is this seat taken? (4) Help yourself, please.

D. 괄호 안에서 문맥에 맞는 단어를 골라라.

(1) It was very (neighboring, neighborly) of you to do her shopping for her.

(2) He is an (officious, official) little man and widely disliked in the company.

(3) He is a (specious, spacious) hypocrite.

(4) He was an (urban, urbane), kindly, and generous man.

(5) Red wine often has a (wooden, woody) taste.

E. 다음의 영문 (a), (b)에서 어느 하나를 고르고, 그 이유를 약 30어 정도의 영문으로 써라.

(a) I would rather live in the country than in a large city.

(b) I would rather live in a large city than in the country.

F. 두 문장이 같은 뜻이 되도록 공란을 메워라.

(1) It is expected that he will broadcast a statement tonight.
He is expected ______________________________ tonight.

(2) I'm sure you were surprised to hear of her remarriage.
You ______________________ to hear of her remarriage.

(3) Christopher Columbus was the man who discovered America.
Christopher Columbus is well known for __________________.

(4) He suggested having a sandwich in a cafeteria.
He said, "_________________________________".

(5) They weren't wearing life-jackets; perhaps that's why they drowned.
If they ____.

(6) Only a fool would do such an idiotic thing.
A wise man ________________________.

(7) You were foolish to hope that he would change his mind.
It was ____.

Answer: D. (1) neighborly (2) officious (3) specious (4) urbane (5) woody

E. (a) In the country, we can live a healthy life, free from environmental pollution. Besides, the country people are simpler and more honest than those who live in a large city. (b) To live in a large city has many advantages. There are many schools, hospitals, museums, libraries and department stores. In short, we can enjoy everything modern civilization can give us.

F. (1) to broadcast a statement (2) are sure to have been surprised 혹은 were surely surprised (3) having discovered America 혹은 his discovery of America (4) Let's have a sandwich in a cafeteria (5) had been wearing life-jackets, they would not have drowned (6) would not do such an idiotic thing (7) foolish of you to hope that he would change his mind

어 휘 · 발 음

A. 다음 단어를 동사형으로 변화시켜 알맞은 공란에 써 넣어라.

symbol, association, proof, count, dear, distinctive, process, conviction

(1) She is unlikely to (   ) herself to her colleagues with such an aggressive approach to the problem.
(2) The lighting of the Olympic torch (   ) peace and friendship among the nations of the world.
(3) The name of Darwin is (   ) with the doctrine of evolution.
(4) Ability to talk (   ) human beings from animals.
(5) I am (   ) that death does not end all.
(6) This book is (   ) among his best works.
(7) He will (   ), on a closer acquaintance, a very warm-hearted man.
(8) We should (   ) with extreme vigilance.

B. 주어진 글자로 시작하는 적당한 단어로 공란을 메워라.
(1) I bought a *b*_____ of bananas in the market on the way home.
(2) I'm going to *p*_____ some water from this pitcher into this glass.
(3) How much money did the drugstore *c*_____ for these pills?
(4) He seemed honest but his story turned out to be a *d*_____ lie.
(5) After putting sugar and cream into my coffee, I always *s*_____ it.
(6) Are you going to *d*_____ your paycheck in the bank?
(7) In order to help plants grow, farmers *c*_____ their land.
(8) If we *d*_____ the Italian team, we'll be through to the final.
(9) Those are not real flowers; they are *a*_____ flowers.
(10) In the end he will be the final *c*_____ for mayor.

C. 다음의 이탤릭체 부분을 한 단어로 바꾸어라.
(1) The proposal was accepted *with the agreement of everyone present*.
(2) Some fishermen believe that the sea-god is *able to do everything*.
(3) He undertook the work *of his own free will*.
(4) The Music Festival is held *every year*.

Answer: A. (1) endear (2) symbolizes (3) associated (4) distinguishes (5) convinced (6) counted (7) prove (8) proceed
B. (1) bunch (2) pour (3) charge (4) downright (5) stir (6) deposit (7) cultivate (8) defeat (9) artificial (10) candidate
C. (1) unanimously (2) omnipotent (3) voluntarily (4) annually

D. 다음 각 문장의 공란에 들어갈 적당한 단어를 고르시오.

(1) When a doctor ______ a patient, he is looking for symptoms.
① consults ② examines ③ investigates ④ views

(2) The newspaper increased its ______ by fifty thousand copies.
① circulation ② amount ③ figures ④ quantity

(3) The weather forecast promises a sunny morning, but there may be a ______ or two in the afternoon.
① rain ② fall ③ shower ④ drop

(4) He is a man of his word. He is ______ .
① eloquent ② talkative ③ reserved ④ trustworthy

E. 빈칸에 공통으로 들어갈 단어를 쓰시오.

(1) ⓐ As vegetables rot, spoilage is ( ) in the grocery business.
ⓑ Because of the ( ) fog, the visibility was down to 20 meters.
ⓒ The conflict caused ( ) casualties on both sides.

(2) ⓐ Have you got the ( ) you need to make the rug?
ⓑ I left some of my ( ) in the attic.
ⓒ Don't ( ) anything else in, or the bag will burst.

(3) ⓐ ( ) it in your computer so it won't be lost.
ⓑ You can ( ) fuel if you drive at a regular speed.
ⓒ Did the firefighter ( ) the child from the burning house?

F. 품사가 변해도 액센트의 위치가 변하지 않는 단어 5개를 골라라.

(1) minute (2) record (3) frequent (4) convict (5) perfect
(6) control (7) protest (8) comfort (9) conduct (10) surprise
(11) object (12) subject (13) attribute (14) support (15) offer

G. 액센트의 위치가 변하지 않는 쌍을 골라라.

(1) { memory / memorial } (2) { comparable / comparative } (3) { accident / accidental }
(4) { photograph / photographer } (5) { commerce / commercial } (6) { courage / courageous }
(7) { preferable / prefer } (8) { admire / admirable } (9) { ignorant / ignorance }

Answer: D. (1) ② (2) ① (3) ③ (4) ④ E. (1) heavy (2) stuff (3) save
F. (6), (8), (10), (14), (15) G. (9)

숙 어

(1) **free from[of]** (=without) ~이 없는
☞ Keep all parts of the machine *free from* dust and dirt.

(2) **from time to time** (=occasionally, once in a while) 가끔
☞ *From time to time* this old house gives me the creeps.

(3) **gain ground** (=advance ; move closer to) 전진하다 ; 따라붙다
☞ The soldiers *gained ground* toward the enemy position inch by inch.
To *gain ground* on his opponent, the politician promised to cut taxes.

(4) **get a load of** (=look at) 보다
☞ *Get a load of* Mary breastfeeding her baby.

(5) **get a move on** (=hurry up) 서두르다
☞ We'd better *get a move on* or we'll be late.

(6) **get across** (=cause to be understood) (생각 따위를) 전달하다, 이해시키다
☞ He's not very good at *getting* his ideas *across* to people.

(7) **get at** (=reach ; discover) 도달하다 ; 이해하다
☞ The book is on the top shelf and I can't *get at* it.
It is no easy thing to *get at* the meaning of every idiom.

(8) **get away** (=escape ; leave) 도망치다 ; 떠나다, 빠져 나오다
☞ The suspect ran down the street and *got away*.
I wanted to come but couldn't *get away* from the office.

(9) **get down to** (=begin doing seriously) ~에 착수하다, 시작하다
☞ After talking about the job in general, we *got down to* the specifics, such as the salary.

(10) **get even with one** (=get one's revenge on) ~에게 앙갚음하다
☞ She swore she would *get even with* him if it took ten years.

(11) **get going (on)** (=begin) (~에) 나서다, 착수하다
☞ If we don't *get going on* this work soon, it'll never be ready in time.

(12) **get[take] hold of** (=grasp) 붙잡다
☞ He shouted from above, "*Get hold of* this rope, and I'll pull you up."

⒀ **get in touch with** (=communicate with) ~와 접촉하다, ~와 연락하다
☞ I'm trying to *get in touch with* my nephew who emigrated to Spain.

⒁ **get on in the world** (=succeed in life) 출세하다
get on[along] with (=live in a friendly way with) 사이좋게 지내다
☞ Tell me how he has *got on in the world*.
He is *getting on[along] with* his neighbors.

⒂ **get over** (=recover from ; overcome, tide over) 회복하다 ; 극복하다
☞ He finally *got over* his illness. He *got over* the difficulty.

⒃ **get rid of** (=eliminate, discard, become free of) 제거하다, 없애다
☞ I used weedkiller to *get rid of* the weeds in the garden.

⒄ **get the better of** (=defeat, beat, vanquish) 이기다
☞ I finally *got the better of* him, and he took his defeat without resistance.

⒅ **get through** (=finish) 끝마치다
☞ Can you *get through* with your work by the end of the day?

⒆ **give away** (=give freely, distribute ; disclose) 주다, 분배하다 ; 폭로하다
☞ They are *giving away* prizes at the new store.
The criminal was determined not to *give* his accomplices *away*.

⒇ **give birth to** (=bear ; produce, give rise to) (아기를) 낳다 ; 야기시키다
☞ She *gave birth to* her first baby-girl exactly at midnight.
The new economic policy *gave birth to* widespread dissatisfaction.

Exercise

▶▶ 주어진 단어들을 포함한 글을 지어라. 필요하면 어형을 변화시켜라.

1. drinks / free / artificial
2. come / see / time
3. get / move / late
4. speaker / get / point / audience
5. burglar / away / police
6. I / down / sort / papers
7. get / shock / death
8. company / rid / salesman
9. get / work / bed
10. cat / birth / kitten

8. 법 (Mood)

기본 문법 설명

A. 법의 종류	(1) I **know** you **are** against his proposal. (2) **Make** yourself at home. (3) I wish I **could** speak Japanese as well as you.
B. 주의해야할 명령법	(1) ⓐ **Keep** complaining, **and** they'll soon solve your problem. ⓑ **Be** here on time, **or** we'll leave without you. (2) ⓐ **Come when** you **may**, you are welcome. ⓑ **Be** it **ever so** humble, there is no place like home. ⓒ **Hurry as** you **will**, you are sure to be late. ⓓ **Be** they rich **or** poor, all men are equal before the law. (3) **Let's** order pizza for dinner. **Let's not** (**Don't let's**) talk about it any more. **Let** young men bear these facts in mind.
C. 가정법현재	(1) If your report **be**[**is**] true, I **will** employ him. (2) The doctor **insisted** that the patient **remain** in bed. (3) God **bless** you!
D. 가정법미래	(1) If it **should** rain tomorrow, what **will**[**would**] you do? What **will**[**would**] I do if I **should** lose my sight? (2) If he **were to** tell his wife the secret, what **would** she say? Even if the sun **were to** rise in the west, I **would** never change my mind. (3) If you **would** succeed, you **would** have to work harder.

A. 법의 종류

말하는 사람의 심리 태도에 의한 동사의 표현 형식을 **법**이라 하며, **직설법**, **명령법**, **가정법**이 있다.

(1) 직설법
(난 네가 그의 제안에 반대하는 것을 안다.)

(2) 명령법 (편히 하십시오.)

(3) 가정법
(내가 너 만큼 일본어를 잘할 수 있으면 좋으련만.) = I am sorry I cannot speak Japanese as well as you.

B. 주의해야 할 명령법

(1) 조건을 나타내는 경우
명령법은 접속사 and, or와 함께 쓰여 조건을 나타내는 용법이 있다.

ⓐ「**명령법 + and**」
= If you keep complaining, they'll soon solve your problem.

ⓑ「**명령법 + or**」
= If you aren't here on time, we'll leave without you.
= Unless you are here on time, we'll leave without you.

(2) 양보를 나타내는 경우

ⓐ「**명령법 + 의문사 + 주어 + 조동사**」
(= Whenever[No matter when] you (may) come, ~.)

ⓑ「**명령법 + 주어 + ever so + 형용사**」
(= However[No matter how] humble it may be[is], ~.)

ⓒ「**명령법 + as + 주어 + 조동사**」
(= However[No matter how] you (may) hurry, ~.)

ⓓ「**명령법 + A or B**」
(= Whether they are rich or poor, ~.)

(3) Let을 사용하는 권유의 명령법
「Let's + 동사원형」으로 상대방에게 권유할 때 사용한다.
Let's의 부정형은 Let's not 혹은 Don't let's
(젊은이들은 이런 사실들을 명심해야 할 것이다.)

C. 가정법 현재

현재의 불확실한 일이나 **미래에 대한 가정·상상**을 나타내는 것으로 조건절 외에 명사절이나 기원문에 쓰인다.

(1) 조건절에 쓰이는 경우
현대영어에서는 조건절에 가정법 현재(동사원형)를 쓰는 일은 거의 없고 대신 직설법 현재(현재형 동사)를 쓴다.
즉 「If your report *is* true, ~.」로 쓴다.

(2) 명사절에 쓰이는 경우
주장, 명령, 희망, 요구, 기대, 제안 등을 나타내는 동사 뒤의 명사절에서 should를 생략하고 동사 원형만을 쓸 수 있다.
The doctor *insisted* that the patient (should) *remain* in bed.
Our ardent wish is that she soon *recover*.
(그녀의 조속한 회복이 우리의 진정한 소망이다.)

(3) 기원문에 쓰이는 경우
미래에 대한 기원으로 앞에 may를 붙여 May God bless you! (신의 축복이 있으시기를!)과 같은 형식으로 사용되기도 한다.
Long *live* the King! (국왕만세!)

D. 가정법 미래

미래의 실현 곤란한 가정·상상을 표현

(1) 조건절에 should가 쓰이는 경우

(2) 조건절에 were to가 쓰이는 경우

☞ should를 쓰는 경우에는 주절의 조동사가 현재형, 과거형이 모두 쓰일 수 있으나 were to를 쓰는 경우에는 반드시 과거형 조동사만 쓸 수 있다.

☞ 원칙적으로 were to는 should에 비해서 「일어날 것 같지 않다」는 불가능성이 강조된 표현이다. 그러나 현대 영어에서는 should와 were to의 근본적인 차이가 없이 사용되고 있다.

(3) 조건절에 would가 쓰이는 경우
조건절에 would가 쓰이는 경우가 있는데, 이때는 주어의 의지를 나타낸다.
(성공하려면 더 열심히 일해야 할 것이다.)
He could do so if he *would*.

E. 가정법 과거	(1) ⓐ If I **had** the book, I **could** lend it to you. ⓑ **Were** I in his place, I **would** do the same thing. ⓒ Perhaps it **would** be better if you **told** him the facts. (2) ⓐ I wish I **were** the winner of the lottery. ⓑ If I **could** only go with you! (3) ⓐ He talks **as if** he **knew** everything about the new plan. He talked **as if** he **knew** everything about the new plan. * He talks **as if** he **had read** the great novel by Tolstoy. * He talked **as if** he **had read** the great novel by Tolstoy. ⓑ It is time (that) you **started** work on the project. ⓒ You **had better** give it up. ⓓ I **would rather** die **than** surrender. ⓔ He is, **as it were**, a walking encyclopedia.
F. 가정법 과거완료	(1) You **could have done** it if you **had tried**. (2) **If it had not been for** your help, I **would have failed**. (3) ⓐ I wish I **had worked** harder in my youth. ⓑ I wished I **had worked** harder in my youth. (4) If it **had** not **rained** last night, the road **would** not **be** so muddy this morning.
G. **if** 대용어	(1) **Unless** you pay me the money you owe me, I will sue you. (2) **In case** I forget, please remind me of it. (3) **Suppose** (**that**) I were to leave, would you miss me? (4) **Granted** (**that**) it is true, it does not concern me. (5) I agreed to employ him, **provided** (**that**) he had a strong knowledge of sales skills. (6) You may borrow the book **so**[**as**] **long as** you keep it clean. (7) I'll accept the position **on condition** (**that**) you assist me.

E. 가정법 과거

현재의 사실에 반대되는 가정·상상을 나타낸다.

be동사는 원칙적으로 인칭·수에 상관없이 were가 쓰이지만 구어에서는 was도 쓰인다.

What would Alec say if he *was* here?

(1) 조건절에 쓰이는 경우

ⓐ (그 책이 있으면 너에게 빌려 줄텐데.) 즉「As I don't have the book, I can not lend it to you.」의 뜻이다.

ⓑ (내가 그의 입장이라면 나도 그처럼 할 것이다.)
… If가 생략되어 were가 앞에 나왔다.

ⓒ 겸손한 말씨
(그에게 사실을 말씀드리는 것이 좋을 것 같습니다만.)

(2) **I wish … 가정법**

ⓐ I am sorry I am not the winner of the lottery.

ⓑ 소망을 나타내는 감탄문의 대용.
예문은「If I could only go with you, how glad I would be.」의 뜻.
= I wish I could go with you.

(3) **가정법을 포함하는 관용 표현**

ⓐ **as if … 가정법**
예문의 뜻은 각각 다음과 같다.
In fact he does not know everything about the new plan.
In fact he didn't know everything about the new plan.
* In fact he has not read the great novel by Tolstoy.
* In fact he had not read the great novel by Tolstoy.

ⓑ **It is time** 다음에 계속되는 형용사절에 **가정법 과거**를 써「당연·필요」를 나타낸다.
= It is time (that) you should start work on the project.

ⓒ **had better**는「~해야한다 (= should, ought to)」는 충고의 뜻이며, 뒤에는 원형 부정사가 온다.
= You should [ought to] give it up.

ⓓ **I would rather ~, I had rather ~**:「차라리 ~하고 싶다」

ⓔ **as it were**:「말하자면(=so to speak)」

F. 가정법 과거완료

과거의 사실에 반대되는 가정·상상을 나타낸다.

(1) 조건절에 쓰이는 경우
= As you did not try, you could not do it.

(2) **If it had not been for~**
=「~이 없었다면, ~이 아니었다면」
If it were not for~
=「~이 없다면, ~이 아니라면」

(3) **I wish** 다음에 **가정법 과거완료**를 쓰면 과거에 실현하지 못한 소망을 표시한다.

ⓐ = I am sorry I did not work harder in my youth.

ⓑ = I was sorry I had not worked harder in my youth.

(4) 조건절은 **가정법 과거완료**이지만 주절이 **가정법 과거**가 되는 경우가 있다.
이는, 가정은 과거 사실의 반대지만 그 결과가 현재에 미칠 수 있기 때문이다.
= As it rained last night, the road is so muddy this morning.

G. if 대용어

unless = if ~ not, in case = if
suppose[supposing] (that)
= (what will[would] happen) if
granted (that) = even if
provided[providing] (that) = if, only if
so[as] long as = if, if only
on condition (that) = if

(1) (나에게 빚진 그 돈을 갚지 않으면 당신을 고소하겠다.)

(2) (내가 혹시 잊어버리면 그것을 생각나게 해 주십시오.)

(3) (만약이라도 내가 떠난다면 당신은 날 그리워 할 겁니까?)

(4) (비록 그것이 사실이라고 해도 나에게는 관계가 없다.)

(5) (판매 기술에 대한 많은 지식이 있다면 그를 채용하기로 동의했다.)

(6) (네가 그 책을 깨끗이 보기만 하면 빌려주마.)

(7) (네가 돕는다면 그 자리를 받아들이겠다.)

H. if 이외의 조건을 나타내는 형식

(1) ⓐ **But for** the heat of the sun, nothing *could live*.

ⓑ **Without** your timely advice, he *would have been ruined*.

(2) ⓐ **To look** at him, you *could* hardly *help* laughing.

ⓑ The same thing, **happening** in wartime, *would amount* to disaster.

(3) ⓐ **A true friend** *would* not *say* such a thing.

ⓑ A man **who had common sense** *would* not *do* that.

(4) ⓐ He *could* easily *have done* it **with your help**.

One minute later, we *might have been crushed* to death.

ⓑ I went at once; **otherwise** I *would have missed* the flight.

(5) ⓐ That **would** seem strange.

ⓑ **I would like to** take a trip around the world.

ⓒ **Would** you mind lending me your car?

※ 다음을 If-Clause를 사용하여 바꿔 쓰시오.

(1) It would be delightful to me for us to work together.

(2) An ordinary man could not do such a thing.

(3) An impartial judge would have pardoned them.

(4) To rely on such a traitor as that would be foolish.

(5) He would have been a failure in that field.

(6) In his place I would act differently.

(7) With a little more capital, you would be sure to succeed.

(8) Do what you are told; otherwise you will be punished.

Answer: ※ (1) It would be delightful to me if we were to work together.

(2) If he were an ordinary man, he could not do such a thing.

(3) If he had been an impartial judge, he would have pardoned them.

(4) If we were to rely on such a traitor as that, it would be foolish.

(5) He would have been a failure if he had worked in that field.

(6) If I were in his place, I would act differently.

(7) If you had a little more capital, you would be sure to succeed.

(8) If you don't do what you are told, you will be punished.

H. if 이외의 조건을 나타내는 형식

(1) **But for, Without**

ⓐ But for[Without]~, 가정법 과거
= If it were not for~, 가정법 과거
「~이 없으면」
(태양열이 없으면 아무것도 살 수 없을 것이다.)
If it were not for language, there would be no thought.
(언어가 없으면 사상도 없을 것이다.)

ⓑ But for[Without]~, 가정법 과거완료
= If it had not been for~, 가정법 과거완료
「~이 없었더라면」
(당신의 시기 적절한 충고가 없었더라면, 그는 파멸했을 것이다.)
If it had not been for the accident, we would have arrived earlier.
(사고가 없었더라면 더 일찍 도착했을텐데)
☞ But for, Without의 뜻은 주절에 의하여 결정된다.
But for his help, I *couldn't* succeed. … 가정법 과거
But for his help, I *couldn't have succeeded.* … 가정법 과거완료

(2) **조건의 뜻을 포함하는 부정사와 분사**

ⓐ (그를 보면 당신은 웃지 않을 수 없을 것이다.)
To look at him [부정사]
= If you *looked* at him

ⓑ (이와 같은 일이 만약 전시에 일어난다면 큰 재난이 될 것이다.)
happening in wartime [분사구문]
= if it *happened* in wartime

(3) **주어, 형용사절에 조건의 뜻이 내포되어 있는 경우**

ⓐ (참된 친구라면, 그런 것을 말하지 않을 것이다.)
= If he *were*[*was*] a true friend, he *would* not say such a thing.

ⓑ (상식이 있는 사람이라면 그런 짓은 안 할 것이다.)
= A man, if he *had* common sense, *would* not *do* that.

(4) **조건의 뜻을 포함하는 부사어구**

ⓐ (너의 도움이 있었다면 그는 쉽게 그것을 할 수 있었을 텐데.)
… with your help가 조건절 대용
= He could easily have done it *if he had had your help.*
(1분만 늦게 떠났더라면 우리는 압사 당했을는지도 모른다.)
= *If we had left one minute later*, we might have been crushed to death.

ⓑ (나는 곧 갔다. 그렇지 않았다면 나는 그 비행기를 놓쳤을 것이다.)
= I went at once; *if I had not gone at once*, I would have missed the flight.

(5) **언외(言外)에 가정의 뜻을 포함하는 고정된 표현어구** : 이들은 주로 사양하는 겸손한 완곡 어법이다.

ⓐ (그것은 아마 이상하게 보일 것입니다.)
… If you did not know the truth, 「진상을 모르시면」의 뜻이 내포되어 있다.
I am so hungry I *could* eat a horse.
(하도 배가 고파 말고기라도 먹을 수 있을 것 같다.)

ⓑ (나는 세계 일주 여행을 하고 싶다.)
… 「If I could」의 뜻이 내포되어 있다.
would like to~ : 「~하고 싶다」

ⓒ (미안하지만, 당신의 차를 좀 빌려 주시겠습니까?)
…「If I could ask you」의 뜻이 내포되어 있다.
☞ Would you mind doing it?에 대한 대답(네, 좋습니다.)은 No, not at all. 혹은 Certainly not. 그러나 구어에서는 Sure, Surely를 많이 쓴다.

문법 · 작문

A. 괄호 안의 동사를 적당한 어형으로 바꾸어라.

(1) If my father (be) alive, I could go abroad for study.
(2) We might have missed the train, if we (walk) more slowly.
(3) I wish I (be) a bit taller.
(4) I wish you (go) there with us that day.
(5) He looked as if he (be) sick for a long time.
(6) (Be) you in my place, what would you do?
(7) (Be) it not for your help, I would fail.
(8) A member proposed that the bill (reject).
(9) He spoke French as well as if he (be) a Frenchman.
(10) Had it not been for the loan, we (go) bankrupt.

B. 다음 각 문장을 If 나 I wish를 사용하여 다시 써라.

(1) You didn't help me, and so I couldn't do it.
(2) I don't have enough money, so I cannot replace my old car.
(3) As I did not know his phone number, I could not call him.
(4) I am sorry I cannot speak English as well as you.
(5) I am sorry she was not at the party.
(6) As the watch was very expensive, I could not buy it.
(7) In case of his death, how could I bring up my two children?
(8) I worked hard; otherwise I would have failed.
(9) But for the teacher's assistance, he would have failed the exam.
(10) Without immediate surgery, the patient would die.
(11) It is a pity that you cannot visit us more often.
(12) He treated me like a mere child.
(13) One step further, and you would have fallen over the cliff.
(14) Thanks to her tender care, I have become as strong as I am.
(15) A closer examination of it might have revealed a new fact.
(16) Stormy weather prevented me from continuing my journey.
(17) With two more levers we could have removed the rock.
(18) It would be wrong to reveal his secret.

C. 괄호 속의 동사의 어형을 바로 잡아라.

(1) It's time you (submit) the final report.
(2) One week later, we (may starve) to death. But we were lucky enough to be rescued.

(3) The party was awful, and we all wished we (go) to it.
(4) It was such a sorrowful sight that anyone who had seen it (will cry).
(5) It is fortunate that we are not all molded after one pattern, otherwise life (will be) very monotonous.
(6) If his son hadn't been killed in the war, he (be) about 40 now.

D. 적당한 단어 하나로 공란을 채워라.
(1) Had it not ______ for your help, I could not have done it.
(2) Keep away from those high tension wires, ______ you'll be electrocuted.
(3) I move that the question ______ put to a vote.
(4) He seldom, ______ ever, goes to church.
(5) Had I had time, I could have gone. ______ it was, I had not even a moment at my disposal.

E. Translate the following into English:
(1) 2분 전에 도착했더라면 너는 그 기차를 잡았을 텐데.

____

(2) 그때 그 의사의 충고를 받아 들였다면 나는 지금쯤은 건강할텐데.

____

(3) 내가 너처럼 빨리 달릴 수 있다면 좋겠는데.

____

(4) 그가 신체적으로 건강하기만 하면 그는 완전 할텐데.

____

(5) 그가 영어로 말하는 것을 들으면, 당신은 그가 미국인이라고 생각할 것이다.

____

(6) 참된 신사라면 그런 짓을 하지 않았을 것이다.

____

(7) 그는 파리에 가본 적이 없다. 그러나, 갔었던 것처럼 이야기한다.

____

(8) 너의 도움이 없었더라면 난 역사 시험에 낙제했을 것이다.

____

(9) 만약 태양이 달과 충돌한다면, 지구는 어떻게 될 것인가?

____

'Time'이라는 제목으로 60어 내외의 글을 지어라.

● 단 문 독 해 ●

If he **were** honest, I **would** employ him.
If he **had been** honest, I **would have employed** him.
If it **should** rain tomorrow, I **will** put off my departure.

1. When people live in a community they cannot do exactly as they please. Motorists, for example, cannot drive wherever they like without creating disorder; neither can men kill nor rob whomever they please without causing society to collapse. **If** men **were** not thus restricted, **if** they **had**, in name, the liberty to do what they liked, they **would**, in fact, have very little liberty.

notes :
*exactly as they please = 자기 멋대로
*cannot … without ~ing = …하면 반드시 ~하다
*collapse 무너지다
*thus 이렇게
*in name = 명목상

▶▶Which of the following is most appropriate for the main topic of the above paragraph?

① In a free society we can do as we wish without any restriction.
② Restricted liberty is liable to destroy human dignity.
③ We can't enjoy liberty without having responsibility for it.
④ Every motorist should observe the traffic laws.
⑤ Without burglary and robbery we could enjoy more freedom in our daily life.

▶▶영작하시오.
너를 보면 꼭 너의 어머님 생각이 난다.

2. When she had gone Macbeth looked with horror at his red hands. "Will all the water in the ocean wash this blood from my hands?" he muttered, and, after a pause, sadly answered his own question. "No, if I **were to** wash in the ocean my hands **would** turn the whole sea red."

notes :
*his red hands = 그의 피묻은 손
*mutter 중얼거리다
*after a pause = 잠시 후

▶▶Which of the following is most suitable to describe Macbeth's emotion?

① cheerful and joyful ② contented and delighted
③ cynical and sneering ④ agonized and despairing
⑤ determined and obstinate

▶▶영작하시오.
비록 해가 서쪽에서 뜨더라도 내 마음을 바꾸지 않겠다.

Come what may, we must not lose courage.
I **propose** that the necessary action **be** taken immediately.

3. He knows now that there are, in the air he breathes every day, sounds that his ears cannot discern, **listen as** he **may**, and lights that his eyes cannot distinguish, **strain** them **as** he **may**.

notes :
*discern 식별하다
*strain 긴장시키다
*strain them에서 them = his eyes

▶▶He has come to know the (   ) of human sensibility.
[lessons, drawbacks, limitations]

▶▶영작하시오.
어디에 가든 너는 이곳보다 더 아름다운 곳을 찾지 못할 것이다.

4. The young Newton proved to be totally inadequate at farming. Instead of paying attention to his duties, he would read or daydream or make wooden models. His mother at last agreed that Isaac **be prepared** to enter college.

notes :
*inadequate 부적합한
*would ~ = ~하곤 했다
*daydream 몽상에 잠기다

▶▶윗글의 내용과 일치하도록 아래 빈 칸에 가장 적당한 것은?
According to the above paragraph, the young Newton had no (   ) for farming.
① ability ② aptitude ③ altitude ④ skill ⑤ experience

▶▶영작하시오.
그를 즉시 여기에 불러 올 것을 요구합니다.

Should you meet him, tell him to come here.
Were I rich, I **could** go abroad.

5. You want for a friend someone whom you would like to have with you in trouble, **should** you meet it, as well as in sport; such a one is one who has your respect.

notes :
*for a friend = as a friend
*in sport = 즐거울 때
*such a one의 one = friend

▶▶A friend in (   ) is a friend indeed.
[need, want, fair]

▶▶영작하시오.
그 여자는 친구로서 그를 원한다.

6. Even **had** he **possessed** the poetic faculty, of which, as far as we can judge, he was utterly destitute, the want of a language would have prevented him from being a great poet.

notes :
*faculty 재능
*destitute 부족한
*want = lack

▶▶ Which of the following corresponds with the underlined he?

① He possessed everything that was necessary to be a great poet.
② He stood almost no chance of being a great poet due to his lack of poetic sense and linguistic skills.
③ He was considered a born poet and attained fame in poetic circles.
④ He was a promising young man who was expected to be a great poet.
⑤ He had both poetic ability and linguistic sense.

▶▶ 영작하시오.
그는 동정심이 전혀 없는 사람이다.

But for your help, I could not succeed.
If it were not for your help, I could not succeed.

7. Man would have remained a savage, **but for** the results of the useful labors of those who preceded him. They discovered art and science, and we succeed to the useful effects of their labors.

notes :
*savage 야만인
*precede 선행하다
*succeed to ~ = ~을 계승하다

▶▶ 문맥으로 보아 다음 빈칸에 들어갈 수 없는 말은?
We would have still been uncivilized without the (   ) of our ancestors.

① artistic creations ② age-old superstitions
③ laborious farming ④ cultural inheritance
⑤ scientific discoveries

▶▶ 영작하시오.
그는 뒤를 이을 자식이 없다.

8. **If it were not for** books, **for** the written record of man's most profound thoughts, his loftiest achievements, each generation would have to rediscover by itself the truths of the past, with only the inadequate help of oral tradition.

notes :
*profound 심오한
*lofty 고상한
*by itself = 혼자 힘으로
*oral tradition = 구전(口傳)

▶▶The writer of this passage attributes the extensive knowledge of the human race to (　　) materials rather than to oral (　　).

[reading, written, heritage, information, method]

▶▶영작하시오.

그 갓난아기는 아직 혼자 서지 못한다.

Hurry up, and you will be on time.
Hurry up, or you will be late.

9. Above all, **make** your study a habit, like getting dressed or undressed, combing your hair or brushing your teeth, **and** it will become so much a part of your life that you will feel guilty if you skip a single time.

notes :
*comb (머리를) 빗다
*and it will에서 it = your study
*so ~ that … = 너무 ~하여 …하다

▶▶Which of the following is most related to the above paragraph?

① Like father, like son. ② It never rains but it pours.
③ Habit is a second nature. ④ Nothing comes from nothing.
⑤ Slow and steady wins the race.

▶▶영작하시오.

무엇보다도 그것에 관해 아무에게도 말하지 말아라.

10. **Say** all you have to say in the fewest possible words, **or** your reader will be sure to skip them; and in the plainest possible words, **or** he will certainly misunderstand them.

notes :
*in the fewest possible words에서 possible은 최상급의 뜻을 강조
*plain 평이한

▶▶Which of the following does **not** correspond with the above paragraph?

① You should use the fewest possible words in expressing your opinion.
② Generally speaking, readers cannot derive any satisfaction from books that are too easy to read.
③ Some readers are not likely to read all of your words if there are too many of them.
④ Too academic and difficult words will ultimately result in the readers' misunderstanding.
⑤ You should write books using the most brief and easiest words possible.

▶▶영작하시오.

그는 틀림없이 입학 시험에 합격할 것이다.

If we are not rich, we have good friends.

11. **If** all mankind minus one were of one opinion, and only one person were of the contrary opinion, mankind would be no more justified in silencing that one person, than he, **if** he had the power, would be justified in silencing mankind.

notes :
*If = Even if
*no more … than ~ = … 하지 않는 것은 ~하지 않는 것과 같다
*justify 정당화하다
*silence 침묵케하다

▶▶Which of the following is most suitable for the main topic of the above paragraph?

① Democracy is a political system where the opinions of the majorities should be respected.

② The views of minorities should be absolutely subordinate to those of the majorities.

③ Frequently, some tyrants would make the mistake of suppressing public opinions.

④ The opinions of the minorities should be thought highly of, not to speak of the opinions of the majorities.

⑤ It is natural to ignore one man's view if the others except him are of the same opinion.

▶▶영작하시오.

목적이 수단을 정당화하지 못한다는 것이 나의 굳은 믿음이다.

In case it rains, I will bring an umbrella.
Granted that it is true, it does not concern me.
I will go there, **provided** you go with me.
Suppose it should rain, what will you do?
Unless you are good, you cannot be happy.

12. It was the custom in those barbarous times that wherever the king slept, two armed men slept in the same chamber in order to defend his person **in case** he should be attacked by anyone during the night.

notes :
*It = that wherever ~ the night
*chamber 방, 침실
*his person = 그의 신변

▶▶In savage times, kings would sleep under (   ) for protection lest they should be attacked.

[unless, offense, allowing, guard]

▶▶영작하시오.

만일 제가 잊어버릴 경우 그것을 깨우쳐 주세요.

13. **Granted that** your principle is right, I think that the means to the end is the question. Therefore, I suggest that the plan should be postponed for the time being.

notes :
*the means to the end = 목적을 달성하는 수단
*postpone 연기하다

▶▶According to the above passage, which is correct?

① Not only your means but your principle is wrong.
② The writer admits that the end justifies the means.
③ The plan should be carried out right now.
④ The writer admits only the rightfulness of the principle.
⑤ The plan was delayed for the time being.

▶▶영작하시오.

가격이 적당한 호텔을 찾기까지 당분간 나는 삼촌댁에 있을 것이다.

14. The selfish boy is one who loves himself solely, and nobody else. He does not care whom he deprives of enjoyment, **provided that** he can obtain it.

notes :
*solely = only
*deprive A of B = A에게서 B를 빼앗다

▶▶We can consider the underlined He a(n) (   ).

[altruist, eccentric man, egotist]

▶▶영작하시오.

그들은 그의 모든 재산을 빼앗았다.

15. **Supposing** you are in one of the London parks, and there happens to be a bird singing, and you stop to enjoy the song, the fact that some one else stops to enjoy it does not diminish your pleasure, it increases it, but if some one throws a stone at the bird, he destroys your pleasure.

notes :
*it increases it에서 앞의 it = the fact ~ enjoy it, 뒤의 it = your pleasure

▶▶밑줄친 your pleasure가 가리키는 구체적인 내용을 우리말로 쓰시오.

▶▶영작하시오.

어쩌다 양가(良家)에 태어났다는 사실이 남들의 존경을 받을 권리를 반드시 주지는 않는다.

16. **Unless** your college education leads you to continue learning all through your life, it will have failed to play its part to develop you as an individual.

notes :
*lead A to ~ = A가 ~하도록 이끌어주다
*part 역할

▶▶The success of college education depends on whether it can lead an individual to (   ).

[lifelong learning, learning lessons, successful work]

▶▶영작하시오.

그는 그 회사를 일으키는 데 큰 몫을 했다.

17. As a weapon of collective bargaining in a trade dispute, a strike in itself is not now illegal, **on condition that** preliminary notice of the dispute has been given by the workers' trade union.

notes :
*collective bargaining = (노사의) 단체 교섭
*trade dispute = 노동 분쟁
*Trade Union = 노동 조합

▶▶ 윗글과 일치하도록 다음 빈칸에 가장 적절한 것은?

The strike is legal as long as the trade union (   ) the authorities of it in advance.

① notices ② reports ③ explains ④ mentions ⑤ notifies

▶▶ 영작하시오.

그는 계획의 일부 변경을 알렸다.

An honest man would not do such a thing.
I am engaged, **otherwise** I would accept it.
Without water, nothing could live.
It would be wrong **to tell** a lie.
I would not do so **in your place.**
You **could have offered** to help me.

18. Not long ago, I had a chance to watch a surgeon perform a delicate brain operation. **A slight slip of his hand** *would have meant* instant death for the patient. What impressed me about the doctor was not his skill but his amazing calmness.

notes :
*operation 수술
*If his hand had slipped slightly, it would have meant ~.

▶▶ Which of the following does **not** correspond with the above paragraph?

① The writer saw a doctor perform a brain operation calmly and skillfully.

② The brain operation required concentration and great skill.

③ The doctor came close to killing the patient by a slight mistake.

④ The writer was deeply impressed by the doctor's amazing composure.

⑤ In a delicate surgical operation, a doctor's calmness as well as his skill is crucially required.

▶▶ 영작하시오.

좀더 능숙한 선생이었다면 그를 달리 다루었을 것이다.

19. There are people who have a talent for writing, just as there are people who are born with a gift for music or painting. It is fortunate that we are not all from the same mold, **otherwise** life *would* be very monotonous.

notes :
*gift = talent
*otherwise = if we were all from the same mold

▶▶Which of the following proverbs is related to the above paragraph?
① A friend in need is a friend indeed.
② So many men, so many minds.
③ All legitimate trades are equally honorable.
④ One should stick to one's occupation.
⑤ After a storm comes a calm.

▶▶영작하시오.
나는 곧 갔다. 그렇지 않았다면 기차를 놓쳤을 것이다.

20. "Please" is a very little word, but it makes a good many requests sound pleasant that **without** it *would* sound harsh, as with "Thank you".

notes :
*that의 선행사는 requests
*would의 주어는 that
*harsh 거친

▶▶The word "Please" seems little but it plays an important (　　　) in making many requests sound pleasant.
[piece, presence, part]

▶▶영작하시오.
그 회의에 참석한 사람들은 상당히 많았다.

21. Let me utter one practical word in conclusion—take care of your health. There have been men who **by wise attention to this point** *might have risen* to any eminence, but by unwise neglect of this point have come to nothing.

notes :
*if they had paid wise attention to this point
*have come의 주어는 who

▶▶Take care of your health, (　　　　　　　　　　).
[or you will become eminent, or you will come to nothing, and you will become wise, and you will become practical]

▶▶영작하시오.
이런 상황이었다면 당신은 어떻게 했겠습니까?

22. There was nobody near when he found the gold, and he **could have kept** it all to himself. Such a heap of gold **would have made** him a rich man, but he did not think of being rich. He thought of being honest.

notes :
*he might have kept it all to himself (if he had been so minded)
*(If he had had such a heap of gold,) it would have made him a rich man.

▶▶Which of the following can be used to describe his nature?

① greedy ② desperate ③ confused
④ anguished ⑤ upright

▶▶영작하시오.

그는 그 돈을 모두 혼자 차지했다.

I wish I **were** a bird.
He talks **as if** he knew everything.
What if I should fail the examination?

23. You may have heard grown-ups say, "**I wish I had learned** that in school," or "**I wish I had** more education." Why do you suppose they <u>feel that way?</u> Perhaps it's because they think life might be more interesting, or they might have had better jobs, if they had learned just a little more or had learned a little better.

notes :
*may have p.p. = 아마 ~했을 것이다
*grown-up 성인
*suppose = think

▶▶Which of the following does the underlined phrase, <u>feel that way</u>, imply?

① regret for their lower level of education
② hope to get a lifelong education
③ despair of having no education
④ are troubled by unreliable school education
⑤ are uninterested in getting advanced education

▶▶영작하시오.

왜 그가 브라질로 이민갔다고 생각하십니까?

24. The workman who drops his tools at the stroke of twelve, as suddenly **as if** he had been struck by lightning, may be doing his duty — but he is doing nothing more. No man has made a great success of his life by doing merely his duty. He must do that — and more. If he puts love into his work, the "more" will be easy.

notes :
*at the stroke of twelve = (시계가) 12시를 치자
*as suddenly as if ~ = 마치 ~이기나 한 것처럼 갑자기
*merely = only

▶▶Your success in an occupation can be achieved by having (　　　) for it above all things, not to mention the fulfillment of your duty.

[indifference, resentment, affection]

▶▶영작하시오.

이 책은 당신의 인생 성공법을 가르쳐 준다.

25. It was a sharp sword and it was hung by only a single horsehair. **What if** the hair should break? There was danger every moment that it would do so.

notes :
*horsehair 말총
*it would do so에서 it = the hair do so = break

▶▶Which is most suitable to describe the mood of the above paragraph?

① peaceful　② gloomy　③ strained
④ monotonous　⑤ delightful

▶▶영작하시오.

그가 약속을 어기면 어떻게 하나?

You **had better** go there at once.
He is, **as it were**, a walking encyclopedia.

26. You **had better** be alone than in mean company. Let your companions be such as yourself or superior; for the worth of a man will always be measured by that of his company.

notes :
*be in mean company = 나쁜 친구들과 어울리다
*such as (are) yourself or superior (to you)

▶▶A man is known by the (　　　) he keeps.

[company, people, corporation]

▶▶영작하시오.

그와 같이 있으면 결코 지루하지 않다.

27. I am a perfect enthusiast in my admiration of nature; and I have looked upon, and **as it were** conversed with, the objects which this country has presented to my views so long, and with such pleasure, that the idea of parting from them oppresses me with a sadness similar to what I have always felt in quitting a beloved friend.

notes :
*the objects는 upon과 with에 공통으로 걸림
*that the idea of parting에서 that는 셋째 줄의 so와 such에 공통으로 걸림
*has presented to my views = has shown me
*quit = leave

▶▶I have loved the nature of this country so passionately that the mere (　　　) of parting with it makes me feel sad, as if I were leaving my best (　　　).

[thought, fact, mention, feelings, friend, faith]

▶▶영작하시오.

그들과 같이 하도 오래 살아와서 이제 헤어지려니 너무나 섭섭하다.

He spent more than half the money, **if not** all. He seldom, **if ever**, goes to church. There is little, **if any**, difference between them. He is little, **if at all**, better than a beggar.

28. Many people, **if not** most, look on literary taste as an elegant accomplishment, by acquiring which they will complete themselves, and make themselves finally fit as members of correct society.

notes :
*look on A as B = A를 B로 간주하다
*accomplishment 교양, 소양

▶▶Many people regard literary taste as a (   ) for civilized members of society.

[quality, qualification, quest]

▶▶영작하시오.

모두가 그의 이름은 몰랐지만, 그의 얼굴은 알았다.

29. Napoleon was rarely, **if ever**, deceived in regard to a man's actual ability, whether the other had demonstrated his ability or not.

notes :
*if ever = if he was ever deceived = 속는 일이 있다 하더라도
*in regard to ~ = ~에 관해

▶▶Which of the following best describes Napoleon's character?

① generous ② shrewd ③ biased
④ humorous ⑤ cynical

▶▶영작하시오.

이 문제에 관해 뭔가 의견이 있으십니까?

30. People divide off vice and virtue as though they were two things, neither of which had with it anything of the other. This is not so. There is no useful virtue which has not some alloy of vice, and hardly any vice, **if any**, which carries not with it a little dash of virtue.

notes :
*divide off = 갈라놓다
*vice 악덕 ↔ virtue 미덕
*had with it은 '포함하다'의 의미
*alloy 합금, <비유> 혼합물
*carries not = does not carry
*a little dash of = 약간의

▶▶Which of the following corresponds with the above paragraph?

① Vice and virtue have nothing to do with each other.
② Both vice and virtue cannot be absolutely pure.
③ Most people know the difference between vice and virtue.
④ The writer thinks vice is entirely different from virtue.
⑤ There is no essential difference between vice and virtue.

▶▶영작하시오.

뭔가 우리에게 유용하지 않은 것은 이 세상에 아무것도 없다는 것이 그의 주장이다.

31. Though the French are little, **if at all**, inferior to the English in either boating or sailing, their tastes for these two pursuits are extremely limited.

notes :
*little, if at all = little or no
*pursuits 직업, 일
*extremely 지극히

▶▶There are very (　　) Frenchmen who are interested in boating or sailing.
[few, many, little]

▶▶영작하시오.
그는 학급에서 영어 성적이 누구에게도 뒤지지 않는다.

32. There are two virtues much needed in modern life, **if** it is **ever** to become sweet. These virtues are honesty, and simplicity of life, and it must be noted that the practice of either of these virtues will make the other easier to us.

notes :
*note 주목하다
*He is a hero, *if ever* there was one.

▶▶If you live a (　　) life, you are more likely to be (　　) because you are easily satisfied with what little you have.
[easy, difficult, simple, satisfied, happy, honest]

▶▶영작하시오.
나는 달걀은 반숙이 좋다.

33. In a scientific inquiry, a fallacy, great or small, is always of importance, and is sure to be in the long run constantly productive of mischievous, **if not** fatal, results.

notes :
*fallacy 오류
*be productive of ~ : ~을 낳다(=produce)
*mischievous 유해한, 해로운

▶▶Which of the following is related to the above paragraph?

① It is perhaps inevitable that scientists make mistakes in their investigations.

② In science accidental elements may prove to be of benefit to us.

③ Scientists can carry out their research more effectively through trial and error.

④ In scientific research any error will affect the outcome.

⑤ We may ignore small mistakes made in scientific investigations, because they won't bring fatal results.

▶▶영작하시오.
질이 좋은 상품을 사는 것이 결국에는 이득이 된다.

● 장 문 독 해 ●

Warming-up

I **cannot** thank you **too** much for your kind help.
The man who **would** succeed in life without making efforts would be like a man seeking a fish in a tree.
His untiring industry **resulted in** his glorious success.
His success in the work is **more than** just a credit to him; it is a benefit to mankind.

1 The fact is that we cannot have too much Temptation in the world. Without contact with Temptation, Virtue is worthless, and even a meaningless term. Temptation is an essential form of that Conflict which is of the essence of Life. Without the fire of perpetual Temptation no human spirit can ever be tempered and fortified. The zeal of the Moral Reformers who would sweep away all Temptation and place every young creature from the outset in a Temptation-free vacuum, even if it could be achieved (and the achievement would not only annihilate the whole environment but eviscerate the human heart of its vital passions), would merely result in the creation of a race of useless weaklings. For Temptation is even more than a stimulus to conflict. It is itself, in as far as it is related to passion, the ferment of Life. To face and reject Temptation may be to fortify life. To face and accept Temptation may be to enrich Life. He who can do neither is not fit to live.

***Havelock Ellis:** Impressions and Comments*

Notes

temptation 유혹 / term 말, 용어 / conflict 투쟁, 갈등 / perpetual 영원한 / temper 부드럽게 하다 / fortify 강화하다 / zeal 열성 *zeal은 11행의 would merely의 주어 / sweep away 일소하다 / outset 시초 / vacuum 진공 상태 / annihilate 전멸시키다 / eviscerate A of B = A로부터 B를 빼 버리다 / weakling 약골 / stimulus 자극 / ferment 효소

Question

1. 본문의 다음 두 문장을 아래와 같이 하나의 문장으로 쓰고자 한다. 알맞은 어구를 쓰시오.

> For Temptation is even more than a stimulus to conflict. It is itself, in as far as it is related to passion, the ferment of Life.

→ For Temptation is (　　)(　　) a stimulus to conflict (　　)(　　) the ferment of Life in as far as it is related to passion.
[not only, if just, but merely, insofar as, but also, only as]

2. Which does the underlined phrase, <u>the ferment of Life</u>, imply?
① Temptation as a factor to destroy the spirit of the man
② Temptation as a factor to vitalize the life of man
③ Temptation as an element to reduce the enjoyment of life
④ Temptation as an element to improve the weakness of the human race
⑤ Temptation as a factor to terminate the conflict of man

3. Which does this passage mainly discuss?
① how to confront the Temptations of life
② the meaninglessness of Virtue
③ how to avoid Temptation
④ the necessity of Temptation for an enriched life
⑤ the useless efforts of the Moral Reformers

4. Which of the following is **not** correct?
① Temptation can strengthen human spirit.
② The rejection of Temptation can strengthen our lives.
③ Without Temptation, the passions within human beings would not exist.
④ Moral Reformers will finally bring a peaceful and sinless life to us.
⑤ An environment cleared of Temptation weakens human beings.

Production

(1) 도덕 교육의 중요성은 아무리 과대 평가해도 지나치지 않다.
(2) 외래 문화와의 접촉 없이 우리의 고유 문화를 풍요롭게 하는 것은 기대할 수 없다.
(3) 남을 사랑하는 것이 곧 남한테 사랑을 받는 길이다.

● 장 문 독 해 ●

Warming-up

What would I not do to make her happy?
I **could have done** so then.
I have never been **happier** in my life.
There is nothing half **as** sweet in life as love.
He left his home **a peddler** and came back **a millionaire**.

2 What noble deeds were we not ripe for in the days when we loved? ⓐWhat noble lives could we not have lived for her sake? Our love was a religion we could have died for. It was no mere human creature like ourselves that we adored. It was a queen that we paid homage to, a goddess that we worshipped. And how madly we did worship! And how sweet it was to worship! ⓑAh, lad, cherish love's young dream while it lasts! You will know, too soon, how truly Tom Moore sang, when he said that there was nothing half as sweet in life. Even when it brings misery, it is a wild, romantic misery, all unlike the dull, worldly pain of after sorrows. When you have lost her—when the light is gone out from your life, and the world stretches before you a long, dark horror, even then a half enchantment mingles with your despair. Ah, those foolish days, those foolish days, when we were unselfish, and pure-minded; those foolish days, when our simple hearts were full of truth, and faith, and reverence!

J. K. Jerome: *On Being in Love*

Notes

be ripe for = be ready for / adore 경모하다 / pay homage to ~에게 경의를 표하다 / worship 숭배하다 / lad 젊은이 ↔ lass / worldly 세속적인 / after 후의(=later) / enchantment 매력, 황홀 / mingle 뒤섞이다 / unselfish 무사(無私)한 / pure-minded 순정(純情)의/ reverence 존경, 경의

Question

1. 본문의 밑줄친 ⓐ와 같은 뜻이 되도록 아래에서 골라 쓰시오.

> We could (   ) live every noble life for her sake.

[easily, willingly, justly]

2. Which of the following proverbs is related to the underlined sentence ⓑ?
   ① The sparrow near a school sings the primer.
   ② One cannot love and be wise.
   ③ The quarrel of lovers is the renewal of love.
   ④ Make hay while the sun shines.
   ⑤ Out of sight, out of mind.

3. Which of the following is most suitable for the tone of the passage?
   ① critical　② gloomy　③ informative
   ④ objective　⑤ sentimental

4. 본문의 내용에 맞도록 다음 글의 빈칸에 들어갈 말이 가장 잘 짝지어진 것은?

> Although we were (   ) when we loved each other, we were not only (   ) but (   ) as far as love was concerned.

① selfish — foolish — innocent
② foolish — egotistical — pure
③ true — simple — selfish
④ foolish — unselfish — innocent
⑤ simple — selfish — faithful

Production

(1) 열심히 공부하지 않고 누가 영어를 마스터 할 수 있겠는가?
(2) 나는 그것을 그 때 할 수 있었고, 또 지금 그것을 할 수도 있다.
(3) 사랑할 때가 인생에서 가장 행복한 때이다.
(4) 나는 깊이 사랑하는 사람은 결코 늙지 않는다는 것을 어느 책에서 읽은 적이 있다.

실력체크 I

1 다음 글을 읽고 아래 물음에 간결하게 답하여라.

What do we mean when we say that one country is richer than another? Or ⓐ that we are better off now than we were fifty years ago? ⓑ It is much easier to say what we do not mean than what we do. We certainly do not mean that a richer country is necessarily happier or better or lives a nobler or more satisfactory life than the poorer one, for ⓒ these are things that we cannot define or measure. When we talk about wealth — or economic welfare — we are referring only to those goods and services which are customarily exchanged for money. It is important to be clear about ⓓ this point, because ⓔ confusion here leads to a good deal of discussion at cross purposes. When two people disagree about whether there has been progress in the world or not, you may find that one is talking about food and clothes and houses and the other is talking about happiness and virtue.

notes :
be better off 보다 잘 살다 / measure 측정하다 / refer to 언급하다, 가리키다 / customarily 관례상으로 / at cross purposes 서로 상반되게

(1) 밑줄 친 ⓐ의 that은 앞의 어느 말에 연결되는가?
(2) 밑줄 친 ⓑ를 번역하시오.
(3) ⓒ these가 가리키는 것은?
(4) 우리가 흔히 말하는 부(富)는 통상 무엇을 의미하는가?
(5) ⓓ this point는 윗 글의 어느 부분을 가리키는가?
(6) 밑줄 친 ⓔ를 번역하시오.
(7) 세계의 진보에 대한 두 견해의 차이를 구체적으로 설명하시오.

2 글의 흐름으로 보아 주어진 문장이 들어갈 가장 알맞은 곳은?

Man has long cherished the illusion of omnipotence. (①) It is flattering and comforting to his ego. (②) In days gone by, man has believed that he could control the weather; countless primitive peoples have had rituals for making rain, stilling high winds, or averting storms. (③) Many have had ceremonies by means of which the course of the sun in heavens could be controlled. (④) But he still believes that he can control his civilization. (⑤)

notes :
omnipotence 전능함 / flattering 기쁘게 하는 / ego 자아 / ritual 종교적 의식 / still 멎게하다

With the advance of science, however, man's faith in his omnipotence has diminished.

3 다음 글을 읽고 질문에 답하여라.

I want to point out that clean English has its limits; cleanness is not the only virtue of prose. When we consider style in the larger sense of the word as the voice of the author's personality, we must admit the importance of qualities that go beyond the plain and the simple. This is particularly true of creative writing. The novelist or essayist who has something that he passionately wants to say may communicate it effectively in spite of mixing his styles or not calling a spade a spade. The power of writing creatively is a greater gift than the power of writing cleanly. Many of us can see the obvious faults in the novels of Scott and Hardy. We could correct and improve their clumsy and stilted English, but we cannot write novels as good as theirs; indeed we probably cannot write novels at all.

notes :
the plain = plainness / the simple = simplicity / call a spade a spade 직언하다 (= speak plainly), 정확히 말하다 / clumsy 어색한 / stilted 과장된

(1) 윗 글의 주제문(Topic sentence)을 본문에서 골라라.
(2) 밑줄 친 부분을 번역하시오.
(3) 윗 글에서 Scott와 Hardy의 소설을 언급한 이유를 적어라.
(4) What are the two qualities of clean English?
They are ________ and ________ .

4 다음 글을 읽고 필자가 말하는 요지로 가장 적합한 것을 골라라.

The mental world of the ordinary man consists of beliefs which he has accepted without questioning and to which he is firmly attached; he is instinctively hostile to anything which would upset the established order of this familiar world. A new idea, inconsistent with some of the beliefs which he holds, means the necessity of rearranging his mind; and this process is laborious, requiring a painful expenditure of brain energy.

notes :
be attached to = ~에 애착을 느끼게 되다 / hostile 적대적인 / inconsistent 일치하지 않는 / labo-rious 힘든

① Human beings are naturally resistant to an established order.
② Human beings accept new beliefs without questioning.
③ People in general are progressive in their thoughts.
④ Human beings are by nature conservative.
⑤ Human brains need to be trained.

실력체크 II

A. 다음 (a)~(d)를 뜻이 통하도록 재구성하여 주어진 문장에 연결하여라.

Water, earth, fire, and air which the ancient Greeks considered as the basic elements of Nature are not necessarily given freely in abundance to everyone.

(a) Considering these facts, we must acknowledge that Earth is a finite globe.

(b) But the other two—earth(land for agriculture, residence, and recreation) and fire(energy resources)—are much less freely available.

(c) Water also is almost as free, at least in most of the world.

(d) The only one still relatively free for everyone is air, but even here problems of air pollution set limits to the freedom of the air.

B. Fill in each blank with a suitable word:

(1) You _____ not have come at a more convenient time.

(2) _____ a little more creativity, he could have written a better novel.

(3) _____ we fail in retrieving the lost parcel, what would happen?

(4) No _____ how long it takes, I'll finish the job.

(5) There was a dead silence; you _____ have heard a pin drop.

C. 공란에 공통적으로 들어갈 말을 적어라.

(1) (a) You should _____ health above every other consideration.

(b) Now Korea holds an important _____ among the countries of the world.

(c) What would you do if you were in my _____?

(2) (a) They will _____ the winner's name from the barrel.

(b) Cover the food so it won't _____ the flies.

(c) The game ended in a _____, with a score of 2 to 2.

(3) (a) She's completely at _____ with computers.

(b) I don't feel at _____ with that man.

(c) Are these cars made for the _____ market or for export?

(4) (a) He has _____ the risk of being captured.

(b) The play had a long _____ of seventy nights.

(c) The soldiers have _____ short of food rations.

Answer: A. (d)-(c)-(b)-(a) B. (1) could (2) With (3) Should (4) matter (5) could
C. (1) place (2) draw (3) home (4) run

D. 다음 (a)~(g)는 Baker 교수의 저서에 관한 여러 서평이다. 그 가치를 인정하는 것을 3개 골라라.

(a) On page after page of Professor Baker's book I found statements which my own experience in this field would certainly lead me to question.

(b) It is difficult to see how anyone could find Professor Baker's book anything but completely satisfying.

(c) Since Professor Baker gathered the material for his book, a wealth of new evidence has been found which clearly shows how unsound the judgments that he makes are.

(d) Although no one could find fault with Professor Baker's style, the theory which he advances in his book leaves a great deal to be desired.

(e) After reading Professor Baker's book with the greatest care, I simply cannot understand why some reviewers have found fault with the position which this distinguished teacher has taken.

(f) I would be very much surprised, indeed, if Professor Baker's book did not soon become the standard work in this field.

(g) Although I have the highest personal regard for Professor Baker, I must confess that I find few major points in this book on which he and I agree.

E. 다음 (1), (2)의 문장 중에는, 올바르지 않은 것이 하나씩 있다. 그것을 골라 고쳐라.

(1) ⓐ If you should have any trouble, don't hesitate to come to me.

ⓑ If he had taken my advice, he would be a rich man now.

ⓒ He looks as though he hasn't had a decent meal for a month.

ⓓ He wished he had been a bird so that he could fly to his native land.

(2) ⓐ The chairman recommended that the meeting not last more than two hours.

ⓑ The boy seems not to have understood the instructions that were given to him.

ⓒ There are many trucks and machines here, because a new mammoth building is built just across the street now.

ⓓ They are going to have an air conditioner installed tomorrow.

Answer: D. (b), (e), (f)
E. (1) ⓓ (had been → were[was]) (2) ⓒ (is built → is being built)

어 휘 · 발 음

A. 왼쪽 두 단어의 관계와 같이 되도록 오른쪽의 공란을 메워라.

(1) Spain	Spaniard	Denmark	( )
(2) pig	pork	sheep	( )
(3) America	Congress	England	( )
(4) golf	links	skating	( )
(5) construction	construct	demolition	( )
(6) police	policeman	gang	( )
(7) sun	solar	moon	( )
(8) father	paternal	mother	( )

B. 공란에 알맞은 말을 주어진 단어에서 골라 옳은 어형으로 바꾸어 넣으시오.

denial, easy, analyze, confer, carbon, exit, exhaust

(1) Chemical ______ shows that water is a compound of hydrogen and oxygen.

(2) They felt quite ______ when they reached the top of the mountain.

(3) She is a linguist, speaking five languages with fluency and ______ .

(4) There is no ______ the fact that you have been careless.

(5) Many international ______ have been held at Geneva.

C. 다음 각 문장의 good의 뜻과 같은 것을 아래 ⓐ~ⓟ에서 골라라.

(1) It's a *good* two hours' drive from here.

(2) He says he's leaving the country for *good*.

(3) It's no *good* talking to such a fellow.

(4) I'm telling you this for your own *good*.

(5) Fish does not stay *good* in hot weather.

(6) It was very *good* of you to help them.

(7) I didn't know that you were so *good* at swimming.

(8) Your driver's license is *good* for three years.

(9) I'll lend him ten dollars because I know he's *good* for the money.

ⓐ actual	ⓑ almost	ⓒ benefit	ⓓ effective
ⓔ ever	ⓕ excellent	ⓖ favorable	ⓗ fresh
ⓘ full	ⓙ kind	ⓚ pleasant	ⓛ real
ⓜ reliable	ⓝ skilled	ⓞ use	ⓟ considerable

Answer: A. (1) Dane (2) mutton (3) Parliament (4) rink (5) demolish (6) gangster (7) lunar (8) maternal
B. (1) analysis (2) exhausted (3) ease (4) denying (5) conferences
C. (1) ⓘ (2) ⓔ (3) ⓞ (4) ⓒ (5) ⓗ (6) ⓙ (7) ⓝ (8) ⓓ (9) ⓜ

D. 다음 각 문장의 (   ) 안에 들어가기에 적합하지 않은 한 단어를 고르시오.

(1) It seems that the planes deliberately (   ) the cease-fire agreement.
① violated ② broke ③ averted ④ disobeyed

(2) Lilies have a wonderful (   ).
① scent ② odor ③ aroma ④ stench

(3) He held his mother in his arms and (   ) her on the sudden death of her sister.
① consoled ② condoned ③ soothed ④ calmed

(4) The chameleon (   ) to its surroundings by changing color.
① adapts ② adjusts ③ accommodates ④ accustoms

(5) The fighting has greatly (   ) weapons technology.
① stimulated ② heightened ③ aroused ④ prompted

(6) Napoleon's decision to invade Russia was a (   ) mistake.
① valuable ② costly ③ disastrous ④ catastrophic

(7) Don't scratch ; you'll only (   ) the itch.
① aggravate ② deteriorate ③ worsen ④ irritate

(8) Our dress code about what to wear at work is (   ) in the summer.
① relaxed ② eased ③ appeased ④ loosened

(9) (   ) politicians must be thrown out of office.
① Crooked ② Corrupt ③ Credible ④ Unethical

E. 다음 각 문장의 빈칸에 알맞은 낱말을 [보기]에서 고르시오.

(1) Each day before class begins, the teacher always calls the (   ).
(2) Any information given during the interview will be treated in strict (   ).
(3) The police left no (   ) unturned to solve the crime.
(4) New facts about ancient Egypt have recently come to (   ).
(5) This was the best room we could get at a moment's (   ).
(6) May I ask you a (   ) question?
(7) The doctor told her to take a (   ) of medicine every four hours.
(8) What's the (   ) of snarling at each other like this?

[보기] ① record ② light ③ roll ④ notice ⑤ dose
⑥ confidence ⑦ top ⑧ use ⑨ point-blank ⑩ stone

Answer: D. (1) ③ (2) ④ (3) ② (4) ④ (5) ② (6) ① (7) ② (8) ③ (9) ③
E. (1) ③ (2) ⑥ (3) ⑩ (4) ② (5) ④ (6) ⑨ (7) ⑤ (8) ⑧

숙 어

(1) **give in** (=hand in ; surrender, yield) 제출하다 ; 굴복[항복]하다
☞ The professor required his students to *give in* their term papers on time.
I won't *give in* to threats or intimidation.

(2) **give off** (=emit, send out) (빛, 가스, 냄새, 열 따위를) 내다, 발(산)하다
☞ Substances such as ammonia *give off* heat when they evaporate.

(3) **give out** (=become exhausted ; distribute) (힘이) 다하다 ; 배부하다
☞ Bob's legs *gave out* and he couldn't run any further.
A clerk stood at the entrance *giving out* leaflets.

(4) **give rise to** (=bring about, cause) 일으키다, 초래하다
☞ The minister's comments *gave rise to* rumors that he would soon resign.

(5) **go about** (=begin, start, undertake) ~을 착수[시작]하다
☞ I cut out the article from the paper to learn how to *go about* finding a job.

(6) **go ahead** (=go before) 먼저 가다
☞ My brother *went ahead* of us and made hotel reservations.

(7) **go back on** (=break, fail to keep) (약속, 협정 등을) 어기다
☞ He *went back on* his word and didn't pay back my money.

(8) **go halves with A on B** (=share the cost of B with A)
B를 사는데 A하고 반씩 부담하다
☞ I *went halves with* my roommate *on* a new TV.

(9) **go in for** (=take pleasure in ; take part in)
~에 취미가 있다, 좋아하다 ; ~에 참가하다
☞ He *goes in for* tennis, while his wife *goes in for* painting.
I won't *go in for* the competition next year.

(10) **go off** (=explode ; ring) 폭발하다 ; (소리 등이) 울리다
☞ A bomb *went off* in central London this morning.
The alarm *went off* when the thieves broke in.

(11) **go on** (=happen ; continue) 생기다, 일어나다 ; 계속하다[되다]
☞ What's *going on* here? *Go on* with your work.
It looks like this argument could *go on* for hours.

(12) **go out of one's way** (=travel an indirect route to do)
(~하기 위하여) 길을 돌아서 가다
☞ He *went out of his way* to pick me up to go there.

(13) **go over** (=repeat ; examine closely, look at carefully)
반복하다, 되풀이하다 ; 자세히 조사[검토]하다
☞ Let's *go over* the English exercises together.
Don't sign anything until you've *gone over* it thoroughly.

(14) **go through** (=suffer or experience) (고통을) 겪다, 경험하다
☞ You'll never know what she *went through* to educate her children.

(15) **hand down** (=give or leave to people who come later)
후세에 전하다, 유산으로 남기다, 물려주다
☞ This strange custom has been *handed down* since the 17th century.

(16) **hand over** (=give control of, transfer) 넘겨주다, 양도하다
☞ He *handed over* all his property to his only daughter.

(17) **have a crush on** (=be infatuated with someone)
(대개 연상의 사람에게) 홀딱 반하다
☞ I had an experience of *having a crush on* one of my teachers.

Exercise

▶▶ 주어진 단어들을 포함한 글을 지어라. 필요하면 어형을 변화시켜라.

1. give / papers / teacher
2. garbage / give / smell
3. give / books / children
4. unhygienic / give / disease
5. go / on / promise
6. go / for / cooking / restaurant
7. go / work / accident
8. parent / hand / house / son
9. robber / clerk / hand / money
10. girl / crush / brother

9. 명　사(Noun) I

기본 문법 설명

A. 명사의 종류	(1) **A horse** used to be a useful animal for transportation. **The horse** used to be a useful animal for transportation. **Horses** used to be useful animals for transportation. (2) **The pen** is mightier than **the sword**. (3) ⓐ There *was* **a** large **audience** at the rock concert. **The audience** *were* all greatly moved by his speech. ⓑ He supports **a** large **family**. Two **families** live in this house. (4) ⓐ **The police** *are* looking into the suspect's past record. ⓑ **Cattle** *are* raised in great numbers here. ⓒ **Furniture** *is* mainly made of wood. **A few pieces of** furniture *were* lost when we moved. (5) The grocery store sells **a pound of** sugar for $2.
B. 명사의 전용	(1) **The water** in this thermos never freezes. (2) ⓐ Do you know that Chinese girl who's dressed in **silks**? ⓑ This is **an** excellent **coffee**, isn't it? ⓒ Waiter, give us two **coffees** and three green **teas,** please. (3) ⓐ She's trying frantically to maintain her **youth**. ⓑ He's an ambitious **youth**. ⓒ **Youth** should respect **age**. (4) ⓐ As a computer programmer he's **a success**. ⓑ Let me give you **a piece of** advice on the matter. (5) ⓐ He's a man **of** great **experience** in software development. ⓑ They're expected to win the election **with ease**. (6) She is **all smiles**. She is **all kindness**. She is **beauty itself**. (7) ⓐ He was going to marry a woman who was **a Stuart**. ⓑ There are three **Marys** in my class. ⓒ **The Bakers** donate money to several charities regularly. (8) ⓐ I want to be **a Shakespeare**. ⓑ I'm going to replace my old car with **a** new **Ford**. ⓒ I've never heard of **a Mr. Jones** around here.

A. 명사의 종류와 주의할 용법

● 명사
- 보통명사, 집합명사 } 가산명사 < 단수 / 복수
- 고유명사, 물질명사, 추상명사 } 불가산명사 (관사 못 붙임. 복수 없음.)

(1) **a, the+단수 보통명사** (대표 단수)
복수 보통명사 (대표 복수)

(2) **the+단수 보통명사=추상명사의 뜻**
(문(文)은 무(武)보다 강하다.)
He forgot *the judge* in *the father*.(그는 부정 때문에 판사의 직분을 망각했다.)

(3) **집합명사**
ⓐ 하나의 단위로 단수취급 (→was)
군집명사로 복수취급 (→were)
ⓑ family, nation, army, people(민족), party 등은 집합체를 단위로 셀 수 있으므로, 단수도 되고 복수도 된다.
*a people(한 민족), peoples(여러 민족들)

(4) 부정관사를 붙일 수 없고, 복수형을 쓸 수 없는 **집합명사 :**
ⓐ **Police**형 집합명사 : police, clergy, aristocracy, gentry, nobility, peasantry 등: 보통 the와 함께 쓰며, 복수 취급.
*a police (×) a policeman (○)
ⓑ **Cattle**형 집합명사 : cattle, people (사람들), vermin, poultry등은 단지 약간수의 모임이며, 집합의 한계가 없다. 단지 그대로 복수 취급.
*cattle : an ox, a cow
a *herd* of cattle, a *flock* of sheep
ⓒ 물질집합명사 : furniture, clothing, machinery, produce, game, baggage, merchandise 등은 물건의 집합체이지만 양으로 다루므로 부정관사가 안 붙고, 항상 단수 취급. 이들은 a piece of, an article of, much, little 등으로 양표시를 한다.

(5) **물질명사의 수량 표시** : a cup of, a piece of, a pound of 등을 쓴다.

B. 명사의 전용

불가산명사라 하더라도 그 직분에 따라 가산명사로 전용되어 관사도 붙이고, 복수로도 할 수 있다.

(1) 물질명사도 **한정**되면 관사를 붙인다.

(2) **물질명사 ⇨ 보통명사**
ⓐ 제품 : 비단옷
ⓑ 종류 : 훌륭한[좋은] 커피
ⓒ 개체[단위] : 커피 두잔, 녹차 세잔

(3) ⓐ 추상명사 (청춘)
ⓑ 보통명사 (야심있는 청년)
ⓒ 집합명사 (젊은이들, 늙은이들)

(4) **추상명사 ⇨ 보통명사**
ⓐ a success (성공한 사람)
ⓑ a piece of advice (한 마디의 충고)
물질명사처럼 조수사(a piece of)를 써서 개별화하는 추상명사도 있다.

(5) ⓐ **of + 추상명사 = 형용사구**
of experience = experienced
of use = useful
of value = valuable
of importance = important
ⓑ **전치사 + 추상명사 = 부사구**
with ease = easily
with patience = patiently
on purpose = purposely

(6) **all+복수보통명사** / **all+추상명사** / **추상명사+itself** } = very+형용사
all smiles = very smiling
all kindness = very kind
beauty itself = very beautiful

(7) **고유명사 ⇨ 보통명사**
ⓐ ~집안 사람 : a Stuart
ⓑ ~이라는 이름의 사람 : three Marys
ⓒ ~집 사람들, 부부 : the Bakers

(8) ⓐ ~과 같은 사람 : Shakespeare와 같은 문학가
ⓑ 제품 : Ford 자동차 한 대
ⓒ ~이라는 사람 : Jones씨라는 사람

문 법 · 작 문

A. Correct the errors in the following sentences:

(1) Whale is not a fish, but a mammal.
(2) What is learned in cradle is carried to tomb.
(3) The crowd was running in all directions when the police arrived.
(4) Milk in this bottle has gone bad.
(5) Much clothing are needed in cold countries.
(6) They sell various wine at that store.
(7) The greater part of my books is in my library.
(8) We saw a herd of cattles in the meadow.
(9) I'm going to get rid of my old car and buy new Ford.
(10) We need a few soaps in the bathroom.
(11) The spacious room has small furnitures.
(12) My father gave me an advice to solve the problem.
(13) The thief picked up stone and threw it at the dog.
(14) Your clothes is a perfect fit.

B. Fill in each blank with a suitable word:

① a _______ of sugar
② a _______ of meat
③ a _______ of pants
④ a _______ of sheep
⑤ a _______ of fish
⑥ a _______ of clothes
⑦ a _______ of cigarettes
⑧ five _______ of oxen

C. Choose a suitable one :

(1) When one is reduced to poverty, (a, the) beggar will come out.
(2) This is (a white, white) wine directly imported from France.
(3) As a diplomat he was (failure, a failure).
(4) I don't want to take much (baggage, baggages) on this trip.
(5) It is absurd that the clergy (is, are) opposed to religious education in schools.
(6) Each student must write (a paper, paper) on a special subject.
(7) The committee (was, were) divided in (its, their) opinions.
(8) A man who is wanted by (a, the) police can have little peace of mind.
(9) Those chimneys spoil (a beautiful, beautiful) scenery.
(10) (A speech, Speech) is to be given by the President.
(11) He wrote a great number of (poetries, poems).

D. Rewrite the following, beginning with the given:

(1) The movie star appeared briefly at the party and then left.
The movie star made ________________________________.

(2) After such a long walk, I have a good appetite.
Such a long walk ________________________________.

(3) It will be difficult for him to prove that they are guilty.
He will have ________________________________.

(4) Why has she left her husband and gone to live with another man?
What ________________________________?

(5) He failed the bar exam and was greatly disappointed.
To ________________________________.

(6) They pressured the mayor to lower taxes or be voted out of office.
They put ________________________________.

(7) The river is so polluted that we cannot drink water from it.
The pollution ________________________________.

(8) Thanks to computerization we can cut production costs by half.
Computerization ________________________________.

(9) I don't know what all this fuss is about at all.
I have ________________________________.

E. Translate the following into English.

(1) 우리 국기를 보고, 나는 가슴 속에서 애국심이 솟아오르는 것을 느꼈다.

____

(2) 집에 화재가 일어나는 경우를 대비하여 소화기를 비치해둬라.

____

(3) 그는 사업가로서는 성공했지만 정치가로서는 실패했다.

____

(4) 그는 경험과 학식을 겸비한 사람이다.

____

(5) 그의 방에는 4, 5점의 가구가 있는데, 모두가 그의 세련된 취미를 보여 주고 있다.

____

(6) 그 소년이 담 너머로 돌을 몇 개 던져 유리창을 두 장 깼다.

____

(7) 역(驛)으로부터 2시간 버스를 타면 그의 고향 마을에 닿는다.

____

'My Best Friend' 라는 제목으로 70어 내외의 글을 지어라.

● 단 문 독 해 ●

The dog is a faithful animal.

1. **The dog** ordinarily remains loyal to a considerate master. Class distinctions between people have no part in **a dog**'s life. It can be a faithful companion to either rich or poor. **Dogs** have endeared themselves to many over the years.

notes :
*loyal 충성스러운
*considerate 인정있는, 사려깊은
*class distinctions 계급차별
*endear oneself to ~ = ~에게 귀여움을 받다

▶▶According to the above paragraph, which of the following is **not** suitable to describe dogs?

① faithful ② considerate
③ loyal ④ impartial
⑤ devoted

▶▶영작하시오.
그녀는 미국 대중들의 사랑을 받아 왔다.

2. It is not easy to be **a patriot** these days—not because it is difficult to love one's country. The difficulty lies in loving one's country the right way.

notes :
*not because ~때문이 아니라
*lie in (책임 등이) ~에게 있다

▶▶It is not easy to be a patriot these days — not because it is difficult to love one's country, (   ) (   ) it is difficult to love one's country in the right way.
[but if, but really, but because]

▶▶영작하시오.
가난하다고 해서 사람을 멸시해서는 안 된다.

The pen is mightier than **the sword**.

3. Here I was in contact with what I most wanted, life in the raw. In those three years I must have witnessed pretty well every emotion of which man is capable. It appealed to my dramatic instinct. It excited **the novelist** in me.

notes :
*in contact with ~과 접촉하여
*pretty = fairly
*the novelist 소설가 적 소질

▶▶Judging from the context, the writer wanted to be a _______.

① politician ② lawyer ③ farmer
④ literary man ⑤ salesman

▶▶영작하시오.
그녀는 그 고아를 보고 그녀의 가슴에 모성애가 우러나는 것을 느꼈다.

A **Newton** cannot become **a Shakespeare**.

4. Teach your children to worship God by doing some useful work, to live honestly and cheerfully, and love their country with an unselfish love. Although they may not all become **Washingtons**, they will surely be such men as will choose **a Washington** to be their ruler and leader.

notes :
*worship 숭배하다
*not all은 부분부정
*unselfish 이기심이 없는

▶▶윗글의 밑줄친 부분이 나타내는 뜻으로 가장 알맞은 것은?

① excellent statesmen
② ambitious politicians
③ good citizens of a democracy
④ distinguished leaders
⑤ obedient subjects of a kingdom

▶▶영작하시오.

미국에는 앤더슨과 존슨 성을 가진 사람이 많다.

The English are **a** practical **people**.

5. Few **peoples** have been more discussed than the English. In the history of human society for several centuries England has been among the principal world energies: Englishmen have often, and in a variety of fields, been either leaders or valuable contributors of noteworthy progress.

notes :
*principal 주요한 ; *principle* 원칙
*world energies 세계 열강
*contributor 공헌자

▶▶윗글의 내용과 일치하지 않는 것은?

① Of all the nations in the world, the English have been the most often discussed.
② England has been one of the world powers for several hundred years.
③ Few people have ever talked about the English.
④ In many ways, the English have contributed to the progress of the world.
⑤ The English have been one of the most important races of the world.

▶▶영작하시오.

그 식당에서는 매우 다양한 음식을 먹을 수 있다.

He is a man **of ability.**
He did it **with ease.**

6. I heartily wish that in my youth I had had someone **of** good **sense** to direct my reading. I sigh when I reflect on the amount of time I have wasted on books that were **of no** great **profit** to me.

notes :
* wish ~ had had는 가정법 과거완료
*of no profit = profitless

▶▶윗 글의 내용과 일치하는 것은?

① In my youth a sensible man guided my reading.
② When young, I was lucky enough to have a wise man to guide my reading.
③ I regret I wasted much time in reading worthless books in my youth.
④ I truly wish I had read books that helped me to make a good profit in business.
⑤ It is unavoidable to read worthless books in one's youth.

▶▶영작하시오.

이 책은 역사 학도들에게 매우 귀중하다.

7. One who has overcome one difficulty is ready to meet the next **with confidence**. See how much such a person has gained. In later life, while others are hesitating what to do, or whether to do anything, he accomplishes what he undertakes.

notes :
*be ready to ~ = ~할 각오가 되어 있다
*with confidence = confidently
*hesitate 주저하다

▶▶다음 중 윗글의 내용에 부합되지 않는 것을 고르시오.

① First of all you must have confidence to accomplish what you undertake.
② Those who are confident can achieve their goals more quickly
③ The overcoming of the first difficulty is important to develop your confidence.
④ If other people are hesitating what to do, you are likely to lose your confidence.
⑤ Your confidence in something ensures a drive to cope with possible future hardships.

▶▶영작하시오.

누가 창문을 일부러 열어 놓았다.

> 8. There are many people who believe themselves to be fundamentally humane and actually behave as humanitarians, but who, if changed circumstances offered occasions for being cruel, would give way to the temptation **with enthusiasm**. Hence the vital necessity of avoiding war, whether international or civil.

notes :
*fundamentally 본질적으로
*humane 인정있는
*humanitarian 박애[인도]주의자
*hence 따라서

▶▶Why does the writer maintain that every kind of war should be avoided? Answer in Korean.

▶▶영작하시오.
이런 종류의 유혹에 굴복하느니 차라리 죽겠다.

> She is **all smiles**.
> She is **all kindness**.
> She is **kindness itself**.

> 9. When I was a boy, I knew an old gentleman who used to say the most ferocious things about his landlady behind her back, but who was **all smiles** and **obeisance** as soon as she came into the room.

notes :
*ferocious 지독한
*behind one's back 안 보는 데서
*obeisance 존경, 복종

▶▶윗글의 밑줄 친 인물에 대한 성격 묘사로 알맞는 것은?
① upright ② warm-hearted ③ trustworthy
④ consistent ⑤ two-faced

▶▶영작하시오.
등 뒤에서 남을 험담하지 말아라.

> 10. Seated in his family arm chair, and looking around him like the sun of the solar system, beaming warmth and gladness to every heart, the old gentleman was **hospitality itself.**

notes :
*solar 태양의
*beam (빛 따위를) 발하다
*hospitality 친절한 접대, 환대

▶▶다음글의 공란에 들어 갈 알맞은 말을 고르시오.
The old gentleman seems to be a kind and (   ) person happy with his comfortable later life.
① sentimental ② handicapped ③ hospitalized
④ hospitable ⑤ capricious

▶▶영작하시오.
손자들에 둘러싸여 그 노인은 만면에 웃음이 가득했다.

● 장 문 독 해 ●

Warming-up

Only a few of them attended the meeting.

If you **would** understand a nation, you must learn its language.

They exchanged New Year's **greetings** with each other by e-mail.

The energy and perseverance **which** you bring to your work will surely light your future.

Do **not** hate him, **but** try to understand him.

May I **ask** a favor **of** you?

1 In the long history of the world, only a few generations have been granted the role of defending freedom in its hour of maximum danger. I do not shrink from ⓐ this responsibility — I welcome it. I do not believe that any of us would ⓑ exchange places with any other people or any other generation. The energy, the faith, the devotion which we bring to ⓒ this endeavor will light our country and ⓓ all who serve it — and the glow from that fire can truly light the world. And so, my fellow Americans: Ask not what your country can do for you — ask what you can do for your country. My fellow citizens of the world: Ask not what America will do for you, but what together we can do for the freedom of man. Finally, whether you are citizens of America or of the world, ask of us the same high standards of strength and sacrifice that we shall ask of you.

John F. Kennedy: *Inaugural Address*

Notes

generation 세대 / be granted 부여받다 / maximum 최대한; *minimum* 최소한 / shrink from 회피하다, 겁내다 / responsibility 책임 / exchange places with (~) (~)와 자리를 바꾸다 / devotion 헌신 / endeavor 노력(=effort) / light-lit-lit / standard 수준(=level) / sacrifice 희생 / I asked him a favor. = I asked a favor of him. / inaugural address 취임사

Question

1. 본문의 밑줄 친 ⓐthis responsibility의 구체적인 내용을 7자 이내의 한글로 쓰시오.

2. 본문의 밑줄 친 ⓑ가 뜻하는 궁극적인 의미는?
   ① understand fully the situations of each other
   ② depend on each other for livelihood
   ③ evade our responsibility and position
   ④ be jealous of the others' situation
   ⑤ reach an agreement through concession

3. 본문의 ⓒ와 ⓓ가 의미하는 것을 알맞게 짝지은 것은?

	ⓒ	ⓓ
①	being granted the responsibility	— Americans
②	defending freedom	— Americans
③	shrinking from the responsibility	— any other generation
④	trading places	— citizens of the world
⑤	lighting the world	— any other people

4. Which of the following is **not** correct?
   ① The speaker wants Americans to fulfill the responsibility to defend freedom.
   ② The speaker urges his countrymen to be devoted and patriotic.
   ③ According to the speaker, the contemporary world is in great peril.
   ④ The speaker asks the citizens of the world to do something for America.
   ⑤ The speaker urges that we should do our best to defend freedom.

Production

(1) 중요한 것은 사람됨이지 재산이 아니다.
(what you are, what you have)
(2) 케네디 대통령과 그의 세계 평화에 대한 염원은 우리의 기억에 영원히 간직될 것이다.
(3) 그는 그 회의에 참가할 귀중한 특권을 받았다.
(4) 네가 좋아하든 아니하든 그것을 해야 한다. 그것은 너의 책임이다.
(5) 그의 많은 급우가 그 대학에 지망했으나, 단지 몇 명만이 입학했다.

● 장 문 독 해 ●

Warming-up

We must recognize that our own prosperity **is bound up with** that of our neighbors.
I **owe** what I am **to** my uncle.
The girl, **if left** alone, would have gone astray.
He succeeded **by virtue of** his industry.
His emotion is **not so much** a feeling of anger, **but rather** that of frustration.

2 When we survey our lives and endeavors we soon observe that almost the whole of our actions and desires are bound up with the existence of other human beings. We see that our whole nature resembles that of the social animals. We eat food that others have grown, wear clothes that others have made, live in houses that others have built. The greater part of our knowledge and beliefs has been communicated to us by other people through the medium of a language which others have created. We have, therefore, to admit that we owe our principal advantage over the beasts to the fact of living in human society. The individual, if left alone from birth, would remain primitive and beast-like in his thoughts and feelings to a degree that we can hardly conceive. The individual is what he is and has the significance that he has, not so much by virtue of his individuality, but rather as a member of a great human society, which directs his material and spiritual existence from the cradle to the grave. A man's value to the community depends primarily on how far his feelings, thoughts, and actions are directed towards promoting the good of his fellows.

Albert Einstein: *The World as I See It*

Notes

survey 되돌아보다; 조사하다 / endeavor 노력 / observe 깨닫다 / be bound up with (~) (~)와 얽혀 있다 / nature 본성 / 7행의 our knowledge and beliefs를 하나의 추상관념(abstract idea)으로 생각하여 has로 받았다. 물론 이것을 have로 받는 작가도 있을 것이다. / medium 매개물 / advantage 우월성 / conceive 상상하다 / significance 중요성 / by virtue of (~) (~)의 덕분으로 / cradle 요람 / grave 무덤 / good 이익

Question

1. 본문의 밑줄친 부분을 다음과 같이 고칠 때, 빈 칸에 들어갈 수 없는 것은?

would remain (   ) in his thoughts and feelings

   ① uncivilized ② barbarous ③ savage
   ④ sophisticated ⑤ uncultivated

2. According to this passage, why are human beings superior to the beasts? Write in Korean.

3. According to the author, what is the standard by which we can estimate the worth of man? Write in Korean.

4. According to this passage, which of the following is **not** correct?
   ① There are some animals that live in a kind of society like ours.
   ② Without human society, men would be no better than animals.
   ③ What is important to a man is not his harmonious living in community but his unique individuality.
   ④ We would have much trouble in enjoying our life without the help of our fellow men.
   ⑤ A man is valuable only when he contributes toward the common good.

5. Which of the following is the main idea of this passage?
   ① The significance of man as an individual
   ② The difference between man and beast
   ③ The importance of human society to man
   ④ Men's exceptional abilities over animals
   ⑤ The similarity between social animals

Production

(1) 그 사건은 그들의 이해 관계와 매우 밀접하게 얽혀 있는 것 같다.
(2) 사람의 가치는 그의 재산에 있는 것이 아니라 그의 인격에 놓여 있다.
(3) 인생의 성공은 자신의 노력에 전적으로 달려 있다는 것을 너는 명심해야 한다.

실 력 체 크 I

1 다음 글의 제목이 될 수 있는 문장을 본문에서 골라라.

English grammar is very difficult and few writers have avoided making mistakes in it. So heedful a writer as Henry James, for instance, on occasion wrote so ungrammatically that a schoolmaster, finding such errors in a schoolboy's essay, would be justly indignant. It is necessary to know grammar, and it is better to write grammatically than not, but it is well to remember that grammar is common speech formulated. Usage is the only test. I would prefer a phrase that was easy and unaffected to a phrase that was grammatical.

notes:
heedful 주의깊은 / justly 당연히 / indignant 분개한 / formulate 공식화하다 / test 척도(尺度) / that was는 과거가 아니라 가정법이다 / unaffected=natural

2 다음 글을 읽고 아래의 질문에 답하여라.

The Englishman appears to be cold and unemotional because he is really slow. When an event happens, he may understand it quickly enough with his mind, but he takes quite a while to feel it. Once upon a time a coach, containing some Englishmen and some Frenchmen, was driving over the Alps. The horses ran away, and as they were dashing across a bridge the coach caught on the stone-work, tottered, and nearly fell into the ravine below. The Frenchmen were frantic with terror: they screamed and gesticulated and flung themselves about, as Frenchmen would. The Englishmen sat quite calm. An hour later the coach drew up at an inn to change horses, and by that time, (ㄱ)<u>the situations were exactly reversed</u>. The Frenchmen had forgot all about the danger, and were chattering gaily; the Englishmen had just begun to feel it, and one had a nervous breakdown and was obliged to go to bed. We have here a clear physical difference between the two races—a difference that goes deep into character. The Frenchmen responded at once; the Englishmen responded in time. They were slow and (ㄴ)<u>they were also practical</u>. Their instinct forbade them to throw themselves about in the coach, because it was more likely to tip over if they did.

notes:
catch on ~에 걸리다 / ravine 계곡 / draw up (마차가) 서다 / tip over 전복하다

(1) (ㄱ) 밑줄 친 부분에 대해 누가 어떻게 했는지, 구체적으로 설명하여라.

(2) (ㄴ) 영국인들이 practical했던 점을 구체적으로 설명하여라.

notes :
in reply to=~의 대답으로 / subsequent 그 이후의, 다음의 / slingshot 고무줄새총

3 다음 글을 읽고 Einstein 박사가 진정으로 하고 싶었던 이야기가 무엇인지 우리말로 적으시오.

> It was, I think, Dr. Einstein who, in reply to the question "What weapons will be used in a third world war?", answered that he didn't know, and added that what he knew was which weapons would be used in a subsequent fourth world war — a slingshot.

notes :
tackle (문제 등을) 다루다 / modernization 현대화 / push 열정, 노력 / forsake 저버리다 / humanity 인간애 / fervor 열정

4 (A)의 내용을 (B)와 같이 요약할 때, 각각의 빈칸에 알맞은 한 단어를 쓰시오.

> (A)
> Like other recent Korean films, this tackles the theme of modernization and the idea that the country, in its push to wealth, has forsaken some of its humanity; in the process, there are people left by the wayside.
>
> (B)
> This film also shows how we have made (ⓐ) of humanity in the wild fervor of making our country quickly (ⓑ) and (ⓒ).

notes :
inflict (해를) 끼치다 / famine 기근 / be due to=~에 기인하다 / starvation 기아 / contribute to=~의 한 원인이 되다 / switch over to=~로 돌리다 / malevolence 악의

5 다음 글의 핵심을 요약하는 문장 하나를 골라 적어라.

> The misfortunes of human beings may be divided into two classes: first, those inflicted by the non-human environment, and, second, those inflicted by other people. As mankind have progressed in knowledge and technique, the second class has become a continually increasing percentage of the total. In olden times, famine, for example, was due to natural causes, and, although people did their best to combat it, large numbers of them died of starvation. At the present moment large parts of the world are faced with the threat of famine, but although natural causes have contributed to the situation, the principal causes are human. For a long time the civilized nations of the world devoted all their best energies to killing each other, and they find it difficult suddenly to switch over to keeping each other alive. It is now man that is man's worst enemy. For the future, therefore, it may be taken that the most important evils that mankind have to consider are those which they inflict upon each other through stupidity or malevolence or both.

실 력 체 크 II

A. Choose a proper word:

(1) The (climate, weather) of the island is good for growing grapes.
(2) Come and sit on my (knee, lap) and I'll read you a story.
(3) We walked along the (coast, shore) of the lake.
(4) I phoned the (customer, guest) service department to protest against it.
(5) (Diversity, Diversification) into software markets will help our firm.
(6) Frequent heavy snow was the (reason, cause) of many delayed planes.
(7) We purchased new farm (machine, machinery).
(8) The mountainous area was known for its beautiful (scene, scenery).
(9) He took the elevator to the 33rd (floor, story).

B. 다음 단어의 올바른 어형을 공란에 써 넣어라.

seem,	regret,	see,	give,	take

When Nazism came to Germany I felt duty-bound to oppose it, for I clearly (1) that it could only lead to slavery. Going all the way against it (2) me to an SS prison, where my wife and I spent a cheerless silver wedding anniversary. But I never (3) my stand. The sense of having done what (4) to me my complete duty (5) me an inner serenity more precious than any physical comfort.

C. Give a response that includes a two-word verb:

(1) Did they postpone the exhibition? Yes, they ______________.
(2) Did they cancel the contract? Yes, they ______________.
(3) Did he appear on time? No, he ______________.
(4) Who phoned me while I was away? Jim ______________.
(5) Did you reject his offer of help? Yes, I ______________.

D. Fill in each blank with a suitable word:

(1) Time and _____ wait for no man.
(2) We call the greatest work of an artist his _____.
(3) He looks the very _____ of health.
(4) To make up for lost _____ I had to run as fast as I could.

Answer: A. (1) climate (2) lap (3) shore (4) customer (5) Diversification (6) cause (7) machinery (8) scenery (9) floor B. (1) saw (2) took (3) regretted (4) seemed (5) gave C. (1) put it off (2) called it off (3) didn't turn[show] up (4) called you up (5) turned it down D. (1) tide (2) masterpiece (3) picture (4) time

(5) His argument was rational and I had to confess I was in the _____.
(6) The plan is absurd from a practical point of _____.
(7) This is a most extraordinary thing, I have never seen the _____.
(8) If today is March 4, this time next _____ will be March 11.
(9) Cucumbers are expensive in winter, because they are out of _____.
(10) Running up to the hilltop, he was completely out of _____.
(11) I couldn't for the _____ of me make _____ the inscription on the gravestone.
(12) So many men, so many _____.
(13) Necessity is the mother of _____ .

E. Fill in the blanks:

(1) star	astronomer	:	land	_______
(2) animals	zoology	:	plants	_______
(3) desk	furniture	:	notebook	_______
(4) music	musician	:	athletics	_______
(5) German	Germany	:	Dutch	_______
(6) novel	novelist	:	politics	_______
(7) man	male	:	woman	_______
(8) Buddha	Buddhism	:	Jesus	_______

F. (1)~(10)의 영문과 가장 가까운 뜻의 문장을 (a)~(j)에서 골라라.

(1) Help yourself.	(a) How stupid of you!
(2) Think nothing of it.	(b) That's good enough.
(3) It doesn't matter.	(c) Take what you want.
(4) Happy birthday to you!	(d) It was all in vain.
(5) We got nowhere.	(e) It's of no importance.
(6) That'll do.	(f) Enjoy yourself.
(7) Have a good time.	(g) Many happy returns!
(8) You should know better.	(h) You deserve to be punished.
(9) It's all over.	(i) There's nothing more to do.
(10) It serves you right!	(j) Don't mention it.

Answer: D. (5) wrong (6) view (7) like (8) week (9) season (10) breath (11) life, out (12) minds (13) invention E. (1) geographer (2) botany (3) stationery (4) athlete (5) Holland 혹은 the Netherlands (6) politician (7) female (8) Christianity
F. (1) — (c) (2) — (j) (3) — (e) (4) — (g) (5) — (d)
(6) — (b) (7) — (f) (8) — (a) (9) — (i) (10) — (h)

어 휘 · 발 음

A. 밑줄 친 단어를, 글 끝에 지시한 품사로 바꿔 두 문장의 뜻을 같게 하라.

(1) (a) John was much <u>pleased</u> with your kind invitation. (명사)
    (b) Your kind invitation was _____ _____ _____ to John.

(2) (a) Betty <u>responded</u> briefly to the question. (명사)
    (b) Betty gave _____ _____ _____ to the question.

(3) (a) The jury <u>concluded</u> unanimously from the evidence that the defendant was innocent. (명사)
    (b) The jury reached ____ ____ ____ from the evidence that the defendant was innocent.

(4) (a) The doctor <u>explored</u> the child's injuries carefully. (명사)
    (b) The doctor made a _____ _____ _____ the child's injuries.

B. 다음의 명사형을 써라.

(1) high __________	(2) long __________
(3) wide __________	(4) deep __________
(5) hate __________	(6) fly __________
(7) give __________	(8) try __________
(9) bury __________	(10) serve __________
(11) pursue __________	(12) strong __________
(13) famous __________	(14) remember __________
(15) enter __________	(16) repeat __________
(17) pronounce __________	(18) curious __________
(19) receive __________	(20) deny __________

C. 다음 (　　　)에 들어갈 적당한 단어를 고르시오.

(1) The theater has a seating (capacity, admission, accommodation) of 2,000.

(2) What is the gas (prices, cost, fee, rate) this month?

(3) That movie isn't to my (hobby, taste, interest, favor).

(4) Her husband gave her roses on the (occasion, present, honor, reception) of her birthday.

(5) These days the Internet is an effective (measure, vehicle, subject, object) for consistent information about a wide range of subjects.

Answer: A. (1) a great pleasure (2) a brief response (3) a unanimous conclusion (4) careful exploration of B. (1) height (2) length (3) width (4) depth (5) hatred (6) flight (7) gift (8) trial (9) burial (10) service (11) pursuit (12) strength (13) fame (14) remembrance (15) entrance (16) repetition (17) pronunciation혹은 pronouncement (18) curiosity (19) receipt 혹은 reception (20) denial C. (1) capacity (2) rate (3) taste (4) occasion (5) vehicle

D. 주어진 문장의 밑줄친 단어와 같은 의미로 쓰인 것을 고르시오.

(1) The students wrote an appreciation of the play they had just seen.
① These flowers are a token of my appreciation for all your help.
② She has an appreciation of painting and sculpture.
③ The magazine published an appreciation about her performance.
④ There has been little appreciation in the value of our house recently.

(2) The suspect was arrested on a charge of murder.
① What is the charge for a night in that hotel?
② The charge in my cellular phone battery is low.
③ He's in charge of our marketing department.
④ What is the charge? — The charge is drunk driving.

(3) It is not a good practice to interrupt your reading in order to consult a dictionary.
① Is Doctor Jones still in practice here?
② It is a practice with him never to speak in a friendly way to strangers.
③ The new methods were not put into practice until last year.
④ We must do much practice for the coming match.

E. 문장 끝에 주어진 단어의 옳은 어형을 빈칸에 써넣어라.

(1) The ______ of his lengthy talk was that he might resign soon. (essential)
(2) The ______ at class was over 50 last Monday. (attend)
(3) Every mother feels a deep ______ for her children. (affect)
(4) There is a striking ______ between the two tunes. (similar)
(5) They needed just a few words of ______. (encourage)
(6) Do you know the theory of the ______ of the fittest? (survive)
(7) Mary's ______ as an architect made her very successful.(original)
(8) It took a lot of ______ to convince him to vote for me. (persuade)
(9) The seed catalogue featured a disease-resistant potato ______. (various)
(10) The company has a ______ on supplying electricity. (monopolize)
(11) The rabbi offered words of ______ at the funeral. (console)
(12) He hit me, and in ______, I hit him back. (retaliate)

Answer: D. (1) ③ (2) ④ (3) ②
E. (1) essence (2) attendance (3) affection (4) similarity (5) encouragement
(6) survival (7) originality (8) persuasion (9) variety (10) monopoly
(11) consolation (12) retaliation

숙 어

(1) **have a way with** (=be good at dealing with) ~을 잘 다루다
☞ The new mechanic *has a way with* intricate machinery.

(2) **have ~ at one's fingertips** (=be thoroughly familiar with) ~을 훤히 알다
☞ With the aid of a computer, I *have* all the information I need *at my fingertips*.

(3) **have had it with** (=have reached one's limit, be fed up with)
(모든 것을 다 겪어) ~에 진절머리가 나다, 싫증나다
☞ I'*ve had it with* this old car breaking down all the time!

(4) **have it in for** (=wish or mean to harm, have a bitter feeling against)
~에게 앙심[악의]를 품다
☞ After he hit her for being disobedient, she always *had it in for* him.

(5) **have[get] one's own way** (=do whatever one wants) 마음대로 하다
☞ The boy is spoiled because his parents have always let him *have his own way*.

(6) **have to do with** (=have a connection with) ~와 관계가 있다
☞ Her job *has to do with* looking after the disabled.

(7) **hear out** (=listen from beginning to end) ~의 말을 끝까지 듣다
☞ Don't interrupt, just *hear* me *out* before you start talking.

(8) **hit on** (=think of suddenly or by chance) 갑자기 머리에 떠오르다, 생각나다
☞ The writer *hit on* the perfect title for his new novel.

(9) **hit the ceiling[roof]** (=become very angry) 몹시 화를 내다
☞ Our boss *hit the ceiling[roof]* when we lost an important contract.

(10) **hold[keep] back** (=restrain oneself) 참다, 억제하다
☞ I wanted to denounce him right there, but I *held[kept] back* for fear of making a scene.

(11) **hold good** (=remain valid, be effective) 유효하다
☞ The contract we signed 10 years ago still *holds good*.

(12) **hold off** (=delay, postpone) 유보[보류]하다, 연기하다, 미루다
☞ Could you *hold off* making your decision for a few days?

(13) **hold on** (=wait ; grasp) (특히 전화를 끊지 않고) 기다리다 ; 붙잡다
☞ Please, *hold on* a minute; I'll just see if she's in.
Could you *hold on* to this? My hands are full.

(14) **hold out** (=offer ; resist, last) 제공하다, (손 따위를) 내밀다 ; 저항하다, 버티다
☞ These plans *hold out* the prospect of new jobs for the area.
He *held out* his hand and shook hands with everyone.
The city *held out* for six months under siege.

(15) **hold up** (=support ; rob ; delay) 지지하다 ; 강탈하다 ; 연기하다, 미루다
☞ This pole will *hold up* the wall temporarily.
They *held up* the same bank twice in one week.
The construction of the new road has been *held up* by heavy snow.

(16) **hot under the collar** (=angry) 화가 난
☞ He easily gets *hot under the collar*, but once the problem is ironed out, he forgets it entirely.

(17) **ill at ease** (=uncomfortable) 불안한, 불편한
☞ I'm having my son keep the books, but I'm always *ill at ease*.

(18) **in behalf of** (=for the benefit of) ~을 위하여
on behalf of (=as the representative of) ~을 대표[대신]하여
☞ He gave the prize money to a charitable organization *in behalf of* disabled children.
On behalf of everyone here, I'd like to thank our special guest, Professor Smith.

Exercise

▶▶ 주어진 단어들을 포함한 글을 지어라. 필요하면 어형을 변화시켜라.

1. teacher / way / children
2. necessary / information / fingertips
3. job / have / with / banking
4. angry / hear / out
5. ceiling / get / bonus
6. contract / hold / years
7. hold / buy / prices / down
8. work / hold / weather
9. feel / ease / formal
10. lawyer / act / behalf

10. 명 사(Noun) Ⅱ

수 · 성 · 격
기본 문법 설명

A. 다음 단어들을 복수형으로 만들어라.	***Regular formation*** (1) book, pen, horse, mouth (2) bus, glass, box, dish, bench, monarch (3) lady, boy (4) potato, bamboo, piano (5) calf, wife, chief (6) R, 8, M.P. ***Irregular formation*** (1) foot, child (2) datum, stimulus, formula (3) oasis, phenomenon (4) bureau, monsieur (5) brother, genius (6) sheep, species (7) looker-on, stepmother, manservant (8) forget-me-not, have-not, touch-me-not
B. 복수형의 용법	(1) scissors, glasses, trousers (a pair of trousers) (2) economics, ethics (3) brains, billiards, measles, suburbs, works, means, belongings (4) airs, advices, arms, manners (5) waters, sands
C. 어형과 의미	(1) a ten-**year**-old boy, a **goods** train (2) three **dozen**, two **score** of eggs, **dozens** of eggs (3) two **pair(s)** of shoes, four **yoke** of oxen (4) 4,000 **foot** and 5,000 **horse** (5) Sad **news was** brought to her. **Physics is** his favorite subject. **Measles causes** a high fever and a skin rash. (6) Three **miles is** a suitable distance for jogging. I exercise at the health club **every three days**.

A. 명사의 복수

■ 규칙변화 : 어미에 **-s, -es**를 붙임.

(1) books, pens, horses, mouths
무성음 [p, t, k, f, θ 등] 다음에서는 어미 s가 [s]로 발음되고, 유성음 다음에서는 [z]로 발음된다.
단모음+ths months [θs]
장모음, 이중모음+ths [ðz]
baths, mouths

(2) 어미가 s, x, sh, ch [tʃ]로 끝나면 **-es**를 붙인다. 발음은 [iz]이다.
buses, glasses, boxes, dishes, benches
※ monar**chs**[-ks]

(3)「자음+y」는 y를 **i**로 고치고 **-es**를 붙인다.
ladies, cities, babies ※ boys

(4)「자음+o」는 **-es**를 붙인다.
potatoes, heroes ※ bamboos
(예외) pianos, photos, solos, autos

(5) 어미가 f, fe로 끝나면 **-ves**
calves, wives, leaves
(예외) chiefs, roofs, cliffs, dwarfs, safes, griefs, proofs, strifes

(6) 문자, 숫자, 약어는 보통 **'s**를 붙임.
R's, 8's, M.P.'s (혹은 MPs)

■ 불규칙변화

(1) 모음을 변화시키거나 **-en**을 붙임.
feet, children,
men, geese, oxen, teeth

(2) 라틴어 변화
data, stimuli
formulae (또는 formulas)
memorandum ⇨ memoranda
focus ⇨ foci, focuses
fungus (곰팡이) ⇨ fungi
antenna ⇨ antennas (안테나)
antennae (촉각)

(3) 희랍어 변화
oases, phenomena (현상들)
analysis ⇨ analyses
crisis ⇨ crises
parenthesis (삽입구) ⇨ parentheses

(4) 프랑스어 변화
bureau ⇨ bureaux [-rouz]
monsieur [məsjə́ːr] ⇨ messieurs [mesjə́ːrz]

(5) 뜻에 따라 두 개의 복수형이 있다.
brothers (형제) ; brethren (동포)
geniuses (천재) ; genii (수호신)
pennies (낱동전) ; pence (가격)
cloths (천의 종류) ; clothes (옷)

(6) 단수·복수가 같은 형인 것
sheep, species, deer, swine, trout, salmon, series, Chinese, Swiss, corps

(7) 복합어는 그 중요한 것을 복수로 한다.
lookers-on, stepmothers
(예외) menservants

(8) 명사를 포함하지 않는 복합어는 **-s**를 어미에 붙인다.
forget-me-nots, have-nots,
touch-me-nots

B. 복수형의 용법

(1) 짝을 이루는 것은 복수형이다.
셀 때는 **a pair of** glasses

(2) 어떤 학과 이름
physics, politics, mathematics

(3) 기타 항상 복수로 쓰이는 예
(두뇌), (당구), (홍역), (교외), (공장), (수단), (소유물)

(4) 복수가 되면 뜻이 달라지는 예
(잘난체함), (통지), (무기), (예의범절)

(5) 강조의 뜻이 있는 복수
(바다), (사막)

C. 어형과 의미

(1) 수사 다음에 와서 형용사적으로 쓰일 때 대개 단수형으로 한다. a four-act play. 단, 항상 복수형으로 쓰이는 goods는 그대로 형용사의 역할.

(2) dozen, score, hundred, thousand 등이 수사 다음에 올 때 단수형으로 한다. 단, 막연히 단독으로「많음」을 나타낼 때는 복수로 한다.
hundreds [*thousands*] of people

(3) pair, couple, yoke 등이 짝을 나타낼 때 단수로도, 복수로도 쓸 수 있다.

(4) (보병 4천과 기병 5천)「복수의 뜻」

(5) 형태는 복수지만 단수 취급을 한다.

(6) 한 개의 단위로 생각해 단수 취급
every three *days*=every third *day*
(난 사흘마다 헬스클럽에서 운동한다.)

D. **Gender(성)**	(1) 다음 단어의 **반대되는 성**(性)을 적어라. ⓐ husband, nephew, witch, cow, monk ⓑ lion, tiger, god, duke, widow, hero ⓒ bull-calf, billy goat, manservant (2) 다음 **통성명사**에 대한 **남성명사**와 **여성명사**를 적어라. parent, monarch, spouse (3) 다음 **무성명사**가 **의인화**(擬人化)될 때의 성을 적어라. sun, moon, anger, mercy, fear, liberty
E. **Case(격)**	(1) 다음의 **소유격**(所有格)을 설명하여라. ⓐ a man's stick, men's books, girls' rings ⓑ St. James's Palace, Dickens's novels Moses' Ten Commandments, Hercules' power ⓒ my father-in-law's hat, the Queen of England's son, half an hour's walk ⓓ This is Mr. Kim, our new teacher's room. ⓔ Tom's and Mary's condominiums Tom and Mary's condominium (2) **소유격의 의미** ⓐ Tom's book ⓑ Shakespeare's plays ⓒ My *brother's rescue* came just in time. ⓓ I hurried to my *brother's rescue.* ⓔ a girls' school (3) **소유격의 용법** ⓐ my uncle's car, the legs *of* the table ⓑ Fortune's smile, truth's triumph ⓒ today's paper, ten miles' distance, a pound's weight, a dollar's worth of sugar ⓓ for mercy's sake ⓔ This book is my brother's (book). ⓕ St. Paul's (Cathedral), my uncle's (house) ⓖ { (○) *a* friend of *mine* / (×) a my friend } { (○) *this* book of *hers* / (×) her this book }

D. 성

(1) **성(性)의 표시법**

ⓐ 다른 말을 사용하는 방법
wife, niece, wizard, bull, nun

ⓑ **어미**를 **변경**하는 방법
lioness, tigress, goddess, duchess, widower, heroine

ⓒ **성을 나타내는 말**을 붙이는 방법
cow-calf, nanny goat, maidservant

(2) **통성명사**

parent { father / mother　　monarch { king / queen

spouse { husband / wife　　friend { boyfriend / girlfriend

(3) **무생물의 성**

남성 : sun, anger, fear, day, ocean, war, winter 등

여성 : moon, mercy, liberty, ship, country, peace, spring 등

남성은 강하고 맹렬하고 위대한 것.
여성은 아름답고 우아하고 가련한 것.

* *England* is justly proud of **her** poets. (국가:여성)
America is rich in **its** natural resources. (국토:중성)

E. 격

(1) 소유격의 형성

ⓐ 생물인 명사 어미에 **'s**를 첨가한다. s로 끝나는 복수는 '(apostrophe)만 붙인다.

ⓑ 고유명사는 s로 끝나도 **'s**를 붙이나 예외가 있다.
Jesus' disciples (예수님의 제자들)
Columbus' discovery of America
Venus' beauty (Venus의 아름다움)
Socrates' death (Socrates의 죽음)

ⓒ 복합명사는 마지막에 **'s**를 붙인다.

ⓓ 동격 명사의 경우

ⓔ 각자 소유와 공동 소유
(Tom과 Mary가 각각 소유하는 별개의 아파트)
(Tom과 Mary가 공유하는 아파트)

(2) **소유격의 의미**

ⓐ 소유자 : (Tom 소유의 책)

ⓑ 저자, 발명가 (Shakespeare의 극)
Edison's phonograph

ⓒ 주격 관계
(형님**의** 구조가 때마침 왔다.)
Mother's love of children

ⓓ 목적관계
(나는 서둘러 형님**을** 구조하러 갔다.)
Caesar's murderers
= those who murdered Caesar
Shakespeare's admirers
= those who admire Shakespeare

ⓔ 대상 : 「~를 위한」
(여학교 = a school for girls)
children's clothing (아동복)
= clothing for children

(3) **소유격의 용법**

ⓐ **사람** 또는 **동물**에 한해서 원칙적으로 **'s** 소유격을 만든다.
무생물은 「**of+명사**」로 표시한다.

ⓑ 의인화된 명사
Nature's lessons (자연의 교훈)
Heaven's will (하늘의 뜻)

ⓒ 시간, 거리, 가격, 무게는 **'s** 소유격으로 표시한다.
a day's journey
within a stone's throw of
(엎드리면 코 닿을 데 있는)

ⓓ sake 앞과 관용구
(제발) = for pity's sake
for conscience' sake (양심상)
at one's wits' [wit's] end
(어찌할 바를 몰라)
~ at one's fingers' ends (~에 정통한)

ⓔ 명사의 중복을 피하기 위한 용법

ⓕ 공공 건물, 집, 상점 등의 생략
St. James's (Palace)
the bookseller's (shop)

ⓖ 이중소유격
관사, this, that, some, any, no 등과 같이 쓸 때 소유격은 of 뒤에 놓인다.
that big house of *John's*
It is *no* fault of the *doctor's*.

문 법 · 작 문

A. 다음 명사의 복수형을 적어라.

brush, patriarch, soliloquy, volcano, dynamo, lens, thief, mischief, gulf, Mr., P.T.A., mouse, passer-by, crisis, deer, index, Japanese

B. 다음 각 쌍의 뜻을 적어라.

ⓐ {custom / customs}　ⓑ {provision / provisions}　ⓒ {pain / pains}　ⓓ {good / goods}

ⓔ {content / contents}　ⓕ {ruin / ruins}　ⓖ {quarter / quarters}　ⓗ {perishable / perishables}

C. 다음 단어의 반대되는 성을 써라.

widow, lad, uncle, horse, cock, master, emperor, count, landlord, waiter, heir, bride

D. 다음 단어가 의인화될 때 취하는 성은 무엇인가?

death, law, nature, war, art, love, ship, ocean, charity, country

E. Compare the difference:

(1) ⓐ a portrait of the queen　ⓑ a portrait of the queen's
(2) ⓐ Eve's daughters　ⓑ the daughters of Eve
(3) ⓐ Tom and Mary's cottage　ⓑ Tom's and Mary's cottages
(4) ⓐ His help is needed.　ⓑ They came to his help.
(5) ⓐ Nothing is more precious than the treasure of a child.
　ⓑ Nothing is more precious than the treasure of the family.

F. Choose the wrong ones and correct them:

(1) James's book　(2) Columbus's discovery of America
(3) the mans' hats　(4) the dog's tail
(5) today's paper　(6) a John's book
(7) someone else's hat　(8) at one's fingers' tips

G. Choose a line which has no mistake in plural forms:

(1) oases, pence, goats, monarches, species
(2) trout, fathers-in-law, theses, pianoes, roofs
(3) mice, series, growns-up, saleswomen, goods
(4) echoes, Chinese, solos, clothings, bamboos
(5) phenomena, zeroes, bacteria, alumni, by-standers

H. Correct the errors in the following sentences:

(1) Take his that coat to him in case it gets cold.
(2) About five thousands people inhabit that island.
(3) He is on good term with the people he works with.
(4) She made friend with some of her co-workers.
(5) I have bought two dozens handkerchieves.
(6) They took great pain to accomplish the work.
(7) His bad manner hurt me a lot.
(8) His father is in his late forty or early fifty.
(9) Don't put on air with me!
(10) The queen shook hand with the delegates of the natives.
(11) Through his books he reached million of people.
(12) This house's owner is as good as bankrupt.
(13) I will do it if it is for the country sake.
(14) At what bus stop do I have to change bus?
(15) Do you happen to know where my glasses is?

I. Translate the following into English:

(1) 저의 학교는 집에서 걸어서 5분이면 갑니다.

____

(2) 너의 가족들이 모두 건강하다니 기쁘다.

____

(3) 우리 집은 정거장에서 엎드리면 코닿을 데 있다.

____

(4) 내가 안경을 어디에 두었을까?

____

(5) 돈만 있으면 된다고 생각하는 사람들이 많다.

____

(6) 수천 명이 매년 이 병으로 죽는다.

____

(7) 그 여자는 아침식사로 빵 두 조각을 먹었을 뿐이다.

____

(8) 내 아내의 친구면 누구나 환영이다.

____

어떤 미국 학생에게 e-mail을 보내라.

● 단 문 독 해 ●

Five minutes' walk brought me to the station.
No amount of wealth can satisfy him.

1. **Her musical talent** kept her in touch with a certain number of artistic people, and I enjoyed listening to her play and going to the theater, concerts and the opera with her.

notes :
*talent 재능
*keep ~ in touch with … = ~를 … 와 접촉시키다

▶▶윗글의 분위기를 가장 잘 나타낸 말은?

① perplexed ② calm ③ concerned
④ stunned ⑤ pleasurable

▶▶영작하시오.

인내심 때문에 그는 자기 목적을 달성할 수 있었다.

2. **A glance at the map** is sufficient to explain how it was that Greece became civilized before the other European lands. It is nearest to those countries in which civilization first arose. It is the border line of the East and West.

notes :
*glance 흘긋 봄 (一見)
*how it was that = why
*civilize 개화하다
*the border line 경계선

▶▶윗글의 내용과 일치하도록 다음 빈칸에 가장 적절한 것은?

Because of its (   ) advantage, Greece became civilized before the other European lands.

① ecological ② geographical ③ meteorological
④ geological ⑤ geometric

▶▶영작하시오.

그를 한 번 흘긋 보고 나는 그가 결코 만족하고 있지 않다는 것을 알았다.

3. Luck or the grace of Heaven may seem to take part in many happenings in life, but **a little deeper looking into the causes of them** reveals that one's own efforts were by far more responsible for them than most people imagine.

notes :
*grace 은총
*look into = 조사하다
*be respónsible for~ = ~의 원인이 되다

▶▶Our fate is (   ) of our own making rather than it is (   ) to be.

[luck, destiny, destined, efforts, largely]

▶▶영작하시오.

세월이 흐르면 우리 중 누가 옳고 그른지 알 것이다.

4. Many years ago I was thrown by accident among a company of Englishmen who, when they were all together, never talked about anything worth talking about. I concluded, as young men so easily conclude, that these twenty or thirty gentlemen had not half a dozen ideas among them. **A little reflection** might have reminded me that my own talk was no better than theirs.

notes :
*throw (어떤 상태에) 빠지게 하다
*by accident = 우연히(= by chance)
*company 일행
*reflection 숙고

▶▶Which does **not** correspond with the above paragraph?

① The writer encountered a group of Englishmen many years ago.

② The writer thought that the topics the Englishmen were talking about were worthless.

③ Like most young men, the writer judged people he met too rashly.

④ The writer realized immediately that his own ideas were no better than those of the Englishmen.

⑤ The Englishmen he met were, the writer thought, lacking in ideas.

▶▶영작하시오.

5년 만에 고향에 돌아 왔을 때, 그는 거지나 다름없었다.

His death is **Heaven's** will.
Let peace forever hold **her** sway.

5. If my **life's** journey is to be along an easy road to success, I will have no objection; if, however, it is to be along a hard one, let it be ever so rough, I will make it smooth and gain my object nevertheless.

notes :
*is to는 <예정>을 나타냄
*objection 반대
*let it be ever so rough = however rough it is
*nevertheless 그럼에도 불구하고, 역시

▶▶Which is most suitable to describe the writer of the above paragraph?

① unmanly and cowardly

② carefree and idle

③ ambitious and easygoing

④ determined and confident

⑤ amiable and generous

▶▶영작하시오.

아무리 위험해도 그들은 등산을 계속 즐겼다.

6. **Nature's** way in fashion is exactly opposite to Mankind's. In summer **she** wears **her** heaviest <u>clothing</u>, but in winter **she** goes naked.

notes :
*fashion 옷, 유행
*go naked = 벌거벗고 지내다

▶▶Which is **not** suitable for the meaning of the underlined word <u>clothing</u>?

① leaf ② grass ③ undergrowth ④ frost ⑤ bush

▶▶영작하시오.

그 배는 처녀 항해로 시드니에 도착했다.

He has no **manners** at all.
No **news** is good news.

7. It is a matter of general agreement that the war has had an undesirable effect upon those little everyday **manners** that sweeten the general air. We must restore them if we are to make life pleasant and tolerable for each other.

notes :
*restore 회복하다
*are to = intend to
*tolerable 참을 수 있는

▶▶What does the writer think is the worst outcome of the war?

① a rise in prices
② the continuing recession
③ lack of moral sense
④ high unemployment rate
⑤ the gap between rich and poor

▶▶영작하시오.

네가 사업에 성공하려거든 열심히 일하고 크게 생각해야 한다.

8. Three months later he was able to announce with certainty that **rabies**, one of the worst diseases known to mankind, **was** at last conquered. This **piece** of good **news** soon traveled around the world and added greatly to the reputation of the young scientist.

notes :
*rabies 공수병
*add to = increase
*reputation 평판, 명성

▶▶What is the occupation of the above-mentioned man?

① a botanist ② a naturalist
③ a bacteriologist ④ a zoologist
⑤ an ecologist

▶▶영작하시오.

공공 요금의 인상으로 우리의 어려움은 가중되었다.

Antony defeated **Caesar's murderers**.
We mourn the loss **of** our best friend.

9. For such actions as are prejudicial to the interests of others, the individual is accountable, and may be subject to either social or legal punishment, if society is of opinion that the one or the other is requisite for **its** protection.

notes :
*prejudicial 해로운 (= hurtful)
*be accountable for = be responsible for
*be subject to ~= ~을 받다[당하다]
*requisite 필수의(= indispensable)
*protection 보호

▶▶According to the above paragraph, which of the following is **not** correct?

① An individual is responsible for his or her hurtful behavior toward others.
② The man doing harm to others can be legally punished if necessary.
③ Legal punishment is considered more effective than social punishment.
④ The aim of punishment is the conservation of society.
⑤ A man cannot escape punishment, social or legal, if it is unavoidable for the maintenance of society.

▶▶영작하시오.

그 일이 지체된 것은 그의 책임이다.

10. If by his vices or follies a person does no direct harm to others, he is nevertheless (it may be said) injurious by his example, and ought to be compelled to control himself for the sake of those whom the sight or knowledge **of** his conduct might corrupt or mislead.

notes :
*if = though
*do harm = 해를 끼치다
*be compelled to ~ = ~해야 한다
*corrupt 타락시키다

▶▶윗글의 내용과 일치하도록 빈칸에 들어갈 말이 알맞게 짝지어진 것은?

Although your (　　) may not harm others directly, it could have a(n) (　　) influence on others' conduct.

① good deed — beneficial
② misbehavior — indirect
③ good behavior — detrimental
④ misconduct — helpful
⑤ corruption — good

▶▶영작하시오.

조국을 위해 목숨을 바칠 준비가 되어 있어야 한다.

● 장 문 독 해 ●

Warming-up

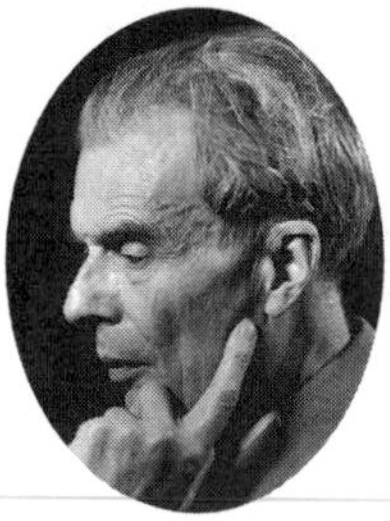

That he will arrive on Tuesday is doubtful.
He **gave his assent to** my proposal.
She always **acts on** his advice.
Every man **cannot** be a poet.
I will attend the meeting **at any rate**.
She talks **as though** she knew all about it.
He **is** too **ready to** promise.

1 That all men are equal is a proposition to which, at ordinary times, no sane human being has ever given his assent. A man who has to undergo a dangerous operation does not act on the assumption that one doctor is just as good as another. Editors do not print every contribution that reaches them. And when they require civil servants, even the most democratic governments make a careful selection among their theoretically equal subjects. At ordinary times, then, we are perfectly certain that ⓐmen are not equal. But, when, in a democratic country, we think or act politically we are no less certain that men are equal. Or at any rate — which comes to the same thing in practice — we behave as though we were certain of men's equality. Similarly, the pious medieval nobleman who, in church, believed in forgiving enemies and turning the other cheek, was ready, ⓑas soon as he had emerged again into the light of day, to draw his sword at the slightest provocation. The human mind has an almost infinite capacity for being inconsistent.

Aldous Huxley: *Proper Studies*

Notes

proposition 명제 / give one's assent to ~에 동의하다 / sane 제정신의 / undergo ~을 받다 / operation 수술 / assumption 가정 / contribution 기고 / civil servants 공무원 / subjects 국민 / no less certain that men are equal (than we are certain that men are not equal); no less … than ~=~에 못지않게[~와 마찬가지로] …이다 / at any rate 어쨌든 / in practice 실제상 / pious 경건한 / medieval 중세의 / be ready to 기꺼이 ~하다 / emerge 나타나다 / provocation 성나게 함 / inconsistent 모순되는

Question

1. 본문에서 언급된 밑줄 친 ⓐmen are not equal의 구체적인 보기 3가지를 우리말로 간단히 쓰시오.

2. Which of the following does the underlined phrase ⓑ imply?
   ① as soon as he escaped from the pressure of religion
   ② as soon as he walked out of the church
   ③ as soon as he was facing an emergency
   ④ as soon as sunlight shone again
   ⑤ as soon as the sun appeared from behind the clouds

3. Which of the following is most suitable for the main topic of the passage?
   ① A proposition that all men are equal is the prerequisite of democracy.
   ② It is absolutely certain that all men are theoretically equal.
   ③ We shouldn't behave as though we are certain of man's equality.
   ④ Forgive enemies and turn the other cheek.
   ⑤ There is an infinite capacity of inconsistency in the human mind.

4. According to the passage, which is **not** correct?
   ① In reality no one agrees that all men are equally treated without discrimination.
   ② The author maintains that all men are too capricious.
   ③ In public life we pretend to ensure men's equality.
   ④ The reason the author refers to the pious medieval nobleman is to support his argument over men's equality.
   ⑤ Judging from a political view, all human beings basically have the right to equality and opportunity.

Production

(1) 당신은 그 사고를 자세히 조사해야 한다.
(2) 네가 입학 시험에 합격할 것을 나는 확신한다.
(3) 그는 아주 사소한 일에도 불끈 성을 낸다. (flare up)

● 장 문 독 해 ●

Warming-up

You must do the work whether you **regard** it **as** your duty or not.

Your argument **rests on** a statement that can't be proved.

Accidents **will** happen.

I **am inclined to** think so.

I trust that, **in the long run**, I will not be a loser.

I will do so **provided** you help me.

2 The democratic doctrine of freedom of speech and of the press, whether we regard it as a natural and inalienable right or not, rests upon certain assumptions. One of these is that men desire to know the truth and will be inclined to be guided by it. Another is that the sole method of arriving at the truth in the long run is ⓐ by the free competition of opinions in the open market. Another is that, since men will inevitably differ in their opinions, each man must be permitted to urge, freely and even strenuously, his own opinion, provided he accords to others ⓑ the same right. And the final assumption is that from this mutual tolerance and comparison of diverse opinions the one that seems the most rational will emerge and be generally accepted.

Carl L. Becker: *Freedom of Speech and Press*

Notes

doctrine 원리(原理) / freedom of speech and of the press 언론과 출판의 자유 / inalienable 양도할 수 없는 / right 권리 / rest on ~에 토대를 두다 / assumption 가정(假定) / be inclined to ~하고 싶은 기분이다 / sole=only / in the long run 결국에 / competition 경쟁 / the open market 공개 시장, 공개 토론장 / since=as / inevitably 불가피하게 / urge 주장하다, 권하다 / strenuously 열렬하게 / provided=if / accord 주다, 허용하다 / mutual tolerance 상호 아량 / comparison 비교 / diverse 다양한 / rational 이성적(理性的)인 / emerge 나타나다

Question

1. 본문의 밑줄친 ⓐ가 가리키는 내용으로 가장 알맞은 것은?
   ① by adopting the opinion of the majority at open sessions
   ② through the decision-making at free conferences
   ③ by discussing various opinions at open forums
   ④ by respecting the views of the minorities at open meetings
   ⑤ by listening to prevailing opinions at open meetings

2. 본문의 밑줄친 ⓑ가 의미하는 바를 우리말로 간단히 쓰시오.

3. Which of the following is **not** referred to in this passage?
   ① The opinions of the minorities should be respected, not to mention those of the majorities.
   ② Human beings are naturally eager to know facts.
   ③ We should adopt a resolution by free discussion.
   ④ Democratic decision-making is possible by mutual tolerance and comparison.
   ⑤ Free speech should be guaranteed to all of us regardless of our position.

4. Which is **not** a prerequisite for freedom of speech?
   ① Every man has a thirst for the truth.
   ② Free exchange of opinions should be ensured.
   ③ All members have to recognize various views among them.
   ④ Freedom of speech and of the press is justifiably restricted in an emergency.
   ⑤ A reasonable conclusion can be reached by mutual respect.

Production

(1) 우리들이 평화롭게 살 수 있는 한 방법은 남의 의견과 소망을 아량 있게 받아들이는 것이다.
(2) 민주 국가에서는 누구나 자신의 의견을 자유롭게 발표하도록 허용해야 한다.
(3) 어떤 의견이 아무리 어리석게 보일지라도 그것의 발표를 막아서는 안 된다.

실 력 체 크 I

1 아래 단어 중에서 알맞은 것을 공란에 써넣되 필요하면 어형을 변화시켜라.

Human nature does not change, or, at any rate, history is too short for any changes to be ___(1)___ . The earliest specimens of art and literature are still ___(2)___ . The fact that we can understand them all and can recognize in some of them an unsurpassed artistic ___(3)___ is proof enough that not only men's feelings and instincts, but also their ___(4)___ and imaginative powers, were in the remotest times precisely ___(5)___ they are now. In the fine arts it is only the convention, the form, the incidentals that change : the fundamentals of passion, of intellect and imagination ___(6)___ unaltered.

ⓐ excellent ⓑ what ⓒ perceive
ⓓ comprehend ⓔ remain ⓕ intellect

notes :
specimen 견본, 예 / in the remotest times =아무리 먼 옛날이라도 / the fine arts 미술, 예술 / incidental 부수적인 일[것]

2 (A), (B)에 각각 넣을, 세 단어로 된 어구를 본문에서 골라라.

The good life is one inspired by love and guided by knowledge. Knowledge and love are both indefinitely extensible; therefore, however good a life may be, a better life can be imagined. Neither love without knowledge nor knowledge without love can produce a good life. In the Middle Ages, when pestilence appeared in a country, holy men advised the population to assemble in churches and pray for deliverance; the result was that the infection spread with extraordinary rapidity among the crowded masses of supplicants. This was an example of (A) . The late war afforded an example of (B) . In each case, the result was death on a large scale.

notes :
indefinitely 무한하게 / extensible 넓힐 수 있는 / pestilence 페스트 / deliverance 구원 / infection 전염병 / with rapidity=rapidly / supplicant 탄원자 / afford 제공하다

3 다음 글의 제목으로 적당한 것을 골라라.

"Mr. Hargrove, I really don't understand this provision in your will," said his lawyer.
"Which provision is that?"
"The one that stipulates that your wife must remarry before receiving any part of your estate. Why do you insist she remarry?"
"Well," replied Hargrove, "it's a pity for a man to go unmourned. I want somebody to be sorry I died."

① 선량한 남편 ② 악처 ③ 불쌍한 아내
④ 다정한 부부 ⑤ 교활한 변호사

notes :
provision 조항, 규정 / will 유언장 / stipulate (계약서, 조항 따위를) 규정하다, 명기하다 / estate 재산, 유산 / insist she (should) remarry

4 다음 글의 흐름으로 보아 빈칸에 가장 적절한 것은?

notes :
dwarf 위축시키다 / docile 유순한, 다루기 쉬운 / machinery 정부통치기구 / it=state(국가) / avail ~에 도움이 되다, ~을 이롭게 하다 (=profit)
※ 이글은 John Stuart Mill의 "On Liberty"의 마지막 부분이다.

A state which dwarfs its men, in order that they may be more docile instruments in its hands even for beneficial purposes, will find that with small men no great thing can really be accomplished; and that the perfection of machinery to which it has sacrificed everything, will in the end avail it nothing, for want of the vital power which, in order that the machine might work more smoothly, it has preferred to ________.

① maintain ② banish ③ increase
④ support ⑤ vitalize

5 다음 글의 주제가 될 수 있는 부분을 본문 속에서 골라라.

notes :
superficial 피상적인 / ethical 윤리적인 / in that ~이라는 점에 있어서 / radically 근본적으로 / permanently 영원히 / prior 먼저의, 앞서의

Though a superficial understanding of science often causes men to arrive at the hasty conclusion that science has no connection with moral judgments, this conclusion is not sustained by careful analysis. It is true that the scientific question is not the same as the ethical question, in that "Why did I do it?" is radically different from "Should I have done it?" but the scientific question is not even possible except upon an ethical basis. Science cannot be divorced from ethics, because science would not be permanently possible except upon a prior basis of trustworthiness.

6 다음 글의 제목으로 가장 알맞은 것을 고르시오.

notes :
by means of ~에 의하여 / soft-treading 가볍게 걷는 / erect 똑바로 선 / in connection with ~와 관련하여

When the very young child begins to notice things he becomes physically aware of them by means of his senses of sight, touch, hearing, and smell. He recognizes a certain black, smooth-furred, soft-treading shape, with an erect tail. He then becomes aware that those around him frequently make the sound 'cat' in connection with the appearance of this creature, and so he gradually gets the conviction that the black, smooth-furred shape is called a cat.

① The First Step to Language Learning
② The Physical Recognition of a Cat
③ The Gradual Conviction of a Young Child
④ The Frequent Appearance of the Creature
⑤ The Step to Socialization

실 력 체 크 II

A. 제시된 문장과 비슷한 뜻이 되도록 주어진 철자로 시작하는 단어를 써 넣어라.

(1) It is no concern of yours.

(a) It is n______ of your business.

(b) M______ your own business.

(c) You have n______ to do with it.

(2) I'm very sorry I have to leave so early.

(a) I wish I d______ have to go so soon.

(b) What a pity I can't stay a______ longer!

(c) I wish I c______ stay much longer.

(3) Will you please show me the way to the station?

(a) May I a______ you the way to the station?

(b) W______ you mind telling me the way to the station?

(c) Be good e______ to direct me to the station.

(4) The task is too difficult for him.

(a) He is not e______ to the task.

(b) The task is b______ his ability.

(c) His ability falls s______ of the task.

B. 괄호안의 낱말들의 어순을 바로잡아 글 전체의 뜻이 통하게 하여라.

The English language which we speak (1)(from, of, is, words, up, languages, many, made, really), and that is one reason why it is spoken in more and more places every year; and is also the reason why many people believe that at some time the English language (2)(that, be, the, of, will, world).

C. 다음의 이탤릭체 부분을 명사가 들어가는 구로 바꾸어라.

(1) I want to ask a favor of you *privately*.

(2) He bears his misfortune *very patiently*.

(3) The soldiers marched off *triumphantly*.

(4) *Luckily* he escaped the danger.

(5) I can recommend him *confidently*.

(6) Did you make that mistake *purposely* or *accidentally*?

Answer: A. (1) none, Mind, nothing (2) didn't, any, could (3) ask, Would, enough (4) equal, beyond, short
B. (1) is really made up of words from many languages (2) will be that of the world
C. (1) in private (2) with great patience (3) in triumph (4) By (good) luck (5) with confidence (6) on purpose, by accident

D. 다음 각 문장을 끝에 주어진 단어로 시작하여 다시 쓰시오.

(1) An hour's walk will take you to the park. (If)
(2) The year 1967 witnessed the publication of this book. (We)
(3) The payment of his debts left him broke. (As)
(4) A closer examination of it will reveal the fact. (If)
(5) The cry brought her to the window. (When)

E. 다음 10개의 문장 중 같은 취지를 나타내는 문장을 서로 짝지어라.

(1) Prevention is better than cure.
(2) Misfortunes never come single.
(3) Look before you leap.
(4) Make hay while the sun shines.
(5) It is no use crying over spilt milk.
(6) Don't judge a man by his looks.
(7) It never rains but it pours.
(8) What is done cannot be undone.
(9) Strike while the iron is hot.
(10) All that glitters is not gold.

F. 다음을 우리말로 옮겨라.

(1) They deceived the old man into this belief.
(2) Darkness is the absence of light.
(3) He married without the knowledge of his parents.
(4) A refusal to compromise kept him out of office.
(5) His admiration for her beauty blinded him to her faults.
(6) Everynight found him poring over his books.
(7) Insurance statistics show women outlive men by years.

Answer: D. (1) If you walk an hour, you will get to the park. (2) We witnessed the publication of this book in the year 1967. (3) As he paid his debts, he was left broke. (4) If you examine it more closely, it will reveal the fact. (5) When she heard the cry, she came to the window.

E. (1)-(3), (2)-(7), (4)-(9), (5)-(8), (6)-(10)

F. (1) 그들은 그 노인을 속여 이것을 믿게 했다. (2) 어둠은 빛이 없는 것이다. (3) 그는 부모님 모르게 결혼했다. (4) 그는 타협을 거부했기 때문에 직[보직]을 잃었다. (5) 그녀의 미모에 현혹되어 그는 그녀의 결점을 보지 못했다. (6) 매일 밤 그는 열심히 책을 읽고 있었다. (7) 보험통계에 의하면 여자들이 남자들보다 여러 해 더 산다.

어 휘 · 발 음

A. 밑줄 친 부분에 들어갈 가장 적합한 단어를 골라라.

(1) Flowers will not thrive without ______.

ⓐ sunshine ⓑ botanist ⓒ greenhouse ⓓ gardener

(2) A man who gives advice is ______.

ⓐ a sponsor ⓑ an instructor ⓒ a counselor ⓓ a commander

(3) The mayor vowed to reduce ______ among the city's residents.

ⓐ wealth ⓑ success ⓒ prosperity ⓓ poverty

(4) When you see something that really doesn't exist, you are having an optical ______.

ⓐ illusion ⓑ allusion ⓒ delusion ⓓ illumination

B. 글 끝에 주어진 단어를 적절한 어형으로 바꾸어 공란을 채워라.

(1) He is a ______ young statesman. (promise)

(2) Our ______ is called a democracy because power is in the hands not of a ______ but of the whole people. (constitute, minor)

(3) Their hearts glow with genuine ______. (patriot)

(4) He is known to be an ______ person. (influence)

(5) Staying in the country will be ______ to his respiratory problem. (benefit)

(6) My political ideal is democracy. Everyone should be respected as an individual, but no one ______. (idol)

(7) Ellen's ______ with pop music is astonishing. (familiar)

(8) Once the sun is harnessed, the supply of energy will be ______. (exhaust)

(9) I expect all players to show complete ______ of the rules of the game. (observe)

C. 괄호 안에서 적당한 단어를 골라라.

(1) In his (contact, relation, company, friendship) you never get bored.

(2) (Geography, Geometry, Geology) is a branch of mathematics.

(3) Prisoners went on (hunger, fast, starvation) strike for better conditions.

(4) One who owes something to another is called a (creditor, debtor, owner).

Answer: A. (1) ⓐ (2) ⓒ (3) ⓓ (4) ⓐ
B. (1) promising (2) constitution, minority (3) patriotism (4) influential (5) beneficial (6) idolized (7) familiarity (8) inexhaustible (9) observance
C. (1) company (2) Geometry (3) hunger (4) debtor

D. 주어진 정의에 알맞은 단어를 주어진 철자로 쓰시오.

(1) the smallest particle of a chemical element (=a)

(2) a building on the campus for public gatherings of the students (=a)

(3) a sum of money paid as a punishment for breaking a law or a rule (=f)

(4) animals kept on a farm, such as cattle or sheep (=l)

(5) a building in a college, where students live and sleep (=d)

(6) the line at which the earth or sea and sky appear to meet (=h)

(7) an optical instrument for making distant objects appear nearer and larger (=t)

(8) a book written by oneself about one's own life (=a)

(9) a bag-like part of the body which receives and digests food (=s)

(10) someone who is not a member of the military or police forces (=c)

E. 다음의 (1)에서는 발음이 같은 짝을 고르고, (2)에서는 밑줄 친 부분의 발음이 같은 짝을 골라라.

(1) ㉠ live / leave ㉡ walk / work ㉢ pull / pool ㉣ color / collar ㉤ pole / poll

(2) ㉠ south / southern ㉡ pleasure / soldier ㉢ epoch / chorus ㉣ lose / loose ㉤ singer / anger

F. ( ) 안에 들어갈 적당한 단어를 고르시오.

(1) The earth is not a true ( ) but is slightly larger near the equator.

① globe ② grove ③ glove ④ grave

(2) An eclipse of the sun is called a ( ) eclipse.

① sonar ② solar ③ cellular ④ lunar

(3) We thought this necklace was expensive, but it turned out to be ( ).

① priceless ② valueless ③ invaluable ④ precious

(4) A Celsius or Fahrenheit thermometer is used to measure ( ).

① temperance ② temper ③ temperament ④ temperature

Answer: D. (1) atom (2) auditorium (3) fine (4) livestock (5) dormitory (6) horizon (7) telescope (8) autobiography (9) stomach (10) civilian
E. (1) ㉤ (2) ㉢
F. (1) ① (2) ② (3) ② (4) ④

숙 어

(1) **in favor of** (=approving of, in support of) ~에 찬성[지지]하여, ~에게 유리한
in one's favor (=to one's advantage) ~에게 유리하도록
in favor with (=be favored by) ~의 마음에 들어
☞ So far there's no evidence *in favor of* the defendant.
Both teams claimed the point, but the referee decided *in our favor*.
He stands high *in favor with* his boss.

(2) **in force** (=in effect[operation], effective ; in large numbers)
효력을 발생하여, 시행하여 ; 대거, 전원
☞ The new telephone charges aren't *in force* yet.
Protesters turned out *in force* for the demonstration.

(3) **in high[low] spirits** (=pleasantly[unpleasantly]) 기분좋게[불쾌하게]
☞ He came home *in high spirits* satisfied with the result.

(4) **in honor of** (=in celebration of) ~에게 경의를 표하여, ~을 기념하여
☞ A rose bush was planted *in honor of* the Queen Mother's birthday.

(5) **in line for** (=likely to get, destined for) ~이 될 예정인, ~하게 되어 있는
☞ He is an excellent employee and is *in line for* a promotion.

(6) **in line with** (=in agreement with) ~과 일치하여
☞ Students' behavior at school parties must be *in line with* school rules.

(7) **in no case** (=never, under no circumstances) 결코 ~아닌
☞ He should *in no case* be told that he has a terminal illness.

(8) **in no time** (=quickly, fast) 즉시, 신속히
☞ I asked my secretary to do the task, and she did it *in no time*.

(9) **in one ear and out the other** (=quickly forgotten)
한쪽 귀로 듣고 한쪽 귀로 흘려버리는
☞ My advice to him went *in one ear and* straight *out the other*.

(10) **in one's face** (=straight against) 정면으로
☞ A cold wind was blowing *in our faces*.

(11) **in proportion to** (=according to, relative to) ~에 비례하여[따라]
☞ The tax increases *in proportion to* the amount you earn.

(12) **in place of[in one's place]** (=instead of) ~의 대신에

☞ *In place of* regular programs, there was a special news broadcast.
He sent his son to attend the ceremony *in his place*.

(13) **in pursuit of** (=pursuing, seeking) ~을 추구하여, ~을 쫓아, ~을 찾아

☞ They emigrated to Australia *in pursuit of* a better life.

(14) **in regard to** (=with regard to, in respect to) ~에 관하여

☞ What is your opinion *in regard to* this subject?

(15) **in season** (=readily available) 제철의 ↔ **out of season** 제철이 아닌

☞ Oranges are *in season* now but grapes are *out of season*.

(16) **inside out** (=with the inner surface turned out) (안과 밖이) 뒤집어진
upside down (=in a position with the bottom being above the top) 거꾸로

☞ He had one of his socks on *inside out*.
The picture was hung *upside down* on the wall, so I got it down to turn it right side up.

(17) **in sight** (=able to be seen, within view) 보이는
out of sight (=unable to be seen, out of view) 안 보이는

☞ The land is still *in sight*. The plane is *out of sight* behind a cloud.

(18) **in terms of** (=from the standpoint of) ~의 관점[견지]에서

☞ *In terms of* money, how much do you think you are worth to our company?
If computed *in terms of* tonnage, it will aggregate 100 tons.

Exercise

▶▶ 주어진 단어들을 포함한 글을 지어라. 필요하면 어형을 변화시켜라.

1. favor / tax / increases
2. law / force / year
3. farewell / hold / honor
4. sun / shine / face
5. sick / go / place
6. advice / ear / out / other
7. police / run / pursuit / thief
8. strawberry / now / season
9. stand / upside / on / hands
10. terms / sales / successful

11. 관 사(Article)

기본 문법 설명

A. 부정관사	(1) It is **a** universal problem. I stood there for **an** hour. (2) **A** fox is a cunning animal. (3) I have **an** Israeli friend here. (4) Birds of **a** feather flock together. (5) It is true in **a** sense. (6) Please give me a call at least once **a** day. (7) Oil paintings look better at **a** distance.
B. 정관사	(1) I bought a new shirt on my way home; **the** shirt fits me very well. (2) **The** arrest of some leaders touched off the student riots. (3) I went to **the** airport to see her off. (4) **The** dog is a faithful animal. (5) Gas is sold by **the** gallon. (6) He caught me by **the** hand. (7) I am positive that I was in **the** right. (8) **The** sun is the center of our solar system.
C. 정관사와 고유명사	(1) **the** Thames, **the** Pacific (Ocean) (2) **the** Korean Peninsula, **the** Philippines **the** English Channel, **the** Alps (3) **the** United States of America, **the** Sahara (Desert) (4) **the** State Department, **the** White House Seoul Station, Pagoda Park (5) **the** Mayflower, **The** transcontinental railroad **the** Gyeongbu line (6) **the** Royal Society, **the** British Broadcasting Corporation (7) **The** Times, **The** Economist (8) **the** ambitious Caesar honest Dick (9) **the** Chinese language (=Chinese) What is **the** French for **the** English 'yes'?

A. 부정관사

(1) 자음 발음 앞에서는 a
모음 발음 앞에서는 an

(2) 종족 대표 (a=any)
(여우는 교활한 동물이다.)

(3) a=one (나는 여기에 이스라엘인 친구 한 사람이 있다.)

(4) a=the same (깃이 같은 새는 끼리끼리 모인다 : 유유상종)
We are of *an* age. (우리는 동갑이다.)

(5) a=a certain (그것은 어떤 의미에서 사실이다.)

(6) a=per (하루에 한 번)

(7) a=some
to *a* degree (어느 정도)
for *a* time (잠깐,얼마동안)

B. 정관사

(1) 앞에 나온 명사를 반복할 때

(2) 수식어구로 한정될 때

(3) 전후 관계로 누구나 알 수 있을 때

(4) 종족 대표
(개는 충실한 동물이다.)
(=Dogs are faithful animals.)

(5) 시간·수량의 단위를 나타낼 때
I hired a boat by *the* hour.
They sell it by *the* yard.

(6) 소유격 대신 관용적으로 쓰이는 the. 예문과 같이 신체의 부분을 나타낼때는 전치사 다음에 the를 붙인다.
look one in *the* face
pull one by *the* sleeve
strike one on *the* head
pat one on *the* back

(7) 관용구
in the morning (*or* afternoon)
in the wrong
in the light
in the shade

(8) 유일한 것에는 the를 붙인다.
the moon, the universe, the sky,
the south, the right (오른쪽)

C. 정관사와 고유명사

(1) 강·바다의 이름
the Han River (*or* river)
the Atlantic (Ocean) (대서양)

(2) 반도·군도·해협·산맥의 이름
the Malay Peninsula
the West Indies
the Magellan Strait
the Rocky Mountains

(3) 어떤 나라의 이름이나 지명은 일반적으로 무관사이지만 일부 나라 (주로 복수형 국명) 혹은 일부 지명 앞에는 the를 쓴다.
the Far East, *the* Riviera
the Netherlands = Holland
The Hague
the Bronx (뉴욕시 북부의 한 구 5개 구 중에서)

(4) 관공서, 공공 건물
the Red Cross
the British Museum
☞역, 항구, 호수, 다리, 공항, 공원(폭포, 광장)에는 일반적으로 the를 붙이지 않는다. at Grand Central Sta
at Busan Harbor at Pearl Harbor (진주만) Times Square
Lake Michigan Niagara Falls
Ruby Falls
Waterloo Bridge at Central Park
Incheon International Airport at O'Hare International Airport
at Hartsfield-Jackson Atlanta International Airport

(5) 배·열차·항공기·철로의 이름
the Queen Mary
The Spirit of St. Louis

(6) 학회·협회·연구소의 이름
(영국 학술원), (영국 방송 협회)
the Royal Academy (영국 미술원)

(7) 신문·잡지의 이름
the New York Times
☞*Time, Newsweek*

(8) 성질을 나타내는 형용사가 인명에 붙을 때는 the를 붙인다.
그러나 old, young, dear, great, good 등 흔한 형용사가 올 때는 the를 붙이지 않는다.

(9) 국어 이름과 특정한 말을 나타낼 때
the Spanish language=Spanish
(영어의 'yes'는 프랑스어로 무엇이라 합니까?)

D. 관사의 위치	(1) **Such a** work cannot be done in **so short a** time. **What a** wonderful organ the human brain is! **How** wonderful **an** organ the human brain is! He wasn't **as** rich **a** man as he was reputed to be. It is **too** good **a** chance to be lost. (2) She is **quite a** good painter. It is **rather a** cold day. (3) Lend me **all the** money you've got. **Both the** contestants were given a prize. I paid **double the** price for it.
E. 관사의 생략	(1) **Waiter**, bring me a cup of coffee, please. (2) What time will **uncle** come back this evening? (3) **President** Bush, **General** MacArthur, **Professor** Smith (4) When I'm busy, I often skip **lunch**. (5) On average, **woman** lives longer than **man**. (6) Washington was twice elected **president**. (7) I used a folded newspaper as **a kind of hat** to keep the rain off. (8) They are cousins, not **brother and sister**. They are now living **from hand to mouth**. (9) go to **school**, at **school** (10) **by train**, **take place**
F. 관사의 생략과 반복	(1) **A** poet and novelist **is** present. **A** poet and **a** novelist **are** present. (2) **The** King and Queen attended the banquet.

◈ ***Riddles*** ◈

What is the longest word in the English language?
Answer—SMILES, for there is a mile between the first and last letters.

Should a man stir his coffee with his right or his left hand?
Answer—Neither; he should use a spoon.

D. 관사의 위치

(1) so / as / too / how / however } +형용사+부정관사+명사의 순서이다.

(2) 일반적으로 quite, rather 다음에 부정관사가 온다.

(3) all, both, double이 오면 그 다음에 대개 정관사가 온다.

* I have had *so* good *a* time.
He is *as* diligent *a* man as ever lived.
It was *too* difficult *a* problem for me to solve.
How difficult *a* problem this is!
We went *quite a* long way.
I know *all the* people there.
Both the boys are my acquaintances.
Many a time have I seen it.
It is *half a* mile from here.
☞ *rather a* cold day [영국식]
a rather cold day [미국식]

E. 관사의 생략

(1) 호격

(2) 가족 관계
Father is looking for you, John.

(3) 고유명사 앞에 붙는 관직, 칭호, 신분을 나타내는 말

(4) 식사·질병·운동의 이름
He is suffering from *fever.*
They are playing *tennis.*

(5) man (인간·남성), woman (여성)

(6) 관직 혹은 신분을 나타내는 말이 보어로 쓰였을 때
Mr. Kim was appointed *principal* of our school.

(7) a kind of, a sort of 다음에는 일반적으로 관사가 없다.
It is a sort of *flower.*

(8) 짝을 이루는 두 개의 명사가 전치사 혹은 접속사로 밀접하게 연결될 때
man and *wife*, *father* and *son*, *mother* and *child*, *body* and *soul*, *teacher* and *student*, *east* and *west*, *knife* and *fork*, *young* and *old*
짝을 이루는 두 개의 명사로 된 관용구
The lord wrote a letter with *pen and ink.*
They bound him *hand and foot.*
They are walking *arm in arm.*
The butterflies are flying *from flower to flower.*

(9) 공공 건물이 본래의 목적으로 쓰일 때 (학교에 공부하러 가다) (수업중)
in school : 재학중
go to church : 예배보러 가다
go to (the) hospital : 입원하다
go to prison : 징역살이하다
at church : 예배중
*go to sea : 선원이 되다
go to bed : 잠자리에 들다
at table : 식사중
at sea : 항해중

(10) 관용구
㉠ 전치사+명사
at *home*, by *sea*, on *foot*, by *mistake*, at *noon*, at *hand*, by *e-mail*
㉡ 동사+명사
take *place* : 일어나다
take *part* in : ~에 참가하다
lose *sight* of : 시야에서 놓치다
keep *house* : 살림을 하다
take *hold* of : 잡다, 쥐다

F. 관사의 생략과 반복

(1) (시인이며 소설가인 분이 참석했다.)
…동일인이기 때문에 and 다음에 관사가 없다.
(한 시인과 한 소설가가 참석했다.)
…두 사람이기 때문에 and 다음에 관사가 있다.

(2) 불가분의 관계가 있을 때는 두 사람이라도 and 다음에는 관사를 안 붙인다. 첫 명사에만 관사를 붙인다.

문 법 · 작 문

A. 필요한 곳에 관사를 넣어라.

(1) There is jacket in the closet. Jacket is my brother's.
(2) I walked up to her house, rang bell and opened door.
(3) Amsterdam is capital of Netherlands.
(4) Unlike Pacific, Atlantic Ocean has only a few islands.
(5) Thames flows through the heart of London.
(6) The mountain climber got lost in Himalayas.
(7) Meat is usually sold by pound.
(8) She patted me gently on shoulder.
(9) We saw an ancient Egyptian mummy at British Museum.
(10) Thank you for playing violin for us.
(11) It is such lovely cat. I have never seen so lovely cat.
(12) Six months is too short time to learn a foreign language.
(13) What intelligent animal the dolphin is!
(14) My pious mother goes to church twice week.
(15) He'll go to church to see the poet's grave before long.
(16) The sinking ship sent out SOS signal over the radio.

B. 관사의 용법을 바로잡고, 필요한 관사를 넣어라.

(1) What's the total circulation of an Economist?
(2) The Hyde Park is a very fashionable place in London.
(3) The guilty criminal was sent to the prison.
(4) Between ourselves, they'll choose him the chairman of the political rally.
(5) Portuguese language is very hard to learn.
(6) It was in the days of the King Alfred.
(7) Two of trade seldom agree.
(8) Let me know the result by an e-mail.
(9) He possesses a 18th century edition of Shakespeare's works.
(10) Full moon changes to crescent moon every month.
(11) The man is mortal and God is immortal.
(12) I prefer a life in a country to a life in town by nature.
(13) Many little makes a mickle.
(14) He gave up a sword for a pen.
(15) This is one of the most dangerous substances known to the man.

C. 공란을 적당한 관사로 메워라. 필요 없는 곳에는 X표를 하여라.

(1) The house is rented by _____ year to Miss Sweet.

(2) He held me by _____ sleeve.

(3) "Will you pass me _____ salt, please?" "Here you are."

(4) Towards _____ end of _____ 1950's he visited _____ Philippines.

(5) She will make an angel of ________ wife.

(6) Philip was lying on the sofa, ________ book in hand.

(7) The couple never fail to go out ________ arm in arm.

(8) The great discovery came in 1492 when (㉠) Italian sailor, Christopher Columbus, sailed three tiny ships under the flag of Spain all (㉡) way across the Atlantic Ocean to the Caribbean Sea. He did not expect to find (㉢) new world. When, after an eternity of sailing across the ocean, he sighted land on (㉣) morning of 12 October 1492, he thought he had reached the Indies. To this day we call the islands that he discovered (㉤) West Indies, and we still call the copper-colored natives of (㉥) New World Indians.

D. Translate the following into English:

(1) 나는 한 달에 두서너 번 그를 방문하기로 하고 있다.

(2) 그 여자는 독실한 기독교인이다. 일요일마다 꼭 예배보러 간다.

(3) 앤더슨 시장이 개회사를 했다.

(4) 그는 나의 팔을 붙잡고 도와 달라고 했다.

(5) 그는 친절하게도 정거장으로 가는 길을 가르쳐 주었다.

(6) 심한 강우 때문에 한강 물이 4피트 불었다.

(7) 그는 아주 신뢰할 만한 사람이어서 틀림없이 제때 그 프로젝트를 완수할 수 있을 것이다.

(8) 얼룩소 한 마리가 풀밭에서 풀을 뜯고 있다.

오늘의 일기를 영어로 써라.

● 단 문 독 해 ●

Birds of **a** feather flock together.
She is **an angel of a** girl.
I e-mail her twice **a** week.

1. We had met at college; and though there was not much liking between us, nor even much intimacy, we were so nearly **of a humor** that we could get along with ease.

notes :
*liking 좋아함 (=fondness)
*intimacy 친근함
*humor 기질
*with ease =easily

▶▶According to the above passage, which of the following does **not** correspond with the underlined We?

① They were contemporaries and of the same age.
② They were not that fond of each other.
③ They were not quite on intimate terms with each other when they met.
④ They got along with each other thanks to their similar disposition.
⑤ They took lessons at the same college.

▶▶영작하시오.

그들은 그 문제 해결에 관해 모두 같은 의견이었다.

2. Livingstone was **a mere skeleton of a man**, his clothes in rags, when he returned to civilization. Only the most wonderful courage and perseverance could have carried him through. After having spent sixteen years in Africa, he sailed for England.

notes :
*skeleton 해골
*in rags = 너덜너덜 해어져
*carry ~ through = ~을 버티어 나가게 하다

▶▶According to the above passage, which does **not** correspond with the underlined he?

① He was skinny when he returned to civilization.
② He explored Africa for 16 years.
③ He was courageous and very patient, we guess.
④ He went back to England by ship from Africa.
⑤ He was very thin because of an endemic disease in Africa.

▶▶영작하시오.

그는 건장한 체질 때문에 오랜 병을 견디어 냈다.

3. Many times **a day** I realize how much my outer and inner life is built upon the labors of my fellow men, both living and dead, and how earnestly I must exert myself in order to give in return as much as I have received. My peace of mind is often troubled by the depressing sense that I have borrowed too heavily from the work of other men.

notes :
*how much ~ have received 는 realize 의 목적어가 되는 명사절
*exert oneself = 노력하다
*in return = 보답으로
*depressing 침울한

▶▶According to the above paragraph, which of the following is most suitable to describe the above-mentioned man?

① He is sticking to the past and is depressed.
② He is earnest and a workaholic.
③ He is humble and too conscious of his inability.
④ He is grateful for others' help but he does not think of doing something for them.
⑤ He attributes his existence largely to other people's help and he is anxious to return what he owes.

▶▶영작하시오.

모두의 이익을 위해 각자는 노력해야 한다.

He caught her **by the hand.**

4. Mother held me **by the hand** and we were kneeling by the bedside of my brother, two years older than I, who lay dead, and the tears were flowing down her cheeks unchecked, and she was moaning. That dumb sign of anguish made upon me a very strong impression which holds its place still with her picture.

notes :
*kneel 무릎을 꿇다
*unchecked 제지되고 않고
*moan 신음하다
*that dumb sign of anguish = 소리내지 않고 괴로워하며 울던 모습

▶▶Which of the following is **not** correct?

① The tone of the paragraph is miserable and sad.
② The writer's mother got a serious illness because of the sadness caused by the death of her son.
③ The aspect of the writer's mother in deep grief has left an indelible impression in his mind.
④ Whenever the writer thinks of his mother, he vividly remembers her moaning at the bedside of his dead brother.
⑤ The writer's mother was shedding tears without wiping them away.

▶▶영작하시오.

그녀는 두 눈에 눈물을 글썽이며 그의 얼굴을 응시했다.

Man is a rational animal.
He **had the kindness to** show me the way.

5. **Man** is a rational animal, — so at least I have been told. Throughout a long life, I have looked diligently for evidence in favor of this statement, but so far I have not **had the fortune to** come across it, though I have searched in many countries spread over three continents. On the contrary, I have seen the world plunging continually further into madness.

notes :
*look for = 찾다
*in favor of = ~을 찬성하여
*so far = 지금까지
*come across = 우연히 마주치다(=meet ~ by chance)
*on the contrary = 그 반대로
*plunge 뛰어 들어가다

▶▶ According to the above paragraph, which of the following is **not** correct?

① The writer made efforts to find the evidence to support the statement that man is rational.
② In spite of much searching, the writer has found no evidence that man is reasonable.
③ The writer has traveled to many countries, only to find the growing madness of man.
④ Unfortunately the writer hasn't found any grounds for the belief that man is a sensible creature.
⑤ The writer has expected the madness of man to improve sooner or later through his efforts.

▶▶ 영작하시오.
그는 불행하게도 무장한 비행기 납치범들에 의해 납치되었다.

She is **such a beautiful girl.**

6. With most men the knowledge that they must ultimately die doesn't weaken the pleasure in being alive at present. To the poet the world appears still more beautiful as he gazes at flowers that are doomed to wither, at spring that comes to **too speedy an** end.

notes :
*ultimately 결국 (= finally)
*be doomed to = ~할 운명을 지니다
*come to an end = 끝나다

▶▶ According to the writer, the (   ) of all living things adds to the pleasure of our life rather than (   ) it.
[mortality, majesty, death, removes, reduces, enhances]

▶▶ 영작하시오.
이것은 놓치기에는 너무 아까운 기회다.

While a boy he **went to sea.**
They live **from hand to mouth.**

7. As for me, having some money in my pocket, I traveled to London **by land**; and there, as well as on the road, had many struggles with myself, what course of life I should take, and whether I should go home, or **go to sea**.

notes :
*As for me = 나로서는(= For my part)
*(as to) what course of life

▶▶Which is most appropriate to describe the writer?

① Owing to his wanderlust, he was very fond of traveling to different places.
② He was not only anguished but also indecisive about what to do in the future.
③ He was extravagant with money and he couldn't stand being tied to anything.
④ After serious consideration of all the situations, he determined to be a sailor.
⑤ Because of his strong homing instinct, he made up his mind to return home.

▶▶영작하시오.

실제적인 면에서만 아니라 이론상으로도 그의 생각은 터무니없다.

8. Today, if a man were to know something about everything, the allotment of time would give one minute to each subject, and he would flit **from topic to topic** as a butterfly **from flower to flower**. Today commercial, literary, or inventive success means concentration.

notes :
*allotment 할당
*flit 날아 옮겨 다니다
*inventive 발명의 ; 독창적인
*concentration (정신) 집중

▶▶Which of the following proverbs is most related with the above paragraph?

① A drowning man will catch at a straw.
② A rolling stone gathers no moss.
③ One swallow does not make a summer.
④ Make hay while the sun shines.
⑤ It is an ill wind that blows nobody good.

▶▶영작하시오.

그 불쌍한 노인은 지팡이를 들고 이집 저집 구걸하고 다녔다.

● 장 문 독 해 ●

Warming-up

He has **taken pains** to show me how to do the work.
He **not only** sings, **but** plays the guitar very well.
She cooked the dinner **herself**.
Will you help me **with** my work?
I was **waited on** by the waitress in the restaurant.

1 A characteristic of American culture that has become almost a tradition is the glorification of the self-made man — the man who has risen to the top through his own efforts, usually beginning by <u>working with his hands</u>. The leader in business or industry or the college professor may take pains to point out that his father started life in America as a farm hand or worker of some sort.

This attitude toward manual labor is seen in many aspects of American life. One is invited to dinner at a home that is not only comfortably but even luxuriously furnished; yet the hostess probably will cook the dinner herself, will serve it herself, and will wash the dishes afterward. And even though her husband may be a professional man he talks about washing the car, digging in his flower beds, painting the house, or laying tiles on the floor of the recreation room in the basement. His wife may even help him with these things, just as he often helps her with the dish washing. The son who is away at college may wait on tables and wash dishes for his board, or during the summer he may work with a construction gang on a new highway in order to earn his next year's school expenses.

G. Doty & J. Ross: *Language and Life in the U.S.A.*

Notes

characteristic 특징 / culture 문화 / tradition 전통 / glorification 찬미 / self-made 자수성가한 / attitude 태도 / manual labor 육체 노동; *mental labor* 정신 노동 / aspect 면(面) / luxuriously 사치스럽게 / furnish 가구를 설비하다 / professional man 지적(知的) 직업인 / recreation room 휴게실 / basement 지하실 / wait on 시중들다(=serve) / board 식사(=meal) / gang=group / school expenses 학비

Question

1. 본문의 밑줄친 부분을 다음과 같이 바꿔 쓸 때, 빈칸에 들어갈 말을 본문에서 찾아 쓰시오.

   doing (　　) (　　)

2. 본문의 내용과 일치하도록 다음 빈 칸에 공통으로 들어갈 말을 골라 쓰시오.

   * Some successful Americans try to emphasize the fact that they are (　　) of their family's assistance.
   * Young American people try to be financially (　　) of their parents.

   [indifferent, independent, insolvent]

3. Which of the following is **not** correct?

   ① Young Americans are encouraged to earn their school expenses without their parents' help.

   ② Most Americans are apt to glorify the self-made man.

   ③ The people living in an elegant house hardly ever do their routine chores.

   ④ Even a professional man often shares household duties with his wife.

   ⑤ Many American leaders are proud of their parents who started their lives as manual workers.

4. Which of the following is the main idea of the passage?

   ① The changing of roles between husband and wife

   ② Social problems caused by the tradition of glorifying the self-made man

   ③ How to accept an invitation in America

   ④ Americans' positive attitude to manual labor

   ⑤ How to earn school expenses in America

Production

(1) 미국 사람들은 노동으로 시작하여 인생에서 성공한 것을 자랑으로 여긴다.

(2) 나는 그 계약을 따내기 위해서 열심히 노력할 것이다.

(3) 대부분의 미국 가정에서는 남편이 식사 후에 아내의 설거지를 돕는다.

● 장 문 독 해 ●

Warming-up

It **bears no relation to** the problem.
It was in the park **that** I met her for the first time.
His words have some **bearing on** the problem.
To make good progress in English, you must practice it regularly every day.
The man **turned out** to be an enemy agent.

2 Questions of education are frequently discussed as if they bore no relation to the social system in which and for which the education is carried on. ⓐ This is one of the most common reasons for the unsatisfactoriness of the answers. It is only within a particular social system that a system of education has any meaning. If education today seems to deteriorate, if it seems to become more and more chaotic and meaningless, it is primarily because we have no settled and satisfactory arrangement of society, and because we have both vague and diverse opinions about the kind of society we want. ⓑ Education is a subject which cannot be discussed in a void: our questions raise other questions, social, economic, financial and political. And the bearings are on more ultimate problems even than these: to know what we want in education we must know what we want in general; we must derive our theory of education from our philosophy of life. The problem turns out to be a religious problem.

***T. S. Eliot:** Selected Essays*

Notes

bear relation to (~) (~)에 관계가 있다 / carry on 경영하다, 행하다 / deteriorate 악화하다, 타락하다 / chaotic 혼란한 / settled 확고한 / arrangement of society 사회 기구 / vague 막연한 / diverse 다양한 / void 공간 / financial 재정적인 / bearing 관계 / ultimate 궁극적인 / derive 뽑다, 끌어내다 / turn out=prove

Question

1. 본문의 ⓐ가 가리키는 구체적인 내용을 우리말로 쓰시오.

2. Which does the underlined sentence ⓑ imply?
   ① We can't discuss the problem of education in a void.
   ② Education should be discussed at a forum for debate.
   ③ Education is a comprehensive subject that should be discussed with other problems.
   ④ We have to discuss education apart from political or social problems.
   ⑤ Generally speaking, the reform of education should be based on the majority opinion.

3. Which of the following does **not** correspond with the passage?
   ① Education must go hand in hand with the social system in which it is carried on.
   ② A tendency to separate education from the social system doesn't help solve educational problems satisfactorily.
   ③ A proper organization of society is necessary to cope with current educational problems.
   ④ The solutions of educational problems are far more important than those of other social problems.
   ⑤ Educational problems are ultimately related to religion.

4. According to the passage, which is **not** the prerequisite for educational improvement?
   ① a settled and satisfactory arrangement of society
   ② definite and unified opinions about the kind of society we want
   ③ a reinforced teacher-training program and increased financial assistance to educational facilities
   ④ an educational theory derived from the philosophy of life
   ⑤ dealing with educational problems in connection with other social problems

Production

(1) 그는 마치 아무 일도 없었던 것처럼 방 안에 들어왔다.
(2) 내가 그와 알게 된 것은, 작년에 런던에 있을 때였다.
(3) 나는 그를 성실한 사람으로 생각했으나, 알고 보니 사기꾼이었다.

실력체크 I

1 다음 글을 읽고 본문의 내용과 일치하지 않는 것을 골라라.

In the memories which I retain of my early childhood my father appears clearly as the central figure around whom our family life revolved, whereas my mother's image is far less distinct. In fact the clearest recollection I have of her from that period, is of a quiet person who moved around slowly in the kitchen as she prepared our meals, and who was always present in time of crisis—such as waiting on my father during his periodical attacks of gout and tending my frequent cuts and bruises with calm efficiency. Complete calmness and apparent lack of emotion under any circumstances, in spite of almost constant discomfort, remained with her throughout her life. This resolute placidity was almost frightening at times.

notes:
retain 잊지 않고 있다 / recollection 회상, 추억 / periodical 주기적인 / resolute 결연한 / placidity 평온함, 침착 / gout 통풍(痛風) / tend 돌보다, 간호하다

① 필자의 어머니에 대한 기억은 아버지에 대한 기억보다 분명하지 않다.
② 필자의 어머니는 육체적으로 힘든 생활을 했다.
③ 필자의 아버지는 때때로 필자의 어머니를 윽박질렀다.
④ 필자의 어머니는 때때로 필자가 두려워할 정도로 침착하였다.
⑤ 필자의 어머니는 집안에 어려운 일이 생겼을 때 항상 침착히 대처했다.

2 다음 글의 빈 곳에 들어갈 것을 골라라.

One day the manager of a well-known hotel in New York was called on ___(1)___ of a very irate lady. "I can't bear it another minute," she told him indignantly. "You must tell ___(2)___ making that horrible noise on the piano." And ___(3)___ on the manager's face, she added, "If you don't make him stop, I will leave immediately."
"I'm sorry it's disturbing you," the manager said patiently. "That's Paderewski." It was ___(4)___ surprised. "What?" she stammered, much embarrassed. "The great pianist Paderewski?"
She was silent for a moment. "Well, of course, that's different. Please don't say a word to him."
Two days later the manager ___(5)___ to another visitor in the lobby. "It's so wonderful," she was saying, "I can open my door every morning and hear Paderewski practice."

notes:
irate 성난, 화난 / indignantly 분연히, 화가나서 / disturb 괴롭히다, 어지럽히다 / stammer 말을 더듬다

① the man across the hall to stop
② overheard her talking
③ seeing the look of astonishment
④ the lady's turn to look
⑤ to deal with the complaint

3 한 나라를 부강하게 하는 중요한 요소 셋을 영어로 적어라.

A country's capacity to produce wealth depends on many factors, most of which have an effect on one another. Wealth depends to a great extent upon a country's natural resources, such as coal, gold, and other minerals, water-supply, and so on. Some regions of the world are well supplied with coal and minerals, and have a fertile soil and a favorable climate; other regions possess perhaps only one of these things, and some regions possess none of them. The U.S.A. is one of the wealthiest regions of the world because she has vast natural resources within her borders, her soil is fertile, and her climate is varied. The Sahara Desert, on the other hand, is one of the least wealthy. Next to natural resources comes the social and political ability to turn them to use. China is perhaps as well off as the U.S.A. in natural resources, but has suffered for many years from civil and external wars, and for this and other reasons has been unable to develop its natural resources peacefully and steadily, and to produce more wealth than another country equally well served by nature. Another important factor is the technical efficiency of a country's people. Old countries that have, through many centuries, trained up numerous skilled craftsmen and technicians are better placed to produce wealth than those countries whose workers are largely unskilled.

notes :
capacity 능력 / natural resources 천연자원 / minerals 광물 / and so on=and so forth 기타 등등 / fertile 비옥한 / be well off=be fortunately situated / civil wars 내란 / external 외부의 / efficiency 능률 / craftsman 직공, 일꾼 / technician 기술자

4 다음 글을 읽고 문맥상 공란에 넣어 글의 뜻이 완성되도록 3단어 이내의 영어로 써라.

Mrs. Bennet rang the bell, and Miss Elizabeth was called in. "Come here, child," cried her father as she appeared. "I understand that Mr. Collins made you an offer of marriage. Is it true?" Elizabeth replied that it was.

"Very well, and this offer of marriage you have refused?" "I have, father." "Very well. We now come to the point. Your mother insists upon your accepting it. Is it not so, dearest?"

"Yes, or I will never see her again." "An unhappy choice is before you, Elizabeth. From this day you must be a stranger to one of your parents. Your mother will never see you again if you do not marry Mr. Collins, and I will never see you again ______."

notes :
call in 불러들이다 / offer 제안, 신청 / come to the point 문제의 요점에 들어가다

실 력 체 크 II

A. 밑줄 친 단어의 명사형을 사용하여, 다음 문장을 단문으로 고쳐써라.

(1) It was right after breakfast that he departed.
(2) If you permit, I'd like to do it.
(3) As it snowed heavily, their arrival was delayed.
(4) If he had attended the party, it would have encouraged them.
(5) Her father died suddenly, and she had to give up school.
(6) He can't walk because he is disabled.
(7) Compare them carefully, and you will see the difference.

B. 다음과 같은 경우, 영어로 어떻게 표현할 것인가?

(1) 계산은 제가 하겠습니다.
(2) 512-5172로 전화를 하려고 하는데 통화 중 신호만 자꾸 들리는데요.
(3) 전화한 김에 부탁 하나 더 드려도 되겠습니까?
(4) 우리는 맞벌이 부부입니다.
(5) 그것이 나하고 무슨 상관이 있지요?

C. Fill in each blank with a suitable word :

(1) He firmly believed (   ) it was (   ) to learn it.
He was convinced (   ) the necessity of (   ) it.
(2) I knew Tom's character. I had confidence in Tom.
With my (   ) of Tom's character, I had confidence in him.
(3) He had been treated unfairly. He complained about it.
He complained about his (   ) (   ).
(4) She is (   ) proud to do such a mean thing.
Her (   ) will not allow her to do such a mean thing.
(5) She made a detailed (   ) of the scene.
She described the scene in (   ).

Answer: A. (1) His departure was directly after breakfast. (2) With your permission I would like to do it. (3) The heavy snow delayed their arrival. (4) His attendance at the party would have encouraged them. (5) Her father's sudden death forced her to give up school. (6) His disability prevents him from walking (7) A careful comparison of them will show you the difference.
B. (1) I'll pick up the tab. (2) I'm trying to reach 512-5172, but all I get is a busy signal. (3) While I've got you on the phone, could I ask you another favor? (4) We are a two-paycheck couple. 혹은 We are a two-income family. (5) What does that have to do with me?
C. (1) that, necessary, of, learning (2) knowledge (3) unfair, treatment (4) too, pride (5) description, detail

D. 밑줄 친 단어를 뜻이 통하게 바른 순서로 배열하여라.

(1) I have (good, of, deal, a, it, read).
(2) He didn't know (to, matter, how, deal, the, with).
(3) No reference (what, was, to, had, made, happened).
(4) Some of the workers (earn, on, don't, live, to, enough).
(5) I'm not going to have (a, fool, make, of, you, yourself).
(6) A (better, feel, long, make, much, sleep, will, you).

E. 다음 단어를 적당한 형으로 고쳐 공란에 써 넣어라.

arrive,	depend,	drive,	excellent,	food,
patriot,	prove,	refer,	resist,	idiot

(1) Because you ( ) your dog on cakes, it's not surprising he's so fat.
(2) He is an ( ) person who can't distinguish vice from virtue.
(3) Vitamin A helps to build ( ) to infection.
(4) ( ) to my aunt, he said that she reminded him of his mother.
(5) We were unable to establish ( ) of his innocence.
(6) All ( ) people are willing to fight for their country.
(7) Switzerland has been an ( ) country for hundreds of years.
(8) There's nothing ( ) dislike more than traffic congestion.
(9) We received a welcome from our friends on our ( ).
(10) This part of France is famous for the ( ) of its wine.

F. Tom이 Jack에게, 음악회에 가자고 권유하는 편지를 40~60단어의 영문으로 쓰시오. (단, 다음의 5가지 내용을 반드시 넣을 것.)

다음주 토요일 ; 세계적인 바이올리니스트 ; 오후 6시부터 ; 누이동생을 데리고 ; 여유시간이 있으면

Answer: D. (1) read a good deal of it (2) how to deal with the matter (3) was made to what had happened (4) don't earn enough to live on (5) you make a fool of yourself (6) long sleep will make you feel much better

E. (1) feed (2) idiotic (3) resistance (4) Referring (5) proof (6) patriotic (7) independent (8) drivers (9) arrival (10) excellence

F. Dear Jack,
I think you are getting along quite well. Won't you come and enjoy a recital by a world-famous violinist, which is to be given at the Town Hall at six in the evening next Saturday? I'll be very happy if you are free and can come with your sister.
Yours sincerely
Tom

어 휘 · 발 음

A. 다음 ( )에 공통으로 들어갈 단어를 쓰시오.

(1) (a) This machine takes ( )s instead of money.
(b) The release of two out of the twenty hostages is being seen as ( ) gesture of goodwill.
(c) Please accept this small gift as a ( ) of our gratitude.

(2) (a) ( ) liquids must be kept in very tightly closed containers.
(b) The situation in the Middle East is ( ).
(c) Richard is too ( ) to stay in one job for very long.

(3) (a) Spread the map out ( ) on the floor.
(b) Have you got a ( ) tire?
(c) The couple moved into a new three-room ( ).

(4) (a) She has a certain ( ) of sadness all the time.
(b) Stop putting on ( )s with us! You're just human like the rest of us.
(c) They put commercial programs off the ( ).

(5) (a) The company makes a large ( ) of its products to poor families.
(b) All ( )s, however small, will be greatly appreciated.
(c) He made an important ( ) to the Korean automotive industry.

B. 다음 밑줄친 단어의 어미 ed의 발음은 ㉠ [d] ㉡ [id] ㉢ [t] 중 어느 것인가?

(1) The natives <u>used</u> ( ) to go <u>naked</u> ( ).
(2) Her face was <u>bathed</u> ( ) in tears.
(3) The <u>learned</u> ( ) man <u>laughed</u> ( ) at his silly remark.
(4) An <u>aged</u> ( ) farmer <u>purchased</u> ( ) a <u>used</u> ( ) car.

C. ( ) 속의 단어를 문맥에 맞게 적당한 형태로 고쳐라.

(1) British (athletics) won five gold medals in the Olympics.
(2) The curator of the museum discovered the Greek vase was a (forge).
(3) Fortunately, my suspicions proved (ground).
(4) A sword often (symbol) power gained by violence.
(5) It was a (deceive) attempt to persuade people that they would make a large profit.

Answer: A. (1) token (2) volatile (3) flat (4) air (5) contribution
B. (1) ㉢, ㉡ (2) ㉠ (3) ㉡, ㉢ (4) ㉡, ㉢, ㉠
C. (1) athletes (2) forgery (3) groundless (4) symbolizes (5) deceitful

파생어 만들기

파생어는, 말 내부의 음 변화에 의하는 것 (speak ⇨ speech, feed ⇨ food)과, 접두사·접미사를 붙여 만드는 것 (large ⇨ enlarge, kind ⇨ kindness)이 있는데, 이런 접사가 매우 많으므로 이를 모두 다루는 혼잡을 피하고, 그 중 중요한 것을 들어 파생어 만들기 연습을 해 보자.

A. 명사 만들기

(1) ***Verb* ⇨ *Noun***

(a) -tion, -sion	satisfy ⇨ satisfaction; allude ⇨ allusion
(b) -al, -ment, -ure, -ance, -ence	arrive ⇨ arrival; attain ⇨ attainment; seize ⇨ seizure; assist ⇨ assistance; depend ⇨ dependence
(c) -er, -or, -ant, -ent	do ⇨ doer; act ⇨ actor; serve ⇨ servant; depend ⇨ dependent

(2) ***Adjective* ⇨ *Noun***

-ness, -ity, -ce, -cy	good ⇨ goodness; responsible ⇨ responsibility; fragrant ⇨ fragrance; accurate ⇨ accuracy

B. 형용사 만들기

(1) ***Noun* ⇨ *Adjective***

(a) -ful, -less, -ious; -y	hope ⇨ hopeful; end ⇨ endless; ambition ⇨ ambitious; peril ⇨ perilous; chill ⇨ chilly
(b) -ed, -ic, -ish, -an, -ary	wing ⇨ winged; artist ⇨ artistic; fever ⇨ feverish; America ⇨American; imagination ⇨ imaginary

(2) ***Verb* ⇨ *Adjective***

-able, -ible, -ive	change ⇨ changeable; reverse ⇨ reversible; compare ⇨ comparable, comparative

C. 동사 만들기

(1) ***Noun* ⇨ *Verb***

-ize, en-, em-, in-, be-	memory ⇨ memorize; slave ⇨ enslave; body ⇨ embody; flame ⇨ inflame; prison ⇨ imprison; friend ⇨ befriend

(2) ***Adjective* ⇨ *Verb***

-ize, -en, -fy	fertile ⇨ fertilize; thick ⇨ thicken; beautiful ⇨ beautify

숙 어

(1) **in the absence of** (=for lack of) ~이 없어서, ~이 없을 경우
☞ He was set free *in the absence of* definite evidence.

(2) **in[into] the bargain** (=as well, in addition) 게다가, 그 위에
☞ He looked after a house, his sick wife, and 4 children *into the bargain*.

(3) **in the face of** (=despite, in spite of) ~에도 불구하고
☞ *In the face of* great hardship, she managed to keep her sense of humor.

(4) **in the flesh** (=in real life, in person) 실물로, 직접
☞ I saw my favorite movie star *in the flesh*.
I've seen him perform on TV, but never *in the flesh*.

(5) **in (the) light of** (=in view of) ~의 견지에서, ~에 비추어(서)
☞ Capital punishment should be done away with *in the light of* the dignity of life.

(6) **in the name of** (=with the authority of) ~의 이름으로
☞ I really hate any cruel animal experiments that are conducted *in the name of* science.

(7) **in the nick of time** (=just in time) 꼭 알맞은 때에, 때마침
☞ The police arrived at the crime scene *in the nick of time*.

(8) **in the presence of** (=in front of) ~의 면전에서, ~의 앞에서
☞ At every opportunity Tom made fun of him *in the presence of* Mary.

(9) **in truth** (=in fact, really) 사실은
☞ *In truth*, the doctor feared rejection with the transplant surgery.

(10) **in turn** (=one after the other) 차례로
☞ We watched over our sick mother *in turn* during the night.

(11) **in vain** (=without success) 헛되이, 성과없이
☞ The criminal tried *in vain* to bribe the policeman.

(12) **in view of** (=considering) ~의 견지에서, ~을 고려하여
☞ *In view of* rising labor costs, many companies have turned to computerization.

(13) **in vogue** (=fashionable or popular) 유행하는
☞ Blue jeans are still *in* great *vogue* among teenagers.

(14) **jot down** (=make a note of) 메모하다
☞ His instructions made no sense, but I *jotted* them *down*.

(15) **just about** (=almost) 거의
☞ At *just about* midnight we'll uncork the champagne for celebration.

(16) **(just) between the two of us** (=between ourselves) 우리끼리 이야기인데
☞ *Just between the two of us*, John is considering breaking up with his wife.

(17) **just in case** (=because of the possibility of something happening) 만약의 경우에 대비하여
☞ I don't think I'll need any money, but I'll bring some *just in case*.

(18) **jump to one's feet** (=quickly rise to a standing position) 펄쩍 뛰다
☞ He *jumped to his feet* the moment he heard the news.

(19) **keep an eye on** (=have one's eye on, watch, guard) 지키다, 감시하다
☞ *Keep an eye on* my suitcase while I buy my ticket.

(20) **keep away from** (=avoid going or coming near) ~에 가까이 가지 않다[않게 하다]
☞ *Keep away from* the edge of the cliff.
Keep your children *away from* the stove.

(21) **keep after** (=constantly remind, nag) (계속해서) 잔소리하다
☞ He won't get anything done unless you *keep after* him.

Exercise

▶▶ 주어진 단어들을 포함한 글을 지어라. 필요하면 어형을 변화시켜라.

1. fever / runny / nose / bargain
2. light / behavior / leave / company
3. crimes / commit / name / justice
4. candidates / interview / turn
5. try / vain / change / mind
6. miniskirts / back / vogue
7. jot / address / notebook
8. take / umbrella / case
9. teacher / eye / boys / row
10. keep / children / clean

12. 대 명 사(Pronoun) I

기본 문법 설명

A. 인칭대명사

(1) **We** always have bad weather at this time of the year.
They raise lots of sheep in Australia.

(2) **It**

ⓐ **It**'s been raining on and off since this morning.
Do you have the time? — **It**'s a few minutes after two.
It is about an hour's walk to the nearest station.
How is **it** going with you?

ⓑ **It** is natural for a child *to fear injection.*
It is no use *trying to escape.*
It is certain *that he will come here.*
It doesn't matter *whether he agrees or not.*
He thought **it** interesting *to play the part of Hamlet.*
I thought **it** natural *that he should get angry.*
You will find **it** pleasant *talking with her.*

ⓒ **It** is you **that** are wrong.

(3) ⓐ You have your point of view, and I have **mine**.
ⓑ He is sending e-mails to **some friends of his**.
ⓒ What I do with my spare time is **my own** business!

(4) ⓐ I cut **myself** while I was shaving.
He laughed at **himself**.
ⓑ I did it **myself**.
The house **itself** was humble, but the garden was wonderful.
ⓒ He completed the work **by himself**.

B. 지시대명사

(1) **This, that**

ⓐ The climate of Seoul is similar to **that** of Chicago.
This year's fashions are quite different from **those** of last year.

ⓑ He's crazy about gambling, and **this** absorbs most of the family income.

ⓒ **Those who** like borrowing dislike paying.

A. 인칭대명사

(1) **일반인**을 나타낸다. (we, you, they)
(일년 중 이맘때면 언제나 날씨가 좋지 않다.)
(호주에서는 많은 양을 기른다.)

(2) **It의 용법**

ⓐ 날씨, 시간, 거리, 막연한 상황 등을 나타낸다. — 비인칭대명사
It is all over with him.
(그는 이제 끝장이다.)
I had a good time (of *it*).

ⓑ **It의 기타 용법** : 예문의 it은 각각 이탤릭체 부분을 받는다.
(아이가 주사를 두려워하는 것은 당연하다.)
… it은 가주어, to 이하가 진주어
(탈출하려고 해봐야 소용없다.)
… it은 가주어, trying 이하가 진주어
(그가 여기 올 것은 확실하다.)
… it은 가주어, that절이 진주어
(그가 동의하든 안하든 중요하지 않다.)
… it은 가주어, whether절이 진주어
(그는 Hamlet역을 한다는 것이 흥미롭다고 생각했다.)
… it은 가목적어, to 이하가 진목적어
(그가 화를 내는 것도 당연하다고 생각했다.)
… it은 가목적어, that절이 진목적어
(그 여자와 이야기하는 것이 즐겁다는 것을 알게 될 것이다.)
… it은 가목적어, talking 이하가 진목적어

ⓒ **It is ~ that의 강조구문**
(잘못한 것은 바로 너다.)
☞ The man met her there yesterday.
It was **the man** that met her there yesterday. (the man의 강조 구문)
It was **her** that the man met there yesterday. (her의 강조 구문)
It was **there** that the man met her yesterday. (there의 강조 구문)
It was **yesterday** that the man met her there. (yesterday의 강조 구문)

(3) **소유대명사**

ⓐ 소유대명사 (mine, yours, his, hers, ours, theirs)는 독립적으로 쓰인다.

ⓑ 명사의 소유격과 마찬가지로 a, some, any, no, this, that 따위와 같이 인칭대명사의 소유격을 쓸 때는 이중소유격으로 **a friend of mine** 형이 된다.
this book of *his* (그의 이 책)
another book of *yours*

ⓒ **own**은 소유격의 의미를 강조한다.

(4) **재귀대명사**

ⓐ 목적어가 되는 경우
(면도하다 비었다.) … 동사의 목적어
(자조(自嘲)했다.) … 전치사의 목적어

ⓑ 강조용법
(내가 직접 그것을 했다.) … I를 강조
(그집 자체는 초라했지만 정원은 아주 훌륭했다.) … The house를 강조

ⓒ 관용구
(그는 그 일을 혼자 힘으로 끝냈다.)
by oneself : 혼자서, 홀로 (= alone) ; 혼자 힘으로 (= without help from others)
☞ for oneself : 자기 자신을 위하여 (= for one's own sake)
in itself : 본질적으로, 그 자체로는
of itself : 저절로 (= by itself)
beside oneself (with ~) : (~으로) (거의) 제정신이 아닌
pride oneself on = take pride in
present oneself at = be present at
avail oneself of = utilize

B. 지시대명사

(1) **This, that**

ⓐ that = the climate
those = the fashions

ⓑ this는 앞 문장 전체를 받는다.
(그는 도박에 미쳤다. 이것으로 인해 가정수입의 대부분이 날아간다.)

ⓒ Those who : ~하는 사람들
(빌리기를 좋아하는 사람은 갚기를 싫어한다.)
He who : ~하는 사람

(2) **Such**

ⓐ **Such** was my reward.

ⓑ He is only a child and should be treated **as such**.

ⓒ **Such** men **as** Washington and Lincoln are rare.

Autumn gives us fruits, **such as** pears, persimmons, and apples.

ⓓ Jane is **such** a polite girl **that** everybody loves her.

(3) **the same**

ⓐ He'll do **the same** again.

ⓑ This is **the same** watch **as** I gave her.

This is **the same** watch **that** I gave her.

ⓒ Are these **the same** people **who** came here yesterday?

ⓓ They do not think **the same as** we do.

(4) **So**

ⓐ Is he coming? I think **so**.

ⓑ He is rich. **So** he ís. **So** is shé.

C. 부정대명사

(1) **One**

ⓐ **One** should obey **one's** parents.

ⓑ I'm looking for a house. I'd like **one** with a beautiful garden.

ⓒ This story is more interesting than the preceding **ones**.

ⓓ I received a phone call from **one** Mr. Jones.

(2) **Other, another**

ⓐ **One** of their children is 15 years old, and **the other** is 12.

ⓑ This is not good enough. Show me **another**.

ⓒ Some people like wrestling; **others** do not.

ⓓ Mary's here. Where are **the others**?

ⓔ To love is **one thing**, and to marry is **another**.

ⓕ They help **one another** (*or* **each other**).

ⓖ They keep horses and cattle; **the one** for riding, **the other** for food.

ⓗ **One** is red, **another** is white, and **a third** is green.

(2) **Such**

ⓐ Such는 보어이다.
이것은 단수·복수에 두루 쓰인다.
(내가 받은 보답은 이런 것이었다.)

ⓑ (그는 단지 어린아이이므로 그렇게 취급되야 한다.) such = a child

ⓒ such~as… = …과 같은 ~
such as~ = 가령 ~과 같은
(Washington과 Lincoln 같은 이는 드물다.)
(가을은 우리에게 배, 감, 사과 같은 과일을 준다.)

ⓓ (Jane은 매우 예의바른 소녀여서 누구나 귀여워한다.)
such+명사+that } 너무 ~하므로
so+형용사[부사]+that }
He had *such* a fever *that* he nearly died. = He was *so* feverish *that* he nearly died.

(3) **the same**

ⓐ 이 same에는 항상 the가 따른다.
여기서는 do의 목적어이다.
(그는 또 같은 짓을 할 것이다.)

ⓑ 이 same은 형용사이다.
the same ~ as : 동일 종류
the same ~ that : 동일물
(이것은 내가 그 여자에게 준 것과 같은 종류의 시계이다) — 동일 종류
(이것은 내가 그 여자에게 준 바로 그 시계이다.) — 동일물

ⓒ the same은 that 이외의 관계대명사나 관계부사와도 같이 쓰인다.
the same ~ where[when, who, as]

ⓓ 부사로서의 the same
(그들은 우리처럼 생각지 않는다.)
the same = in like manner

(4) **So**

ⓐ 목적어로서의 so
(그가 올까요? 나는 그가 오리라고 생각합니다.)

ⓑ 보어로서의 so
(그는 부자입니다.)
(**예,** 그는 정말 부자입니다. [= yes])
(그 여자도 **역시** 부자입니다. [= also])

C. **부정대명사**

(1) **One**

ⓐ 일반인 one은 대개 one으로 받는다.

ⓑ one = a house : 명사의 반복을 피함

ⓒ ones = stories
(이 이야기는 먼저 이야기들보다 더 흥미가 있다.)

ⓓ one = a certain (어떤)

(주의) one을 쓸 수 없는 경우

☞ 불가산명사에는 사용할 수 없다.
I like red wine better than *white*.

☞ 「소유격+own」 다음에는 사용할 수 없다. This bed is *my own*.

☞ 수사 다음에는 사용할 수 없다.
He has three cars and I have *two*.

☞ 최상급의 형용사, 「the+비교급」 뒤에는 사용할 수 없다.
He has two sisters; *the elder* is more beautiful than *the younger*.

(2) **Other, another**

ⓐ (그들 아이들 중 한 아이는 15살이고, 나머지 한 아이는 12살이다.)

ⓑ another = an+other
(이것은 그리 좋지 않다. 다른 것을 하나 보여 주시오.) — 다른 또 하나

ⓒ others : 지정되지 않은 다른 사람들
(어떤 사람들은 레슬링을 좋아하는데, 다른 사람들은 싫어한다.)

ⓓ the others : 지정된 다른 사람들
(Mary는 여기 있는데, 나머지 다른 사람들은 어디에 있느냐?)

ⓔ one thing ~ another (관용표현)
= A와 B는 별개의 것이다
(사랑하는 것과 결혼하는 것은 별개의 것이다.)

ⓕ 상호대명사

ⓖ the one ~ the other
전자 (혹은 후자) ~ 후자 (혹은 전자)
(그들은 말과 소를 키우는데, 전자는 승마용이고 후자는 식용이다.)

ⓗ 많은 것을 열거할 때
(하나는 붉고, 또 하나는 희고, 다음 것은 녹색이다.)

☞ 셋일 때 : one, another, *the* third

(3) **Some, any**

ⓐ Is there **any** wine left in the bottle? No, there isn't **any**.
If you have **any** money with you, please lend me **some**.
Would you like **some** more cheese?

ⓑ You can get the book at **any** bookseller's.

ⓒ The event occurred **some** twenty years ago.
He's living at **some** place in South America.

(4) **None, no**

ⓐ **None** have succeeded in solving the problem.
I looked for some jam, but there was **none** left.

ⓑ I have **no** children.
There were **no** clouds in the sky.
He is **no** genius.

(5) **Each, every, all**

ⓐ **Each** of the guests tried to flatter her.

ⓑ **Not every** good man will prosper.

ⓒ Write your answer on **every other** line.

ⓓ **All** of the students *were* present.
All of the money *was* stolen.

ⓔ I do not know him **at all**.
If you do it **at all**, do it well.
Do you know him **at all**?
I am surprised that he has succeeded **at all**.

(6) **-thing, -body**

ⓐ Is there **anything** interesting in today's paper?
Is **anybody** in the room?
I saw **something white** moving in the dark.

ⓑ Money is **everything** to her.
He thinks himself **something**.
If you want to be **anybody**, you must make efforts.
He's **nothing** here, but I suppose he's **somebody** in his native village.

(7) **Either, neither, both**

ⓐ Do you know **either** of the two sisters?
Either of the two sisters are beautiful, but if given a choice, I prefer the younger.

ⓑ If you don't go, I won't **either**.
If you will not do so, **neither** will I.

ⓒ I do **not** know **both** of the sisters.

(3) **Some, any**

ⓐ 의문문, 부정문, 조건문에서는 any를 쓰고, 긍정문에서는 some을 쓴다. 그러나, 긍정의 답을 예측하거나 남에게 권유, 의뢰할 때는 some을 의문문에 쓸 수 있다.

ⓑ 긍정문의 any : 「어떤 ~이라도」
(그 책은 어떤 서점에서도 구입할 수 있다.)

ⓒ some = about; a certain
(그 사건은 약 20년 전에 일어났다.)
(그는 남미 어딘가에 살고 있다.)

(4) **None, no**

none : 단독으로 쓰여 부정대명사.
no : 명사에 붙어 형용사로 쓰임.

none은 원래 no one의 뜻으로 대명사로서 단수·복수 어느 쪽에나 쓰이지만, 가산명사를 나타낼 때는 보통 복수 취급을 한다.

no는 I have~, There is~ 문형에서 not any 대신에 쓰여 「조금도 ~아닌」의 뜻을 나타낸다.

ⓐ (아무도 그 문제를 풀지 못했다.)
(나는 잼을 찾았지만, 전혀 남아 있지 않았다.)

ⓑ (나는 아이가 없다.)
(하늘에는 구름 한점 없었다.)
(그는 결코 천재가 아니다.)
☞ He is no genius.는 He is not a genius. 보다 강한 뜻이다.

(5) **Each, every, all**

ⓐ each : 「각자」, every : 「누구나 다」
(그 손님들 각자가 다 그녀에게 잘 보이려고 애썼다.)

ⓑ (선량한 사람이 모두 잘되란 법은 없다)
— 부분부정
☞ every, both, all 등이 부정어와 같이 쓰이면 **부분부정**이 된다.
Every man is **not** polite.
(모든 사람이 다 공손한 것은 아니다.)
I do **not** know **both** of them.
= I know one of them.
(난 그들 둘을 다 알지는 못한다.)
All of them will **not** come.
(그들 모두 다 오지는 않을 것이다.)

ⓒ (답을 한줄 건너[두줄마다] 써라.)
☞ every five days = every fifth day (닷새마다)

ⓓ (학생들은 전원 출석했다.)
— 사람 : 복수취급
(돈을 전부 도둑 맞았다.)
— 사물 : 단수취급

ⓔ (나는 그를 전혀 모른다.)
(기왕에 그것을 하려거든 잘 해라.)
(도대체 너는 그를 아느냐?)
(어쨌든 그가 성공했다니 놀랍다.)

(6) **-thing, -body**

any와 some의 용법에 준한다.

ⓐ (오늘 신문에 재미있는 게 있니?)
(방 안에 누가 있느냐?)
(나는 어둠 속에서 움직이는 흰 무엇을 보았다.)
☞ -thing의 대명사를 수식하는 형용사는 대개 그 뒤에 온다.

ⓑ everything : 「가장 중요한 것[사람]」
something : 「상당한 것[사람]」
anybody[somebody] : 「중요인물」
nothing : 「하찮은 것[사람]」
(돈이 그 여자에게는 가장 중요한 것이다.)
(그는 자신을 대단한 사람으로 여긴다.)
(유명인사가 되고 싶으면 노력을 해야한다.)
(그는 여기서는 아무것도 아니지만 자기 고향에서는 대단한 인물인 것 같다.)

(7) **Either, neither, both**

ⓐ (그 두 자매 중 어느 한 사람을 아니?)
…either : 「둘 중의 하나」
(그 두 자매 중 어느 쪽도 예쁘지만 선택하라면 동생이 더 낫다.)
…either : 「둘 중의 어느 쪽이든」

ⓑ (네가 가지 않으면 나도 역시 안 가겠다.)
…not 과 too는 같이 못 쓰며, too 대신 either를 쓴다.
(네가 그렇게 하지 않으면 나도 역시 안 하겠다.)
…not either = neither
☞ *neither* will I = *nor* will I

ⓒ (그 두 자매를 다 알지는 못한다.)
…not+both = 부분부정

문 법 · 작 문

A. Fill in each blank with a suitable word:

(1) _____ often have heavy rain in this part of the country.

(2) I took _____ for granted that his naughty son would misbehave again.

(3) _____ must be nice to have all your sons and daughters around you.

(4) Where was _____ that you left your briefcase?

(5) The cells of the body, especially _____ of the brain, can live only minutes without circulating blood.

(6) He is _____ an honest man that everybody trusts him.

(7) You won't find _____ easy to get a taxi.

(8) He overworked _____ to sickness.

(9) He is doing his usual work, and she is doing _____.

(10) If you want a true friend, you will find _____ in him.

(11) The twins are so alike that it is impossible to distinguish _____ from _____ _____ .

(12) She prides _____ on her loyalty to her family.

(13) He was so rich and didn't know what _____ was to be poor.

(14) To call oneself a patriot is one thing, and to be one is _____ .

B. Correct the errors in the following sentences:

(1) I have lost my electric shaver; I think I must buy it.

(2) I have no bookcase, and so I am going to have it made.

(3) I like jasmine tea better than lemon one.

(4) Some of my books are English and others are all Korean.

(5) She was more attractive than either of her three sisters.

(6) They are brothers; one is an accountant and another a veterinarian.

(7) Nobody except you and she saw him enter the room.

(8) His all novels are easy and interesting to read.

(9) His point of view is quite different from me.

C. 이탤릭체 부분을 대명사로 바꾸어라.

(1) His dress is *the dress* of a gentleman, but his speech and conduct are *the speech and conduct* of a clown.

(2) The new buildings are not yet finished, and the old *buildings* are still in use.

(3) If you are a lady, you must behave as *a lady*.

(4) This notebook is *my notebook*. That is *your notebook*.

D. 전체부정은 부분부정으로, 부분부정은 전체부정으로 바꿔 써라.

(1) I don't understand any of his speech.

(2) Everybody cannot be an Edison.

(3) None of his family are happy.

(4) I did not invite both of them.

(5) Neither of his parents is at home.

E. 괄호 안에서 맞는 것을 골라라.

(1) It was (he, him) who gave to charity regularly.

(2) These shoes of (him, his) are already worn out.

(3) He studied law in America, and (so, that) at Yale.

(4) His speech left a deep impression on (that, those) present.

(5) (Anybody couldn't, Nobody could) solve the crime before the end of the book.

(6) He asked (we, us) boys to report it to the police.

F. Translate the following into English:

(1) 여기서 학교까지의 거리는 2마일이며, 걸어서 약 30분 걸립니다.

(2) 내가 그 여자를 공원에서 만난 것은 가을의 어느 맑은 아침이었다.

(3) 그를 설득하려고 애써도 아무 소용이 없다.

(4) 그가 올지 안 올지는 아직 확실하지 않다.

(5) 너의 공부에 부지런한 것이 너의 의무라고 생각한다.

(6) 그 모임에 참석 못한다는 양해를 구하고 싶군요.

(7) 금년 추위는 작년 추위보다 심하다.

(8) 아무도 그런 계획에 동의하지 않을 것이다.

(9) 나는 그 문제들을 다 풀지는 못했다.

'My Father'라는 제목으로 70어 내외의 글을 지어라.

● 단 문 독 해 ●

One should respect one's superiors.

1. As **one** grows older **one** becomes more silent. In one's youth one is ready to pour oneself out to the world; one feels an intense fellowship with other people, one wants to throw oneself in their arms and one feels that they will receive one; one wants to penetrate into them; one's life seems to overflow into the lives of others and become one with theirs as the waters of rivers become one in the sea.

notes :
*In one's youth= When one is young
*be ready to= 기꺼이 ~하다
*intense 강렬한
*penetrate into= ~에 스며들다
*become one= 하나가 되다
*theirs=their lives

▶▶According to the above paragraph, which is incorrect?

① Most young people open their hearts when they are talking to each other.
② A sense of unity is easily formed between young people.
③ The young want to share their joys and sorrows with each other.
④ Many a young man tends to poke his nose into other people's business.
⑤ Young people tend to socialize with others very intensely.

▶▶영작하시오.

우리 직원들은 필요하면 늘 기꺼이 시간외 근무를 한다.

It is you that are wrong.

2. Those who have read everything are thought to understand everything too: but it is not always so. Reading furnishes the mind only with materials of knowledge: **it** is thinking **that** makes what we read ours.

notes :
*not always는 부분부정
*furnish A with B = A에게 B를 공급하다
*materials of knowledge = 지식의 재료들

▶▶윗글에서 언급되지 않은 것을 하나 골라라.

① A person of wide reading is not always wise.
② A person who reads everything does not know everything.
③ Random reading does more harm than good.
④ We can make what we read ours through our deep thinking.
⑤ Reading books provides us with only materials of knowledge.

▶▶영작하시오.

많이 배운 사람이 반드시 인생에서 성공하는 것은 아니다.

He has done it **by himself.**

3. Letters **in themselves** are not language, but merely symbols which are used for the sounds of which language is composed. There is no life or meaning in written symbols **by themselves**.

notes :
*letters 문자
*symbol 부호, 기호
*be composed of =consist of

▶▶Which of the following is the writer's ultimate argument?

① Letters are the most important among means by which we can express our thoughts.
② Any sound without letters to communicate is useless in a daily conversation.
③ The current letters we have are not perfect enough to describe all the sounds in the world.
④ Not until letters are combined together with sounds are they meaningful as a language.
⑤ Spoken language is more changeable than written language.

▶▶영작하시오.
유엔군은 다국적 군으로 구성될 것이다.

To be, or not to be: **that** is the question.

4. When we went there they had no sense of sin at all. They broke the commandments one after the other and never knew they were doing wrong. And I think **that** was the most difficult part of my work, to instill into the natives the sense of sin.

notes :
*commandment 계율 ; *the Ten Commandments* 십계명
*one after the other =one after another
*instill 불어넣다.

▶▶According to the above passage, which does the underlined word that imply?

① to compel the natives to obey the commandments
② to criticize the natives' faults
③ to educate the natives to be aware of their sins
④ to relieve the natives of their extreme sense of sin
⑤ to make the natives fully understand the commandments

▶▶영작하시오.
우리는 용감하게 헌신적으로 곤경에 차례차례 대처했다.

His behavior is **that** of a clown.
He was a child and treated **as such**.

5. I used to judge the worth of a person by his intellectual power and attainment. I could see no good where there was no logic, no charm where there was no learning. Now I think that one has to distinguish between the two forms of intelligence, **that** of the brain, and **that** of the heart, and I have come to regard the second as by far the more important.

notes :
*attainment 학식
*distinguish between=~을 구별하다
*by far=훨씬

▶▶Which of the following can we **not** reason from the above paragraph?

① It is not desirable to judge a man only by his intellectual power and academic achievements.
② The writer used to think highly of man's logic and level of education.
③ The intelligence of the heart can be complete through the help of academic training.
④ The writer now places the heart above the brain in valuing a person.
⑤ In the past the writer tended to consider an uneducated man worthless.

▶▶영작하시오.

서울의 교통 체증은 세계 어느 도시보다 심각하다.

6. His opinion may be summarized like **this**. Love of power, like vanity, is a strong element in normal human nature, and **as such** is to be accepted; it becomes deplorable only when it is excessive.

notes :
*summarize 요약하다(=sum up)
*human nature =인간의 본성
*is to be=must be
*deplorable 개탄할 만한

▶▶윗글의 내용과 일치하도록 다음 빈칸에 알맞은 말끼리 짝지어진 것은?

Like vanity, love of power should be accepted as a (　　) factor in human nature. But if it goes beyond what is (　　), the situation can become lamentable.

① strong — weak　② negligible — sensible
③ powerful — reasonable　④ poisonous — extreme
⑤ insignificant — uncontrollable

▶▶영작하시오.

권력욕은 거의 우리들 모두에게 있다. 그러나 권력만을 쫓는 사람은 멸시를 받아야 한다.

> Virtue and vice are before you; **the former** leads to happiness, **the latter** to misery.

7. Public men are nearly always being overblamed or overpraised, and the more knowledge they have of themselves, the less likely they are to be unduly depressed by ⓐ**the former** or to be unduly elated by ⓑ**the latter**.

notes :
*overblame 과도하게 비난하다
*overpraise 과찬하다
*be likely to = ~할 것 같다
*unduly 부당하게
*be depressed = 의기소침하다
*be elated = 우쭐하다

▶▶윗글의 밑줄친 ⓐthe former와 ⓑthe latter가 가리키는 것을 우리말로 구체적으로 쓰시오.

ⓐ the former ______________________.

ⓑ the latter ______________________.

▶▶영작하시오.

그 미국인은 서울을 잘 알고 있다.

> **It** is wrong **to cheat** on the examination.
> **It** is true **that** right is might.

8. No young man can possibly see immediately the qualities of a great book. Remember that in many cases **it** has taken mankind hundreds of years **to find** out all that is in such a book. But **it** depends upon a man's knowledge and experience of life, **whether** the text will unfold new meanings to him.

notes :
*possibly는 can과 함께 쓰여 강조의 뜻
*quality 내용, 질
*unfold = open

▶▶According to the above paragraph, which of the following is **not** correct?

① As for young men, it is too difficult to recognize all the qualities of a great book at once.

② In many cases it has taken us hundreds of years to realize exactly what is in a great book.

③ A great book may not be very helpful to a man if he doesn't have enough experience of life to understand it.

④ The reader's experience is more important than his knowledge in the comprehension of a great book.

⑤ How fully one can understand a great book depends on his knowledge and experience.

▶▶영작하시오.

그 산의 정상에 오르는데 우리는 3시간이 걸렸다.

● 장 문 독 해 ●

Warming-up

We **are inclined to** forget our gratitude to our teachers.
You may not go out until you **finish** your homework.
He has knowledge, and experience **as well**.
Few people ever made a great success of life without being industrious.
For companionship there are **none** I would place above good books.

1 A good farmer is always one of the most intelligent and best educated men in our society. We have been inclined in our wild industrial development, to forget that agriculture is the base of our whole economy and that in the economic structure of the nation ⓐ<u>it</u> is always the cornerstone. It has always been so throughout history and ⓑ<u>it will continue to be so</u> until there are no more men on this earth. We are apt to forget that the man who owns land and cherishes it and works it well is the source of our stability as a nation, not only in the economic but the social sense as well. Few great leaders ever came out of city slums or even suburbs. In every country most of the men who have molded the destinies of the nation have come off the land or from small towns. The great majority of leaders, even in the world of industry and finance, have come from ⓒ<u>there</u>. I have known all kinds of people, many of them celebrated in many countries, but for companionship, good conversation, intelligence and the power of stimulating one's mind there are none I would place above the good farmer.

Louis Bromfield: *Pleasant Valley*

Notes

be inclined to ~하는 경향이 있다 / structure 구조 / cornerstone 초석(礎石) / work=cultivate / stability 안정 / as well=also / slum 빈민굴 / suburbs 교외 주택 지역 / come off the land 농촌 출신이다 / celebrated 유명한 / stimulate 자극하다 / *I would place love above knowledge.*

Question

1. 본문의 밑줄 친 ⓐIt과 ⓒthere가 가리키는 것을 우리말로 쓰시오.

2. 본문의 밑줄 친 ⓑit will continue to be so를 다음과 같이 풀어 쓸 때, 빈칸에 적절한 말을 골라 쓰시오.

( ) is still going to be the ( ) of the national economic structure in the future.

[agriculture, technology, founder, foundation]

3. According to the passage, which is **not** correct?
   ① It is a good farmer who is the very essence of a nation and keeps it stable and going.
   ② We, living in an industrial society, are liable to forget the importance of agriculture.
   ③ The majority of great leaders in the field of business and industry got an advanced education in the country.
   ④ The author has been acquainted with all kinds of people who are honored and famous in many nations.
   ⑤ The author thinks very highly of the good farmer for companionship.

4. Which is most suitable for the main topic of the passage?
   ① The excessive development of industry and finance tends to damage the prestige the farmers have enjoyed.
   ② We cannot but allow ourselves to get carried away in the wild stream of industrial development to the ruin of our agriculture.
   ③ More positions should be open to many talented men living in the country.
   ④ We should keep in mind that agriculture is the essence to maintain the stability of our economy and society.
   ⑤ Compared with people from urban areas, those from rural areas are more likely to get ahead in every field.

Production

(1) 식사를 많이 한 후에는 졸음이 오는 경향이 있다.
(2) 90세까지 사는 사람은 드물다.
(3) 나 자신의 이익을 위해서 나는 이것을 하지, 딴 이유는 전혀 없다.
(4) 농업이 국가의 근본이라는 것을 우리는 망각하기 쉽다.

● 장 문 독 해 ●

Warming-up

You may stay here **as long as** you keep quiet.
His sincerity **led** me **to** agree to his proposal.
It is hard for us **not to** betray our intention by our behavior.
He has **done**, and will continue to **do his best** in his work.

2 It is a common saying that thought is free. A man can never be hindered from thinking whatever he chooses as long as he conceals what he thinks. The working of his mind is limited only by the bounds of his experience and the power of his imagination. But this natural liberty of private thinking is of little value. It is unsatisfactory and even painful to the thinker himself, if he is not permitted to communicate his thoughts to others, and it is obviously of no value to his neighbors. Moreover it is extremely difficult to hide thoughts that have any power over the mind. If a man's thinking leads him to call in question ideas and customs which regulate the behavior of those about him, to reject beliefs which they hold, to see better ways of life than those they follow, it is almost impossible for him, if he is convinced of the truth of his own reasoning, not to betray by silence, chance words, or general attitude that he is different from them and does not share their opinions. Some have preferred, like Socrates, some would prefer today, to face death rather than conceal their thoughts. Thus freedom of thought, in any valuable sense, includes freedom of speech.

***John B. Bury:** A History of Freedom of Thought*

Notes

bound 제한, 범위 / of little value, of no value 가치가 없는(=valueless) / have any power over ~을 다소라도 지배하다 / call in question 의심하다(=doubt) / to reject, to see는 leads him에 걸린다 / that he is의 that는 betray에 걸리는 접속사 / reasoning 추리 / prefer … rather than ~=~보다 …를 택하다 / conceal 감추다

Question

1. 본문의 8행의 밑줄친 it이 가리키는 것을 써라.

2. 본문과 일치하도록 다음 빈칸에 적절한 어구를 찾아 쓰시오.

Without freedom of (   ), freedom of (   ) is meaningless and even painful to the thinker.

[action, imagination, thought, life, speech, movement]

3. According to the passage, which does **not** correspond with it?
   ① Whatever a man thinks can not be restricted by others if it is not exposed to them.
   ② Someone's thought can be useful to his neighbors only when it is expressed.
   ③ Many people, like Socrates, have confidently revealed their thoughts at the risk of their death.
   ④ If a man's ideas are confidently expressed, they will be definitely helpful to the development of society.
   ⑤ Only man's experience and imaginative power can limit the working of his mind.

4. Which is most suitable for the main topic of the passage?
   ① The main function of freedom of speech is to make people resist established ideas and customs.
   ② Everyone should be allowed to express himself or herself regardless of others' reactions.
   ③ Freedom of thought in a sense must be based on freedom of speech.
   ④ We should be ready to die for the further extension of freedom of speech.
   ⑤ Freedom of thought is not compatible with freedom of speech.

Production

(1) 그렇게 좋은 아이디어라도 그것을 실천할 수 없으면 가치가 없다는 것은 명백하다.(put into practice)
(2) 그녀의 미소에 끌려서 그는 약속을 하고 말았다.
(3) 그는 자기 이론의 진리를 확신했고, 그 진리를 부인하기보다는 차라리 죽음을 맞이했다.

실 력 체 크 I

1 다음 글을 읽고 아래 물음에 답하여라.

There are many ways in which we can be peacemakers. One way is to tolerate the opinions and desires of others. Many quarrels result from arguments in which men become angry at the opinions others express. Many religious wars have arisen because one party would not tolerate the beliefs of others. Every man has a right to his opinion. However foolish an opinion may seem, we should allow it to be expressed and should not (ㄱ)take offense because others don't think as we do. Quarrels arise because our desires conflict with those of others. At home two children sometimes desire the same thing, and neither will give way to the other. We should be willing to give in to many of the desires of others. Unselfishness promotes peace. If all of us are willing to let others have their fair share of things, and their own places in games at home and at school, we can live in (ㄴ)__________.

notes :
those of others에서 those=desires / give way=give in 양보하다 / unselfishness 이타적임, 헌신적임

(1) 밑줄친 (ㄱ)을 우리말로 옮겨라.
(2) (ㄴ)의 빈칸에 알맞은 단어 하나를 써 넣어라.
(3) 윗글의 대의를 간단히 적어라.

2 다음 글을 읽고 물음에 답하여라.

In men, as a rule, love is but an episode which takes its place among the other affairs of the day, and ①the emphasis laid on it in novels gives it an importance which is untrue to life. There are few men to whom it is the most important thing in the world, and (ㄱ)they are not very interesting ones; even women, with whom ②the subject is of paramount interest, have a contempt for (ㄴ)them. (ㄷ)They are pleased and excited by (ㄹ)them, but have an uneasy feeling that (ㅁ)they are poor creatures. But even during the brief intervals in which ③they are in love, men do other things which turn their minds aside; they are absorbed in sport; they can interest themselves in art.

notes :
but = only / paramount 최고의 / have a contempt for = ~을 경멸하다 / uneasy 불안한 / interest oneself in = be interested in / (ㄷ)의 they = women

(1) ①의 내용이 무엇인지 간단히 우리말로 적어라.
(2) ②의 밑줄 친 부분을 한 단어로 바꾸어라.
(3) ③의 they가 가리키는 것은?
(4) (ㄱ)~(ㅁ)의 대명사중 가리키는 것이 나머지와 다른 것을 하나 골라라.

3 다음 글을 읽고 아래의 물음에 답하여라.

When we are asked to specify the debt which civilization owes to the Greeks, their achievements in literature and art naturally occur to us first of all. But a truer answer may be that our deepest gratitude is due to ⓐ <u>them</u> as the originators of liberty of thought and discussion. For this freedom of spirit was not only the condition of their speculations in philosophy, their progress in science, their experiments in political institutions; ⓑ <u>it</u> was also a condition of their literary and artistic excellence. Their literature, for instance, could not have been what it is if they had been prevented from free criticism of life. But apart from what they actually accomplished, even if they had not achieved the wonderful things they did in most of the fields of human activity, their assertion of the principle of liberty would place them in the highest rank among the benefactors of the race; for ⓒ <u>it</u> was one of the greatest steps in human progress.

notes :
specify 상술하다 / debt 은혜 / occur to =(머리에) 떠오르다 / be due to=응당 치러져야 하다 / originator 창시자 / speculation 사색 / apart from=~은 별도로 하고 / field 분야 / assertion 주장 / benefactor 은인

(1) 밑줄친 ⓐ, ⓑ, ⓒ는 본문 중의 어느 어구를 받는가?

(2) 윗글에 의하면 그리스인이 인류문명에 기여한 가장 큰 공헌은?
① 위대한 문학예술의 업적 ② 여러 정치제도의 운용
③ 심오한 철학적인 사색 ④ 과학의 찬란한 진보
⑤ 사상과 토론의 자유를 창시한 것

4 다음 글을 읽고 아래 물음에 답하여라.

It has recently been remarked by Dr. William Russel that "Too much leisure with too much money has been the dread of societies across the ages. That is when nations cave in from within. That is when they fall." Too much of a good thing is, of course, never any good, and since work is a necessity of existence, an unhealthy disproportion of ⓐ <u>one</u> in relation to ⓑ <u>the other</u> is likely to have undesirable consequences. As every man who has lived long enough to learn ⓒ <u>it</u> knows, the principal, the most enduring, and the most reliable source of happiness is work.

notes :
dread 공포, 걱정, 불안 / existence 존재, 생존 / disproportion 불균형 / in relation to ~=~에 관하여 / consequence 결과 / principal 근원적인, 근본적인 / enduring 지속적인 / reliable 확실한, 의지할 수 있는

(1) 국가가 내부적으로 붕괴하는 때는 어느 때인가?
(2) 밑줄친 ⓐone과 ⓑthe other는 무엇을 가리키는가?
(3) 밑줄친 ⓒit이 가리키는 내용을 우리말로 써라.

실 력 체 크 Ⅱ

A. 두 문장의 뜻이 같아지도록 공란을 메워라.

(1) I know why he refused the offer.
I know ______ made him refuse the offer.

(2) Your pronunciation is far from perfect.
Your pronunciation leaves ______ to be desired.

(3) He will recover his health soon.
It will not be long ______ he gets well.

(4) It makes me sick to see him.
The ______ of him makes me sick.

(5) I disliked him at first, but I've grown to like him.
I didn't like him at first, but he's grown ______ me.

(6) Everybody kept silent.
Nobody seemed to know ______ to say.

(7) Your proposal can not be accepted.
I find your proposal ______ .

(8) They did not understand what I meant.
I could not make myself ______ .

(9) He will never con you into buying such useless junk.
He is the ______ person to con you into buying such useless junk.

(10) I think he is a man of high character.
I have nothing to say ______ his character.

B. 두 문장의 뜻이 같아지도록 공란을 메워라.

(1) The bomb threat ______ to be a hoax.
The bomb threat ______ out to be a hoax.

(2) They're not so ______ friends as lovers.
They're lovers ______ than friends.

(3) The policeman knew ______ than to argue with a drunken man.
The policeman was not ______ a fool as to argue with a drunken man.

(4) If you want to learn, you must not be ______ asking questions.
If you want to learn, you must not be ______ proud to ask questions.

(5) He is ______ as the highest authority on biochemistry.
He is looked ______ as the highest authority on biochemistry.

Answer: A. (1) what (2) much (3) before (4) sight (5) on (6) what (7) unacceptable (8) understood (9) last (10) against
B. (1) proved, turned (2) much, rather (3) better, such (4) above, too (5) regarded, on

C. 각 문장 안의 적당한 곳에 한 단어를 넣어 문장을 완성하여라.

(1) If anyone commits something illegal, he will be punished it.
(2) He was taken advantage of a phony salesman and suffered a fatal loss.
(3) However much she spends her dresses, she still doesn't look any good.
(4) Mr. Jones was really looked up by all the students.
(5) Things we are familiar are apt to escape our notice.
(6) Please help to the cakes and pass them around.
(7) Every student should look all the new words in his dictionary.
(8) On my last visit to Rome I enjoyed very much.
(9) Never did I expect such misfortune would fall on us.
(10) He was a timid man and not easy to talk.

D. 공란을 적당한 단어로 메워라.

(1) His concerns come down _______ worries about losing money.
(2) The attorney general promised to come down hard _______ drug dealers.
(3) He started as an office boy and ended _______ as president of the company.
(4) She talked her husband _______ buying a new car.
(5) He is a good doctor, _______ doctors go nowadays.
(6) I have found a true friend _______ him.

E. 다음 (1), (2) 대화에 각각 공통으로 들어갈 낱말 하나씩을 써라.

(1) A: I use the same airline everytime I (   ). What airline do you use?
B: I usually (   ) Singapore Airlines.
A: Do you (   ) economy class?
B: Sometimes I (   ) economy, sometimes business class.

(2) A: Mary told me that her husband had bought her a new diamond ring for her birthday.
B: Really? (   ) consideration!
A: That's not all. She also said that he had bought her a new Mercedes Benz as well.
B: Wow, that's amazing, but (   )'s a new Mercedes Benz to a billionaire like him?

Answer: C. (1) for it (2) of by (3) spends on (4) up to (5) familiar with (6) help yourself (7) look up (8) enjoyed myself (9) such a (10) talk to
D. (1) to (2) on (3) up (4) into (5) as (6) in
E. (1) fly (2) what

어 휘 · 발 음

A. 이탤릭체 부분의 뜻과 가장 가까운 추상명사를, [　　　] 안에 주어진 철자로 시작하여 완성하여라.

(1) I *met him halfway* and lent him $100. [com______]
(2) The boy *made believe* that he was lame. [pre______]
(3) Charles was *out of spirits*. [dep______]
(4) Patricia *has no interest* in politics. [ind______]
(5) We were kept *in the dark* as to future plans. [ig______]
(6) Please move aside; you are *in the way*. [obs______]
(7) He likes to *put his nose* into his neighbor's affairs. [int______]

B. Replace the underlined part by a word:

(1) The disaster was <u>of the kind that nothing could help</u>.
(2) The author is a master of <u>serious plays with unhappy endings</u>.
(3) They left on a well-equipped ship to <u>travel in and investigate</u> the antarctic regions.
(4) He is a <u>man who believes everything will turn out for the worst</u>.

C. Give a word corresponding in meaning to the underlined part:

(1) <u>Many nations</u> took part in the conference; it was an (　　) conference.
(2) He is <u>fond of inquiring into other people's affairs</u>; he is an (　　) person.
(3) He is <u>shamelessly rude</u>; he is an (　　) person.
(4) His strength seems <u>more than human</u>; he has (　　) strength.

D. Connect the words on [A] with those on [B]:

[A] (1) juvenile (2) top (3) sour (4) artificial (5) stray
(6) narrow (7) first (8) golden (9) necessary (10) tropical

[B] ⓐ sheep ⓑ aid ⓒ delinquency ⓓ zone ⓔ satellites
ⓕ age ⓖ grapes ⓗ evil ⓘ secret ⓙ escape

Answer: A. (1) compromise (2) pretense (3) depression (4) indifference (5) ignorance (6) obstruction (7) interference
B. (1) unavoidable (2) tragedies (3) explore (4) pessimist
C. (1) international (2) inquisitive (3) impudent [insolent, impertinent] (4) superhuman
D. (1) ⓒ (2) ⓘ (3) ⓖ (4) ⓔ (5) ⓐ (6) ⓙ (7) ⓑ (8) ⓕ (9) ⓗ (10) ⓓ

동철이음이의어 (Heteronym)

발음에 따라 의미가 변하는 단어

A. abuse [əbjúːs] *n.* 남용
[əbjúːz] *v.* 남용하다
attribute [ǽtribjuːt] *n.* 속성, 성질
[ətríbjuːt] *v.* ~으로 돌리다
bow [bou] *n.* 활
[bau] *v.* 인사하다
conduct [kándʌkt] *n.* 행위
[kəndʌ́kt] *v.* 행동하다
desert [dézərt] *n.* 사막
[dizə́ːrt] *v.*도망치다, 버리다
digest [dáidʒest] *n.* 요약
[daidʒést] *v.* 소화하다
excuse [ikskjúːs] *n.* 구실
[ikskjúːz] *v.* 변명하다
extract [ékstrækt] *n.* 발췌
[ikstrǽkt] *v.* 발췌하다
lead [led] *n.* 납
[liːd] *v.* 인도하다
mouth [mauθ] *n.* 입
[mauð] *v.* 입에 넣다
object [ábdʒikt] *n.* 물건
[əbdʒékt] *v.* 반대하다
project [prádʒekt] *n.* 계획
[prədʒékt] *v.* 계획하다
protest [próutest] *n.* 항의
[prətést] *v.* 항의하다
rebel [rébl] *n.* 반역자
[ribél] *v.* 반역하다
record [rékɔːrd] *n.* 기록
[rikɔ́ːrd] *v.* 기록하다
sow [sau] *n.* 암돼지
[sou] *v.* 종자를 뿌리다
tear [tiər] *n.* 눈물
[tɛər] *v.* 찢다
wind [wind] *n.* 바람
[waind] *v.* 감다
use [juːs] *n.* 사용
[juːz] *v.* 사용하다

B. absent [ǽbs(ə)nt] *a.* 부재의
[æbsént] *v.* 결석하다
close [klous] *a.* 밀접한
[klouz] *v.* 닫다 *n.* 끝
converse [kánvəːrs] *a.* 반대의
[kənvə́ːrs] *v.* 담화하다
frequent [fríːkwənt] *a.* 빈번한
[frikwént] *v.* 자주 가다
intimate [íntəmit] *a.* 친근한
[íntəmeit] *v.* 암시하다
live [laiv] *a.* 살아있는
[liv] *v.* 살다
minute [mínit] *n.* 분, 잠시
[mainjúːt] *a.* 세밀한
moderate [mádərit] *a.* 적당한
[mádəreit] *v.* 조절하다
perfect [pə́ːrfikt] *a.* 완전한
[pərfékt] *v.* 완성하다
present [préznt] *a.*현재의 *n.*선물
[prizént] *v.* 선물하다
separate [sépərit] *a.* 분리된
[sépəreit] *v.* 분리하다
subject [sʌ́bdʒikt] *n.*주제 *a.*종속의
[səbdʒékt] *v.* 종속시키다

C. drawer [drɔ́ːər] *n.* 끄는 사람
[drɔːr] *n.* 서랍
mankind [mænkáind] *n.* 인류
[mǽnkaind] *n.* 남성
prayer [prɛər] *n.* 기도
[préiər] *n.* 기도하는 사람
recollect [rekəlékt] *v.*회상하다
re-collect [ríːkəlékt] *v.*다시 모으다
row [rou] *n.* 열, *v.*노젓다
[rau] *n.v.* 소동(을 피우다)
sewer [sóuər] *n.* 재봉사
[sjúər] *n.* 하수구
shower [ʃóuər] *n.* 보여주는것(사람)
[ʃáuər] *n.*소나기

숙 어

(1) **keep company with** (=associate with, be friendly with) ~와 사귀다
☞ They had *kept company with* each other for ages before they married.

(2) **keep from** (=refrain from) ~을 삼가다
☞ I can't *keep from* laughing. *Keep* your dog *from* running here.

(3) **keep[bear] ~ in mind** (=remember) 명심하다, 기억하다
☞ *Keep*[*Bear*] your voters *in mind* when you deliver your speech.
Keep[*Bear*] *in mind* that I can't walk as fast as you.

(4) **keep in touch with** (=continue in communication with) 접촉을 유지하다
☞ He promised to *keep in touch with* us while he was abroad.

(5) **keep late hours** (=stay awake until late at night) 늦게까지 자지 않다
☞ Keeping early hours is better than *keeping late hours* for health.

(6) **keep[ward] off** (=avert) 가까이 오지 못하게 하다, 막다
☞ She used a bug spray to *keep*[*ward*] *off* the mosquitoes.

(7) **keep one's cool** (=retain one's composure) 침착하다, 냉정을 유지하다
☞ You have to *keep your cool*, no matter what the boss says.

(8) **keep up with** (=keep abreast with *or* of) ~에 뒤떨어지지 않다
☞ You walk so fast that I cannot *keep up with* you.
I tried to *keep up with* the times.

(9) **know ~ by sight[name]** (=know one's face[name]) ~얼굴[이름]을 알다
☞ I *know* the man who died of lung cancer *by sight*, but not *by name*.

(10) **know[tell] ~ from** (=distinguish ~ from) 구별하다
☞ I've met her several times, but she says she still doesn't *know*[*tell*] me *from* my brother.

(11) **know the ropes** (=know one's job very well) (요령·사정 등을) 잘 알다
☞ Never argue with him!; he's worked here for 25 years, so he really *knows the ropes*.

(12) **lacking in** (=wanting in) ~이 부족한
☞ I'm afraid she's somewhat *lacking in* intelligence.

(13) **land on one's feet** (=get oneself out of trouble without damage) 무사히 궁지를 벗어나다
☞ He lost his job but *landed on his feet* by finding a better one.

(14) **lash out** (=hit someone suddenly ; offer harsh criticism) (갑자기 달려들어) 때리다, 구타하다 ; 폭언을 퍼붓다
☞ The prisoner *lashed out* at the guard.
She *lashes out* at anyone who finds fault with her.

(15) **lay off** (=stop employing temporarily) (일시) 해고시키다
☞ When they lost the contract, they had to *lay off* about a hundred workers.

(16) **lay out** (=arrange) 배열하다, 배치하다
☞ They *laid out* the tables in style for the party.

(17) **learn[know] ~ by heart** (=memorize) 암기하다
☞ I make a point of *learning*[*knowing*] at least 10 English idioms *by heart* a day.

(18) **leave out** (=omit, fail to include) 빠뜨리다
☞ This sentence doesn't make sense; a key word has been *left out*.

(19) **let on** (=reveal) (비밀을) 누설하다
☞ Don't *let on* to Helen that we are going to the movies.

(20) **let go of** (=release) (쥐고 있던 것을) 놓다
☞ Don't *let go of* the rope until I tell you.

Exercise

▶▶ 주어진 단어들을 포함한 글을 지어라. 필요하면 어형을 변화시켜라.

1. mind / interested / buy
2. call / keep / sleep / morning
3. do / ropes / show
4. food / lacking / vitamin / health
5. opposition / lash / policy
6. recession / lay / month
7. son / learn / multiplication
8. leave / name / list
9. ask / where / let
10. let / of / arm

13. 대 명 사(Pronoun) Ⅱ

기본 문법 설명

A. 의문대명사

(1) **Who** is that woman over there? She is Susan, my aunt.
What is she? She is a dentist.

(2) **Who** sent you the e-mail about the new plan?
What made you change your mind?

(3) What does his secretary do in his absence?
He doesn't care **what his secretary does** in his absence.

(4) What is his job?
Do you know **what his job is**?
What do you think **his job is**?

(5) **Who did it** is a question to me.
The question is **who did it**.
Tell me **who did it**.
There is no doubt *as to* **who did it**.

(6) You have no idea **how depressed it made me**.

B. 관계대명사

Ⅰ. 종류와 용법

(1) **who**

ⓐ The man **who** called yesterday wants to buy the house.

ⓑ The guy **whom** you met there is my brother.
The man *to* **whom** I gave the present thanked me.

ⓒ That's the man **whose** house was burnt down.
The man **whose** car you borrowed needs it tomorrow.

ⓓ I picked up a man **who** I thought was honest.
I picked up a man **whom** I thought to be honest.

(2) **which**

ⓐ He has a dog **which** barks furiously.
Please give me a room **which** commands a fine view.

ⓑ The mountain **whose** top[the top **of which**, **of which** the top] is covered with snow is Kilimanjaro.

ⓒ There was some reason **which** he could not understand.
The paint on the seat *on* **which** you're sitting is still wet.

A. 의문대명사

(1) Who는 사람의 성명, 혈족 관계.
What은 사람의 직업, 신분 및 물건.

(2) 의문대명사가 주어일 때는 do, did와 같은 조동사가 필요 없다.
(누가 너에게 그 새로운 계획에 대한 이메일을 보냈느냐?)
(무엇 때문에 너의 생각을 바꿨느냐?)

(3) 의문문이 다른 문장의 종속절이 될 때는 평서문의 어순이 된다.
What does he want?
Ask him *what he wants*.
What did you do?
He asked me *what I had done*.

(4) Do you know what his job is?
(그의 직업이 무엇인지 아십니까?)
의 대답은 yes, no로 할 수 있으나,
What do you think his job is?
(그의 직업이 무엇이라 생각합니까?)
의 대답은 yes, no로 할 수가 없다.
이런 경우 의문사는 문두에 나간다.
이런 동사는 think, suppose, believe, imagine, guess등이다.
What do you suppose he did?

(5) 의문사절은 명사처럼 글의 주어, 목적어, 보어의 역할을 한다.
(누가 그것을 했는지가 나에게 문제가 된다.) … 주어의 역할
(문제는 누가 그것을 했느냐이다.) … 보어의 역할
(누가 그것을 했는지 말해다오.) … 동사의 목적어
(누가 그것을 했는지에 대해 의심할 바 없다.) … 전치사의 목적어

(6) 의문사절이 전치사의 목적어가 될 때, 전치사가 생략되는 경우가 있다.
(그것이 나를 얼마나 우울하게 했었는지 넌 전혀 모른다.)
… *of*가 생략된 것이다.
= You have no idea *of* how depressed it made me.

B. 관계대명사

Ⅰ. 종류와 용법

(1) **who**

ⓐ (어제 전화했던 남자가 그 집을 사고 싶어한다.) … 주격
I see some boys in the room *who* are reading books
She has an adopted child *who* she says was an orphan.
Who(=He who) steals my purse steals trash. (돈은 잃어도 아깝지 않다.)

ⓑ (네가 거기서 만난 사람은 나의 동생이다.) … 동사의 목적격
(내가 그 선물을 준 그 남자는 내게 감사했다.) … 전치사의 목적격
The girl *who* you met is my sister.
구어에서는 whom 대신에 who를 쓰기도 한다.
Whom(=Those whom) the gods love die young. (才士短命)-Byron

ⓒ (저 사람이 자기 집이 다 타버린 그 사람이다.) … 소유격
(당신이 빌린 차의 주인이 내일 그 차가 필요하다고 한다.)

ⓓ (나는 정직하다고 생각하는 사람을 골랐다.)
첫째 글의 I thought는 삽입절이며 who는 was의 주어이다.
둘째 글의 whom은 thought의 목적어이다.

(2) **which**

ⓐ (그에게는 심하게 짖는 개가 한 마리 있다.) … 주격[동물]
(전망이 좋은 방 하나 주세요.)[사물]
He is not the man *which* his father wants him to be. (그는 그의 아버지가 바라는 그런 성품의 사람은 아니다.)

ⓑ (꼭대기가 눈으로 덮여 있는 저 산은 Kilimanjaro 이다.)… 소유격

ⓒ (그가 이해할 수 없는 어떤 이유가 있었다.)… 목적격[동사의 목적어]
(네가 앉아 있는 자리의 페인트는 아직 덜 말랐다.) [전치사의 목적어]

ⓓ They thought him dull, **which** he was not.
She said nothing, **which** made him more angry.

(3) **that**

ⓐ He is *the only* friend **that** I have.

ⓑ *Who* **that** has common sense can believe such a thing?

ⓒ He spoke of *the men and the things* **that** he had seen.

ⓓ This is the book **that** I spoke *of*.

(4) **what**

ⓐ **What** he said was lost in the applause that greeted him.

ⓑ Are you doing **what** you think is right?

ⓒ My uncle has made me **what** I am today.

ⓓ She is **what you call** a talented woman.
Reading **is to** the mind **what** food **is to** the body.
He is clever, and **what is better still**, very brave.
What with illness **and** (**what with**) poverty, she is unhappy.

Ⅱ. 제한적 용법과 계속적 용법

(1) He had four sons **who** became doctors.
He had four sons, **who** became doctors.

(2) I hate Jack, **who** habitually tells lies.
I met a boy, **who** told me the news.
The farmer, **who** is poor, is honest.

Ⅲ. 관계대명사의 생략

(1) The women (**whom**) you mentioned are all former employees.
He has no friend (**whom**) he can depend *on*.
This is the problem (**which**) he alone has to deal *with*.

(2) ⓐ He is not the man (**that**) he was.
She is not the cheerful woman (**that**) she used to be.

ⓑ He is one of the greatest scholars (**that**) there are in the world.

ⓒ There is a lady (**who**) wants to see you.
It was Wilson (**that**) told me this.
Who was it (**that**) told you the matter?

ⓓ 명사, 대명사 이외에 형용사, 구, 절을 선행사로 가질 수 있다.
(그들은 그를 어리석다고 생각했지만, 그는 그렇지가 않았다.)
… which의 선행사는 dull
(그녀는 아무말도 하지 않았는데, 그것이 그를 더욱 화나게 했다.)
… which의 선행사는 She said nothing
I beckoned her to come here, *which* she did not. (그녀에게 이리로 오라고 손짓했지만 오지 않았다.)
… which의 선행사는 come here

(3) **that**

ⓐ that은 who 대신에 사용되나 한정의 뜻이 강하므로 선행사에 최상급의 형용사, 서수사, the only, the very, all 등이 올 때 흔히 쓰인다.
ⓑ 선행사가 who 일때 (상식이 있는 사람이라면 누가 그런 것을 믿겠는가?)
ⓒ 선행사가 「사람과 사물[동물]」인 경우
ⓓ that 앞에는 전치사를 못 쓴다.

(4) **what**

ⓐ (그의 말은 그를 환영하는 박수소리에 묻혀 들리지 않았다.) … 주어
ⓑ (당신은 옳다고 생각하는 것을 하고 있는 겁니까?) … 목적어
ⓒ (나의 아저씨가 나를 오늘날의 나로 만드셨다.) … 보어
ⓓ (그녀는 소위 재능있는 여자이다.)
what we[you, they] call
= what is[are] called (소위)
(독서가 정신에 대한 관계는 음식이 신체에 대한 관계와 같다.)
A is to B what C is to D
= A가 B에 대한 관계는 C가 D에 대한 관계와 같다.
(그는 영리하다. 더욱 좋은 것은 매우 용감하다.)
(한편으로는 병 또 한편으로는 가난으로 인해 그 여자는 불행하다.)

II. 제한적 용법과 계속적 [비제한적] 용법

(1) (그는 의사가 된 네 아들이 있었다.)
… 제한적 용법—의사가 아닌 아들이 또 있었는지도 모른다.
(그는 아들이 넷 있었는데, 모두 의사가 되었다.) … 계속적 용법

(2) (나는 Jack을 싫어하는데 왜냐하면 그는 습관적으로 거짓말을 하기 때문이다.)
<, who = for he>
(나는 한 소년을 만났는데, 그가 그 소식을 내게 말했다.)
<, who = and he>
(그 농부는 비록 가난하지만 정직하다.)
<, who = though he>

III. 관계대명사의 생략

(1) 관계대명사는 동사의 목적어나 전치사의 목적어가 될 때 생략할 수 있다.
(네가 언급했던 그 여자들은 모두 이전 직원들이다.) … 동사의 목적어
(그는 의지할 친구가 없다.)
… 전치사의 목적어
(이것은 그가 혼자 처리해야 하는 문제다) … 관계대명사를 생략할 때, 관계대명사 앞에 있는 전치사는 뒤에 온다.

(2) 주격 관계대명사의 생략

ⓐ 관계대명사가 보어가 될 때
(그는 옛날의 그가 아니다.)
(그 여자는 이제 옛날 처럼의 쾌활한 여자는 아니다.)
ⓑ 관계대명사 다음에 there is[are]가 계속될 때
(그는 세계적인 대학자의 한 분이다.)
He taught me the difference (that) there is between right and wrong.
(선악의 차이를 가르쳐 주었다.)
ⓒ There is ~ , It is ~ 의 구문
(너를 만나고자 하는 부인이 있다.)
(이것을 내게 이야기한 사람은 Wilson 이었다.)
(그 일을 너에게 이야기한 사람은 누구였느냐?)

Ⅳ. 복합관계대명사

(1) ⓐ Could I speak to **whoever** is in charge of sales?
ⓑ Give it to **whomever** you please.
ⓒ Choose **whichever** you like.
ⓓ I eat **whatever** I want and still don't gain weight.

(2) ⓐ You may read **whatever** book you like.
ⓑ Choose **whichever** day is best for you.
ⓒ **Whosever** horse comes in first wins the prize.

(3) **Whoever** comes, they will be welcome.
Whatever you do, do it well.

Ⅴ. 의사관계대명사

(1) ⓐ Choose **such** friends **as** will benefit you.
ⓑ I have **the same** trouble **as** you have.
ⓒ **As** many men **as** came were caught.
ⓓ He often loses his temper, **as** is often the case with impatient young men.

(2) There is no rule **but** has some exceptions.

(3) The next war will be more cruel **than** can be imagined.

Ⅵ. 관계형용사

(1) He spoke to me in French, **which** language I could not understand.

(2) I gave them **what** money I had.

(3) I will approve **whichever** (*or* **whatever**) course you decide on.

▶ 명 언 ◀

You can fool all the people some of the time, and some of the people all the time, but you cannot fool all the people all the time.

-Abraham Lincoln-

I disapprove of what you say, but I will defend to the death your right to say it.

-Voltaire-

Humanitarianism consists in never sacrificing a human being to a purpose.

-Schweitzer-

Ⅳ. 복합관계대명사

(1) 명사용법

ⓐ (판매를 담당하는 분 누구하고나 이야기를 할 수 있을까요?)
whoever = anyone who

ⓑ (그것을 네가 좋아하는 사람 누구에게나 주어라.)
whomever = anyone whom

ⓒ (마음에 드는 어느 쪽이나 고르시오.)
whichever = anything that

ⓓ (나는 원하는 것을 무엇이나 먹어도 체중이 늘지 않는다.)
whatever = anything that

(2) 형용사용법

ⓐ (어떤 책이나 네가 좋아하는 것을 읽어도 된다.)
whatever book = any book that

ⓑ (어느 쪽이든 너에게 가장 좋은 날을 선택해라.)
whichever day = any of the days that

ⓒ (누구의 말이건 맨 먼저 들어오는 쪽이 그 상을 탄다.)
whosever = anyone whose

☞ whosever는 거의 쓰이지 않고 anyone whose가 쓰인다.

(3) 부사용법 (양보의 부사절 유도)
(누가 오든 환영을 받을 것이다.)
Whoever = No matter who
(무엇을 하든 그것을 잘 하여라.)
Whatever = No matter what

☞ Whatever는 부정문 · 의문문에서 강조어로 쓰인다.
There can be no doubt *whatever* about it.
(그것에 관해서는 의심의 여지가 전혀 있을 수 없다.)
Is there any chance *whatever*?
(조금이라도 가망이 있습니까?)

Ⅴ. 의사관계대명사

(1) 관계대명사로서의 as
선행사에 such, the same, as가 있을 때, 뒤의 as는 관계대명사로 본다.

ⓐ (너에게 이익이 될 친구를 선택하여라.) … will의 주어 ; 주격

ⓑ (나도 너와 같은 괴로움이 있다.) … have의 목적어 ; 목적격

ⓒ (온 사람은 다 붙잡혔다.) … 주격

ⓓ (그는 참을성 없는 젊은이들이 흔히 그러하듯이 화를 잘낸다.)
… as의 선행사는 He often loses his temper

He was an American, *as* I knew from his accent. (그의 말투로 안 일이지만, 그는 미국인이었다.)
As was the custom with him, he went out for a walk after supper.
(여느때처럼 저녁식사 후 산책 나갔다.)

(2) but = that ~ not
= There is no rule *that* has *not* some exceptions.
There was no one *but* admired his courage. (그의 용기를 찬탄하지 않는 사람이 아무도 없었다.)

(3) 관계대명사로서의 than
(다음 전쟁은 상상 이상으로 잔인할 것이다.) … can be의 주어

Ⅵ. 관계형용사

(1) (그는 나에게 불어로 말하였는데, 나는 그 언어를 이해할 수 없었다.)
… 관계대명사로서의 which가 명사 language를 수식한다.

(2) (나는 내가 가지고 있던 모든 돈을 그들에게 줬다.)
…what은 money를 수식하는 동시에 I had를 형용사절로 money에 연결시킴.
= I gave them *all the* money *that* I had. (what = all the … that)

(3) (네가 결정하는 어느 과정이나 나는 동의하겠다.) … 복합관계형용사

문 법 · 작 문

A. 다음의 두 문장을 연결하여 한 문장으로 만들어라.

(1) I wanted to know …	How much will this cost?
(2) Do you remember?	When did horse-drawn carriages disappear?
(3) Do you know?	What is the matter with him?
(4) Do you suppose?	What time will he be arriving?

B. 두 문장을 관계대명사를 사용하여 연결하여라.

(1) You are clearly one of those men.
Everything goes wrong with them.

(2) All this was done by the man.
We thought he was a mere dreamer.

(3) She was a well-known singer.
Her voice delighted the whole world.

(4) This is the car.
The engine of the car is of the latest type.

(5) I was unable to find out the man's name.
He called on me yesterday.

(6) I bought many books.
I have not read all of them.

(7) We went to the seashore.
We found many shells there.

C. 다음 문장의 틀린 것을 고쳐라.

(1) One of the men have made a great contribution to world peace is Bertrand Russell.

(2) How became of that nice girl you used to share an apartment with?

(3) That one likes, one will do well.

(4) We visited Jinhae where is noted for its cherry blossoms.

(5) He offered me a considerable sum, but which I declined.

(6) I dislike such a girl who is proud and coy.

(7) A free gift will be given to whomever completes the questionnaire.

(8) Who do you know was the mastermind of the crime?

(9) Whoever that gets the job will be responsible for the annual budget for the department.

(10) To sum up, this is the argument he told me yesterday.

D. Fill in each blank with a suitable word:

(1) He _____ tries to please everybody pleases nobody.

(2) I met a man _____ I thought was a gardener.

(3) He is so diligent that he succeeds in _____ he undertakes.

(4) I tried to persuade him, _____ I found impossible.

(5) Who _____ has a sense of honor can do such a thing?

(6) It was more difficult _____ had been expected.

(7) I'd like to introduce to you the lady of _____ I spoke.

(8) His father suddenly passed away, and, _____ was worse, his mother was taken ill.

(9) It may be cold, in _____ case you must put on your coat.

(10) They robbed him of _____ little money he had.

(11) There is no one that I know of, _____ deserves to love you.

(12) We drove on to the hotel, from _____ balcony we could look down at the town.

E. Translate the following into English:

(1) 그가 무엇을 했다고 생각하느냐?

(2) 옳다고 믿는 바를 행하여라.

(3) 이 분이 그 어려운 일을 맡았다고 하는 Johnson씨이다.

(4) 내가 가지고 있는 모든 돈을 그에게 주었다. (what money)

(5) 나는 자전거 한 대를 샀는데 그 다음날 그것을 도난당했다.

(6) 그 여자는 예전처럼 그리 쾌활한 여자는 아니다.

(7) 그녀는 친절하며 더욱 좋은 것은 아주 예쁘다.

(8) 그는 이 문제를 해결할 유일한 사람이다.

(9) 누구나 이 문제를 먼저 푸는 사람이 그 상품을 탄다.

'My Mother' 라는 제목으로 90어 내외의 글을 지어라.

● 단 문 독 해 ●

I want a man **who** can speak English.
I will engage the man, **who** can speak English.

1. I have encountered nothing on Apollo 15 or in this age of space and science **that** dilutes my faith in God. While I was on the moon, in fact, I felt a sense of inspiration, a feeling that someone was with me, watching over me, protecting me. There were several times when tasks seemed to be impossible — but they worked out all right every time.

notes :
*encounter (우연히) 만나다
*that의 선행사는 nothing
*dilute 희박하게 하다
*inspiration 영감(靈感)

▶▶Which of the following does **not** correspond with the above paragraph?

① The writer's occupation is an astronaut.
② While he was carrying out his duties on the moon, he felt that God was helping him.
③ The writer believed that apparently impossible tasks were accomplished by the help of a spiritual being.
④ The writer was very confident of the existence of God and found definite evidence to support his belief.
⑤ No matter how much scientific technology has advanced, his firm belief in God hasn't weakened.

▶▶영작하시오.

이것이 내가 찾고 있던 바로 그 책이다.

2. His father, **who** had been a great general of the armies of Athens, died when the boy was very young, and left his money in the care of some bad men, **who** spent it.

notes :
*leave A in the care of B = A를 B에게 맡기다
*who spent it에서 who = but they

▶▶According to the above paragraph, which is most suitable to describe the underlined His father?

① generous and altruistic
② suspicious and skeptical
③ credulous and trusting
④ careful and cunning
⑤ extravagant and lavish

▶▶영작하시오.

이번 여름 집을 떠나 있는 동안 우리는 집을 친구에게 맡길 것이다.

This is the **book he wrote**.
I am not the **man I was**.

3. I would not claim for a moment that **those years I spent** at that hospital as a doctor gave me a complete knowledge of human nature. I do not suppose anyone can hope to have that. I have been studying it, consciously or unconsciously, for forty years and I still find men unaccountable; **people I know** intimately can surprise me by some action of which I never thought them capable.

notes :
*would = wish to
*those years (which or that) I spent
*unaccountable 설명할 수 없는
*intimately 친밀하게
*capable of ~ = ~ 할 수 있는

▶▶Which does **not** correspond with the above passage?

① Even an intimate friend is impossible to understand fully.
② Man's nature is too complicated and changeable to comprehend.
③ The writer began his study of human nature 40 years ago.
④ Despite his lengthy research, the writer hasn't still gained a perfect knowledge of human nature.
⑤ The writer was surprised to find some people acting as he thought they would.

▶▶영작하시오.

그는 어떤 범죄도 저지를 사람이라고 나는 생각한다.

4. I had stepped into a new life. Between the **man I had been** and that which I now became there was a very notable difference. In a single day I had matured astonishingly; which means, no doubt, that I suddenly entered into conscious enjoyment of powers and sensibilities which had been developing unknown to me.

notes :
*the man (which) I had been
*that which = the man which
*notable 주목할 만한
*mature 성숙하다
*astonishingly 놀랍도록
*which means에서 which=and it

▶▶본문과 부합하도록 다음 빈칸에 들어갈 말이 가장 잘 짝지어진 것은?

Suddenly the writer recognized his (　　) maturity. In other words he began enjoying consciously his (　　) capacities and senses.

① physical — established　② mental — limited
③ bodily — confined　④ inner — potential
⑤ intellectual — finite

▶▶영작하시오.

경제학자들은 경기침체의 원인에 대해 논의를 시작했다.

This is the person **of whom** I spoke.
I have no house **in which to live**.

5. The circumstances **of which** so many complain should be regarded as the very tools **with which** we are to work, and the steppingstones we are to mount **by**. They are the wind and tide in the voyage of life, which the skillful mariner generally either takes advantage of or overcomes.

notes :
*are to = should
*steppingstones (which) we
*steppingstone 디딤돌, 발판
*mariner 선원
*overcome 극복하다

▶▶Which of the following is most suitable for the main topic of the above paragraph?

① One should lead one's life without complaining of the given circumstances.
② The circumstances we are faced with, good or bad, are sure to influence our success in life.
③ One should prepare for the wind and tide in the voyage of life.
④ Those who tide over adverse circumstances they are thrown into are the very people who succeed in life.
⑤ To be an excellent sailor one should learn many skills to cope with difficult situations at sea.

▶▶영작하시오.
곤경에 처한 사람들을 이용해 먹는 것은 바람직하지 않다.

6. When the subtle influence of spring has awakened almost all forms of vegetation, and millions of hidden plants that pass the winter beneath the soil have broken through the thick covering of dead leaves, there is no sweeter place **in which to pass** a few hours of idleness than the woodland.

notes :
*when ~ leaves 종속절, there is no ~ 주절
*subtle 미묘한
*vegetation 식물
*idleness 한가함

▶▶Which is most appropriate to describe the tone of the above paragraph?

① subtle and distracting
② active and tranquil
③ desolate and lonesome
④ noisy and disordered
⑤ quiet and indolent

▶▶영작하시오.
무더운 오후에 우리는 휴식할 그늘을 찾았다.

He says he saw me there, **which** is a lie.
She was proud, **which** he never was.
They tried to catch the fish, **which** was deemed impossible.

7. There is a story of a clergyman who, preferring not to wear the usual clerical dress, said: "I will wear no clothes which will distinguish me from my fellow men." But when his remark was reported in the newspapers, a comma was put in by mistake, and the sentence then read: 'I will wear no clothes, **which** will distinguish me from my fellow men.'

notes :
*clergyman 목사
*preferring ~ dress 이유를 나타내는 분사구문
*clerical 목사의
*read (~라고) 써있다
*which=and it

▶▶Which of the following is **not** suitable to describe the above-mentioned clergyman?

① He tried to avoid wearing his clerical dress if possible.
② He didn't wish to be distinguished from his fellow men by his clothes.
③ His remark was sent to newspaper offices and printed in the newspapers.
④ The papers reported that he would go naked because he wanted to distinguish himself from his fellow men.
⑤ The articles about his remark were just as he intended.

▶▶영작하시오.
그는 너무 어려서 옳고 그름을 판단할 수 없었다.

He gave me **what** I wanted.
He asked me **what** I wanted.

8. The whole world of art and literature and learning is international; **what** is done in one country is not done for that country alone, but for mankind. If we ask ourselves **what** are the things that make us think the human race more valuable than any species of animals, we will find that all are things in which the whole world can share.

notes :
*첫번째 what는 관계대명사, 두번째 what는 의문대명사
*not A but B =A가 아니라 B다
*species 종(種)

▶▶What makes human beings more valuable than other animals? Write in Korean.

▶▶영작하시오.
그는 기쁨뿐 아니라 슬픔도 나와 함께 했다.

What with hunger **and what with** fatigue, he fell down.
Reading **is to** the mind **what** exercise **is to** the body.
She is intelligent, and **what is better still**, very beautiful.

9. **What with** heat **and what with** thirst, I became so impatient to get ashore, that when at last we glided towards the shore, I stood up in the bow of the boat ready to jump.

notes :
*impatient 조바심하는
*glide 미끄러지듯이 나아가다
*bow [bau] 뱃머리; *stern* 선미(船尾)

▶▶When the writer got ashore he was very (   ).
[hot and thirsty, tired and sore, bored and hungry]

▶▶영작하시오.
그는 죽을 각오를 하고 거기에 갔다.

10. Society is like a building, which stands firm when its foundations are strong and all its timbers are sound. The man who can not be trusted **is to** society **what** a piece of rotten timber **is to** a house.

notes :
*foundation 기초
*timber 재목
*sound 건전한
*rotten 썩은

▶▶본문의 내용과 일치하도록 다음 빈칸에 들어가기에 가장 적절한 것은?
Society is likely to (   ) if its members are not trustworthy.
① stand firm ② collapse ③ thrive
④ flourish ⑤ prosper

▶▶영작하시오.
나뭇잎이 식물에 대한 관계는 허파가 동물에 대한 것과 같다.

11. As the world grew older, men became more and more quarrelsome. They quarrelled more sadly than ever over the possession of the bright yellow gold they had found; and, **what was worst of all**, they made sharp knives and other weapons out of iron, and fought fiercely with each other.

notes :
*sadly = badly, severely
*possession 소유
*make ~ out of = make ~ of

▶▶As the world grew older, men's quarreling became more and more (   ).
[vigorous, violent, tame]

▶▶영작하시오.
우리는 종이로 많은 종이학을 만들었다.

As many men **as** came were caught.
There is no rule **but** has some exceptions.
You have more money **than** is necessary.

12. He who would do some great thing in this short life must apply himself to work with **such** a concentration of his forces **as** to idle spectators, who live only to amuse themselves, looks like madness.

notes :
*would = wish to
*apply oneself to = ~에 전념하다
*concentration 집중
*idle spectators = 게으른 방관자
*amuse oneself = 즐기다

▶▶He who would succeed in life should work like mad and ( ) all his ( ) on accomplishing his goals.
[concern, concentrate, spread, efforts, insanity]

▶▶영작하시오.
필요한 만큼의 인원을 소집해야 한다.

13. There was not a line in her countenance, not a note in her soft and sleepy voice, **but** spoke of an entire contentment with her life. It would have been fatuous arrogance to pity such a woman.

notes :
*countenance 용모, 안색
*that의 선행사는 line과 note
*note 음조(音調)
*to pity = if one had pitied
*fatuous arrogance = 어리석은 교만

▶▶Which does **not** correspond with the above paragraph?
① The woman's facial expression showed signs of contentment.
② The woman's face had wrinkles.
③ The woman had a soft and sleepy voice.
④ The writer felt pity for her because of her wrinkled face and harsh voice.
⑤ The woman was not so miserable as to be sympathized with.

▶▶영작하시오.
그의 책에서 시종일관 그는 정부의 권력 남용에 대해 말했다.

14. I found the first two years of the curriculum very dull and gave my work no more attention **than** was necessary to scrape through the examinations. I was an unsatisfactory student.

notes :
*curriculum 교과과정
*attention 주의(력)
*scrape through = 겨우 통과하다
*unsatisfactory 성적이 나쁜

▶▶The writer was an unsatisfactory student because he found no ( ) in his schoolwork and didn't do his ( ).
[interest, excitement, challenge, part, best, share]

▶▶영작하시오.
요즘은 부모들이 자식들에게 필요 이상의 돈을 주는 것 같다.

I gave him **what** money I had.
We stayed there for a month, during **which** time I often visited her.

15. One day when the President was riding in a car with General Bradley and me, he fell to discussing the future of some of our war leaders. I told him that I had no ambition except to retire to a quiet home and from there do **what** little I could to help our people understand some of the great changes the war had brought to the world.

notes :
*fall to ~ing = ~하기 시작하다
*ambition 야망, 야심
*I could (do)

▶▶Which does **not** correspond with the above paragraph?
① The writer was riding in a car with the President and General Bradley one day.
② The President began discussing the future of war leaders including the writer.
③ General Bradley had no ambition except to retire to his hometown.
④ The writer wanted to retire from public service and to live a quiet life.
⑤ The writer was ready to do what little he could to enlighten people about the postwar changes.

▶▶영작하시오.
당신을 돕기 위해 미력이나마 다하겠습니다.

16. He now plainly saw that he was no better than a murderer; the extreme anguish of **which** discovery made life insupportable, and drove him to fall on his sword.

notes :
*no better than = as good as
*fall on one's sword = 자결하다
*sword 검(劍)

▶▶According to the above paragraph, which is **not** correct?
① He realized his behavior was as good as murder.
② He was suspected of murder by the police.
③ He was consumed with severe mental torment caused by a sense of guilt.
④ His mental pain was too acute for him to endure.
⑤ After all he preferred death to a painful life of guilt.

▶▶영작하시오.
사람들은 그를 마치 짐승과 다름없는 것처럼 취급했다.

There was nothing **that** he wished **which** he was denied.

17. There is no man **that** carries guilt about him **who** does not receive a sting into his soul. A guilty conscience needs no accuser, while a clear one fears none.

notes :
*sting 양심의 가책
*guilty conscience 죄의식
*accuser 비난자, 고발자

▶▶윗글의 내용에 언급되지 않은 것을 골라라.

① Those who commit crimes always have a sense of guilt.
② Criminals always suffer from a guilty conscience.
③ An innocent man has nothing to fear.
④ A criminal's accuser is his own conscience.
⑤ Some criminals escape from their legal accusers.

▶▶영작하시오.

우리가 아는 사람으로서 그 만큼 재능 있는 사람이 있습니까?

18. I cannot recall a case of man or woman **who** ever occupied any considerable part of my thoughts **that** did not contribute towards my moral or physical welfare.

notes :
*recall 회상하다
*case 경우
*occupy 차지하다
*considerable 상당한
*contribute towards ~ = ~에 기여하다

▶▶Now I realize that (   ) occupied my mind for some time in my life has always made a (   ) to my well-being.

[what, which, whoever, contribution, consideration]

▶▶영작하시오.

소유할 가치가 있는 것으로서 노력없이 얻을 수 있는 것은 아무것도 없다.

Whoever wishes to succeed must work hard.

19. **Whoever** has to deal with young children soon learns that too much sympathy is a mistake. Too little sympathy is, of course, a worse mistake, but in this, as in everything else, each extreme is bad.

notes :
*sympathy 동정, 연민
*each extreme = 각 극단(極端), 즉 너무 동정하거나 너무 동정을 아니하는 것

▶▶윗글의 밑줄친 each extreme is bad의 구체적인 내용설명이 될 수 있도록 밑의 빈칸을 두 단어 이상으로 채우시오.

(   ) as well as (   ) is not desirable.

▶▶영작하시오.

누구나 범죄를 저지르면 곧 잡혀 처벌을 받을 것이다.

● 장 문 독 해 ●

Warming-up

While it is true that you have a right to do that, there is an obligation you must follow.

His poor health **compelled** him **to give up** the task.

The first requirement is that you **should** have a good command of English.

Pleasant smiles keep our life **oils and running** sweetly.

He **would** not listen to my advice and **would** have his own way.

1 While it is true that there is no law that compels us to say "Please," there is a social practice much older and more sacred than any law which enjoins us to be civil. And the first requirement of civility is that we should acknowledge a service. "Please" and "Thank you" are the small change with which we pay our way as social beings. They are the little courtesies by which we keep the machine of life oiled and running sweetly. They put our intercourse upon the basis of a friendly cooperation, an easy give and take, instead of on the basis of superiors dictating to inferiors. It is a very vulgar mind that would wish to command where he can have the service for the asking, and have it with willingness and good feeling instead of resentment.

Alfred Gardiner: *Many Furrows*

Notes

compel 강요하다 / practice 관습 / sacred 신성한 / which의 선행사는 practice / enjoin 명령하다(=order, direct) / requirement 필요조건 / civility 공손함 / change 잔돈 / pay one's way 빚지지 않고 살아가다 / courtesy 예의 / intercourse 교제 / give-and-take 상호 양보(=mutual concession) / on the basis of ~의 토대 위에 / dictate 지시하다 / vulgar 저속한 / for the asking=if only he asks for it 부탁하기만 하면 / resentment 분노, 원한

Question

1. 본문의 밑줄친 <u>They</u>가 궁극적으로 가리키는 내용을 본문에 찾아 쓰시오.

2. What does the author compare the little courtesies to, saying they are means to compensate for others' services?

3. According to the passage, which is **not** correct?
   ① There is no legislation that forces us to say "Please".
   ② Not a rule but a social practice regulates us to be courteous.
   ③ An acknowledgement of others' services and gratitude for them make our society run smoothly.
   ④ With the help of the little courtesies, like "Thank you" and "Please", we can get along with others on the basis of cooperation and mutual concession.
   ⑤ In an organization where the order between ranks is necessary, the little politenesses such as "Please" and "Excuse me" are rarely found.

4. Which best represents the main idea of the passage?
   ① We should impose a legal responsibility on those who don't follow social practices.
   ② We should cooperate to eliminate the social disharmony between superiors and inferiors.
   ③ "Thank you" and "Please" are natural and common expressions to show your appreciation of others' services.
   ④ Daily thoughtful expressions such as "Please" and "Thank you" are lubricants to keep our life more comfortable and tolerable.
   ⑤ The resentment that can cause a strong repulsion among subordinates should be controlled.

Production

(1) 당신이 제안하는 것은 이론적으로는 가능하지만, 실제로 그것을 수행하기는 불가능하다.
(2) 내 이름을 뒤에서 부르는 소리가 들렸다.
(3) 그 문이 아무리 해도 열리지 않았다. 그래서, 우리는 그것을 부셔서 억지로 열지 않을 수 없었다.

● 장 문 독 해 ●

Warming-up

We **ascribe** omnipotence **to** the Lord.
Uneasy and frightened, we approached the deserted house.
It **rests in** you to finish the work.
It suddenly occurs to me that my retirement is near **at hand**.
Having finished his assignment, he went to bed.
He **may well** be proud of his son.

2 Less than fifty years after his death, the door of nature was unlocked and we were offered the dreadful burden of choice. We have usurped many of the powers we once ascribed to God. Fearful and unprepared, we have assumed the lordship over the life and death of the whole world of all living things. The danger and the glory and the choice rest finally in man. The test of his perfectibility is at hand.

Having taken God-like power, we must seek in ourselves for the responsibility and the wisdom we once prayed some deity might have. ⓐ Man himself has become our greatest hazard and our only hope. So that today, St. John the Apostle may well be paraphrased: In the end is the *word*, and the word is *man*, and the ⓑ word is *with* man.

John Steinbeck: *Nobel Prize Acceptance Speech*

Notes

his death에서 his는 Alfred Nobel을 가리킨다 / unlock 자물쇠를 열다 / burden 무거운 짐 / usurp 빼앗다, 강탈하다 / assume (책임을) 지다, (권력을) 잡다 / lordship over ~에 대한 지배권 / rest in ~에 달려있다(=rest on=depend on) / perfectibility 완전성 / seek for 찾다 / responsibility 책임 / wisdom (that) we once / deity 신(성) / hazard 위험 / so that 그래서 / St. John the Apostle 사도 성 요한 / paraphrase 바꾸어 말하다[쓰다] / *In the beginning was the Word, and the Word was with God, and the Word was God. (요한복음 첫 시작 부분)

Question

1. 본문의 밑줄친 문장 ⓐ와 같은 뜻이 되도록 다음 빈칸에 들어갈 말이 알맞게 짝지어진 것은?

Man's advanced scientific technology and weapons can either (   ) us completely or help us to (   ). The choice between the two is up to (   ).

① eradicate — thrive — God
② eliminate — exterminate — human beings
③ obliterate — flourish — our science
④ annihilate — prosper — ourselves
⑤ demolish — develop — our leaders

2. 본문의 밑줄친 ⓑword를 다음과 같이 풀어 쓸 때, 빈칸에 가장 알맞은 말을 골라 쓰시오.

final outcome of man's (   )

[end, world, future]

3. 본문의 내용과 일치하도록 다음 빈칸에 들어갈 말을 쓰시오.
The author maintains that we should be (r   ) for our advanced technology and deadly weapons as well as (w   ) enough to use them properly.

4. According to the passage, which is **not** correct?
① Before human beings secured the power which could cause mass destruction, we thought only God had it.
② When human beings first took the power to dominate all life on the earth, they were well prepared and fearless.
③ The author holds the opinion that the choice to make between death and glory lies in man himself.
④ Before the scientific age, only God was considered to have the lordship over the life and death of all creatures on the earth.
⑤ The author maintains that we have finally come to a crucial point to determine whether we are rational or not, whether we will die or live on.

Production

(1) 그는 실패를 운명의 탓으로 돌렸다.
(2) 이 상(賞)은 연중 가장 우수한 소설에 수여된다.
(3) 그녀의 아들이 일등상을 탔다. 그녀가 아들을 자랑하는 것도 당연하다.

실력체크 I

1 다음 글을 읽고 아래의 물음에 답하여라.

Some people think they have an answer to the troubles of automobile crowding and dirty air in large cities. Their answer is the bicycle, or 'bike'.

In a great many cities, hundreds of people ride bicycles to work everyday. In New York City, some bike riders have even formed a group called Bike for a Better City. They claim that if more people rode bicycles to work there would be fewer cars in the downtown section of the city and therefore less dirty air from car engines.

For several years this group has been trying to get the city government to help bicycle riders. For example, they want the city to draw special lanes—for bicycles only—on some of the main streets, because when bicycle riders must use the same lanes as cars, there are accidents.

But no bicycle lanes have been drawn. Not everyone thinks they are a good idea. Taxi drivers don't like the idea—they say it will slow traffic. Some store owners on the main streets don't like the idea—they say that if there is less traffic, they will have less business. And most people live too far from downtown to travel by bike.

The city government has not yet decided what to do. It wants to keep everyone happy. On weekends, Central Park—the largest piece of open ground in New York—is closed to cars, and the roads may be used by bicycles only. But Bike for a Better City says that this is not enough and keeps fighting to get bicycle lanes downtown.

notes:
an answer to~ = ~에 대한 대답 / claim 주장하다, 요구하다 / section 구분, 구역 / draw (drew-drawn) (선을) 긋다 / lane (도로의) 차선 / traffic 교통(량) / the city government 시 당국 / piece (거리·지면 따위의) 일부, 1구획 / open 널찍한, 탁 트인 / keep ~ing = 계속 ~하다

(1) Bike for a Better City의 주장을 50자 이내의 우리말로 적어라.

(2) Which does **not** correspond with the above passage?

① Some people believe that bikes could eliminate the problems of inner city traffic congestion and pollution.

② The bike riders have succeeded in getting Central Park closed to cars on weekends.

③ The 'Bike for a Better City' group has designated special lanes for bicycles in the downtown area.

④ Some taxi drivers and store owners are not in favor of bicycle lanes because of their own interests.

⑤ The New York city government has exerted considerable efforts to work out an all-pleasing policy.

2 다음 글을 읽고 물음에 답하여라.

To other Europeans the best known quality of the English is 'reserve'. A reserved person is one who does not talk very much to strangers, does not show much emotion, and seldom gets excited. It is difficult to get to know a reserved person: he never tells you anything about himself, and you may work with him for years without ever knowing where he lives, how many children he has, and what his interests are. English people tend to be like that. If they are making a journey by bus, they will do their best to find an empty seat. If they have to share the seat with a stranger, they may travel many miles without starting a conversation. This reluctance to talk with others is an unfortunate quality in some ways, since it tends to give the impression of coldness, and it is true that the English are not noted for their generosity and hospitality. On the other hand, they are perfectly human behind their barrier of reserve, and may be quite pleased when a friendly stranger or foreigner succeeds for a time in breaking the barrier down.

notes :
reserve 자제, 사양, 마음에 숨김 / reserved 내성적인 / get to ~하게 되다 / reluctance 싫어함 / tend to ~하기 쉽다 / be noted for = be famous for / generosity 아량, 인심이 좋음 / hospitality 환대 / barrier 장벽

(1) 영국인의 가장 잘 알려진 특성은 여행할 때 어떻게 나타나는가?
(2) 이런 특성 때문에 영국인은 어떤 오해를 받기 쉬운가?
(3) 필자는 영국인의 참된 모습을 어떻게 나타냈는가?

3 다음 글의 문맥상 글의 마지막에 들어갈 내용을 골라라.

Those who have not distinguished themselves at school should not on that account be discouraged. The greatest minds do not necessarily ripen the quickest. If, indeed, you have not taken pains, then, though I will not say that you should be discouraged, still you should be ashamed; but if you have done your best, you have only to persevere; for many of those who have never been able to distinguish themselves at school, have _____.

notes :
distinguish oneself 두각을 나타내다 / on that account 그 때문에 / mind 정신의 소유자, 사람 / persevere 참다, 견디다

① tried in vain to succeed in life
② been very successful in after life
③ hardly done anything great in life
④ lived a comfortable and contented life
⑤ been discouraged and ashamed of themselves

실 력 체 크 II

A. 다음 문장을 복문으로 고쳐라.

(1) He had three sons, but I knew that one of them was missing.

(2) He was a young gardener of her acquaintance.

(3) Rats do much damage. They multiply very fast.

(4) It is a profession of his own choosing.

B. 다음 세 글의 공란에 같은 단어를 써 넣어 문장을 완성시켜라.

(1) He gave up his _____ on account of his failing health.
It may not be out of _____ to examine it here.
A big fire took _____ near the station last night.

(2) Blue does not go _____ green.
He sat reading, _____ his wife sewing beside him.
She was almost beside herself _____ joy.

(3) We got the news at second _____ .
He is a good _____ at all sorts of games.
Practice should go hand in _____ with theory.

(4) I can _____ no sense of what he says.
You don't have to _____ so much of such an unimportant thing.
I could not _____ up my mind which to choose.

(5) I can hardly make _____ the number on the door.
The women set _____ their chickens and ducks on the market stalls.
The firemen made desperate efforts to put the fire _____ .

C. 두 문장의 뜻이 같아지도록 공란에 적당한 단어를 써라.

(1) Every day he read the Bible.
Not a day passed _____ his reading the Bible.

(2) I supported him as much as I could.
I supported him to the best of my _____ .

(3) To our great relief we learned that the child was safe.
We were greatly _____ to learn that the child was safe.

Answer: A. (1) He had three sons, one of whom I knew was missing. (2) He was a young gardener with whom she was acquainted. (3) Rats, which multiply very fast, do much damage. (4) It is a profession that he himself has chosen.
B. (1) place (2) with (3) hand (4) make (5) out
C. (1) without (2) ability (3) relieved

D. 적당한 관계대명사로 밑줄 친 곳을 메워라.

(1) The snow prevented her from coming, _____ gave us much trouble.

(2) Charles Lamb, a charming, gentle, witty creature _____ to know was to love, has always appealed to the affections of his readers.

(3) They thought him diligent, _____ he was, and intelligent, _____ he was not.

(4) That was _____ Richard wanted to know chiefly about his sisters.

E. 다음 문장의 공란을 「전치사+관계대명사」로 메워라.

(1) Consult the dictionary whenever you meet with any word the meaning _____ _____ you don't understand.

(2) He is a jolly youth, each minute of company _____ _____ makes me delightful.

(3) It is unfortunately too true that many people, when they have achieved success, forget the very friends _____ _____ help and advice they were able to do so.

(4) Of course I am quite unable to judge the attitude of her mind, but I think, _____ _____ I knew of her, that there has been a misunderstanding between you and her.

(5) She occupied a house the rent _____ _____ absurdly exceeded the due proportion of her income.

(6) One writer _____ _____ I had taken an interest was Stephen King.

F. 밑줄 친 부분이 주절이 되게 관계대명사를 써서 두 문장을 연결하여라.

(1) He lives in a house. I see the house over there.

(2) I hear he is going to marry a girl.
The girl happens to be a friend of my wife's.

(3) They say he is very clever. I cannot believe it.

(4) He made a witty remark. I doubted the truth of it.

(5) You used the word in a sense. The sense is not familiar to us.

Answer: D. (1) which (2) whom (3) which, which (4) what
E. (1) of which (2) with whom (3) by whose (4) from what (5) of which (6) in whom
F. (1) I see over there the house in which he lives. (2) The girl, whom I hear he is going to marry, happens to be a friend of my wife's. (3) They say he is very clever, which I cannot believe. (4) He made a witty remark, the truth of which I doubted. (5) The sense in which you used the word is not familiar to us.

어 휘 · 발 음

A. 두 문장의 뜻이 같아지도록 공란을 한 단어로 메워라.

(1) He has received a good education.
He is a ______ man.

(2) People know this artist well.
This man is a ______ artist.

(3) There was not a break in the line of people.
The people were standing in an ______ line.

(4) They made these shoes by hand.
These shoes are ______ .

(5) He is unable to see things clearly at a distance.
He is ______ .

B. 공란에 맞는 말을 고르고, 셋 전체를 대표할 수 있는 공통어를 써라.

(1) The soldiers were ready to die at the ______ from the king.
Everything is kept in proper ______ .
The name of an applicant is enrolled in the ______ in which it is received.

① sequence ② arrangement ③ command
④ application ⑤ agreement 공통어 : ______

(2) Men are ______ to temptation.
I have nothing more to say on the ______ .
Your conduct will ______ you to public ridicule.

① matter ② expose ③ close
④ open ⑤ dispose 공통어 : ______

C. 밑줄 친 단어를 적절한 어형으로 바꾸어 공란에 써 넣어라.

(1) She grew more anxious. Her (   ) increased.

(2) We must make our city modern. We must (   ) our city.

(3) He often offended men who might have been useful friends.
We are prohibited from manufacturing (   ) weapons.

(4) Last night I was disturbed by a terrible dream.
The (   ) on the campus have been quieted.

Answer: A. (1) well-educated (2) well-known (3) endless (4) hand-made (5) near-sighted [short-sighted] B. (1) ③, ②, ① : order (2) ④, ①, ② : subject
C. (1) anxiety (2) modernize (3) offensive (4) disturbances

동음이의어 (Homonym)

[εər]…air, heir, ere
[əláud]…allowed, aloud
[ɔ́:ltər]…altar, alter
[əsént]…ascent, assent
[bæd]…bad, bade
[beis]…base, bass
[bə:rθ]…berth, birth
[bεər]…bear, bare
[béri]…berry, bury
[blu:]…blew, blue
[bau]…bow, bough
[breik]…break, brake
[sait]…cite, site
[klaim]…clime, climb
[kɔ:rs]…coarse, course
[kɔ:r]…core, corps
[diər]…dear, deer
[dju:]…dew, due
[dai]…die, dye
[ə:rn]…earn, urn
[feint]…faint, feint
[fεər]…fair, fare
[fi:t]…feat, feet
[fláuər]…flour, flower
[fɔ:rθ]…forth, fourth
[faul]…fowl, foul
[groun]…grown, groan
[gest]…guest, guessed
[hεər]…hair, hare
[hɔ́:l]…hall, haul
[hiər]…hear, here
[hi:l]…heal, heel
[hju:]…hew, hue
[háiər]…hire, higher
[him]…him, hymn
[houl]…hole, whole
[áidl]…idle, idol
[ail]…isle, aisle
[ki:]…key, quay
[kə́:rnəl]…kernel, colonel
[nju:]…knew, new
[lésn]…lesson, lessen
[meid]…made, maid
[meil]…male, mail
[máinər]…minor, miner
[nʌn]…nun, none
[ɔ:r]…oar, or
[ɔ:t]…ought, aught
[auər]…our, hour
[peil]…pail, pale
[pεər]…pear, pair
[pi:l]…peal, peel
[plein]…plain, plane
[pi:s]…peace, piece
[piər]…pier, peer
[poul]…pole, poll
[prei]…pray, prey
[reiz]…raise, raze
[rein]…rain, rein
[rait]…right, rite, write
[ru:t]…root, route
[seil]…sail, sale
[sent]…scent, cent
[sou]…sew, sow
[said]…side, sighed
[slei]…slay, sleigh
[soul]…sole, soul
[steik]…stake, steak
[stεər]…stare, stair
[sti:l]…steal, steel
[streit]…strait, straight
[swi:t]…sweet, suite
[sʌm]…sum, some
[sɔ:rd]…sword, soared
[teil]…tail, tale
[ti:m]…team, teem
[θru:]…threw, through
[θroun]…thrown, throne
[taid]…tide, tied
[tou]…tow, toe
[veil]…vale, veil
[vein]…vain, vein
[wεər]…ware, wear
[weist]…waste, waist
[wei]…weigh, way
[weit]…weight, wait
[jouk]…yoke, yolk

숙 어

(1) **lie down on the job** (=be lazy and work little) 일을 게을리 하다
☞ She *lies down on the job* by talking all the time.

(2) **little[no] better than** (=almost the same as) ~나 다름없는
☞ People treated him as if he was *little better than* an animal.

(3) **live beyond one's means** (=spend more than one can afford) 분수에 맞지 않게 살다
☞ She's an extravagant woman who *lives beyond her means*.

(4) **live it up** (=enjoy life by spending money freely) 흥청망청 즐기다
☞ There is no reason why I can't *live it up* from time to time.

(5) **live (from) hand to mouth** (=live a hand-to-mouth existence) 하루 벌어 하루 먹고 살다, 먹고 살기 급급하다
☞ We've been *living from hand to mouth* ever since I lost my job.

(6) **live up to** (=satisfy, meet) 만족[충족]시키다
(=fulfill, carry out) (책임, 의무 등을) 수행[이행]하다
☞ This new technology has not *lived up to* our expectations.
Tom *lived up to* his promises and paid the money he owed.

(7) **look back at[on]** (=view in retrospect) 회상하다, 회고하다
☞ When I *look back at* my childhood I realize how happy I was then.

(8) **look down on** (=consider ~ inferior to oneself) 얕잡아 보다, 깔보다
☞ He always *looks down on* everyone; he thinks he's so special.

(9) **look forward to** (=anticipate with pleasure) 학수고대하다
☞ I'm *looking forward to* the day when I will see her.

(10) **look on** (=be a spectator ; regard) 방관하다 ; 간주하다 (as)
☞ Why don't you play football instead of just *looking on*?
We *look on* him *as* an authority on the subject.

(11) **look over** (=examine, inspect) 조사하다, 검토하다
☞ We *looked over* several kinds of new cars before deciding.

(12) **look to A for B** (=depend on A for B) A에게 B를 의존하다
☞ Korea mainly *looks to* Arab countries *for* oil.

(13) **look up** (=search for ; visit, call on) 찾아 보다 ; 방문하다
☞ I *looked up* your address in the personnel file.
Do *look* me *up* the next time you're in London.

(14) **look up to** (=respect) 존경하다
☞ He's a respectable man everybody *looks up to*.

(15) **lose heart** (=become discouraged) 낙담하다, 상심하다
☞ The team had won no games and it *lost heart*.

(16) **lose no time in ~ing** (=do without any hesitation) 곧 ~하다
☞ The police *lost no time in sending* the injured man to the hospital.

(17) **lose one's head** (=become uncontrolled) 이성을 잃다, 흥분하다
☞ He *lost his head* and started yelling at me.

(18) **lose one's temper** (=get very angry) 화를 내다
☞ The basketball coach *lost his temper* and shouted at his players.

(19) **lose one's touch** (=fail at what one used to do well) 기량이[솜씨가] 떨어지다
☞ He's lost another game; he must be *losing his touch*.

(20) **lose oneself in** (=become engrossed in) 몰두하다
☞ She *lost herself in* rewriting her new novel for television.

Exercise

▶▶ 주어진 단어들을 포함한 글을 지어라. 필요하면 어형을 변화시켜라.

1. he / dismiss / lie / job
2. We / live / up / vacation
3. machine / live / to / expectations
4. like / look / on / days
5. look / on / man / because / poor
6. he / celebrity / look / to
7. lose / time / homework
8. patient / never / temper
9. she / mistake / lose / touch
10. lose / write / novel

14. 형 용 사(Adjective) Ⅰ

기본 문법 설명

A. 형용사의 용법	(1) ⓐ We have many problems of **black** people living here. There's something **sharp** in my shoe. ⓑ Life is **short**, art is **long**. (2) ⓐ The damage to the car was a **mere** scratch. ⓑ She's **afraid** of going there on her own. ⓒ We cannot comment on that at the **present** time. How many people were **present** at the meeting? (3) ⓐ She is a lady **beautiful**, **kind** and **rich**. ⓑ I have nothing **special** to tell you. ⓒ This is a loss **too heavy for me to bear**. ⓓ You have to use the latest information **available**. ⓔ a boy **ten years old** / a letter **written in English** ⓕ Look at **those two large old stone** buildings. ⓖ from time **immemorial** / China **Proper** (4) It's a film that's really **worth** seeing. (5) It's an urgent problem to narrow an income gap between **the rich** and **the poor**. **The true, the good** and **the beautiful** were their ideals.
B. 수 사	(1) five **hundred** / five **thousand** / five **million** **hundreds** of people / five **million** inhabitants (2) \$2,358 = two thousand three hundred (**and**) fifty-eight dollars (the year) 1981 = nineteen eighty-one (at) 7 : 55 a.m. = seven fifty-five [éiém] a girl in her teens 2003 = two thousand **and** three (3) ⓐ He was **the first** president of the university. Do it **a second** time. ⓑ **Two-thirds** of the apples **were** rotten. **Two-thirds** of the land **was** uncultivated. (4) I had to pay **double** the usual price. There are **twice as** many houses here **as** there used to be.

A. 형용사의 용법

(1) **한정용법과 서술용법**

ⓐ 한정용법—명사의 앞 또는 뒤에서 수식
ⓑ 서술용법—보어(주격 보어, 목적격 보어)
I found an *empty* cage. [한정용법]
I found the cage *empty*. [서술용법]

(2) **용법상의 주의**

ⓐ 한정용법에만 쓰이는 형용사
woolen, elder, former, latter, only, inner, outer, lone, mere, live[laiv], upper, utmost, utter, very, wooden, sole, this, that, etc.

ⓑ 서술용법에만 쓰이는 형용사
afraid, alike, alive, alone, asleep, ashamed, awake, aware, content, fond, unable, liable, worth, etc.

ⓒ 같은 말이라도 한정용법, 서술용법에 따라 뜻이 달라지는 단어가 있다.
(우리는 현 시점에서는 그것에 대해 논평할 수 없다.)
(몇 사람이 그 모임에 참석했습니까?)
{ a *certain* lady (어떤 부인)
{ It is quite *certain*. (확실하다)
{ Mr. Brown is *late*. (늦다)
{ the *late* Mr. Brown (故 Brown씨)

(3) **형용사의 어순**

ⓐ 여러 형용사들이 겹칠 때는 명사 뒤에 두는 경우가 있다.
ⓑ -thing, -body를 수식하는 형용사는 대개 그 뒤에 온다.
(너에게 말해 줄 특별한 것이 없다.)
ⓒ 형용사가 다른 요소를 동반하여 길어질 때는 뒤에 온다.
ⓓ 최상급, all, every 등을 한정하는 형용사는 대개 뒤에 온다.
I will try every means *possible*.
ⓔ 형용사절의 who is, which is가 생략된 형식
a boy (who is) ten years old
a letter (which is) written in English
ⓕ 「지시+수량+대소+성상+신구+재료」의 순서
ⓖ 관용구 (옛날부터) (중국본토)
the sum *total* (합계)
the authorities *concerned* (관계당국)

(4) **목적어를 취하는 형용사**

My house is *near* the lake.
They sat *opposite* each other.
They are very *like* each other.

(5) **the+형용사**

the rich = rich people [복수 보통명사]
the true = truth [추상명사]

B. 수 사

(1) hundred, thousand, million은 앞에 숫자가 있는 경우는 단수로 쓰이나, 단독으로 쓰일 경우에는 복수로도 사용되어 불특정 다수의 의미를 갖는다.
☞ hundreds[thousands, millions] of
= 수백의[수천의, 수백만의]

(2) hundred 다음에 *and*를 빼고 읽기도 한다. 3021처럼 100 단위가 없을 때는 「three thousand *and* twenty-one」으로 읽는다. 연대는 둘씩 나누어 읽는다.
<*cf.*> 1900 : nineteen hundred
1801 : eighteen O[ou] one

(3) ⓐ 서수사 : 서수사에는 the를 붙임.
first, second, third 이외에는 기수사에 -th를 붙여 서수사를 만든다.
☞ 철자에 주의 : fifth, eighth, ninth, twelfth, twentieth, fourteenth, fortieth
a second time = again
☞ Napoleon Ⅲ = Napoleon the Third
World War Ⅱ = World War Two
혹은 the Second World War
a third world war

ⓑ 분수 읽기 (분자 : 기수 / 분모 : 서수)

$\frac{1}{2}$ = a half [one half]

$\frac{2}{3}$ = two thirds　　$\frac{1}{3}$ = one third

$4\frac{2}{7}$ = four and two sevenths

분수의 수는 그 뒤의 말에 따라 결정됨.
☞ one and a half 는 단수로 받는다.
2.34 = two point three four

(4) **배수사**

This is three *times as* large *as* that.
= This is three times the size of that.

C. 고유형용사	(1) Most **English** subjects are loyal to the queen. the **Americans** / the **French** / the **Swiss** (2) The English **are** proud of their country and its traditions.
D. 주의할 수량형용사	(1) ⓐ **Many a** man *has* repeated the same mistake. ⓑ **A great many** people think that money is everything. ⓒ They worked **like so many** bees. ⓓ I waited for fifteen minutes; it seemed **as many** hours to me.
	(2) ⓐ **Few** people showed up for the party. I'm sorry I've made **a few** mistakes. ⓑ **Quite a few** passengers were killed in the airplane crash. **Only a few** members agreed with his opinion. (3) ⓐ I was not in the least surprised; I had expected **as much**. I tried **as much as** I could to control my temper. ⓑ He even went **as much as to say** that all money should be abolished. ⓒ I do **not so much** dislike him **as** feel sorry for him. ⓓ He can**not so much as** write his own name. ⓔ At sea he proved to be **not much** of a sailor. Although we were good friends, I have**n't** seen **much** of him lately. (4) ⓐ There is still **a little** time to prepare for the exams. As I have **little** money with me, I can't join you for dinner. There's **little** hope of an agreement being reached. ⓑ She knows **quite a little** about Korean art. He understood **only a little** of her speech. ⓒ **Little** *did* I dream that such a terrible accident would happen to my family. ⓓ I did **what little** I could. ⓔ The cancer patient's recovery was **little short of** a miracle.

C. 고유형용사

국 명	고유형용사	국민 한 사람 a, an	국민의 복수	국민전체 the
England	English	Englishman	Englishmen	English
France	French	Frenchman	Frenchmen	French
America	American	American	Americans	Americans
Germany	German	German	Germans	Germans
Spain	Spanish	Spaniard	Spaniards	Spanish

☞ the Engli**sh**, the Fren**ch**, the Swi**ss**, the Japan**ese** 등은 어미에 s가 붙지 않지만, the Korean**s**, the American**s**, the Greek**s**는 s가 붙는다. 국민은 복수로 받는다.

D. 주의할 수량형용사

(1) ⓐ **many a**는 복수의 의미지만 단수 취급을 한다. 「many a+단수명사」
(같은 실수를 반복한 사람들이 많다.)

ⓑ **a great many** = 매우 많은
a good many = 상당히 많은
(돈이 제일이라고 생각하는 사람이 매우 많다.)

ⓒ **like so many** : 문자 그대로의 뜻은 「같은 수의 ~처럼」인데, 「마치 ~처럼」으로 해석하면 무방하다.
(그들은 마치 벌처럼 열심히 일했다.)

ⓓ **as many** = 같은 수의
(나는 15분 기다렸는데, 그 15분이 내게는 15시간 처럼 느껴졌다.)

(2) ⓐ **few**는 부정, **a few**는 긍정의 뜻
(그 파티에 참석한 사람은 거의 없었다.)
(몇 가지 실수를 해서 죄송합니다.)

ⓑ **quite a few** = many
(많은 승객들이 그 비행기 추락사고로 숨졌다.)
only a few = not many
(몇 명의 회원들만이 그의 의견에 동의했다)

(3) ⓐ **as much** = 같은 양의
(나는 조금도 놀라지 않았다. 나는 그쯤은 기대했었기 때문이었다.)
(나는 화를 참기 위해 가능한 한 많이 애썼다.)

ⓑ **as much as to say** = as if to say
(그는 심지어 돈은 모두 없어져야만 한다고까지 말했다.)

ⓒ **not so much A as B**
= A라기 보다는 차라리 B이다
(난 그를 싫어한다기 보다는 차라리 동정한다.)
= I feel sorry for him *rather than* dislike him.

ⓓ **not so much as** = not even
= ~조차도 못 한다
(그는 자기 이름조차 못 쓴다.)

ⓔ **not much** = 너무 ~은 아니다
(바다에서 그는 대단한 뱃사람은 아니라는 것이 판명되었다.)
(비록 우린 친한 친구였지만 요즈음은 그를 자주 만나지 않는다.)

(4) ⓐ **little**은 부정, **a little**은 긍정의 뜻
(아직도 시험 준비할 약간의 시간이 있다.)
(수중에 돈이 거의 없기 때문에 저녁 식사하러 너와 함께 갈 수 없다.)
(합의에 도달할 희망은 거의 없다.)

ⓑ **quite a little** = much
(그녀는 한국 미술에 관해 많이 안다.)
only a little = not much
(그는 그녀의 연설을 겨우 몇 마디만 알아 들었다.)

ⓒ **little**은 부정어로 도치구문을 이끈다.
(그런 끔직한 사고가 나의 가족에게 일어나리라고는 꿈에도 생각을 못했다.)

ⓓ **what little** = all the little that
(나는 미력이나마 전력을 다했다.)

ⓔ **little short of** = almost
(그 암 환자의 회복은 거의 기적이었다.)

문 법 · 작 문

A. Choose a proper word:

(1) To take too (more, many, much) sugar is not good for the health.
(2) There are (little, few) things in this world that give me more pleasure than a long bath.
(3) He is not much better, but there is still (a little, little) hope.
(4) It may sound (strange, strangely); nevertheless, it is true.
(5) The government set the prisoners (freely, free).
(6) How (sweet, sweetly) the rose smells!
(7) Latin is not (an alive, a living) language.
(8) It's all over. There's nothing to be (awful, afraid) of now.
(9) He is (like, similar) his father in many respects.
(10) You should be (satisfactory, content) with a small salary at the beginning.
(11) His conduct is (worthy, worth) of praise.
(12) Is there anything you're not (sure, sure of)?
(13) Cherry trees are planted on (both, either) side.
(14) The work was (good, well) planned; therefore, the results were (good, well).

B. Correct errors:

(1) More doctors were urgently required to tend sick and wounded.
(2) Little care would have prevented the accident.
(3) She is thin and high with light brown hair.
(4) As I was thirsty, I wanted cold something to drink.
(5) He spends twice as more money as I do every day.
(6) An old kind gentleman gave me this book.
(7) Many a careless climbers has been killed here.
(8) I have great many English novels.
(9) There seems to be a little hope of a ceasefire, and even less hope of peace.
(10) He has made little mistakes in his composition.
(11) The distressed is not always unhappy.
(12) He is possible to run for Parliament next year.
(13) The two first days of the week are most hectic for me.
(14) He bought the CD, and there was no left money in his wallet.
(15) In more six months, you'll be able to speak fluent English.

C. Read the following:

(1) March 10th ; March 10

(2) Queen Elizabeth Ⅱ

(3) Chapter V

(4) 6:05 p.m.

(5) the year 1880 ; the year 1600

(6) 205 ; 1,028 ; 263,975 ; 7,524,876

(7) $\frac{1}{5}$; $7\frac{3}{8}$; $\frac{319}{456}$

(8) 475-7272

D. Fill in each blank with a suitable word:

(1) You'll get the feel of it in two hours, but it'll take me as ______ days.

(2) ______ did I dream that I would fall in love with her.

(3) Consult your dictionary as often as ______ .

(4) He was always as ______ as his word.

(5) There are ______, if any, people who believe it.

E. 밑줄 친 부분을 형용사로 바꾸어라.

(1) The stealth fighter is <u>not to be seen</u> to the radar.

(2) The lecturer's speech was <u>not to be heard</u> at the back of the hall.

(3) The testimony of the witness is <u>not to be denied</u>.

(4) His innocence is <u>not to be questioned</u>.

F. Translate the following into English:

(1) 수만 명의 관객이 그 국제 축구 경기를 보러 왔다.

____

(2) 나는 너무 늦게 일어났기 때문에 아침 6시 기차를 놓쳤다.

____

(3) 내 급우들 중 3분의 2가 졸업 후 직장을 구하려고 한다.

____

(4) 그는 화가 나서 얼굴이 빨개졌다.

____

(5) 나는 그가 결점이 없어서가 아니라 결점이 약간 있어서 그를 좋아한다.

____

(6) 현재 그 나라에는 자동차의 수가 전쟁 전의 30배나 된다.

____

(7) 1930년 대에 그의 양친이 사망했을 때 그는 10대 중반이었다.

____

'My Hometown'이라는 제목으로 80어 내외의 글을 지어라.

● 단 문 독 해 ●

The rich are not always happy.
The graceful is better than **the beautiful**.

1. Many a man, no doubt, has been ruined by money, and on the whole, probably **the rich** are more anxious about money matters than **the poor**. To none but **the wise** can wealth bring happiness. The man who is too eager to be rich will always be a poor fellow.

notes :
*be anxious about = 근심하다
*but = except
*wealth는 주어
*be eager to ~ = ~하고 싶어하다

▶▶Which does **not** correspond with the above paragraph?

① Money has undoubtedly destroyed many men's lives.
② The more money we have, the more likely we are to be anxious about it.
③ We can obtain happiness from wealth by using it wisely.
④ One's excessive eagerness to possess more money will result in one's downfall.
⑤ Money is a prerequisite for the happiness of man.

▶▶영작하시오.
많은 사람들이 그들의 미래가 어떻게 될까 걱정한다.

2. The most beautiful and most profound emotion we can experience is the sensation of **the mystical**. It is the source of all true art and science. He to whom this emotion is a stranger, who can no longer pause to wonder and stand rapt in awe, is as good as dead: his eyes are closed.

notes :
*profound 심오한
*mystical 신비적인
*be a stranger to ~ 을 모르다
*rapt in awe 경외심에 넋을 잃고
*as good as = nearly, almost

▶▶According to the above passage, which is **not** correct?

① The experience of a mystical sensation is more profound and beautiful than any other emotion.
② The source of all true art and science is derived from the sensation of the mystical.
③ Those who can't admire mystical experiences are no better than dead men.
④ He who doesn't stand in awe of the mystical experience is like a stranger from another world.
⑤ Those who don't feel the sense of the mystical are emotionally blind.

▶▶영작하시오.
나는 음악에 문외한이다.

The wall was about ten feet high, and **as many** feet thick. The five children began to work **like so many** ants.

3. It is of far greater importance to a man in public life to make one friend who will hold out with him for twenty years, than to find twenty followers in each year, losing **as many** or even a tenth part **as many**.

notes :
*hold out = endure, last
*as many = twenty (followers)
*a tenth part as many = two

▶▶Which of the following is the main topic of the above paragraph?

① When it comes to a man in public life, a wide circle of friends is very helpful for success in his career.

② The more followers a man has in public life, the more useful they are to him.

③ To advance in his field an officeholder had better get acquainted with many people in high places.

④ A true and old friend is more valuable than those many who merely follow.

⑤ The man in public life should try to be everybody's friend to pave a smooth way to success.

▶▶영작하시오.

그는 시험에서 열 줄에 열 개의 실수를 했다.

4. All our streets are lined with trees, and, **like so many** stars among the leaves and branches, the street lamps shed their light. When we pass under them we notice how the light tinges the foliage that is nearest to it with a greenish ash-color.

notes :
*shed 빛을 내다
*tinge … with ~= …을 ~로 물들이다
*foliage = leaves
*it = the light

▶▶Which of the following is most suitable to describe the tone of the above paragraph?

① monotonous and boring

② informative and critical

③ descriptive and poetic

④ persuasive and encouraging

⑤ sarcastic and instructive

▶▶영작하시오.

나무는 가을에 잎이 떨어진다.

> I am **sure that** he will succeed.
> I am **sure of** his success.
> He is **sure to** succeed.

5. La Cachirra asked the boy if he had a novia, a sweetheart, **aware that** so attractive a youth must <u>enjoy the smiles of women</u>, and she knew he lied when he swore he spent his evenings at work.

notes :
*novia (스페인어) = sweetheart 연인
*attractive 매력적인
*swear-swore-sworn 맹세하다

▶▶Which of the following does the underlined phrase imply?
① be fond of women ② be popular with women
③ like making women smile ④ like smiling at women
⑤ be fond of the smiles of women

▶▶영작하시오.
댁의 차가 불법으로 주차되어 있다는 것을 아십니까?

6. The number of countries **capable of** developing nuclear weapons has increased to more than 20 in recent years. If the countries possessing the deadly weapons increase, the control of the weapons will become so much more difficult, resulting in the emergence of nuclear anarchy and increasing the danger of a nuclear war.

notes :
*so much = 그만큼
*result in = 결국 ~이 되다, 결국 ~을 초래하다
*emergence 출현
*anarchy 무정부 상태

▶▶다음 빈칸에 들어갈 가장 알맞은 말을 순서 대로 고르시오.
The writer of the above paragraph maintains that the ( ) of nuclear weapons will inevitably grow out of control and increase the ( ) of a nuclear war.
① capability ② proliferation ③ destructivity
④ emergence ⑤ possibility

▶▶영작하시오.
그의 피곤은 수면 부족 탓이었고 결국 자동차 사고를 초래했다.

> Apples are sold at **so much** a piece.
> Apples are sold at **so many** for ten thousand won.

7. While the dog is generally intelligent, one must remember that he has his limitations, can absorb only **so much** at a time, and must not be forced in his training.

notes :
*While = Though
*absorb 흡수하다
*so much = 일정한 양

▶▶Which of the following is most appropriate for the main idea of the paragraph?

① Great intelligence of a dog
② Physical development of a dog
③ Faithfulness of a dog
④ Difficulties in training a dog
⑤ Proper training of a dog

▶▶영작하시오.

나는 그녀에게 동의는 하지만, 그녀의 계획이 최고라고 믿지는 않는다.

8. We work **so many** hours a day, and, when we have allowed the necessary minimum for such activities as eating and shopping, the rest we spend in various activities which are known as recreations.

notes :
*so many hours = 몇 시간, 일정한 시간
*allow A for B = A를 B에 할당하다

▶▶Which of the following titles would be the most suitable for the above paragraph?

① The Value of Time ② The Preciousness of Time
③ The Allotment of Time ④ The Definition of Time
⑤ The Definition of Recreation

▶▶영작하시오.

그의 아버지는 그에게 용돈으로 월 100달러씩 주신다.

It is getting **colder** day by day.
The scenery struck him **speechless**.

9. Since our power on the earth's surface is entirely dependent on the supply of energy which the earth derives from the sun, we are necessarily dependent upon the sun, and could hardly realize any of our wishes if the sun grew **cold**.

notes :
*power 동력
*derive A from B = B에서 A를 얻다
*realize 실현하다

▶▶The sun is the only (   ) of the earth's energy supply and mankind simply could not (   ) without it.

[destination, source, provision, survive, stand, succeed]

▶▶영작하시오.

너의 성공은 전적으로 너의 노력 여하에 달려 있다.

> 10. I was never afraid of being alone at these times; for I had been brought up in such an out-of-the way place that the lack of human beings at night made me less **fearful** than the sight of them.

notes :
*bring up = 기르다 (= rear)
*out-of-the-way = 외딴(= remote)
*lack 부족, 없는 것
*the sight of them = 사람들을 보는 것

▶▶According to the above paragraph, which of the following is **not** correct?

① The sight of human beings at night made the writer fearful.

② The writer was raised in a remote place.

③ The writer was accustomed to seeing human beings at night.

④ The writer was not afraid when left alone at night.

⑤ It seems that only a few people used to get around at night where the writer grew up.

▶▶영작하시오.

나는 시골에서 자랐기 때문에 항상 전원 생활을 그리워한다.

few, **a** few, **quite a** few little, **a** little, **only a** little

> 11. The French have always been regarded, and rightly, as the thriftiest of people. **Few** Frenchmen live up to their incomes: they manage to put something aside for a rainy day, or better still, add to or found a little family fortune.

notes :
*live up to their incomes = 그들의 수입을 모두 쓰며 살다
*manage to ~ = 이럭저럭 ~하다
*put aside = 저축하다
*add to = increase
*found 설립하다

▶▶Which of the following does **not** correspond with the above paragraph?

① The French have always been considered to be very economical people.

② Quite a few Frenchmen often have difficulties in making both ends meet.

③ Frenchmen usually save their money in preparation for future adversities.

④ Some Frenchmen are thrifty enough to develop a family fortune.

⑤ Frenchmen generally lead a frugal life.

▶▶영작하시오.

우리는 불행한 때를 대비해 매달 약간의 돈을 저축한다.

notes :
*hundreds of thousands of = 수십만의
*inside each (star)
*leave room to spare = 여분의 공간을 남기다

12. **A few** stars are known which are hardly bigger than the earth, but the majority are so large that hundreds of thousands of earths could be packed inside each and leave room to spare.

▶▶The writer describes the (   ) of the universe.
[variety, size, vastness]

▶▶영작하시오.
미안해요, 이 차에는 당신이 탈 자리가 없군요.

notes :
*rely upon = depend upon = be dependent upon
*look out for = search for

13. It is important to learn early to rely upon yourself; for **little** has been done in the world by those who are always looking out for someone to help them.

▶▶윗글의 내용과 일치하도록 할 때, 다음 빈칸에 알맞지 않은 것은?
The earlier you learn to be (   ), the better you are.
① self-reliant ② independent ③ self-sufficient
④ subordinate ⑤ self-supporting

▶▶영작하시오.
항상 남에게 의존하는 사람은 인생의 성공을 기대할 수 없다.

notes :
*by accident = 우연히(= by chance)
*set out = start
*in one's way = 도중에
*chance upon = 우연히 ~을 만나다
*by-product 부산물(副産物)

14. Among the greatest discoveries of science, **quite a few** have been made by accident. Setting out to reach a certain goal, the investigator chances in his way upon a law, or an element, that had no place in his purpose. The discovery is a by-product of his activity.

▶▶According to the above paragraph, which is correct?
① Scientists think highly of only facts and never expect anything to come by a mere chance.
② All our great scientific discoveries have some accidental elements unknown to us.
③ Chance is an indispensable factor in completing a scientific accomplishment.
④ There are many great discoveries in science which have been made accidentally.
⑤ Strictly speaking, a discovery caused by an accidental element can not be scientific.

▶▶영작하시오.
가끔 우리는 우연히 길거리에서 만나곤 했다.

He is **not** a teacher **but** a policeman. He is **not so much** a novelist **as** a poet.

15. A little learning is not dangerous as long as you know that it is little. Danger begins with thinking you know much more than you do. It is **not** knowledge, be it great or small, **but** the conceit of knowledge, that misleads men.

▶▶ According to the above paragraph, which of the following is the writer's ultimate argument?

① A little knowledge is very dangerous under any circumstances.

② You should bear in mind the saying that pride goes before a fall.

③ A man who knows a little is more dangerous than a man who knows nothing.

④ What misleads you is not knowledge itself but your arrogant attitude toward knowledge.

⑤ One's intellectual conceit can be useful only when one is confident in one's knowledge.

▶▶ 영작하시오.

그녀를 당황하게 한 것은 그의 거절이 아니라 그의 무례함이었다.

notes :
*so long as = ~하는 한
*be it great or small = whether it is great or small
*마지막 문장은 It… that의 강조 구문
*conceit 자부심
*mislead 잘못 인도하다

16. I find the great thing in this world is, **not so much** where we stand, **as** in what direction we are moving. To reach the port we must sail sometimes with the wind and sometimes against it, — but we must sail, and not drift, nor lie at anchor.

▶▶ According to the above paragraph, which is correct?

① We must make sure where we stand before moving in a certain direction to achieve our goals.

② To proceed toward our destination at sea we must have certain sailing skills.

③ To reach our goals in life, we must push on through times of good and bad but never remain idle.

④ We must not make an error in choosing the course of our life.

⑤ To stay in one place and wait for your fortune to come is the wisest way to approach your goals in life.

▶▶ 영작하시오.

그는 연주는 고사하고 악기를 제대로 들지도 못했다.

notes :
*the great thing = the important thing
*with the wind = 순풍을 타고
*against it = 역풍을 거슬러서
*drift 표류하다
*lie at anchor = 정박하다

I will try **every** means **possible**.
Give me **something hot** to drink.

17. He could not look her straight in the face. She, observant of this, kept a very steady eye on him, and spoke with **all** calmness **possible**.

notes :
*look ~ in the face = ~의 얼굴을 (똑바로) 쳐다보다
*observant 주의 깊은, 관찰력이 날카로운
*keep an eye on ~ = ~을 지켜보다, ~을 응시하다
*with calmness = calmly

▶▶Which of the following is most appropriate to describe the emotion of the underlined He?

① proud and bold
② impudent and barefaced
③ daring and manly
④ timid and shy
⑤ considerate and discreet

▶▶영작하시오.

그 날카로운 형사는 그의 얼굴을 똑바로 쳐다보고는 무언가 중요한 것을 찾아냈다.

18. Accustomed to playing the host in the highest circles, he charmed and dominated all whom he approached; there was **something** at once **winning** and **authoritative** in his address; and his extraordinary coolness gave him yet another distinction in this society.

notes :
*As he was accustomed to playing ~
*the highest circles = 저명 인사들의 모임
*at once ~ and …= both ~ and …
*authoritative 권위 있는
*address 사람 접대
*distinction 특징, 명성

▶▶According to the above paragraph, which of the following is **not** correct?

① It was quite natural for him to host social gatherings for people of high status.
② He received many celebrities with confidence and authority.
③ His exceptional calmness distinguished him from other people in high society.
④ Many people were fascinated by his particular style of making speeches.
⑤ He was a sociable, charismatic and popular man in his society.

▶▶영작하시오.

(1) 나는 피곤했으므로 평소보다 일찍 잠자리에 들었다.
(2) 그는 엄격한 동시에 다정하다.

● 장 문 독 해 ●

Warming-up

In so far as her education is concerned, I spare no expense.
There is no country where freedom of speech is **more** enjoyed **than** England.
His ill health **interfered with** his work.
You may go if you want **to**.
Do not **associate with** men of low standards.
The job **brings** me **into** constant **touch with** youngsters.

1 It used to be said that ⓐ the Englishman's home is his castle. In as far as this saying creates the impression that there is something defensive and inhospitable about the Englishman's home, it is quite misleading; for there is no country where family life has always been more readily thrown open to friends, and even to strangers, than England. ⓑ It represents a certain truth, however, in the sense that the Englishman hates to be interfered with, and prefers to live without too close a contact with his neighbors. He likes to be able to ⓒ keep himself to himself if he wants to. He readily associates with those who are sympathetic to him, but has no love for the kind of communal life which brings him into constant touch with everybody and anybody. Hence his preference for living in a house to living in a flat.

Philip Carr: *The English Are Like That*

Notes

castle 성 / in as far as ~하는 한(限) / defensive 방어적인 / inhospitable 무뚝뚝한, 불친절한 / misleading 그릇된 인상을 주는 / readily 기꺼이 / represent 나타내다 / in the sense that ~이라는 의미에 있어서 / interfere with 방해하다 / keep oneself to oneself 남들과 어울리지 않다 / associate with ~와 교제하다 / sympathetic 마음이 맞는, 공감을 나타내는 / communal life 공동 생활 / bring into … touch with~=…를 ~와 접촉하게 하다 / hence 그러므로(=for this reason) / preference 선호(=liking) / flat=apartment

Question

1. 본문의 전체내용으로 미루어 밑줄친 ⓐthe Englishman's home is his castle.가 의미하는 바를 20자 이내의 우리말로 쓰시오.

2. 본문의 밑줄친 ⓑit 의 구체적 내용을 본문에서 찾아 쓰시오.

3. 본문의 밑줄친 ⓒ를 다음과 같이 바꿨을 때 빈 칸에 적절한 한 단어를 골라 쓰시오.

remain (   ) from his neighbors

[aloof, segregated, integrated]

4. According to the passage, which of the following is **not** correct?
   ① The Englishman is usually kind and open-hearted to his friends.
   ② The Englishman is fond of keeping on good terms with close friends.
   ③ The English don't want their privacy invaded by other people.
   ④ The Englishman feels rather uncomfortable when he comes into too much close contact with his acquaintances.
   ⑤ The reason the Englishman prefers to live in a house is that it is more comfortable than a flat.

5. Which is most suitable for the main idea of the passage?
   ① Englishmen's reluctance to live a communal life
   ② Englishmen's defensive and hostile attitude
   ③ Englishmen's favorite style of residence
   ④ Englishmen's disposition to enjoy their private life
   ⑤ Englishmen's excessive unsociability

Production

(1) 네 학업에 방해가 되지않으면 일자리를 얻어도 된다.

(2) 영국보다 더 사생활의 권리가 존중되는 나라는 없다.

(3) 그녀는 그 비밀을 남에게 알리지 않았다.

● 장 문 독 해 ●

Warming-up

Such things do **not** happen **every** day.
Pleasure must **be subordinate to** work.
You had better **leave** it **untouched**.
It is not what you have, but what you are **that** matters.
If you do not sign this contract, **others will**.
Cupid, **the god of love**, is the son of Venus.

2 We cannot travel every path. Success must be won along one line. We must make our business the one life purpose to which every other must be subordinate. I hate a thing done by halves. If it is right, do it boldly; if it is wrong, leave it undone.

To live with an ideal is a successful life. It is not what one does, but ⓐ what one tries to do, that makes a man strong. "Eternal vigilance," it has been said, "is the price of liberty." With equal truth it may be said, "Unceasing effort is the price of success." ⓑ If we do not work with all our might, others will; and they will defeat us in the race, and pick the prize from our grasp. Success grows less and less dependent on luck and chance. Self-distrust is the cause of most of our failures. The great and indispensable help to success is character. Character is crystallized habit, the result of training and conviction.

Ernest Hemingway: *Advice to a Young Man*

Notes

path 길 / line 분야 / be subordinate to ~에 종속되다 / by halves 어중간하게 / eternal 영원한 / vigilance 경계 / unceasing 끊임없는 / might 힘 / defeat 패배시키다 / self-distrust 자기 불신 / crystallize 결정(結晶) 시키다 / conviction 신념

Question

1. 본문의 밑줄친 ⓐ<u>what one tries to do</u> 가 가리키는 말을 본문에서 찾아 쓰시오.

2. 본문의 밑줄친 ⓑ를 다음과 같이 바꿔 쓸 때, 빈칸에 적절한 한 단어를 골라 쓰시오.

Unless we do our (　　)

[utterance, utmost, ultimate]

3. Which does **not** correspond with the passage?
① It would be better to do nothing rather than to do things by halves.
② An ideal is a very important element which one needs to lead a successful life.
③ Success doesn't depend on luck and chance but on one's endeavor.
④ The author maintains that because character is inherent in man, it can't be acquired by training and conviction.
⑤ Our failures are likely to be caused by self-distrust.

4. Which of the following is **not** the author's main argument?
① To gain success in life we should concentrate on only one aim.
② Once your sole purpose in life is set up, all your activities should be centered on the accomplishment of it.
③ If we are to preserve our liberty, we should always be vigilant about oncoming dangers.
④ Constant efforts are indispensable to win the competition for success among rivals.
⑤ Character is one of the most crucial factors to decide a man's success in life.

Production

(1) 모든 운동선수들이 다 대중의 영웅이 될 수는 없다.
(2) 일을 어중간하게 하지 말아라.
(3) 인생에 성공하기 위해 전력을 다해 일해야 한다.
(4) 너의 성공은 운이나 기회보다는 차라리 자신의 노력에 달려 있다.

실력체크 I

1 다음 글을 읽고 아래 물음에 답하여라.

ⓐ Good writing is frequently a matter of rewriting. Some people are so gifted that they can put down in the first manuscript exactly what they want to say, and say it very closely to the best possible way of saying it. They do not have to labor over the manuscript afterward, correcting, recasting sentences, rewriting. Some writers work slowly, getting everything right the first time. Others type rapidly, turning out pages and pages, as fast as their fingers can fly over the keys. For nearly all a lot of sweat is required. Don't let any professional writer tell you it isn't hard work. He knows better. My advice is to write as fast as you can, as fast as your mind will function. Then, when you have time, when your mind is clear and rested, go back over it. ⓑ In the cold light of the next day, when you have had time to think over some of the things you have said, you can improve what you have put on paper. There never was a piece of writing that couldn't be improved by rewriting.

notes :
manuscript 원고 / recast 다시 뜯어고치다 / function 작용하다

(1) 윗 글의 밑줄 친 ⓐ와 같은 취지의 문장을 본문에서 찾아 적어라.
(2) 밑줄 친 ⓑ와 같은 의미를 갖는 부분을 본문에서 찾아 적어라.

2 다음 글을 읽고 물음에 답하여라.

Professor Urey regards the flight of Apollo 11 as still one more humbling experience for mankind. "The idea of man as a special creation is out," he said last week. "Man's attitude toward himself is changing rapidly. Man is now capable of seeing himself as a small organism in the universe. The farther out he goes, the smaller and frailer he seems to become." True in one sense but wide of the mark in another. If the flight of Apollo 11 demonstrated one triumphant truth above all other revelations, it is the discovery of how great and powerful the image of man becomes, the farther out he goes. The pre-eminent figures, of course, are Armstrong, Aldrin, Collins...... and their families. But all of us rode with them.

notes :
is out = is no longer valid / frail 나약한 / wide of the mark 빗나간, 적중하지 못한 / demonstrate 시위하다, 과시하다, 나타내다 / triumph 승리 (triumphant 의기양양한) / reveal 나타내다 (revelation 폭로, 놀라운 발견)

(1) Apollo 11호의 비행에 대한 두 견해를 간단히 요약하여라.
(2) 밑줄 친 부분을 구체적으로 설명하여라.

3 다음 글을 읽고 아래 제시된 문장 뒤에 이어질 알맞은 말을 골라라.

Creative thinking is a process of attacking a problem by studying all the available facts, then finding previously unknown or unrecognized relationships among them, and coming up with a solution. It applies equally to the mental process of a Thomas Edison, a space scientist, or a housewife hitting upon a new and faster way to iron a shirt. The business world pays generously for ideas, for productive creative thinking. Leaders in many fields have said that a good part of the world's future depends on the creative ideas developed and proposed for every aspect of living. Anyone can improve his chances of making a contribution.

notes :
attack 착수하다 / come up with (해답 등을) 생각해 내다 / hit upon ~을 생각해 내다 / in good part 상당히 / make a contribution 기여하다

(1) In creative thinking we (　　　).
① make anything that may be necessary for life
② solve a problem by merely examining the facts
③ attack a problem that cannot be solved by science
④ discover connections hidden under the surface of the facts
⑤ come up with an idea which will make us rich

(2) The processes of creative thinking are found in (　　　).
① an inventive mind ② spiritual vitality ③ a practical mind
④ exact calculation ⑤ scientific data

4 다음 글을 읽고 아래 질문에 답하여라.

How difficult it is even for a grown and reasonable man to do his fellow beings justice without reference to their external appearance! Beauty is a letter of recommendation which it is almost impossible to ignore; and we attribute too often the ugliness of the face to the character. Or, to be more precise, we make no attempt to get beyond the mask of the face to the realities behind it, but run away from the ugly at sight without even trying to find out (　　　).

notes :
reasonable 분별있는, 합리적인 / do+사람[사물]+justice = ~을 올바르게 평가하다 / external 외부의 / to be precise = 엄밀히 말하면

(1) 글 끝의 (　　) 안에 들어갈 가장 적당한 어구를 고르시오.
① how they look to others ② what they are really like
③ how miserable they feel ④ what others think of them

(2) What does the writer advise us to do? Answer in English.

실력체크 II

A. Choose a suitable word:

(1) He had a (heavy, big, serious) illness for ages.
(2) Mary had a (slight, light) cold for a time.
(3) The traffic was (busy, crowded) on the road this morning.
(4) I prefer my coffee (thin, weak) especially first thing in the morning.
(5) For God's sake, try to be more (healthful, healthy).
(6) He was (famous, notorious) as a dictator.
(7) These oranges taste (nicely, nice).
(8) He is one of my (far, distant) cousins on my father's side.
(9) The railway strike caused many workers to be (lazy, idle).
(10) Lincoln made his (historic, historical) speech at Gettysburg.
(11) The price of oil is twice as (high, expensive) as it was last year.
(12) As the speech was dull, many of them were (boring, bored).
(13) She's very (exciting, excited) about getting the part in the film.
(14) He has acquired a (practical, practicable) knowledge of English.
(15) She is very (economic, economical) and has saved much money.
(16) Mr. and Mrs. Russell are staying at a (luxurious, luxuriant) hotel.
(17) The mother always pampers her (bad, spoiled) child.
(18) He is a (desirable, desirous) person; I am (desirable, desirous) of employing him.
(19) Is the baby (able, possible) to walk yet?
(20) The (industrial, industrious) farmer works from dawn to dark.
(21) You are (welcome, welcomed) to any book in my library.

B. Fill in the blanks:

(1) as _______ as a lion
(2) as _______ as a bat
(3) as _______ as a hawk
(4) as _______ as a beaver
(5) as _______ as a fox
(6) as _______ as a king
(7) as _______ as a sheet
(8) as _______ as a bee
(9) as _______ as a cucumber
(10) as _______ as a peacock

Answer: A. (1) serious (2) slight (3) busy (4) weak (5) healthy (6) notorious (7) nice (8) distant (9) idle (10) historic (11) high (12) bored (13) excited (14) practical (15) economical (16) luxurious (17) spoiled (18) desirable, desirous (19) able (20) industrious (21) welcome
B. (1) brave (2) blind (3) hungry (4) busy (5) sly 혹은 cunning (6) happy (7) white (8) busy (9) cool (10) proud

C. 각 쌍의 두 글의 차이를 말하여라.

(1) ⓐ He left his son rich. ⓑ He left his rich son.

(2) ⓐ He shot the dead tiger. ⓑ He shot the tiger dead.

(3) ⓐ The present members are in favor of his suggestion.
ⓑ The members present are in favor of his suggestion.

D. 다음을 문장 끝의 지시대로 바꿔 쓰시오.

(1) Mr. Green was foolish to agree to the proposal. (It을 주어로)

(2) Will the examination be hard to pass? (it을 주어로)

(3) I'm sorry that I have caused all this trouble. (단문으로)

(4) This room is pleasant to work in. (This를 주어로)

(5) We are all anxious that you should return. (부정사를 사용하여)

E. 공란을 적당한 형용사로 메워라.

(1) One who is easily impressed is an ______ person.
One who impresses others deeply is an ______ person.

(2) A girl who shows love for someone is a ______ girl.
A girl who inspires love is a ______ girl.

(3) An event which deserves one's memory is a ______ event.
An arch built in memory of a person is a ______ arch.

F. 이탤릭체 단어를 형용사로 바꾸어 다음 문장을 다시 써라.

(1) She *narrowly* escaped drowning.

(2) You will *surely* need more money.

(3) The old couple lived *happily*.

(4) He *envied* me my trip around the world.

(5) Are you *attending* to what I am saying?

(6) You must study mathematics *systematically*.

(7) A day with the *sun* shining cheers us up.

Answer: C. (1) ⓐ 그는 자식에게 큰 유산을 남겼다. ⓑ 그는 부자인 자식 곁을 떠났다. (2) ⓐ 그는 죽은 호랑이를 쏘았다. ⓑ 그는 그 호랑이를 쏘아 죽였다. (3) ⓐ 현재의 회원들은 그의 제안에 찬성한다. ⓑ 참석한 회원들은 그의 제안에 찬성한다. D. (1) It was foolish of Mr. Green to agree to the proposal. (2) Will it be hard to pass the examination? (3) I'm sorry to have caused all this trouble. (4) This is a pleasant room to work in. (5) We are all anxious for you to return. E. (1) impressionable, impressive (2) loving, lovable (3) memorable, memorial F. (1) She had a narrow escape from drowning. (2) I am sure that you will need more money. (3) The old couple lived a happy life. (4) He was envious of my trip around the world. (5) Are you attentive to what I am saying? (6) You must make a systematic study of mathematics. (7) A sunny day cheers us up.

어 휘 · 발 음

A. Choose a suitable word:

(1) The medication was (beneficial, beneficent) to him in curing the disease.

(2) No other power is (comparable, comparative) to that of the printed word.

(3) We should be (considerable, considerate) of the comfort of the old people.

(4) He is (contemptible, contemptuous) for his rude behavior.

(5) I'm very (pleasant, pleased) you've decided to come.

(6) All the characters in this book are (imaginable, imaginary).

(7) An (ingenious, ingenuous) smile brightened her lovely face.

(8) This book is (intelligible, intelligent) to the initiated.

(9) The solution of the problem is very (momentary, momentous) to the development of our economy.

(10) I have no (object, objection) to your proposal.

(11) He is an expert in physics. He is a (physician, physicist).

(12) Success as a lawyer was her (principal, principle) goal.

(13) He is (regretful, regrettable) for what he has done.

(14) You should be (respectable, respectful) towards seniors.

(15) It was very (sensible, sensitive) of her to follow his advice.

(16) The school team has won five (successive, successful) games.

B. 밑줄 친 단어와 같은 뜻의 단어를 골라라.

(1) He expressed a **candid** opinion.

① candidate ② thoughtful ③ outspoken ④ valuable

(2) One should learn the **judicious** use of time and money.

① various ② lawful ③ prudent ④ habitual

(3) It was a very **desolate** garden.

① separate ② impolite ③ determined ④ lonely

(4) The **assiduous** student worked hard to earn her degree.

① sincere ② cordial ③ insolent ④ industrious

Answer: A. (1) beneficial (2) comparable (3) considerate (4) contemptible (5) pleased (6) imaginary (7) ingenuous (8) intelligible (9) momentous (10) objection (11) physicist (12) principal (13) regretful (14) respectful (15) sensible (16) successive B. (1) ③ (2) ③ (3) ④ (4) ④

C. 밑줄 친 단어와 의미가 다른 것은?

(1) His report on the higher education was **ambiguous**.

① vague ② explicit ③ equivocal ④ indefinite

(2) In later years he came to be a **prominent** statesman.

① inconspicuous ② eminent ③ leading ④ outstanding

(3) In dealing with others, it is the **discreet** man who is less likely to give offense.

① careful ② wary ③ cautious ④ rash

(4) He is **keen** to find out the solution.

① eager ② intent ③ anxious ④ apathetic

D. 밑줄 친 단어의 발음이 같은 짝을 하나 고르시오.

(1) ⓐ She tears the cloth to pieces.
ⓑ Tears ran down her cheeks.

(2) ⓐ He will present you with a book.
ⓑ He was present at the meeting.

(3) ⓐ Do not desert me in misfortune.
ⓑ The camel lives in the desert.

(4) ⓐ His conduct is worthy of praise.
ⓑ He will conduct you to the place.

(5) ⓐ His house is quite close.
ⓑ Please close the door.

(6) ⓐ What's this tool used for?
ⓑ That's where I used to live.

(7) ⓐ Twenty lives were lost in the battle.
ⓑ He lives in the country.

(8) ⓐ The dog licked its wound.
ⓑ The river wound its way to the sea.

(9) ⓐ He is a quite perfect gentleman.
ⓑ They perfect their plans.

(10) ⓐ I received a slight bow of recognition from her.
ⓑ We must bow to the universal law.

Answer: C. (1) ② (2) ① (3) ④ (4) ④ D. (10)

숙 어

(1) **make a difference** (=be significant, matter) 중요하다, 문제가 되다
☞ One false step will *make* a great *difference* to us.
It doesn't *make any difference* whether he agrees or not.

(2) **make a face** (=frown, grimace) 얼굴을 찡그리다
☞ Opening the door, he *made a face* at the stinking smell.

(3) **make a fool of oneself** (=make an ass of oneself) 놀림감이 되다
☞ He *made a fool of himself* by turning up drunk to a TV talk show.

(4) **make a fuss** (=cause a needless commotion) 야단법석을 떨다
☞ I'm sure she'll be here soon, so please don't *make a fuss* over it.

(5) **make a note of** (=write down so as to remember) ~을 적어두다
☞ I'll *make a note of* the fact that I must visit the prospective client sooner or later.

(6) **make allowance(s) for** (=take into consideration) ~을 참작[감안]하다
☞ You have to *make allowances for* her inexperience in the task.

(7) **make amends for** (=give compensation) 보상하다
☞ He must *make amends for* the harm he has caused you.

(8) **make away[off] with** (=steal and carry away) 훔쳐 달아나다
☞ The cashier *made away with* all the money in the safe.

(9) **make believe** (=pretend) ~인체하다
☞ The spoiled boy *made believe* he didn't hear his father calling.

(10) **make (both) ends meet** (=balance one's income and expenditure) 수입과 지출을 맞추다, 빚 안지고 살아가다
☞ These days I scarcely earn enough money to *make ends meet.*

(11) **make do with** (=manage with) 그럭저럭 때우다[해나가다]
☞ There wasn't much food, but we *made do with* it.

(12) **make for** (=go toward ; make possible) 향해가다 ; 가능하게 하다

☞ They took their ice skates and *made for* the frozen pond.
The new computers *make for* much greater productivity.

(13) **make good** (=succeed) 성공하다

☞ She graduated from college, then *made good* as an attorney.

(14) **make head or tail of** (=understand) 이해하다

☞ Can you *make head or tail of* the letter written so badly?

(15) **make it** (=arrive in time ; succeed) 시간에 대다 ; 성공하다

☞ The flight leaves in ten minutes—I'll never *make it*.
He owns a good business and has *made it* big in life.

(16) **make light[little] of** (=treat as unimportant) 경시하다, 무시하다

☞ I thought the problem was serious, but he *made light of* it.

(17) **make much of** (=consider as very important) 중요시하다

☞ Why are you *making* so *much of* such a trivial matter?

(18) **make nothing of** (=fail to understand ; treat lightly)
이해하지 못하다 ; 아무렇지 않게 여기다

☞ I could *make nothing of* what the speaker said.
He *made nothing of* walking three miles to buy a newspaper.

(19) **make one's mark** (=become famous) 유명해지다

☞ It was not long at college before he *made his mark*.

Exercise

▶▶ 주어진 단어들을 포함한 글을 지어라. 필요하면 어형을 변화시켜라.

1. exercise / difference / state / health
2. they / fuss / play / it / success
3. make / allowances / lack / experience
4. burglars / off / with / money / jewelry
5. He / believe / not / hear
6. due / recession / people / make / meet
7. We / do / little
8. sure / good / job / new
9. I / make / tail / she
10. much / advice / father / give

15. 형 용 사(Adjective) Ⅱ

기본 문법 설명

A. 형용사의 비교 변화	(1) Regular exercise made him **healthier** than before. (2) This knife is so blunt it's **more useless** than a spoon. (3) The movie is the **worst** one I've ever seen! (4) Our product is **inferior to** our competitor's.
B. 비교법의 종류	(1) ⓐ He is **as meticulous as** his father. Johnson is **as** cunning **as** wicked. ⓑ He was **not as stingy as** he was thought to be. (2) ⓐ Water is **heavier than** oil. ⓑ The new edition is **less expensive** than the old one. ⓒ She and her husband are both forgetful, but she is *the* more forgetful **of the two**. I like him all *the* better **because** he has faults. ⓓ **The more** one gets, **the more** one wants. ⓔ I think he is **more** sly than clever. This book is for *the younger generation.* (3) ⓐ Smith is **the tallest** of all the students here. Of all those boys he ran (**the**) **fastest**. ⓑ She is **the greatest** poet *that has ever lived.* He is **the greatest** poet *that Korea has ever had.* ⓒ **The wisest** man doesn't always make a right decision. ⓓ The lake is **deepest** at this point. These flowers are **most beautiful** at this time of the year. ⓔ He was standing there with **a most** peculiar expression on his face. ⓕ He is **the last** man to break a promise. (4) ⓐ **No** (**other**) mountain in the world is **as** (혹은 **so**) **high as** Mt. Everest. ⓑ **No** (**other**) mountain in the world is **higher than** Mt. Everest. ⓒ Mt. Everest is **higher than any other** *mountain* in the world. ⓓ Mt. Everest is **the highest of all** (**the**) *mountains* in the world.

A. 형용사의 비교 변화

(1) **비교의 변화 형식**

단음절어와 흔히 쓰는 2음절어(-er, -ow, -le, -y, -ly 등으로 끝나는 것)는 원급에 **-er, -est**를 붙여 비교급, 최상급을 만든다.

fine	finer	finest
big	bigger	biggest
easy	easier	easiest

(2) **more, most**를 붙일 때 : 대다수의 2음절어와 3음절어 이상의 말

active *more* active *most* active

(3) **불규칙변화 형식**

good / well	better	best
bad / ill	worse	worst
many / much	more	most
little	less	least
far	farther / further	farthest / furthest

☞ far의 경우, 거리를 뜻할 때는「farther, farthest」와「further, furthest」가 혼용되고, 정도를 뜻할 때는「further, furthest」

We walked a mile *farther*[*further*] down the road.

Let's consider this point *further*.

late	later / latter	latest (시간) / last (순서)

☞ the *latest* news (최근의 소식)
the *last* news (마지막 소식)

(4) **라틴어 비교급** : 어미가 -or인 형용사의 비교급은 than이 아닌 *to*를 쓴다.

<*ex.*> superior, inferior, senior, junior 등

He is three years *senior to* me.

B. 비교법의 종류

(1) **원급에 의한 비교**

ⓐ 동등비교 (아버지처럼 꼼꼼하다.)
(사악하기도 하고 교활하기도 하다.)

ⓑ 열등비교
(생각한 것처럼 그렇게 인색하지 않았다.)

(2) **비교급에 의한 비교**

ⓐ 우등비교 (물은 기름보다 무겁다.)

ⓑ 열등비교
= The new edition is *not as* expensive *as* the old one.

ⓒ the 비교급+ of the two
all the 비교급 + for[because]
= I like him *all the better for* his faults.

ⓓ The 비교급, the 비교급
= ~하면 할수록, …하다
The more haste, *the less* speed.
(급할수록 돌아가라.)

ⓔ 동일인의 성질비교는 -er을 쓰지 않고 more를 쓴다. 여기서 more는 rather의 뜻이다. (나는 그가 영리하기 보다는 교활하다고 생각한다.)
She is *more* mother than wife.

☞ 비교의 상대없이 비교급을 쓰는 절대비교급
the *higher* classes
the *greater* part of = ~의 대부분

(3) **최상급에 의한 비교**

ⓐ 형용사의 최상급에 the를 붙인다.
of, among은「~중에서」의 뜻이다.
부사의 최상급에는 원칙적으로 the를 안쓰나, 구어에서는 쓰기도 한다.

ⓑ 최상급의 뜻을 강조하여 that has ever lived, that Korea has ever had

ⓒ even의 뜻을 가지는 최상급
(아무리 현명한 사람이라도 언제나 옳은 결정을 하는 것은 아니다.)

ⓓ (the) 최상급의 의미상 차이
The lake is *the deepest* (one) in Korea.
These flowers are *the most beautiful* (ones) in the garden.

ⓔ 절대최상급
a most = a very
☞ at best = 기껏해야, at most = 많아야

ⓔ (그는 약속을 어길 사람이 절대 아니다.)
= He is *the most* unlikely man to break a promise.

(4) **같은 내용을 나타내는 비교 형식**

Mt. Everest is the highest mountain in the world. 의 내용을 네 가지로 달리 나타낼 수 있다.

ⓐ 부정 주어+as (혹은 so)+원급+as~

ⓑ 부정 주어+비교급+than~

ⓒ 주어+비교급+than any other+단수 명사

ⓓ 주어+최상급+of all (the)+복수 명사

문 법 · 작 문

A. 공란을 메워라.

[원급]	[비교급]	[최상급]
(1) dry	________	________
(2) ________	worse	________
(3) ________	later	________
(4) ________	________	last
(5) thin	________	________
(6) famous	________	________

B. 다음 각 문장의 틀린 것을 고쳐라.

(1) Which do you like, soccer or basketball?
(2) This is superior than that in both quality and quantity.
(3) Of the two girls, she is prettier.
(4) Solomon was the wisest of all the other Jewish kings.
(5) She is the wealthiest of any woman here.
(6) He is the most hardworking of his class.
(7) The sooner I try to finish my report, the more it becomes difficult.
(8) Jane is the most beautiful of the two women.
(9) You can't get its repair free of charge, still more its free replacement.
(10) He is shier than humble.
(11) The job you applied for is junior than your current position.
(12) I prefer to stay at home than to go out on such a rainy day.
(13) This bridge has been under construction since the later part of last month.
(14) I always put little sugar into tea than into coffee.
(15) Any farther heated discussion on this matter would be pointless.
(16) For a growing child a small town seems to be more preferable to a large city.
(17) As you grow old, you will realize the truth of this saying all the more clearly.
(18) He gave me no more than $500,000; it was a huge sum to me.
(19) The army suffered very heavier casualties than in the last battle.
(20) This lake is the deepest at this point.
(21) He is as rich, or even richer than, his uncle.
(22) Give me a coke, or something to drink.
(23) There is no richer man in this town than he is.

C. 공란에 적당한 말을 넣어 문장을 완성하여라.

(1) _____ people can afford to pay those prices for clothes these days than a few years ago.

(2) There's very little coal, less iron than _____ and still less oil than _____.

(3) The number of the wounded is much _____ than might be supposed.

(4) On account of a heavy loss in business, he is _____ off than ever.

(5) Time is more valuable than anything _____ , but nothing is _____ valued.

(6) You are all _____ better for your faults.

(7) I don't even suggest that he's negligent, still _____ that he's dishonest.

(8) The sun sets _____ in summer than in winter.

(9) Although I was freezing I gave the wine to the poor beggar, for I thought he wanted something to warm up his inside far _____ than I did.

(10) As a working mother she felt she had all the problems of motherhood with very _____ of the benefits.

D. 다음 각 문장을 '셰익스피어는 가장 유명한 극작가다.'라는 뜻이 되도록 공란에 적합한 말을 넣어라.

(1) Shakespeare is the _____ famous _____ all playwrights.

(2) Shakespeare is _____ famous than any _____ _____ .

(3) No other playwright is _____ famous _____ Shakespeare.

(4) No other playwright is _____ famous as Shakespeare.

E. 각 문장 끝의 지시대로 다음 문장을 고쳐 써라.

(1) No period of life is happier than one's school days. <원 급>

(2) Perhaps Big Ben is the largest clock in the world. <비교급>

(3) Busan is the best seaport in Korea. <원 급>

(4) I have never seen a more beautiful sight than this. <최상급>

(5) He was as brave a soldier as ever shouldered a gun. <최상급>

(6) Nothing is as precious as health. <비교급>

(7) It seems less difficult than before. <원 급>

(8) She is no less lovely than her sister. <원 급>

(9) There is nothing more dangerous than to try to appear what one is not. <최상급>

F. Translate the following sentences:

(1) *No more than* ten people applied for the job.
No less than ten people applied for the job.

(2) There were *not more than* a hundred people at the political rally.
There were *not less than* a hundred people at the political rally.

(3) A whale is *no more* a fish *than* a horse is.
= A whale is *not* a fish *any more than* a horse is.

(4) He is *no less* energetic *than* his brothers.
He is *not less* energetic *than* his brothers.

(5) He is *not more* intelligent *than* any other student in his class.
He is *no more* intelligent *than* any other student in his class.

(6) He is *no better than* a beggar.
He *knows better than to* do such an offensive thing.

(7) Every one has a right to enjoy his liberties, *still more* his life.
I can hardly walk, *much less* run.

(8) He studied all *the harder*, because his teacher praised him.
I love him *none the less* for his faults.

(9) I was *more than* pleased with the news.

(10) I had *no sooner* started mowing the lawn *than* it started raining.
= *No sooner* had I started mowing the lawn *than* it started raining.

(11) Anything will do, *so long as* it is interesting.
You'll want for nothing *as long as* I live.

(12) He is *the last* man to walk out on his wife and children.
I was *the last* person in line to get tickets for the concert.

(13) She has a cat *as well as* two dogs as pets.
= She has *not only* two dogs, *but also* a cat as pets.

(14) The movie is *at once* educational *and* humorous.

(15) She is *as* proud *as anything*.

(16) I will go with you *as far as* Suwon.

(17) He was *as* good an officer *as ever* served this country.
He was *as* hard-working *as any* student in his class.

(18) As the deadline for our client's order drew nearer, we were *as* busy *as possible*.

(19) *The wisest* man sometimes makes a mistake.

(20) *As* rust eats iron, *so* care eats the heart.

(21) She is *as* kind *as* can be.

G. Translate the following into English:

(1) 너는 영어와 수학 중 어느 쪽을 더 좋아하니?

(2) Tom과 Judy 중에서 Tom이 키가 더 크다.

(3) 그는 나보다 3배나 더 많은 책을 가지고 있다.

(4) 그 여자는 보기만큼 그리 젊지 않다.

(5) 날씨가 점점 추워지고, 해가 점점 짧아진다.

(6) 그가 겸손하기 때문에, 나는 그를 더욱 더 좋아한다.

(7) 강아지와 마찬가지로, 튼튼하고 건강한 어린애는 가만히 앉아 있질 못한다.

(8) 나는 이것보다 더 아름다운 그림을 본 적이 없다.

(9) 외국인과 접할 기회가 많아짐에 따라, 외국어 공부가 더 필요해진다.

(10) 그는 이 학급의 어느 학생 못지 않게 총명하다.

(11) 그 여자는 허영심이 있다기보다 오히려 거만하다.

(12) 그는 불어를 말할 수 있다. 하물며 영어는 더 잘 한다.

(13) 그는 자신이 그 여자보다 못하다고 생각하고 있다.

(14) 그는 친구를 배반할 사람이 절대 아니다.

(15) 그 약을 먹었는데도 전혀 차도가 없다.

(16) 화창한 봄날 해변가를 따라 걷는 것보다 더 기분좋은 일은 없다.

(17) 이 학급의 가장 어린 학생도 너의 형보다 두세 살 위다.

'My Family' 라는 제목으로 70어 내외의 글을 지어라.

● 단 문 독 해 ●

동등비교 · 우등비교 · 열등비교

1. I was only five years old when my mother died, but her image is **as** fresh in my mind, now that twenty years have elapsed, **as** it was at the time of her death. I remember her, as a pale, gentle being, with a sweet smile, and a voice soft and cheerful.

notes :
*elapse (시간이) 지나가다
*pale 창백한
*cheerful 즐거운, 명랑한

▶▶Though many years have passed, the image of my mother is still (　　　) in my mind.
[vain, vague, vivid]

▶▶영작하시오.
그 사건이 일어났을 때, 나는 한낱 어린애에 불과했다.

2. In the daily lives of most men and women, <u>fear</u> plays a great**er** part **than** hope: they are **more** filled with the thought of the possessions that others may take from them, **than** of the joy that they might create in their own lives and in the lives with which they come in contact.

notes :
*possession 소유물
*take A from B = B에게서 A를 빼앗다
*than (the thought) of the joy

▶▶윗글의 밑줄친 <u>fear</u>의 구체적 내용을 우리말로 간단히 쓰시오.

▶▶영작하시오.
최근에 당신의 변호사하고 접촉한 일이 있습니까?

3. The destiny of Man is not limited to his existence on earth. He exists **less** by the actions performed during his life **than** by the wake he leaves behind him like a shooting star.

notes :
*less A than B = rather B than A
*wake 자국
*a shooting star = 유성

▶▶Though our life here on the earth is temporary, we can live an (　　　) life by what we leave behind us.
[eternal, extra, exclusive]

▶▶영작하시오.
신판 브리테니커 백과 사전이 구판보다 비싸지 않다.

4. Often the people instinctively choose the right man; sometimes, unfortunately, their choice is determined by emotional tests unrelated to the hero's capacity for ruling, and they find too late that they have picked the wrong man and now cannot get rid of him **as** easily **as** they adopted him.

notes :
*test 시금석, 척도
*unrelated 관계가 없는
*get rid of = remove

▶▶Which is the main topic of the above paragraph?
① We have the instinct by which we can decide the most qualified man.
② It is impossible for us to judge our leader without an emotional bias.
③ The ability for ruling is the only thing by which we can judge our leader.
④ We should choose our leader reasonably, not emotionally.
⑤ We should devise simpler procedures to depose our leaders we've wrongly chosen.

▶▶영작하시오.
너는 너의 그 나쁜 습관을 될 수 있는 대로 빨리 없애야 한다.

5. There is **no** love **as** unselfish **as** parental love. There is nothing which true parents have **more** at heart **than** the highest welfare of their children. There is no way in which a child can please father and mother **better than** by doing that which is for its own highest good.

notes :
*welfare 복지, 행복
*please 즐겁게 하다
*good 이익
*A child can please father and mother best by doing that which is for its own highest good.

▶▶What pleases our parents most? Answer in Korean.
▶▶영작하시오.
사업에서 신용만큼 중요한 것은 없다.

As far as the eye can see, the plain is covered with snow.

6. In some parts of the world there are great tracts of country called deserts. In these deserts nothing can be seen but sand, and stones and rocks, **as far as** the eye can see.

notes :
*tract 넓은 면적
*country 지역

▶▶In deserts, the (   ) things we can (   ) are sand, stones and rocks.
[older, open, only, send, save, see]
▶▶영작하시오.
그 도시는 눈길이 미치는 한 온통 불바다였다.

7. Language is a product of the human mind, and reflects its operations. **In as far**, then, **as** the human mind is one and the same all the world over, human speech is bound to exhibit some common features wherever it comes into being.

notes :
*one and the same = exactly the same
*come into being = exist

▶▶윗글의 내용에 부합하도록 아래 빈칸에 들어가기에 가장 적절한 것은?

Human speech, being a product of the human mind, inevitably shows some (   ) characteristics all over the world.

① simple ② complicated ③ similar
④ fundamental ⑤ reflective

▶▶영작하시오.

집에 문제가 있으면 틀림없이 너의 일에 영향을 미칠 것이다.

A whale is **no more** a fish **than** a horse is.
A whale is **not** a fish **any more than** a horse is.
He has **no more than** a hundred dollars.

8. We may sometimes think our country has done us personally an injury, but that gives us **no more** a right not to love our country **than** does an injury received from our father or mother gives us a right to hate our father or mother.

notes :
*do ~ an injury = ~에게 피해를 주다
*but that에서 that은 앞문장 전체를 가리킴.

▶▶Which does **not** correspond with the above paragraph?

① The writer inspires the readers to be patriotic.
② According to the writer our allegiance to our nation should be unconditional.
③ Although we may be injured by our country, our loyalty to it should remain unchanged.
④ We should be faithful to our nation, let alone to our parents.
⑤ The only justification for a government's existence is the improvement of the people's welfare and therefore it could be overthrown if it fails to provide it.

▶▶영작하시오.

사랑이 없는 가정이 가정이 아닌 것은, 영혼이 없는 육체가 사람이 아닌 것과 같다.

9. We are **never more** in danger **than** when we think ourselves most secure, **nor** in reality **more** secure **than** when we seem to be in danger.

notes :
*most = very
*nor = and ~ not

▶▶The writer claims that our (   ) can be our enemy.
[secrets, security, savings]

▶▶영작하시오.
그 노인은 어린애들한테 둘러싸일 때만큼 행복한 적이 없었다.

10. John was eight years older than she and for many years he paid her scanty attention, though he took it for granted that eventually they would marry; the engagement papers had been signed while he was only a child and Judith **no more than** a baby.

notes :
*take it for granted that ~=~을 당연한 것으로 여기다
*engagement papers = 약혼증서

▶▶Which does **not** correspond with the above paragraph?
① John had been born eight years before Judith was born.
② For ages Judith was paid little attention to by John.
③ John looked forward to the day when he would marry Judith.
④ Two people were engaged to each other in their childhood.
⑤ There was a document to verify their engagement.

▶▶영작하시오.
나는 으레 그가 우리를 도와 주리라고 여겼다.

11. We can**not** create an observing faculty **any more than** we can create a memory, but we may do much to develop both.

notes :
*faculty 능력, 재능
*memory 기억력
*may = can

▶▶Though observation and memory are (   ), they can be (   ) by our efforts.
[indifferent, inherent, destined, developed]

▶▶영작하시오.
운이 항상 좋을 수 없듯이 나쁠 수도 없다.

He can speak French, and **much more** English.
He can't speak English, **still less** French.

12. It is a familiar saying that the only school where fools learn is the school of experience. If the lessons of experience are profitable to foolish students, **much more** must they be to the wise.

notes :
*It = that~ experience
*saying 속담, 격언
*profitable 유익한

▶▶윗 글의 요지가 되도록 빈 칸에 알맞은 단어를 써 넣으시오.
The (   ) of experience

▶▶영작하시오.
세월은 사람을 기다리지 않는다는 옛 말이 있다.

13. Culture is not an ornament to decorate a phrase, **still less** to show off your knowledge, but a means, painfully acquired, to enrich the soul.

notes :
*ornament 장식품
*show off = 자랑하다
*acquired는 means를 수식

▶▶We painfully acquire (   ) not to decorate our outer surface but to enrich our inner soul.
[culture, knowledge, decoration]

▶▶영작하시오.
그는 해외 여행으로 견문을 넓혔다.

The more we have, **the more** we want.
I like him all **the** better **for** his faults.

14. Length of years is no proper test of length of life. A man's life is to be measured by what he does in it, and what he feels in it. **The more** useful work the man does and **the more** he thinks and feels, **the more** he really lives. The idle, useless man, no matter to what extent his life may be prolonged, merely vegetates.

notes :
*proper test = 적당한 척도
*life is to be에서 is to = should
*prolong 연장하다
*vegetate 무위도식하다

▶▶Which is the main topic of the above paragraph?
① One's age is the standard by which we can judge the value of his experiences.
② The judgment of one's life depends on the achievements and contributions he has made in life.
③ The old should be respected by the young regardless of their attainments.
④ The harder we work, the longer we live.
⑤ There is a proportional relation between one's value and age.

▶▶영작하시오.
그의 제안을 생각할수록 나는 더욱 그것이 싫다.

15. The political freedom we have today will never be too easy to preserve. It came out of struggle, and it may still demand struggle. It came out of wisdom and patience. We may honor the fathers of the Declaration all **the** more **because** now that we ourselves live in a time of peril we can understand their danger and their courage.

notes :
*too = very
*honor 존경하다
*peril 위험

▶▶Write the three main elements by which we can get political freedom. Answer in Korean.

▶▶영작하시오.
아무리 늙어도 배울 수 있다.

The wisest man cannot know everything. He is **the last** man to tell a lie.

16. "**The weakest man**," says Carlyle, "by concentrating his powers on a single object, can accomplish something; whereas **the strongest**, by dispersing his over many, may fail to accomplish anything."

notes :
*concentrate 집중하다
*dispersing his (powers) over many (objects)

▶▶While you can accomplish something with (   ) efforts, you can attain nothing with your efforts (   ).
[strengthened, concentrated, dividing, dispersed]

▶▶영작하시오.
아무리 수영을 잘 하는 사람이라도 익사할 수 있다.

17. It was early and there was only one other person in the library. He was seated in a big leather chair absorbed in a book. I was surprised to see it was Larry. He was **the last** person I had expected to find in such a place.

notes :
*leather 가죽
*absorbed in = ~에 몰두하여

▶▶Which of the following does **not** correspond with the above paragraph?
① He had been reading a book before the writer entered the library.
② Surprisingly the writer found him lost in reading a book.
③ The writer was surprised to recognize his acquaintance in the library.
④ He was the last person the writer had seen in the library.
⑤ He had been considered to be uninterested in books.

▶▶영작하시오.
그는 생각에 잠겨 공원을 걷고 있었다.

She is **no less** beautiful **than** her sister.
She is **not less** beautiful **than** her sister.
He has **no less than** a million dollars.

18. Resignation, however, has also its part to play in the conquest of happiness, and it is a part **no less** essential **than** that played by effort. The wise man, though he will not sit down under preventable misfortunes, will not waste time and emotion upon such as are unavoidable.

notes :
*its part to play 자기가 해야 할 역할
*that = the part
*such (misfortunes) as

▶▶윗글의 문맥으로 보아 윗글 바로 앞에 올 수 있는 내용은?
① How to overcome misfortunes
② Importance of resignation in achieving our happiness
③ Significance of our efforts in seeking our happiness
④ The wise man's conquest of happiness
⑤ A role played by resignation in approaching happiness

▶▶영작하시오.
그는 그 분쟁 해결에 있어서 중요한 역할을 했다.

19. Houses should be built so as to admit plenty of light as well as fresh air. The former is **not less** necessary **than** the latter to a healthy condition of body. Just as plants, when deprived of light, become white in their stalks and leaves, so man becomes pale and unhealthy when he lives underground.

notes :
*so as to = ~하도록
*as well as (plenty of) fresh air
*stalk 줄기

▶▶According to the above paragraph, which of the following is **not** correct?
① In choosing a place to live in, we should always consider fresh air and sunshine.
② Our houses should be well ventilated.
③ Fresh air is more important to our health than plenty of light.
④ Plants will wither if they don't get enough air and light.
⑤ Air and light keep us healthy and alive.

▶▶영작하시오.
그들은 신문뿐만 아니라 책도 판다.

He is **as** diligent **as any** student in his class.
He was **as** good an officer **as ever** served his country.

20. Poor as the family were, young Sam Johnson had **as** much pride **as any** nobleman's son in England. The fact was, he felt conscious of uncommon sense and ability, which, in his opinion, entitled him to great respect from the world.

notes :
*Poor as에서 as = though의 의미
*entitle 자격을 주다
*the world = 세상사람들

▶▶According to the above paragraph, which of the following does **not** correspond with the above-mentioned man?

① His poverty couldn't harm his pride.
② He thought himself extraordinarily competent and sensible.
③ He believed that he deserved others' respect.
④ Most of his contemporaries agreed that he was a capable man.
⑤ He was well aware of his uncommon sense and ability, and regarded himself as capable as any nobleman's son.

▶▶영작하시오.

비록 가난하지만 그는 정직하다.

21. As <u>he</u> had admitted he was in the wrong, there was nothing for it but to write an apology, the composition of which was **as** disagreeable a task **as ever** had fallen to his lot.

notes :
*own 자백하다
*there is nothing for it but to~ = ~하는 수 밖에 없다
*lot 운명(=destiny)

▶▶Which of the following is most suitable to describe the underlined <u>he</u>?

① He was repentant and willingly sent his letter of apology.
② He couldn't bring himself to write an apology.
③ He blamed others for his own mistakes, instead of admitting them.
④ He ascribed his poor situation to his destiny.
⑤ He had recognized his fault and reluctantly wrote a letter of apology.

▶▶영작하시오.

잘못했다고 인정하는 수밖에 없었다.

I will take care of him **as long as** I live.
Any book will do, **so long as** it is interesting.

22. My family was by no means wealthy when I was born, and many decades were to pass before my father felt he was standing on firm ground. For **as long as** I remember my parents had to struggle with heavy financial problems that overshadowed my entire youth.

notes :
*by no means = 결코 ~이 아닌
*decade 10년간

▶▶According to the above paragraph, which of the following is **not** correct?

① The writer's father had to struggle for a living for many years.
② The writer's family suffered great difficulties because of money problems.
③ The writer was born with a silver spoon in his mouth.
④ The writer never enjoyed an easy life in his youth.
⑤ His family was not well off in the past.

▶▶영작하시오.
외국어를 배우기란 결코 쉬운 일은 아니다.

23. Animals are happy **so long as** they have health and enough to eat. Human beings, one feels, ought to be, but they are not, at least in a great majority of cases.

notes :
*enough n. 충분한 양
*ought to be (happy)
*at least = 적어도

▶▶( ) animals, just meeting physical ( ) can't bring happiness to all of us.
[Until, Unlike, Unless, desires, health, urgency]

▶▶영작하시오.
결백하기만 하면 너는 두려울 것이 없다.

I have never been **happier** in my life.
As bees love sweetness, **so** flies love rottenness.

24. The island of Sicily lies as a triangle across the center of the Middle Sea. Few islands have been **better** favored by nature. Its climate is mild and its scenery beautiful. But man has not been as kind to the island. Geography placed it to be an inevitable battle ground between the forces of Europe and Africa.

notes :
*triangle 삼각형
*favored by nature = 자연의 혜택을 받은
*nature (than the island of Sicily)
*island (as nature)

▶▶Fill in the blank with a suitable word.
Few islands have been better favored by nature than (   ).

▶▶영작하시오.
때마침 오셨습니다.

25. **As** bad manners are infectious, **so** also are good manners. if we encounter incivility most of us are apt to become uncivil, but there is no one who can be disagreeable with sunny people. **It is with** manners **as with** the weather.

notes :
*infectious 전염성의, 옮기 쉬운
*encounter (우연히) ~에 마주치다
*incivility 무례함
*disagreeable 불쾌한
*It is with A as with B = A is like B

▶▶다음은 윗글에 계속되는 문장이다. 빈칸에 적당한 단어를 쓰시오.
"Nothing clears up my spirits like a (f   ) day," said Keats.

▶▶영작하시오.
너무 자주 나무라면 요즘 십대들은 반항하기 쉽다.

As soon as I met her, I took to her.
No sooner had I met her **than** I took to her.
I had **hardly** [**scarcely**] met her **when** I took to her.

26. The world is a very pleasant place to live in **as soon as** we accept the fact that other people have a right to live as well as ourselves and that the people who get in our way in the streets do not do so on purpose or out of malice.

notes :
*get in our way = 우리에게 방해가 되다
*malice 악의

▶▶The world becomes a nicer place to live in when we (   ) others have an equal right to live and that they do not get in our way on the streets (   ).
[remember, recognize, impatiently, intentionally]

▶▶영작하시오.
그는 항상 나의 방해만 된다.

27. **No sooner** had word spread that the white doctor had arrived, **than** he was surrounded with natives suffering from various kinds of diseases.

notes :
*word (관사없이 쓰여) 소식, 소문
*native 원주민

▶▶As soon as the natives (   ) that the white doctor had arrived, they surrounded him to have their diseases (   ).
[heard, recognized, listened, seen, curing, treated]

▶▶영작하시오.
나를 보자마자 그는 도망쳤다.

● 장 문 독 해 ●

Warming-up

What is it that has happened to her?
I won't do so if I can **help** it.
The train was so crowded that I **was compelled to** stand for five hours on end.
A new novel is **being** written by her.
Human beings **are turned into** parcels at rush hour.
Here and there over the grass **stood** beautiful flowers.

1 What is it that makes people grumble about the crowded Tubes and swear they will never travel underground again if they can help it? Most of them seem to imagine it is ordinary discomfort, but I fancy ⓐ<u>it</u> is really a sense of indignity. After all, to be compelled to stand ten minutes or so is no great hardship to most of us, especially when we know that we are being hurled towards our destinations at a tremendous speed. The indignity of these rush hours, however, is undoubtedly unpleasant. Human beings, yourself included, are suddenly turned into parcels. ⓑ<u>Labels</u> are pushed into their hands; trains are promptly loaded with them to the full capacity; doors are opened and shut to admit them; they are hustled out, shot up in lifts, and only then, when the sweet cold rush of real air comes to meet them, are they allowed to turn back into ordinary men and women.

John B. Priestley: *Man Underground*

Notes

grumble 투덜대다 / tube=subway / help=avoid / indignity 모욕감 / be compelled to ~ 강제로 ~하다(=be forced to) / hurl 집어던지다 / destination 목적지 / parcel 짐짝 / label 꼬리표 / promptly 신속하게 / capacity 수용력 / hustle out 밀어내다 / lift=elevator

Question

1. 본문의 밑줄친 ⓐit 이 가리키는 것을 우리말로 간단히 쓰시오.

2. The author of the passage compares human beings to parcels. What does he mean by the underlined ⓑLabels?

3. 다음 글이 저자의 주장이 되도록 할 때, 빈칸에 들어가기에 적절한 말끼리 짝지어진 것은?

People should recognize that the crowded subway at rush hour causes (   ) as well as (   ).

① dehumanization — considerable comfort
② a sense of inferiority — many grumbles
③ a sense of indignity — annoying discomfort
④ the recovery of humanity — slight discomfort
⑤ a sense of humiliation — jammed traffic

4. Which of the following does **not** correspond with the passage?

① Most people are likely to consider the problems caused by the subway as simple physical inconveniences.
② As soon as a man gets out of the subway, he can escape from the feeling of being treated like a parcel.
③ If we consider the swiftness of the subway, we can endure passing trivial inconveniences.
④ All types of public transportation tend to damage man's dignity.
⑤ In the process of getting on and off the subway, human beings are treated as nothing but packages being sent.

Production

(1) 이렇게 비가 심하게 올 때는 나는 될 수 있으면 외출하고 싶지 않다.
(2) 그는 그 회의에 참석하지 않겠다고 했는데, 결국은 참석했다.
(3) 그는 한 주일 가량 우리 집에 머물 것이다.
(4) 우리는 하루 일이 끝나고 집에 돌아오고 나서야 보통의 인간으로 돌아온다.

● 장 문 독 해 ●

Warming-up

Idleness leads **not only** to poverty, **but also** to moral degradation.

They lived constantly **threatened** by external invasions.

The idea **suggested** by him was approved unanimously.

The time has come **when** we must all come to the aid of our country.

2 I think that the advocates of peace should emphasize, not only the unspeakable disasters to which existing policies must lead, but also, and just as much, ⓐ the new world of unexampled happiness which is opened to us if we can forget our quarrels. Man has risen slowly from a rare and hunted species, constantly threatened by wild beasts that were his superiors in strength, periodically decimated by disastrous famines, haunted by terrors generated by the spectacle of an apparently hostile world of nature. Man has risen to mastery over ⓑ the external dangers, but he has not risen to mastery over the internal dangers generated by his own passions of hate and envy and pride. The time has come when he must master these internal perils or recognize that he is himself a more dangerous wild beast than the lion or the tiger. It is unbearable to think that all the immense progress since the days of primitive man may be thrown away because we cannot acquire that last step in mastery which is the mastery over our own passions.

Bertrand Russell: *Fact and Fiction*

Notes

advocate 옹호자 / emphasize 강조하다 / existing 현존하는 / unexampled 유례가 없는 / species 종족 / periodically 정기적으로 / decimate 대량으로 죽이다 / famine 기근 / haunt 괴롭히다 / generate 발생하다 / hostile 적대적인 / external 외부의; *internal* 내부의 / primitive man 원시인

Question

1. 밑줄친 ⓐ를 다음과 같이 바꿔 쓸 때, 빈칸에 가장 적절한 것은?

the new world of (   ) happiness

① routine ② usual ③ unprecedented
④ typical ⑤ ordinary

2. 본문에서 밑줄친 ⓑ의 예를 찾아 우리말로 쓰시오.

3. According to the passage, which is **not** correct?
① The author's attitude to the existing policies is very critical.
② We must realize that our current policies must lead to the end of our existence on the planet.
③ Compared with other creatures, human beings were an originally weak and rare species.
④ The population growth of human beings used to be restricted by natural disasters.
⑤ In spite of the development of our modern science and technology, we are still under the sway of the force of nature.

4. Which of the following is the author's ultimate argument?
① The government should make new policies to cope with tremendous natural calamity.
② We should not be too pessimistic about our future, but continue our efforts to keep peace among countries.
③ Though man has mastered external dangers, he is still the servant of his instincts.
④ If we cannot conquer our adverse passions of hate, envy and pride, we are sure to be exterminated from the earth.
⑤ Our adverse passions are likely to strengthen us to win the struggle for survival in our society.

Production

(1) 그는 그 결과에 만족하여 성공을 희망하며 돌아왔다.
(2) 그들은 조국을 방어하기 위해 필요한 어떤 희생도 할 결심을 하고서 다가오는 전쟁을 준비했다.
(3) 그의 모든 노력에도 불구하고 그가 실패했다니, 생각만 해도 참을 수 없다.

실 력 체 크 I

1 다음 글을 읽고 아래 물음에 답하여라.

notes :
verdict 평결 / be bound to V = 틀림없이 ~하다 / incredibly 믿을 수 없을 만큼 / inventive 재능있는 / disdainful of ~ = ~을 무시한 / superficial 피상적인 / cheapen 경시하다 / result from ~ = ~에서 기인하다 / astounding 매우 놀라게 하는 / attach the importance to ~ = ~에 중요성을 부여하다 / filth 불결 / enterprise 기업체 / odor 냄새 / emanate from ~ = ~에서 나오다 / deodorant 탈(방)취제

> Any verdict on man — modern man — is bound to show him as incredibly inventive but just as disdainful of the connection between cause and effect. He has devised ways of turning wheels faster and doing things more efficiently than (1)they have ever been done before, but he has given only the most superficial attention to the cheapening of human life that sometimes results from (2)the process. Most astounding of all is the importance he attaches to individual cleanliness even as he creates a total environment of poison and filth. Parents teach their children to clean their fingernails but are apparently unworried about the dangerous layers of dirt that get into their bodies. Vast enterprises are developed to kill off body odors and make the human being a sweet-smelling delight. But what about the horrible odors and poisonous gases that emanate from the backs of buses, trucks and cars? How is it that the passion for daily baths and deodorants has not been extended to the environment itself?

(1) 밑줄친 they는 무엇을 가리키는가?
(2) 밑줄친 the process의 내용을 구체적으로 설명하시오.
(3) 윗글의 첫 밑줄친 부분의 내용을 예를 들어 설명하시오.

2 아래 보기 중 다음 글의 제목이 될 수 있는 것을 골라라.

notes :
vocation 직업 / advantage 장점 / motivation 자극, 동기 / say 가령 / breadth 폭 / culture 교양 / specialize 전공하다 / overlook 간과하다

> There is a difference of opinion as to whether a person should choose his vocation in high school or wait until he is older. The advantages of choosing one's vocation in high school are early preparation and better motivation to master one's studies. Generally speaking, students who have chosen their vocation do better in their studies than those who have not. The advantages of waiting until older, say, until the second year in college, are greater opportunity to learn about various vocations and about one's own interests and abilities. The breadth of culture that comes from not specializing too early should not be overlooked.

① 고등학교와 대학에서의 직업 교육
② 전문가가 되는 직업 선택 방법
③ 직업의 기회 균등과 연령의 관계
④ 직업 선택의 시기와 그 장점
⑤ 고등학교와 대학에서의 직업 선택

3 다음 글의 밑줄친 부분에서 작자가 하고자 하는 말은 무엇인가?

notes :
never A without B = A하면 반드시 B 한다 / apologetic 미안해 하는 / be unworthy of ~ = ~할 만한 자격[가치]이 없다 / shabby 초라한 / fortnight = two weeks / contents 내용물 / loose change = 잔돈 / to say nothing of ~ = ~은 말할 것도 없이 / properly 제대로 / baggy 불룩한

I never walk into my tailor's without feeling apologetic. I know I am unworthy of their efforts. I am the kind of man who can make any suit of clothes look shabby after about a fortnight's wear. Perhaps, the fact that I always carry about with me most of the contents of my desk, odd keys and loose change, to say nothing of old letters, may have something to do with it. <u>I can never understand how a man can manage to look neat and smart and do anything else.</u> Wearing clothes properly seems to me to be a full-time job, and I always have a great many other more important and amusing things to do. I cheerfully wear my suits baggy and look as if I had slept in them. I can say this cheerfully here, but once I am inside my tailor's I immediately begin to feel apologetic.

4 다음 글을 읽고 아래의 물음에 답하여라.

On the Continent, you will sometimes see two people run into each other in the street and then start a violent quarrel, calling each other names, usually of a zoological character. Such a thing is almost unimaginable in England. (1)<u>Should such an event occur</u>, the two people concerned will say, "Sorry," to each other and proceed on their way. If there develops any argument at all, it will be to establish whose fault it was — (2)<u>each party</u> stoutly maintaining that "it was my fault." This is not to say that the English are never rude. They are sometimes. But even rudeness is expressed only in undertones. (3)<u>That</u> is why visitors often do not even realize that they have, in fact, been told off and roughly treated. Coarse expressions are hardly ever used. English discourtesy is, as a rule, phrased in brief, acid, or incredulous questions. Yes, even the newcomer will be struck by the fact that life in England is less noisy and — he will be led to believe — less colorful than on the Continent or on (4)<u>the other side of the Atlantic</u>. Rudeness is not so rude, colors are not so loud, the expression of passions is not so free, love is not so warm, and laughter is not so abandoned in England as in other parts of the world.

notes :
run into ~ = ~와 충돌하다 / violent 격렬한 / name (보통 복수로) 욕설 / zoological 동물학(상)의 / party 당사자 / stoutly 완강하게 / be told off 욕을 먹다 / acid 신랄한, 시큼한

(1)의 어순을 정상으로 되돌려라. (2)가 뜻하는 것을 우리말로 써라.
(3)이 뜻하는 것을 우리말로 써라. (4)는 어디를 말하는가?

실력체크 II

A. 다음 각 문장을 지시대로 바꿔 써라.

(1) Nothing in the world is sweeter than the cute behavior of little children. (최상급)

(2) This is the most beautiful scenery I have ever seen. (비교급)

(3) The bird was half the size of an eagle. (large를 사용하여)

(4) Of all the European cities I like Rome best. (비교급)

(5) With the coming of darkness, the wind blew harder. (The 비교급, the 비교급으로)

B. 이탤릭체 부분을 하나의 형용사로 나타내도록 괄호 안을 채워라.

(1) He is *a student from Holland* (a ______ student).

(2) *The train without stopping* (The ______ train) is very fast.

(3) Drinking of a boy under age is *against the law* (______).

C. 이탤릭체 부분과 뜻이 같도록 괄호 안의 공란을 한 단어로 채워라.

(1) I was trying to arrange these books on the top shelf, when the damned chair *collapsed*. (gave ______)

(2) The art of making these bowls *is no longer in existence*. (has died ______)

(3) I must *collect my thoughts* before I take up my pen to write to the mayor. (put my ideas ______)

(4) Social unrest may *happen* as a result of the endless rising of prices. (come ______)

(5) It never *struck* me that he would swindle me out of my money. (occurred ______)

D. 문장 끝의 지시대로 바꿔써라.

(1) Who doesn't desire to promote the welfare of society? (평서문)

(2) Who ever would have thought that the chimpanzee could understand sign language so well? (평서문)

(3) Ten years have passed since he died. (He를 주어로)

Answer: A. (1) The cute behavior of little children is the sweetest thing in the world. (2) I have never seen more beautiful scenery than this. (3) The bird was half as large as an eagle. (4) I like Rome better than any other European city. (5) The darker it grew, the harder the wind blew. B. (1) Dutch (2) nonstop (3) illegal C. (1) way (2) out (3) together (4) about (5) to D. (1) Everybody desires to promote the welfare of society. (2) Nobody would have thought that the chimpanzee could understand sign language so well. (3) He has been dead for ten years. 혹은 He died ten years ago.

(4) These two are widely different from each other.
(A wide difference를 주어로)

(5) His house was burnt down in the late fire. (He had로 시작)

(6) He may well be proud of his son. (He has로 시작)

(7) Every time you read a good book, you will be the better for it.
(You can으로 시작)

(8) If we are honest, diligent and steadfast, we'll be able to succeed.
(Our success를 주어로)

E. 각 문장의 뜻이 같아지도록 공란을 한 단어로 메워라.

(1) As my father grows older, his hearing becomes worse.
As my father grows older, he becomes ______ of hearing.

(2) This elevator is out of order.
There is something ______ with this elevator.

(3) These documents are of no worth to our present study.
These documents are ______ to our present study.

(4) He refused to listen to her friendly advice.
He turned a ______ ear to her friendly advice.

(5) It was almost impossible to read his microscopic handwriting.
It was ______ to impossible to read his microscopic handwriting.

F. 다음 괄호 안의 단어들을 바른 순서로 배열하여라.

(1) Who built (stone, white, big, the) building?

(2) There are (old, her, cloth, several, large) dolls on the desk.

(3) (golden, her, soft, long) hair

(4) I like (two, silk, those, blue) dresses.

(5) I have never seen (sailing, such, beautiful, a, old) ship before.

Answer: D. (4) A wide difference lies between these two. (5) He had his house burnt down in the late fire. (6) He has good reason to be proud of his son. (7) You can never read a good book without being the better for it. (8) Our success depends on our honesty, diligence and steadfastness.
E. (1) hard (2) wrong (3) worthless (4) deaf (5) next
F. (1) the big white stone (2) her several large old cloth (3) her long soft golden (4) those two blue silk (5) such a beautiful old sailing

어휘 · 발음

A. 다음의 반의어를 각각 적어라. (단, (1)은 접두사를 사용함.)

(1) ⓐ dependent ⓑ regular ⓒ logical ⓓ mortal
ⓔ existent ⓕ satisfy ⓖ comfort ⓗ successful

(2) ⓐ Oriental ⓑ offend ⓒ smooth ⓓ indifferent
ⓔ supply ⓕ quantity ⓖ majority ⓗ domestic
ⓘ objective ⓙ junior ⓚ internal ⓛ superior
ⓜ victory ⓝ generous ⓞ fertile ⓟ abstract

B. s로 시작하는 반의어를 적어라.

(1) clever (2) dangerous (3) doubtful (4) familiar
(5) deep (6) fluid (7) gradual (8) round

C. 공란을 적당한 형용사로 메워라.

(1) He smokes very much. He is a _____ smoker.
(2) I like to play tennis. Tennis is my _____ sport.
(3) Dinosaurs have been _____ for tens of millions of years.
(4) Anxiety kept her _____ all night.
(5) It's never too _____ to mend.

D. 이탤릭체로 된 형용사의 반의어를 적어라.

(1) a *short* person (2) a *dull* knife (3) a *thin* cow (4) a *heavy* heart
a *short* journey a *dull* story a *thin* book a *heavy* rain

E. 이탤릭체로 된 단어의 반의어를 공란에 써 넣어 문장을 완성하여라.

(1) Everything that happens has *cause* and _____.
(2) Better to be a good _____ than a bad *winner*.
(3) Food *production* in this country is solely for domestic _____.
(4) Bear in mind that the best *defense* is a good _____.
(5) *Virtue* itself, being misapplied, may turn into _____.

Answer: A. (1) ⓐ independent ⓑ irregular ⓒ illogical ⓓ immortal ⓔ nonexistent ⓕ dissatisfy ⓖ discomfort ⓗ unsuccessful (2) ⓐ Occidental ⓑ please ⓒ rough ⓓ interested ⓔ demand ⓕ quality ⓖ minority ⓗ foreign ⓘ subjective ⓙ senior ⓚ external ⓛ inferior ⓜ defeat ⓝ mean ⓞ barren ⓟ concrete
B. (1) stupid, silly (2) safe (3) sure (4) strange (5) shallow (6) solid (7) sudden (8) square
C. (1) heavy (2) favorite (3) extinct (4) awake (5) late
D. (1) tall, long (2) sharp, interesting (3) fat, thick (4) happy, light
E. (1) effect (2) loser (3) consumption (4) offense (5) vice

F. 주어진 문장의 밑줄 친 단어와 같은 의미로 쓰인 것은?

(1) His intention was plain to everyone.

ⓐ The book is written in plain English.
ⓑ He never complains about his plain life.
ⓒ The footprints were plain in the snow.
ⓓ She was a plain girl with no education.

(2) The rotten log was alive with ants.

ⓐ He is alive to his own interests.
ⓑ My grandmother is more alive than lots of young people.
ⓒ The dead animal is alive with insects.
ⓓ The weight of the snow collapsed the roof and buried them alive.

G. 빈 곳에 그 문장 안의 어느 낱말과 같은 발음을 가진 낱말을 적어라.

(1) The daughters were not allowed to talk _____ .
(2) The girl in the blue dress _____ out the candle.
(3) The birds seem to bow on the _____ .
(4) The plane landed safely on the green _____ .
(5) The squirrel _____ a lot of berries under the ground.

H. 다음 명사를 형용사로 바꾸고, 액센트의 위치를 표시하여라.

(1) ágriculture	__________	(2) Éurope	__________
(3) cómfort	__________	(4) índustry	__________
(5) ecónomy	__________	(6) énergy	__________
(7) necéssity	__________	(8) sýmpathy	__________
(9) órigin	__________	(10) prógress	__________

I. 다음 각 단어에서 발음되지 않는 철자(묵자)를 적어라.

(1) bomber	(2) debt	(3) handsome	(4) sovereign
(5) gnarl	(6) exhibit	(7) knight	(8) calf
(9) stalk	(10) palm	(11) solemn	(12) aisle
(13) castle	(14) wreath	(15) sword	(16) indict
(17) subtle	(18) receipt	(19) muscle	(20) heir

Answer: F. (1) ⓒ (2) ⓒ G. (1) aloud (2) blew (3) bough (4) plain (5) buries
H. (1) agricúltural (2) Européan (3) cómfortable (4) indústrious 혹은 indústrial (5) económic 혹은 económical (6) energétic (7) nécessary (8) sympathétic (9) oríginal (10) progréssive I. (1) 뒤의 b (2) b (3) d (4) g (5) g (6) h (7) k (8) l (9) l (10) l (11) n (12) s (13) t (14) w (15) w (16) c (17) b (18) p (19) c (20) h

숙 어

(1) **make out** (=understand ; draw up ; pretend) 이해하다 ; 작성하다 ; ~인 체하다
☞ No one could *make out* what he was talking about.
☞ He *made out* a check and handed it to her.
☞ Helen tried to *make out* that she was sick.

(2) **make over** (=transfer the ownership ; change, renovate)
양도하다 ; 바꾸다, 고치다
☞ The land was *made over* to its rightful possessor.
The garage has been *made over* into a playroom.

(3) **make room for** (=create space for) 자리를[공간을] 마련하다
☞ How can we *make room for* all the furniture?

(4) **make sure** (=ascertain) 확인하다
☞ I want you to *make sure* that all of the reports are done on time.

(5) **make the best of** (=do as well as one can in a poor situation)
(열악한 상황에서) ~을 최대한 활용하다
☞ It rained a lot during our vacation, but we *made the best of* it.

(6) **make the grade** (=succeed by reaching a particular standard)
성공하다, 어느 정도 단계에 오르다
☞ He has *made the grade* in the insurance business.

(7) **make the most of** (=use to the greatest advantage)
~을 최대한 이용[활용]하다
☞ He planned to *make the most of* his trip to Europe.

(8) **make up** (=resolve a quarrel ; invent ; apply cosmetics)
화해하다 ; (이야기를) 꾸며내다 ; 화장하다
☞ The couple had a fight, but then *made up* and kissed.
Is that story true or did you *make* it *up*?
He watched his sister *make up* her face for her date.

(9) **map out** (=plan in detail) 상세한 계획을 세우다
☞ I spent many weeks on *mapping out* his election campaign.

(10) **measure up to** (=reach the same level as) ~에 필적하다
☞ The exhibition didn't *measure up to* last year's.

(11) **meet ~ halfway** (=compromise with) 타협하다
☞ If you can drop your price a little, I'll *meet* you *halfway*.

(12) **meet with** (=meet one for something ; unexpectedly experience)
(특히 토론 등을 위해) 만나다 ; ~을 당하다, 경험하다
☞ The President *met with* senior White House aides for discussions.
They *met with* an accident on their way back.

(13) **more or less** (=almost ; approximately, about) 거의 ; 대략
☞ It took *more or less* a whole day to paint the ceiling.
The trip will take ten days, *more or less*.

(14) **next[second] to none** (=the best) 최고의
☞ In English he is *next to none* in his class.

(15) **none other than** (=no one else but) 다름아닌 바로~
☞ It turned out to be *none other than* Bill in a clown costume.

(16) **none the less** (=nevertheless) 그럼에도 불구하고
☞ It's not cheap but I think we should buy it *none the less*.

(17) **not on your life** (=not for the world) 절대[결코] ~아닌
☞ Shall we spend the holiday at home?—*Not on your life*!

(18) **nothing to speak of** (=nothing worth mentioning) 대수롭지 않은, 사소한
☞ What's been happening in the stock market?—*Nothing to speak of*.

Exercise

▶▶ 주어진 단어들을 포함한 글을 지어라. 필요하면 어형을 변화시켜라.

1. I / make / what / he / try / say
2. basement / will / make / into / office
3. we / make / best / what / have
4. she / grade / as / lawyer
5. class / make / teacher
6. story / make / deceive
7. her / job / measure / to / expectation
8. math / second / none / class
9. guest / none / than / Smith
10. injuries / nothing / speak / scratch

16. 부 사(Adverb)

기본 문법 설명

A. 부사의 용법	(1) ⓐ The doctor examined his patient **carefully**. Be **careful** to look both ways when you cross the street. ⓑ The wind blew **hard** during the storm. Poverty is a **hard** problem to solve. ⓒ The bus arrived 10 minutes **late**. I have not seen her **lately**. ⓓ I ran as **quick (=quickly)** as I could. Mr. Kim speaks **loud** (=**loudly**). (2) ⓐ He *came* **late** for work. ⓑ That investment is **too** risky for us. ⓒ The traffic was moving **very** *slowly*. ⓓ I am **quite** a stranger here. ⓔ She **alone** knew his real identity. ⓕ The chartered plane arrived **just** on time. ⓖ I had arrived **long** *before* he came. ⓗ **Fortunately**, the damage was only slight.
B. 부사의 위치	(1) ⓐ She laughed **heartily** at the joke. ⓑ Drive your car **carefully** on those icy roads. ⓒ **Little** did I dream I'd meet her here. (2) ⓐ He'll **always** remember the day he graduated. My car **nearly** crashed into the truck. ⓑ These birds are **rarely** seen around here. I've **also** seen a few of his early films. (3) ⓐ She got up and put **on** her coat. She got up and put her coat **on**. ⓑ Drop me **off** at that corner. (O) Drop **off** me at that corner. (X)

A. 부사의 용법

(1) **부사와 형용사**

ⓐ 형용사+-ly로 부사를 만든다.

☞ 어미 y는 i로 바꿔 -ly를 붙임.
happy ⇨ happily
어미 ue는 e를 빼고 -ly를 붙임
true ⇨ truly; due ⇨ duly
어미 le는 ly로 함. noble ⇨ nobly
단, sole ⇨ solely, whole ⇨ wholly
어미 ll은 lly로 함. full ⇨ fully
어미 ic는 ically로 함.
dramatic ⇨ dramatically
basic ⇨ basically

ⓑ 형용사와 형태가 같은 부사 :
hard, long, high, early, enough, near, much, well, ill 등.

ⓒ 형용사와 같은 형태의 부사에 -ly를 붙여 다른 뜻의 부사가 되는 예 :
high (높이) highly (매우)
near (가까이) nearly (거의)
late (늦게) lately (최근에)
hard (열심히) hardly (거의 ~않다)
(버스가 10분 늦게 도착했다.)
(나는 최근 그녀를 보지 못했다.)

ⓓ 어미 ly가 있는 부사와 없는 부사의 뜻이 같을 때 : go slow = go slowly
(김선생은 목소리가 크다.)

(2) **부사의 기능**

ⓐ 부사 late는 동사 came을 수식
ⓑ 부사 too는 형용사 risky를 수식
ⓒ 부사 very는 부사 slowly를 수식
ⓓ 부사 quite는 명사 stranger를 수식, the *then* king (당시의 왕)
ⓔ 부사 alone은 대명사 She를 수식
ⓕ 부사 just는 부사구 on time를 수식
ⓖ 부사 long은 절 before he came을 수식
ⓗ 부사 fortunately는 문장 전체를 수식
(다행히 피해는 경미할 뿐이었다.)
= It was fortunate that the damage was only slight.
He lived *happily* ever after.
(그는 그 이후에는 (내내) 행복하게 살았다.) … happily는 *lived*를 수식

☞ She will *certainly* come.
= It is certain that she will come.
He *naturally* got angry.
= It was natural that he should have got angry.

B. 부사의 위치

(1) **양태 부사**

ⓐ 일반적으로 동사의 뒤에 놓는다.

ⓑ 목적어가 있으면 목적어 뒤에 놓는다. 동사 앞에 둘 때도 있다.
I *gladly* accepted the invitation.
☞ 수동태에서 부사의 이동에 주의
They speak *well* of him.
⇨He is *well* spoken of.

ⓒ 강조하기 위해 부사를 문두에 놓았다. 그리고, 리듬을 맞추려고 I dreamt를 did I dream으로 했다.

(2) **횟수(빈도)·정도 부사**

always, generally, often, ever, sometimes, scarcely, hardly, forever, never, rarely, seldom, nearly, almost, also 등.

ⓐ 「횟수·정도부사+일반동사」
I *seldom* get up before nine o'clock.

ⓑ 「be, 조동사+횟수·정도부사」
It is *never* too late to mend.

☞ 횟수·정도부사는 문두에도 온다.
Sometimes I walk to work.

(3) **「타동사+부사」의 결합**

ⓐ 명사가 목적어일 때:
「타동사+부사+목적어」, 또는
「타동사+목적어+부사」로 된다.

ⓑ 대명사가 목적어일 때 :
「타동사+대명사+부사」의 어순
She put it *ón*. (○)
She put *on* it. (×)
Take it *out*. Give it *up*.
☞ 「자동사+전치사」의 결합형과 혼동하지 말 것.
look at the boy / look at him

	(4) ⓐ I've lived **here for ten years**. ⓑ They drove **downtown quickly this morning**. He was working **hard there then**. ⓒ I'll call on you **at ten o'clock next Wednesday**. ⓓ Despite a blizzard we arrived **safely at the station**. (5) ⓐ You're not improving because you don't practice **enough**. ⓑ He's old **enough** to make his own decisions. ⓒ He was kind **enough** to take me to the airport. (6) ⓐ **Only** five people were hurt in the accident. ⓑ We **only** waited a few minutes but it seemed like hours. ⓒ I could see **only** him in the room. ⓓ They arrive **only** on Thursday.
C. 의문부사와 관계부사	(1) ⓐ I don't know **when** to take these pills. ⓑ **Where** do you think we will be if we fail it? ⓒ I wonder **why** he was kidnapped. ⓓ Tell me **how** it is to be attained. (2) ⓐ I like to climb the mountain **where** there is some snow. ⓑ Monday is the day **when** we work (the) hardest. ⓒ The reason **why** grass is green was a mystery to the child. ⓓ Do it **how** you can. (3) ⓐ He died on the day **that** I arrived. ⓑ Is that the reason (**that**) you went there? (4) ⓐ He lived in Rome for two years, **where** he taught English. ⓑ I was about to ask after his wife, **when** I suddenly remembered that they were getting a divorce. (5) ⓐ That's **where** I often go after work. ⓑ He has changed a great deal from **when** I used to know him. ⓒ That is **why** I was so mad at him. ⓓ That's **how** I have been treated.

(4) **부사가 두 개 이상 겹칠 때**

ⓐ「장소·시간」

ⓑ「장소·양태·시간」

「양태·장소·시간」

ⓒ「시간(작은단위)·시간(큰 단위)」

ⓓ「짧은 부사(구)·긴 부사(구)」

(5) **enough** : 수식하는 말의 뒤에 둔다.

ⓐ enough는 practice를 수식

ⓑ enough는 old를 수식

ⓒ enough는 kind를 수식

=He was so kind as to take me to the airport.

=He kindly took me to the airport.

(6) **only** : 그 위치가 자유롭게 변한다.

관계가 가장 밀접한 말 가까이에 놓는 것이 원칙이다.

ⓐ only는 five people을 수식

ⓑ only는 waited를 수식

ⓒ only는 him을 수식

ⓓ only는 on Thursday를 수식

(그들은 목요일이 되야 도착한다.)

C. 의문부사와 관계부사

(1) **의문부사의 접속 용법**

의문문을 유도하는 의문부사가 종속절 혹은 종속구를 유도하는 접속의 역할을 한다.

ⓐ I don't know when.

+ I should take these pills.

ⓑ Where will we be if we fail it?

+ Do you think?

(그것에 실패하면, 우리는 어떻게 될 것이라고 생각하는가?)

ⓒ Why was he kidnapped? + I wonder.

ⓓ Tell me. + How is it to be attained?

(2) **관계부사의 용법**

관계부사 where, when, why, how는 부사와 접속사의 역할을 하는데, 「**전치사+which**」로 바꿔 쓸 수 있다.

ⓐ where = 장소의 관계부사

= in which, on which 등

선행사는 the mountain

ⓑ when = 시간의 관계부사

= on [at] which 등. 선행사는 the day

The *day* has come *when* I must say goodbye to her.

ⓒ why = 이유의 관계부사 = for which

선행사는 the reason

ⓓ how = 방법의 관계부사

the way how는 피해야 할 용법이다. the way 혹은 how 만을 쓰든지, the way that 혹은 the way in which를 쓴다.

Do it *the way* you can.

(3) **관계부사로서의 that**

that는 관계부사로서 when, how, why, where 대신 쓰이며, 형용사절을 유도한다. 이 that는 때로 생략된다.

ⓐ that는 when의 대용

ⓑ that는 why의 대용

…that를 생략할 수 있다.

(4) **관계부사의 계속적 용법**

관계부사 when, where는 관계대명사와 마찬가지로 계속적 용법이 있다.

~, where = ~, and there

~, when = ~, and then

ⓐ (그는 로마에 2년간 살았는데, 거기서 그는 영어를 가르쳤다.)

ⓑ (나는 막 그의 아내 안부를 물어보려고 했는데, 그때 갑자기 그들이 이혼할 것이라는 것이 기억났다.)

(5) **명사절을 유도하는 관계부사**

관계부사는 선행사를 갖지 않고 명사절을 유도한다.

ⓐ where I often go ~ 는 보어로 명사절

ⓑ when I used to know him은 from의 목적어가 되는 명사절

ⓒ why I was so mad at him은 보어가 되는 명사절

ⓓ how I have ~ 는 보어로 명사절

(나는 이렇게 취급당해 왔다.)

	(6) ⓐ You may go **wherever** you like. ⓑ **Wherever** I go, I always seem to bump into him. ⓒ The roof leaks **whenever** it rains. ⓓ **However** cold it is, he always goes fishing.
D. 부사의 비교	(1) ⓐ The lake was frozen **hard**. The lake was frozen **harder** than any other lake in the area. The lake was frozen **hardest** of all the lakes in the area. ⓑ I drive **carefully** at night. I drive **more carefully** at night than any other time. I drive **most carefully** at night. ⓒ He behaves **well**. He behaves **better** than any other boy in his class. He behaves **best** of all his friends. (2)ⓐ **The more** I thought about it, **the more** depressed I became. **The less** we say about the problem, **the bigger** it will become. ⓑ **The sooner the better**.
E. 주의할 부사의 용법	(1) ⓐ My father has had a **very** interesting life. ⓑ Thank you for the offer, but I'm not **much** interested. (2) ⓐ **There** *was* a drunken man lying on the road as I passed. ⓑ **There** *appeared* to be nobody willing to help me. (3) ⓐ Do you think he will apologize? — I think **not**. ⓑ **Every** rock singer can**not** be the king of rock' n' roll. (4) ⓐ I invited Bill to the party, and David, **too**. ⓑ I **don't** like the zoo, and I don't like the museum, **either**.

(6) **복합관계부사** : wherever, whenever, however는 그 자체가 선행사를 포함하여, 부사절을 이끈다.

ⓐ wherever = to any place that
(네가 가고 싶은 곳 어디나 가도 좋다.)

ⓑ = No matter where I go,
(어디로 가든지 난 늘 그와 마주치는 것 같다.)

ⓒ whenever = at any time when
(그 지붕은 비가 올 때마다 샌다.)

ⓓ However cold it is,
= No matter how cold it is,
(아무리 추워도 그는 늘 낚시를 간다.)

D. 부사의 비교

(1) ⓐ **단음절어의 부사**는 -er, -est를 붙여 비교급, 최상급을 표시한다.
(그 호수는 꽁꽁 얼어붙었다.)

ⓑ -ly로 끝나면 more, most를 붙여 비교급, 최상급을 표시한다.

ⓒ **불규칙 변화**

well	better	best
ill, badly	worse	worst
little	less	least
much	more	most

☞ 부사의 최상급 앞에는 the를 안 붙여도 된다.

(2) **the+비교급, the+비교급**
…하면 할 수록 그 만큼 더~

ⓐ (난 그것에 대해 생각하면 할수록 그 만큼 더 우울해 졌다.)
(그 문제에 대해 덜 이야기할수록 그 만큼 더 그 문제가 커질 것이다.)

ⓑ (빠를수록 더욱 좋다.)
The more the better.
(많을 수록 더욱 좋다.)

E. 주의할 부사의 용법

(1) **very**와 **much**

ⓐ very는 원급, 현재분사를 수식한다.

ⓑ much는 비교급, 과거분사 그리고 동사를 수식한다.

☞ 과거분사가 동사적 성격을 잃고 완전히 형용사화한 것은 very로 수식한다. 즉 tired, pleased, delighted, surprised, satisfied, disappointed 등이 그렇다.

(2) **유도부사 There**
문두에서 동사를 이끄는 역할을 한다.
be 동사의 경우가 흔하다.

ⓐ (내가 지나갈 때 길위에 술취한 사람이 누워있었다.))
= A drunken man was lying on the road as I passed.

ⓑ be 동사 외에도 유도부사 There를 쓰는 예가 있다.
(기꺼이 날 도와줄 사람은 아무도 없는 것 같았다.)
There *used to* be a bridge here.
(여기 예전에 다리가 하나 있었다.)

(3) **not**

ⓐ I think *not*.
= I think he will not apologize.

☞ 이런 용법은 believe, think, hope, fear, suppose 등의 동사에 많다.
Will he fail? I hope **not**.
Will he recover? I am afraid **not**.

ⓑ **부분부정**
(모든 록가수가 다 로큰롤의 황제가 될 수는 없다.)
부정어+all, both, every, always, necessarily, quite, fully, altogether 등.
The rich are *not always* happy.
All books are *not* good.
I do *not* believe him *fully*.
I do *not quite* agree.
(내가 전적으로 동의하는 것은 아니다.)
Food that looks good does *not necessarily* taste good.
(보기에 좋은 음식이 반드시 맛이 좋은것은 아니다.)
It's *not altogether* a bad idea.
(그것이 전적으로 나쁜 생각은 아니다.)

(4) **too**와 **either**

ⓐ too는 긍정문

ⓑ either는 부정문에 쓴다.

문 법 · 작 문

A. 어법이 맞는 단어를 골라라.

(1) The party lasted (late, lately) into the night.
(2) Mary talks much, and Susie talks (very, even) more.
(3) He hasn't done much work (yet, already) but she has (yet, already) finished.
(4) A (much, very) celebrated neurological surgeon will perform the operation.
(5) "Aren't you tired?" "(Yes, No), a little."
(6) I think I did (pretty, prettily) well on the exam.
(7) I care very (few, little) for your problems, and you care (fewer, less) for mine.
(8) It was the answer she (less, least) wanted to hear.

B. 틀린 것을 고쳐라.

(1) How quickly does the soap opera begin?
(2) I like this jacket much than the one I saw in the other shop.
(3) He hadn't scarcely time to get dressed.
(4) You'll never know how she went through to educate her children.
(5) When years went on, he grew duller.
(6) It was near ten o'clock when he came home.
(7) The dollar stayed highly after a busy day on the foreign exchanges.
(8) Babies are allowed to travel freely on buses.
(9) She had a much annoyed look on her face.
(10) He was in such an ecstasy of delight that he could get hardly a wink of sleep.

C. 공란을 적당한 단어로 메워라.

(1) We must camp ______ we can easily get water.
(2) That is ______ he named her as ambassador to France.
(3) ______ do you say he is living now?
(4) Can you imagine ______ glad I was when I won the one million dollar lottery?
(5) No matter ______ hard he listened, he could hear nothing.

D. 보기에 따라 다음 문장들을 다시 써라.

<Ex.> She runs fast. ⇨ She is a fast runner.

(1) She dances well.
(2) She cooks well.
(3) Mary plays the violin well.
(4) He teaches earnestly.
(5) He rises late.
(6) She answered politely.

E. 문미의 부사 혹은 부사구를 적당한 곳에, 또는 옳게 배열하여라.
(1) Our busy office manager leaves work before 7:00 P.M. (seldom)
(2) He takes his dog for a walk after dinner. (often)
(3) The water was warm for us to swim in. (enough)
(4) I was moved by the composer's romantic music. (deeply)
(5) They stayed (all day, quietly, there).
(6) He played (in the concert, at the Town Hall, last night, beautifully).
(7) Sam went (with Tom, to the concert, last night).
(8) The most important question has not been asked. (perhaps)
(9) Bullying is a problem in some schools. (quite)

F. 이탤릭체로 된 절은 무슨 절인가?
(1) *Wherever you look* there are pictures.
(2) He is welcomed *wherever he goes*.
(3) I don't know *where he comes from*.
(4) The police found out the place *where the criminal was hiding out*.

G. 두 문장을 관계부사를 써서 연결하여라.
(1) He visited the village after ten years' absence.
He was born in that village.
(2) This is the way. He managed to do it in this way.
(3) He was praised for a certain thing. Do you know the reason?

H. Translate the following into English:
(1) 그가 고향을 떠난 이유는 아무에게도 알려져 있지 않다.

(2) 이것이 그 시인이 소년기를 보낸 집이다.

(3) 최근에 물가가 상당히 올랐다.

(4) 그는 항상 일찍 일어나고 늦게 잔다.

(5) 그 우유 배달부는 항상 아침 일찍 이곳을 지나간다. (milkman)

(6) 그는 칭찬을 받았기 때문에 더 열심히 일했다.

(7) 너의 어리석음을 후회할 날이 꼭 올 것이다.

(8) 어디에 가든, 자기 집보다 더 좋은 곳을 찾지 못할 것이다.

(9) 왜 그가 그 여자에게 성을 냈다고 생각하느냐?

'Love' 라는 제목으로 150어 내외의 글을 지어라.

● 단 문 독 해 ●

I don't know the exact time **when** it happened.
We went to Seoul, **where** we stayed for a week.
This is **where** I was born.
This is the way (**that**) he did it.
I will follow you **wherever** you (may) go

1. In these days **when** so many human beings are compelled to live in enormous cities **where** they so easily forget the fact that nature is greater than man, that love of nature is more necessary than ever.

notes :
*be compelled to 부정사 = ~하지 않을 수 없다
*enormous 거대한, 막대한(= huge, immense)

▶▶Which of the following is the writer's main argument?
① We prefer living in large cities to living in small towns.
② In our scientific age nature is still greater than man.
③ We should go back to a rural way of life.
④ Rural people love nature more than urban people.
⑤ We should remember that man is greater than nature.

▶▶영작하시오.
나는 할 수 없이 그의 요구에 응하지 않을 수 없었다.

2. No doubt it is true that a genius is born, not made. But while it is a mistake to try and discover reasons for a man being a genius, it is proper and most interesting to note **how** his genius has taken on a certain shape and direction as a result of his environment.

notes :
*try and discover = try to discover
*reasons for a man being a genius = reasons why a man is a genius
*take on = assume (모습, 성격을) 띠다
*environment 환경

▶▶Which can **not** be inferred from the above paragraph?
① A genius is born with a hidden talent.
② It's wrong to try to find out why someone is a genius.
③ Our environment affects us as a character-building element.
④ A genius is born but is also subject to his environment.
⑤ A man can become a genius through special training.

▶▶영작하시오.
오늘 저녁 나한테 놀러 오너라.

3. To many the movies offered an escape from drab reality into the unreal world of romance, **where** wickedness was always punished and virtue always rewarded, **where** all women were beautiful and all men handsome, **where** riches brought happiness and poverty contentment, and **where** all stories had a happy ending.

notes :
*escape 도피구
*drab 따분한, 단조로운
*wickedness 사악, 부정
*contentment 만족

▶▶윗글의 내용과 일치하도록 할 때, 빈칸에 알맞지 않는 것은?

By showing the fantastic world, movies often provided us with a refuge, where (   ).

① we could forget our tedious reality
② the wicked would not go unpunished
③ all men and women were gorgeous and attractive
④ good deeds were followed by a financial compensation
⑤ people were satisfied though they were poor

▶▶영작하시오.

화요일까지 기다려 주십시오. 그 때 모든 것을 말씀드리겠습니다.

4. An amusing story is told of Sir Walter Raleigh, who brought tobacco from America to England, where it had seldom or never been seen before. He was fond of smoking, and it is reported that **the first time** his servant saw smoke coming from his master's lips he thought Raleigh was on fire, and poured a bucket of water over him to put the fire out.

notes :
*it is reported that = they report that
*the first time (when) his servant saw
*put the fire out = put out the fire = extinguish the fire

▶▶Which of the following corresponds with the above passage?

① Tobacco was already prevalent in England before Raleigh brought it from America.
② Sir Walter Raleigh was not interested in tobacco.
③ The first time Raleigh smoked, he accidentally caught on fire.
④ When the servant first saw his master smoking, he thought his master was on fire.
⑤ Raleigh was engaged in the tobacco business between England and America.

▶▶영작하시오.

그 집이 불타고 있다. 불을 끄기 위해 소방차들이 오고 있다.

5. It goes without saying that the most necessary thing in business is capital. But **however big** your capital may be, if you employ it in a wrong way, you cannot hope to succeed. Besides, you must know that in doing business credit is almost as important as capital.

notes :
*It goes without saying that ~ = It is needless to say that~
*employ = use

▶▶ In doing business, gaining the (   ) of others is just as important as capital and its proper (   ).
[faith, trust, respect, service, use, benefit]

▶▶ 영작하시오.
폐에 문제가 있는 사람은 담배를 피우지 말아야 한다는 것은 말할 나위조차 없다.

All that glitters is **not** gold.
The rich are **not always** happy.

6. Since you can**not** read **all** the books which you may possess, it is enough to possess only as many books as you can read. You should always read standard authors; and when you long for a change, fall back upon those whom you have read before.

notes :
*standard authors 권위있는 작가의 책
*fall back upon [on] ~ = ~에 의지하다

▶▶ 윗글의 내용과 일치하지 않는 것은?
① 항상 양서를 가려서 읽어야 한다.
② 책은 읽을 만큼만 가지면 된다.
③ 장서는 많을수록 좋다.
④ 양서는 되풀이해 읽을 가치가 있다.
⑤ 기분 전환을 위하여서도 가치 없는 책은 읽지 말아야 한다.

▶▶ 영작하시오.
긴급할 때 우리는 저금에 의지할 수 있다.

7. It must be clearly understood that the 'fittest' which survive are **not necessarily** the best or highest on any absolute standard, but simply fittest for the given conditions.

notes :
*the fittest 최적자
*on any absolute standard = 어떤 절대적인 기준에서

▶▶ The fittest are not the ones which are absolutely (   ) in all respects but the ones which are best adapted to the given (   ).
[inferior, superior, average, air, country, surroundings]

▶▶ 영작하시오.
적자생존과 자연도태에 대해 아십니까?

You cannot be too diligent

8. A book may be compared to the life of your neighbor. If it is good, it **cannot** last **too** long; if bad, you **cannot** get rid of it **too** early.

notes :
*be compared to~ = ~에 비유[비교]되다
*get rid of = remove

▶▶The (　　) you remove a bad book, the (　　) it will be.
[sooner, more, less, greater, finer, better]

▶▶영작하시오.
이 감기가 도무지 낫지 않는다.

There used to be a bridge here.

9. **There** has come about a situation which is novel in the history of the world. The essence of it is that, for the first time, the six continents of the world really matter to one another. For at least a good time to come bad harvest or economic depression in any one of them will affect all the others; a war beginning anywhere can soon become a war which is happening everywhere.

notes :
*novel 새로운
*for a good time to come = 앞으로 오랜 동안
*depression 불경기

▶▶According to the above passage, the world has now become a (　　) village.
[global, greater, good]

▶▶영작하시오.
앞으로 오랜 동안 너의 지각없는 이 행동을 너는 후회할 것이다.

10. **There** is much to support the belief that **there** is a struggle for existence among ideas, and that those which correspond with the changing conditions of humanity tend to prevail. But it does not follow necessarily that the ideas which prevail are better morally, or even truer to the laws of Nature, than those which fail.

notes :
*prevail 우세하다
*not ~ necessarily … 부분부정

▶▶In a struggle for existence some ideas which can best (　　) the demands of the changing times can survive. Nevertheless they are not necessarily (　　) than their competitors in every respect.
[make, meet, change, bigger, superior, greater]

▶▶영작하시오.
돈이 반드시 우리에게 행복을 가져다 주는 것은 아니다.

● 장 문 독 해 ●

Warming-up

We are likely to **set too much value on** the material side of our life.

We are all **in pursuit of** small things which are really worthless and will soon be forgotten.

A sudden end might be **brought to** our life on earth at any moment.

You must **take account of** his youth and inexperience.

1 If we were perpetually conscious of the insecurity of life and happiness we might easily become morbid, and lose our ardor alike in work and in pleasure. If we are never conscious of it, however, we are likely to set a false value on what is really valueless, and to waste our years in pursuit of things that are not worth pursuing. Hence, it is an excellent medicine for the mind that we should occasionally realize that we are traveling through space on a fragile crust of earth that may one day subside, bringing a sudden end to ourselves, our possessions and our ambitions. Many of the philosophers, at least, have thought so, and have made it their business to remind us that we build up our business and pursue our dreams ⓐunder the shadow of death. We are all condemned to die, it has been said, but under an indefinite reprieve, and we cannot measure the worth of anything in life by a standard which takes no account of ⓑthis.

Robert Lynd: *The Earthquake*

Notes

perpetually 영원히 / insecurity 불안정성 / morbid 병적인 / ardor 열의 / fragile 망가지기 쉬운 / crust 껍질 / subside 함몰하다 / condemn ~에게 형을 선고하다 / but (we are all condemned to die) under ~ / reprieve 집행유예 / take no account of ~을 고려하지 않다

Question

1. 본문의 밑줄친 ⓐunder the shadow of death가 함축하는 바를 다음과 같이 쓸 때, 빈칸에 알맞은 말을 골라 쓰시오.

   knowing that death could (   ) to us at any moment

   [call, approach, come]

2. 본문의 밑줄친 ⓑthis 가 가리키는 구체적인 내용을 우리말로 쓰시오.

3. 다음이 본문의 요지가 되도록, 빈칸에 적절한 말이 가장 잘 짝지어진 것은?

   Our occasional (   ) that we are all doomed to die some day could be an excellent medicine to cure us of our (   ) diseases caused by materialism prevalent in our age and to stimulate us to live a (   ) life.

   ① awareness — physical — valuable
   ② consciousness — moral — fleeting
   ③ realization — mental — worthy
   ④ discovery — spiritual — meaningful
   ⑤ acknowledgment — worldly — short

4. 본문의 내용과 일치하지 않는 것을 하나 고르시오.

   ① We should not spend our precious life worrying about trivial things.
   ② Our happiness is too easily affected by the death of our close friends.
   ③ We must lead our life, always keeping death in mind.
   ④ If we are too conscious of the insecurity of life, we are likely to be pessimistic about life.
   ⑤ Death comes to all, rich or poor, high or low.

Production

(1) 그녀는 그의 그림을 높이 평가한다.
(2) 우리는 모두 행복을 추구하고 있다. 그래서, 행복을 달성할 기회는 우리 모두에게 균등하게 열려야 한다.
(3) 그 시도는 자금 부족 때문에 결실 없이 끝났다.
(4) 흡연은 이곳에서 안 된다는 것을 여러분께 다시 한번 상기시켜 드립니다.

● 장 문 독 해 ●

Warming-up

I know of nothing which gives **more** pleasure and peace of mind **than reading**.

Once he has made a promise, he keeps it.

You may use my car, **such as it is**.

He grew **interested** in the work.

I regret to say that his work does not come up to the standard.

I have read two novels **at a stretch**.

2 Painting is complete as a distraction. I know of nothing which, without exhausting the body, more entirely absorbs the mind. Whatever the worries of the hour or the threats of the future, once the picture has begun to flow along, there is no room for them in the mental screen. ⓐThey pass out into shadow and darkness. All one's mental light, such as it is, becomes concentrated on the ⓑtask. ⓒTime stands respectfully aside, and it is only after many hesitations that luncheon knocks gruffly at the door. When I have had to stand up on parade, or even, I regret to say, in church, for half an hour at a time, I have always felt that the erect position is not natural to man, has only been painfully acquired, and is only with fatigue and difficulty maintained. But no one who is fond of painting finds the slightest inconvenience, as long as the interest holds, in standing to paint for three or four hours at a stretch.

Winston Churchill: *Painting as a Pastime*

Notes

distraction 기분 전환, 오락 / the hour=the present / the threats of the future (are), / flow 흐르다 / room 여유, 공간 / concentrate 집중하다 / gruffly 무뚝뚝하게 / parade 열병식 / erect 직립의, 똑바로 선 / at a stretch 단숨에

Question

1. 밑줄 친 ⓐ와 같은 뜻이 되도록 다음 글의 빈칸을 한 단어로 채우시오.

   One soon (f   ) one's daily anxieties.

2. 본문의 밑줄 친 ⓑ가 가리키는 것을 한 단어로 쓰시오.

3. Choose an appropriate word for the blank to replace the underlined phrase, ⓒTime stands respectfully aside.

One seems to lose (   ) of time

   [pace, track, lots]

4. According to the passage, which is **not** correct?

   ① Painting is a favorite pastime of the author.

   ② While painting, the author doesn't feel exhausted.

   ③ The author is so concentrated on the painting that he often forgets about lunch.

   ④ When the author stands on parade for an hour, he feels it natural to be in an upright position.

   ⑤ When painting, the author may stand willingly for more than three hours.

5. What makes the author tolerate fatigue and inconvenience caused by painting? Write one word mentioned in the passage.

6. Which is the main idea of the passage?

   ① The painting skills

   ② The advantage of painting compared to other hobbies

   ③ The right position when painting

   ④ The admiration for painting as a hobby

   ⑤ The obsession of a task

Production

(1) 일단 그 강을 건너가기만 하면, 너는 안심이다.
(2) 결과가 무엇이 되든, 나는 내 계획을 수행할 결심이다.
(3) 너의 흥미가 지속되는 한, 너는 공부에 틀림없이 진보가 있을 것이다.
(4) 여러 번 망설이고 나서야 나는 그의 문을 두드렸다.

실력체크 I

1 다음 글의 제목으로 가장 적합한 것을 고르시오.

> Universities have by tradition aimed at providing a liberal education in depth. Specialized study is thought necessary in order that graduates may know enough on leaving the university to take up posts in the professions, in the public services, and in industry and commerce. They need to be experts, and the vastness of modern knowledge prevents them from being experts in more than one or two subjects. Again, the intensive study of a limited field is believed to be the best way, some would say the only way, of training the mind.
>
> But specialization should come only after some acquaintance with what a philosopher has called 'the system of vital ideas which every age possesses and by which it lives,' a sense at least of the whole range of human achievement. The greater the need of specialization, the greater the need to give it a solid basis of general culture. And only with the experience of different subjects can anyone make an intelligent choice of specialization in the first place, let alone be able to see his subjects in any kind of perspective.

notes :
by tradition = 전통적으로 / liberal education = 일반 교양 교육 / in depth = 깊이 있게, 철저히 / specialized 전문화된 / take up = (일자리를) 얻다 / post 지위, 직 / industry 산업(계) / commerce 상업(계) / intensive 집중적인 / specialization 전문화 / acquaintance 지식, 숙지 / general culture = 일반 교양 / let alone ~ = ~은 말할 것도 없이 / perspective 원근감, 균형

① Necessity of specialization in modern society
② General culture and university education
③ University and importance of specialization
④ How to cope with the vastness of modern knowledge
⑤ Philosophy and university education

2 공란에 들어갈 말을 골라라.

> Learning a foreign language consists not in learning about the language but in developing a new set of habits. One may have a great deal of information about a language without being able to use the language at all. The "grammar" lessons here set forth, therefore, consist basically of exercises to _______, not explanations or talk about the language.

notes :
consist in ~에 놓여있다(=lie in) / consist of =~으로 구성되다 / a new set of~=새로운 일련의~(set=series) / set forth=explain

① increase knowledge
② give information
③ develop habits
④ use the language
⑤ explain the language

3 다음 공란에 들어갈 어구를 첫 단어의 대소문자 구분없이 ①~⑦에서 골라라.

The age (1)_____ has been called the machine age, the age of science, and even the atomic age. It could as reasonably be called the verbal age. For today words are the mightiest and yet the commonest tools in the world. (2)_____, electric and atomic power are relatively unimportant in our daily lives. This, of course, has been true of other ages. There has never been a time when civilized men could do much without words. But (3)_____, the more its existence depends on the power of words. And today their power is immense. We often fail to understand this (4)_____. Familiarity breeds, if not contempt, at least indifference. Yet, stop a moment and consider how much we live in a verbal world. The university education, (5)______, is almost entirely a verbal experience. You read books, you listen to lectures, you formulate your outlook on life—with words.

notes :
reasonably 당연히 / verbal 말의, 구두의 / mighty 강력한 / be true of ~=~에 들어맞다 / do much without ~=~없이 잘지내다 / familiarity 너무 잘 아는 것 / breed 낳다 / outlook on life 인생관

① contrasted with the power of words
② the greater progress men make
③ the more complex a civilization becomes
④ because we take words for granted
⑤ we live in
⑥ because we set great value on the power of words
⑦ which, you feel, has so much importance to your future

4 다음 글의 주제를 20자 내외의 우리말로 적어라.

To an extent never known, instability has become our way of life and colors our attitude profoundly. Instead of relying on what has proved itself in the past, we look eagerly to the new. The stream of advertisements to which we are daily exposed shows that to be new is the most recommendable. What is the good of making suits which will last for twenty years, if the fashion will change next spring? Is there any point in producing cars with engines which will not wear out quickly, if next year's model will have attractive innovations? This means that the durability of consumer goods, based on high quality material and careful finishing, is no concern of ours.

notes :
instability 끊임없는 변화 / color 영향을 미치다 / look to=기대를 걸다 / wear out=마모되다 / durability 내구성 / finishing 끝손질, 마무리

실 력 체 크 Ⅱ

A. 다음의 각 대화가 이루어지도록 ( )에 알맞은 것을 보기에서 골라라.

(1) A : I'm sorry I've dropped a spoon again. I'm all ( ) today.
B : That's all right. Nobody is perfect.

(2) A : I've something to tell you.
B : I'm all ( ). Go ahead.

(3) A : Congratulations on your son's passing the bar exam. Like father, like son. It must be in the ( ).
B : Thank you.

(4) A : I don't think I can go through with this.
B : I think it's a bit late for you to ( ) out now.

(5) A : May I speak to Mr. Cooper?
B : He is on another ( ). Do you mind holding or calling back later?

B. 다음 각 항에서 옳은 문장을 골라라.

(1) ① Having read the book, it was thrown aside.
② His father is resembled by him.
③ There being no seat left in the bus, I kept standing all the way.
④ You had better do not such a thing.

(2) ① Romeo and Juliet are one of my favorite plays.
② His salary is lower than his wife's.
③ A white and grey rabbit have run across the field.
④ A thousand dollars are the maximum sum I can lend you.

(3) ① I was made do it at once.
② Please bring this letter to your father when you go home.
③ The marriage was objected by his parents.
④ Never let this misbehavior happen again.

(4) ① When only a baby, our house was sold.
② They woke up at six, and so do I.
③ I wish I were with you at that time.
④ Had he not died in the war, he would be 30 years old now.

Answer: A. (1) thumbs (2) ears (3) genes (4) chicken (5) line
B. (1)—③ (2)—② (3)—④ (4)—④

C. 괄호 속의 동사의 어형을 바로 잡아라.

(1) This is a brand new computer! I wish we (have) one like this in our office last month, when we were so busy. Then I (can do) that large amount of work in a week.

(2) When I got to the office, all the desks, chairs, and bookshelves (already carry) out by my men.

(3) The man the policeman found (act) suspiciously in the shop doorway was charged with (loiter) with intent to sell drugs.

(4) There is a tide in the affairs of all of us, which, (take) at its flood, leads on to fortune, and (not take), may lead on to failure or misfortune.

(5) He does nothing but (complain) when he is asked (do) anything that he doesn't feel like (do).

D. 빈 부분을 10단어 이상을 써서 완성하여라.

(1) There was nothing I__________________________________.

(2) The holiday I____________________________________.

(3) The town my parents________________________________.

E. 괄호 안에 공통으로 들어갈 단어를 쓰시오.

(1) ⓐ It is in our (　　) to have a good command of English.
　ⓑ She seems to take a great (　　) in modern art.

(2) ⓐ He cut a brilliant (　　) among them.
　ⓑ Plato was the central (　　) in Greek philosophy.

(3) ⓐ He contributed an (　　) to the magazine every month.
　ⓑ Every (　　) on the shop is on sale.

(4) ⓐ We're faced with the (　　) of buying a new car.
　ⓑ He was forced by (　　) to steal a loaf of bread.

(5) ⓐ He lost his (　　) and fell off his bicycle.
　ⓑ My bank (　　) isn't very large.

(6) ⓐ Life at college seemed (　　), and the student longed for a change.
　ⓑ There's a lot of (　　) on the radio.
　ⓒ Friction generates (　　) electricity.

Answer: C. (1) had had, could have done (2) had already been carried (3) acting, loitering (4) taken, not taken (5) complain, to do, doing
D. (1) could do to help him to solve the difficult problem
(2) spent with my friend in Jeju will never be forgotten in my memory
(3) live in is in the southern part of our country
E. (1) interest (2) figure (3) article (4) necessity (5) balance (6) static

어 휘 · 발 음

A. 이탤릭체 부분을 대신할 수 있는 동사를 하나 적어라.

(1) The kite *rose high in the air* above the houses.
(2) The sailing boat *moved smoothly* through the water.
(3) The man with the injured foot *walked painfully* from the field.
(4) The thief *quickly took* the woman's bag from her hand.
(5) The stone *broke* the window *into many pieces*.

B. 주어진 낱말에서 적당한 것을 골라, 그 형태를 변화시켜 빈칸에 써라.

oppose, normal, effect, early, modest, moment, lose

(1) You should not waste time seeking after _____ joys.
(2) Never take an unfair advantage of any weakness which your _____ may have.
(3) He suffered an irreparable _____ on account of the fire.
(4) Inferior work is most _____ remedied when we know why it is poor.
(5) It is _____ for a baby to have teeth at the age of two weeks.
(6) If an appointment must be broken, notification should be given at the _____ possible moment.
(7) Her _____ prevented her from making her real feelings known to him.

C. (1)은 offend, (2)는 succeed, (3)은 origin의 파생어를 적어라.

(1) ⓐ He was not aware that he had committed an ______.
ⓑ He was arrested for using ______ language in public.
ⓒ He was a first ______, so he was not given a prison sentence.
(2) ⓐ Elizabeth Ⅱ succeeded George Ⅵ. She was his ______.
ⓑ After graduation he took a ______ of low-paid jobs.
ⓒ This concept has been applied ______ to painting, architecture, and sculpture.
(3) ⓐ The strike ______ from a dispute between two workers.
ⓑ ______ it was a bedroom, but we turned it into a study.
ⓒ The proposed route of the railway line has been changed twice since the ______ announcement.

Answer: A. (1) soared (2) glided (3) limped (4) snatched (5) shattered
B. (1) momentary (2) opponent (3) loss (4) effectively (5) abnormal (6) earliest (7) modesty
C. (1) ⓐ offense ⓑoffensive ⓒ offender (2) ⓐ successor ⓑ succession ⓒ successively (3) ⓐ originated ⓑ Originally ⓒ original

D. 아래 주어진 단어들을 문맥에 맞게 어형을 고쳐 빈칸에 써넣어라.
(단, 한번씩만 사용할 것.)

due, whole, noble, true, sole, high, dramatic, near

(1) For our country to remain competitive, we need a (　　　)-skilled, (　　　)-educated workforce.

(2) She was (　　　) born into a wealthy and aristocratic family.

(3) I was so annoyed that I (　　　) said something, but I managed to stop myself.

(4) She asked for his autograph and he (　　　) obliged by signing her program.

(5) This is a desperate situation which requires a (　　　) radical solution.

(6) I wasn't (　　　) convinced by her explanation.

(7) "I'll relinquish my claim to the throne", he announced (　　　).

(8) You shouldn't judge people (　　　) by their appearance.

E. 다음의 각 정의에 해당되는 단어를 ①~⑭에서 골라라.

① astronomy	② astrology	③ ethics	④ physics	⑤ geography
⑥ psychology	⑦ anarchy	⑧ chronic	⑨ chronicle	⑩ anachronism
⑪ operating system		⑫ geology	⑬ geometry	⑭ physiology

(1) a principle of right or good conduct, or a body of such principles

(2) the science of the sun, stars, and the planet

(3) the science of the earth's crust, esp. rock formations

(4) the science concerned with the study of how the bodies of living things, and their various parts, work

(5) a record of historical events, arranged in order of time

(6) absence of government or control

(7) the software that tells the parts of a computer how to work together and what to do

(8) the study of the movement of the stars and planets and how some people think they influence people's characters and lives

(9) the study of the earth's physical features and the people, plants, and animals that live in different regions of the world

Answer: D. (1) highly, highly (2) nobly (3) nearly (4) duly (5) truly (6) wholly (7) dramatically (8) solely
E. (1) ③ (2) ① (3) ⑫ (4) ⑭ (5) ⑨ (6) ⑦ (7) ⑪ (8) ② (9) ⑤

숙 어

(1) **odds and ends** (=miscellaneous items) 자질구레한 것, 잡동사니

☞ I've finished putting everything away, except for a few *odds and ends*.

(2) **off the record** (=unofficial(ly)) 비공식의[으로], 비공개의[로]

☞ He told the reporters that his remarks were strictly *off the record*.

(3) **off the top of one's head** (=quickly, without much thought) 즉석에서, 깊이 생각하지 않고

☞ It was the best answer I could think of *off the top of my head*.

(4) **of one's own accord** (=by one's own choice, voluntarily) 자발적으로

☞ Do you think he resigned his directorship *of his own accord*?

(5) **on the air** (=being broadcast) 방송중인[방송되는]

off the air (=not being broadcast) 방송중이 아닌[방송이 끝난]

☞ That soap opera has been *on the air* for over ten years.

All broadcasts with a political theme went *off the air*.

(6) **on the ball** (=alert, quick) 빈틈없고 재빠른

☞ He does his work fast and accurately; he is really *on the ball*.

(7) **on the blink** (=not working well, out of order) 고장인

☞ The vacuum cleaner is *on the blink* again; we should buy a new one.

(8) **on the job** (=at work) 일하는 중에[일하고 있는, 근무중인]

☞ Junior doctors are sometimes so tired they fall asleep *on the job*.

(9) **on the level** (=honest, sincere) 정직한, 진솔한

☞ How can I be sure you're *on the level* with me?

(10) **on the line** (=at risk) (지위·명성 등이) 위태로운

☞ If you don't stop being so lazy, your job will be *on the line*.

(11) **on the spot** (=at once ; at the scene of action) 즉시 ; 현장에서

☞ Anyone breaking the rules will be asked to leave *on the spot*.

If you get caught littering, you'll be fined *on the spot*.

⑿ **on the tip of one's tongue** (=about to be recalled)
(입안에서 맴돌 뿐) 생각이 안 나는
☞ His cellular phone number was *on the tip of my tongue*.

⒀ **once in a blue moon** (=very rarely) 어쩌다가 한번, 좀처럼 ~ 않는
☞ He works all the time and takes a vacation *once in a blue moon*.

⒁ **out of shape** (=in poor physical condition) 몸이 불편한
☞ I haven't had any exercise for weeks, and I'm really *out of shape*.

⒂ **pass out** (=faint, lose consciousness) 기절하다, 의식을 잃다
☞ Today is so hot that I feel as if I may *pass out* at any moment.

⒃ **pave the way for** (=make possible or easier) 길을 열다, 토대를 닦다
☞ The negotiations will *pave the way for* restoring economic ties.

⒄ **pay off** (=bribe ; produce good results ; pay in full)
매수하다 ; 좋은 결과를 낳다, 보상받다 ; 다 갚다, 청산하다
☞ The man wouldn't give evidence; I think someone *paid* him *off*.
His hard work *paid off* when he got a big raise in salary.
He finally *paid off* the 30-year mortgage on his house.

⒅ **pick up on** (=understand, catch on to) 이해하다, 알아차리다
☞ He failed to *pick up on* the humor in my remark.

⒆ **play along with** (=pretend to agree with) ~에 동의하는 척하다
☞ He pretended to be a celebrity and his friends *played along with* him.

⒇ **play down** (=make little of) 경시하다, 가볍게 여기다
☞ At first the authorities *played down* the threat to public health.

Exercise

▶▶ 주어진 단어들을 포함한 글을 지어라. 필요하면 어형을 변화시켜라.

1. there / lot / odd / end / attic
2. tell / comments / record
3. think / answer / top / head
4. He / army / of / accord
5. machine / on / blink
6. trust / she / on / level
7. agreement / pave / peace
8. put / prison / pay / cop
9. pick / on / what / mean
10. minister / down / disaster

17. 일치와 화법(Agreement & Narration)

기본 문법 설명

▶▶▶ 일치의 법칙 ◀◀◀

A. 주어와 술어동사의 일치

(1) ⓐ *Bread and butter* **was** given to the travelers.

ⓑ *Slow and steady* **wins** the race.

(2) ⓐ *The crew* **consists** of about 200 people.

ⓑ *The crew* **were** all saved.

(3) ⓐ *Either* Sam *or* Jim **is** responsible for it.

ⓑ *Neither* you *nor* I **am** wrong.

(4) ⓐ *Not only* he *but also* they **are** dependable.

ⓑ They *as well as* he **are** dependable.

(5) ⓐ *Twenty dollars* **is** a reasonable price for the shoes.

ⓑ About *three-fourths* of his property **is** already lost.

(6) ⓐ The politician and diplomat **is** present at the meeting.

ⓑ The politician and the diplomat **are** present at the meeting.

(7) ⓐ Every boy and girl **is** taught to read and write.

ⓑ Neither of the musicians **play(s)** the violin well.

B. 시제의 일치

(1) ⓐ Your eyes **are saying** that you **love** me as well.

Your eyes **were saying** that you **loved** me as well.

ⓑ I **hope** you **will** soon get well.

I **hoped** you **would** soon get well.

ⓒ She **says** that she **has refused** his proposal.

She **said** that she **had refused** his proposal.

ⓓ I **think** that he **was** an electrician.

I **thought** that he **had been** an electrician.

(2) ⓐ He **said** that honesty **is** the best policy.

ⓑ He **said** that he always **keeps** early hours.

ⓒ The guide **told** us that the roads in this city **are** still under repair.

▶▶▶ 일치의 법칙 ◀◀◀

A. 주어와 술어동사의 일치

(1) 주어가 and로 결합되어 있지만 단수취급

ⓐ Bread and butter는 「버터를 바른 빵」이라는 한 개의 단위
brandy and water (물 탄 브랜디)
*Bread and butter *have* risen in price. (버터와 빵값이 올랐다.)

ⓑ Slow and steady는 「천천히 그리고 꾸준한 것」이라는 단일 개념

(2) ⓐ 집합명사 — 단수취급
(승무원은 약 200명으로 구성되어 있다.)
ⓑ 군집명사 — 복수취급
(승무원들은 모두 구조되었다.)

(3) Either A or B, Neither A nor B는 B에 술부 동사가 일치한다.

(4) not only A but (also) B는 술부동사가 뒤의 B에 일치하고, B as well as A일 때는 앞의 B에 일치한다.
(그뿐만 아니라, 그들도 믿을만 하다.)

(5) 복수형 주어가 단수 취급되는 경우
ⓐ twenty dollars 전체를 한 단위로 생각한다.
ⓑ 분수는 뒤에 오는 말에 따라서 수가 결정된다.
(그의 재산 중 약 4분의 3이 이미 없어졌다.)

(6) ⓐ 동일인
(정치가이며 외교관인 그 사람이 모임에 참석하고 있다.)
ⓑ 다른 사람
(그 정치가와 그 외교관이 모임에 참석하고 있다.)

(7) ⓐ Every, each는 원칙적으로단수
Everybody *has* a way of *their* own.
(누구에게나 자기나름의 방식이 있다.)
ⓑ Neither는 단수 혹은 복수
Neither of them is (*or* are) alive.

B. 시제의 일치

(1) ⓐ 주절의 are saying이 과거시제 were saying이 되면, 종속절의 love는 loved로 되어야 한다. 이때의 변화는 의미의 변화가 아니라 형식상의 변화에 불과하다. "너 또한 나를 사랑**했다**고 네 눈은 말해주고 있었다"가 아니라 "너 또한 나를 사랑**한다**고 네 눈은 말해주고 있었다."로 번역해야 한다.

ⓑ hope ⇨ hoped에 일치하여
will ⇨ would가 되었다.

ⓒ says ⇨ said에 맞추어
has refused ⇨ had refused

ⓓ think ⇨ thought에 맞추어
was ⇨ had been

◎ 주절의 술부동사가 과거, 과거완료가 되면 종속절의 시제는 다음의 변화를 받는다.

현재	⇨	과거
현재완료, 과거	⇨	과거완료
shall, will / can, may	⇨	should, would / could, might

(2) 시제의 일치의 예외

ⓐ 보편적인 진리
(정직은 최선의 방책이라고 그는 말했다.) — 정직이 최선의 방책이라는 것은 보편적인 진리이다.
The ancients didn't know the earth *is* round.

ⓑ 현재의 습관 · 사실
(그는 늘 일찍 자고 일찍 일어난다고 말했다.)
He said that New Zealand *is* an island country.
She didn't know that mercury *is* poisonous.

ⓒ 과거부터 현재 혹은 미래에 계속 관계가 미칠 때
He told us that his school *begins* at 8.

	ⓓ The teacher **told** us that World War Ⅱ **broke** out in 1939. ⓔ He **said** that he **would** go with them if he **were** not sick. ⓕ He **said** he **must** go to the bank to withdraw some money. I **told** her that she **ought to** be ashamed of herself.
	▶▶▶ 화 법 ◀◀◀
A. 평서문의 전달	(1) My aunt always says to me, "You are a modest girl." My aunt always **tells me that I am** a modest girl. (2) He said, "I will be back tomorrow." He said that he **would** be back **the next day**. (3) He said to me, "I have received this e-mail today." He **told** me that he **had received that** e-mail **that day**. (4) They said, "We saw him here yesterday." They said that they **had seen** him **there the day before**. (5) He promised, "I will come, if I can." He promised that he **would** come if he **could**. (6) He said, "If I were rich, I would buy a luxurious car." He said that if he **were** rich he **would** buy a luxurious car.
B. 의문문의 전달	(1) He said to me, "What do you think of the speaker's talk?" He **asked** me **what** I thought of the speaker's talk. (2) She said to me, "When will your brother go to America?" She **asked** me **when** my brother **would go** to America. (3) I said to him, "How long have you been studying French?" I **asked** him **how** long he **had been studying** French.

ⓓ 역사적 사실은 항상 과거 시제
We learned that America *was discovered* in 1492.

ⓔ 가정법
= He said, "I *would* go with them, if I *were* not sick."
I said, "It *might* be true."
= I said that it *might* be true."

ⓕ must, ought to 는 시제 일치에 영향을 받지 않는다. 그러나 had to로 바꿔 쓸 수는 있다.
= He said he *had to* go to the bank～.
= I told her that she *had to* be ashamed～.
☞ 추측을 나타내는 must는 그대로.
He said, "I *must* be sick."
=He said (that) he *must* be sick.

▶▶▶ 화 법 ◀◀◀

A. 평서문의 전달

· 전달동사: say ⇨ say,
say to ⇨ tell,
이외의 동사는 그대로.
· 피전달문: that-Clause로 한다.
· 인칭, 지시대명사, 부사(구)는 전달자의 입장에서 적절히 바꾼다.
· 시제의 일치에 따른다.

☞ 화법전환에 따르는 어구 변화
now ⇨ then today ⇨ that day,
tomorrow ⇨ the next day
혹은 the following day
yesterday ⇨ the day before
혹은 the previous day
last night ⇨ the night before
혹은 the previous night
ago ⇨ before this ⇨ that
these ⇨ those here ⇨ there

(1) says to ⇨ tells, that을 보충,
You are ⇨ I am

(2) said ⇨ said, I will ⇨ he would
tomorrow ⇨ the next day

(3) said to ⇨ told,
have received ⇨ had received,
this ⇨ that, today ⇨ that day

(4) We ⇨ they, saw ⇨ had seen,
here ⇨ there,
yesterday ⇨ the day before

(5) 가정법이 아니라 조건문이다.
전달동사는 그대로 promised,
I will ⇨ he would

(6) 이 문장은 가정법이므로 시제는 그대로 쓰고, 인칭만 내용에 따라 바꾸었다.
You said, "I wish I *were* a bird."
=You said you wished you *were* a bird.

☞ 다음의 화법을 바꾸어라.
This morning he said to me *here*, "My father will come here tomorrow."
= This morning he told me here that his father would come *here tomorrow*.
This morning과 here라는 조건이 주어졌기 때문에 내용에 따라 간접화법에 그대로 쓰였다. 이와 같이 간접화법으로 고칠 때, 어구를 공식적으로 무조건 바꾸는게 아니라 그 때의 조건에 맞추어 바꾸어야 한다.
Yesterday he said *here*, "I like *this* room very much."
= Yesterday he said here that he liked *this* room very much."

B. 의문문의 전달

· 전달동사는 ask, inquire로.
· 피전달문은 다음과 같이 한다.
의문사가 있는 의문문은「의문사+평서문」
의문사가 없는 의문문은「if(혹은 whether)+평서문」

☞ **의문사가 있는 의문문**

(1) "What do you think of ～?"
⇨ what I thought of ～

(2) "When will your brother ～?"
⇨ when my brother would ～

(3) "How long have you been ～?"
⇨ how long he had been ～

	(4) He said to me, "What is the matter with you?" He **asked** me **what was** the matter with me.
	(5) He said to me, "Do you know her e-mail address?" He **asked** me **if** I knew her e-mail address.
	(6) Mary said to her mother, "May I go out with Helen?" Mary **asked** her mother **if** she might go out with Helen.
	(7) He said to the doctor, "Will I get well soon?" He **asked** the doctor **if he would** get well soon.
	(8) He said to me, "Shall I mail this letter?" He **asked** me **if he should** mail that letter.
C. 명령문의 전달	(1) The pilot said to his copilot, "Take over the controls." The pilot **told** his copilot **to take** over the controls.
	(2) The old man said to me, "Please help me with this luggage." The old man **asked** me **to help** him with that luggage.
	(3) The officer said to his men, "Stay where you are." The officer **commanded** his men **to stay** where they were.
	(4) She said to me, "Don't quit this job before you find a new one." She **advised** me **not to** quit that job before I found a new one.
	(5) He said, "Let's play baseball." He **suggested** that we (**should**) play baseball. He **suggested** playing baseball.
	(6) "Let me show you the way," he said. He **offered** to show me the way.
	(7) He said, "Let me go and say goodbye to John." He **asked to be allowed to** go and say goodbye to John.
D. 감탄문의 전달	(1) She said, "What a lovely flower it is!" She **exclaimed** what a lovely flower it was.

(4) "What is the matter with you?"
what was the matter with me

☞ 이 예문과 같이 의문사가 주어 또는 보어이고, be동사가 오되 그 뒷 부분이 길 때는 be를 뒤로 돌리지 않고, 글의 안정감을 위해 어순을 그대로 한다.

He said to me, "Which is the shortest cut across the field?"
⇨ He asked me which was the shortest cut across the field.

☞ **의문사가 없는 의문문**

(5) 평서문 I knew her e-mail address.를 if가 연결했다.
(6) May I go ~?가 if she might go ~로 됨.
(7) Will I ~?는 if he would ~가 되었다.
(8) Shall I ~? = Do you want me to ~?
… 상대방의 의지를 묻는다. 그래서 그대로 받아 if he should

☞ I said to myself, "Where can I find him?"
⇨ I wondered where I could find him.

☞ He said to me, "Could you give me a lift [ride]?"
⇨ He asked me to give him a lift [ride]. (그는 차를 태워달라고 내게 부탁했다.)

C. 명령문의 전달

· 전달동사는 피전달문의 내용에 따라서 tell, ask, beg, order, command, bid, advise, request, forbid 등으로 하여 그 다음에「**목적어+to부정사**」를 붙인다.
·「Let이 유도하는 명령문」은 그 내용에 따라서 suggest (*or propose*) that ~ should…,혹은 offer, ask to be allowed 등을 쓴다.

(1)「**tell+목적어+to 부정사**」를 썼다.
(2) **의뢰**를 나타낼 때:
「**ask[beg]+목적어+to 부정사**」
(3) **지시, 명령**을 할 때:
「**command[order]+목적어+to 부정사**」
(4) **충고**를 나타낼 때
충고의 뜻이 포함될 때는 대개 전달동사를 advise로 한다. 특히 피전달문에 had better가 있으면 advise를 쓴다.
The doctor said to me, "You *had better* not drink."
⇨ The doctor *advised* me not to drink.
(5) **제안**을 할 때: 전달동사를 suggest 혹은 propose로 바꾸고, 전달 내용을 that절로 하여 should를 넣는다 이 should를 빼고 동사원형을 써도 된다.
(6) "Let me show you the way."의 뜻은「길을 안내**해 드리겠습니다**」이므로, 이때 전달 동사는 offered로 바꾼다.
(7) "Let me go and say ~."는「하도록 **해 주십시오**」의 뜻으로, 상대방의 허가를 구하는 형식이다. 이 때 전달동사는 asked to be allowed이다.

D. 감탄문의 전달

감탄문을 간접화법으로 바꿀 때는 피전달문의 원뜻에 가깝도록 해야 한다. 따라서, 감탄문의 화법 전환은 다음과 같이 형식이 각각 달라지게 되며, 그때 그때 보아서 가장 알맞은 표현을 하면 된다. 감탄문의 화법 전환은 차라리 작문의 영역에 속한다.

전달동사는 say, cry (out), exclaim, shout 등으로 바꾸고 다음처럼 한다.
· 감탄문 어순을 그대로 놓는 방법.
· 부사 very를 보충하고 평서문의 순으로 하는 방법.
· 감탄사를 부사구로 바꾸고, 평서문의 순으로 하는 방법

(1) 감탄문의 어순을 그대로 옮겨 쓴 것이다. said를 exclaimed로 바꾼 것은 감탄의 감정을 돕기 위해서이다.
She said, "How happy I am!"
⇨ She *exclaimed* how happy she was.

	(2) He said, "How foolish I was to believe her!" He said that he had been **very** foolish to believe her. (3) He said, "Hurrah! I've won!" He **shouted with joy** that he had won. (4) The spectators said, "Bravo! Wonderful!" The spectators **cried out with applause** that it was wonderful. (5) Father said, "God bless my child!" Father **prayed** that God **might** bless his child. (6) He said to us, "May you have a long and happy life!" He **expressed the wish** that we might have a long and happy life.
E. 중문, 복문, 두 문장 이상의 전달	(1) She said, "The ruby is very expensive, and I cannot buy it." She said (that) the ruby was very expensive, **and that** she could not buy it. (2) He said, "It will rain, **for** the barometer is falling." He said that it would rain, **for** the barometer was falling. (3) He said to me, "Hurry up, and you will be on time." He told me to hurry up **and** I would be on time. He told me that if I hurried up I would be on time. (4) He said, "Let's wait here until the rain stops." He suggested that we (should) wait there until the rain **stopped**. (5) She said, "It is hot in this room, why don't you turn on the air conditioner?" She **said** that it was hot in that room **and asked** why I didn't turn on the air conditioner. (6) He said to me, "Listen! Can you hear someone talking?" He **told** me to listen **and asked** if I could hear someone talking. (7) She said, "Oh, how wonderful! I'd simply love to go with you." She **exclaimed with delight** that she would simply love to go with me.

(2) 감탄의 내용을 평서문으로 바꾸고 very를 덧붙였다.
(내가 그 여자를 믿다니 정말 바보였구나!)
He said, "What a charming girl!"
He said that she was a *very* charming girl.

(3) Hurrah!와 같은 감탄사를 포함할 때는 그 내용만 나타내면 된다. 즉, 여기서는 shouted with joy로 Hurrah의 뜻을 나타냈다. 그리고, I've won은 that he had won으로 하여 shouted의 목적어가 되었다.

(4) Bravo!는 박수치는 뜻이 있는 감탄사이므로, cried out with applause로 표현하였다. 또한, Wonderful!은 It is wonderful!의 생략문으로 생각하여서 that it was wonderful로 했다.

(5) 기원문은 prayed that God might ~의 형식을 쓴다.
= Father prayed God to bless his child.

(6) May you have ~!는 기원문이지만, 신에 대한 기원이 아니라 말하는 사람의 소망이다. 그래서 expressed the wish that we might have ~라고 했다.

E. 중문, 복문, 두 문장이상의 전달

- 피전달문이 and, but로 연결되는 등위절로 될 때는 that를 그 뒤에 놓는다.
- 피전달문이 복문일 때는 단문의 경우와 마찬가지다. 다만, 일치의 법칙이 종속절에도 미친다.
- 피전달문이 두 개 혹은 그 이상의 문장으로 될 때는 and로 연결하며, 文의 종류가 다를 때는 각각 거기에 맞는 전달 동사를 반복하여 사용한다.

(1) **중문** : 피전달문이 and로 연결 된 중문이다. 등위접속사 and 다음에 that를 놓는다.

(2) **중문**: for도 등위접속사이지만 that를 그 뒤에 놓지 않는다. as, because 같은 종속접속사 뒤에도 놓지 않는다.

(3) 「**명령법+and[or]**」 : and [or]를 그대로 남겨 두어도 된다.

(4) **복문**: 종속절의 시제도 바뀌었다.

(5) 「**평서문+의문문**」 : 이때는 전달동사를 두번 사용해 양자를 and로 연결한다.

(6) 「**명령문+의문문**」 : 이때도 역시 전달동사를 두번 쓰고, and로 연결한다.

(7) 「**감탄문+평서문**」 : 이런 경우는 작문의 분야에 속하게 된다. 그 때의 환경에 따라 알맞은 표현을 하는 수밖에 없다.

☞ **묘출화법 [중간화법]**

직접화법과 간접화법의 중간적 성격을 가지는 화법을 묘출화법(Represented Speech)이라 한다. 이것은 소설 등에서 많이 볼 수 있으며, 생생한 표현이 된다.
He asked me *would I go to the concert*.
I was wondering *could she be our new teacher*.
She whispered something, and asked *was that enough*.
She asked her next-door neighbor if she knew Lady Mickleham by sight, and *had she seen her lately*.

☞ **다음 문장들을 간접화법으로 고쳐보자.**

He said to me, "Hello!"
⇨ He *greeted* me.
He said to me, "Goodbye."
⇨ He *bade* me goodbye.
He said to her, "Thank you."
⇨ He *thanked* her.
He said to me, "Congratulations!"
⇨ He *congratulated* me.
He said to me, "Good luck to you!"
⇨ He *wished* me good luck.

문 법 · 작 문

A. 괄호 안에서 맞는 것을 골라라.

(1) He as well as Mary and Tom (is, are) coming to the party.
(2) Either you or he (is, are) aware of it.
(3) About two-thirds of my books (is, are) novels.
(4) The number of cars (has, have) been remarkably increasing.
(5) All work and no play (make, makes) Jack a dull boy.
(6) There (was, were) lots of people suffering from tuberculosis.
(7) Mary is one of those women who (believe, believes) that the success of any marriage depends entirely on the husband.
(8) The English (is, are) often said to be a practical people.
(9) A needle and thread (was, were) needed to sew the button.
(10) Any pants to go with this jacket (is, are) OK.
(11) He said that he (came, had come) back the day before.
(12) They climbed higher so that they (can, could) get a better view.
(13) He said that Europe (is, was) separated from America by the Atlantic Ocean.
(14) Not only the general but all his soldiers (was, were) annihilated.
(15) Then the United States (was, were) ready for war.
(16) There (seems, seem) to have been a mistake; my name isn't on the list.
(17) In my opinion, physics (is, are) badly taught in our schools.
(18) The news that he's suffered from lung cancer (is, are) a shock to us.
(19) Many a boat (have, has) been wrecked here.
(20) It is not you but he that (is, are) to blame for it.
(21) Ham and eggs (is, are) my favorite breakfast.
(22) The Olympic Games (was, were) held in Seoul in 1988.
(23) According to religious people the soul and the body (are, is) one.
(24) Plain living and high thinking (is, are) a great ideal.
(25) There (are, is) more than one reason to believe that he is innocent.
(26) Measles (is, are) much less common now than it used to be.
(27) A year and a half (have, has) passed since he died.
(28) Johnson's Lives of the Poets (is, are) a work of great interest.
(29) I, your sergeant, (order, orders) you to clean your guns.
(30) Every policeman and official (is, are) on the alert.
(31) Trial and error (is, are) the source of our knowledge.
(32) On the expressway car after car (was, were) driving at breakneck speed.
(33) A large supply of toys (is, are) expected.

(34) Early to bed and early to rise (make, makes) a man healthy.
(35) You have said that you (would, will) leave here tomorrow.
(36) He is the only one of the boys that (speaks, speak) English well.
(37) Most marines lost their (life, lives) at the landing battle.
(38) The beautiful (do, does) not always go hand in hand with the good.

B. 다음 문장의 화법(話法)을 바꾸어라.
(1) He said, "I'll pay you double if you get the work finished by tomorrow."
(2) She said, "I will keep my promise."
(3) He said to me, "I have been reading this book since last night."
(4) Last night she said to me, "My mother wants to see you tomorrow."
(5) He said, "Yes." He said, "No."
(6) He said, "I wish I were rich enough to buy a private plane."
(7) He refused to attend the meeting.
(8) He said, "I'll be back as soon as I can."
(9) She said to me, "What can I do for you?"
(10) I said to the clerk, "Can I use this telephone?"
(11) She asked a girl at the post office how many days it takes a parcel to reach Chicago by air mail.
(12) He invited me to lunch with him the following day.
(13) He said, "The flu is an infectious disease, but cancer isn't."
(14) He said to himself, "Should I ever forget her?"
(15) She said, "If I can get permission, I'll come."
(16) He told me that if he was me he would not worry about it.
(17) He said, "It is a holiday today, and we have no school."
(18) "What about going for a swim?" he said.
(19) He said to her, "Help me, or you will be sorry."
(20) "He went to the barber's an hour ago," his wife said to me, "and I think he will be back very soon. Will you please step in and wait?"
(21) He said to me, "Go and see who it is."
(22) Father said to me, "Don't forget to leave a space."
(23) He said to me, "Disinfect the wound before you bandage it."
(24) He said to us, "Let's have a cup of coffee."
(25) He told me not to speak until I was spoken to.
(26) I suggested to her that we should eat out at a posh restaurant the following Sunday.

(27) The boys said, "Hurrah! We have won the race!"
(28) He said, "Alas! I have failed again!"
(29) He said to me, "How pretty your picture is!"
(30) He said, "Oh, what a disaster it is!"
(31) He said, "God help the poor!"
(32) She exclaimed with joy that she had beaten him.
(33) He said to me, "What a glorious day it is! Let's go out for a drive."
(34) Mother said, "Please be quiet, boys. The baby has just gone to sleep."
(35) She said, "I was very busy some days ago, but I am presently quite free."
(36) He said to me, "Which do you like better, this or that?"
(37) The clerk denied that he had refused to help the obnoxious customer.

C. Translate the following into English:

(1) 그 당시는 아무도 지구가 공처럼 둥글다는 것을 믿지 않았다.

(2) 나는 한두 시간이면 그가 돌아오리라고 생각하고 세 시간이나 기다렸으나 그는 결국 돌아오지 않았다.

(3) 그 버스는 대개 몇 시에 여기에 도착하느냐고 나는 그에게 물었다.

(4) 그는 나에게 미국에 가 본적이 있느냐고 물었다.

(5) "당신이 편리할 때 그 돈을 돌려 줘도 좋습니다."라고 그는 내게 말했다.

(6) 그 여자를 전송하려고 공항에 갔다오는 길이라고 그는 나에게 말했다.

(7) "오, 나는 정말 어리석었구나!"하고 그는 말했다.

(8) "아직 오늘 신문을 읽지 않았습니다. 뭐 좋은 소식이 있습니까?"하고 그는 나에게 말했다.

(9) 아버지께서 입학시험에 합격하도록 열심히 공부하라고 내게 말씀하셨다.

'Winter'이라는 제목으로 90어 내외의 글을 지어라.

● 단 문 독 해 ●

She **said** that she **was** happy.
I **asked** her **if** she **was** happy.
He said **that** he was poor **and that** he couldn't buy it.
He **said** that he **would** go with them if he **were** not ill.
Columbus **proved** that the earth **is** round.
She whispered something, and asked **was that enough**.

1. When I reached Paris the taxi-driver **told** me that all the hotels **were** full, and that I **would** have a great deal of difficulty in finding a room, unless I **went** out into the suburbs.

notes :
*have (a great deal of) difficulty in ~ing = ~하는 것이 (무척) 어렵다[힘들다]

▶▶윗글의 내용과 일치하도록 다음 빈칸에 들어갈 말을 고르시오.
The taxi-driver said that all the hotels in (　　) area were full and advised me to find one in the (　　).
[Paris, outskirts, residential, home, downtown]

▶▶영작하시오.
(1) 힘 안 들이고 나는 그의 집을 찾았다.
(2) 내가 즉시 오지 않으면 혼자 떠나겠다고 그는 나에게 전화했다.

2. I asked a physician **whether** he **agreed** with those of his profession who **held** the view that salt **was** unnecessary and even harmful. He replied with great energy in the negative. He would not admit that the foods we **eat** contain enough salt required by the human body.

notes :
*those of his profession에서 those = physicians
*with great energy = 매우 힘차게(= very energetically)

▶▶According to the above paragraph, the underlined a physician maintained that salt was absolutely (　　) and not harmful, and that sometimes we should absorb (　　) salt besides the foods we eat.
[correct, necessary, better, additional]

▶▶영작하시오.
기차는 매 30분마다 떠난다고, 그는 나에게 말했다.

3. In the course of that letter I told her **that** I needed a hundred dollars, **and that** if she could lend me that sum until I could repay it, I would be very much obliged to her, and would tell her afterward what I had wanted it for.

notes :
*be obliged to+명사[대명사] = ~에 감사하다

▶▶According to the above passage, which is correct?

① The writer explained in detail why he needed the money.
② The writer sent her a thank-you letter for her help.
③ The writer didn't mention when he could repay the money.
④ The writer asked her to repay him a hundred dollars.
⑤ The writer said he would not be able to repay the money.

▶▶영작하시오.

(1) 너는 무엇때문에 그것을 원하느냐?
(2) 친절한 도움에 대단히 감사드립니다.

4. One of the most disgraceful features of life in the country, Father often declared, was the general inefficiency and slackness of small village tradesmen. He said he had originally supposed that such men were interested in business, **and that** that was why they had opened their shops and sunk capital in them, but no, they never used them for anything but gossip and sleep. They took no interest in civilized ways. Hadn't heard of them, probably.

notes :
*disgraceful 수치스러운
*feature 특징
*inefficiency 비능률
*slackness 느슨함
*tradesman 장사꾼(= shopkeeper)
*capital 자본금

▶▶Which of the following does **not** correspond with the above paragraph?

① The shopkeepers were inefficient and idle.
② Small village shopkeepers made ends meet in spite of their inefficient ways of trading.
③ The writer's father thought at first that the shopkeepers opened their shops because they were interested in business.
④ The shopkeepers ran their shops in an inefficient manner.
⑤ The shopkeepers wasted their time in dozing or gossiping.

▶▶영작하시오.

나는 그것 이외에는 어떤 일이라도 하겠다.

5. Recently I became acquainted with an old gentleman of eighty who seemed to look at least twenty years younger. He **told** me that if doctors **had to** depend on people like him for patients, they **would** all go out of business, for he had never been sick a single day in his life.

notes :
*depend on A for B = turn to A for B
*go out of business = 폐업하다
*(for) a single day

▶▶The old gentleman, who looked very young for his (　　), said that doctors would have to stop (　　) if there were only healthy people like him.
[age, youth, wife, working, trying, practicing]

▶▶영작하시오.
고아이기 때문에 그는 도움을 의존할 사람이 없다.

6. Newton **found** that the planets, including the Earth, **go** around the sun by what he called the law of gravitation, and his reward for making his great discovery about the Universe was that he was blamed for being an atheist.

notes :
*the law of gravitation = 인력의 법칙
*atheist 무신론자

▶▶Most of Newton's contemporaries didn't fully recognize the greatness of his discovery, because it (　　) with their religious beliefs.
[disagreed, debated, denied]

▶▶영작하시오.
그 선생님은 학생들에게 지구는 1년에 한 번 태양 주위를 돈다고 말했다.

7. A letter from Sam informed her that he had been unexpectedly fortunate in obtaining the shop. He was in possession of it; it was the largest in the town, combining fruit with vegetables, and he thought it would form a home worthy even of her some day. **Might he not run up to town to see her**?

notes :
*묘출화법 / May I not run up to town to see you?
*town (관사 없이) 수도 (주로 '런던'을 의미함)

▶▶Having finally overcome his (　　) problems, Sam was thinking of making a (　　) to her.
[fiscal, physical, financial, proposal]

▶▶영작하시오.
나는 다음 주 하루 쉬겠다고 사장에게 통보했다.

● 장 문 독 해 ●

Warming-up

Mine is a silk umbrella.
I have known him **ever since** he was in diapers.
We have reached **the certainty that** the negotiations will be successful.
Whatever **is**, is right.
I have not seen him **since**.
No matter what happens, you must do it.

1 Mine has been ⓐthe limited experience of one who lives in a world without color and without sound. But ever since my student days I have had a joyous certainty that my physical handicaps were not an essential part of my being, since they were not in any way a part of my mind. ⓑThis faith was confirmed when I came to Descartes' maxim, "I think, therefore I am."
Those five emphatic words woke something in me that has never slept since. I knew then that my mind could be a positive instrument of happiness, bridging over the dark, silent void with concepts of a vibrant, light-flooded happiness. I learned that it is possible for us to create light and sound and order within us, no matter what calamity befalls us in the outer world.

***Helen Keller:** The Story of My Life*

Note Mine=My experience / certainty 확신 / being 존재 / not in any way=in no way / maxim 격언, 금언 / I am=I exist / emphatic 힘있는 / positive 적극적인 / void 공간 / concept 개념 / vibrant 활기에 넘친 / light-flooded 빛이 가득한 / calamity 재난 / befall (재난이) 떨어지다

Question

1. Which is **not** included in the examples of the underlined phrase ⓐ?
   ① She had trouble communicating with an ordinary man.
   ② She couldn't enjoy the works of classical composers.
   ③ She had a difficult time reading normal books.
   ④ She couldn't properly appreciate Picasso's works.
   ⑤ She couldn't feel the sense of touching the fur of a cat.

2. 본문의 밑줄친 ⓑThis faith의 내용을 다음과 같이 정리할 때 빈칸에 알맞은 말을 골라 쓰시오.
   Our genuine happiness lies in the (　　　). Therefore physical handicaps are not (　　　) to our happiness.
   [mental, mind, mercy, obstacles, objects, options]

3. Which is most appropriate to describe the author?
   ① determined and strong-willed
   ② pessimistic and desperate
   ③ miserable and pitiful
   ④ aggressive and competent
   ⑤ indecisive and optimistic

4. Which does **not** correspond with this passage?
   ① The author's experiences were limited because of her handicaps.
   ② The author would not let her physical disabilities prey on her mind.
   ③ The author suffered a lot from depression because of her physical handicaps.
   ④ The author affirmed her faith on finding truth in the Descartes' maxim.
   ⑤ The author got over many adversities with a strong will.

Production

(1) 내가 여기에 온지 10년이다.
(2) 그녀가 불어로 말했으므로, 나는 그녀의 말을 이해할 수 없었다.
(3) 너의 생일에 너와 함께 있지 못할 것 같다.
(4) 비록 프랭클린 루즈벨트는 신체적인 장애자였으나, 미국의 가장 위대한 대통령 중의 한 분이 되었다.

● 장 문 독 해 ●

Warming-up

He is absolutely **devoid of** musical sense.

There was **nothing** left **to indicate** that he had been in the room.

A tower **shows** (itself) above the forest.

I **could** do it now and I **could have done** it then.

I **am convinced that** we have to place greater emphasis on economic stability.

2 The moon was so desolate, so uninviting, so completely devoid of life or anything to indicate that there ever had been life.

The view of the earth from the moon fascinated me — a small disk, 240,000 miles away. It was hard to think that little thing held so many problems, so many frustrations. Raging nationalistic interests, famines, wars, pestilence don't show from that distance.

I'm convinced that some wayward stranger in a spacecraft, coming from some other part of the heavens, could look at the earth and never know it was inhabited at all. But the same wayward stranger would certainly know instinctively that if the earth were inhabited, then the destinies of all who lived on it must inevitably be interwoven and joined. We are one hunk of ground, water, air, clouds, floating around in space. From out there it really is "one world."

***Frank Borman**: The Travel to the Moon*

Note

desolate 황량한 / uninviting 마음이 끌리지 않는, 매력없는 / devoid of ~이 없는 / indicate 나타내다 / fascinate 매혹시키다 / disk 원반(圓盤) / frustration 좌절 / raging 맹렬한 / nationalistic interests 국가 이익 / famines 기근 / pestilence 질병 / wayward 정처 없는 / spacecraft 우주선 / some=a certain / it was inhabited의 was는 가정법 / instinctively 본능적으로 / inhabit 서식하다 / destiny 운명 / inevitably 불가피하게 / interweave 섞어 짜다 / hunk 큰 덩어리 / float 떠돌다

Question

1. 본문에서 the earth를 가리키는 말을 3개 찾아 쓰시오.
(대명사 it 제외)

2. 본문의 내용으로 보아 아래 빈칸에 적절하지 않은 말은?
Seen from the moon, raging nationalistic interests and wars are (   ) matters.
① trivial and meaningless
② insignificant and worthless
③ unimportant and useless
④ fatal and momentous
⑤ negligible and trifling

3. Which is most appropriate to describe the tone of the underlined sentence?
① eloquent
② ironic
③ instructive
④ scornful
⑤ constructive

4. Which of the following is the author's ultimate argument?
① We should invest more money in a space development project.
② Some conflicts caused by limited resources are unavoidable.
③ We should take steps to cope with the global calamities.
④ We, living in the small planet, should cooperate with each other, living as one.
⑤ Compared with the whole universe, the earth is too small for us to live on.

Production

(1) 태양이 지평선 위에 그 모습을 나타냈다.
(2) 나는, 그가 그 죄가 없다고 확신한다.
(3) 우리의 지구는 이 끝없는 우주에서 하나의 작은 점에 불과하다.
(4) 그렇게 행동하다니 그는 미쳤음에 틀림없다.

실 력 체 크 I

1 다음 글을 읽고 아래 물음에 답하여라.

ⓐA great many worries can be diminished by realizing the unimportance of the matter which is causing the anxiety. I have done in my time a considerable amount of public speaking; at first every audience terrified me, and nervousness made me speak very badly; I dreaded the ordeal so much that I always hoped I might break my leg before I had to make a speech, and when it was over I was exhausted from my nervousness. Gradually I taught myself to feel that it did not matter whether I spoke well or badly; the universe would remain much the same ⓑin either case. I found that the less I cared whether I spoke well or badly, the less badly I spoke, and the nervousness diminished almost to a vanishing point. A great deal of nervous fatigue can be dealt with in this way.

notes :
terrify 겁나게 하다 / nervousness 신경과민 / dread 두려워하다 / ordeal 시련 / the less badly = the more well / vanish 사라지다

(1) 밑줄 친 ⓐ의 내용을 작자는 어떻게 설명하고 있는가?
(2) 밑줄 친 ⓑ의 내용을 구체적으로 설명하여라.

2 다음은 서로 주고받는 대화이다. 빠진 인용부호를 넣고, 아래 물음에 답하여라.

How pleasant to have travelled the world as you have, Mr. Renvil! Six months here, a year there—always moving on! We parsons are tied to our parishes like watchdogs to their kennels, barking once a week, as best we can. Well, Mr. Dodd, I would not mind being tied to such a spot as this. I would like it very much; one gets weary of wandering. I am hoping to be able to stay here permanently; I hope it will turn out that way. Go back to your chair, Patricia. Mr. Renvil did not come here to be bothered by a little girl. He came here to have tea with your father and me. Oh, please, Mummy, let me sit with Mr. Renvil. Patricia, you heard your mother; sit in your place and show how well-behaved you can be. Oh, but please, Mr. Dodd, don't disturb your little daughter on my account.

notes :
parson 교구의 목사 / parish 교구 / kennel 개집 / weary 피로한, 싫증이 난 / permanently 영원히 / disturb 방해하다

* 윗 이야기의 무대는 (1)(직업명)(2)(인명)의 응접실이며, 등장 인물의 총수는 (3)(명)이다. 방문객은 (4)(인명)이고, (5)(인명)는 (6)(인명)의 딸이다.

3 다음 글의 공란을 적당한 단어로 메워라.

The other day I read in the newspaper about a man who was killed while going to the aid of a boy whose bicycle had been stolen. The man saw the boy crying and asked him (1) was the matter. The boy pointed in the direction of a youth making off (2) the bicycle. When the man gave chase, the youth stabbed him to death.
It is a heart-rending story, but the greater pity of it is that the newspapers, by playing it up, will (3) doubt dissuade countless others from going to the aid of someone (4) trouble. "Leave well enough alone." "Play it safe." "Don't go asking for trouble." These are the cowardly words that many people live (5), and our society is the weaker (6) it. If every citizen made it a practice to answer a cry for (7), gangsters would have to think twice about attacking people on the street and we'd live in a safer world. But (8) it is, most gangsters know that they can generally attack people, even in daylight, (9) impunity. Onlookers and bystanders will do just that: look (10) and stand by. They don't want to be involved.

notes :
stab one to death = ~을 찔러 죽이다 / heart-rending 가슴이 찢어지는 듯한 / play up 강조하다, ~을 잘 이용하다 / Leave well enough alone. 긁어 부스럼 내지 말라. / Play it safe. 위험한 짓을 하지 말라. / ask for trouble 고생을 사서 하다 / impunity 벌받지 않음

4 다음 글을 읽고 아래 질문에 답하여라.

Miss Smith's landlady, Mrs. Baker, admitted Charley without surprise. She was a big woman with very large arms and looked as though she would not hesitate to use them <u>if called on to do so</u>. Yes, she said, Miss Smith was in. He'd better go straight up. Number 12 was on the top floor. He must excuse her for not going up first to tell Miss Smith, but she had trouble with her feet and couldn't be expected to wear them out running up and downstairs after her lodger's friends. Charley sympathized with her over her feet and started briskly up the stairs. Mrs. Baker remained standing in the hall for a moment and, as he reached the first floor, called out sharply, "No male visitors after eleven. That's my rule and Miss Smith doesn't need to be reminded of it."

notes :
admit 받아들이다 / call on ~ to … = ~에게 … 하도록 요구하다 / wear out = 지치게하다 / lodger 하숙인 / briskly 기운차게

(1) 밑줄 친 부분을 번역하여라. (so의 내용을 밝힐 것)
(2) 여주인이 ⓐ 누구에게, ⓑ 무엇이라고 변명했는가?
그리고, ⓒ 그 이유는 무엇인가?
(3) 이 하숙집의 규칙을 말하여라.

실 력 체 크 II

A. 다음의 빈 곳을 우리말을 참고하여 알맞은 단어로 채워라.

(1) 의사는 내 흉부 엑스레이를 찍고 혈압을 쟀다.
The doctor _______ me a chest X-ray and _______ my blood pressure.

(2) 어디 봅시다. 아…, 네, 어금니 중의 한 개에 충치가 있군요.
Let me look at it. Ah…, yes, you have a _______ in one of your molars.

(3) 소변을 볼 때 힘드세요? Do you have any trouble _______ urine?

(4) 국소 마취를 하겠습니다. I'll give you a _______ anesthetic.

(5) 가래가 나옵니까? Do you _______ phlegm?

(6) 배가 아파 죽겠어요. My stomach is _______ me.

(7) 선생님, 불안하고 초조하고 불면증으로 고생하고 있는데요.
Doctor, I've been suffering from _______, _______, and _______ .

B. A와 B간에 대화가 이루어지도록 공란을 한 단어로 메워라.

(1) A: Do you mind if I smoke here?
B: ( ). My throat is sore.

(2) A: Thank you very much, Mr. Park. I can't thank you ( ).
B: You're quite welcome. Don't ( ) it, Mr. Smith.

(3) A: How's your business?
B: It couldn't be ( ). How about yours?
A: Oh, it couldn't be ( ).
B: Really? That's too bad.

(4) A: May I take your order?
B: Not yet, I'm expecting ( ).

(5) A: Excuse me, but ( ) calls.
B: OK. The men's room is out in the hallway to your right.

(6) A: Yesterday was my wife's birthday and I forgot about it.
B: Oh, Yeah? Why don't you buy her a nice present today? ( ) late than ( ).

(7) A: Honey, can I buy that expensive sapphire?
B: Sure. Money is no ( ).

(8) A: He charged into the boss' room and demanded a raise.
B: Really? He has quite a ( ).

Answer: A. (1) gave, took [measured, tested] (2) cavity (3) passing (4) local (5) raise *phlegm[flem] (6) killing (7) anxiety, nervousness, insomnia
B. (1) Yes (2) enough, mention (3) better, worse (4) company (5) nature (6) Better, never (7) object (8) nerve

C. 다음 (　　　) 속에 있는 낱말을 문법적인 기능에 맞도록 고쳐서 완전한 문장이 되도록 하여라.

(1) Doctors encourage people to have complete physical examinations regularly and (*not, wait*) until illnesses have become serious before having them (*treat*).

(2) Dislike of the dentist's drill seems to be universal, and many people put off (*go*) to the dentist until they (*force*).

(3) Some social insects, it is true, go out to fight in armies; but their attacks (*always direct*) against members of another species. Man is unique in (*organize*) the mass murder of his own species.

(4) Packages (*mail*) to addresses in the United States have (*vary*) costs, (*depend*) on the weight and the distance they must be sent.

(5) With older children, who (*go*) to school for some years, there may be deeper problems, which need (*handle*) sensitively.

D. 다음 글의 밑줄 친 우리 글을 영어로 옮겨라.

Compared with those living in the country, the people living in cities are not blessed with fresh air and forests. ㉠도시가 더 바빠지고 혼잡해질수록 휴식공간은 좁아지고 공기는 더 오염이 된다. There are few places where we can stroll and find pleasure in beautiful flowering plants or in the lushness of trees as we can in rural areas. ㉡더구나 도시의 어린이들을 위한 넓은 놀이터가 없어서 그들은 위험한 거리에서 논다. For this reason, the number of children who are run over by cars and motorcycles, who are hurt and killed is by no means small. ㉢그래서 도시에는 많은 공원이 있어야 한다. However, we have very few parks in Seoul. The authorities concerned should try to provide citizens with more parks. ㉣공원은 모든 도시인의 레크리에이션 장소이며, 그들의 마음을 위안해 주는 정원이다.

Answer: C. (1) not to wait, treated (2) going, are forced (3) are always directed, organizing
(4) mailed, varying, depending
(5) have been going, need handling [need to be handled]

D. ㉠ The busier and more crowded cities become, the narrower the places to rest become and the more polluted the air becomes.
㉡ Moreover, there are no spacious playgrounds for city children, so they play on the dangerous streets.
㉢ So, there must be many parks in the cities.
㉣ A park is a recreation place for all the people of the city and a garden that consoles their spirits.

어 휘 · 발 음

A. 각 단어의 동의어를 2개씩 고르고, 접두어를 이용하여 반의어를 만드시오.

(1) connect ① join ② unfasten ③ detach ④ correlate ⑤ erect
반의어 : ______

(2) pure ① mixed ② genuine ③ purge ④ core ⑤ clean
반의어 : ______

(3) relevant ① reliable ② vulgar ③ pertinent ④ appropriate ⑤ ruthless
반의어 : ______

B. 공란에 넣어 문장의 뜻을 완성시킬 수 있는 단어를 골라라.

(1) Don't worry about all the details as long as you get the ______ of it.
① gist ② girth ③ gibberish ④ hoard

(2) The sudden cold spell served to ______ his already weakened condition.
① aggregate ② agitate ③ aggravate ④ agonize

(3) As you get older your bones become increasingly ______ .
① brittle ② plastic ③ facile ④ elastic

(4) Realization of ignorance is a step toward ______ .
① courage ② knowledge ③ darkness ④ sympathy

C. 주어진 단어의 바른 어형을 써 넣어 문장의 뜻을 완성하여라.

rich, exceed, enclosure, moderate, obey, cherish

(1) Post cards and greeting cards with only a signature, _____ in unsealed envelopes, may be sent for one dollar.

(2) Having a fine library doesn't prove that its owner has a mind ______ by books.

(3) Another type of restaurant offering _____ priced meals is the cafeteria.

(4) Purely physical fatigue, provided it is not ______, tends if anything to be a cause of happiness.

(5) There can be no question that without law, and men and nations ______ to law, what we know as civilization, cannot exist.

(6) After hard struggle, he finally fulfilled his long ______ desire.

Answer: A. (1) ①, ④, disconnect (2) ②, ⑤, impure (3) ③, ④, irrelevant
B. (1) ① (2) ③ (3) ① (4) ②
C. (1) enclosed (2) enriched (3) moderately (4) excessive (5) obedient (6) cherished

D. 밑줄 친 단어와 같은 뜻의 단어를 골라라.

(1) As it is, the situation in that part of the world is a real <u>menace</u> to world peace.

① hope ② threat ③ realization ④ rectification

(2) After the executive meeting, we came to a <u>tentative</u> conclusion from the discussion.

① temporary ② theoretical ③ inductive ④ descriptive

(3) Nancy has had a <u>perverted</u> sense of righteousness since her childhood.

① good ② idealistic ③ right ④ twisted

(4) He felt a lot of <u>malice</u> toward his mean and cunning roommate.

① evil spirit ② anger ③ graciousness ④ ill will

(5) Mrs. Smith <u>chastised</u> her daughter for arriving home late.

① conversed ② scolded ③ scoffed ④ complimented

E. 다음과 같이 끊어 읽을 때의 의미의 차이를 나타내어라.

(1) John treated her roughly / in the same way.

(2) John treated her / roughly in the same way.

F. 다음 각 문제에서 ⓐ, ⓑ, ⓒ 세 개의 문장의 빈 칸에 공통적으로 들어가는 1음절어를 써 넣으시오.

(1) ⓐ The ( ) rattled in and pulled up sharply.

ⓑ This will bring an unending ( ) of misfortunes.

ⓒ His father's desire was to ( ) him to be a doctor.

(2) ⓐ Hold the ( ), please.

ⓑ Mrs. Green thought the repairman's charge was out of ( ).

ⓒ Please drop a ( ) to me when you get to Chicago.

(3) ⓐ We call him Monty for ( ), his real name being Montgomery.

ⓑ Since we didn't want to run ( ) of food on the trip, we each carried extra rations.

ⓒ All our efforts, in ( ), resulted in nothing.

Answer: D. (1) ② (2) ① (3) ④ (4) ④ (5) ②
E. (1) John은 같은 방법으로 그 여자를 난폭하게 다루었다.
(2) John은 대개 같은 방법으로 그 여자를 다루었다.
F. (1) train (2) line (3) short

숙 어

(1) **play it by ear** (=do as a situation develops) 임기응변으로 대처하다
☞ I can't give you any advice, so you'll have to *play it by ear*.

(2) **play up to** (=flatter, seek favor with) 아부[아첨]하다
☞ He always *plays up to* his boss to get promoted.

(3) **poke fun at** (=make fun of, mock, tease) 놀리다, 조롱하다
☞ Most of his novels *poke fun at* the upper class.

(4) **pop into one's head** (=suddenly think of) 갑자기 생각나다[떠오르다]
☞ While I was taking a shower, a good idea *popped into my head*.

(5) **prevail on** (=persuade) 설득하다
☞ He *prevailed on* me to believe in his innocence.

(6) **pull[tear] down** (=demolish, destroy) (건물 등을) 부수다, 헐다
☞ They *pulled*[*tore*] *down* several old office buildings downtown.

(7) **pull in** (=drive in and stop, arrive) 차를 대다[멈추다], 도착하다
☞ We'd better *pull in* at the next gas station to refill the gas tank.

(8) **pull off** (=succeed in a difficult task) (어려운 일을) 잘해내다
☞ The task seemed impossible, but he managed to *pull* it *off*.

(9) **pull one's leg** (=fool, play a trick on) (남을) 놀리다, 속이다
☞ He was *pulling my leg* when he said he had won the lottery.

(10) **pull oneself together** (=become emotionally stable) 마음을 가라앉히다
☞ After crying for an hour, she began to *pull herself together*.

(11) **pull over** (=drive to the side of the road to stop) 차를 길가로 붙이다
☞ We *pulled over* to ask a passerby for directions.

(12) **pull through** (=survive a crisis or an illness) (난관, 병 등을) 이겨내다
☞ If we just stick together, we can *pull through* this hardship.

(13) **put in for** (=officially ask for) ~을 공식적으로 요구하다
☞ The labor union *put in for* a pay raise of 20%.

(14) **put the cart before the horse** (=reverse the logical order of things)
앞뒤가 뒤바뀌다, 본말(本末)을 전도하다
☞ When the salesman wanted money for goods he hadn't delivered, I told him he was *putting the cart before the horse*.

(15) **put through** (=connect by telephone ; cause to suffer)
(전화를) 연결하다 ; (시련 등을) 겪게 하다
☞ If he's not in, can you *put* me *through* to his secretary?
We *put* all new recruits *through* a very rigorous training.

(16) **read A into B** (=believe A to be meant though not expressed by B)
B를 A의 뜻으로 (확대) 해석하다[추측하다, 짐작하다]
☞ Please don't *read* any criticism *into* what I'm about to say to you.

(17) **recall to one's mind** (=recall to one's memory) 기억[회상, 상기]하다
☞ I can't *recall to my mind* where I have seen him before.

(18) **refer A to B** (=send A to B for help, information or advice)
(도움, 정보, 조언 등을 얻기 위해) A를 B에게 보내다
☞ They should have *referred* you *to* the personnel department.

(19) **reflect on** (=think deeply about ; affect the quality or reputation of)
~에 대해 숙고하다 ; ~의 자질[평판]에 영향을 미치다
☞ I need time to *reflect on* what you've offered.
These exam results *reflect* badly (*or* well) *on* your school.

Exercise

▶▶ 주어진 단어들을 포함한 글을 지어라. 필요하면 어형을 변화시켜라.

1. know / anything / play / ear
2. play / up / boss / raise
3. kids / poke / ridiculous
4. prevail / drive / airport
5. pull / shop / on / party
6. trick / impossible / pull
7. sure / mother / pull / illness
8. put / me / number
9. read / criticism / what / say
10. guard / refer / information

18. 전 치 사(Preposition)

기본 문법 설명

A. 전치사의 용법	(1) ⓐ She walked **to** the *couch* and sat down **with** *him*. ⓑ My brother is fond **of** *pointing* out my mistakes. ⓒ The plumber came out **from** *under the sink*. ⓓ He will not work **except** *when he is pleased*. (2) ⓐ Where do you come **from**? Who(m) are you speaking **of**? **By** whom was this computer program written? ⓑ There was nothing to sit **on**. (3) ⓐ We adopted a baby boy **instead of** a baby girl. ⓑ **On account of** bad weather, the picnic was canceled. ⓒ Seat belts must be worn, **in accordance with** the law. (4) ⓐ That is a site **of** archaeological **importance**. ⓑ It is **of no use** to speculate without more information. ⓒ Put the carrot peelings **in the garbage can**. ⓓ He walked **ten miles** without getting tired. ⓔ This is **the same size as that**.
B. 장소의 전치사	(1) He's just arrived **at** the station. The plane arrived **in** Chicago. (2) We have a beautiful Oriental rug **on** the floor. The sky **above** us was clear and blue. A formation of jet planes thundered **over** the city. (3) The ice gave way **beneath** [**under**] our feet. He lives in the apartment **below** me. Let's shelter **under** those trees. (4) Stay close **behind** me in the crowd. The lion ran **after** the zebra. (5) The town lies half-way **between** Rome and Florence. There were several private yachts **among** the fishing boats.

A. 전치사의 용법

(1) **전치사의 목적어**

전치사 뒤에 오는 말은 모두 **목적격**이 되어야 한다.

전치사의 목적어는 명사, 대명사 외에 명사 상당어구가 된다.

ⓐ **명 사** : couch는 to의 목적어
대명사 : him은 with의 목적어

ⓑ **동명사** : pointing은 of의 목적어

ⓒ **구** : under the sink는 from의 목적어

ⓓ **절** : when he is pleased는 except의 목적어
(그는 마음이 내켜야 일을 한다.)

☞ It is far **from** *here*.
It is far **from** *possible*.

(2) **전치사의 위치**

전치사는 그 목적어 앞에 오는 것이 정상적인 위치이지만 가끔 그 목적어에서 떨어지는 경우가 있다.

ⓐ 의문사가 전치사의 목적어가 될 때, 전치사는 보통 문미에 놓는다.

☞ 의문사를 문두에 둘 때는 주격을 쓰는 경향이 강하다. 특히 미구어(美口語)에서 그렇다.

☞ 수동태의 의문문에서는 By whom을 문두에 놓는 것이 보통이다.

ⓑ nothing to sit on
= nothing on which to sit

☞ 관계대명사를 생략하면 전치사는 뒤로 돌린다.
This is the house I live *in*.

(3) **합성전치사(전치사구)**

낱말이 둘 이상 모여 한 개의 전치사에 해당하는 구실을 한다.

ⓐ instead of ~ = ~ 대신에
(우리는 여자아기 대신에 남자 아기를 입양했다.)

ⓑ on account of ~ = ~ 때문에
(나쁜 날씨 때문에 소풍이 취소 되었다.)

ⓒ in accordance with ~ = ~에 따라
(안전벨트는 법에 따라 반드시 착용해야 한다.)

(4) **「전치사+목적어」의 역할**

ⓐ of importance = important
… site를 수식하는 형용사구
(그곳은 고고학상 중요한 장소이다.)

ⓑ of no use = useless
…보어가 되는 형용사구
(더 이상의 정보없이 추측하는 것은 아무 소용없다.)

ⓒ in the garbage can [부사구] …put 수식
(그 당근 껍질 벗겨 놓은 것을 쓰레기 통에 넣어라.)

ⓓ ten miles = **for** ten miles [부사구]

☞ **시간, 거리, 방법, 정도**를 나타낼 때는 전치사 없이 부사구의 역할을 한다. 이런 부사구를 **부사적 대격**이라 한다.
I awaited him (*for*) a long time.
He walked (*for*) two miles.
You can do it (*in*) that way.
Is your father (*at*) home?
I saw him (*on*) Tuesday.
(*At*) What time do you get up?

ⓔ the same size as that는 그 앞에 전치사 of가 생략되어 있다.

☞ **연령, 크기, 모양, 색채** 등을 나타낼 때는 of를 생략할 때가 많다. 이것을 **형용사적 대격**이라 한다.
We are (*of*) the same age.
These rooms are all (*of*) the same size.
The earth is (*of*) the shape of an orange.
The door is (*of*) dark brown.

B. 장소의 전치사

(1) **at** : 좁은 장소 **in** : 넓은 장소

(2) **on** : 표면에 접촉한 「위에」
above : 보다 높은 「위에, 위쪽에」
(= higher than)
over : 떨어져 「바로 위에」

(3) **beneath** : 접해서 「바로 밑에」
☞ beneath 대신 **under**도 쓴다.
below : 보다 낮은 「아래 (쪽)에」
(= lower than)
under : 떨어져 「바로 아래에」
(저 나무 아래로 피(신)합시다.)

(4) **behind** : 「~의 뒤에」
after : 「뒤를 좇아」

(5) **between** : 둘 「사이에」
among : 셋 이상 「사이에」
하지만, 현대영어에서는 서로 혼용된다.

	(6) We put the gift-wrapped gloves **in** the closet. I saw him go **into** the living room to watch TV. Don't put your head **out of** the window. (7) The trees are planted **along** the street. We went **across** the street when the light turned green. We could hear cries **through** the noise of the machines. (8) He flew **to** San Francisco by way of Hawaii. Our plane is headed **for** Paris. This beer is imported **from** Germany.
C. 때의 전치사	(1) **at** eight o'clock, **at** midnight, **at** noon, **at** the age of fifty **on** the tenth of August, **on** the morning of May 1 **in** March, **in** spring, **in** the 21st century, **in** the morning (2) You'll get the hang of how to do word-processing **in** a few weeks. The bill is due **within** 10 days. He let me know his resignation **after** a few days. (3) We stayed at the bar **till** 5:00 A.M. We must read the next chapter **by** tomorrow. (4) It's been raining on and off **since** last Sunday. Three weeks **from** today is summer vacation. (5) He's been holding a grudge against his ex-wife **for** years. **During** the night the rain changed to snow. He dozed off **through** the class.
D. 원인•이유의 전치사	(1) He was taken ill **from** overwork. (2) He lost his position **through** his idleness. (3) Many needy people died **of** malnutrition. Your illness comes **of** drinking too much. (4) We were very surprised **at** the result. He got angry **at** my words. (5) My professor and I talked **over** my research project. She's been agonizing **over** whether to accept his offer. (6) He has long been sick **with** asthma. (7) He is famous **for** his contribution to bioengineering.

(6) **in** :「~의 안에」(상태)
into :「~의 안으로」(운동)
out of :「(안)에서 밖으로」(운동)
(7) **along** : 긴 것을「따라서」
across :「횡단(교차)하여」(운동)
through :「관통하여, 꿰뚫고」
(8) **to** :「~으로」
for :「~을 목표로 하여」
from :「~으로부터」

C. 때의 전치사

(1) **at** : 몇 시 몇 분, 밤, 정오, 시각
on : 날짜, 정한 시간
in : 월, 계절, 해, 세기 등 비교적 긴 시간에 쓰일 뿐 아니라 아침, 저녁에도 쓰인다.
(2) **in** :「(현재부터) ~이 지나면」
(넌 몇주일 지나면 워드프로세싱하는 요령을 터득하게 될 것이다.)
within :「~이내에」
after :「(과거부터) ~후에」
(3) **till** :「~까지」(계속)
(우리는 오전 5시까지 그 술집에 있었다.)
by :「~까지는 (완료)」
(우리는 내일까지는 다음장을 읽어야 한다.)
(4) **since** :「~이래 죽」 (과거부터 현재까지의 계속)
from :「~부터」(어느 때의 기점)
☞ School begins *at* eight o'clock.
(begins *from* 하면 틀린다.)
School begins *on* the tenth.
School begins *in* March.
(5) **for** :「~동안」(기간)
(그는 여러해 동안 자기의 전 아내에 대해 원한을 품고 있다.)
during :「~중에」(상태의 계속)
through :「~동안 죽」(처음부터 끝까지)
(그는 수업내내 꾸벅꾸벅 졸았다.)
He was asleep *during* the lecture.
Dogs barked *through* the night.

D. 원인·이유의 전치사

(1) **from** : 직접적인 원인
(2) **through** : 간접적, 소극적인 원인
Through his help, I got over the difficulty.
(3) die **of** :「~으로 죽다」(사망 병의 원인)
come **of** :「~의 결과다」
(4) **at** :「~을 보고, 듣고」(기쁘다, 슬프다, 놀라다 등의 감정의 원인)
The whole nation rejoiced *at* the news of victory.
(5) **over** :「~에 대하여」(기뻐하다, 슬퍼하다, 웃다, 울다 등의 감정의 원인)
He is troubled *over* his health.
(6) **with** :「~으로」
(그는 오랫동안 천식을 앓고 있다.)
Are you shivering *with* cold?
I am tired *with* work.
(7) **for** :「~때문에」
(그는 생명공학에 대한 공헌으로[공헌 때문에] 유명하다.)
I could not speak *for* fear.
He was scolded *for* being late.
I admire him *for* his success.
☞ 뜻의 차이를 생각해 보시오.

I *met* a friend on the street.
He *met with* an accident.

He *consulted* his doctor about his health.
I *consulted with* him about the problem.

He *reached* London yesterday.
He *reached for* the dictionary.

A: Please look over my English composition.
B: With pleasure.

A: How do you like eggs?
B: Sunny-side up, please.

A: Can I help you with your baggage?
B: No, thank you. I can manage.

A: Do you work on Saturday?
B: No, that's my day off.

A: Let me pay the bill.
B: No, let's go halves.

E. 원료•재료 의 전치사	(1) This bridge is built **of** wood. (2) Beer is made **from** barley. (3) This picture is painted **in** oils.
F. 수단•도구 의 전치사	(1) Stir the mixture of the milk and chocolate **with** a spoon. (2) **Through** hard training the team has achieved remarkable success. (3) His parents arrived in Hong Kong **by** air.
G. 보어를 가지는 전치사	(1) Don't speak **with** your mouth *full.* (2) He was standing **with** his hands *in his* pockets. (3) **With** an eye *bandaged,* he could not write properly. It was a misty morning, **with** little wind *blowing.* (4) I will be lonely **with** you *away.* (5) He was sitting **with** his hat *on,* not **with** his hat *off.* (6) The doctor lay back in his long chair, **his head against a cushion**.

◈ Superstitions ◈

* If the palm of your left hand itches, you are going to receive a present.
(왼손 바닥이 간지러우면 선물을 받는다.)

* If you find a horse shoe, you will have good luck.
(말굽을 찾으면 행운이 온다.)

* If a black cat runs across a road in front of you, you will meet with an accident.
(검은 고양이가 네 앞을 가로지르면 너는 사고를 당한다.)

* If a task be begun on Friday, it will not be successfully done.
(일을 금요일에 시작하면 잘 이루어지지 않는다.)

* It is unlucky if a hare runs across a road in front of a traveler.
(산토끼가 여행자 앞을 가로지르면 재수없다.)

* To find a four-leafed clover, good luck; five-leaved, bad.
(네잎 클로버를 찾으면 행운, 다섯 잎 클로버는 불운.)

* If your nose itches, a friend is coming: if it itches on the left side, a boy is coming; if right, a girl.
(코가 간지러우면 친구가 오는데, 왼쪽이 간지러우면 남자 친구, 오른쪽이면 여자 친구.)

E. 원료·재료의 전치사

(1) **of** : 재료가 제품이 되어도 원형을 잃지 않을 때 쓰인다.

Springs are made *of* steel.

This bridge is built *of* stone.

(2) **from** : 재료가 제품이 되어 원형을 잃어버릴 때 쓰인다.

Wine is made *from* grapes.

What is nylon made *from*?

(3) **in** : write, speak, paint, carve 등의 동사와 같이 쓰여 재료를 나타낸다.

The old letter was written *in* ink.

Answer *in* English.

The woman was dressed *in* white.

F. 수단·도구의 전치사

(1) **with** : 사용되는 도구를 나타낸다.

He was killed *with* a sword.

The city was destroyed *with* fire.

<*cf.*> The city was destroyed *by fire*.
(동작의 주체)
= Fire destroyed the city.

(2) **through** : 수단·중개를 나타낸다.

He spoke *through* an interpreter.

I gained permission *through* a friend.

(3) **by** : 수단을 나타낸다.

Did you inform him *by* e-mail or *by* fax?

He took her *by* the hand.

G. 보어를 가지는 전치사

전치사 with는 having의 뜻으로 그 목적어를 설명하는 보어를 동반하여 부대상황을 나타내는 부사구를 만든다.

(1) (입에 가득 넣고 이야기하지 말아라.)
…보어로서 형용사 full이 쓰였다.

(2) (그는 호주머니에 두 손을 넣고 서 있었다.)
… 보어로서 구(in his pockets)가 쓰였다. his hands는 그 보어(in his pockets)에 대해 의미상 주어이다.

(3) (한 눈을 붕대로 감았기 때문에 그는 글을 잘 쓸 수 없었다.)
… 보어는 과거분사 bandaged이다
= As an eye was bandaged, he could not write properly.

(거의 바람이 불지 않는 안개 낀 아침이었다.)
… 현재분사(blowing)가 보어로 쓰였다.
with little wind blowing
= and little wind was blowing
… with를 빼면, little wind blowing은 독립분사구문이 된다.

(4) (네가 가 버리면 나는 외로울 것이다)
… 보어로 부사(away)가 쓰였다.
with you away = when you are away

(5) (그는 모자를 벗지 않고 쓴채 앉아 있었다.) … 보어로 부사(on,off)가 쓰였다.

(6) (머리를 쿠션에 기대고 그 의사는 긴 의자에 누워 있었다.) … with의 생략

◈ 名 言 ◈

As for me, all I know is that I know nothing.

— Socrates —

If you want people to think well of you, do not speak well of yourself.

— Pascal —

Strength does not come from physical capacity; it comes from an indomitable will.

— Mahatma Gandhi —

We must learn to live together as brothers or perish together as fools.

— Martin Luther King, Jr. —

문 법 · 작 문

A. Fill in each blank with a suitable word:

(1) I went to Miami ______ the vacation and stayed there ______ a week.
(2) Urban problems often stretch ______ city limits ______ the suburbs.
(3) Patients are angry ______ the increase ______ the cost of medicines.
(4) I got stuck ______ a traffic jam for half an hour.
(5) ______ our regret, our economic revolution, ______ itself, bore no fruit.
(6) The company decided to relocate ______ the suburbs because the rent was much cheaper.
(7) Who did you order it ______?
(8) John went fishing ______ a river.
(9) She has provided us ______ food for weeks ______ end.
(10) His explanation is very much ______ the point.
(11) I'd love to congratulate you ______ your remarriage.
(12) Korea is ______ the east of Asia, and China is ______ the west of Korea.
(13) He was accused ______ robbery.
(14) We sang Old Black Joe ______ her piano.
(15) The bullet hit me ______ the arm.
(16) Make yourself ______ home and help yourself ______ the cake.

B. Fill in each blank with a suitable word:

(1) If a meeting is called ______, it is canceled.
(2) To get ______ something is to overcome it.
(3) To look ______ something is to examine it.
(4) If I put ______ my cigarette, I extinguish it.
(5) If they are sure to stand ______ us, they will support us.
(6) If they go well ______ each other, they match well.
(7) If something stands ______ reason, it is clear and logical.
(8) To let go ______ something is to release it.
(9) If a bomb goes ______, it explodes.
(10) If I hand ______ a report, I submit it.
(11) To take something ______ granted is to accept it without investigation.

Answer: A. (1) during, for (2) beyond, into (3) at, in (4) in (5) To, in (6) to (7) from (8) at (9) with, on (10) to (11) on (12) in, to (13) of (14) to (15) in (16) at, to B. (1) off (2) over (3) over (4) out (5) by (6) with (7) to (8) of (9) off (10) in (11) for

(12) If I tell you something once and ______ all, I tell it to you in a final and definite manner.
(13) If I get along ______ someone, I live or work harmoniously with him.
(14) If someone breaks ______ your house, he enters by force.
(15) To come ______ something is to obtain it.
(16) To make up ______ something is to atone for it.
(17) To look ______ to someone is to respect him.
(18) To look ______ on someone is to consider him inferior to yourself.
(19) If someone drops ______ on me, he visits me casually.
(20) To stand ______ is to be prominent or outstanding.
(21) To let ______ something is to reveal it.
(22) To do away ______ something is to abolish it.
(23) If someone is taken ______ , he is deceived.
(24) To beat ______ the bush is to be indirect in approaching something.
(25) If the rain lets ______, it lessens.
(26) To correspond ______ something is to be in agreement with it.
(27) If two men make ______ after a quarrel, they become reconciled.
(28) If I carried ______ something, I executed it.
(29) ______ the time being means for the present.
(30) If something is ______ of order, it is not in working condition.
(31) If you leave ______ something, you omit it.
(32) If someone is ______ my way, he is blocking my way.
(33) If I cannot put up ______ something, I cannot stand it.
(34) To cheer someone ______ is to make him happier.

C. 공란에 적당한 말을 써라.
(1) Thoughts are expressed by ______ of words.
(2) They wouldn't let their cat run around outside ______ fear that it would get run over by a car.
(3) The children were quarreling as ______ which was the stronger.
(4) Thanks ______ his timely rescue, the child escaped death.
(5) A man will succeed ______ proportion to his efforts.

Answer: B. (12) for (13) with (14) into (15) by (16) for (17) up (18) down (19) in (20) out (21) on (22) with (23) in (24) around[about] (25) up (26) to[with] (27) up (28) out (29) For (30) out (31) out (32) in (33) with (34) up
C. (1) means (2) for (3) to (4) to (5) in

(6) I made the opening address on ______ of my class.
(7) He came late due ______ an accident.
(8) I will keep silence in regard ______ your secret.
(9) As ______ the style his novels leave nothing to be desired.
(10) I dare not enter for fear ______ the dog.
(11) Society exists for the sake ______ the individual.
(12) I must say a few words ______ connection with this subject.
(13) I cannot start in consequence ______ his sudden illness.
(14) We gave him 50 dollars in consideration ______ his labors.
(15) ______ the course of his remarks, he made this statement.
(16) The decision is in favor ______ the defendant.
(17) A farewell party was held in honor ______ Mr. Jones.
(18) Mr. Jones is sick and Mr. Brown teaches in his ______ today.
(19) The judge laughed ______ spite of himself.
(20) Close the shop in the event ______ my absence.
(21) They went forward ______ the face of many obstacles.
(22) She was educated ______ a view to becoming a lawyer.
(23) The secret was ______ the brink of discovery.
(24) He wishes to resign ______ the grounds of ill health.
(25) He muttered something ______ way of apology.
(26) The ship was drifting ______ the mercy of the waves.
(27) He saved the child ______ the risk of his own life.
(28) He did everything for the good ______ others.

D. 공란을 적당한 전치사로 채워라.

(1) She is always anxious ______ her son's health.
We are all anxious ______ peace.
(2) She waited ______ him for two hours in the park.
The waitress waited ______ him in the restaurant.
(3) She succeeded ______ getting a place at the art school.
He succeeded ______ the throne of the kingdom.

Answer: C. (6) behalf (7) to (8) to (9) for (10) of (11) of (12) in (13) of (14) of (15) In (16) of (17) of (18) place (19) in (20) of (21) in (22) with (23) on (24) on (25) by (26) at (27) at (28) of
D. (1) about, for (2) for, on (3) in, to

(4) His diligence resulted _____ his success.
His success resulted _____ his diligence.
(5) I am tired _____ doing the same thing over and over again.
I am tired _____ working all day.
(6) He spends most of his time _____ reading.
He spends most of his money _____ books.
(7) He caught me _____ the hand.
He looked me _____ the face.
He patted me _____ the shoulder.
(8) He went to search _____ the missing child.
He went in search _____ the missing child.
(9) A man is known _____ the company he keeps.
He is known _____ his athletic ability.
He is known _____ everybody in this town.
(10) He is possessed _____ a large fortune.
He is possessed _____ the devil.
(11) Life is compared _____ a voyage.
Compare your translation _____ the original.
(12) Happiness consists _____ contentment.
Water consists _____ oxygen and hydrogen.
(13) He is good _____ tennis.
What is this medicine good _____?
(14) He put up _____ the motel on the way.
I cannot put up _____ his insolence any longer.
(15) I inquired _____ the affair immediately.
I inquired _____ a sick friend.
I inquired _____ him if he would come.
I inquired _____ the book at the shop.
(16) You think me lazy, but _____ the contrary I am very busy.
He holds an opinion, contrary _____ mine.
(17) Please don't be concerned _____ me.
He is said to have been concerned _____ the crime.

Answer: D. (4) in, from (5) of, from[with] (6) in, on (7) by, in, on (8) for, of (9) by, for, to (10) of, with (11) to, with (12) in, of (13) at, for (14) at, with (15) into, after, of, for (16) on, to (17) about, in [with]

E. 공란을 메워라.

(1) You'll have to answer ______ your violent behavior in court
(2) Mr. Kim asked ______ some money yesterday.
(3) My digital watch keeps good time ______ the minute.
(4) Please inform us ______ any changes in your circumstances.
(5) This rule can be applied ______ every case.
(6) With his accent and flamboyant gesture I took him ______ an Italian.
(7) Ten men voted for the motion and two ______ it.
(8) She was dressed ______ the western fashion.
(9) The continuous traffic noise got ______ my nerves.
(10) Can you tell wheat ______ barley?
(11) He ascribed his success ______ good luck.
(12) You are liable ______ the damage.
(13) The whole of crime is ______ the gradual decrease, but the juvenile delinquency is rather ______ the increase.
(14) Perhaps that's why he took ______ opium.
(15) Such a difficult task was quite ______ me.
(16) Idleness leads ______ poverty.
(17) This story is ______ far the most interesting of all.
(18) It started raining so they made ______ the nearest shelter.
(19) As soon as he saw me, he sprang ______ his feet.
(20) I presented her ______ a Rolex watch for our wedding anniversary.
(21) He lay ______ his back looking up at the blue sky.
(22) The room smells ______ paint.
(23) Isn't it warm ______ the season right now?
(24) The thief robbed me ______ all my money.
(25) You can have it ______ nothing.
(26) This picture is not ______ my taste.
(27) The same is true ______ the nation.
(28) Hunger makes a thief ______ any man.
(29) I wouldn't do such a thing ______ the world.
(30) He banged his head ______ the low ceiling when he stood up.

Answer: E. (1) for (2) for (3) to (4) of (5) to (6) for (7) against (8) after (9) on (10) from (11) to (12) for (13) on, on (14) to (15) above[beyond] (16) to (17) by (18) for (19) to (20) with (21) on (22) of (23) for (24) of (25) for (26) to (27) of (28) of (29) for (30) on

(31) I bought this book ______ ten dollars.
(32) He took ______ his heels at the sight of a policeman.
(33) Specimen copies of these textbooks may be obtained ______ application to the publisher.
(34) He felt no pride ______ his vast knowledge.
(35) His face seems familiar ______ me.
(36) The cardinal urged people not to resort ______ violence.
(37) The fields are cleared ______ the insects.
(38) This hot summer reminds me ______ my years in Kenya as a nurse.
(39) A shot of morphine relieved me ______ my acute pain.
(40) This tool is good ______ nothing.
(41) You must check ______ when you arrive at a hotel.
(42) ______ a certain point of view, you are right.
(43) The athlete prides himself ______ winning all the races he entered.
(44) You must refrain ______ judging others hastily.
(45) Do you know what NASDAQ stands ______?
(46) The pill will work ______ him.
(47) They avenged themselves ______ their enemy by killing the hostages.
(48) You may leave the room, but must stay ______ call.
(49) I like him ______ that he is honest and candid.
(50) I knocked ______ the door several times.
(51) We must conform ______ all the rules of the game.
(52) Try to look ______ the bright side of things.
(53) It is ______ to you to decide where to go on vacation.
(54) The study which he specializes ______ is economics.
(55) He didn't know ______ certain how the accident had happened.
(56) She was leaning ______ the wall with her arms crossed.
(57) Temperatures tomorrow will be ______ the mid twenties.
(58) Do that exercise ______ until it is perfect.
(59) Knowledge without common sense counts ______ little.
(60) He has applied to the bank ______ a loan.

Answer: E. (31) for (32) to (33) (up)on (34) in (35) to (36) to (37) of (38) of (39) of (40) for (41) in (42) From (43) on (44) from (45) for (46) on (47) on (48) within (49) in (50) at (51) to (52) on (53) up (54) in (55) for (56) against (57) in (58) over (59) for (60) for

F. Fill in each blank with a suitable word.

The schoolhouse is a low structure made (1) logs, having only one room. It stands (2) a rather lonely but pleasant situation, just (3) the foot of a gently rising green hill, with a stream running close (4). From there the sound of students' voices could be heard while learning their lessons, interrupted now and then (5) the voice of the master, (6) a tone of threat and command. But he is not one (7) those cruel masters who take pleasure (8) punishing their students. He carefully distinguishes (9) right and wrong. He regards discipline (10) doing his duty, and he never punishes a student (11) telling him that "he would remember it and someday thank him (12) it."

G. Translate the following into English:

(1) 나는 8시까지 그를 기다렸으나, 그는 결국 오지 않았다.

(2) 오늘 아침 학교 가는 길에, 나는 초등학교 시절의 선생님을 한 분 만났다.

(3) 요즈음은 많은 여성들이 첫 아이를 가지는 것이 20대 후반이나 30대 초반이다.

(4) 면전에서 아첨하는 사람은 뒤에서 욕하기 쉽다.

(5) 그의 성공은 전적으로 내조의 덕이다.

(6) 양심을 희생하여 돈과 권력을 얻으면, 그것은 오히려 인생의 커다란 실패다.

(7) 그 사건을 기념하여 기념탑을 세웠다.

(8) 사람은 그의 인내에 비례하여 성공한다.

(9) 붉은 신호등이 켜졌는데도 길을 횡단해서는 안 된다.

(10) 다른 학생들은 시간을 허송하는데, 이 학생은 꾸준히 자기 학업을 계속한다.

(11) 친구가 친절하게 너의 과오를 깨우쳐 주면, 그가 하는 말을 고맙게 받아들여라.

'Which country would you like to visit, and why?'
라는 제목으로 70어 내외의 글을 지어라.

● 단 문 독 해 ●

He was standing **with** a hat on.
He lay **face down**.
She **reasoned** the boy **out of** doing it.

1. The men whom I have seen succeed best in life have always been cheerful and hopeful men, who went about their business **with** a smile on their faces, and took the changes and chances of this mortal life like men, facing success and failure alike as it came.

notes :
*go about ~ = 부지런히 ~하다
*changes and chances = 인생변천(浮沈;부침)
*mortal 인간의; 죽어야할 운명의
*this mortal life = 인생

▶▶윗글의 밑줄친 부분을 아래와 같이 바꿔 쓸 때, 빈칸에 적절한 말을 쓰시오.
confronted the (u　　) and (d　　) of life bravely

▶▶영작하시오.
인생에는 좋은 일도 궂은 일도 있다. 그것이 인생이다.

2. He pulled the blanket over his shoulders and then over his back and legs and he slept **face down** on the newspapers **with** his arms **out** straight and the palms of his hands **up**.

notes :
*face down on the newspapers = 신문지 위에 엎드려
*palm 손바닥

▶▶윗글의 밑줄친 부분을 다음과 같이 바꿀 때, 빈칸에 알맞은 어구를 쓰시오.
he slept lying on his (s　　)

▶▶영작하시오.
창문을 열어 놓고 자지 말아라.

3. He had not been a week at school when he grew homesick. Both his teacher and his friends did all they could, but his grief was too deep to be **reasoned away**.

notes :
*grow homesick = 향수병이 나다
*reason ~ away = 타일러 ~을 없애다

▶▶윗글의 내용으로 보아 다음 빈칸에 들어갈 수 없는 것은?
According to the above paragraph, it was impossible to (　　) him by words.
① console　② comfort　③ solace
④ soothe　⑤ sympathize

▶▶영작하시오.
나는 잠을 자 여독을 풀었다.

They **deprived** him **of** his property.

4. What added, no doubt, to my hatred of the beast was the discovering, on the morning after I brought it home, that it had **been deprived of** one of its eyes. This circumstance, however, only endeared it to my wife.

notes :
*deprive A of B = A로부터 B를 빼앗다
*endear A to B = cause A to be loved by B = A로 하여금 B의 사랑을 받도록 하다

▶▶Which of the following does the underlined phrase imply?
① The fact that I brought the beast home
② The fact that I hated the beast very much
③ The fact that the beast had only one eye
④ The fact that my wife liked the beast very much
⑤ The fact that the beast liked my wife very much

▶▶영작하시오.
그 여자는 친절한 마음씨 때문에 모두의 사랑을 받는다.

5. A good way of **ridding** yourself **of** certain kinds of dogmatism is to become aware of opinions held in circles different from your own. If you cannot travel, seek out people with whom you disagree, and read a newspaper belonging to a party that is not yours.

notes :
*rid A of B = A에게서 B를 제거하다
*dogmatism 독단주의
*travel 교제가 있다, 사귀고 있다
*seek out = 찾아내다
*party 단체, 정파

▶▶In a democracy we should not be so (　　) as to reject any beliefs and ideas that are (　　) from ours.
[free-minded, dogmatic, friendly, opposite, different]

▶▶영작하시오.
그는 자기 의견에 동조하지 않는 사람은 누구든지 미워한다.

전 치 사 구

6. The custom of making New Year resolutions may not be popular today. But in many countries people used to make New Year pledges **for the purpose of** having a better year or conquering their bad habits.

notes :
*resolution 결심, 결의
*pledge 맹세, 서약

▶▶윗글의 내용에 맞도록 할 때, 다음 빈칸에 알맞지 않은 것은?
Some people made New Year resolutions to (　　) their bad habits.
① quit ② give up ③ forsake ④ maintain ⑤ abandon

▶▶영작하시오.
그는 사옥을 짓기 위해 그 땅을 샀다.

7. **In spite of** the great advance of European culture, there is no reason to think that the African Negro or the Eskimo is less intelligent than dwellers in more temperate lands. The Eskimo remains uncivilized because he lacks the materials for making tools, without which civilized life is impossible.

notes :
*dweller 거주인 (= inhabitant)
*temperate(기후·온도 따위가) 온화한

▶▶The uncivilized life of the Eskimo is the result of a lack of (　　), not of the lower level of his (　　).
[race, resources, rain, intelligence, interest, igloos]

▶▶영작하시오.
그가 기분 나빠할 이유가 얼마든지 있다.

8. The best way to read fiction is to mix one's reading, neither to favor the present **at the expense of** the past nor to favor the past **at the expense of** the present. And don't think that if this policy is pursued, contemporary works will appear thin and trivial beside the great works of the past. It isn't necessarily so at all.

notes :
*at the expense of ~ = ~을 희생하여, ~의 대가로
*contemporary 현대의

▶▶윗글의 내용에 맞는 것을 하나 고르시오.
① The great works of the past dwarf contemporary works.
② We should read past novels because they give us valuable lessons.
③ We should read present novels because they represent the age we live in.
④ As we live in the present age, contemporary novels look too ordinary to us.
⑤ The best way is to read contemporary works as well as the great works of the past.

▶▶영작하시오.
그 여우는 한쪽 다리를 잃고 덫에서 빠져나왔다.

To my joy, he passed the entrance examination.

9. At the age of sixteen he managed to be allowed to fight a bull on horseback, and **to the admiration** of the public, killed it with one thrust of his lance.

notes :
*thrust 쿡 찌름, 습격
*lance 창

▶▶What do you suppose is the above-mentioned man's occupation?

▶▶영작하시오.
내가 실망하게도 그는 시험에 떨어졌다.

● 장 문 독 해 ●

Warming-up

It does not necessarily **follow that** all criminals come from a deprived home.

His new film **deals with** the relationship between a boy and an alien.

A clerk told me it was brand-new and I was stupid **enough to** believe him.

They discussed the **distinction between** Chinese history **and** Japanese history.

1 I cannot conceive education as a training in so many separate subjects. Education is integral: it is the encouragement of the growth of the whole man, the complete man. It follows that it is not entirely, nor even mainly, an affair of book learning, for that is only the education of one part of our nature — that part of the mind which deals with concepts and abstractions. In the child, who is not yet mature enough to think by these shortcut methods, it should be largely an education of the senses — the sense of sight, touch and hearing: in one word, the education of the sensibility. From this point of view there is no valid distinction between art and science: there is only the whole man with his diverse interests and faculties, and the aim of education should be to develop all these in harmony and completeness.

Herbert E. Read: *The Politics of the Unpolitical*

Notes

conceive 생각하다 / integral 통합적인 / the whole man 전인(全人) / It follows that ~ ~라는 결론이 되다 / entirely 전적으로 / abstractions 추상적인 내용들 / mature 성숙한(↔ immature 미숙한) / largely 주로 / sensibility 감각(=sense) / valid 뚜렷한 / distinction 구별 / diverse 다양한(=varied) / faculty 능력 / develop 발전시키다 / in harmony 조화롭게 / in completeness 완전하게

Question

1. 본문의 밑줄친 these shortcut methods가 가리키는 내용을 우리말로 쓰시오.

2. 글쓴이는 왜 어린이들의 교육에는 예술과 과학의 뚜렷한 구별이 없다고 했는지 우리말로 간단히 쓰시오.

3. According to the passage, which of the following is **not** correct?
   ① The aim of education is to encourage the growth of the whole man.
   ② The author insists that an education only through books is not enough for the growth of the complete man.
   ③ Because of their immaturity, children need the education of sensibility rather than that of book learning.
   ④ Educators should encourage kids to develop their various abilities harmoniously and completely.
   ⑤ Book learning has been considered to be the shortest and most effective way to our children's education.

4. Which of the following is most appropriate for the main topic of the passage?
   ① The training of sensibility is more urgent and important than any other types of education.
   ② Many adverse effects have been caused by a book-centered education.
   ③ Education should aim to help our children grow into well-balanced people through harmonious learning.
   ④ There is no basic difference between art and science.
   ⑤ Harmonious society is necessary for the success of our education.

Production

(1) 단지 그녀가 부자라고 해서, 반드시 그녀가 행복하다는 결론이 되는 것은 아니다.
(2) 컴퓨터 소프트웨어 사용법은 4장에 좀더 상세히 다루어져 있다.
(3) 일란성 쌍둥이의 겉모습에는 거의 차이점이 없다.

● 장 문 독 해 ●

Warming-up

This book is **intended for** the general reader rather than the student.

If our company **is to** survive in the world market, we must invest more money into our business.

The number of youngsters **involved** in crime was frightening.

The president of our firm went to America **for the purpose of** making business contracts.

2 It might be useful for men at the summit to consider why a summit meeting should be necessary in the first place. If the machinery of the United Nations had been able to do the job intended for it, there would be no need for top-level meetings. If the U.N. is to survive, what is necessary is not so much the willingness of the individual nations to refer matters to the U.N. but the absolute authority of the U.N. that can act whether the nations like it or not. At present, the U.N. acts when it has the consent of the parties involved. Thus, it becomes an arbitration agency instead of a law-making and law-enforcing agency. Any policeman who is required to obtain the consent of a law-breaker before he, the policeman, can do his job is not a policeman but a supplicant. The men who lead the nations have the obligation to agree to a revision conference of the U.N. for the purpose of converting it from <u>an arena of unlimited options</u> to an organization of binding obligations.

Norman Cousins: *In Place of Folly*

Notes

summit (국가의) 수뇌 / a summit meeting 정상회담 / machinery 기관, 기구 / not so much A but B = A라기 보다는 B / absolute 절대적인 / consent 동의(하다) / involved 관계있는 / arbitration agency 중재 기관 / law-enforcing agency 법집행 기관 / supplicant 탄원자(= suppliant) / obligation 의무, 책무 / revision 개편 / convert 바꾸다 / arena 장소; 경기장 / organization 기구 / binding obligation 구속력

Question

1. 이 글의 저자가 U.N.이 갖추었으면 하는 기능 두 가지를 찾아 우리말로 쓰시오.

2. According to the passage, what does the author compare the feeble U.N. to?

3. Which does the underlined phrase, <u>an arena of unlimited options</u>, ultimately imply?
   ① The U.N. where opposite views are freely expressed
   ② The U.N. where every nation can go its own way
   ③ The U.N. having the power to intervene in the international disputes
   ④ The U.N. acting as an international government
   ⑤ The U.N. which member nations willingly bring troublesome problems to

4. Which of the following is the author's main argument?
   ① Basically the summit meeting should have more power to settle conflicts among nations.
   ② Arbitration should be the main function of the U.N.
   ③ The authorities in every member nation should cooperate to maintain world peace.
   ④ The U.N. should be reorganized to become a much more powerful organization.
   ⑤ The authority of the Security Council should be weakened.

Production

(1) 이 세금은 관광산업의 발전을 위한 것이다.
(2) 만약 그녀를 다시 보고 싶다면, 그녀에게 진실되게 사과해야 한다.
(3) 그 범인은 살인사건에 관련된 또 다른 용의자의 이름을 대는 것을 거부했다.
(4) 시장은 대중 교통 근무자들의 파업에 대비하기 위한 목적으로 비상위원회를 소집할 것이다.

실 력 체 크 Ⅰ

1 다음 글을 읽고 아래 물음에 답하여라.

Twenty-one years ago we climbed Mont Blanc together to watch the sunset from the summit. A year ago we observed ⓐthe same phenomenon from the foot of the mountain. The intervening years have probably made little difference in the sunset. If ⓑ they have made some difference in our powers of reaching the best point of view, they have, I hope, diminished neither our admiration of such spectacles, nor our pleasure in each other's companionship. If I have retained my love of the Alps, it has been in no small degree owing to you. Many walks in your company, some of ⓒ which are described in this book, have confirmed both our friendship and our common worship of the mountains. I wish, therefore, to connect your name with this new edition of my old attempt to set forth the delights of Alpine rambling.

notes:
phenómenon 현상 / foot(산의) 기슭 / make little difference 차이가 거의 없다 / diminish 줄이다 / describe 서술하다 ; *description* / set forth 설명하다 / the delights of Alpine rambling = 알프스 산을 여기저기 다녀보는 즐거움

(1) 밑줄 친 ⓐ가 의미하는 바를 영어로 써라.

(2) 밑줄 친 ⓑ와 같은 일이 생긴 이유는? 그리고, the best point of view의 구체적인 뜻을 영어로 써라.

(3) ⓒ which의 선행사는 무엇인가?

(4) 이 글의 필자는 글 속의 you에게 이 책을 바치고 있는데, 그 사실을 나타내는 문장을 찾아라.

2 다음 글을 읽고 최종 답을 적어라.

Do you know the small gun gangsters use in the movies? Yes, the word for it begins with a P and ends in an L. It is composed of six letters in all. Write down this word in capital letters. Now, replace the second letter with an A and substitute an R for the S. Of course you still have six letters there, but they don't seem to form any word familiar to us. So let's reverse the order of the two letters in the center. Well, here we have a new word, don't we? But, since the gangsters wouldn't like this word very much, let's go on changing it. I think we had better do without the T. But we must put something in its place. Oh, yes, the fifth letter of the alphabet will do, for it is one of the most useful letters. And where shall we put it? Why don't we just add it at the very end? There, we have another word now. And this is our final answer.

notes:
in capital letters = 대문자로 / replace A with B = substitute B for A / do without = dispense with (~없이 지내다) / at the very end=바로 맨끝에

3 [B]는 [A]를 요약한 글이다. (a)~(e)에 들어갈 적당한 것을 ①~⑩에서 골라라.

[A] Many people are worried about what television has done to the generation of children who have grown up watching it. For one thing, recent studies tend to show that TV stifles creative imagination. Some teachers feel that television has taken away the child's ability to form mental pictures in his own mind, resulting in children who cannot understand a simple story without visual illustrations. Secondly, too much TV too early tends to cause children to withdraw from real-life experiences. Thus, they grow up to be passive spectators who can respond to action, but not initiate it. The third area for concern is the serious complaint frequently made by elementary school teachers that children exhibit a low tolerance for the frustrations of learning. Because they have been conditioned to see all problems resolved in 30 or 60 minutes on TV, they are quickly discouraged by any activity that promises less than instant gratification. But perhaps the most serious result is the impact of television violence on children, who have come to regard it as an everyday thing. Not only does this increase their tolerance of violent behavior in others, but most authorities now concede that under certain conditions, some children will imitate anti-social acts that they witness on television.

notes :
For one thing 우선 첫째로 / stifle 억누르다 / visual 시각적인 / illustration 실례, 보기 / initiate 스스로 시작하다, 창시하다 / tolerance 인내심 / frustration 좌절, 욕구불만 / condition 길들이다 / gratification 만족 / impact 영향 / authorities 관계당국 / concede 인정하다 / imitate 모방하다 / witness 목격하다 / consequence 결과

[B] Television causes children to have the following (a): children lose (b) because they watch so much TV; the (c) is a consequence of too much TV; children develop (d) the frustrations of learning because they expect every problem to be solved in a short time; and children have come to regard (e) as an everyday thing because they see it on TV.

① a tolerance for
② an impatience towards
③ bad effects
④ creative ability
⑤ good effects
⑥ passive spectators
⑦ passivity of children
⑧ tolerance of children
⑨ visual illustrations
⑩ violence

실력체크 II

A. 다음 공란을 적당한 단어로 메워라.

(1) I told the taxi driver to pull ______, and I got out.
(2) The song caught ______ with the public.
(3) I'm not really cut out ______ this kind of work.
(4) You almost caused a crash by cutting ______ like that!
(5) He really goes ______ for traveling and sightseeing.
(6) He couldn't bring himself ______ tell her the news.
(7) I gave you credit ______ being more polite.
(8) A little kindness will go a long ______ with some people.
(9) The ambulance arrived at the accident scene ______ no time.
(10) I left the firm, because I wanted to be ______ my own.
(11) All my kindness was lost ______ that man.
(12) Another trip abroad this year is out of the ______ .
(13) The news of his assassination came as a shock to ______ and all.
(14) ______ second thoughts she decided to join the party.
(15) My grandmother passed ______ in her sleep at the age of eighty-four.
(16) It's the weekend, so I can sleep ______ my heart's content.
(17) We must keep some of these in store ______ next year.
(18) I have never had the pleasure of meeting him ______ person.
(19) This new law is, ______ effect, a rise in income taxes.

B. 다음 각 항의 어군을 적당한 순서로 배열하여 거기에 한 낱말만 더 추가하면 우리말과 같은 뜻이 된다. 그 추가할 말을 적어라.

(1) 나는 주객전도(主客顚倒)를 하지 않을 정도의 분별력은 있다.
[know, to, than, for, I, the, end, mistake, the, means]
(2) 말할 필요도 없이 학생에게는 예습이 필요하다.
[students, preparatory, is, say, needless, required, work, of]
(3) 그는 아무리 보아도 장사에 성공할 사람 같아 보이지 않았다.
[business, be, expected, he, I, in, successful, person, the, to, was]
(4) 아버지가 되어야 비로소 어버이의 사랑을 안다.
[your, father, appreciate, a, love, become, little, you, parents', you'll]

Answer: A. (1) up (2) on (3) for (4) in (5) in (6) to (7) for (8) way (9) in (10) on (11) on (12) question (13) one (14) On (15) away[on] (16) to (17) for (18) in (19) in
B. (1) better(I know **better** than to mistake the means for the end.) (2) to(Needless **to** say, preparatory work is required of students.) (3) last(I expected he was the **last** person to be successful in business.) (4) until(You'll little appreciate your parents' love **until** you become a father.)

C. 다음 영문의 (1)~(6)에 들어갈 가장 적당한 것을, 아래에서 고르시오.
(단 같은 단어를 2번 사용해서는 안된다.)

Transplanted (1) the American world, the political and legal institutions that had been brought from England gradually diverged (2) those of the mother country, but the Americans retained, (3) some modifications, the essential political habits and attitudes of their English ancestors. They became a more gregarious people than the English, but they were equally insistent (4) their right (5) individual freedom and independence, and they were even more inclined towards pragmatic and empirical ways (6) thinking.

① as	② of	③ from	④ by	⑤ into	⑥ with
⑦ on	⑧ to	⑨ without	⑩ about	⑪ at	⑫ over

D. 문장 끝의 지시에 따라 다음 문장들을 다시 써라.

(1) Her traditional Korean dress made her look fantastic. (She looked로 시작)

(2) Why not try to expand our European market if we are to increase our sales? (How로 시작)

(3) This laptop computer is indispensable to me. (I cannot로 시작)

(4) The union assured the new owner that their members would be loyal to the company. (loyal의 명사형을 이용해 단문으로)

(5) The baby is awake thanks to your shouting. (Your shouting을 주어로)

(6) The death of his father in the car crash would have brought a great misfortune to his family. (복문으로)

(7) It's useless trying to convince her of not needing to lose any weight. (복문으로)

(8) They were charged by the police because they stole bikes in a house in the vicinity. (police를 주어로한 단문으로)

(9) The word itself is so rare that it is almost obsolete. (단문으로)

(10) The tornado has lifted my house and moved it down miles away. (I 로 시작)

Answer: C. (1) ⑤ (2) ③ (3) ⑥ (4) ⑦ (5) ⑧ (6) ② D. (1) She looked fantastic in her ~ dress. (2) How about trying to expand our European market if ~ sales? (3) I cannot do without this laptop computer. (4) The union assured the new owner of their members' loyalty to the company. (5) Your shouting has awoken[woken (up)] the baby. (6) If his father had died in the car crash, it would have brought ~ family. (7) It is useless trying to convince her that she doesn't need to ~ weight. (8) The police charged them with stealing bikes ~ vicinity. (9) The word itself is so rare as to be almost obsolete. (10) I have had my house lifted and moved down miles away by the tornado.

어 휘 · 발 음

A. 다음 각 항에 풀이한 어구의 뜻을 한 단어로 나타내어라.

(1) The story of a person's life written by others

(2) An actor who amuses an audience with funny talk or actions

(3) A building in which a collection of objects illustrating science, ancient life, art, or other objects is kept

(4) A paper or a book giving a person official permission to travel abroad under the protection of his own government

(5) A drug or other substance very dangerous to life and health

(6) Strong desire for fame or honor, or seeking after a high position or great power in life

B. Choose a proper word:

(1) He was in an auto accident but was not (injured, wounded).

(2) The calm sea (glinted, shimmered) in the moonlight.

(3) I was (sprinkled, spattered) with mud by passing cars.

(4) The man on his bicycle (wobbled, staggered) along the street.

(5) A light from a distant house (flickered, glimmered) through the mist.

(6) Embarrassment caused the blood to (flush, flash) her cheeks.

(7) He is a successful lawyer with hundreds of (customers, clients).

C. 다음 보기에서 알맞은 것을 찾아 각 (　)에 쓰고 무엇의 약어인지 [　　]에 쓰시오.

> CPA, NASA, AIDS, CEO, ATM

(1) (　　)s are found in business districts and shopping malls of all American cities. [　　　　　　]

(2) The new (　　) will preside at the meeting of the board of directors. [　　　　　　]

(3) My (　　) did my federal income tax return. [　　　　　　]

(4) The first case of (　　) was found in the early 1980s. [　　　　　　]

(5) (　　) has announced that the launch of the new communication satellite will proceed next month. [　　　　　　]

Answer: A. (1) biography (2) comedian (3) museum (4) passport (5) poison (6) ambition
B. (1) injured (2) shimmered (3) spattered (4) wobbled (5) glimmered (6) flush (7) clients　C. (1) ATM(Automated Teller Machine) (2) CEO(Chief Executive Officer) (3) CPA(Certified Public Accountant) (4) AIDS(Acquired Immune Deficiency Syndrome) (5) NASA(National Aeronautics and Space Administration)

D. 다음 각 문장의 빈칸에 들어갈 가장 적당한 말을 골라 어형을 변화시키시오.

(1) Last night a sharp earthquake (   ) china and glass crashing to the floor.

[drop, fall, fly, run, send]

(2) Instead of making an effort to resist the temptation he tried to find excuses for (   ) to it.

[agree, comply, obey, subdue, yield]

(3) I discussed the matter with him many times and finally (   ) him round to my point of view.

[allow, bring, catch, lull, succeed]

(4) We were about a quarter of a mile away from the top of the mountain pass when we (   ) first snow.

[grow, long, stand, strike, travel]

(5) The hurricane has (   ) many people to living without food or housing for days.

[leave, reduce, keep, bring, take]

E. 다음 경우에 맞는 응답을 골라라.(고딕체 단어는 강세가 있다.)

(1) Why didn't you tell me?

① **You** didn't ask me. ② You **didn't** ask me.

③ You didn't **ask** me. ④ You didn't ask **me**.

(2) I can't do it.

① **You** aren't even trying. ② You **aren't** even trying.

③ You aren't **even** trying. ④ You aren't even **trying**.

(3) How about the Moonlight Sonata?

① Good! **I'm** passionately fond of Beethoven.

② Good! I'm **passionately** fond of Beethoven.

③ Good! I'm passionately **fond** of Beethoven.

④ Good! I'm passionately fond of **Beethoven**.

F. 다음과 같이 끊어 읽을 경우의 의미의 차이를 말하여라.

(1) They decorated / the soldier with an admirable uniform.

(2) They decorated the soldier / with an admirable uniform.

Answer: D. (1) sent (2) yielding (3) brought (4) struck (5) reduced E. (1) ③ (2) ④ (3) ②
F. (1) 그들은 아주 멋진 군복을 입은 그 병사에게 훈장을 주었다. (2) 그들은 그 병사를 아주 멋진 군복으로 꾸며주었다.

숙 어

(1) **regardless of** (=irrespective of) ~에 상관없이
☞ That's a film that can be enjoyed by anyone, *regardless of* age.

(2) **resign oneself to** (=reluctantly accept) 마지못해 받아들이다, 감수하다
☞ I had to *resign myself to* making a loss on the sale.

(3) **rest assured** (=be sure, be certain) 확신하다, 안심하다
☞ You can *rest assured* that I'll never tell anyone the truth.

(4) **rise to one's feet** (=stand up) 일어서다
☞ The congregation *rose to their feet* when the priest walked down the aisle.

(5) **rise to the occasion** (=deal successfully with) (어려운 일을) 잘해내다
☞ It's not an easy task, but I'm sure he will *rise to the occasion*.

(6) **rub ~ the wrong way** (=annoy, irritate) ~을 화나게[짜증나게] 하다
☞ His impolite comments *rubbed* his father *the wrong way*.

(7) **rule out** (=exclude) 제외하다, 배제하다
☞ The investigators said the possibility of arson could not be *ruled out*.

(8) **run into** (=run across ; collide with) 우연히 만나다 ; 충돌하다
☞ On the way to the shop I *ran into* my old friend, Tom.
The taxi went too fast around the corner and *ran into* a streetlight.

(9) **run out of** (=exhaust, use up) 다 써버리다, ~이 다 떨어지다
☞ The troops *ran out of* ammunition and had to withdraw.

(10) **run short of** (=use up almost all of) ~이 부족하다
☞ Due to the recession our company is beginning to *run short of* funds.

(11) **see about** (=find out about, inquire about) ~에 대해 알아보다[검토하다]
☞ I'm not sure, but I'll *see about* the cost of renting a van.

(12) **see fit to** (=decide to) ~하기로 결정[결심]하다
☞ I didn't *see fit to* apologize to him for my mistakes.

(13) **see red** (=become very angry) 몹시 화내다, 격분하다
☞ My father will *see red* when I tell him I wrecked his new car.

(14) **see through** (=recognize the truth ; do something until it is finished)
꿰뚫어 보다, 간파하다 ; (일을) 끝까지 해내다

☞ I could *see through* him from the start; he was obviously an impostor.
You must *see* this task *through* now that you've started it.

(15) **see to** (=deal with, take charge of) 처리하다, 책임지다
see to it that (=make sure) 확인하다, ~을 확실히[분명히] 하다

☞ Will you *see to* the arrangements for the next meeting?
Can you *see to it that* the fax goes this afternoon?

(16) **send away for** (=order ~ by mail) ~을 우편으로 주문하다

☞ I *sent away for* some books last month but they haven't arrived yet.

(17) **send out** (=distribute ; emit, send forth) 배포하다 ; 내뿜다, 방출하다

☞ I *sent out* 100 invitations to my gallery opening.
The factory *sends out* toxic gases into the surrounding countryside.

(18) **serve one right** (=be the right punishment for) 벌받아 마땅하다, 그래도 싸다

☞ It *serves you right* to have lost your purse; you were always too careless with it.

(19) **set about** (=go about, begin, start) 시작[착수, 개시]하다

☞ The sooner we *set about* it the sooner we'll finish it.

(20) **set in** (=start to happen) 시작되다

☞ Shortly after I started my new business, a long economic downturn *set in*.

Exercise

▶▶ 주어진 단어들을 포함한 글을 지어라. 필요하면 어형을 변화시켜라.

1. had / resign / to / wait
2. assured / break / promise
3. task / sure / you / occasion
4. behavior / rub / wrong
5. truck / run / streetlight
6. car / run / gas / mile / town
7. fit / late / help / him / work
8. see / lies / from / start
9. see / it / bill / paid
10. winter / set / early / north

19. 접 속 사(Conjunction)

기본 문법 설명

A. 등위 접속사	(1) This isn't the main reason, **nor** is the most important. (2) Bill tended to overeat, **for** he was a glutton. (3) Bill won the lottery, **so** he quit his job. (4) He said he would be late, **yet** he arrived on the dot.
B. 상관 접속사	(1) **Both** the captain **and** the crew were very tired. (2) The furnishings in the shop are **at once** elegant **and** practical. (3) He **not only** took me home **but also** gave me some money. (4) He **as well as** his father became a mortician. (5) I needed to discuss the problem with **either** Tom **or** Mary. (6) My doctor told me I should **neither** smoke **nor** drink.
C. 종속 접속사	(1) **When** I'm finished with my homework, let's go see a movie. (2) I'll accompany you **as far as** Chicago. (3) You should not despise me **because** I'm only a secretary. (4) I always keep fruit in the refrigerator **so** (**that**) the insects **will** keep off it. (5) He spoke English **so** fast **that** I couldn't follow him. It was **such** a lovely day **that** we decided to go for a picnic. (6) **If** I were you, I would fire a lazy guy like him. (7) *Coward* **as** he was, he had the conscience to say so. (8) Do in Rome **as** the Romans do.
D. 종속상관 접속사	(1) **No sooner** had the game begun **than** it started raining. **Hardly** [**Scarcely, Barely**] had the game begun **when** it started raining. (2) I'll drive to New York tomorrow **whether** it snows **or not**.
E. 접속사구	(1) I fell asleep **as soon as** I lay down. (2) I can eat anything **as** [**so**] **long as** it is edible. (3) He's spending money **as if** he were a millionaire. (4) **In case** you need any money, I can lend you some. Bring a map **in case** you get lost.

A. 등위접속사

단어·구·절을 문법상 대등의 관계로 결합시키는 접속사로 and, but, or, nor(…도 또 ~아니다), for(왜냐하면 ~이니까), so(그래서, 그러므로), yet(그럼에도 불구하고) 등.

(1) nor 다음에 절이 올 때는 「nor+be 동사+주어」또는 「nor+조동사+주어」의 어순이 된다. (이것이 주된 이유는 아니며 또한 가장 중요한 이유도 아니다.)
I can't go, **nor** *do I want to*. (나는 갈 수 없고, 또한 가고 싶지도 않다.)

(2) for는 앞말에 대한 이유를 부가적으로 기술한다. (Bill은 과식하는 경향이 있었다. 왜냐하면 그는 대식가였으니까.)

(3) so는 원래 부사였으므로 and so로 사용되기도 한다. (Bill은 복권에 당첨되었다. 그래서 직장을 그만 두었다.)

(4) yet은 and yet, but yet의 형태로 사용될 때도 있다. (그는 늦겠다고 말했지만 정각에 도착했다.)

B. 상관접속사

등위접속사를 포함하는 상관접속사에는 다음과 같은 것들이 있다.

(1) **both A and B** : A와 B 둘다
(2) **at once A and B** : A하기도 하고 또 B하기도 하다 (그 상점의 비품들은 우아하기도 하고 또 실용적이기도 하다.)
(3) **not only A but (also) B** : A뿐만 아니라 B도 (그는 나를 집에 데려다 주었을 뿐만 아니라 돈까지 주었다.)
(4) **B as well as A** : A뿐만 아니라 B도
(5) **either A or B** : A든가 B든가 (어느 쪽이든 한쪽)
(6) **neither A nor B** : A도 B도 어느쪽도 아니다

C. 종속접속사

(1) **때** : when, as, after, since, till, as long as, the moment 등
(2) **장소** : as far as (~까지), where 등
(3) **원인·이유** : because, since, now that 등
(내가 비서에 지나지 않는다고 나를 멸시해서는 안된다.) — not … because ~ = ~라고 해서 …하지 않다
(4) **목적** : so that+주어+조동사 : 구어체에서는 that을 생략하는 경향이 있다.
so 대신에 in order를 써 「in order that+주어+조동사」형태로 쓰이기도 한다.
(난 벌레가 닿지 않도록 과일을 항상 냉장고에 보관한다.)
(5) **결과** : so ~ that, such ~ that 등
(6) **조건** : if, unless, in case, granted (that), provided[providing] (= if 혹은 if only), suppose[supposing] (= if) 등
(7) **양보** : though, although, (even) if 등
☞ as 앞에 관사가 없는 명사, 형용사, 부사가 오면 대개 양보의 뜻이 된다.
Though he was **a** coward, ~ (비록 그는 겁쟁이였지만 그렇게 말할 양심은 있었다.)
Rich **as** he is, he is very modest.
Much **as** I liked her, I couldn't love her.
(8) **비교·양태** :
as (~과 같이, ~ 그대로), as if [though] 등.
Leave it *as* it is.

D. 종속상관접속사

(1) **no sooner ~ than = hardly [scarcely, barely] ~ when [before]** (경기가 시작되자마자 비가 오기 시작했다.)
He had *hardly* got to the station *when* the train started.
(2) **whether ~ or not** : ~이든 아니든

E. 접속사구

(1) **as soon as** : ~하자마자
(2) **as[so] long as** : ~하는 한 (먹을 수 있는 것이라면 난 무엇이든 먹을 수 있다.)
(3) **as if** : 마치 ~인 것 처럼
(4) **in case** : ~라면(= if); ~할 경우에 대비하여

F. 접속사 상당어구	(1) **The moment** I saw her, I was dazed in perplexity. (2) **The instant** I saw him, I knew he was Bill. (3) **Immediately** your application is accepted, you will be informed by e-mail. (4) **Now(that)** he is gone, we miss him very badly.
G. 중요 접속사	1. **And** : (1) It is hard to give up my **bread and butter**, but I feel now is the time to retire. (2) My colleague **and** best friend Tom died suddenly. (3) Try **and** get some tickets for tonight's performance. (4) Make sure the water is **nice and** hot. (5) I tried **and** tried, but I couldn't finish it on time. (6) Analyze it in detail, **and** you'll be able to find the cause. 2. **But** : (1) He is not so old **but** he can work. (2) I don't doubt **but that** you're telling the truth. (3) She would have fallen down **but that** he caught her. (4) She has no goal **but** to win the tennis match. (5) **Indeed** it was the worst disaster, **but** we could get over it. (6) **Excuse me**, **but** haven't we met somewhere before? 3. **As** : (1) He treats me **as** a child. (2) **As** he grew older, he became more forgetful. (3) **As** I didn't know how to operate the machine, I asked for his help. (4) I filled out the form **as** I had been instructed to do. (5) Tired **as** I was, I was determined to get the job finished. (6) The voting results are **as follows**. 4. **Or** : (1) He is an authority on botany, **or** the study of plants. (2) Rain **or** snow, the game will never be called off. (3) Take these pills, **or** your symptoms will become worse. 5. **That** : (1) If I complain, it is **that** I want fairness. (2) He must be mad **that** he should cry out at this time of night. (3) **That** he is guilty is certain. (4) He realized the fact **that** he had made a blunder. (5) **That** he should betray me! O **that** I were young again!

F. 접속사 상당어구

(1) **the moment** : ~하자마자, ~하는 순간 (난 그녀를 본 순간 너무 당황하여 멍했다.)
(2) **the instant** : ~하자마자, ~하는 즉시
(3) **immediately** : ~하자마자, ~하는 즉시 (당신의 신청[지원]이 받아들여지는 즉시 이메일로 통보될 것입니다.)
(4) **Now(that)** : Since ~, Seeing that ~ (그가 가고나니 우리는 그가 몹시 그립다.)

G. 중요접속사

1. And :

(1) **bread and butter**[brédnbʌ́tər]는 「버터를 바른 빵」이라는 뜻 이외에도 「생계, 수입, 중요한(bread-and-butter)」이란 뜻으로도 사용된다. (수입을 포기하는 것이 어렵지만 난 지금이 은퇴할 시기라고 느낀다.)
(2) **and**는 부가의 뜻을 나타낸다.
He was a great poet *and* novelist.
(3) **and**는 부정사의 to 대신에 쓰인다.
— try and get은 try to get의 의미
(4) **nice [good] and**는 very라는 부사의 뜻으로 사용된다. I felt *good and* tired.
(5) **and**는 강조의 뜻을 나타낸다.
(6) 명령문+**and** = …해라, 그러면 ~할 것이다 (그것을 상세히 분석해 보아라, 그러면 그 원인을 찾아낼 수 있을 것이다.)

2. But :

(1) **but** = that … not (그는 일을 할 수 없을 만큼 그렇게 늙은 것은 아니다.)
(2) **but that**은 부정문 다음에서 that의 의미로 쓰일 때가 있다.
(3) **but that** = unless = if ~ not (만약 그가 그녀를 잡지 않았더라면, 그녀는 넘어졌을 것이다.)
(4) **but** = other than = ~이외에는
(5) **Indeed** … **but** ~ = It is true (that) … but ~ = 과연 …이지만 그러나 ~ (과연 그것은 최악의 재난이었지만, 우리는 그것을 극복할 수 있었다.)
(6) **Excuse me, but** ~ = 죄송하지만 ~, 실례지만 ~ (실례지만 우리 전에 어디서 만난 일이 없었던가요?)

3. As :

(1) **as**는 「~처럼」의 뜻을 갖는다.
He treats me *as* if I am a child.
Do *as* you like.
(2) **as**는 「~함에 따라, ~에 비례하여」의 뜻을 갖는다. (나이를 먹어감에 따라 그는 점점 더 건망증이 심해졌다.)
(3) **as** = because, since (그 기계의 작동법을 몰랐으므로, 나는 그의 도움을 요청했다.)
(4) **as**는 「~하는 대로」의 뜻을 갖는다. (지시받은 대로 난 그 양식에 기재했다.)
(5) **as**는 양보의 뜻을 갖는다. (비록 피곤했지만, 난 그 일을 기어코 마칠 결심이었다.)
(6) **as follows**는 관용구 (그 투표결과는 다음과 같다.)

4. Or :

(1) **or**는 「즉, 다시 말해 (that is (to say)」의 뜻을 갖는다. (그는 식물학, 다시 말해 식물의 연구에 권위자이다.)
(2) **or**는 양보의 뜻을 갖는다. (비가 오든 눈이 오든 그 경기는 결코 취소되지 않을 것이다.) rain *or* shine
(3) **명령문+or** = …해라, 그렇지 않으면 ~할 것이다. (이 알약을 복용해라, 그렇지 않으면 병세가 악화될 것이다.)

5. That :

(1) **that** = because (내가 불평한다면 그것은 공평함을 원하기 때문이다.)
(2) **that**은 「판단의 기준」을 나타낸다. (이런 밤 시간에 소리를 지르다니 그는 미친 것이 틀림없다.)
(3) **that**은 명사절을 유도한다.
It is certain *that* he is guilty.
(4) **that**은 동격의 명사절을 유도한다.
(5) 놀람, 슬픔, 소망 등을 타나냄.

문법 · 작문

A. 공란을 적당한 단어로 메워라.

(1) The employees talked about bread _____ butter issues, like a wage increase and vacation time.
(2) Clever _____ you are, you can't do that.
(3) She had _____ heard the news when she cried out.
(4) _____ that everyone is here, we can start the meeting.
(5) He does it only _____ he thinks it is right.
(6) _____ or not he is coming hasn't been decided yet.
(7) I had not walked a mile _____ I got tired.
(8) He is not so much a businessman _____ a politician.
(9) I asked him by phone _____ he would attend the meeting.
(10) It was not _____ he warned me that I became aware of the danger.
(11) I am not rich, _____ do I wish to be.
(12) I am an eager, _____ not a skillful, sportsman.
(13) There is little, _____ any, hope of his recovery.
(14) I went out in disguise _____ someone should recognize me.
(15) Hard _____ I tried, I could not understand it.
(16) I was ignorant _____ the task was so difficult.
(17) I would rather die _____ suffer disgrace.
(18) I am more grateful to you _____ I can tell you.
(19) One step further, _____ you will fall over the precipice.
(20) The cows must eat grains, _____ they will not grow fat.
(21) The dense fog will have cleared away by _____ _____ day breaks.
(22) Don't waste your money on silly things _____ your brother does.

B. 틀린 부분을 고쳐라.

(1) The refugees neither had food nor shelter.
(2) It will not be long until the terrible recession ends.
(3) He refused to go except I went with him.
(4) I am merely questioning that we have the money to fund such a project.
(5) Although I left after Tom, I had arrived till he did.
(6) It was six years when I saw him again.
(7) I treated her not only to a delicious lunch but also tea and muffins.

C. 다음 글 속에 있는 that이 유도하는 절은 무슨 절인가?

(1) This could not hide the fact that he was growing old.

(2) Bring it closer so that I can see it better.

(3) Who are you in the world that you should say such a thing?

(4) That time is money was rarely realized in the Oriental society.

(5) Given that you haven't had much time to do this, I think you've done it very well.

(6) He ran so fast that I could not catch up with him.

(7) He cooperated with his abductor for fear that something might happen to the child.

D. Translate the following into English:

(1) 바보는 진리를 무시하는 반면에, 현명한 사람은 진리를 추구한다.

(2) 그 여자는 대답하지 않고 그 책을 책상 위에 놓고 가 버렸다.

(3) 그는 늦지 않도록 서둘렀다.

(4) 좀더 천천히 말씀하지 않으면 알아듣지 못하겠습니다.

(5) 김씨는 영국에도 미국에도 가 보지 못했지만 영어를 썩 잘 한다.

(6) 우리는 앉자마자 가야 할 시간이라는 것을 알았다.

(7) 사람은 심신(心身)이 아울러 건전해야 한다.

(8) 그들은 결혼한지 한 달도 못 되어서 싸우기 시작했다.

(9) 사람은 건강을 잃고 나서야 비로소 건강의 중요성을 안다.

(10) 다른 사람들이 단지 어떤 책을 읽는다고 해서 그 책을 읽지는 말아라.

(11) 시간이 지나감에 따라 사태가 더 악화되는 것처럼 보였다.

'My Hobby' 라는 제목으로 90어 내외의 글을 지어라.

● 단 문 독 해 ●

Stupid **as** he is, he is honest.
Hero **as** he was, he was actually a hypocrite.
Dearly **as** he loved his native land, he loved liberty even more.
Old **as** he is, he is not equal to the task.

1. Dull **as** a student may be, and difficult **as** a subject may seem to be at first sight, he will find the study becomes easier or at least less difficult, if he can persevere and does not neglect it.

notes :
*Dull as a student may be = Though a student may be dull
*persevere 인내하다, 참다

▶▶The writer stresses that the most important thing for a student is diligence and (　　).
[progress, perseverance, proverbs]

▶▶영작하시오.
그는 첫눈에 그 여자한테 반해 버렸다.

2. Much **as** I once loved Thoreau, I confess I have never looked upon money as a cause of enslavement. I have always felt freer when I had a dollar in my pocket rather than just a quarter. To be able to take a taxi instead of a bus is to me a desirable kind of freedom.

notes :
*look (up)on A as B = regard A as B
*enslavement 노예화

▶▶Which can **not** be inferred from the above paragraph?
① Thoreau maintained money caused men's enslavement.
② The writer thinks money is everything.
③ The writer feels more comfortable with more money.
④ The writer disagrees with Thoreau's opinion of money.
⑤ The writer would rather take a taxi than a bus.

▶▶영작하시오.
네가 할 일을 따분한 의무로 여기지 말고 흥미를 갖도록 해라.

3. If our science were perfect it would represent the essence of the human spirit. Imperfect **as** it is, it can give us only a few glimpses of the essence, mixed with many more glimpses of the human flesh.

notes :
*represent 설명하다
*essence 본질
*glimpse 흘끗 봄

▶▶Our science, as it is imperfect, has discovered (　　) about the human (　　) than about the human (　　).
[more, less, spirit, much, body]

▶▶영작하시오.
나는 기차의 창문을 통해 그 집을 흘끗 보았다.

4. Great physicist **as** he is, he is still greater as a man. He achieved a fame greater than that of any other scientist, although no other man is as indifferent to fame and as uncomfortable about publicity as he is. Fame or external circumstances can change him very little.

notes :
*Great physicist as he is, = Though he is a great physicist,
*publicity 남한테 알려지는 것
*external 외부의 ; internal 내부의

▶▶Which does **not** correspond with the underlined he?
① He has achieved many great tasks associated with physics.
② He gained great publicity for which he was eager.
③ The worldly fame others long for doesn't count for him.
④ His personality was rarely affected by outside influence.
⑤ He is not interested in being respected as a celebrity.

▶▶영작하시오.
그는 정치 문제에 무관심한데 그 여자는 관심이 크다.

Once you have made a promise, you should keep it.

5. A young man who has passed through a course of university training should discipline himself at an early date never to read for mere amusement. And **once** the habit of the discipline has been formed, he will find it impossible to read for mere amusement.

notes :
*discipline oneself to ~하도록 자신을 훈련시키다
*discipline 훈련

▶▶윗 글의 밑줄친 the discipline 의 구체적인 내용을 우리말로 쓰시오.
▶▶영작하시오.
일단 네가 그 섬에 가보면 내가 왜 그렇게 그 섬을 좋아하는지 넌 이해하게 될 것이다.

Whether you like it or not, you must do it.
However rich he **may** be, he never wastes his money.
No matter what you are going to do, you must do your best.

6. Every man in the world is better than somebody else. **Whether** one of my students is rich or poor, white, black or yellow, bright or slow, it is no matter to me if there is humanity in him — if he has a heart — if he loves truth and honor.

notes :
*slow 둔한
*matter 중대한 것
*humanity 인간미
*heart 열의, 애정

▶▶The teacher thinks highly of his students' personality and passion, regardless of their (　　) situation, race and (　　).
[financial, functional, intelligence, integrity]
▶▶영작하시오.
왼쪽으로 돌든 오른쪽으로 돌든 상관없다. 양쪽길 다 공원에 이른다.

7. Men sometimes speak as if the study of the classics would at length make way for more modern and practical studies; but the adventurous students will always study classics, in **whatever** language they **may** be written and **however** ancient they **may** be. For what are the classics but the noblest recorded thoughts of man?

notes :
*classics 고전
*at length = at last
*make way for ~ = ~에게 길을 내주다

▶▶Why does the writer maintain that it is desirable for students to study classics? Answer in Korean.

▶▶영작하시오.
나는 후진을 위해 자리를 내 주겠다.

8. A house without books is a mindless and characterless house, **no matter how** rich the Persian carpets and **how** elegant the furniture. The Persian carpets only tell you that the owner has got money, but the books will tell you whether he has got a mind as well.

notes :
*the furniture (may be)
*has got = has
*as well = also

▶▶According to the above passage, which is **not** correct?
① A standard by which we can judge if someone has a mind is whether he has books.
② The richness of a man is not related to his mind.
③ Household furnishings just mean that a man is wealthy enough to buy them.
④ A richly furnished house is preferable to a humble house with books.
⑤ The possession of books may imply that someone has not only money but also intelligence.

▶▶영작하시오.
아무리 재능이 있을지라도 노력 없이 성공을 기대할 수 없다.

I do not deny (**but**) **that** he is idle.
No one is **so** old **that** he can not learn.

9. There is no denying (**but**) **that** the earth must have been somewhat sweeter in that dewy morning of creation, when it was young and fresh, when the feet of the trampling millions had not trodden its grass to dust.

notes :
*There is no ~ing = It is impossible to ~
*but that = that
*trample 짓밟다
*tread 밟다

▶▶According to the above passage, what is the main cause of environmental destruction? Write a word.

▶▶영작하시오.
앞으로 무엇이 일어날는지 알 수 없다.

10. A newspaper is the only kind of reading that is almost universal. **No** one is **so** occupied with the business of his calling **that** he can't find time to read a newspaper.

notes :
*universal 보편적인
*reading 읽을 거리
*calling 직업, 천직

▶▶밑줄 친 부분과 같은 뜻이 되도록 빈칸을 채워라.
However much we are (t) up with business, we can still find time to read a newspaper.

▶▶영작하시오.
그 기자는 월드컵에 관한 기사를 쓰느라 여전히 바쁘다.

Indeed he is young, **but** he is careful.
I can speak **neither** French **nor** German.

11. **Indeed** science is a good thing, **but** it is not an end in itself; it is a means toward an end and that end is human improvement. As scientists keep insisting, there is **neither** good **nor** bad in any scientific discovery; it is the use to which it is put which makes it beneficial or dangerous; and the decision does not lie with the scientists themselves but with society.

notes :
*put ~ to use = ~을 이용하다
*lie with ~ = (책임 등이) ~에게 있다

▶▶According to the above paragraph, which is incorrect?
① Human well-being is the ultimate aim of science.
② Science can be considered a means by which we can achieve the advancement of human beings.
③ The writer maintains that scientists should be legally responsible for the results of their research.
④ Science itself can not be regarded as good or bad.
⑤ The use of a scientific discovery will determine if it is beneficial or harmful.

▶▶영작하시오.
무슨 조치를 취할 것인지를 결정하는 것은 우리의 몫이다.

12. Until now <u>he</u> has been an insignificant member of the school, one of those boys who excel **neither** at games **nor** at lessons, of whom nothing is expected, and rarely, if ever, get into trouble.

notes :
*insignificant 대수롭지 않은
*if ever 비록 ~한다고 해도

▶▶Which is **not** appropriate to describe the underlined <u>he</u>?
① negligible ② average ③ ordinary
④ plain ⑤ delinquent

▶▶영작하시오.
그는 실수를 한다고 해도 좀처럼 하지 않는다.

He is **so** honest **that** he cannot tell a lie. He is **such** an honest fellow **that** he cannot tell a lie.

13. Mass media have referred **so** much to the atomic bomb and the possibility that a far more forcible H-bomb will come into use, **that** one is apt to forget what atomic energy can do for our well-being and health by using it properly.

notes :
*refer to = mention 언급하다
*H-bomb 수소폭탄
*well-being = welfare 복지

▶▶다음 빈칸에 적절한 말끼리 가장 잘 짝지어진 것은?

The atomic energy often mentioned in mass media tends to remind us only of the ( ) power of the atomic bomb. In fact, its right use can be ( ) human welfare and health.

① harmful - undesirable to ② constructive - helpful to
③ devastating - detrimental to ④ destructive - good for
⑤ productive - useful to

▶▶영작하시오.

이 기계는 최근에 일반적으로 사용하게 되었다.

14. Photography has been brought to **such** a degree of perfection **that** there is scarcely an object in nature that is beyond the reach of the camera.

notes :
*photography 사진술
*object 사물
*that의 선행사는 object

▶▶Photography has been ( ) so much that now there is almost nothing we cannot take a ( ) of.

[painting, picture, pleasure, developed, reached]

▶▶영작하시오.

그것은 보통 사람으로는 이해할 수 없다.

15. The world is **so** made **that** it probably never happens that a person lives who has not, or has never had, any one to love him. There is the love of parents, of brothers and sisters, of relatives and companions.

notes :
*so가 동사(made)를 수식. 뒤에서부터 해석한다; so made that~ = ~하도록 만들어져
*relatives 친척

▶▶There is ( ) one in the world that is ( ) loved by someone else.

[always, ever, no, just, not, maybe]

▶▶영작하시오.

그 다리는 가운데가 열리도록 만들어져 있다.

You should **not** scorn a man **because** he is uneducated.
He does it **only because** he thinks it is right.
I like him **not because** he has few faults **but because** he has a few faults.
Not that I loved Caesar less, **but that** I loved Rome more.

16. One of the gifts which many people have but few use to the full is the gift of expression. **Because** you have never tried to write anything other than letters, or essays when you were at school, there is **no** reason for believing that you don't have literary ability.

notes :
*gifts 재능
*to the full 충분히
*expression 표현
*other than = except
*essay 논문
*literary ability 문학적 재능

▶▶Which is the main idea of the above paragraph?
① The ability to express oneself is important in our society.
② There are many people who are endowed with literary gifts but do not fully develop them.
③ Writing only letters and essays is enough to develop literary ability.
④ Our current education can fully develop students' literary ability.
⑤ Few men and women are making full use of their inborn gifts.

▶▶영작하시오.
사람이 유식하다고 해서 반드시 존경받을 가치가 있는 것은 아니다.

17. I would like to see children taught that they should not say they like things which they do not like, **merely because** certain other people say they like them, and how foolish it is to say they believe this or that when they understand nothing about it.

notes :
*I have never heard it *sung* in Italian.
*merely because = only because, simply because
*how foolish 이하는 명사절로서 taught의 목적어

▶▶The writer maintains that students should be educated to (   ).
① be careful in accepting others' ideas
② remain neutral about the issues they don't know very well
③ be careful of others' feelings in objecting to their views
④ be decisive in expressing their own opinions
⑤ act as they've been taught in school

▶▶영작하시오.
나는 당신이 실망하는 것을 보고 싶지 않다.

18. Those men of genius choose a particular profession **not because** they consider it the best, **because** it promises the most glory, money or happiness, **but because** they cannot help it and for the same reason they stick to it while life lasts.

▶▶Which of the following is most suitable to explain the above-mentioned geniuses?

① They always make the best choice when they decide on their profession.

② As far as they are concerned, the financial condition is the most important factor for choosing an occupation.

③ Once they have made up their minds, they think that their choice is correct.

④ Their choice of occupation is likely to be beyond their control.

⑤ They are apt to change their occupations more frequently than ordinary people.

▶▶영작하시오.

그는 무슨 일이라도 끝까지 버티어 끝낸다.

notes :

*not because …, because …, but because 의 두 번째 because는 not에 걸린다

*it = the particular profession

*cannot help it(어쩔 수 없다)의 help는 avoid의 뜻

*for the same reason 같은 이유로

*stick to 고수하다, 집착하다

19. Birds are naturally the most joyous creatures in the world. **Not that** when you see or hear them they always give you pleasure, **but that** they feel joy more than any other animal. The other animals commonly look serious and grave; and many of them even appear melancholy. But birds for the most part show themselves to be extremely joyous by their movements and by their aspects.

▶▶Why are birds the most joyous animals in the world?

① Because they give us pleasure through their songs.

② Because they seem to make other creatures joyful by their appearance.

③ Because they look more cheerful through their behavior and appearance than other animals.

④ Because they can't fully express their melancholic emotions.

⑤ Because there are no serious and sorrowful things in their lives.

▶▶영작하시오.

우리는 박물관을 돌아보면서 그날의 대부분을 보냈다.

notes :

*creature 생물, 동물

*Not that …, but that ~ = Not because …, but because ~

*grave 근엄한, 엄숙한

*melancholy 우울한

*extremely 매우

Now that I am a man, I think otherwise.

20. In our time, science has placed in human hands the power to destroy entire life on earth. **Now that** the people of the world find themselves facing one another with deadly weapons in their hands, the virtues of prudence, tolerance, wisdom and — far above all these — love have become necessities of life in the literal sense.

notes :
*virtue 미덕
*deadly 치명적
*prudence 신중
*literal 글자 그대로의
*necessity 필수품

▶▶Which of the following is **not** correct?
① Our science has given us the power to annihilate all life on the earth.
② It is possible for people to use their lethal weapons when confronted with war.
③ The virtues such as prudence and love are necessary to prevent the mass destruction of the earth.
④ Many powers in the world tend to reduce the armaments according to their peace treaties.
⑤ Among many factors, love is the most essential to maintain world peace.

▶▶영작하시오.
그들의 결혼 생활은 어느 의미로 보나 행복한 것이었다.

The moment she heard the news, she burst into tears.

21. There is one all-important law of human conduct. If we obey that law, we will almost never get into trouble. In fact, that law, if obeyed, will bring us countless friends and constant happiness. But **the very instant** we break that law, we will get into endless trouble. The law is this: Always make the other person feel important.

notes :
*all-important 극히 중요한
*if (it is) obeyed
*constant 변함 없는

▶▶Which does **not** correspond with the above-mentioned law?
① The law is a kind of oil that makes our society run smoothly.
② The ignorance of the law is punished according to the existing laws.
③ As soon as we violate the law, the relationships between our peers get worse.
④ Our happiness depends on the observance of the law.
⑤ The law is to praise and encourage others.

▶▶영작하시오.
그 규칙을 위반하는 순간 너는 곤경에 처하게 될 것이다.

장 문 독 해

Warming-up

The country **was subject to** Roman rule.

Poverty often **leads to** crime.

We **were made to realize** that a nuclear war is a way of mutual suicide.

I met him then **for the first time**.

1 Intelligence alone is dangerous if it is not subject to the intuitive or rational perception of moral values. It has led, not only to materialism, but to monstrosities. All of a sudden the public at large was made to realize that a wonderful triumph of science brutally challenged the security of all mankind. And at once, the so-called civilized countries understood that only a moral union could protect them against ⓐthe threat. Time was so short that the only possible protection had to be sought in written agreements, but every man knows that written agreements are only as good and as trustworthy as the man who signs them, and that unless this man is honest and sincere, unless he really represents a nation who will back his word of honor, they mean absolutely nothing. For the first time in the history of man, the conflict between pure intelligence and moral values has become a matter of life and death. All we can do is to hope that humanity will profit by this lesson. Alas, we doubt it.

Lecomte Du Noüy: *Human Destiny*

Notes

be subject to=be controlled by / intuitive or rational perception 직관적인 혹은 이성적인 지각 / moral values 도덕적 가치/ monstrosity 괴물 / at large=in general / challenge 도전하다 / security 안전 / trustworthy=dependable / back=support / his word of honor 그의 명예를 건 약속 / humanity=mankind / profit 이익을 얻다

Question

1. 본문의 밑줄친 ⓐthe threat의 구체적 내용을 우리말로 쓰시오.

2. Which is an appropriate tone of the last underlined sentence?
   ① positive ② skeptical ③ descriptive
   ④ informative ⑤ satirical

3. According to the passage, which is **not** correct?
   ① Modern materialism is caused by the extreme advancement of technology.
   ② Nothing but our moral union can save us from human extinction.
   ③ Underdeveloped countries haven't yet recognized the oncoming global calamities.
   ④ Written agreements are the only means of protection we can seek because of the urgency of the matter.
   ⑤ To secure the validity of a treaty each party should be qualified, honest and sincere.

4. Which of the following is most suitable for the main topic of the passage?
   ① Only the advancement of technology can make up for the decline of moral values.
   ② The details to support a treaty concluded by nations should be urgently prepared.
   ③ The unbalanced development of pure intelligence and moral values can be a danger to the survival of mankind.
   ④ A wonderful development in science will eventually bring infinite happiness to human beings.
   ⑤ We should push ahead with plans to hold summit meetings in order to settle international conflicts.

Production

(1) 그 협정이 실패하면, 양국뿐만 아니라 전 세계에 커다란 재난을 초래할 것이다.
(2) 우리는 누구나 나라의 법에 복종해야 한다. 법을 그저 몰랐다는 것만으로 범법이 정당화되지는 못한다.
(3) 이번 일요일에 무슨 특별한 것을 생각하고 있습니까? 없으면 저희들과 같이 소풍을 가는 게 어떻습니까?

장 문 독 해

Warming-up

Among the pastimes of teenagers **there is nothing as** popular **as** computer games.

The crew of the ship gave me **nothing but** bread to eat.

The sale of defective goods **exposed** the company **to** widespread criticism.

The villagers **are dependent on** this stream **for** their water supply.

2 There is nothing as degrading as the constant anxiety about one's means of livelihood. I have nothing but contempt for the people who despise money. They are hypocrites or fools. Money is like a sixth sense without which you cannot make a complete use of the other five. Without an adequate income half the possibilities of life are shut off. The only thing to be careful about is that ⓐ<u>you do not pay more than a dollar for the dollar you earn</u>. You will hear people say that poverty is the best spur to the artist. They have never felt the iron of it in their flesh. They do not know how mean it makes you. It exposes you to endless humiliation, it cuts your wings, it eats into your soul like a cancer. It is not wealth one asks for, but just enough to preserve one's dignity, to work unhampered, to be generous, frank, and independent. I pity with all my heart ⓑ<u>the artist</u>, whether he writes or paints, who is entirely dependent for subsistence upon his art.

W. Somerset Maugham: *Of Human Bondage*

Notes

degrading 품위를 낮추는, 창피한 / contempt 경멸 / despise 경멸[멸시]하다 / hypocrite 위선자 / adequate 적당한 / poverty 빈곤, 가난 / spur 자극 / the iron of it 가난의 쓰라림[혹독함] / in one's flesh 직접, 몸소 / expose ~ to humiliation ~로 하여금 수모를 겪게 하다 / eat into (~) (~)를 갉아먹다 / enough (*n*) 충분한 양 / preserve 유지[보존]하다 / dignity 위신[품위] / unhampered 방해[구속]받지 않는 / entirely 완전히 / be dependent for … upon[on] ~ ~에게 …를 의존하다 / subsistence 생계

Question

1. What does the underlined part of the passage ⓐ ultimately imply? Write in Korean.

2. Why does the author feel pity for ⓑthe artist?

Because a poor artist can't fully (　　) himself to creative activities owing to (　　) problems.

[devote, devour, divide, family, familiar, financial]

3. According to the passage, which of the following is **not** the author's argument?
   ① It is desirable that artists should be free of financial worries in order to produce better works.
   ② Poverty encourages the artists to create their best works.
   ③ Money can be considered a sixth sense.
   ④ Poverty-stricken artists are driven to earn their bread and butter, which influences their mental activities.
   ⑤ Poverty withers our potentialities, depriving us of half of the opportunities in life.

4. Which of the following does **not** correspond with the passage?
   ① Continuous worries about one's livelihood make a man miserable.
   ② Those who say that money is not important in our lives are nothing but hypocrites.
   ③ It is poor artists who often produce masterpieces.
   ④ Those who have never felt humiliated by being poor often ignore the influence of money.
   ⑤ Money is indispensable for us to completely utilize our five senses.

Production

(1) 싼 물건을 찾아 다니지만 싸게 비지떡이라는 것을 너는 곧 알 것이다.
(2) 그가 죽었다는 그녀의 이메일은 거짓에 지나지 않았다.
(3) 그 지휘관의 부주의한 명령 때문에 많은 군인들이 방사능에 노출되었다.
(4) 수질 오염때문에 많은 어부들이 생계를 의지하는 수백만의 물고기가 죽었다.

실력체크 I

1 다음 글을 읽고 아래 물음에 답하여라.

The Oxford English Dictionary defines Biography as 'the history of the lives of individual men, as a branch of literature'. This excellent definition contains within itself the three principles that any serious biographer should observe. A biography must be 'history', in the sense that it must be accurate and depict a person in relation to his times. It must describe an 'individual' with all the gradual changes of human character, and not merely present a type of virtue or of vice. And it must be composed as 'a branch of literature', in that it must be written in grammatical English and with an adequate feeling for style.
A biography combining all these three principles can be classed as a pure biography: a biography that violates any one of these principles or combines them in incorrect proportions, must be classed as an 'impure' biography. A pure biography is written with no purpose other than that of conveying to the reader an authentic portrait of the individual whose life is being narrated. A biography is rendered impure when some extraneous purpose intrudes to distort the accuracy of presentation.

notes :
define 정의하다 / depict 묘사하다 / and (it must) not merely~ / present 나타내다, 묘사하다 / compose 작성하다 / in that~=~라는 점에 있어서 / class 분류하다 / other than =except / convey 전달하다 / authentic 믿을 만한 / render=make / extraneous 외부의 / intrude 침입하다 / distort 왜곡하다 / presentation 묘사, 제시

(1) 전기문에는 세 개의 요소가 필요하다고 하는데, 그것이 무엇인지 각각 20자 정도의 우리말로 설명하여라.
(2) 전기문은 'pure'한 것과 'impure'한 것으로 구별된다고 하는데, 각각 어떤 내용을 가지게 되는지 30자 정도의 우리말로 설명하여라.

2 다음 글을 읽고 아래 질문에 답하여라.

ⓐ<u>In the organization of industrial life the influence of the factory upon the physiological and mental state of the workers has been completely neglected.</u> Modern industry is based on the conception of the maximum production at the lowest cost, in order that an individual or a group of individuals may earn as much money as possible. It has expanded without any idea of the true nature of the human beings who run the machines, and without giving any consideration to the effects produced on the individuals and on their descendants by the artificial mode of existence

notes :
physiological 생리학상의 / impose (의무 따위를) 부과하다 / mode 방식 / existence 생활 / with no regard for (~) =(~을) 전혀 고려하지 않고 / dimension (주로 복수로) 면적, 용적 / tenant 세입자 / mass 집단 / banal 진부한, 평범한 / monstrous 괴물같은 / lorry 화물트럭 / congregate ~에 모여들다

imposed by the factory. The great cities have been built with no regard for us. The shape and dimensions of the skyscrapers depend entirely on the necessity of obtaining the maximum income per square foot of ground, and of offering to the tenants offices and apartments that please them. This caused ⓑthe construction of gigantic buildings where too large masses of human beings are crowded together. Civilized men like such a way of living. While they enjoy the comfort and banal luxury of their dwelling, they do not realize that they are deprived of the necessities of life. The modern city consists of monstrous buildings and of dark, narrow streets full of petrol fumes, coal dust, and poisonous gases, torn by the noise of the taxi-cabs, lorries and buses, and congregated ceaselessly by great crowds. Obviously, it has not been planned for the good of its inhabitants.

(1) 윗 글을 내용상 두 **paragraph**로 나누고 각 **paragraph**의 요지를 가장 잘 나타내는 문장을 하나씩 골라라.

(2) 밑줄 친 ⓐ와 같은 상황은 근대 산업의 어떤 성격에서 나오는가? 본문에 입각하여 간단히 우리글로 적어라.

(3) 밑줄 친 ⓑ와 같은 건물을 건설하게 된 이유는 무엇이냐? 본문에 입각하여 간단히 우리글로 적어라.

3 다음 글의 끝 부분을 7단어 이내로 완성하여라.

notes :
think of A as B = A를 B로 간주하다, 여기다 / engaged in ~ = ~에 관련된 / depend on ~ = ~에 의지하다 / well-being 복지, 행복 / observe 지키다, 따르다 / consideration 이해, 배려 / state 말하다 / carry out = 실행하다 / in deeds = 실제로 / the like = 그와 같은 것 / earthly 이 세상의, 속세의

We should not think of ourselves as individuals engaged in a Darwinian struggle for survival, behaving like wolves to each other. We should rather think of ourselves as brothers, united in one human family, and depending on each other for our well-being. What we expect of them, in their behavior to us, should be the rule we observe in our behavior to them. As we naturally wish them to show kindness and consideration to us, so we should be ready in turn to show kindness and consideration to them. It is so simple, when stated in words; yet somehow so difficult to carry out in deeds. If everyone followed this simple rule, it would be a real social revolution, the like of which has never been heard; and this world would immediately become an earthly paradise. The simple rule is this: Do to others as ________________________________.

실 력 체 크 Ⅱ

A. 주어진 부분으로 시작하여 다음 문장을 다시 쓰시오.

(1) Though his business is not doing well, he never cheats on taxes.
In ________________________________.

(2) Yesterday's heavy rain caused the river to rise.
As ________________________________.

(3) I am sure that the exhibition will be popular.
The exhibition ________________________________.

(4) Knowing is one thing and doing is quite another.
Knowing is quite ________________________________.

(5) He will recover from leukemia before long.
It will ________________________________.

(6) I was so astonished that I could hardly speak.
Astonishment almost ________________________________.

(7) It is impossible that he has done the work by himself.
He ________________________________.

(8) This is the most touching story that I have ever been told.
I have never ________________________________.

(9) To even his closest friends' great surprise, he disappeared suddenly.
His ________________________________.

(10) Nothing gives such a good appetite as hunger.
Hunger ________________________________.

B. 다음 (　　) 안의 동사를 적당한 어형으로 바꾸어라.

(1) I will keep you (inform) of the state of affairs.

(2) Cancer can be treated if (discover) in time.

(3) Mary stood there motionless with her hand (shade) her eyes.

(4) I saw their houses (carry) away by the flood.

(5) If we are (escape) unimaginable catastrophes, we must find a way of avoiding all wars at all costs.

Answer: A. (1) spite of his business not doing well, he never cheats on taxes (2) it rained heavily yesterday, the river rose (3) is sure to be popular (4) different from doing (5) not be long before he recovers from leukemia (6) left me speechless (7) cannot have done the work by himself (8) been told a more touching story than this (9) sudden disappearance surprised even his closest friends greatly (10) is the best sauce

B. (1) informed (2) discovered (3) shading (4) carried (5) to escape

C. 각 문장에서 문미의 단어를 어디에 넣으면 되겠는가?

(1) He turned away his face, and so his father. (did)

(2) The city he wants to live in his old age is Busan. (in)

(3) Tom entered by the door opposite to opening into the garden. (that)

(4) It isn't what he says that annoys me, the way he says it. (but)

(5) He is standing his hand in his pocket. (with)

D. 다음 각 문장 안에 적당한 단어를 하나씩 넣어 뜻이 통하게 하여라.

(1) Please explain me what this word means.

(2) Can that vending machine be ordered now and paid on delivery?

(3) After supper I went on my reading.

(4) How older is your brother than you?

(5) We presented him a souvenir when he left Korea.

E. 다음 문장의 틀린 곳을 고쳐라.

(1) I want that she will be picked up at the airport at about 9 o'clock.

(2) I hope you to come and see us when you're in Seoul.

(3) I wish she will shut up for a moment and let someone else speak.

(4) The doctor suggested the diabetic to refrain from eating sweets.

(5) My another hobby is hang-gliding including aerobics and scuba-diving.

F. A와 B의 대화가 이루어지도록 공란을 적당한 단어로 메워라.

(1) A: You'll never get a raise until the economy recovers.
B: You mean I won't get a raise until the recession ends?
I get the ( ). I'm quitting!

(2) A: What's the big ( ) of parking your car in my drive way?
B: Oh, I'm terribly sorry about that.

(3) A: Why can't your wife, as well as you, go on a trip overseas?
B: Because we can't get over jet ( ).

Answer: C. (1) so did his (2) live in in his (3) to that opening (4) but the way (5) with his hand
D. (1) **to** me (2) paid **for** on (3) on **with** (4) **much** older (5) him **with**
E. (1) I want her to be ~. (2) I hope (that) you will come ~. (3) will→would (4) suggested→advised (5) Another hobby of mine is ~.
F. (1) message (2) idea (3) lag

어 휘 · 발 음

A. 주어진 단어 중 문맥상 가장 적당한 것을 골라라.

(1) Don't keep the windows closed. It is so ______.

ⓐ humid ⓑ cold ⓒ chilly ⓓ windy

(2) There is usually a tendency among older men not to ______ the morals of the younger generation.

ⓐ acquire ⓑ adapt ⓒ amend ⓓ approve

(3) We see from these works of art that their ______ of beauty is different from ours.

ⓐ conception ⓑ deception ⓒ exception ⓓ reception

(4) We'll need to ______ how the new material stands up to wear and tear.

ⓐ value ⓑ evaluate ⓒ devaluate ⓓ eliminate

B. 다음 문장 속의 do의 의미와 가장 가까운 것을 밑에서 골라라.

(a) Go and **do** your hair immediately.

(b) She must **do** the flowers for the party.

(c) It is not hard to **do** three miles on foot.

(d) This room will **do** me quite well.

(e) The task is too difficult for me to **do** .

① suit	② arrange	③ solve	④ brush	⑤ cover

C. 접두사를 붙여 반대어를 만들어라.

(1) normal	(2) arctic	(3) order	(4) ordinary
(5) moral	(6) function	(7) literate	(8) comfortable
(9) belief	(10) existent	(11) probable	(12) approve
(13) active	(14) load	(15) fortune	(16) fortunate
(17) balance	(18) convenience	(19) please	(20) infection
(21) perishable	(22) equality	(23) gratitude	(24) modesty

Answer: A. (1) ⓐ (2) ⓓ (3) ⓐ (4) ⓑ B. (a) ④ (b) ② (c) ⑤ (d) ① (e) ③
C. (1) abnormal (2) antarctic (3) disorder (4) extraordinary (5) immoral (6) malfunction (7) illiterate (8) uncomfortable (9) disbelief (10) nonexistent (11) improbable (12) disapprove (13) inactive (14) unload (15) misfortune (16) unfortunate (17) unbalance[imbalance] (18) inconvenience (19) displease (20) disinfection (21) nonperishable (22) inequality (23) ingratitude (24) immodesty

D. 밑줄 친 부분에서 가장 강하게 발음되는 단어를 하나씩 골라라.

A: "Will you please bring it here?"
B: (1)"Johnny will bring it to you."
A: (2)"I want you to bring it to me."
B: "I am engaged now, but he is not busy."
A: (3)"Yes, he is busy. What are you doing now?"
B: "I am putting my coat away."
A: (4)"What coat are you putting away?"
B: (5)"I am putting my black coat away."

E. 괄호 속에 들어갈 낱말 중 나머지와 의미가 다른 한 단어를 골라라.

(1) We could see many vehicles with posters ( ) their new product.
① advertising ② promoting ③ publicizing ④ denouncing

(2) Fingerprints on the gun were ( ) evidence that the suspect was guilty.
① conclusive ② decisive ③ indisputable ④ refutable

(3) As time was short, he ( ) his schedule.
① abbreviated ② prolonged ③ shortened ④ curtailed

(4) Two witnesses must ( ) that this is your signature.
① specify ② certify ③ verify ④ confirm

(5) The multinational corporation ( ) both its domestic and overseas business last year.
① downsized ② expanded ③ enlarged ④ amplified

(6) Although he often disagreed with me, he was a ( ) youth.
① well-mannered ② discourteous ③ mannerly ④ respectful

(7) Our boss's ( ) reply offended our feelings.
① abrupt ② curt ③ gruff ④ point-blank

(8) He delivered a speech ( ) the need for more volunteers.
① emphasizing ② stressing ③ accenting ④ appealing to

Answer: D. (1) Johnny (2) you (3) is (4) What (5) black
E. (1) ④ (2) ④ (3) ② (4) ① (5) ① (6) ② (7) ④ (8) ④

숙 어

(1) **second only to** (=not quite as good as something, but still very good)
~다음으로 첫째
☞ As a soccer player he is *second only to* Tom in skill.

(2) **second to none** (=better than all others, the best) 둘째 가라면 서러운
☞ Their new product is *second to none* in quality.

(3) **settle down** (=become calm; establish residence)
(흥분등이) 가라앉다; 정착하다
☞ After the excitement *settled down*, they decided to *settle down* there.

(4) **shed light on** (=cast[throw] light on) (~의 해결에) 실마리를 주다
☞ These clues *shed* new *light on* the mystery.

(5) **shop around** (=compare prices in different shops for the best price)
여기저기 다니며 값을 비교하다
☞ *We shopped around* before deciding which furniture to buy.

(6) **single out** (=select ~ alone from others) (유독) ~만을 뽑아내다
☞ They were all to blame; why did you *single* him *out* for punishment?

(7) **sleep on** (=think about ~ overnight) ~을 하룻밤 자면서 생각하다
☞ Can I *sleep on* it and let you know my decision in the morning?

(8) **spy into** + 사물 (=collect secret information about) 몰래 조사하다
spy on + 사람 (=watch secretly) 몰래 감시하다
☞ He's always *spying into* my actions.
☞ He's always *spying on* me.

(9) **stand to reason** (=make sense, be logical) 당연하다, 이치에 맞다
☞ If you have a driver's license, it *stands to reason* that you can drive.

(10) **stand up for** (=defend, side with) 옹호하다, (~의) 편을 들다
☞ He always *stands up for* what he thinks is right.

(11) **stir up** (=get ~ into trouble) (분란 따위를) 일으키다
☞ Don't *stir* things *up* again by refusing to go there.

(12) **storm out of** (=walk out of ~ in a very angry manner) 화가 나서 뛰쳐나가다
☞ He tore up the contract and *stormed out of* the room.

⒀ **strike up** (=begin to sing[play]) (노래·연주 따위를) 하기 시작하다
☞ Someone *struck up* a song, and we all joined in.

⒁ **suit oneself** (=do what one likes) 마음[생각]대로 하다
☞ I don't feel like going out tonight.— *Suit yourself.*

⒂ **take a fancy to** (=become fond of) ~을 좋아하게 되다
☞ I've *taken a* sudden *fancy to* those pink pants.

⒃ **take advantage of** + 사물 (=make use of) ~을 이용하다
take advantage of + 사람 (=cheat, deceive) 누구를 속이다
☞ I'll *take advantage of* my business trip to Paris to see the sights.
☞ The salesman *took advantage of* me by charging me too much for it.

⒄ **take one's time** (=act slowly) 천천히 하다
☞ You can *take your time* altering that dress; I don't need it right away.

⒅ **take something out on** (=vent one's anger on a person or object) 어떤 것을 ~에게 화풀이하다
☞ When he's had a bad day he *takes* it *out on* his wife and children.

⒆ **take the bull by the horns** (=face a difficult situation boldly) 용감히 맞서다
☞ I'll have to *take the bull by the horns* and demand a raise from my boss.

⒇ **take the liberty of** (=act on one's own authority without permission from another) (이해해 줄 것을 기대하고) 허락없이 ~하다
☞ I *took the liberty of* helping myself to a drink.

Exercise

▶▶ 주어진 단어들을 포함한 글을 지어라. 필요하면 어형을 변화시켜라.

1. family / settle / Midwest / farming
2. shop / buy / inexpensive
3. sleep / decide / accept / offer
4. job / stand / reason / find
5. storm / shouting / quit
6. can't / tell / what / suit
7. take / advantage / opportunity
8. fast / take / enjoy / meal
9. often / anger / take / out
10. take / liberty / borrow / away

20. 도치, 강조, 생략, 공통관계, 삽입, 동격

(Inversion, Emphasis, Ellipsis, Common Relation, Parenthesis, Apposition)

기본 문법 설명

A. 도치

(1) 구문상의 도치
ⓐ Where **have you** been for the last week?
ⓑ **How tedious** life is! **What courage** he has!
ⓒ There **is** no **royal road** to learning.
ⓓ **May you** succeed!
ⓔ **Had I** known it, I would have told it to you.
ⓕ **Woman as** I am, I may be of great help to you.

(2) 목적어의 도치
ⓐ **Which** of the two secretaries did you talk to?
ⓑ **That mountain** we are going to climb.
What I had given myself to I finally achieved.
ⓒ **Not a word** did she say all day long.

(3) 보어의 도치
ⓐ **Who** are all those people?
ⓑ How **smart** he is!
ⓒ **Happy** is he who is contented with his life.
ⓓ **The more learned** a man is, **the more modest** he usually is.

(4) 부사(구)의 도치
ⓐ **Well** do I remember the scene of carnage.
ⓑ **Here and there over the grass** bloomed wild flowers.
ⓒ She loves animals, and **so does** her husband.
ⓓ **Not till years afterwards** was he able to understand it.

B. 강조

(1) I **do** hope you will help us. Who **did** break the window?
(2) This is the **very** book I have been looking for.
(3) Who **ever** could it be?
(4) I know nothing **whatsoever** about it.
(5) What **on earth** have you done to your hair?
What **in the world** are you doing?
(6) The car was running at the **highest** speed **possible**.

A. 도 치 (Inversion)

- 구문의 성질에 의한 도치
- 뜻을 강조하기 위한 도치
  —목적어, 보어, 부사(구)를 문두에 둔다.

(1) **구문상의 도치**

ⓐ 의문문 What's the matter with you?

ⓑ 감탄문 How fast he runs!

ⓒ There is ~. 의 구문 (학문에 왕도는 없다.)

ⓓ 기원문 (부디 성공하기를!)
May you live long!

ⓔ if가 생략된 조건문
= If I had known it, ~.

ⓕ as를 포함한 양보의 구문
= Though I am a woman, ~.
Poor *as* he is, he is happy.

(2) **목적어의 도치**

ⓐ 의문사가 목적어이다.
(어느쪽 비서에게 이야기 했느냐?)
☞ Who[Whom] do you want to speak with? …의문사가 문두에 나갈 때는, 목적격보다 주격을 쓰는 경향이 강함.

ⓑ 강조하기 위하여 목적어를 문두에 둠.
(저 산을 우리는 오르려고 한다.)
(몰두해왔던 것을 나는 드디어 해냈다.)
= I finally achieved what I had given myself to.

ⓒ 목적어를 문두에 내고 강조하였으며, 조동사 did를 앞에 놓았다.
(한 마디 말도, 그 여자는 하루 종일 하지 않았다.)

(3) **보어의 도치**

ⓐ 의문문 What is this?

ⓑ 감탄문 What a beautiful girl she is!

ⓒ 강조하기 위해 보어를 문두에 놓았다.
(자기 생활에 만족하는 사람은 행복하다.)
Blessed are the poor in spirit.
(마음이 가난한 자는 복이 있다.)

ⓓ 「the+비교급」에 의해 수식될 때 도치됨.
(사람은 배움이 높을수록 대개 더욱 겸손해진다.)
The more dangerous it is, *the more attractive* it becomes.

(4) **부사(구)의 도치**

강조하기 위해 부사어구가 앞에 나가 도치 구문을 만드는 예가 많은데, 특히 부정을 나타내는 어구에 많다.

ⓐ (나는 그 학살현장을 지금도 역력히 기억한다.) … do가 끼어든 도치
On this depends the success of our plan.

ⓑ (풀밭 여기저기 야생화들이 피어 있었다.) …「부사구+V+S」

ⓒ (그녀는 동물을 사랑하는데, 그녀 남편도 그렇다.) …「so+V+S」
You are not wrong, *nor is* he.

ⓓ (수년 후에야 비로소 그는 그것을 이해할 수 있었다.) …부정의 뜻의 부사구가 문두에 나갔다.
☞「부사(구)+조동사(조동사가 없으면 do)+S+V」의 어순일 때가 많다.
Never have I seen such a wonderful sight.
Little did I dream that I would never see her again.
To none but the wise can wealth bring happiness.

B. 강 조 (Emphasis)

- do · very · 부사(구) · 어구반복
- 강조 구문 등에 의한 강조

(1) 강조의 do
Yet the earth dóes move.

(2) 강조의 very
(이것이 바로 내가 찾고 있었던 그 책이다.)

(3) 부사 ever가 강조의 뜻으로 쓰였다.
(도대체 그자가 누구일까요?)

(4) (나는 그것에 관하여 아무것도 모른다.)
[whatsoever = whatever, at all]

(5) on earth, in the world는 강조의 부사구.
(도대체 머리를 어떻게 해 놓은거야?)
(너는 도대체 뭘 하고 있는거니?)
What *the devil* is it all about?
(도대체 이 모든게 웬 소동이냐?)

(6) 최상급에 possible을 붙여 강조했다.
(그 자동차는 그 이상 더 낼 수 없는 속력으로 질주하고 있었다.)

	(7) **It is** you **who** are to blame for the accident. **It is** not until one gets sick **that** one knows how valuable health is. (8) It rained for **hours** and **hours** and **hours**. The door opened **very, very** slowly. (9) I **came**, I **saw**, I **conquered**. (10) I **myself** will resolve the difficult issue. His explanation was simplicity **itself**.
C. 생략	(1) The report was very critical though (it was) fair. (2) To some life is pleasure; to others (life is) suffering. (3) No parking (is allowed here). (If you take) No pains, (you will get) no gains.
D. 공통관계	(1) My sister, not my brother, **went** with me. (2) His energy is not and cannot be **what it was**. (3) We can, and indeed must **help** our needy neighbors. (4) Passions weaken, but habits strengthen, **with age**. (5) **A man** of virtue, and not of wealth, deserves our respect.
E. 삽입	(1) This is, **I am sure**, what he means. (2) When **do you suppose** the riot will be calmed down? This is the policy which **everybody thinks** is very wrong. (3) The judge, **who was honest**, was respected by all the people. He is, **as I said before**, very punctual.
F. 동격	(1) Mr. Smith, **a psychiatrist**, solved her mental problems. (2) I have heard the *news* **of** *our team's victory.* (3) He has but one **aim** in life, **to make money**. (4) The fact **that he is dishonest** is known to everybody. The question arose **who was to receive him**. (5) I am apt to judge my fellow men in comparison with myself, **a wrong and foolish thing to do**.

(7) It is ~ that의 구문 : It is 다음에 놓이는 어구가 강조된다. ☞ 이 때 that은 who나 혹은 which로 대치할 수도 있다.
(그 사고에 책임있는 사람은 바로 너다.)
(사람은 병이 들고 나서야 비로소 건강이 얼마나 귀중한가를 안다.)
(8) 동일 어구를 반복하여 강조했다.
All, all are gone.
(9) 접속사 and를 생략하여 긴박감을 나타냄.
(나는 왔다, 보았다, 정복했다.) - *Caesar*
(10) 재귀대명사의 강조 용법
(내가 직접 그 어려운 문제를 처리하겠다.)
(그의 설명은 매우 단순했다.)
☞ 추상명사 + itself = very + 형용사

C. 생 략 (Ellipsis)

품사가 거의 모두 다 생략될 수 있고, 생략의 경우도 너무 많으니, 여기서는 대표적인 것만 예를 들겠다.

(1) 「S+be동사」의 생략 : 부사절이 as, though, if, when, while 등으로 유도될 때
(그 보고서는 공평했지만 매우 비판적이었다.)
When (I was) a boy, I liked her.
Come with me, if (it is) possible.
(2) 반복을 피하기 위한 생략
(어떤 사람에게는 인생이 즐겁지만 다른 사람에게는 고통이다.)
The sun shines in the daytime and the moon (shines) at night.
Hate breeds hate; violence violence.
(증오는 증오를 낳고, 폭력은 폭력을 낳는다.)
The dimmer economic prospects get in Tokyo, it seems, the brighter Seoul's become.
(일본의 경제전망이 어두워질수록 한국의 경제전망은 더 밝아 보인다.)
(3) 관용적 생략 : 관용어구, 일상적인 인사말, 격언, 게시 용어 등에 많다.
(I wish you a) Good morning.
(It is) Well done!
If only he were here (how happy I would be)!
(If there are) So many men, (there are) so many minds. (각인각색)

D. 공통관계 (Common Relation)

· 주어 · 목적어 · 술어 · 피수식어
· 수식어가 공통어

(1) went는 sister와 brother의 공통어
(2) what it was는 is not과 cannot be에 공통적으로 걸린다.
(그의 체력은 예전과 같지 않으며, 또 그럴 수도 없다.)
(3) help는 can, must와 공통관계
(우리는 가난한 이웃을 도울 수 있고 또 도와야 한다.)
(4) with age(부사구)는 weaken에도 걸리고, strengthen에도 걸린다.
(정열은 연령과 더불어 약해지나, 습관은 연령과 더불어 강해진다.)
(5) 형용사구 of virtue와 of wealth는 a man에 공통적으로 걸린다.
(돈 있는 사람이 아니라 덕망이 있는 사람이 우리의 존경을 받을 가치가 있다.)

E. 삽 입 (Parenthesis)

· 「S+V」 · 구 · 종속절의 삽입

(1) 주절의 삽입 : 대개 comma나 dash를 앞뒤에 찍는다.
(2) 의문문이나 관계사절 안에서 comma의 표시 없이 주절이 삽입되는 경우
(3) 형용사절이나 부사절을 문중에 삽입하여 설명을 부가하는 경우

F. 동 격 (Apposition)

· 명사 · 부정사 · 문장 전체를 받는 어구 · 명사절이 동격어로 쓰임

(1) 명사가 동격의 역할
(2) of에 의해 유도되는 동격어구
the city of Paris (파리시)
(3) 부정사가 동격의 역할
(그는 인생에서 돈을 벌겠다는 목적 외에는 아무것도 없다.)
(4) 고딕체 부분의 문장 전체가 동격어
(누가 그를 접대할 것인가 하는 문제가 생겼다.)
(5) 고딕체 부분은 앞의 문장과 동격어
(내가 동료들을 나 자신과 비교하여 판단하기 쉬운데, 그것은 잘못된 바보짓이다.)

문법 · 작문

A. 다음 각 문장의 주어를 지적하여라.

(1) Side by side in the same city dwell rich and poor.
(2) Wide is the gate, and broad is the way that leads to destruction.
(3) What he meant by that nobody could tell.
(4) Like sunshine after the storm was the peaceful week which followed.
(5) There rose a thick smoke from the volcano.
(6) Those who love Nature she loves in return.
(7) Not until sunrise on the following morning did they see land.
(8) On the table beside me burned a lamp, and near it lay a little box.

B. 다음 각 문장의 이탤릭체 부분을 강조하여라.

(1) I *little dreamed* that I would meet a long-lost relative there.
(2) I *wish* I didn't have to go to work today.
(3) The rain came *down* in torrents.
(4) He arrived *at that moment*. (very를 써서)
(5) *Why* are you so mad? (it ~ that을 써서)
(6) *The runner had no sooner finished the marathon* than he fainted.

C. 다음 각 문장에서 생략할 수 있는 부분을 생략하여라.

(1) The higher the tree is, the stronger is the wind.
(2) The task having been completed, he went to bed.
(3) The bird may abandon the nest, leaving the chicks to die if it is disturbed.
(4) This is the book which was written by the famous novelist.
(5) He looks as he would look if he were ill.
(6) I came here because I wanted to come.
(7) Ten to one he will stay here for an hour or two.
(8) We'll have the party in the garden if the weather's good, but if the weather's not good, it'll have to be inside.

D. 다음 각 문장에서 생략된 부분을 보충하여라.

(1) "Do you predict we'll have rain tomorrow?" "No, I hope not."
(2) Spare the rod and spoil the child.
(3) Don't speak until spoken to.
(4) It matters not how long we live, but how.
(5) If wisely used, money may do much.
(6) Hands off.

E. 보기와 같이 다음 문장 안에서 공통어를 골라 밑줄을 쳐라.

[보기] Knowledge is not, cannot be, <u>everything</u>.

(1) No man can live by and for himself.

(2) Education means development, not only of the brain, but also of the body.

(3) It probably never happens that a person lives who has not, or has never had, anyone to love him.

F. Translate the following into Korean:

(1) *What he lacks in size and strength*, he makes up for in quickness and skill.

(2) To some life is pleasure; *to others*, *everything*. But a man's work must be his life, and *his life his work*, whether it is pleasure or anything else.

(3) The public games of Greece consisted in *athletic contests* of various kinds, generally connected with and forming a part of *a religious festival*.

G. Translate the following into English:

(1) 그는 회의에서 좀처럼 말하지 않지만, 일단 말하면 항상 요령 있게 말한다.

(2) 언제 불행이 닥칠지 알 길이 없다. 그러나, 불행이 일단 올 때 그것을 침착하게 맞을 준비가 되어 있어야 한다.

(3) 어떤 사람들은 자기가 하고 싶은 것을 할 시간을 낼 수 없다고 말하지만, 대부분의 경우 부족한 것은 진정 시간이 아니라 의지이다.

(4) 우리 나라의 경제 자립을 위해서 대외 무역을 증진시키는 것보다 더 필요한 것이 없다는 사실은 두말할 나위가 없다.

(5) 우리가 그것을 해야 할 것인가 하지 말아야 할 것인가 하는 문제가 대두되었다.

(6) 20년 전 고향을 떠날 때, 나는 다시 고향을 못 볼 거라고는 꿈에도 생각지 않았다.

(7) 우리는 큰 일뿐만 아니라 작은 일에도 주의해야 한다.

'Write a Story' — 70어 내외의 이야기를 영문으로 써라.

● 단 문 독 해 ●

Blessed are the merciful. **What I did** I did in honor. **Down** came the shower in torrents.

1. Closely **associated with** the regression in charity **is** the decline in men's regard for truth. At no period of the world's history has organized lying been practiced so shamelessly as by the political and economic dictators of the present century.

notes :
*the decline이 주어
*regression 퇴보
*regard for truth = 진리를 존중하는 마음
*organized lying (조직적인 거짓말)이 주어
*dictator 독재자

▶▶According to the above paragraph, what ultimately causes the regression in charity? Answer in two words.

▶▶영작하시오.
너무 화가 나서 그는 거의 말을 할 수가 없었다.

2. **The vices of others** we keep before our eyes, our own behind our backs; it often happens therefore that a man does not pardon another's faults who has more of his own.

notes :
*our own (vices)
*it happens that ~ = ~한 일이 일어난다

▶▶Which proverb is most suitable to explain the main topic of the above paragraph?
① Don't bite off more than you can chew.
② Don't judge a man until you've walked in his boots.
③ Familiarity breeds contempt.
④ The pot calls the kettle black.
⑤ Actions speak louder than words.

▶▶영작하시오.
그가 그것을 했다고, 나는 굳게 믿는다.

3. **So often** have I removed, **so rough** has been the treatment of my little library at each change of place, and, to tell the truth, **so little care** have I given to its well-being at normal times, that even the most attractive of my books show the results of unfair usage.

notes :
*remove 이사하다
*well-being 보존
*normal times = 평상시
*unfair 부당한
*usage 사용, 취급

▶▶윗글의 밑줄친 unfair usage의 내용을 설명하는 두 단어를 본문에서 찾아 쓰시오.

▶▶영작하시오.
내가 그 상을 타리라고는 꿈에도 생각지 않았다.

If wisely used, money may do much.
Lead always remains lead; **gold gold**.

4. **Though a brother**, he considered himself as my master, and me as his apprentice, and, accordingly, expected the same service from me as he would from **another**, while I thought he required too much of me, who from a brother expected more indulgence.

notes :
*Though (he was) a brother
*(considered) me
*as he would (expect) from another (apprentice)
*apprentice 견습공
*indulgence 관대

▶▶Which does **not** correspond with the above paragraph?
① The writer was learning some skills from his brother.
② The writer's brother regarded and treated him as if he were a subordinate novice.
③ The writer thought his brother expected too much of him.
④ It was the writer that wanted equality between him and the other workers.
⑤ The writer was disappointed at his brother's attitude toward him.

▶▶영작하시오.
혼자 남았을 때 그 여자는 무엇을 해야 할지 몰랐다.

5. Some people give no thought to the value of money until they have come to an end of it, and many do the same with their time. Lost wealth may be regained by industry and economy, **lost knowledge by study, lost health by temperance and medicine**, but lost time is gone forever.

notes :
*give thought to = ~을 생각하다
*temperance 절제

▶▶Lost wealth and health are not as important as lost time because they can be (　　　) by certain efforts, whereas lost time is impossible to (　　　).
[returned, obtained, regained, receive, recover, remain]

▶▶영작하시오.
여름휴가를 산으로 가는 사람들도 있고, 바닷가로 가는 사람들도 있다.

Passions weaken, but habits strengthen, **with age**.

6. The close of a year provides a natural occasion for mental pause and reflection. We survey the past, and we look forward, **resolved**, if we are serious, **to** make the best use of the new year's opportunities, and **to** face with courage its trials and discipline.

notes :
*reflection 반성, 숙고
*be resolved to ~ = ~할 결심이다
*opportunity 기회

▶▶Which of the following is most appropriate to describe the above paragraph?
① Reflection on the past
② Oncoming adversities
③ Making new year resolutions
④ Expectation of success
⑤ Devising a plan to cope with the future

▶▶영작하시오.
그는 새로운 출발을 하겠다고 결심하고 돌아왔다.

7. Art is always as much **concerned with** the way people feel about things as it is **with** the way things really are. Usually, both knowing and feeling go to make up a picture, and so paintings are different from one another, **depending on** whether the artist was more **interested in** what he saw or knew, or **in** what he felt; also **on** how much he saw, and knew, and felt.

notes :
*be concerned with ~ = ~와 관계가 있다
*depending on~ = ~에 따라서

▶▶윗글의 내용과 일치하도록 다음 빈칸에 가장 적절한 것은?
The creation of any art work is likely to depend on (   ).
① both an artist's experience and others' appreciation
② both others' criticisms and the artist's reaction to them
③ others' works as well as critics' views
④ both an artist's knowledge and his impression of objects.
⑤ an artist's sense and reputation

▶▶영작하시오.
인간은 환경의 창조물이 아니라 환경의 창조자이다.

> You can lead a horse to water, **I believe**, but you can't make him drink.
> We cannot deny the fact **that he is dishonest**.

8. My mother married my father largely, **it seems**, to help him out with his five motherless children. Having any child herself was a secondary consideration. Yet first she had a girl, then she had another girl, and it was very nice, **of course**, to have them, but slightly disappointing, because she belonged to the generation and tradition that made a son the really important event; then I came, a fine healthy child.

notes :
*largely = mainly
*she had a girl의 had는 낳았다(bore)의 의미

▶▶Which of the following does **not** correspond with the above paragraph?

① The writer's mother married his father mainly because of her sympathy for him.
② At first the writer's mother gave little thought to having any children herself.
③ The writer's father had previously had five children from another woman before he married the writer's mother.
④ In the generation of the writer's mother, no importance was given to the gender of a baby.
⑤ At last the writer's parents came to have eight children under their care.

▶▶영작하시오.

나는 그를 도와 그의 일을 끝내게 했다.

9. There is **this difference** between man and the lower animals, **that** what man does he has to learn how to do, while animals are able to do the most that they accomplish by what we call instinct; that is, without having to learn how.

notes :
*what man does는 how to do의 목적어
*that is = 즉
*how (to do)

▶▶Man is different from animals in that man has to (　　) the way to do his work, while animals do almost everything (　　).

[list, lead, learn, instinctively, intentionally, impeccably]

▶▶영작하시오.

민주주의는 모든 인간은 동등하게 태어났다는 생각에 바탕을 두고 있다.

● 장 문 독 해 ●

Warming-up

He considered himself a failure and **took to** drink.

The unfamiliarity of the thing makes it more difficult for us to understand it.

The point is that those people lack in responsibility and have low morality.

Our language **is full of** bad habits which must be gotten rid of.

I **am** quite **willing to** do anything for you.

1 A man may take to drink because he feels himself to be a failure, and then fail the more completely because he drinks. It is rather the same thing that is happening to the English language. It becomes ugly and inaccurate because our thoughts are foolish, but the slovenliness of our language makes it easier for us to have foolish thoughts. The point is that the process is reversible. Modern English, especially written English, is full of bad habits which spread by imitation and which can be avoided if one is willing to take the necessary trouble. If one gets rid of these habits one can think more clearly, and to think clearly is a necessary first step towards political regeneration: so that the first fight against bad English is not frivolous and is not the exclusive concern of professional writers.

George Orwell: *Politics and the English Language*

Notes

take to drink [drinking] 술에 빠지다 / slovenliness 단정치 못함 / point 요점 / process 과정 / reversible 뒤집을 수 있는 / imitation 모방 / get rid of = remove / regeneration 갱생, 쇄신 / so that = therefore / frivolous 경솔한, 하찮은 / exclusive 독점적인 / concern 관심사

Question

1. 다음 중 본문의 밑줄친 frivolous 와 바꿔 쓸 수 없는 것은?
   ① insignificant ② inconsiderable ③ invaluable
   ④ negligible ⑤ trivial

2. 밑줄친 the process is reversible의 내용을 구체적인 예를 들어 설명하시오.

3. Which of the following does **not** correspond to the passage?
   ① The author believes that it is necessary to take the trouble to correct the bad habits of the English language that have been spread by imitation.
   ② The fight against bad English is not solely the responsibility of professional writers.
   ③ The careless use of the English language is one of the causes of our political degeneration.
   ④ The messy usage of our English is partly due to the rapid change of our living circumstances.
   ⑤ The author claims that if we were to discard the bad usages of modern English, we could think more clearly and it would bring about a political improvement.

4. 다음 글이 본문의 주제문이 되도록 빈칸에 들어갈 말이 가장 잘 짝지어진 것은?

   The (   ) of our language is a prerequisite to achieving (   ).

   ① change — a social innovation
   ② imitation — a linguistic modernization
   ③ rediscovery — a cultural revolution
   ④ purification — a political renewal
   ⑤ investigation — the language skills

Production

(1) 너의 목표를 달성하지 못했다고 해서 자신을 실패자로 여겨서는 안 된다.
(2) 그는 결점이 조금 있지만, 그래도 여전히 나는 그를 사랑한다.
(3) 너는 그 나쁜 습관을 당장 없애야 한다.
(4) 그는 딱한 입장에 놓인 친구를 언제나 기꺼이 돕는다.

● 장 문 독 해 ●

Warming-up

There once lived a king who had three beautiful daughters.
The man **desirous of** success must work hard.
His health is **being** undermined by his excessive drink.
The dictator **had no idea of** calling in public opinion upon national affairs.
The meeting **came to an end** at last.

2 Why had the Roman Empire grown and why had it so completely decayed? It grew because at first the idea of citizenship held it together. (A) Throughout the day of the expanding republic, and even into the days of the early empire, there remained a great number of men conscious of Roman citizenship, feeling its privilege and an obligation to be a Roman citizen, confident of their rights under the Roman law and willing to make sacrifices in the name of Rome. (B) Citizenship spread indeed but not the idea of citizenship. (C) The Roman Empire did not educate, did not explain itself to its increasing multitudes of citizens, did not invite their cooperation in its decisions. (D) The adventurers who struggled for power had no idea of creating and calling in public opinions upon the imperial affairs. (E) All empires, all states, all organizations of human society are, in the ultimate, things of understanding and will. There remained no will for the Roman Empire in the world and so it came to an end.

H. G. Wells: *A Short History of the World*

Notes

decay 쇠퇴하다 / expanding 팽창하는 / privilege 특권 / obligation 의무 / confident of ~을 확신하는 / right 권리 / willing to 기꺼이 ~하는 / sacrifice 희생 / multitude 다수, 대중 / cooperation 협동 / decision 결정 / adventurer 모험자 / struggle 투쟁하다 / call in 불러들이다 / imperial affairs 국사(國事) / organization 조직체, 기관 / in the ultimate = ultimately 궁극적으로 / will 소망 / come to an end 끝나다

Question

1. 본문의 문맥의 흐름에 맞도록 다음 문장이 들어갈 위치를 고르시오.

But gradually the sense of citizenship was being undermined by the growth of wealth and slavery.

① (A) ② (B) ③ (C) ④ (D) ⑤ (E)

2. 로마의 번성과 로마의 쇠퇴의 근본 원인을 본문에서 무엇이라 지적했는지 우리말로 간단히 쓰시오.

3. Which of the following is **not** correct?
   ① Even though citizens spread greatly throughout the Roman Empire, the idea of citizenship did not.
   ② The author states that all organizations of human society exist only when there are people who understand them and support them.
   ③ The rulers of the Roman Empire had no thought of creating and inviting public opinions on imperial affairs.
   ④ A widening gap between the rulers and the general public of the Roman Empire caused its eventual collapse.
   ⑤ The more territory and people the Roman Empire had under its rule, the stronger it grew.

4. Which of the following is **not** referred to as a cause of the fall of the Roman Empire?
   ① The lack of education to encourage the idea of citizenship
   ② The citizens' exclusion from the national decision-making process
   ③ The rulers' arbitrary administration of the state without any consultation with the public
   ④ The national defense weakened by frequent external aggressions
   ⑤ The weakened sense of citizenship caused by the increase of wealth and slaves

Production

(1) 그 나라는 이웃나라의 도움을 구했다.
(2) 너를 위한다면 기꺼이 무엇이나 하겠다.
(3) 드디어 1학기가 끝나고, 손꼽아 기다리던 여름방학이 시작되었다.
(4) 우리는 요구할 권리뿐만 아니라, 수행해야 할 의무도 있다는 것을 알아야 한다.

실 력 체 크 Ⅰ

1 다음 글을 읽고 아래의 물음에 답하시오.

Now man is beginning to understand that ⓐeach advance to a better life has almost invariably come at the expense of his environment. Automobiles have enabled us to travel short and long distances comfortably, but automobile exhausts poison the air. Chemical insect killers improve crop yields, and chemical weed killers eliminate backbreaking hand labor, but they also pollute the streams and the atmosphere.

We can never get rid of all pollution. To return our natural surroundings to their original purity would involve a return to stone age living conditions. Man can, however, improve the quality of the surroundings if he is willing to pay ⓑthe costs involved. He may have to give up rapid growth; his taxes may rise; and some of the products he buys, now produced cheaply at the expense of his environment, will cost more. At present, the increasing quantity of goods produced put pollutants back into our skies, waterways, and lands at a rate so fast that ⓒthey cannot be assimilated without creating harmful effects.

notes:
invariably 변함없이 / at the expense of ~ = ~을 희생하여 / enable A to V = A가 ~하는 것을 가능하게 하다 / automobile exhausts = 자동차 배기 가스 / poison 오염시키다 / eliminate 제거하다 / backbreaking (육체적으로) 몹시 힘든 / get rid of ~ = ~을 제거하다 / purity 깨끗함, 맑음 / goods 상품 / pollutant 오염물질 / not A without B = A하면 반드시 B한다 / assimilate 흡수시키다

(1) 밑줄친 ⓐ를 우리말로 옮기시오.

(2) 밑줄친 ⓑthe costs involved는 구체적으로 무엇을 나타내는가? 그것을 본문안의 순서에 따라 간략하게 쓰시오.

(3) 밑줄친 ⓒ를 우리말로 옮기시오. (단, they의 내용을 명시할 것.)

2 다음 글의 대의가 될 수 있는 것을 고르시오.

In any matter of which the public has imperfect knowledge, public opinion is as likely to be erroneous as is the opinion of an individual equally uninformed. To hold otherwise is to hold that wisdom can be got by combining many ignorances. A man who knows nothing of algebra cannot be assisted in the solution of an algebraic problem by calling in a neighbor who knows no more than himself, and the solution approved by the unanimous vote of a million such men would count for nothing against that of a competent mathematician.

notes:
erroneous 잘못된 / uninformed 무식한 (=ignorant) / hold 생각하다, 주장하다 / algebra 대수학 / call in = ~을 불러들이다 / unanimous 만장[전원] 일치의 / count for nothing = 아무 가치가 없다 / competent 유능한

① Public opinion should always be valued.
② The opinion of an individual counts for much.
③ Public opinion tends to be erroneous.
④ A unanimous vote is not always right.
⑤ Only a mathematician can solve an algebraic problem.

3 다음은 어느 작가와 어느 부인의 대화이다. 아래 물음에 답하시오.

> "What a bit of luck that I'm placed next to you," said Laura, as we sat down to dinner.
> ⓐ"For me," I replied politely.
> ⓑ"That remains to be seen. I particularly wanted to have the chance of talking to you. I've got a story to tell you."
> ⓒAt this my heart sank a little. ⓓ"I'd sooner you talked about yourself," I answered, "or even about me."
> "Oh, but I must tell you the story. I think you'll be able to use it."
> ⓔ"If you must, you must. But let's look at the menu first."
> ⓕ"Don't you want me to?" she said, somewhat aggrieved. "I thought you'd be pleased."

notes :
be placed = 자리잡다 / particularly 특히 / aggrieve 괴롭히다

(1) 밑줄친 ⓐ의 생략된 부분을 보충하여 완전한 문장으로 만드시오.

(2) 밑줄친 ⓑ, ⓔ를 우리 말로 옮기시오.

(3) 밑줄친 ⓒ의 뜻을 영어로 달리 표현하시오.

(4) 밑줄친 ⓓ와 같은 의미가 되도록 다음 공란을 메우시오.
I want you to talk about yourself rather than _____.

(5) 밑줄친 ⓕ에서 생략된 부분을 보충하시오.
Don't you want me to ____________________?

4 다음 글의 요지를 가장 적절하게 나타낸 것을 하나 고르시오.

> It is unlikely that many of us will be famous or even remembered. But no less important than the brilliant few that lead a nation or a literature to fresh achievements, are the unknown many whose patient efforts keep the world from running backward; who guard and maintain the ancient values, even if they do not conquer new; whose inconspicuous triumph it is to pass on what they inherited from their fathers, unimpaired and undiminished, to their sons. Enough, for almost all of us, if we can hand on the torch, and not let it down; content to win the affection, if possible, of a few who know us, and to be forgotten when they in their turn have vanished.

notes :
the brilliant few = 소수의 유명인 / the unknown many = 다수의 무명인 / ancient values = 조상이 남긴 귀중한 가치[것들] / inconspicuous 눈에 띄지 않는 / triumph 큰 업적 / it is의 it은 가주어, 보어는 triumph / unimpaired 손상되지 않은 / undiminished 감소되지 않은 / hand on ~ = ~을 후세에 전하다 / torch 횃불, 전통 / let it down = 그것을 끄다 / affection 애정 / vanish 사라지다

ⓐ It is a few great men of genius that create civilization.
ⓑ The unknown many are less important than the brilliant few.
ⓒ We must maintain old values and pass them on to our sons.
ⓓ Great men alone cannot keep up a high level of civilization.
ⓔ Our civilization goes on thanks to the efforts of great men.

실 력 체 크 Ⅱ

A. 이탤릭체로 된 동사를 문장 끝에 있는 괄호 안의 동사로 대치하여라.

(1) It is hard to *discriminate* between counterfeit notes and genuine money. (tell)

(2) We sincerely *thank* you for your valuable help. (appreciate)

(3) She *gave* him everything he needed. (provide)

(4) He *used* the last two days to settle his private affairs. (devote)

(5) Within a generation we will *replace* coals and oil with atomic energy. (substitute)

(6) The boss *expressed* deep regret to us for staff reduction. (apologize)

B. 이탤릭체로 된 낱말을 명사로 하여 다음 문장을 다시 써라.

(1) Though he's recently *failed* the driving test, he's still hopeful.

(2) When night *approached*, the street became quiet.

(3) Many people *attended* the meeting yesterday.

(4) They *concluded* hastily about the matter.

(5) No one has informed us that he has *decided* to run for office.

(6) I don't doubt that he will be *able* to carry it through.

(7) It was obvious that she was *anxious* to please him.

(8) You have to *look* at the article carefully before you buy it.

C. 다음 각 문장을 단문으로 고쳐 써라.

(1) The sense of smell seems to diminish as we grow older.

(2) Are you going out when it is raining so heavily?

(3) The boys ran off the moment they saw the owner of the orchard.

(4) If you give me your assistance, my success will be certain.

(5) If you had not encouraged me, I would have given up the plan.

Answer: A. (1) tell counterfeit notes from genuine money (2) appreciate your valuable help (3) provided him with (4) devoted the last two days to settling (5) substitute atomic energy for coals and oil (6) apologized deeply to us for staff reduction
B. (1) In spite of his recent failure in the ~. (2) With the approach of night, the street ~. (3) There was a large attendance at the ~. (4) They came to a hasty conclusion about ~. (5) us of his decision to ~. (6) doubt his ability to ~. (7) Her anxiety to please him was obvious. (8) take a careful look at the article before ~.
C. (1) diminish with age. (2) out in such a heavy rain? (3) off at the sight of the owner ~ (4) With your assistance, my success ~ (5) Without your encouragement, I would ~

D. 주어진 말로 시작해 의미가 가장 잘 통하도록 순서를 배열해 그 번호를 쓰시오.

(1) I believe

① so long as each nation pursues its own interests.

② aspire to peace,

③ trying to establish mutual understanding;

④ that men of good will throughout the world

⑤ but true international cooperation is difficult

⑥ it can be taken for granted

(2) The invention of the pendulum was suggested to Galileo

① he observed a lamp,

② by a circumstance somewhat similar to that

③ when Galileo was standing one day in the Metropolitan Church of Pisa,

④ swing backwards and forwards.

⑤ which was suspended from the ceiling,

⑥ which started Newton's mind to the discovery of the theory of gravitation:

E. 다음 (1)~(5)의 대화를 읽고 밑줄 친 곳에 공통어를 써넣어라.

(1) (a) Could I please take a _____ or two off some time next week?

(b) Sure, no problem. What do you say we finish up here and then call it a _____?

(2) (a) My sister only paid 7 dollars for that CD. I thought that was _____.

(b) Well, _____ prices do not necessarily mean _____ quality.

(3) (a) Could you just wait a _____ while I ask my son who won the race?

(b) It's ok. I already know. Tom came first and Jim finished _____.

(4) (a) Where exactly is the group discussion going to take _____?

(b) I believe that it is planned to start at six o'clock at Tom's _____.

(5) (a) It looks like the soccer match has been put _____ to this week.

(b) Really? What a shame, I was looking _____ to playing next weekend.

F. "English"라는 제목으로 30~40어의 영문을 지으시오.

Answer: D. (1) ⑥-④-②-③-⑤-① (2) ②-⑥-③-①-⑤-④

E. (1) day (2) cheap (3) second (4) place (5) forward

F. Nowadays English is a universal language. It is not too much to say that just as we cannot live without water, we cannot lead a comfortable life without some knowledge of English. (33 words)

어 휘 · 발 음

A. 다음 단어의 올바른 어형을 공란에 써 넣어라.

indulge, relate, obstinate, ignorance, legal, vary

(1) We remained blissfully ______ of the trouble that lay ahead.

(2) English people willingly accept as their national emblem the bulldog, an animal noted for its ______, ugliness, and impenetrable stupidity.

(3) He was posing as a wealthy Las Vegas gambler who wanted lawmakers to ______ casinos in Arizona.

(4) So intimate is the ______ between a language and the people who speak it that the two can scarcely be thought of apart.

(5) All the pleasures and ______ of the weekend are over, and now I have to return to my boring day job.

B. 공란에 들어갈 단어를 골라라.

(1) He turned the ______ softly and pushed open the door.
(a) key (b) keyhole (c) lock (d) lack

(2) Having many children, they want to ______ a nanny.
(a) let (b) lend (c) rent (d) hire

(3) It ______ me that there might be some fault on my part.
(a) struck (b) flashed (c) occurred (d) happened

(4) He failed to get elected ______ to our expectations.
(a) opposed (b) contrary (c) contrasted (d) opposing

(5) The policeman ______ to take the bribe.
(a) defied (b) denied (c) refused (d) accepted

C. 이탤릭체로 된 단어의 동의어를 골라라.

(1) He feared his father's *wrath*.
(a) rage (b) outcry (c) grievance (d) criticism

(2) They lived a very *tranquil* life.
(a) eventful (b) stormy (c) placid (d) monotonous

(3) She *cherishes* his memory still in unforgetting affection.
(a) remembers (b) recollects (c) holds dear (d) revives

(4) *Thrift* is the source of wealth.
(a) Good health (b) Finance (c) Economy (d) Extravagance

Answer: A. (1) ignorant (2) obstinacy (3) legalize (4) relation (5) indulgences
B. (1) (a) (2) (d) (3) (a) (4) (b) (5) (c) C. (1) (a) (2) (c) (3) (c) (4) (c)

D. 아래 ⓐ~ⓘ의 (　　) 속의 단어를 명사형으로 바꾸어, (1)~(9) 문장의 (　　)에 넣으시오.

ⓐ in (acknowledge) of	ⓑ in (compare) with	ⓒ with the (except) of
ⓓ in (oppose) to	ⓔ in (respond) to	ⓕ to the (satisfy) of
ⓖ in (consider) of	ⓗ in (connect) with	ⓘ within (see) of

(1) The green curtains seemed too bright to me (　　) the dull gray wall.

(2) He has worked at the company for thirty years, and the management is going to give him a special bonus (　　) his service.

(3) Sailing in antiquity was a perilous venture, and it was the rule whenever possible to keep (　　) land, and anchor the ships at night.

(4) The unions are (　　) the government over the issue of privatization.

(5) The house was old; under the clean white paint, the woodwork was cracked and worm-eaten. (　　) his uncertain tap with the knocker, a maid came to the door.

(6) (　　) your recent application we are sorry to tell you we are unable to offer you the job.

(7) The experiment was successful (　　) us all.

(8) (　　) John, everyone passed the exam.

(9) (　　) his young age, the judge didn't put him in jail.

E. 다음 (　　) 안에 알맞는 공통어를 써 넣으시오.

(1) (a) Water seeped through the (　　) in the basement wall.
(b) We've worked 24 hours without a (　　).

(2) (a) To be (　　), I don't think you have talent to be a great violinist.
(b) A (　　) photograph is more natural than any other one.

(3) (a) The (　　) of the new subway is scheduled for next year.
(b) There are no (　　)s for secretaries at the company at present.

(4) (a) In the dark room she (　　)d over a stool.
(b) I (　　)d on the answer to the riddle.

(5) (a) Who (　　)ed the slogan 'In consideration of others, No smoking'?
(b) I changed a $5 bill because I needed some (　　)s for the vending machine.

Answer: D. (1) ⓑin comparison with (2) ⓐin acknowledgement of (3) ⓘwithin sight of (4) ⓓin opposition to (5) ⓔIn response to (6) ⓗIn connection with (7) ⓕto the satisfaction of (8) ⓒWith the exception of (9) ⓖIn consideration of
E. (1) break (2) candid (3) opening (4) stumble (5) coin

숙 어

(1) **take the place of** (=act instead of) ~을 대신하다, ~의 자리를 차지하다
☞ Robots have now *taken the place of* workers in some factories.

(2) **take to** (=get into the habit of) ~의 습관이 붙다
☞ The insane old man has *taken to* hiding his socks under the carpet.

(3) **take turns ~ing** (=do something by turns) 교대로 ~하다
☞ They *took turns driving* so no one would be too tired.

(4) **take A up with B** (=raise and discuss A with B) A를 B와 의논하다
☞ We'll have to *take* it *up* first *with* our teacher.

(5) **talk someone out of ~ing** (=persuade someone to change his or her mind) 누구를 설득하여 ~하지 않도록 하다
☞ I tried to *talk* him *out of coming*, but all my advice was useless.

(6) **talk over** (=discuss thoroughly) ~에 관해 (상세히) 의논하다
☞ Let's *talk over* the entire plan and see if we discover any flaws.

(7) **tell ~ apart** (=distinguish between) ~을 구별하다
☞ Gold is similar in color to brass; I can't *tell* them *apart* well.

(8) **tell ~ off** (=scold, reprimand, rebuke) ~을 야단치다
☞ It's time someone *told* him *off* about his disrespectful behavior.

(9) **think nothing of** (=give little consideration to) ~를 아무렇지 않게 여기다
☞ He *thinks nothing of* driving 100 miles to see a new movie.

(10) **think over** (=ponder, reflect about) ~을 곰곰이 생각하다, 숙고하다
☞ I'll have to *think* it *over* carefully before I can say yes or no.

(11) **through thick and thin** (=through good and bad times) 좋을 때나 나쁠 때나
☞ His wife faithfully stuck to him *through thick and thin*.

(12) **to one's heart's content** (=as much as one likes) 마음껏
☞ There was so much food on the table that we could eat *to our heart's content*.

(13) **to say the least (of it)** (=at the very least) 아무리 너그럽게 말하더라도
☞ It's a boring novel, *to say the least (of it)*.

(14) **try one's hand at** (=try an unfamiliar task) ~에 (한번) 손 대보다
☞ I'll *try my hand at* bowling although I've never bowled before.

(15) **try out** (=test) ~을 시험해 보다
☞ The biochemists *tried out* the new medicine on real people.

(16) **turn down** (=refuse, reject) 거절하다
☞ I asked her to marry me but she *turned down* my proposal.

(17) **turn[hand] in** (=submit) 제출하다
☞ Don't *turn[hand]* it *in* but send it out by mail.

(18) **turn over a new leaf** (=start again with the intention of doing better) 심기일전하다
☞ He *turned over a new leaf* and behaved himself in class.

(19) **up in the air** (=not settled, undecided, uncertain) 미정인
☞ The proposal to build a golf course next to the airport is still *up in the air*.

(20) **use up** (=consume completely) 다 써버리다
☞ The kids *used up* all their money playing video games.

(21) **up to date** (=modern) 최신식의 ↔ **out of date** (=old-fashioned) 구식의
☞ The equipment here is really *up to date[out of date]*.

(22) **wait on ~ hand and foot** (=serve ~ extremely well) ~을 극진히 시중들다
☞ She *waited on* her sick husband *hand and foot*.

(23) **walk out** (=go on strike) 파업하다
☞ They threatened to *walk out* if their demands were not met.

(24) **wash up** (=do the dishes) 설거지하다
☞ He helped himself to my dinner and then, to add insult to injury, asked me to *wash up*.

(25) **waste one's breath (on)** (=gain nothing by talking (to)) 소용없는 말을 헛되이 지껄이다
☞ He was *wasting his breath on* her; she would not listen to him.

(26) **wear out** (=fatigue ; make ~ useless) 지치게 하다 ; 닳아 해어지게 하다
☞ She *wore* him *out* with her nagging. Those shoes are already *worn out*.

(27) **while away** (=spend time idly or pleasantly) 한가[느긋]하게 보내다
☞ I'm now *whiling away* the hours sunbathing in the garden.

(28) **wipe out** (=destroy) 파괴하다 ; 망하게 하다
☞ The bombing completely *wiped out* the small city.
The large chains are *wiping out* the independent bookstores.

(29) **without fail** (=for certain, without exception) 꼭, 반드시
☞ Each morning, *without fail*, he sits in the park and reads a paper.

(30) **word for word** (=in exactly the same words) 토씨하나 안 틀리게 그대로
☞ Tell me what she said, *word for word*.

(31) **work out** (=accomplish ; exercise) (계획 등을) 완수하다 ; 운동하다
☞ I've drawn up the main outlines and he'll *work out* the details later.
The famous actor keeps fit by *working out* for an hour every morning.

(32) **You bet** (=You can be absolutely sure) 틀림없이 ~하다
☞ "Are you coming?" "*You bet* I am."

(33) **zero in on** (=find out exactly, pinpoint) 정확하게 알아내다[맞히다], 딱 집어내다
☞ The electrician *zeroed in on* the exact cause of the problem.

Exercise

▶▶ 주어진 단어들을 포함한 글을 지어라. 필요하면 어형을 변화시켜라.

1. talk / without / argue
2. boss / tell / finish / time
3. think / nothing / work
4. offer / think / over
5. weekend / sleep / content
6. decide / turn / leaf / study
7. project / up / air
8. soldier / use / ammunition
9. workers / threaten / walk
10. waste / complain / supervisor
11. wear / shoes / months
12. village / wipe / air raid

해 답 편

- 문법 · 작문
- 단문독해
- 장문독해
- 실력체크 I
- 숙어 Exercise

제1장 동사의 종류

문법 · 작문 (p.14)

A.

(1) 완전 자동사	(2) 불완전 자동사
(3) 불완전 자동사	(4) 불완전 타동사
(5) 완전 자동사	(6) 불완전 자동사
(7) 완전 자동사	(8) 불완전 타동사
(9) 완전 자동사	(10) 불완전 자동사
(11) 불완전 자동사	(12) 완전 타동사
(13) 불완전 자동사	(14) 불완전 자동사
(15) 불완전 타동사	(16) 불완전 타동사
(17) 불완전 타동사	(18) 불완전 자동사
(19) 불완전 타동사	(20) 불완전 타동사

B.

(1) at을 뺌 (2) was를 뺌

(3) from을 뺌 (혹은 from ⇨ for로 바꾸거나, left ⇨ departed [started])

(4) lie ⇨ lay (5) did ⇨ made

(6) reminds me ⇨ reminds me of

(7) is belonged to ⇨ belongs to

(8) was를 뺌 (9) about을 뺌

(10) I concern ⇨ I'm concerned

(11) presented at ⇨ presented himself at

(12) well ⇨ good

C.

(1) X	(2) on	(3) to	(4) X
(5) on	(6) X	(7) on	(8) in
(9) X, to	(10) into	(11) X	(12) with
(13) with	(14) X	(15) of	(16) X
(17) X, X			

D.

(1) Last night it blew very hard and I could not sleep well.

(2) That incident which happened in my childhood still remains vivid in my memory.

(3) My father is sixty years old, but he looks very young for his age.

(4) He sighed a deep sigh at the news.

(5) Please lend me the book after you have read it.

(6) The death of her child nearly drove her mad.

(7) She helps her mother (to) wash the dishes every evening.

'What I Did Yesterday'

Yesterday morning I came up to Seoul by train from my home in Busan. At the station my uncle was waiting for me and I was taken by him to his house in Yongsan. All his family were glad to see me and encouraged me to do my best to pass the college entrance examination. In the evening I went to bed earlier than usual to have a good sleep.

단문독해 (p.16)

1. ▶▶해석

나는 미래를 과거보다 더 좋아지게 만들고 싶다. 나는 역사를 가득 채우고 있는 그런 실수와 과오로 미래가 오염되기를 원하지 않는다. 우리는 모두 미래에 대해 걱정해야 한다. 왜냐하면, 그것이 바로 우리가 여생을 보낼 곳이니까.

▶▶정답 ③

▶▶영작

We must not repeat the mistakes with which our history is filled.

2. ▶▶해석

전날 어느 젊은이가 자기의 무지를 한탄하며, 유식해지고 현명해지려면 무슨 책을 읽어야 하며, 무엇을 할 것인지 가르쳐 달라고 요청하면서, 나에게 편지를 보냈다. 나는 그에게 공손한 회신과 나에게 생각나는 그런 충고를 보냈다.

▶▶정답 ④

▶▶영작

A good idea occurred to me when I was just about to turn back.

3. ▶▶해석

젊은이가 자기는 아무것도 모른다는 사실, 그리고 자기는 별로 가치가 없다는 사실을 철저히 깨달았을 때, 그 다음 그가 배워야 할 일은 이 세상은 자기를 조금도 돌봐주지 않는다 — 자기는 자기가 돌봐야 한다는 사실이다.

▶▶정답 modest, self-reliant

▶▶영작

The first thing for you to learn in life is that there is nobody to depend on but yourself.

4. ▶▶해석

과학은, 관찰과 그 관찰에 입각한 추리에 의하여 우선 이 세상에 대한 특별한 사실을 발견하고, 그 다음 여러 사실을 서로 연결시켜 주고, 그리고 다행한 경우에는 미래에 일어나는 일들을 예측해 줄 수 있는 법칙을 발견하려는 시도이다.

▶▶정답 endeavor, through

▶▶영작

The factory set up a new machine that made it possible to perform tasks without workers.

5. ▶▶해석

나의 아버지는 특출하게 분별 있는 분이다. 나의 어린 시절을 돌이켜볼 때, 나는 아버지가 나를 항상 얼마나 잘 다루었는가를 알 수 있다. 아마 나는 한때 다루기가 좀 힘든 애였음에 틀림없다고 생각한다. 그러나, 아버지는 내가 제멋대로 하도록 내버려두지 않았으며, 또 무작정 반대를 하여 내가 화를 내게도 하지 않았다.

▶▶정답 ⑤

▶▶영작

He will always have his own way.

6. ▶▶해석

교육은 대학 교실 안에만 한정될 수 없는 끊임없는 과정이다. 교과서와 교사는 언제나 교육에 필수 불가결할 것이다. 그러나, 오늘날 점점 자기 세대의 다른 사람들과 같이 사는 경험으로부터 나오는 그런 종류의 지적인 발달에 중점을 두어 가고 있다.

▶▶정답 ⑤

▶▶영작

All through his life the butler remained faithful to his master.

7. ▶▶해석

우주비행사가 아무것도 밟지 않고 걸어서, 그가 집이라고 부르는 캡슐로 돌아오는 데 성공했다고 보도되었다. 이 우주의 업적은 종족간의 증오심 혹은 사소한 민족주의를 하잘 것 없는 것으로 만든다. 만약 언젠가 사람들이 우주 공간을 같이 거닐 때, 우주복 안에 있는 피부색이 핑크색이건, 검은색이건, 혹은 갈색이건, 무슨 상관이 있겠느냐?

▶▶정답 ④

▶▶영작

What does it matter whether she is beautiful or not?

8. ▶▶해석

비록 많이 읽었지만 나는 좋은 독서가가 못 된다. 나는 천천히 읽고, 띄어 넘으며 읽는 데도 재주가 없다. 책이 아무리 나쁘고 아무리 나에게 따분해도, 나는 그것을 끝마치지 않고 내버려두는 것이 어렵다는 것을 안다. 내가 처음부터 끝까지 읽지 않은 책을 열 손가락으로 꼽으려면 꼽을 수도 있다.

▶▶정답 widely, through

▶▶영작

You should leave it untouched.

9. ▶▶해석

우리나라를 오늘의 나라로 만든 분들이 바로 우리 조상이었듯이, 우리나라를 세계 자유 우방 속에 떳떳하게 낄 수 있는 나라로 만들 수 있는 사람은 바로 여러분이라고, 나는 진심으로 믿습니다.

▶▶정답 future, ancestors

▶▶영작

It was my uncle who made me what I am.

혹은 I owe what I am to my uncle.

10. ▶▶해석

그는 신사로서 대학에 가지도 않았고, 또 신사로서 돌아오지도 않았다. 그는 대학에 바보로서 갔고, 학자인 체하는 아니꼬운 존재가 되어서 돌아왔다. 그의 원래의 어리석음에 무한히 많은 양의 자부심이 덧붙었다.

▶▶정답 ②

▶▶영작

After ten years' absence he came back a completely changed man.

장문독해 (p.20)

1 ▶▶해석

새로운 문명이 우리 생활에 도래하고 있는데, 세계 도처에서 눈먼 사람들이 이 사실을 숨기려 하고 있다. 대략 1만 년 전의 농업 혁명이 우리가 이 시기를 역사적 변화의 첫 물결이라고 서술할 수 있는 것을 일으켰다. 그 다음 약 300년 전에 시작된 산업혁명이 오늘날 소멸되어 가고 있는 제2의 문명의 물결을 출발시켰다. 오늘 우리는 대변혁의 제3의 물결에 휩쓸려 들어가고 있다. 우리가 가지고 살아온 모든 규칙이 변화하고 있다는 사실을 알아도 놀래서는 안된다. 이와 같은 일은 하나의 시대가 다른 시대로 넘어갈 때는 항상 있는 일이다.

제2의 물결의 문명에서는 우리의 일상생활을 기계의 고동에 맞추었다. 이와 같은 문명에서 성장해왔기 때문에 우리의 부모는 모든 사람이 같은 시간에 직장에 도착해서 일해야 하며 출퇴근 시간의 교통 혼잡은 피할 수 없는 일이며, 식사 시간도 고정되어야 하고, 어린 애들은 시간 엄수에 대한 교육을 받아야 한다는 사실을 당연한 것으로 여긴다. 그들은 자식들이 약속지키는 일에 왜 그렇게 느슨하고 또 9시부터 5시까지 일하는 것이 그들에게는 아주 만족스러웠음에도 불구하고 왜 그것이 갑자기 그들의 아이들에 의해 견딜 수 없는 것으로 여겨져야 하는지를 이해할 수 없다.

그 이유는 제3의 물결이 휩쓸려 들어오면서 전혀 다른 시간 개념을 안고 들어오기 때문이다. 제2의 물결의 시대가 우리 생활을 기계의 속도에 맞추었다면 제3의 물결은 이런 기계적인 (시간) 조절에 도전하여, 우리의 기본적인 사회적 리듬을 변화시키고 또한 그렇게 함으로써 우리를 기계에서 해방시키는 것이다.

▶▶정답

1. careless
2. ⓐ agricultural ⓑ machine ⓒ freedom
3. ④ 4. ③

▶▶영작

(1) You would be surprised to find him doing such a thing.

(2) The next morning we awoke to find ourselves surrounded by natives.

(3) He seems to take it for granted that he will be elected as a representative.

2 ▶▶해석

인간은 약 100만 년 동안 생존해 왔는

데, 과학 기술은 기껏해야 200년 동안이다. 과학 기술이 이미 성취해 온 것을 보건대, 앞으로 그것이 성취할지도 모를 것에 어떤 한계를 짓는다는 것은 너무 성급한 일일 것이다. 그러나, 과학 지식은 사람을 취하게 하는 마취 음료 같은 것이어서, 인류는 이것을 아마 견디어내지 못할지도 모른다. 하늘에 도달하려는 소망으로 바벨탑을 쌓은 사람들처럼 원자의 비밀을 추구하는 사람들은, 인류와 그리고 아마 이 지구상의 모든 생물을 진멸시킬 수단을 우연히 제공함으로 해서 그 불경(不敬) 때문에 벌을 받을는지도 모른다. 어떤 견지로부터 보면, 이런 결말은 전적으로 애통해할 수만은 없다. 그러나, 이런 견해는 지구상의 우리의 견해일 수는 없다. 아마 어떤 먼 성운 가운데 어느 곳에, 어느 대수롭지 않은 별이 이성적인 생물이 사는 대수롭지 않은 혹성을 가지고 있을지도 모른다. 그리고, 아마 100만 년 후에 그들의 과학 기구에 의해, 절멸(絶滅)한 인류의 운명을 알게 되고, 그 결과 그들은 외무부 장관 회의의 협의 사항에 의견의 일치를 보게끔 될 것이다. 그렇게 된다면, 인류가 생존했었던 것은 아마 헛된 일이 아닌 것이 될 것이다.

▶▶정답

1. ④ 2. nuclear warfare
3. 핵전쟁에 의해 멸망하게 된 인류의 운명
4. ④ 5. ⑤

▶▶영작

(1) He went over to America in the hope of making a fortune.
(2) There might be some stars on which life exists.
(3) His sincerity led me to agree to his proposal.
(4) If your life can be a lesson to your children, you will not have lived in vain.

실력체크 I (p.24)

1 ②

2 others than our own

3

(1) ⓐ 문명이 정신적인 면보다 물질적인 면으로 너무 발달하여 균형이 깨어진 것.
ⓑ 우리의 지식과 능력이 아무도 상상할 수 없었던 정도로 부유해지고 증가됨으로 인하여.
ⓒ 우리가 문명의 물질적인 업적만을 너무 높이 평가하고, 정신적인 면을 망각하고 있는 문명에 대한 그릇된 개념.
(2) the importance of the spiritual element in life

4 ④

숙어 Exercise (p.30)

1. All the members of the team abound in courage.
2. His sickness accounts for his absence.
3. I had to stay at work after hours to finish my job.
4. All at once I heard a noise.
5. I can answer for his honesty.
6. Aside from joking, what do you mean by this?
7. We worked around the clock to finish the job.
8. As a rule men should wear tuxedos at formal parties.
9. His house is only a few miles from the lake as the crow flies.
10. He's asking for trouble driving like that.

제2장 동사의 시제

문법 · 작문 (p.38)

A.

(1) began, begun ; beginning
(2) occurred, occurred ; occurring
(3) cried, cried ; crying
(4) lay, lain ; lying (혹은 lied, lied ; lying)
(5) mimicked, mimicked ; mimicking
(6) chose, chosen ; choosing

B.

(1) lay (2) snows (3) will go
(4) have you been doing (5) gets
(6) has been (7) have been
(8) had known, became
(9) had hardly walked
(10) will have climbed

C.

(1) are being (2) will (3) Will
(4) broke (5) hear (6) has proved
(7) gone (8) raise

D.

(1) has the trouble started
⇨ did the trouble start
(2) 've를 뺌
(3) has passed ⇨ is[has been]
(혹은 Many years have passed)
(4) comes ⇨ will come
(5) it rained ⇨ it had rained
(6) will start ⇨ will have started
(7) is usually going ⇨ usually goes
(8) did ⇨ have
(9) was resembling ⇨ resembled
(10) has ⇨ has been
(11) lived ⇨ have lived
(12) gave ⇨ had given
(13) was ⇨ had been
(14) rose ⇨ have risen
(15) hung ⇨ hanged
(16) born ⇨ borne
(17) gone ⇨ been
(18) didn't ⇨ hasn't
(19) has ⇨ had
(20) has died ⇨ has been dead
(21) will break ⇨ breaks
(22) is standing ⇨ stands
(23) falling ⇨ shedding

E.

(1) Wait a little while till I get ready.
(2) Will you please come to my house if you are free?
(3) If I go by train, I will arrive there by noon.
(4) He is now seeing the sights of the city.
(5) Where have you been? I have been looking for you everywhere.
(6) I have never heard him speak well of others.
(7) When he awoke, his family had already finished their breakfast.
(8) As I had met him before, I recognized him at once.
(9) If he takes the entrance examination again this year, he will have taken it three times.

'Our school'

Our school stands on a hill and commands a fine view of our whole city. It has about 900 students and thirty teachers. It was founded 52 years ago and is famous all over the country. Our school boasts of its baseball team, which has won the nation-wide high school baseball championship for several years. As our school is an academic high school, all the students are much concerned with college entrance examinations. We are all studying very hard to keep up the reputation of our school.

단문독해 (p.40

1. ▶▶해석

우리가 단지 노력만 하면, 많은 것이 이루어질 것이다. 자기가 노력해 볼 때까지는 아무도 자기의 능력을 모른다 [노력해 보고 나서야 자기의 능력을 안다]. 그런데, 노력을 하도록 강요당할 때까지 자기의 최선을 다하는 사람은 거의 없다. "내가 이러이러한 일을 할 수만 있다면", 하고 실망에 찬 젊은이는 한숨쉰다. 그러나, 그가 단지 원하기만 해서는 아무것도 이루어지지 않을 것이다.

▶▶정답 ④

▶▶영작

You should try your best in everything [anything].

2. ▶▶해석

태고적부터 바닷물은 나가고 들어왔다. 태고적부터 어둠 다음에는 빛이 오고, 겨울 다음에는 봄이 오고, 죽음 다음에는 생명이 왔다. 지구와 이 끝없는 우주속 만물은 나는 새처럼 가볍고 그리고 새의 노래의 리듬처럼 공간속을 움직인다.

▶▶정답 ④

▶▶영작

He has gone through the ebb and flow of life.

3. ▶▶해석

내 마음은 그녀로 인해 슬펐다. 비록 나는 그녀를 사랑하기를 그쳤지만 위안을 찾지 못했다. 지난날의 쓰라린 고뇌 대신에 괴로운 공허감이 왔다. 이것은 아마 참기가 더 힘들었을 것이다. 사랑은 없어질지 모르지만, 추억은 여전히 남는다. 추억은 없어질지 모르지만, 위안은 그 때에도 오지 않는다.

▶▶정답 ④

▶▶영작

His unrequited love for a married woman gave him unbearable anguish.

4. ▶▶해석

돈을 벌기 위해 여러 방법을 써 온 한 거지가 있었다. 결국 그는 벙어리인 체하겠다고 생각했다. 어느 날, 그 거지의 얼굴을 알고 있는 한 신사가 지나갔다. 그 신사는 그 거지한테로 가서 갑자기 물었다. "벙어리가 된 지 얼마나 되느냐?" 그 거지는 불의의 습격(질문)을 받고 자기가 벙어리 노릇을 하고 있다는 것을 까맣게 잊고, 재빨리 이렇게 대답했다. "오, 선생님 제가 태어나서부터 죽 그랬습니다."

▶▶정답 ④

▶▶영작

I know him only by sight.

5. ▶▶해석

많은 재산을 상속받았으나, 그것을 다 써버릴 때까지 도저히 마음이 편치 않을 것이라고 말하는 한 부인을 나는 만난 적이 있다. 그 여자가 주장하기를, 소유물은 사람을 노예로 만들며, 사람은 소유물의 종이 되지 소유물의 주인은 안 된다는 것이었다.

▶▶정답 ②

▶▶영작

He had to get rid of the car due to financial problems.

6. ▶▶해석

고뇌와 노고로 지쳤으므로 나는 죽음과 같은 깊은 잠에 빠져들었다. 그리고, 그 다음날 아침 해가 뜨고 나서야 비로소 제정신으로 돌아왔다.

▶▶정답 regained, only

▶▶영작

It was not until the chairman appeared that the meeting began.

7. ▶▶해석

우리는 얼마 안가서 다시 우연히 만났다. 나의 집 근처 거리 골목에서 서로 마주쳤다. 나는 그가 변한 데 놀랐다.

▶▶정답 came, changed

▶▶영작

It will not be long before Korea is unified as we wish it to be.

8. ▶▶해석

우리 사이에는 어쩐지 깨지지 않을 것이라고 여긴 침묵이 흘렀다. 그러나, 그 침묵이 몇 초도 못 가서 매우 조용한 속에 급한 발자국 소리가 거리를 따라 점점 가까워지는 것을 나는 분명히 들었다.

▶▶정답 ③

▶▶영작

I had walked quite some distance when I found that my purse had been stolen.

9. ▶▶해석

나는 바다 건너 나의 조국에서 절약이 성공적인 삶의 필수적인 것 중의 하나라고 배워왔다. 우리 가족은 절약으로 유명한 나라(네덜란드)에서 왔다. 그러나 우리가 미국에 온 지 채 며칠도 되지 않아 자식들을 낭비의 나라로 데려왔다는 사실을 아버지는 뼈저리게 느꼈다.

▶▶정답 ④

▶▶영작

In business circles he is noted for his aggressive drive for M&A.

10. ▶▶해석

자연을 더욱 주의깊게 연구할수록, 질서가 더욱 광범하게 지배하고 있다는 것이 발견되었으며 반면에, 무질서하게 보였던 것이 단지 복잡성에 불과하다는 것이 입증되었다. 드디어, 오늘날 어떤 일이 우연히 일어난다든지 혹은 원인 없는 어떤 사고가 정말 있다고 믿을 만큼 그렇게 어리석은 사람은 없다.

▶▶정답 ④

▶▶영작

No one is as foolish as to believe such a lie.

장문독해 (p.44)

1 ▶▶해석

그 개울들은 거의 1년 내내 말라 있었다. 그러나, 말라 있지 않을 때는 물이 소리를 내며 콸콸 흘렀다. 눈이 산에서 녹을 때 이 개울들은 소리를 내기 시작했고, 어디선지 모르게 개구리, 거북, 물뱀, 그리고 물고기들이 여기에 모여 들었다. 봄이면 물살이 빨랐다. 그리고, 그것과 더불어 사람들의 마음도 바빴다. 그러나, 들판이 초록색에서 갈색으로 변하고, 꽃이 열매가 되고, 수줍은 듯 따뜻하던 날씨가 교만한 무더위로 변할 때, 개울의 물도 느려지고 사람의 마음도 게을러졌다. 언덕에서 내려오는 첫물은 차고 빠르고 무서웠다. 그것은 너무 차가워, 애들이 옷을 벗고 그 속에 들어갈 수가 없었다. 한 소년이 혼자서 혹은 애들 틈에 끼어 개울 둑에 서서 오랫동안 물을 지켜보다가 개울물한테 매우 도전을 당했으므로, 옷을 훌떡 벗어 던지고 뛰듯이 물 속으로 다이빙을 하고는 숨을 헐떡이며 물 위로 나와 저쪽 둑으로 헤엄쳐 건너가곤 했다. 만약 그 소년이 또래들 중에서 제일 먼저 물 속으로 뛰어들면, (남들은 물 속에 들어갔는데 너는 비겁해서 못했다는) 수치를 안고 집으로 돌아가지 않기 위해 다른 소년들도 그를 따라 뛰어들곤 했다. 이렇게 된 것은 물이 차가웠기 때문만은 아니었으며, 아니 차라리 개울물이 아이들하고 노닥거릴 시간이 없었기 때문이었다(물살이 빨랐기 때문이었다). 봄철의 물은 매우 비우호적이었다.

▶▶정답

1. 빠른 물살과 더불어 사람들의 마음도 조급해졌다.
2. swift, swim 3. ⑤ 4. ③

▶▶영작

(1) The river was too cold for the boys to swim in.

(2) I got up early in order not to be late for the first train.
(3) He was the first to arrive at the office and the last to leave.

2 ▶▶해석
나의 계획은 명확 간결하고 합리적이었다고 나는 생각한다. 여러 해 동안 나는 세계의 여러 곳을 여행해 왔다. 미국에서 나는 뉴욕에 살고 있다. 가끔 시카고나 샌프란시스코에도 들른다. 그러나, 뉴욕이 미국이 아닌 것은 파리가 프랑스가 아니고, 런던이 영국이 아닌 것과 같다. 이렇게 나는 조국을 모르고 있다는 것을 알았다. 미국에 관해서 쓰고 있는 미국 작가인 나는 기억으로 쓰고 있었다. 그런데, 기억이란 기껏해야 결점 투성이요, 비뚤어진(편견에 찬) 지식의 축적인 것이다. 나는 미국의 언어를 듣지 않았었고, 초목과 하수 오물의 냄새를 맡지 않았었고, 미국의 언덕과 물을 보지 않았었고, 그 색과 빛의 질을 보지 않았었다. 나는 그저 책과 신문으로부터 변화를 알았을 뿐이다. 그러나, 이것 이상으로 나는 이 나라를 25년간이나 느끼지 않고 있었던 것이다. 요컨대, 나도 모르는 무엇에 관해 나는 쓰고 있었으며, 이것은 소위 작가에게 있어서 죄악인 것처럼 생각이 되었다. 나의 기억은 그 동안의 25년간에 의해 비뚤어져 있었다. 이런 연유로 해서, 나는 이 커다란 나라를 다시 한번 보고 재발견하려고 결심하게 되었다.

▶▶정답
1. ④
2. 작가가 자신이 알지 못하는 것에 대해 기억에 의존해 글을 쓰는 것
3. ④ 4. ③

▶▶영작
(1) I am no more crazy than you are.
(2) In short, man is born, suffers, and dies.
(3) It seems to me that you are not really interested in this matter.
(4) Have you decided where you are going to spend your summer vacation?

실력체크 I (p.48)

1
(1) the surface sense of the words themselves
(2) May I help you to change the tire?

2
(1) 소수 지식인의 배출보다 대중의 교육에 중점을 두고 있다.
(2) 미국에서는 같은 지역(공동 사회)에 사는 대부분의 학생들이 그들의 지적인 능력과 가정 환경의 차이에도 불구하고 유치원부터 고등학교를 마칠 때까지 거의 같이 학교에 다닌다.

3
아버님을 생각하면 언제나 카운터 뒤에서 밀가루를 온 머리에 뒤집어 쓰고 연필 끝을 두 입술로 적시며 계산을 하고 있는 모습이 떠오른다.

4 ④

숙어 Exercise (p.54)

1. He described the history of his village at length.
2. The boat was at the mercy of the waves.
3. I'll attend to the problem myself.
4. He attributed his success to good luck.
5. He was soon absorbed in his book.
6. He is anxious about her safety.
7. We are apt to be wasteful of time.
8. She is bound to pass her driving test.
9. His success is entirely due to hard work.
10. He tried to help us but was simply in the way.

제3장 부정사

문법 · 작문 (p.60)

A.

(1) to ask ⇨ ask
(2) not to waste ⇨ not waste
(3) enough mature ⇨ mature enough
(4) enter ⇨ to enter
(5) to carry ⇨ carry
(6) to feel ⇨ feel
(7) smoke ⇨ to smoke
(8) Is it necessary for all of us to be present at the meeting this afternoon?
(9) to cry ⇨ cry
(10) be not ⇨ not be
(11) do ⇨ to do
(12) found advantageous ⇨ found it advantageous
(13) to be killed ⇨ to have been killed
(14) seeing ⇨ to see
(15) to whom ask ⇨ who(m) to ask
(16) to kiss ⇨ to be kissed
(17) to read ⇨ reading
(18) believe ⇨ to believe

B.

(1) 그 여자는 웃으려고 하지 않았다.
그 여자는 웃지 않으려고 애썼다.
(2) 그 여자는 이 도시에서 말할 사람이 없다.
그 여자는 자신에게 말을 걸어주는 사람이 이 도시에 없다.
(3) 쓸 거리가 있느냐?
쓸 도구가 있느냐?
쓸 종이가 있느냐?
(4) 볼 만한 것이 아무것도 없다.
아무것도 보이는 게 없다.
(5) 나는 그를 다시 보고 싶었다.
나는 그를 다시 보고 싶었으나 보지 못했다.

C.

(1) ⓒ (2) ⓑ (3) ⓔ
(4) ⓐ (5) ⓓ (6) ⓑ

D.

(1) to (2) too (3) to, to
(4) to (5) have

E.

(1) with (2) of, you (3) to, in
(4) likely, to (5) for, to (6) not, not

F.

(1) She seems to have been beautiful in her day.
(2) Do you promise never to repeat what I've just said?
(3) I expected you to be promoted to the new position.
(4) I hoped to have finished the work by six.
(5) It is natural for you to get angry.
(6) He is believed to be living a comfortable life.
(7) I firmly believed him to have been innocent of the crime.
(8) I hurried to the station so as not to be late for the train.
(9) It is desirable for the examination results to be made public by then.
(10) I regret to have to inform you of this sad news.
(11) The state-of-the-art equipment was too expensive for us to buy.
(12) He left Korea never to return.
(13) He tried only to fail.
(14) Actors are usually the kind of people to love being the center of attention.
(15) She had no money to send to her son.
(16) They were surprised to see such beautiful scenery.
(17) Tom, it's time for you to wash up and go to bed.

(18) She had no friend to talk about the matter with.
(19) I worked hard only to fail to carry out my plan.
혹은 I worked hard never to carry out my plan.
(20) I would be glad to have the chance to meet her face-to-face.
(21) I was astonished to find him bankrupt.
(22) The colonel ordered all his officers to attend the parade.
(23) I happened to sit beside her in the theater.

G.
(1) Do you wish that I would make a complaint about it?
(2) He believes that I was (*or* have been) in the wrong.
(3) I got to the station so late that I could not catch the train.
(4) He is so tall that he can touch the ceiling.
(5) His bravery was such that it startled the world.
(6) What is the first thing that should be done?
(7) The commander ordered that the deserter should be shot.
(8) We're sure that we will see you again before your departure.

H.
(1) to finish
(2) to persuade, to work
(3) have seen (4) lifted
(5) to grow (6) look
(7) praised, to love
(8) to get
(9) To think
(10) painted
(11) be seen

I.
(1) It is a very bad habit to speak ill of those who are not present.
(2) There are lots of places to visit in this area.
(3) I am sorry to have kept you waiting so long in such a lonely place.
(4) Dr. Kim is to speak on the radio at eight this evening.
(5) You had better read a few good books carefully than read a large number of worthless books.
(6) I advise you to walk at least one hour every day to keep yourself healthy.
(7) I was very happy to find the book that I had given up for lost.
(8) In order to do a thing well, you ought to take real interest in what you do.
(9) English is practically a universal language. It is necessary for us to be able to read, write, and speak it.
(10) I will have him clean your shoes.

'Friendship'

There is a saying that a friend in need is a friend indeed. A true friend helps us when we are in need or in trouble. Sometimes we are disappointed and feel sad to find a man whom we thought to be a true friend fail to come up to our expectations. A true friend is better than twenty followers in our time of prosperity. We wish to have a friend who can share with us sorrows as well as joys.

단문독해 (p.64)

1. ▶▶해석
친절이 하나의 미덕이라는 사실은 아무도 논쟁하지 않을 것이다. 어떤 사람이 친절하다고 말하는 것은, 그가 점잖고 남에게 동정심이 있고 또 자비롭다고 말하는 것과 같다. 그는 타인의 안락을 자기의 편리보다 먼저 생각한다. 우리들이 사귀어 왔고 사랑해 온 사람들을 회고해 볼 때, 그들의 친절로 뛰어났던 어떤 남녀들을 우리는 모두 기억하게 되는 것이다.

▶▶정답 ②

▶▶영작

(In) Looking back on my school days I was rather wild and wayward.

2. ▶▶해석

상상력 그 자체가 벌써 기억의 한 작용이기 때문에, 기억력을 시의 한 기능이라고 말하는 것이 아마 진실일 것이다. 우리가 상상하는 것으로 우리가 이미 모르는 것은 아무것도 없다. 그리고 우리의 상상력은 우리가 한 번 경험해 본 적이 있는 것을 기억하여, 그것을 어떤 다른 상태에 적용하는 우리의 능력이다.

▶▶정답 ③

▶▶영작

Is there anything you want that you don't have?

3. ▶▶해석

인생은 깊고 강해지기 위해 슬픔과 접촉하고, 또 슬픔이 섞여야 한다. 그것은 마치 햇빛이 그늘에 의해 부드러워질 때 가장 온화하고, 음악이 선율이 아름다우려면 그 안에 단조음(短調音)을 가져야 하는 것과 마찬가지다.

▶▶정답 ③

▶▶영작

I got up early to be on time for the first train.

I got up early so as to be on time for the first train.

I got up early in order to be on time for the first train.

4. ▶▶해석

당신은 목욕탕에서 물을 뚝뚝 흘리면서 좇아 나오거나, 식탁에서 밥을 씹으면서 좇아 오거나, 혹은 잠자리에서 일어나 부신 눈을 하고 좇아 나와 수화기를 드니, "당신은 제가 원하는 번호가 아닙니다.(제가 전화 잘못 걸었군요.)"하고 저쪽에서 이야기하는 것을 들어 본 경험이 있습니까?

▶▶정답 ③

▶▶영작

He lived to be ninety years old.

5. ▶▶해석

특별한 음식이나 마실 것은 말할 것도 없이, 같이 모였다는 즐거움에 마음이 흐뭇하여 이글이글 타는 난로 앞에 모여 앉는 것보다 가족들에게 더 즐거운 일은 없다.

▶▶정답 home

▶▶영작

He can speak French very well, not to mention English.

6. ▶▶해석

이승에서 더 살아야 그저 몇 십년 뿐인데, 곧 누구나 다 잊어버리게 될 사소한 것들을 생각하면서 우리는 많은 귀중한 시간을 보낸다. 이런 일을 해서는 안된다. 가치 있는 행동, 감정, 사상에 우리의 생애를 바치자. 왜냐 하면, 인생은 너무 짧아서 사소해질 수 없기 때문이다.

▶▶정답 trivial

▶▶영작

Life is too short for us to be interested in everything, (and) so let us devote all our time to one purpose in life.

7. ▶▶해석

질투심이 강한 사람에게는 공기처럼 가벼운 사소한 일도 성서처럼 확고한 증거가 된다. Cassio의 손에서 본 자기 아내의 손수건은, 속고 있는 Othello에게는 어떻게 해서 Cassio가 그 손수건을 얻게 되었느냐를 단 한 번도 물어 보지 않고 그들 두 사람(부인과 Cassio)에게 사형 선고를 내릴 만큼 충분한 동기가 되었다.

▶▶정답 jealousy

▶▶영작

The man was sentenced to death for the crime.

8. ▶▶해석

비록 애정과 지식이 둘 다 필요하지만, 애정이 어떤 의미에 있어서 더 근본적이다. 그것은, 애정은 총명한 사람들로 하여금 그들이 사랑하는 사람들을 이롭게 할 방법을 찾기 위해 지식을 구하도록 이끌어 줄 것이기 때문이다.

▶▶정답 ④

▶▶영작

His poverty forced him to give up his studies.

9. ▶▶해석

며칠이 지나면 우리의 방학이 시작될 것이다. 모두 이 생각에 기쁨으로 넘쳐 있고, 생기에 가득 차 있다. 그것은 모두 고향으로 갈 것이기 때문이다. 그러나, 나는 방학이 계속되는 닷새 동안 여기 머물러 있어야 하고, 그 동안 나는 매우 외로울 것이라는 것을 알고 있다.

▶▶정답 ⑤

▶▶영작

Is there any prospect of their winning the game?

10. ▶▶해석

유럽인들은 미국인들처럼 어떻게 3차 세계대전을 이길 것인가 하는 문제에 관심이 있는 것이 아니라, 어떻게 그것을 피할까 하는 문제에만 관심이 있다.

▶▶정답 prevent, win

▶▶영작

He is not concerned with the affair.

11. ▶▶해석

하느님에 대한 우리의 중요한 의무 외에, 우리는 우리 나라를 사랑해야 하고 나라의 통치자를 국가를 대표하는 사람으로서 존경해야 한다. 우리의 형제, 즉 동료 기독교인들을 사랑하여야 한다. 그리고, 우리는 모든 인간을 존중하여야 한다.

▶▶정답 worship, dear

▶▶영작

He came home three hours later, that is to say, about eleven o'clock.

12. ▶▶해석

중세기의 암흑을 쫓아 버리고, 결국 이성(理性)을 그 감옥으로부터 해방할 사람들을 위해 길을 준비해 줄 지적인 사회적인 운동이 13세기에 이탈리아에서 시작되었다.

▶▶정답

the darkness of the Middle Ages

▶▶영작

The father and son were never to see each other again.

13. ▶▶해석

음악은 모든 민족들에 의하여 이해되는 만국어이다. 누구나 다 아는 이 말은 진실로 그렇다. 그러나, 우리가 음악을 이해하려면, 어느 정도의 음악의 경험이 필요하다는 사실을 우리는 잊어서는 안 된다.

▶▶정답 ⑤

▶▶영작

If we are to be there before nine, we will have to be quick.

14. ▶▶해석

나는 모든 학생에게 이것을 알게끔 하고 싶은데, 빠르면 빠를 수록 더욱 좋다. 즉, 그 나라의 언어를 정확히 모르고서는 고대 국가건 현대 국가건 그 국가의 문학과 문화의 철저한 이해가 있을 수 없다는 사실을.

▶▶정답 language

▶▶영작

My mother had me hang out the laundry on the clothesline.

15. ▶▶해석

그 여자는 그더러 나가라고 문을 확 열어 버렸다. 그리고, 조용히 그가 나가는 것을 지켜보았다. 그가 나가고 앞문이 닫히는 소리를 들을 때까지, 그 여자는 꼼짝도 하지 않았다. 그러나, 그 다음 그 여자는 소파에 자기 몸을 내던지고 울음을 터뜨렸다.

▶▶정답 ②

▶▶영작

He slammed the door shut and went away without saying a word.

16. ▶▶해석

문명은 역경의 소산물이다. 모든 시대의 위대한 문명은 자연 환경으로 인하여 연중 한철밖에 농사 지을 수 없고, 그리하여 인간이 농사 지을 수 없는 때를 대비하여 일하고 또 저축해야 하는 곳에서 일어났던 것 같다. 인간은 본디 착실히 계속하여 일하고 싶어하지 않는다. 만약 자연 환경으로 인해 착실히 일하는 것을 면할 수만 있다면, 인간은 대개 일하며 진보하는 것보다는 차라리 게으르며 시간을 보내는 데 만족하는 것처럼 보인다.

▶▶정답 ②

▶▶영작

Airplanes enable us to go around the world in a few days.

17. ▶▶해석

비록 읽히는 것이 작가로 하여금 글을 쓰도록 재촉하는 동기가 아니요, 그의 동기는 딴 것이지만, 일단 그가 쓰고 나면 그의 욕망은 읽혀지는 것이다. 그리고, 그것을 달성하기 위하여 그는 자기가 쓰는 것을 읽기 쉽게 만들려고 최선을 다해야 한다.

▶▶정답 ⑤

▶▶영작

Once you have planned something, you must do your best to achieve it.

18. ▶▶해석

약 12살 되어 보이는, 두 눈을 붕대로 감은 한 소녀 외에는 아무도 보이지 않았다. 그런데 한 어린 소년이 조심스럽게 꽃밭 사이로 이 소녀를 인도하고 있었다. 그 소녀는 발걸음을 멈추더니, 지금 들어온 사람이 누구냐고 분명하게 물었다. 그러니까, 그 소년이 나의 모습을 그 소녀에게 이야기하는 것 같았다.

▶▶정답 ②

▶▶영작

He is being watched by his boss.

19. ▶▶해석

지식이 적었던 시기에 우리가 미신적이고 쓸모 없다고 상상했던 많은 것들이, 오늘날 조사해 보니, 인류에게 무한히 가치 있는 것들이었다는 게 입증된다. 아마, 미신 치고 어떤 사회적 가치가 없던 것이 존재한 적은 없었다. 그리고, 외관상 보기 흉하고 잔인한 것들이 가장 귀중한 것들이었다는 게 가끔 증명된다.

▶▶정답 ④

▶▶영작

The rumor has turned out to be false.

20. ▶▶해석

이따금 과거를 돌이켜볼 때 우리는 우리의 과오에 놀라게 되고, 보람없는 옆길에서 그렇게도 많은 시간을 낭비한 것처럼 보이고, 또 흔히 길을 완전히 잘못 들어 모든 세월이 낭비된 것처럼 보인다.

▶▶정답 wandering

▶▶영작

We were appalled at the sight of the horrible atrocity.

21. ▶▶해석

나는 자정이 되기 전에 파티를 떠나려 했으나 꽤 늦게 까지 남아있어야 했다. 왜냐하면 내가 일찍 떠났더라면 그 흥겨운 분위기를 망칠 수도 있었기 때문이었다.

▶▶정답 after, spoil

▶▶영작

We intend to go to Australia next year if all goes well.

장문독해 (p.72)

1 ▶▶해석

현대인의 재앙은 계속하여 자기 파멸의 새로운 가능성에 직면하는 것 같다. 그는 모든 인간 생활을 말살할 수 있는 핵의 힘으로 무장하여 제2차 대전으로부터 출현했다. 그 후로 인구는 세계적인 재난이 닥칠 수도 있는 비율로 늘어났다. 지금 그는 자기 자신이 만든 새 위협에 직면하게 되었다. 즉, 자기의 자연 환경을 해로운 분량의 화학물, 쓰레기, 연기, 소음, 하수 오물, 열기, 추함, 인구의 도시 집중 등으로 오염시켰다. 거의 느끼지도 못하는 사이에 오염이라는 재앙이 벌써 너무나 멀리 퍼져 버려, 이제 근본적인 대책만이 핵파괴와 마찬가지의 철저한 황폐를 막을 수 있다고 하는 과학자들도 있다. 크건 작건 모든 나라들이 이런 환경의 위험(오염)에 직면하고 있다. 그래서, 환경 보존이 금세기의 중요 과제가 될 듯이 보인다. 인간은 탐험의 시대를 가졌으며, 이 지구의 부(자원)를 발견해 내는 데 자신이 명장임을 입증했다. 그는 개발의 시대로 옮아가 이런 부들을 이용하는 데 대단한 기술을 보여주었다. 이제 보존의 시대가 시작되어야 하는데, 벌써 너무 때가 늦었다. 오염과의 싸움이 당장 시작되어야 한다. 그렇지 않으면 너무 늦을 것이다.

▶▶정답

1. ⑤
2. (1) Exploration
   (2) Exploitation
   (3) environment
3. ④
4. ②

▶▶영작

(1) Mobs gathered in twos and threes, armed with clubs, Molotov cocktails, and even rifles.

(2) He proved himself fit for the difficult task.

(3) Now is the time for us all to be up and doing for our country.

2 ▶▶해석

어느 책에서나 최대의 것을 얻기 위해서는 "행간(行間)에 숨은 뜻을 읽어야"한다는 사실을 여러분은 알고 있다. 나는 여러분이 독서하는 도중에 이와 마찬가지로 중요한 일을 하라고 설득하고 싶다. 나는 여러분이 "행간에 글을 적어 넣도록" 권하고 싶다. 이렇게 하지 않으면, 아마 가장 효과적인 독서를 하지 못할 것이다.

책을 소유하는데는 두 방법이 있다. 첫째는, 옷이나 가구 값을 지불하듯이 책값을 지불하여 얻는 소유권이다. 그러나, 이 구매 행위는 소유의 서곡에 불과하다. 완전한 소유는 책을 당신 자신의 일부로 하였을 때에만 온다. 그리고, 당신 자신을 책의 일부로 하는 가장 좋은 방법은 책 안에 글을 적어 넣음으로써 이루어진다. 한 가지 예를 들면 이 점이 명백해질 것이다. 당신이 쇠고기를 사서 푸줏간의 냉장고로부터 당신의 냉장고로 옮긴다. 그러나, 당신이 그것을 소화하여 당신의 혈관 속에 집어 넣을 때까지, 가장 중요한 의미에 있어서 그 쇠고기를 소유하지 않는 것이다. 책도 역시 당신에게 어떤 이익이 되기 위해서는 당신의 혈관 속에 흡수되어야 한다는 것이 나의 주장이다.

▶▶정답

1. hidden 2. ②, ⑤
3. ④ 4. ③

▶▶영작

(1) I could get nothing out of him.
(2) Unless you work harder, you are not likely to succeed.
(3) This medicine will do you good.
(4) He was absorbed in reading the novel.
(5) Full ownership comes only when you have made a book a part of yourself.

실력체크 I (p.76)

1

(1) 시류(時流)에 편승하는 것.
(2) 독창성을 너무 강조하여 기발한 것을 중시하는 피상적인 겉치레에 빠질 위험이 있다고 생각한다.
(3) An atmosphere of intellectual bustle is not favorable to quiet concentration, to unhurried experiments, to brooding over a single problem.

2 (1) ② (2) ①

3

(1) 싫은 사람은 아무리 사랑하려고 해도 소용없는 일이며 무리한 일이니까.
(2) 싫더라도 서로 참으며 관용을 베풂으로써 존속해 나갈 수 있다.

4 궁핍으로 절약이 몸에 밴 기성세대의 제일 목표는 돈을 모아 집을 사고 자식들을 교육시키는 것이었는데, 젊은 세대에게는 돈을 버는 것 만큼 쓰는 것도 중요하다. 집보다 차를 원하고 빚지는 것도 서슴지 않는다. 부모에게는 이 모두가 악습으로만 보인다. (100자)

숙어 Exercise (p.82)

1. I wonder what the little rascal is up to.
2. Stop beating around the bush and get to the point.
3. The prisoner broke away from his guards.
4. Thieves broke into the house through an upstairs window.
5. A fire broke out at the factory.
6. I can't understand why she broke up with her boy-friend.
7. Several days of heavy rain brought about the flood.
8. By degrees their friendship grew into love.
9. They had to tend their sick mother by turns.
10. He was exempt from his military duty by virtue of his disability [illness, deformity].

▶ 명 언 ◀

Nothing can make our life, or the lives of other people, more beautiful than perpetual kindness.
— *Leo Tolstoy*

Short as life is, we make it still shorter by the careless waste of time.
— *Victor Hugo*

Knowing is not enough, we must apply ;
willing is not enough, we must do.
— *Goethe*

제4장 동명사

문법 · 작문 (p.86)

A.
(1) sending (2) doing (3) sitting
(4) to think (5) to call (6) driving
(7) receiving (8) canceling (9) On
(10) sharpening

B.
(1) to go ⇨ on going
(2) to walk ⇨ from walking
(3) to fight ⇨ fighting
(4) being ⇨ to be
(5) to scream ⇨ screaming
(6) he will investigate ~
⇨ his [him] investigating ~
(7) to explain ⇨ in explaining
(8) to try ⇨ trying
(9) to drown ⇨ (to) drowning
(10) running ⇨ to run
(11) look ⇨ looking
(12) to hear ⇨ of hearing
(13) to do ⇨ doing
(14) think ⇨ thinking
(15) being not ⇨ not being

C.
(1) P (2) G (3) G
(4) G (5) P (6) G

D.
(1) ⓐ 나는 거짓말을 싫어한다. (일반적)
ⓑ 나는 지금 거짓말하고 싶지 않다. (일시적)
(2) ⓐ 나는 수영을 좋아한다. (일반적)
ⓑ 나는 지금 수영하고 싶다. (일시적)
(3) ⓐ 그녀는 계속해서 말했다.
ⓑ 그녀는 쉬었다가 계속해서 말했다.
(4) ⓐ 그렇게 하려고 노력하시오.
ⓑ 시험삼아 그렇게 해보시오.
(5) ⓐ 그는 성공을 확신하고 있다.
(= He is sure that he will succeed.)
ⓑ 그는 틀림없이 성공한다.
(= I am sure that he will succeed.)

E.
(1) of (2) having (3) worth
(4) of (5) help (6) handling

F.
(1) reading the Bible every day.
(2) declaring bankruptcy
(3) stealing
(4) saying that the patient needs an immediate blood transfusion

G.
(1) being (2) playing (3) going
(4) having followed (5) to invest
(6) going (7) studying

H.
(1) I'm so proud of my son having been chosen for the national team.
(2) He was not ashamed of having cheated on his wife.
(3) He still insists on having done nothing wrong.
(4) We have no doubt of his [him] being sick in bed.
(5) On her car arriving, the crowd started cheering.
(6) He was nervous because of not having spoken in public before.
(7) I don't like your [you] lying in bed till late on Sunday morning.
(8) Besides holding an important office, he often writes good novels.
(9) Is this also a picture of your own drawing?
(10) I never meet him without thinking of his dead father.
(11) She repented having spanked her child and promised never to do it again.

(12) I remember your [you] promising (*or* having promised) me to do so.
(13) He denied having told a lie.
(14) He always complains of his boss being useless and having too much work.
(15) Having such poor health is against him.
(16) There is no denying that this has been a difficult year for him.
(17) In spite of being very learned, he lacked common sense.
(18) There is every reason for your [you] being displeased.
(19) Would you mind helping me carry this suitcase?
(20) Instead of going myself, I sent my representative.
(21) I cannot help thinking of his being still alive.
(22) His mother scolded him for breaking her favorite vase.
(23) What do you say to taking a walk for a while after dinner?
(24) It is necessary to advance step by step in learning a foreign language.
(25) Be polite in speaking to others.
(26) I've always regretted not having studied harder at school.

I.

(1) I forgot that the doctor advised me not to eat salty foods.
(2) She is proud that she (has) won the first prize in the beauty contest.
(3) He started early so that he could get a good seat.
(4) I am convinced that she will tell [is telling] the truth.
(5) Do you mind if I open the window?
(6) All the lights go out when the clock strikes ten.
(7) I don't think it fair that you should speak ill of him.
(8) Is there any possibility that he will succeed in raising enough funds?

J.

(1) being, be converted
(2) being taught
(3) reading, be read
(4) satisfying
(5) letting, paint
(6) becoming, being poisoned
(7) Going, being sent [to be sent]
(8) being thought

K.

(1) He left the place without saying a word.
(2) It is no use saving money unless one knows how to use it.
(3) Writing letters in English is a good practice in English composition.
(4) Last night I fell asleep without turning off the TV.
(5) There is no knowing how far science may progress by the end of the twenty-first century.
(6) I cannot help thinking that he has told a lie.
(7) Don't be too much afraid of making mistakes, but try to speak boldly.
(8) On returning from my journey, I found my father seriously ill.
(9) There is no staying at home in this fine weather.
(10) He was blamed for neglecting to do the homework.
(11) The rain prevented us from going for a drive yesterday.

'Spring'

I like spring better than any other season of the year, for the trees awake from their long winter sleep and wear the clothes of green leaves and beautiful flowers. Everything around us seems to be smiling and beckoning us to enjoy spring. Spring gives us hope and love.

단문독해 (p.90)

1. ▶▶해석

유사 이전의 인간이 전쟁을 했다는 증거는 없다. 왜냐하면, 거의 모든 석기(石器)는 사냥을 하고, 땅을 파고 혹은 짐승가죽을 벗기는 데 사용하기 위해 고안된 것처럼 보이기 때문이다. 비록 그들이 전쟁을 했다고 해도, 인간 생활의 수렵 시기에 있어서의 집단 간의 싸움은 드물고 또 심하지 않았을 것이라는 것을 우리는 거의 확신할 수 있다.

▶▶정답 survival

▶▶영작

There is no evidence that he is guilty.

2. ▶▶해석

그 여자는, 어린애들이 산(山) 공기의 덕을 보기 위해 온 가족이 여름에 시골로 가야겠다고 생각했다. 그것은 이 무더운 계절에 도시에서는 도저히 살 수가 없었기 때문이었다.

▶▶정답 ②

▶▶영작

I work hard so that my family may live in comfort.

3. ▶▶해석

규율은 너무 지나쳐서는 안 된다. 즉, 우리는 규율을 위한 규율을 원치 않는다. 또, 규율은 변덕스럽게 너무 자주 바뀌어서는 안 된다. 오늘 어떤 것을 금지했다가, 내일 그것을 허용하는 것은 소용없는 일이다.

▶▶정답 ④

▶▶영작

It is no use you [your] trying to deny it.

4. ▶▶해석

Mary의 얼굴이 두 손에 가려져 있었으므로, 조용히 현관으로 들어와 그녀를 보자, 처음에는 마치 뒤로 물러설 듯한 몸짓을 했으나 곧 그 자리에 서서 그녀를 주의해 보는 사람의 모습을, 그녀는 알아차리지 못했다. Mary는 얼마 동안 머리를 들지 않았다. 그러나, 그녀가 고개를 들고 주위를 둘러볼 때 그녀의 얼굴은 젖어 있었고, 두 눈은 눈물에 잠겨 몽롱했다. "Smith씨, 여기 오신지 얼마나 되신 거죠? (언제 여기에 오셨습니까?)"하고 그녀가 말했다.

▶▶정답 ④

▶▶영작

How long have you been in Korea?

5. ▶▶해석

아직 살아있는 사람들의 당혹감을 덜어주기 위해 나는 이 소설에 나오는 사람들에게 내가 직접 지어낸 이름들을 붙여주었다. 그리고 나는 또 달리 여러 방법으로 애를 써 아무도 그들을 알아보지 못하도록 하였다.

▶▶정답 real, lest

▶▶영작

This is a picture of his (own) painting.

6. ▶▶해석

사람은 아무리 남에게 영향을 주고 싶지 않고 혹은 아무리 자기가 지금 영향을 주고 있다는 것을 의식하지 못해도, 타인에게 영향을 주지 않을 수가 없다. 어떤 사람이나 중립일 수는 없다. 그가 좋은 일을 행하지 않으면, 그는 어떤 의미에 있어서 해를 끼치고 있는 것이다.

▶▶정답 ④

▶▶영작

We cannot help influencing others and being influenced by them.

7. ▶▶해석

우리가 위인들의 전기를 읽을 때, 그 자체로서는 되는대로이고 심지어 비참해 보이는 모든 종류의 경험들을 결국에는 이용해 버린 그런 방법에 감동 받지 않을 수 없다는 것은 말할 필요가 없다.

▶▶정답 adversity, success

▶▶영작

She always makes good use of her spare time.

8. ▶▶해석

토마스·A·에디슨의 위대한 발명은 모두 오랜 동안의 고된 노력의 결실이었다. "천재는 1%의 영감과 99%의 땀이다."라고 말하여 그는 자기의 성공을 설명하였다. 그는 또 "나는 어떤 것이나 할 가치가 있는 것을 우연히 한 적이 없고, 나의 발명 가운데 우연히 온 것은 하나도 없다. 모두 노력에 의해 왔다."라고 말했다.

▶▶정답 perspiration, inspiration

▶▶영작

Many books are published, but very few of them are worth reading.

9. ▶▶해석

그녀는 시합을 이 이상 더 즐겨 본 적이 없었다. 중요한 것은 경기 그 자체였지 이기는 것이 아니었다. 심지어 지는 것도 중요하지 않았다.

▶▶정답 Win or lose

▶▶영작

As he was afraid of being punished, he ran away.

10. ▶▶해석

영국 사람들은 자기들 같은 사람들이 없으며, 영국 외에는 다른 세상이 없다고 생각한다. 그들은 잘생긴 외국인을 보면, 그가 영국인처럼 보인다고 반드시 말한다. 그들은 외국인 앞에 맛있는 음식을 차려 놓고는, 이런 것을 당신의 나라에서도 만드느냐고 반드시 묻는다.

▶▶정답 ③

▶▶영작

Everybody but him seems to know it.

11. ▶▶해석

남의 권리를 생각하지 않으면 질서가 가능하지 못한 그런 세계에 우리는 살고 있다. 다시 말해서, 그것은 항상 구속이 있어야 한다는 것을 뜻하며, 또 그것은 다시 말해 단순한 자유는 본래부터의 권리이기는 커녕 명백하게 불합리하다는 뜻이다.

▶▶정답 respect, restrain

▶▶영작

He failed again, which made her mad.

장문독해 (p.94)

1 ▶▶해석

인종 차별의 날카로운 화살을 느껴 보지 못한 사람들이 "기다려라."하고 말하기는 쉬울 것이라고 나는 추측한다. 그러나, 악독한 폭도들이 당신의 부모를 마음대로 린치(私刑)하고, 형제 자매를 기분내키는 대로 물에 빠뜨리는 것을 당신이 보았을 때, 증오심으로 가득 찬 경찰관들이 당신의 흑인 형제 자매를 저주하고 발길로 차고 짐승처럼 취급하고 심지어 죽이는 것을 보았을 때, 당신의 여섯 살 난 딸에게 텔레비전에 방금 광고된 공중 오락 공원에 왜 갈 수 없는지 설명하려고 애쓸 때 갑자기 당신의 혀가 뒤틀리고 말이 더듬어지는 것을 느낄 때, 그리고 흑인 어린애들은 오락 공원(Funtown)에 갈 수 없다는 말을 듣고 당신의 귀여운 딸의 어린 두 눈에서 눈물이 솟아오르는 것을 볼 때, 그리고 열등 의식의 침울한 구름이 당신의 딸의 어린 마음의 하늘에 형성되기 시작하는 것을 볼 때, 백인에 대하여 무의식으로 악의를 일으킴으로 해서 그 어린 마음이 비뚤어지기 시작하는 것을 볼 때, 해가 뜨나 해가 지나 "백인", "유색인"하는 그 괴로운 간판들을 보고 당신이 마음의 굴욕을 느낄 때, 그리고 당신은 항상 발돋움을 한 불안한 자세로 사는 검둥이라는 사실에 낮이면 괴롭고 밤이면 꿈에마저 괴롭힘을 당할 때, 당신은 "보잘것없는 놈"이라는 타락감과 영원히 싸우고 있을 때—그 때 당신은 우리들이 기다리는 것을 어렵다고 생각하는 이유를 알 것이다.

▶▶정답

1. loss 2. ① 3. ③ 4. ⑤

▶▶영작

(1) I have never seen the sun rise as gloriously as on that morning.

(2) The old man used to tell us stories that

would make us laugh.

(3) He stood on a hill and watched migratory birds flying high up in the sky toward the north.

2 ▶▶해석

인생에서 배워야 할 가장 중요한 일은 어떻게 사느냐이다. 자기 인생만큼 사람이 지키려고 애를 쓰는 것도 없으나, 그것을 잘 지키기 위해 그렇게도 수고를 하지 않는 것도 없다. 이것은 단순한 문제가 아니다. Hippocrates는 그의 의학 금언집의 책머리에, "인생은 짧고 예술은 길다. 기회는 달아나고, 실험은 불확실하고, 판단은 어렵다."라고 말했다. 인생에서 행복과 성공은 우리의 환경에 달려 있지 않고 우리 자신에 달려 있다. 다른 사람에 의해서 망한 사람보다는 자기 자신을 망친 사람이 더 많다. 폭풍우와 지진이 파괴한 것보다는 사람의 손에 의해서 더 많은 집과 도시가 파괴되었다. 파멸에는 두 가지가 있는데, 그것은 시간의 작용과 인간 스스로가 하는 일이다. 모든 파멸 중에서 인간 자신이 하는 파멸이 가장 슬프며, 인간의 가장 나쁜 적은 Seneca가 말했듯이 인간의 가슴속에 있는 것이다. 신은 악을 창조하지 않고 자유를 준다. 만약 우리가 자유를 오용하면 우리는 꼭 괴로움을 당하고 이것에 대해 자기밖에 탓할 사람이 없다.

▶▶정답

1. ② 2. ⓐ master ⓑ responsible
3. ③ 4. ②

▶▶영작

(1) I was very anxious to see him then, but an unexpected emergency prevented me from paying him a visit.

(2) Whether you will succeed or not depends on how you make use of what you have.

(3) Of all the students in our class, he is the most intelligent and hard-working.

(4) When you go out of the room, please be sure to close the door.

실력체크 I (p.98)

1

(1) ③

(2) Olivero씨는 30년 전에 영국의 어느 산골의 자기 고향을 떠나 남미(南美)에 가서 살다가 지금 고향으로 돌아오는 길이다.

2 한 사람의 다루기 힘든 위인[영웅]보다는 여러 종류의 선량한 시민을 배출하는 것이 민주주의의 보다 훌륭한 업적이다.

3 (1) ③ (2) ①

4

(1) (a) 이 더 복잡한 컴퓨터는 훨씬 더 복잡한 컴퓨터를 설계할 수도 있을 것이고, 같은 일이 계속 거듭될 것이다. (더 복잡한 컴퓨터가 훨씬 더 복잡한 컴퓨터를, 훨씬 더 복잡한 컴퓨터는 그보다 훨씬 더 복잡한 컴퓨터를 설계하는 일이 계속 거듭될 것이다.)

(c) 지금 인류는 지구 운영을 그다지 훌륭하게 수행하지 못하고 있다.

(2) 컴퓨터가 자신보다 더 복잡한 컴퓨터를 설계하게 되는 시점

(3) 아마 인류는 컴퓨터에게 지구의 운영권을 넘겨야 할 것이다. (기계문명의 발달로 인하여 아마 인류의 종말이 올 것이다.)

숙어 Exercise (p.104)

1. This situation calls for an immediate action.
2. I took her to the ballet to cheer her up.
3. I came across some old books in the attic.
4. The whole family came down with the flu.
5. We threw cold water in his face, and he came to.
6. His hope of becoming a lawyer didn't come true.
7. Can you cope with all this work?
8. You can't count on the weather being fine.
9. How will you deal with the problem?
10. All his family depend on him.

제5장 분 사

문법 · 작문 (p.110)

A.

(1) drowning
(2) known
(3) pestering
(4) embarrassed
(5) exciting, excited
(6) waiting
(7) satisfied
(8) wearing
(9) rolling
(10) done
(11) hanging, torn
(12) containing

B.

(1) Apple-trees covered
(2) girl picking
(3) see a pine tree growing
(4) too tender-hearted to bear
(5) song sung by the children

C.

(1) left
(2) Seen
(3) done
(4) Taking
(5) being
(6) Having
(7) done
(8) does
(9) gone
(10) being
(11) Granting (혹은 Granted)

D.

(1) deliver ⇨ delivered
(2) leaned ⇨ leaning
(3) assuring ⇨ assured
(4) throbbed ⇨ throbbing
(5) it was sold ⇨ I sold it
(6) carry ⇨ carried
(7) wrote ⇨ written
(8) pleasant ⇨ pleased
(9) using ⇨ used
(10) training ⇨ trained
(11) situating ⇨ situated
(12) Comparing ⇨ Compared
(13) understand ⇨ understood
(14) the cold wind drove me indoors
⇨ I was driven indoors by the cold wind
(15) to prepare ⇨ preparing
(16) having not ⇨ not having
(17) Writing ⇨ Written
(18) take my picture
⇨ have my picture taken
(19) reading ⇨ read
(20) followed ⇨ following
(21) came on ⇨ coming on
(22) closing ⇨ closed
(23) his father stood before him
⇨ he found his father standing before him
(24) Telling him the truth, I'm positive he'll keep it under his hat.
(25) (Being) Made of iron, the article will not break.
(26) I had my hat blown off by the wind.
(27) destroying ⇨ destroyed
(28) gushed ⇨ gushing
(29) respecting ⇨ respected
(30) seizing ⇨ seized
(32) expecting ⇨ expected
having ⇨ having been

E.

(1) Being very tired from working, he sat down to take a break.
(2) Having finished my daily task of inputting the sales figures, I had nothing more to do.
(3) It having rained heavily the previous night, part of the road subsided.
(4) There being nothing left to do, he was allowed to go home.
(5) Not knowing what to say, I remained silent.
(6) A ball flew into the room, breaking the vase on the desk.
(7) The car breaking down on the way, the trip took longer than we'd [we had] expected.
(8) Having no keys, they could not enter.

(9) Overtaken by night among the mountains, the traveler did not know which road to follow.
(10) A foreign travel, properly conducted, will serve to broaden our horizons.
(11) I sat reading a novel, (with) my wife drying her hair by me.
(12) They were enjoying skiing on the steep slope, (with) the sun shining brightly overhead.
(13) The woman having always been idle and dishonest, I must dismiss her.
(14) Getting across the river by the sightseeing boat, you'll arrive at the famous spa.
(15) It is difficult to hire an efficient man, the salary being small.
(16) Hearing the cry, she came to the window.
(17) I ran all the way to the station, arriving there breathless.
(18) Having had a long and tiring walk, he sat down to rest a little.

F.
(1) Though he had made an obvious mistake, he still refused to admit it.
(2) While he was jaywalking on the street, he was run over by a taxi.
(3) If we are united, we stand; if we are divided, we fall.
(4) When the game was over, the crowd dispersed.
(5) If he had been born in better times, he would have been a great ruler.
(6) As he had been praised, the boy worked the harder.
(7) Though I admit what you say, I can hardly approve of your proposal.
(8) As he was taken by surprise by the burglar, he was severely wounded.
(9) As the work was finished, she looked happy.

G.
(1) crossed
(2) mentioned, accomplished
(3) passed
(4) been called, working, worrying
(5) observed
(6) Worn, be seen, wrecked

H.
(1) The bus was awfully crowded, so I had to keep standing all the way.
(2) Yesterday was Sunday and was fine, and that having nothing to do in particular, I went fishing.
(3) When I came near her house, I heard her playing the piano.
(4) I have just been to the barber's to have my hair cut.
(5) He went out saying he would be back in an hour or so.
(6) Generally speaking, we Koreans are a little too timid in speaking foreign languages.
(7) The soldiers wounded in the battle were evacuated to the hospital.
(8) Written in plain English, this book is suitable for beginners.
(9) Though living so near (to) his house, I seldom see him.
(10) The sun having set, we hurried home.

'Autumn'

Autumn is a very beautiful season. Most of the trees change color and shed their leaves. Farmers are busy harvesting in the fields. Orchards are beautiful with ripe apples and persimmons. Autumn is said to be a good season for reading. We read far into the night, listening to the melancholy chirpings of the crickets. True, autumn is a season of the clear sky and mellow fruitfulness.

단문독해 (p.114)

1. ▶▶해석

그리고, 시골 초가 지붕 위에서 볼 수 있는 잘 자란 박, 길가를 따라 널려 있는 멍석 위에서 마르고 있는 고추, 크고 작은 상점들 안에서 풍성하게 볼 수 있는 맛있는 사과·배·감들을 나는 역시 생각한다. 그리고, 길옆에 있는 손수레에서 숯불로 굽고 있는, 뿌리칠 수 없는 구수한 밤 냄새가 있다.

▶▶정답 ④

▶▶영작

I received an e-mail from her saying that he died.

2. ▶▶해석

슬픈 얼굴을 한 사람이 어느 날 아침 일찍이 나의 꽃가게로 들어왔다. 나는 조화 주문을 받을 준비를 하고 있었다. 그러나, 이번에는 내 추측이 틀렸다. 그는 한 바구니의 꽃을 결혼 기념으로 자기 아내에게 보내고 싶어했다. "그러면 그 날은 언제입니까?"하고 내가 물었다. 우울하게 그는 "어제요."라고 대답했다.

▶▶정답 ⑤

▶▶영작

I had the florist send a basket of flowers to my wife for the fifth anniversary of our wedding.

3. ▶▶해석

기계를 발명하고 난 후, 인간은 옛날에 자기의 상상력에 의하여 창조된 신들에 의해 노예가 되었듯이 기계의 노예가 되고 말았다. 부녀자들을 공장에 들어가게 한 것도 기계고, 동시에 가족과 가정을 해체시킨 것도 기계다.

▶▶정답 ③

▶▶영작

It was on a fine autumn day that I met her for the first time.

4. ▶▶해석

우리의 감각은 거의 기계적인 작용에 의해, 즐거운 것이건 나쁜 것이건, 외계 사물의 인상을 수동적으로 받아들인다. 그러나, 정신은 자기 통제력을 소유하고 있기 때문에, 자기가 옳다고 생각하는 것 무엇에나 주의를 기울일 수 있다.

▶▶정답 active

▶▶영작

Praised by the teacher, she felt very happy.

5. ▶▶해석

비록 어리석고 상상력이 없지만, 짐승들은 가끔 인간들보다 훨씬 더 지각 있게 행동을 한다. 효과적으로 그리고 본능적으로, 적절한 순간에 옳고 적당한 일을 그들은 한다. 즉, 배가 고플 때 먹고, 갈증이 날 때 물을 찾고, 여가가 있을 때 쉬고 논다.

▶▶정답 instinctively, sensibly

▶▶영작

Admitting what you say, I cannot approve of your proposal.

6. ▶▶해석

억제되지 않으면 자연의 힘은 위험하고 파괴적이 될 수 있으나, 일단 정복되면 인간의 뜻과 소망대로 따를 수 있다. 가령, 오늘날 전기는 엄청난 능률로써 수많은 일을 수행하며 인간에 순종하는 하인이다.

▶▶정답 ③

▶▶영작

At last they bent to my will.

7. ▶▶해석

간단히 말해, 우리는 모두 자기 자신의 취미, 직업, 그리고 편견에 의해 채색된 안경을 끼고, 또 자기의 기준에 의해 이웃을 판단하며, 또 자기 멋대로의 계산에 의해 이웃을 판단하며 인생을 살아간다. 우리는 주관적으로 보며, 객관적으로 보지 못한다. 즉, 우리가 단지 볼 수 있는 것만을 보며, 보아야 할 것은 보지 못한다.

▶▶정답 ②

▶▶영작

He lay awake for a long time, thinking of his future.

8. ▶▶해석

저녁에 제일 처음 나오는 별을 저녁 별(明星)이라고 부른다. 그러나, 엄격히 말해 그것은 별이 아니라 하나의 혹성이다. 혹성은 별과 다르다. 혹성은 그들 자신의 빛을 내지 못하고, 자기에게 비치는 태양의 빛을 반사함으로써 반짝인다. 이런 혹성 9개가 태양 주위를 돌고 있는데, 지구도 그 중의 하나이다.

▶▶정답 ③

▶▶영작

Judging from his accent, he must be an Englishman.

9. ▶▶해석

자기들의 온 정신을 미래에 쏟고 있는 (미래지향적인) 미국인들은 자기들이 광대한 땅과 자원에 둘러싸여 있으나 노동력과 기술의 부족으로 고통을 받고 있음을 절감하였다. 그들은 나라의 풍요한 자원을 개발하여 영광스러운 미래로 나아갈 문을 열어줄 기술지식과 창의성을 높이 평가하였다.

▶▶정답 short, blessed

▶▶영작

He was leaning against a pine tree staring at the ground with his hands in his pockets.

장문독해 (p.118)

1 ▶▶해석

그들이 태어나야 할 곳에 태어나지 못하고 딴 곳에서 태어나는 사람들이 있다는 생각을 나는 가지고 있다. 우연히 이런 사람들은 어떤 환경에 던져지게 된다. 그러나, 그들은 자기들이 모르는 어느 고향에 대하여 항상 어떤 향수를 느끼고 있다. 그들은 자기가 태어난 고장에서 오히려 타인이고, 그들이 어려서부터 알고 있는, 나뭇잎이 우거진 오솔길 혹은 그들이 놀던, 사람들이 북적대는 가로들이 그저 지나가다 잠깐 들른 곳으로밖에 남지 않는다. 그들은 한평생을 자기 친척들 사이에서 타인(異邦人)으로 살며, 그들이 나서부터 알아온 모든 환경에서 격리되어 산다. 아마 이런 소원감(疏遠感)이 바로, 사람들을 자기가 애착을 느낄 영원한 무엇을 찾아 멀리 여러 곳을 헤매게 하는 것인가 보다. 아마 어떤 뿌리 깊이 박힌 격세유전(隔世遺傳)이 이런 방랑자를, 자기의 조상들이 아득한 옛날에 떠나온 고장으로 몰고 가는 것 같다. 가끔, 그는 바로 여기가 내 고장이다 하고 신비롭게 느끼게 되는 곳을 우연히 찾게 된다. 여기가 바로 그가 찾던 고향이다. 그리하여, 그는 자기가 전에 한 번도 본 적이 없고 안 적이 없는 환경과 사람들 틈에, 마치 그들이 자기가 태어나서부터 자기에게 낯익은 것처럼 정착한다. 드디어, 여기서 그는 휴식을 찾는다.

▶▶정답

1. wrong 2. ③ 3. ④ 4. ③

▶▶영작

(1) He pretended as if she were a stranger to him.

(2) It was his sense of responsibility that urged him to undertake the dangerous task for which he eventually sacrificed himself.

(3) Some men have a nostalgia for a home they never know, and spend their whole lives wandering about and searching for something unknown.

2 ▶▶해석

만약 당신이 시골에서 온 겨울을, 상점이나 영화관에서 멀리 떨어져, 대부분의 시간을 방안에 박혀, 비나 진흙 그리고 추위로 떨며 학교에 터벅터벅 걸어다니면서 보낸 적이 있다면, 봄이 왔을 때 얼마나 신기한 마음의 위안이 되는지 당신은 알 것이다. 원시인에게는 그것이 얼마나 더한 위안이었음에 틀림없었겠는가를 상상해보라. 원시인은 하여튼 상점이나 영화관이 없었고, 긴 겨울밤에 읽을 책조차 없었다. 아니 책이 있었다고 해도, 그것을 읽을 등불이 없었다. 무지무지하게 추울 때가 흔히 있었다. 자기가 저장해 둔 식량이 겨울을 지탱해 낼까 근심스러웠다. 가장 나쁜 것은, 여름이 도대체 돌아오려는지 절대적인 확신이 있을 수가 없었다는 것이다. 그래서, 봄의 첫날은 그에게 기적처럼 생각되었던 것이다. 이제 그는 다시 따뜻해질 수 있고, 들에 나갈 수 있고, 굶주림을 두려워할 필요가 없었다. 원시인이 겨울이 끝나길 바라던 그 정열적인 소망, 날씨가 드디어 따뜻해지기 시작할 때의 그 황홀한 안도감이 시를 통하여 우리 자신의 시대까지 메아리치고 있다. 이 기분은 말하자면 우리의 핏속에 스며 있으며, 그것이 바로 모든 시대를 통하여 봄에 관해 그렇게도 많은 훌륭한 시가 쓰여져 온 이유다.

▶▶정답

1. 봄의 도래　2. ②　3. ④　4. ⑤

▶▶영작

(1) Being mistaken for a Chinese, I was spoken to in Chinese.
(2) He had no money to buy the book with.
(3) The success of the scheme depends upon whether you will cooperate.
(4) Worst of all, he had no money and was in poor health.

실력체크 I (p.122)

1

(1) insult : 7째줄 his cab부터 thank him까지의 내용
injury : 5째줄 Dr. Callendar부터 message까지의 내용
(2) ㈁ Aidid씨는 잠깐 동안의 마음의 평화를 찾기 위해 한 Hindu사원에 잠시 들렀다.
㈂ Moore부인도 자기처럼 Callendar씨를 높이 평가하지 [좋게 생각하지] 않았다.
(3) Moore부인이라는 한 영국 부인이 Hindu교의 관습을 존중하여 신을 벗고 사원에 들어온 것.

2

(1) Edward　(2) Isabel을 차지하는 것
(3) Edward와 Isabel

3

(1) 교육이 인위적이 되고 일상 생활의 현실과 유리될 위험이 있다.
(2) 화기(火器)가 전쟁 수단으로 확립되고 난 오랜 후에도 궁술을 관리들의 채용시험으로 삼았다.
(3) 일상 생활과 거의 관계가 없는 교육 형태가 수세기 동안 지속할 수 있었다.
(4) 실생활과 학교를 연결시키는 생활 교육

4

(1) 남의 집을 방문하는 손님이 지금껏 당해 보지 못한 가장 무서운 개한테 정식으로 소개받았다.
(2) 도대체 이 개는 어떤 종류에 속하는 것일까?

숙어 Exercise (p.128)

1. They will do away with the (unpopular) tax soon.
2. I couldn't do without my car.
3. I'll drop in some time next week.
4. My boss is always engaged in his work.
5. He never exerts himself to help other people.
6. In case you fail, you must have something to fall back on.
7. The trip fell short of our expectations.
8. We are far from happy with the results of the election.
9. She felt in her bag for a pen.
10. She's always finding fault with the way I dress.

제6장 조동사

문법 · 작문 (p.136)

A.

(1) must
(2) must
(3) cannot
(4) have [need]
(5) cannot
(6) ought
(7) shall
(8) has
(9) will
(10) dare
(11) used
(12) may [might]
(13) should
(14) did
(15) should
(16) should
(17) May
(18) Can
(19) should
(20) should
(21) will

B.

(1) The statement may not be true.
(2) He cannot have been ignorant of the fact.
(3) What you said cannot be true.
(4) Passengers now must not carry more than one piece of hand baggage onto the aircraft.
(5) Will I be able to reach Mr. Brown at home?
(6) You had to support your family.
(7) Will John have to come here?
(8) Her sickness must be a mere cold.
(9) He may have succeeded.

C.

(1) shall ⇨ will
(2) were ⇨ did
(3) has to ⇨ must
(4) can ⇨ cannot
(5) will ⇨ would [might]
(6) should ⇨ would
(7) to ⇨ will
(8) should ⇨ would
(9) shall ⇨ will
(10) should ⇨ would
(11) should ⇨ would
(12) could ⇨ would
(13) deal ⇨ dealing

D.

(1) You may go out, but you must come home before dark.
(2) It cannot be denied that he is a great man.
(3) He cannot have done such a foolish thing.
(4) I advised him again and again to give up smoking, but he would not listen to me.
(5) I used to play here on the beach when I was a child.
(6) He got up early so that he would not be late for the meeting.
(7) He had to be at home, because his mother was sick yesterday.
(8) One should respect the freedom of others as well as one's own.

'Health'

Health is well said to be better than wealth. Without health we can do nothing. However, we sometimes meet so many silly people who act as if wealth were above health. It is also a pity that some students pay no attention to their precious health to get a few more marks in their examinations. These people realize only too late that health is above everything else in life.

단문독해 (p.138)

1. ▶▶해석

항상 동정을 받는 어린아이는 사소한 고통을 가지고 끊임없이 울어댄다. 보통 성인의 정상적인 자제심은, 어떤 동정도 떠들며 불평을 해서는 얻을 수 없다는 것을 알게됨으로써만 성취할 수 있다.

▶▶정답 (1) knows (2) lest, dependent

▶▶영작

She was crying over her misfortune.

2. ▶▶해석

하느님은, 아담과 이브가 자기에게 복종하지 않은 게 슬펐다. 죄와 두려움이 그들의 친교 관계를 해쳤다. 하느님은 이브에게, "너는 악마의 소리에 귀를 돌리고 나에게 복종치 않았으니, 너는 한평생 고통과 괴로움을 가질지어다."하고 말했다.

▶▶정답 tempted, doomed

▶▶영작

I am sorry that I have not written to you for a long time.

3. ▶▶해석

사람은 빵으로만 살 수가 없으며, 또 생각만을 함으로써 살 수도 없다. 나는 생각하고, 이야기하고, 느끼기를 좋아한다. 그러나, 나에게는 사용되고 싶어 안달하는 손과, 하는 일 없이 그냥 매달려만 있지 않으려는 팔뚝이 있다는 것을, 나는 잊지 않고 있다.

▶▶정답 mind and body

▶▶영작

That computer is lying idle. We have to put it to good use.

4. ▶▶해석

돌이켜볼 때, 나에게는 보통 젊은이들보다 좀 우수한 점이 있었음에 틀림없다고 나는 추측한다. 그렇지 않았더라면, 나보다 연령도 매우 많고 학문적인 지위도 높은, 위에서 말한 사람들이 자기들과 내가 교제하는 것을 허용하지 않았을 것이다.

▶▶정답 ④

▶▶영작

There was something in him a little superior to us.

5. ▶▶해석

인류의 역사는 인간 활동의 역사이다. 인간의 본성과 인간의 물질적 조건이 현재와 같은 한, 그 동안은 경제적·산업적 요소가 우리의 정치적·사회적 생활에 강력한 영향을 미칠 것임에 틀림없다.

▶▶정답 result, affect

▶▶영작

You may stay here as long as you like.

6. ▶▶해석

당신은 황금빛의 태양 그리고 따뜻하고 부드러운 공기의 나라, 이탈리아라고 불리는 저 사랑스러운 나라를 아마 들었을 것입니다. 그 나라에서는 하늘이 거의 항상 푸릅니다 — 너무 신기하게 푸르러, 이탈리아는 "창공의 나라"라고 흔히 불립니다.

▶▶정답 beauty

▶▶영작

I may have met him somewhere before, but I don't remember.

7. ▶▶해석

언어는 생물이다. 단어는 식물이나 동물과 같다. 그것은 생겨나서, 자라고, 그 형태를 바꾸고, 성숙하고 그리고 쇠퇴한다. 그러므로 언어학은 식물학이나 동물학만큼 재미있고 매혹적이다. 그래서 인쇄된 페이지 [책]을 연구하는 언어학자를 표본을 찾기 위해 들판을 헤매는 박물학자에 비유하는 것은 당연한 일이다.

▶▶정답 botanist, zoologist

▶▶영작

You may well think that the rumor is true.

8. ▶▶해석

인생을 어떻게 잘 선용할 것인가 하는 문제에 대하여 이야기해 달라고 나는 부탁을 받았다. 그러나, 그런 것은 조금도 모른다고 즉시 고백하는 게 나을 것이다. 나는 지금까지 내 자신의 인생을 선용해 왔다고 생각할 수 없으며, 또한 나에게 남아 있을 혹은 남아 있지도 않을 인생을 더욱 잘 선용할 것 같지도 않다.

▶▶정답 ⑤

▶▶영작

He was asked to make a speech on air pollution.

9. ▶▶해석

경제 법칙을 피할 수 없는 것은 인력을 피할 수 없는 것과 같다. 산업의 진보를 역행하여 인간을 수공업의 시대로 되돌려 보내려고 시도할 바에는, 지구의 지축 회전을 역행하려고 시도하는 게 낫다.

▶▶정답 ③

▶▶영작

You may [might] as well throw your money away as lend it to him.

10. ▶▶해석

사람은 자기가 잘못했다고 고백하는 것을 부끄러워해서는 안 된다. 왜냐 하면, 그 고백은 단지 자기가 어제보다 더 현명해졌다는 것을 다른 말로 하는 것에 불과하기 때문이다.

▶▶정답 ②

▶▶영작

He admitted that he had done it.

11. ▶▶해석

모든 면에서 보아, 이 세상의 통일과 인류의 조화를 위해 공헌해야만 했던 공중의 정복(비행기의 발명 같은 것)이 오히려 우리의 가장 위협적인 위험이 되었다는 것은 최근의 과학 발달에 있어서 가장 비극적인 사실의 하나이다.

▶▶정답 ③

▶▶영작

He is going to resign on the grounds of ill health.

12. ▶▶해석

즐거운 생각을 마음 속에 품고 호수 위에 떠다니는 백조들을 바라보고 있을 때, 누가 내 팔꿈치를 만지는가 했더니 바로 방금 말한 그 어린 소녀가 아니겠는가!

▶▶정답 than

▶▶영작

Every day she would sit gazing at a distant mountain.

13. ▶▶해석

꽤 좋은 수입이 퍽 중요하다는 것을 나는 안다. 그러나, 사람은 그 직업의 보수가 좋건 좋지 않건, 자기에게 적합한 직업을 택하는 것이 더욱 중요하다.

▶▶정답 ③

▶▶영작

Yesterday I happened to meet an old friend of mine on the bus.

14. ▶▶해석

내가 가장 존경하는, 자기나라를 창시한 저 미국인들은 결코 봉사의 대가를 받지 않았다. 워싱턴은 7년 동안 총사령관으로서 봉급을 받으려고 하지 않았고, 또한 8년 간 대통령으로서도 봉급을 받으려고 하지 않았다.

▶▶정답 ③

▶▶영작

He would not listen to my advice.

15. ▶▶해석

멀리서 산맥을 바라보면, 산봉우리는 하늘을 배경으로 뚜렷이 솟아 있는 것처럼 보인다. 꼭대기까지 오르려는 사람을 방해할 아무 장애물도 없는 것처럼 보인다. 그러나, 가까이 감에 따라 모든 것이 변한다. 멀리서는 그렇게 단순해 보였던 것이, 가까이 다가감에 따라 무한히 복잡해진다. 인생도 역시 그렇다.

▶▶정답 ③

▶▶영작

The trees appeared black against the morning sky.

16. ▶▶해석

하루하루 지나감에 따라 그의 건강은 회복되었다. 그는 나에게 이렇게 말하곤 했다. "아, 섬 생활은 어디에서나 찾아볼 수 없는 매력이 있다. 이세상의 이렇게 아름다운 곳(이 섬)에서 단지 살기만 하면, 의사와 약이 없어도 인류의 질병의 절반은 없어질 것이다."라고.

▶▶정답 ⑤

▶▶영작

I came to realize that my mission in this country came closer to an end with every passing day.

17. ▶▶해석

나의 모든 결점에도 불구하고 나에게는 따뜻한 마음이 있다. 비록 내가 가난하지만, 너그럽지 못한 일을 할 바에는 차라리 생활 필수품마저도 거절하겠다.

▶▶정답 ④

▶▶영작

With all his wealth, he is unhappy.

혹은 Rich as he is, he is unhappy.

18. ▶▶해석

우유 배달부는 이른 아침의 직업에 있어서 라이벌이 하나 있다. 그 라이벌은 신문 배달부이다. 우유와 뉴스는 둘 다 아침식사에 필요하다. 런던의 실업가는, 전자는 신체의 청량제이고 후자는 정신의 청량제이므로, 신문보다는 우유 없이 지내기를 택한다.

▶▶정답 milk than news

▶▶영작

(1) I found it very hard to do without cigarettes.

(2) I would rather walk than go in a crowded bus.

19. ▶▶해석

그녀의 격노는 결코 오래가지 않았다. 겸손하게 자기의 잘못을 실토하고 보다 좋은 일을 하려고 애썼다. 그녀의 누이동생들은 차라리 조(Jo)를 성내게 하는 것이 좋다고 말하곤 했다. 왜냐 하면, 성낸 다음에는 마음씨 착한 천사 같았으니까.

▶▶정답 ⑤

▶▶영작

I'd rather like you to give up doing the work.

20. ▶▶해석

그 섬의 공기는 매우 온화하고 향기로웠으므로, 집 안이 아니라도 잘 잘 수 있었을 정도였다. 그러나, 우리는 밖에서 자는 데 익숙해 있지 않았으므로, 지붕 없이 눕는 것을 그리 달갑게 여기지 않았다.

▶▶정답 roof, accustomed

▶▶영작

I could not have done it without your help.

21. ▶▶해석

방안에 갇혀 방안 일에 묶인 현대인은 자기 생명을 자기가 단축하고 있다는 것을 알고 있다. 그는 운동이 필요하다. 그것은 그도 안다. 그러나, 그가 남에게 지도를 부탁할 때 그는 너무도 상호 모순되는 충고를 많이 받기 때문에, 혹시 가뜩이나 나쁜 것이 더 악화되지 않을까 하여 어떠한 충고도 받아들이기를 두려워한다.

▶▶정답 ④

▶▶영작

Hide it lest he should see it.

22. ▶▶해석

우리가 실업 · 병 · 노령으로 인해 일할 수 없을 경우, 굶거나 남에게 자선을 애걸해야 할 신세가 되지 않도록, 우리는 항상 무엇인가 저축해야 한다.

▶▶정답 ④

▶▶영작

We should put aside something so that we may not be dependent on others in our old age.

23. ▶▶해석

그는, 그것이 비록 습관이라고 하더라도, 개가 이빨을 드러내면 안되니 개한테 접근하기도 두렵고, 또 동시에 겁쟁이로 생각되어서도 안되니 도망가기도 두렵고 하여 그저 개를 바라 보고 서 있었다.

▶▶정답 devil, hard

▶▶영작

He lowered his voice for fear (that) he should [would] be overheard.

24. ▶▶해석

하등동물들은 매우 변한 상태 하에서 생존하기 위해 그들의 신체 조직이 변형되어야 한다. 그들은 새로운 적을 방어하기 위해, 더 강해지거나 더 효과적인 이빨 혹은 발톱을 획득해야 한다. 그렇지 않으면, 탐지와 위험을 피하기 위해 몸의 크기가 줄어들어야 한다.

▶▶정답 ③

▶▶영작

You must have that decayed tooth of yours pulled out immediately.

장문독해 (p.148)

1 ▶▶해석

우리들이 살아가는 동안 매일 이야기하는 언어에 대하여, 아무리 우리가 많이 알아도 지나치지 않다. 물론, 우리들 대부분은 우리의 언어에 대해 많이 알지 않고도 또 수고스럽게 옥스퍼드 대사전을 펴 보지 않고도 잘 살아갈 수는 있다. 그러나, 지식은 힘이다. 올바르게 선택된 말의 힘이란, 그것이 남에게 지식을 전달하기 위해 사용되건 혹은 남을 즐겁게 하기 위해서이건, 또 남을 감동시키기 위해 사용되건 대단히 큰 것이다. 영어는 급속하게 세계적인 의사 전달의 수단이 되어 가고 있다. 영어는 지금 대서양의 양쪽에서 수많은 잘 훈련된 연구가들에 의해 연구되고 있다. 지금까지 영어 연구에 있어서 이루어진 진보를 생각해 보면 매우 고무적인 일이다. 영국인은 모국어에 별로 관심이 없다고 하는, 너무도 자주 되풀이되던 그 주장은 이미 타당하지 못하다. 드디어, 우리 영국인들은 우리 모국어를 살아 있는, 변하는 무엇으로 각성된 흥미를 보여 주고 있다. 이것을 우리는 여러 분야, 즉 중앙 행정부와 지방 자치 단체에서, 사업계와 언론계에서, 영화와 라디오에서, 학교와 대학에서 본다. 우리 모두 이 탐구(모국어 연구)에 아낌없이 가담하자. 그리고, 일상생활에서 찾기만 하면 우리의 것일 수 있는 언어 연구의 그 지적인 기쁨을 즐거이 나누어 가지자.

▶▶정답

1. impossible
2. 영국인들이 모국어에 무관심하다는 주장
3. ③
4. ⑤

▶▶영작

(1) You cannot be too careful in the choice of books to read.

(2) The garden, covered with dead leaves, was a dreary sight.

(3) The boy, it is true, is bright but careless in everything he does.

2 ▶▶해석

그렇게도 많은 대전쟁에서, 이긴 쪽이 패자였었다는 것은 주목할만한 사실이다. 전쟁이 끝났을 때에 최악의 상태로 남은 사람들이, 대개 그 일을 모두 결산하고 나면 최선의 상태로 남은 사람들이었다. 가령, 십자군 전쟁은 그리스도 교도들의 패배로 끝났다. 그러나, 십자군 전쟁은 그리스도 교도들의 쇠망으로 끝나지는 않았다. 십자군 전쟁은 사라센인들의 쇠망으로 끝났다. 기독교국의 도시 바로 위 하늘에 무겁게 드리워 있었던 그 회교도 세력의 거대한 예언의 파도, 그 파도는 깨졌고, 다시 밀려오지 않았다. 십자군 전사들은 불가항력으로 예루살렘을 잃었지만 파리를 구했다. 똑같은 사실이, 우리들 자유당원들이 우리의 정치 신조를 힘입고 있는 18세기 공화국 전쟁의 그 서사시에도 적용된다. 프랑스 혁명은 패배로 끝났다. 국왕들은 워털루에 깔린 시체를 밟고 돌아왔다. 혁명은 최후의 싸움에 패했다. 그러나, 자기의 첫 목표를 달성했다. 혁명은 깊은 틈을 갈라놓았다. 그 이후로 세계는 전과 같지 않았다. 그 이후로, 아무도 가난한 사람들을 단지 발판으로만 여길 수는 없었다.

▶▶정답

1. the Crusades
2. ⑤
3. 가난한 사람들이 인간대접을 받는 것
4. ③
5. ②

▶▶영작

(1) The dead and the dying were scattered on the battlefield.
(2) I owe it to you that I am still alive.
(3) This rule applies in [to] all cases.
(4) Don't treat me like a child.

실력체크 I (p.152)

1

(1) The Population Crisis
(2) 지금은 아이들이 더 오래 살 수 있으며 그들이 커서 또 아이를 낳고, 그리하여 인구폭발을 가져온다.
(3) 인구증가는 현재와 미래의 문명을 파괴한다. 이것을 방지하려면 출생률을 저하시킬 필요가 있다.

2 인간은 만물의 영장이라는 서구의 견해와, 인간은 끝없는 우주 안에서 하나의 생명체에 불과하다는 동양의 견해의 차이

3

(1) limit (2) freedom
(3) protected (4) actions
(5) hurt

4

(1) 하수와 산업 폐기물
(2) sewage and industrial waste must be purified

숙어 Exercise (p.158)

1. He flatters himself that he is the best speaker of English in his class.
2. He raised his glass and I followed suit.
3. The boys fooled around all afternoon in the park.
4. They locked all the doors for fear of thieves.
5. Meals will be provided for free.
6. I clung onto the branch for dear life.
7. My name is David, or Dave for short.
8. The inhabitants are for the most part diligent.
9. She saved money for the sake of her family.
10. The plants died for lack of water.

제 7 장 태

문법 · 작문 (p.164)

A.

(1) by (2) to (3) at
(4) with (5) with (6) to
(7) by, by, into (8) in

B.

(1) was signed (2) is believed
(3) being taught (4) be made
(5) had been found, murdered
(6) are buried (7) brought
(8) be loved (9) been done

C.

(1) A lovely suit will be sent to her (by us).
(2) You could put your money to good use instead of leaving it idle in the bank.
(3) Two little boys were seen wallowing in the mud (by us).
(4) Let the paper be signed and mailed at once.
(5) An opening address is being given by the mayor in the city hall.
(6) It must have been taken away (by someone).
(7) By whom do you think the gold medal will be won?
(8) Don't let it be kept a secret that the money was stolen by him.
(9) Do they sell salt by the pound?
(10) The lilac is said to have originally come from the north of Persia.
(혹은 It is said that the lilac originally came from the north of Persia.)
(11) Your travel arrangements will be taken good care of by my secretary.
(혹은 Good care will be taken of your travel arrangements by my secretary.)
(12) I was never taken for an Italian before (by anyone).
(13) A pin might have been heard to drop. *or* A pin might have been heard dropping.
(14) The problem has never been solved.
(15) Regard these facts as of special importance.
(16) She was allowed to stay out late just that once by her father.
(17) It used to be thought that the sun went around the earth.
(18) He has always been looked up to by scholars as a great benefactor of learning.
(19) What she had said was taken no notice of. (혹은 No notice was taken of what she had said.)
(20) The people speak ill of the stuck-up new manager.
(21) We must endure what we cannot cure.
(22) By what are you made to say such a rude thing?
(23) You have written your composition well.
(24) They asked us no questions.
(혹은 They asked no questions of us.)
(25) Naturally you are expected to be interested in the job you have been offered.

D.

(1) This morning a dog was run over by a truck near my house.
(2) You will be laughed at if you do such a foolish thing.
(3) I was very much surprised when I was abruptly spoken to by a stranger in the dark.
(4) The whole city was flooded because of the heavy rain brought by Typhoon Judy.
(5) He seems to be quite satisfied with his present post.
(6) Though he is young, it is said, he is a very able man and is made much of.

(7) Yesterday I was caught in a shower on my way home from school, and was drenched to the skin.
(8) As the new teacher is a man of character, he is well spoken of by the students.
(9) A man's worth should be estimated not by his position in society but by his character.

'Abraham Lincoln'

Abraham Lincoln, the 16th President of America, was one of the most eager advocators of democracy. In the Civil War he led the army of the northern states to set slaves free. He expressed his ideas most eloquently in his Gettysburg Address. His "the government of the people, by the people, for the people" is frequently quoted to define democracy. Unfortunately, however, he was assassinated.

단문독해 (p.166)

1. ▶▶해석
얼마 안 있어 어떤 사람이 내게, 새 꼬리에 소금을 뿌려서 새를 잡을 수는 없으며, 나를 놀리고 있다고 말해 주었다. 거짓말하는 것은 나쁘다고 믿도록 배워 왔기 때문에, 이것은 나에게 커다란 충격이었다. 이제 내 인생에서 처음으로, 나는 거짓말에도 가지가지가 있으며, 거짓말이 아닌 거짓도 있다는 것을 알았다.
▶▶정답 ③, ④
▶▶영작
As you grow older, you will find that there are lies and lies.

2. ▶▶해석
장래의 사회가 부를 인간 생활의 올바른 목적을 이루는 단순한 수단으로만 간주하게 된다면, 그 사회가 전체적으로 보아 부하건 가난하건, 그 사회의 부는 공평히 분배될 것이며, 그리고 이런 목적을 추구하는 사회는 행복하고 건전할 것이다.
▶▶정답 ③
▶▶영작
We are all in pursuit of happiness.

3. ▶▶해석
드디어 야유회 공원에 도착했다. 곧 점심 도시락을 열고, 어느새 그것을 모두 먹어 버렸다. 아침에 너무 많은 점심을 자기들이 싸고 있다고 확신한 어머니들은 이런 샌드위치와 과자들이 얼마나 빨리 없어지는지 와서 보았으면 좋았을 텐데. 음식을 하나도 남김없이 다 먹어 버렸으며, 그만큼 더 가져 왔었다고 해도 아마 똑같이 없어 졌을 것이다.
▶▶정답 ④
▶▶영작
It is not likely that I will see her again.

4. ▶▶해석
높은 지위에 있는 사람들은, 평범한 일상적인 일에 종사하며 일생을 보내는 사람들보다 물론 더 많이 생각되고, 이야기되고, 그들의 덕망이 더욱 칭송되는 것은 사실이다. 그러나, 이런 평범한 일상적이 일이 얼마나 필요하며, 또 그것이 잘 이루어지는 것이 얼마나 우리에게 중요한가를, 지각 있는 사람이면 누구나 다 안다.
▶▶정답 ③
▶▶영작
We must know how important it is to us that the work should begin immediately.

5. ▶▶해석
어제 어떤 남자가 번화가(High Street)에서 차에 치었다. 그 자동차는 화이트 씨가 운전했다. 구급차를 부르고, 그 사람을 인근 병원으로 데려갔다. 그 부상당한 사람의 신원은 아직 밝혀지지 않았다. 그는 다갈색의 상의와 회색 바지를 입고 있었다. 그의 나이는 약 35세 가량으로 추산된다. 이 사람을 혹시 아는 사람은 경찰에 전화하도록 요망하고 있다.

▶▶정답 ④

▶▶영작

She was dressed in white and looked young for her age.

6. ▶▶해석

웰링턴 공(公)은 부하 장교를 그들의 코와 턱을 보고 선택했다고들 말한다. 공작의 여러 초상화들로 판단하건대, 장교가 되는 코의 표준은 좀 높았음에 틀림없다. 그러나, 틀림없이 에누리는 있었으리라. 어쨌든, 이 방법으로써 그는 자기가 원하는 사람들을 구했다.

▶▶정답 ①

▶▶영작

We must make allowances for his youth.

7. ▶▶해석

그리고 정오 경에, 보운즈의 노예 선이 그 섬 근처에서 목격되었다는 전갈이 왔다. 그 노예 선은 당장이라도 출범할 만반의 준비가 되어 있으므로, 매우 주의해야 한다고 그 전갈은 전하고 있었다. 해군 선박이 몰래 이 노예 무역선을 불의에 덮칠 수 있도록, 모든 선원들은 조용히 하라고 경고되었다.

▶▶정답 ④

▶▶영작

Word came that he could not come.

8. ▶▶해석

모든 것을 자신을 위해 (남들이) 하게끔 하는 것 대신에, 아이는 스스로 일을 하도록 놔 두어야 한다. 모든 그의 결정을 남이 해주는 대신 그 나름의 결정을 할 기회가 주어져야 하고 스스로 생각하도록 권장해야 한다.

▶▶정답 ③

▶▶영작

The general is used to having [getting] everything done by his subordinates.

9. ▶▶해석

공정하게 판결하는 판사가 있고, 누구나 정의를 베풀어 받을 수 있는 법정이 있는 한, 그 나라는 정의가 없는 곳에서 항상 생기는 모든 위험과 불만족으로부터 안전하다.

▶▶정답 fair, danger

▶▶영작

The house had its roof blown off.

장문독해 (p.170)

1 ▶▶해석

자유는 평화 위에 세워지며, 다른 기초를 가질 수 없다. 전쟁과 무질서는 자유의 두 커다란 적이다. 우리가 지금 향유하는 바로서의 자유주의 정치는 폭력 대신에 법을, 육체적 투쟁 대신에 의논을 바꾸어 놓은 것이다. 이것은 여러 세기에 걸쳐 이룩된 업적이다. 이것은, 자유로운 토론이 정의를 행하고 정책에 관한 현명한 결론에 도달할 수 있는 가장 적당한 방법이라는 소신에 기초를 두고 있다. 그러나, 그것은 지켜야 할 자신의 규칙이 있다. 그것은 관용과 상호 자제를 요한다. 그것은 소수파가 의회에서 표결에 졌을 때 당분간 복종하고, 자기들의 견해를 (그들이) 이성과 토론에 의해 우세하게 할 수 있는 장래를 위하여 일하는 것에 만족하는 것을 요구한다. 만약에 이런 전제 조건들이 이루어지지 않으면, 우리의 감정이 문자 그대로 말로 나타낼 수 없을 정도로 너무 강하면, 소수파가 복종하려 들지 않고, 말로부터 주먹으로 날아가면, 혹은 다수파가 그들의 권력을 남용하여 소수파로 하여금 육체적인 저항을 하게끔 몬다면, 그때는 자유는 만사 끝나는 것이다.

▶▶정답

1. ⑤ 2. uncontrollable 3. ⑤ 4. ④

▶▶영작

(1) We can substitute margarine for butter.

(2) All knowledge rests on experience.

(3) I am going to stay at this hotel for the time being.
(4) Her comments were so childish as to be not worth considering.

2 ▶▶해석

우리가 안전하게 하려는 미래에 있어서, 우리는 네 가지의 인간의 기본적인 자유에 입각한 세계가 실현되기를 기대합니다.

첫째는 세계 모든 곳에서의 언론과 표현의 자유입니다.

둘째는 세계 모든 곳에서 자기 마음대로 신을 숭배할 수 있는 신앙의 자유입니다.

셋째는 결핍으로부터의 해방입니다. 그것은, 세계적인 넓은 의미에서 볼 때, 세계 모든 곳에서 모든 국가의 국민들에게 건전한 평화로운 생활을 보장해 줄 수 있는 경제적인 이해를 의미합니다.

넷째는 공포로부터의 해방입니다. 이것은, 세계적인 넓은 의미에서 볼 때, 군비를 세계적으로 철저하게 축소하여 세계 어디에서나 어떤 국가도 다른 국가에게 실제적인 침략을 감행할 입장에 놓이지 못하도록 하는 것입니다.

이런 것은 먼 천년 후에나 생길 꿈이 아닙니다. 그것은 우리 시대, 우리 세대에 이룩할 수 있는 세계의 명확한 토대인 것입니다. 이런 세계는, 오늘날 독재자들이 폭탄의 굉음에 의하여 이룩하려고 하는, 소위 새로운 독재 질서와 정반대입니다.

▶▶정답

1. ③ 2. ⑤ 3. ④
4. ① T ② T ③ F ④ T ⑤ T ⑥ T ⑦ T ⑧ T ⑨ F ⑩ T

▶▶영작

(1) We have been traveling around for two months, and now all are looking forward to going back home.
(2) Some books, read carelessly, will do more harm than good.
(3) This book is written in such easy English that beginners can understand it.

실력체크 I (p.174)

1

(1) 개인차는 유전에 의한다.
(2) 개인차는 유전에 의한다는 여태까지의 설에 대해, 경험이 개인차를 결정하는 요인이라는 설이 주창되기 시작한 것.
(3) 유전과 경험 양쪽이 모두 개인차를 이루는데 중요한 요인이라고 생각되고 있다.
(4) 적성과 지능, 개인적인 기호 혹은 요구 등은 잠재 능력에 있어서는 유전의 영향이 크지만, 이들을 발전시키는데 있어서는 경험에 의존함이 육체적인 특징의 경우보다 훨씬 크다.

2

(1) ⑤
(2) 노상 수시 검문은 교통안전 보장에 도움이 된다는 경찰의 주장에 대해, 그것이 헌법 4조 수정안의 불법적인 수색이나 압류금지 조항을 초월할 수 없다는 것이 미국 연방 대법원의 평결이다.

숙어 Exercise (p.180)

1. They are soft drinks free of artificial coloring.
2. They come to see me from time to time.
3. Get a move on, or you'll be late.
4. The speaker didn't get his point across to the audience.
5. The burglar got away from the police.
6. I got down to sorting out the papers.
7. She still hasn't got over the shock of her mother's death.
8. The company quickly got rid of poor salesmen.
9. After I got through with my work, I went to bed.
10. My cat gave birth to three kittens.

제 8 장 법

문법 · 직문 (p.188)

A.

(1) were [was] (2) had walked
(3) were [was] (4) had gone
(5) had been (6) Were
(7) Were (8) (should) be rejected
(9) were [was] (10) would have gone

B.

(1) If you had helped me, I could have done it.
(2) If I had enough money, I could replace my old car.
(3) If I had known his phone number, I could have called him.
(4) I wish I could speak English as well as you.
(5) I wish she had been at the party.
(6) If the watch had not been very expensive, I could have bought it.
(7) If he should die (혹은 were to die, died), how could I bring up my two children?
(8) I worked hard; if I had not worked hard I would have failed.
(9) If it had not been for the teacher's assistance, he would have failed the exam.
(10) If it were not for immediate surgery, the patient would die.
(11) I wish you could visit us more often.
(12) He treated me as if I were a mere child.
(13) If you had taken one step further, you would have fallen over the cliff.
(14) If it had not been for her tender care, I would not have become as strong as I am.
(15) If you had made a closer examination of it, it might have revealed a new fact.
(16) If the weather had not been stormy, I could have continued my journey.
(17) If we had had two more levers, we could have removed the rock.
(18) It would be wrong if we were to reveal his secret.

C.

(1) submitted (혹은 should submit)
(2) might have starved
(3) hadn't gone (혹은 had never gone)
(4) would have cried
(5) would be
(6) would be

D.

(1) been (2) otherwise [or]
(3) be (4) if (5) As

E.

(1) If you had arrived two minutes earlier, you would have caught the train.
(2) If I had taken the doctor's advice then, I would be well about now.
(3) I wish I could run as fast as you.
(4) If only he were [was] physically strong, he would be perfect.
(5) If you heard him speak English, you would take him for an American.
(6) A true gentleman would not have done such a thing.
(7) He has never been to Paris, but he talks as if he had been.
(8) Without [But for, If it had not been for] your help, I would have failed my history test.
(9) If the sun were to collide with the moon, what would become of the earth?

'Time'

Time passes day and night. Time passes like an arrow. No man can stop it. This is very well known to everybody, but we find too many old people who regret that they did not work harder when they were young. Therefore, we younger people should not waste time; we should make the most of our spare time.

단문독해 (p.190)

1. ▶▶해석

사람이 공동 사회에서 살 때 자기 멋대로 행동할 수 없다. 가령, 자동차를 운전하는 사람이 자기 좋은 대로 아무데로나 차를 운전하면 반드시 혼란이 일어난다. 또한, 사람들이 자기 멋대로 서로 죽이고 빼앗으면 반드시 사회의 붕괴를 야기한다. 이와 같이 사람들이 행동에 제한을 받지 않는다면, 비록 명목상으로나마 그들이 좋아하는 것을 무엇이나 할 수 있는 자유를 갖게 된다고 해도, 사실 그들은 거의 자유를 소유하지 못할 것이다.

▶▶정답 ③

▶▶영작

I cannot see you without thinking of your mother.

2. ▶▶해석

그 여자가 죽었을 때, 맥베드는 두려움으로 몸을 떨며 그의 피 묻은 손을 보았다."대양의 모든 물이 나의 손으로부터 이 피를 씻어 낼 수 있을까?" 하고 그는 중얼거렸다. 그리고 잠시 후, 자신의 물음에 슬프게 대답했다. "아니다. 설사 내가 대양에서 손을 씻는다고해도, 내 손은 온 바다를 붉게 물들일 것이다." 라고.

▶▶정답 ④

▶▶영작

If the sun were to rise in the west, I would not change my mind.

3. ▶▶해석

그는, 자기가 매일 호흡하는 공기 속에 그가 아무리 귀를 기울여도 그의 귀가 분간할 수 없는 음이 있고, 그가 아무리 눈을 긴장하여 떠도 구별할 수 없는 빛이 있다는 것을 이제 안다.

▶▶정답 limitations

▶▶영작

Go where you will, you will never find a place more beautiful than here.

4. ▶▶해석

어린 뉴턴은 농사일에 전혀 적합하지 않다는 것이 입증되었다. 자기 일에 정신을 쏟는 대신에, 그는 책을 읽든지 몽상에 잠기든지 혹은 목제 모형을 만들곤 했다. 드디어, 어머니는 아이작(뉴턴)이 대학 입학 준비를 하는 것에 동의했다.

▶▶정답 ②

▶▶영작

I demand that he be called here immediately.

5. ▶▶해석

당신은 놀 때뿐만 아니라 괴로움을 만나면, 그 괴로울 때에도 같이 있고 싶은 그런 사람을 친구로서 원한다. 그런 친구가 당신이 존경할 수 있는 친구다.

▶▶정답 need

▶▶영작

She wants him for a friend.

6. ▶▶해석

우리가 판단할 수 있는 한, 그에게는 전혀 없는 시적인 재능을 설사 그가 가지고 있더라고 하더라도 언어의 부족 때문에 그는 위대한 시인이 되지 못했을 것이다.

▶▶정답 ②

▶▶영작

He is entirely destitute of sympathy.

7. ▶▶해석

인간은 우리의 선인들의 유용한 노동의 결과가 없었더라면 여전히 야만인으로 남아있었을 것이다. 그 선인들은 예술과 과학을 발견했고, 우리는 그들의 유용한 결과를 이어받는다.

▶▶정답 ②

▶▶영작

He has no children to succeed him.

8. ▶▶해석

책이 없다면, 인간의 가장 심오한 사상과 그의 가장 고매한 업적을 적어 놓은 기록물이 아니라면, 매 세대마다 구전이라는 부적당한 도움만을 가지고 혼자 힘으로 과거의 진리를 재발견해야 할 것이다.

▶▶정답 written, heritage

▶▶영작

The baby still cannot stand by itself.

9. ▶▶해석

무엇보다도 너의 공부를, 옷을 입고 벗는 것처럼, 머리를 빗고 이를 닦는 것처럼 습관으로 만들어라. 그러면, 공부가 아주 네 생활의 일부가 되어, 단 한 번이라도 공부를 빠뜨리면 너는 죄의식을 느낄 것이다.

▶▶정답 ③

▶▶영작

Above all, don't talk to anybody about it.

10. ▶▶해석

네가 이야기하려고 하는 모든 것을, 될 수 있으면 적은 어휘로 간단히 말하여라. 그렇지 않으면, 독자는 틀림없이 그것을 읽지 않고 넘겨 버릴 것이다. 또, 될 수 있는 한 쉬운 말로 하여라. 그렇지 않으면, 독자는 틀림없이 그것들을 오해할 것이다.

▶▶정답 ②

▶▶영작

He is sure to pass the entrance examination.

11. ▶▶해석

비록 한 사람을 제외하고 모든 인류가 같은 의견이고, 한 사람만이 반대 의견을 갖고 있다해도, 인류가 그 한 사람의 의견을 묵살하는 것이 정당화되지 못하는 것은, 그 한사람이 비록 그런 힘이 있다고 해도, 인류의 의견을 묵살하는 것이 정당화되지 못하는 것과 같다.

▶▶정답 ④

▶▶영작

My firm belief is that the end does not justify the means.

12. ▶▶해석

왕이 밤에 잘 때 누구한테 공격을 받을 경우 왕의 신변을 보호하기 위해, 왕이 어디에서 자건, 같은 방에서 두 무장한 병사가 자는 것이 그런 야만 시대의 습관이었다.

▶▶정답 guard

▶▶영작

In case I forget, please remind me about it.

13. ▶▶해석

비록 당신의 원칙은 옳지만, 그 목적을 달성하는 수단이 문제라고 저는 생각합니다. 그러므로, 그 계획을 당분간 연기할 것을 제안합니다.

▶▶정답 ④

▶▶영작

I will stay with my uncle for the time being until I find an affordable hotel.

14. ▶▶해석

이기적인 소년은 아무도 사랑하지 않고 유독 자기만을 사랑하는 소년이다. 그는 자기가 즐거움만 얻을 수 있다면 누구에게서 즐거움을 뺏건 상관하지 않는다.

▶▶정답 egotist

▶▶영작

They deprived him of all his property.

15. ▶▶해석

만약 당신이 런던의 어느 한 공원에 있으며, 어쩌다 새 한 마리가 노래하고 있을 때 당신이 그 소리를 즐기기 위해 선다고 가정할 경우, 어떤 다른 사람이 그 소리를 즐기기 위해 선다고 해도 그것이 당신의 즐거움을 줄이지 않습니다. 아니, 오히려 그것은 당신의 즐거움을 더 합니다. 그러나, 만약에 어떤 사람이 그 새에게 돌을 던지면 그는 당신의 즐거움을 파괴합니다.

▶▶정답

새소리를 다른 사람들과 같이 들으며 나누는 즐거움

▶▶영작

The fact that you happened to be born into a good family does not necessarily entitle you to people's respect.

16. ▶▶해석

당신의 대학 교육이 당신으로 하여금 평생토록 공부를 계속하게끔 이끌어 주지 못한다면, 그것은 한 개인으로서 당신을 발전시키는 그 역할을 다 하지 못한 것이 된다.

▶▶정답 lifelong learning

▶▶영작

He played a large part in building up the company.

17. ▶▶해석

노동 분쟁에 있어서 집단적인 흥정에 쓰이는 하나의 무기로서 동맹 파업 그 자체는, 분쟁을 하겠다는 예비적인 경고가 노동 조합에 의해 주어지면, 오늘날 불법이 아니다.

▶▶정답 ⑤

▶▶영작

He gave notice of some changes in his plan.

18. ▶▶해석

얼마 전에, 나는 어느 외과 의사가 정교한 뇌 수술을 하는 것을 볼 기회가 있었다. 그의 손이 약간만 미끄러졌다면, 그것은 환자에게 즉각적인 죽음을 의미했을 것이다. 그 의사에 관해 내가 감동을 받은 것은, 그의 기술이 아니라 그의 놀라운 침착성이었다.

▶▶정답 ③

▶▶영작

A more skillful teacher would have treated him otherwise.

19. ▶▶해석

태어날 때 음악 혹은 회화의 재능을 부여받은 사람들이 있듯이, 글재주가 있는 사람들이 있다. 우리 모두가 똑같은 틀에서 나오지 않은 것이 다행이다. 그렇지 않다면 (한가지로 만들어져 있다면), 인생은 너무나 단조로울 것이다.

▶▶정답 ②

▶▶영작

I went at once; otherwise, I would have missed the train.

20. ▶▶해석

"Please" 라는 말은 매우 보잘 것 없는 말이다. 그러나 그것은, 그것이 없다면 거칠게 들릴 그런 많은 요청들을 즐겁게 들리게 해 준다. "Thank you." 라는 말도 마찬가지다.

▶▶정답 part

▶▶영작

A good many people attended the meeting.

21. ▶▶해석

결론으로 한 마디 실제적인 말을 하겠습니다. 건강에 주의하시오. 이 점에 현명하게 주의를 하였던들 어떤 높은 지위에도 올라갔을 텐데, 이 점을 현명치 못하게 게을리 했기 때문에 아무것도 안 된 사람들이 많았습니다.

▶▶정답 or you will come to nothing

▶▶영작

What would you have done in such circumstances?

22. ▶▶해석

그가 그 금을 발견했을 때, 아무도 가까이 없었다. 그는 그 금을 모두 자기가 가지려면 가질 수 있었을 것이다. 이런 큰 금덩어리를 가졌다면 그를 부자로 만들었을 것이다. 그러나, 그는 부자가 될 생각은 없었다. 그는 정직하기로 마음먹었다.

▶▶정답 ⑤

▶▶영작

He kept the money all to himself.

23. ▶▶해석

아마 너는 어른들이 이렇게 말하는 것을 들었을 것이다. "그것을 학창 시절에 배웠더라면" 혹은 "좀 더 교육을 받았더라면" 하고. 왜 어른들이 이렇게 느끼리라고 너는 생각하느냐? 그것은 아마, 그들이 좀 더 배웠더라면 혹은 좀더 잘 공부했더라면 인생은 좀더 흥미 있고 혹은 보다 나은 직장을 구했을 텐데 하고, 그들이 생각하기 때문일 것이다.

▶▶정답 ①

▶▶영작

Why do you suppose he emigrated to Brazil?

24. ▶▶해석

12시를 치자 마치 벼락이라도 맞은 사람처럼 빨리 연장을 놓는 일꾼은 자기의 의무를 다하고 있을지는 모르나, 그는 그 이상은 아무것도 안하고 있다. 자기의 의무만을 다함으로써 인생에 성공한 사람은 아무도 없다. 그는 의무도 다해야하고, 또 그 이상을 해야 한다. 그가 자기 일에 사랑을 쏟아 넣으면, 일은 그 만큼 더 쉬워질 것이다.

▶▶정답 affection

▶▶영작

This book teaches you how to make a success of life.

25. ▶▶해석

그것은 날카로운 검이었다. 그것은 단 한 가닥의 말총에 의해 매달려 있었다. 저 말총이 끊어지면 어떡할까? 당장에라도 끊어질 위험이 있었다.

▶▶정답 ③

▶▶영작

What if he should fail to keep his promise?

26. ▶▶해석

너는 나쁜 친구를 사귀기보다는 차라리 혼자 있어야 한다. 친구는 너와 비슷하든지 혹은 뛰어난 사람을 사귀어라. 왜냐하면, 사람의 가치는 그의 친구의 가치에 의하여 측정되기 때문이다.

▶▶정답 company

▶▶영작

In his company I am never bored.

27. ▶▶해석

나는 자연을 찬미하는 데 있어서 매우 열렬하다. 이 나라가 나에게 보여 준 여러 사물들을 그렇게도 오랫동안 또 그렇게도 즐겁게 내가 바라보고, 말하자면 서로 대화를 해 왔기 때문에 그들과 헤어진다는 생각을 하니, 사랑하는 친구와 헤어질 때 항상 느껴 온 것과 비슷한 슬픔이 내 마음을 억누른다.

▶▶정답 thought, friend

▶▶영작

I have lived with them so long that I feel very sorry to part from them.

28. ▶▶해석

대부분의 사람들이 그런 것은 아니지만, 문학 취미를 하나의 우아한 교양으로 간주하는 사람들이 많다. 이 취미를 획득함으로써, 그들은 자기 자신을 완성하고 올바른 사회의 구성원으로서 드디어 자기를 적응시킨다.

▶▶정답 qualification

▶▶영작

Everybody knew him by sight, if not by name.

29. ▶▶해석

나폴레옹은, 다른 사람이 자기의 능력을 증명하건 안 하건 그 사람의 실력에 대해 비록 속는다고 해도, 좀처럼 속는 일이 없었다.

▶▶정답 ②

▶▶영작

Do you have anything to say in regard to this matter?

30. ▶▶해석

사람들은, 악과 미덕이 마치 두 개의 동떨어진 것이며 서로 어느 쪽도 다른 쪽을 조금도 포함하고 있지 않은 것처럼 이들을 구분해 버린다. 이것은 그렇지 않다. 가치 있는 미덕으로서 약간의 악이 섞이지 않은 것이 없으며, 약간의 미덕을 갖고 있지 않은 악이 비록 있다고 해도 거의 없다.

▶▶정답 ②

▶▶영작

He insists that there is nothing in the world that is not of some use to us.

31. ▶▶영작

프랑스 인이 영국인보다 보트나 항해술에 있어서 비록 못하다고 해도 거의 못하지 않지만, 이 두 가지 일에 대한 그들의 취미는 매우 제한되어 있다.

▶▶정답 few

▶▶영작

He is inferior to none in English in his class.

32. ▶▶영작

현대 생활이 적어도 유쾌한 것이 되려면, 매우 필요한 미덕이 둘 있다. 그것은 정직과 생활의 간소화다. 그리고, 이 두 미덕 중에서 어느 하나를 실행하면, 다른 쪽도 우리에게 더 쉬워진다는 사실을 주목해야 하겠다.

▶▶정답 simple, honest

▶▶영작

I like my eggs half boiled.

33. ▶▶해석

과학 조사에 있어서 한 번의 오류는 크건 작건 간에 매우 중요하다. 그리고, 비록 치명적인 결과는 아니지만, 결국에 가서 항상 해로운 결과를 꼭 낳는다.

▶▶정답 ④

▶▶영작

It pays in the long run to buy goods of high quality.

장문독해 (p.202)

1 ▶▶해석

사실은, 우리가 이 세상에서 아무리 유혹이 많아도 지나치지 않다는 것이다. 유혹과 접촉이 없으면 미덕은 가치가 없고, 심지어 뜻없는 낱말이다. 유혹은 인생의 근본을 이루는 투쟁의 한가지 필수 형태이다. 영원한 유혹의 불길이 없으면, 인간 정신은 결코 부드럽게 되고 강화될 수 없다. 모든 유혹을 일소하고 최초부터 유혹이 없는 진공 상태에 모든 젊은이들을 가져다 놓으려는 도덕 개혁가들의 열성은, 비록 그것이 성취될 수 있다해도 (그 성취는 모든 환경을 섬멸할 뿐만 아니라 인간의 마음으로부터 그 중요한 정열을 제거해 버릴 것이다), 아무 쓸모 없는 약골의 무리만을 창조하는 결과가 될 것이다. 왜냐하면, 유혹은 투쟁에 대해 자극 이상의 것이기 때문이다. 유혹은 그것이 정열과 관계되는 한, 그 자체가 인생의 효소다. 유혹에 직면하여 그것을 배척하는 것은, 곧 인생을 강화하는 것이 될 수 있다. 유혹에 직면하여 유혹을 받아들이는 것은 인생을 풍부하게 할 수 있다. 어느 것도 할 수 없는 사람은 사는데 알맞지 않다.

▶▶정답

1. not only, but also 2. ② 3. ④ 4. ④

▶▶영작

(1) We cannot overestimate the importance of moral education.

(2) Without contact with foreign culture we cannot expect to enrich our own.

(3) To love others is the way to be loved by them.

2 ▶▶해석

우리가 사랑을 속삭이던 청춘 시대에는 어떤 고상한 행동이라도 할 마음의 준비가 되어 있지 않았던가? 사랑하는 그 여자를 위해서라면 어떤 고상한 생활이라도 할 수 있지 않았던가? 우리의 사랑은 그것을 위해서 죽을 수도 있었던 종교와도 같은 것이었다. 우리들이 경모한 것은 우리와 같은 하잘것없는 인간은 아니었다. 우리들이 경의를 표한 것은 여왕이었고, 우리들이 숭배한 것은 바로 여신이었다. 그리고, 얼마나 열렬히 숭배했던고! 그리고, 숭배한다는 것이 얼마나 달콤했던고! 아, 젊은이여, 사랑의 꿈이 계속되는 동안 그것을 고이 간직하오! 톰 무어가 인생에 있어서 사랑의 달콤함의 절반도 되는 게 없다고 말했을 때, 그가 얼마나 진실하게 노래했는가를 그대는 곧 알게 될 것이다. 사랑의 젊은 꿈이 불행을 가져올 때라도, 그것은 격정적인 낭만적인 불행이며, 나중에 오는 슬픔의 저 음침한 세속적인 괴로움과는 전혀 다르다. 당신이 사랑하는 여자를 잃었을 때에도, 빛이 당신의 인생으로부터 꺼졌을 때에도, 세상이 당신 앞에 기다란 어두운 공포의 그림자를 던지고 가로놓여 있을 때라도, 심지어 그 때에라도 당신의 실망에는 황홀함이 절반쯤은 섞여 있는 것이다. 아, 저 어리석었던 나날이여, 우리들이 헌신적이고 순수했던 저 어리석었던 나날이여, 우리들의 소박한 마음이 진실과 성실과 존경으로만 가득 찼던 저 어리석었던 나날이여!

▶▶정답

1. willingly 2. ④ 3. ⑤ 4. ④

▶▶영작

(1) Who can master English without working hard?
(2) I could have done it then and I could do it now.
(3) The days when we are in love are the happiest in our life.
(4) I have read it written in some book that those who love deeply never grow old.

실력체크 I (p.206)

1

(1) we say
(2) 우리들이 의미하는 것보다 우리들이 의미하지 않는 것을 말하는 것이 훨씬 쉽다.
(3) happier or better or lives a nobler or more satisfactory life
(4) 보통 돈으로 살 수 있는 물품이나 봉사를 의미한다.
(5) When we talk about wealth ~ for money
(6) 여기서 분명히 해 두지 않으면 서로 목적이 엇갈린 많은 토론을 가져온다.
(7) 한 쪽은 의식주 같은 물질적인 면의 진보를 논하고, 다른 쪽은 행복・도덕등 정신적인 면의 문제를 논하고 있다.

2 ④

3

(1) The power of writing creatively is a greater gift than the power of writing cleanly.
(2) 우리는 그들의 어색하고 과장된 영어를 고치려면 고칠 수도 있고, 개선하려면 개선할 수도 있다.
(3) 영어를 잘 쓴다는 것만으로는 부족하다. 작문력보다는 창작력이 더 위대한 재능이다.
Scott과 Hardy의 문장은 손볼 데가 많지만, 그들의 소설은 창조적인 내용이 담긴 위대한 작품이다.
(4) plainness, simplicity

4 ④

숙어 Exercise (p.212)

1. Give your exam papers in to the teacher.
2. The garbage was giving off a horrible [terrible, nasty] smell.
3. She gave the books out to the children.
4. Unhygienic conditions [surroundings, environment] give rise to disease.
5. I won't go back on my promise.
6. She doesn't go in for cooking; she usually eats in restaurants.
7. He went on working even after his car accident.
8. His parents handed down a big house to their son.
9. The robber threatened the clerk to hand over the money (to him).
10. The girl has had a crush on my brother (for years).

제9장 명사 I

문법 · 작문 (p.216)

A.

1. Whale ⇨ The [혹은 A] whale
   ※The whale은 A whale보다 문어적이다.
2. cradle ⇨ the cradle, tomb ⇨ the tomb
3. was ⇨ were
4. Milk ⇨ The milk
5. are ⇨ is
6. wine ⇨ wines
7. is ⇨ are
8. cattles ⇨ cattle
9. new Ford ⇨ a new Ford
10. soaps ⇨ bars [cakes] of soap
11. small furnitures ⇨ little furniture
12. an advice
    ⇨ a piece [a word] of advice
13. stone ⇨ a stone
14. is ⇨ are

B.

① spoonful 혹은 lump, pound
② piece
③ pair
④ flock
⑤ shoal 혹은 school
⑥ suit
⑦ pack
⑧ head

C.

1. the
2. a white
3. a failure
4. baggage
5. are
6. a paper
7. were, their
8. the
9. beautiful
10. A speech
11. poems

D.

1. a brief appearance at the party and then left
2. gives me a good appetite
3. difficulty (in) proving that they are guilty
4. has made her leave her husband and go to live with another man
5. his great disappointment, he failed the bar exam
6. pressure on the mayor to lower taxes or be voted out of office
7. of the river prevents us from drinking water from it
8. enables us to cut production costs by half
9. no idea what all this fuss is about

E.

1. At the sight of our national flag, I felt the patriot rising up in my heart.
2. Keep an extinguisher in case a fire breaks out in the house.
3. As a businessman he was a success, but a failure as a politician.
4. He is a man of experience and knowledge.
5. There are four or five pieces of furniture in his room, and each of them reflects his refined taste.
6. The boy threw a few stones over the fence and broke two windowpanes.
7. Two hours' bus ride from the station takes you to his native village.

'My Best Friend'

My best friend is Song. He is my classmate. We always visit each other on Saturday afternoons or Sundays. We sometimes go fishing in a river which is about one mile west of our village. During the summer vacation last year we visited Seoul together. Next year we will sit for the entrance examination to the same university. If we pass it, we will go on a sightseeing trip to Jeju.

단문독해 (p.218)

1. ▶▶해석

개는 보통 인정있는 주인에게는 변함없이 충성스럽다. 사람들 사이에 존재하는 계층차이라는 것은 개의 생활과는 조금도 관계가 없다. 개는 부자나 가난한 사람에게나 충실한 벗이 될 수 있다. 개는 오랜 세월에 걸쳐서 많은 사람들에게 귀여움을 받아 왔다.

▶▶정답 ②

▶▶영작

She has endeared herself to the American public.

2. ▶▶해석

요즘은 애국자 되기가 쉽지 않다. 그것은 자기의 조국을 사랑하기가 어렵기 때문에 그런 것은 아니다. 그 어려움은 자기의 조국을 어떻게 올바르게 사랑하느냐에 있다.

▶▶정답 but because

▶▶영작

You must not despise a man because he is poor.

3. ▶▶해석

여기서 나는 내가 가장 원하는 것, 즉 있는 그대로의 인생과 접촉할 수 있었다. 그 3년 동안에 나는 인간에게 가능한 모든 감정을 매우 잘 보아왔음에 틀림없다. 그것은 나의 극작가적인 본능에 호소했으며, 또 나의 소설가적인 소질을 자극했다.

▶▶정답 ④

▶▶영작

At the sight of the orphan, she felt the mother welling up in her breast.

4. ▶▶해석

무엇인가 유용한 일을 함으로써 신을 숭배하고, 정직하고 즐겁게 살며, 사욕을 버리고 조국을 사랑하도록 자식들에게 가르쳐라. 그들이 모두 다 워싱턴 같은 위인은 못 될지라도, 틀림없이 워싱턴 같은 사람을 그들의 통치자와 지도자로 선택하는 그런 사람들은 될 것이다.

▶▶정답 ③

▶▶영작

There are a great number of Andersons and Johnsons in America.

5. ▶▶해석

영국인보다 더 자주 토의되어 온 국민은 거의 없었다. 인간 사회사에서 수세기 동안 영국은 주요한 세계 열강의 일원이었다. 영국인들은 자주, 그리고 다양한 분야에서 지도자였거나, 혹은 주목할 만한 진보의 귀중한 공헌자였다.

▶▶정답 ③

▶▶영작

A wide variety of food is available at the restaurant.

6. ▶▶해석

내가 젊었을 때 나의 독서를 지도할 양식 있는 사람이 나에게 있었더라면 하고, 나는 진심으로 (지금) 바란다. 나에게 그다지 이익이 없는 책에 내가 허비한 많은 시간을 생각할 때 한숨이 나온다.

▶▶정답 ③

▶▶영작

This book is of great value to history students.

7. ▶▶해석

한 가지 어려움을 극복한 사람은 다음의 어려움을 자신 있게 맞이할 각오가 되어 있다. 그런 사람이 얼마나 많은 것을 얻었는가를 보라. 후에 다른 사람들이 무엇을 할 것인가, 혹은 어떤 일을 할 것인가 안 할 것인가 망설일 때, 그는 자기가 시작하는 것을 성취한다.

▶▶정답 ④

▶▶영작

Someone has left the window open on purpose.

8. ▶▶해석

자신들이 본질적으로 인도적이라고 믿고 실제로 박애주의자로 처신하지만, 그러나 만약 변화된 환경이 잔인해 질 수 있는 기회를 제공하면 그러한 유혹에 열정적으로 굴복하는 사람들이 많다. 그러므로 국제전이건 내란이건 전쟁을 피하는 것이 절대로 필요하다.

▶▶정답

전시에는 많은 사람들이 잔인해지기 쉽기 때문에

▶▶영작

I would rather die than give way to this sort of temptation.

9. ▶▶해석

어렸을 때 나는, 안 주인이 안 보이는 데서는 그 여자에 대해 아주 심한 욕을 하다가 그 여자가 방에 들어오자마자 만면에 웃음을 띄우고 매우 굽실거리곤 하던 노신사를 한 분 알고 있었다.

▶▶정답 ⑤

▶▶영작

Don't speak ill of others behind their backs.

10. ▶▶해석

그 노신사는, 대대로 물려받은 팔걸이 의자에 앉아, 태양계의 중심인 태양처럼 주위를 둘러보며, 따뜻한 기쁨의 미소를 모두에게 보내며, 손님대접이 더할 나위 없이 친절했다.

▶▶정답 ④

▶▶영작

Surrounded by his grandchildren, the old man was all smiles.

장문독해 (p.222)

1 ▶▶해석

오랜 세계 역사에 있어서 단지 몇 세대만이 매우 위험한 시각에 자유를 수호할 역할을 부여받아 왔습니다. 나는 이 책임을 회피하지 않습니다. 아니, 오히려 그것을 환영합니다. 나는 우리들 가운데 어떤 분도 다른 나라 사람과 혹은 다른 세대와 자리를 바꾸고 싶어하리라고는 생각하지 않습니다. 이 노력을 위해 우리가 쏟는 힘, 신념, 헌신은 우리나라와 우리나라에 봉사하는 모든 사람의 앞길을 밝힐 것입니다. 그리고, 그 불빛은 참으로 온 세계를 밝힐 수 있습니다.

그러므로, 동포여러분! 여러분의 조국이 여러분을 위해 무엇을 할 것인가를 묻지 말고, 조국을 위해 여러분이 무엇을 할 수 있을 것인가를 물으십시오. 세계의 시민 여러분! 미국이 여러분을 위해 무엇을 해 줄 것인가를 묻지 말고, 우리들이 서로 힘을 합해 인간의 자유를 위해 무엇을 할 수 있는가를 물으십시오.

마지막으로, 여러분이 미국 시민이건 세계의 시민이건, 우리들이 여러분에게 부탁하는 똑같은 정도의 높은 희생과 힘을 우리에게 부탁하십시오.

▶▶정답

1. 자유 수호의 책임 2. ③ 3. ② 4. ④

▶▶영작

(1) The important thing is not what you have but what you are.

(2) President Kennedy and his earnest desire for world peace will forever be cherished in our memory.

(3) He was given the rare privilege of participating in the conference.

(4) Whether you like it or not, you must do it; that's your responsibility.

(5) Many of his classmates applied to the college but only a few of them were admitted.

2 ▶▶해석

우리의 생활과 노력을 돌이켜 보면, 우리의 거의 모든 행동과 소망이 다른 사람들의 존재와 밀접하게 얽혀 있다는 것을 우리는 곧 깨닫는다. 우리 인간의 본성이 모든 점에서 사회적 동물들의 본성과 닮았다는 것을 우리는 안다. 우리는 남이 생산한 음식을 먹고, 남이 만든 옷을 입고, 남이 지은 집에서 산다. 우리의 지식과 신념의 대부분은, 남이 창조한 언어에 의해 남으로부터 우리에게 전달되어 왔다. 그러므로 우리는, 짐승보다 인간이 나은 주된 우월성은, 인간 사회에 산다는 사실 덕분임을 인정해야 한다. 태어나서부터 혼자 내버려두면, 개인은 우리가 상상할 수 없을 정도로 그의 사상과 감정에 있어서 원시적이며 짐승같은 상태에 남아 있을 것이다. 인간이 오늘과 같은 개인이 되고 또 개인으로서 지금과 같은 의의를 갖게 된 것은, 그의 개인성 덕분에 의해서보다는 차라리 태어나서 죽을 때까지 그의 물심 양면의 생활을 이끄는 커다란 인간 사회의 일원으로서이다. 공동 사회에 대한 인간의 가치는 그의 감정, 사상, 행동이 동료의 이익을 증진하는 쪽으로 얼마나 멀리 향했느냐에 주로 달려 있다.

▶▶정답

1. ④
2. 인간 사회의 일원이기 때문에
3. 그의 생각과 행동이 사회 공익에 얼마나 이익이 되느냐의 여부
4. ③ 5. ③

▶▶영작

(1) The affair seems very closely bound up with their interests.
(2) A man's value lies not so much in what he has as in what he is.
(3) You must keep in mind that your success in life entirely depends upon your own efforts.

실력체크 I (p.226)

1 Usage is the only test.

2

(1) (ㄱ) 프랑스인들은 그 위험을 완전히 잊어버리고 즐거운 듯이 잡담을 하기 시작했다. 그러나, 한편 영국인들은 이 때가 되어서야 그 위험을 깨닫기 시작하고, 심지어 한 영국인은 신경이 쇠약해져 몸져 누워야 했다.
(2) (ㄴ) 그들은 본능적으로 마차 안에서 이리 몰리고 저리 몰리고 하지 않았다. 왜냐하면, 그렇게 하면 마차가 더 뒤집힐 것 같았기 때문이었다.

3 3차 세계 대전에 사용될 가공할 무기와 이로 인한 인류의 파멸을 이야기하고 싶었다.

4 ⓐ light ⓑ modernized ⓒ wealthy

5 It is now man that is man's worst enemy.

숙어 Exercise (p.232)

1. The teacher has a way with difficult children.
2. I have all the necessary information at my fingertips.
3. His job has something to do with banking.
4. I was (very) angry, but I heard him out.
5. He hit the ceiling when he didn't get his (usual) bonus.
6. The contract holds good for three years.
7. We held off buying a house until prices came down.
8. The building work was held up by bad weather.
9. I feel ill at ease in such formal clothes.
10. As a lawyer I act on behalf of her.

제10장 명사 II

문법 · 작문 (p.238)

A.

brushes, patriarchs
soliloquies,
volcanoes(*or* volcanos)
dynamos, lenses
thieves, mischiefs
gulfs, Messrs.
P.T.A.'s(*or* PTAs), mice
passers-by, crises
deer, indexes (*or* indices)
Japanese

B.

ⓐ 습관 ; 세관 ⓑ 설비 ; 양식
ⓒ 고통 ; 수고 ⓓ 이익 ; 상품
ⓔ 만족 ; 목차 ⓕ 파멸 ; 폐허
ⓖ 4분의 1 ; 숙소
ⓗ 썩기 쉬운(형용사) ;
썩기 쉬운 것들(명사)

C.

widower, lass,
aunt, mare,
hen, mistress,
empress, countess,
landlady, waitress,
heiress, (bride)groom

D. *남성: death, law, war, love, ocean
*여성: nature, art, ship, charity, country

E.

(1) ⓐ 여왕을 그린 초상화
ⓑ 여왕 소유의 초상화
(2) ⓐ Eve의 딸들
ⓑ 여성
(3) ⓐ Tom과 Mary 공유의 별장
ⓑ Tom과 Mary 각자의 별장
(4) ⓐ 그의 도움이 필요하다
ⓑ 그들은 그를 도우러 왔다.
(5) ⓐ 보물 같은 아기보다 더 귀중한 것은 없다.
ⓑ 가보(家寶)보다 더 귀중한 것은 없다.

F.

(2) Columbus' discovery of America
(3) the men's hats
(6) a book of John's
(8) at one's fingertips (~에 정통한)

G. (5)

H.

(1) that coat of his to him
(2) thousand
(3) terms
(4) friends
(5) dozen handkerchiefs
(*or* handkerchieves)
(6) pains (7) manners
(8) forties, fifties (9) airs
(10) hands (11) millions
(12) The owner of this house
(13) country's (14) buses
(15) is ⇨ are

I.

(1) My school is within five minutes' walk of my house.
(2) I am glad to hear that your family are all well.
(3) Our house is within a stone's throw of the station.
(4) I wonder where I have left my glasses.
(5) Many people think that money is everything.
(6) Thousands of people die of this disease every year.
(7) She had only two slices of bread for breakfast.
(8) Any friend of my wife's is welcome.

To : tom@hero.com
Subject : Hello Tom

Dear Tom,
A few days ago I received your name and e-mail address from your friend Mary who is staying in Korea. Mary thought it would be a great idea if we became friends by e-mail. I am a seventeen-year-old high school boy in Seoul and take a great deal of interest in English. My hobby is playing computer games over the Internet. When I finish my high school, I hope I will enter Seoul National University, and when my four-year study of English literature there is over, I wish to go to your country and continue my study. Perhaps one day we could play a computer game against each other! I am looking forward to your reply.

Regards,
Hong Gil-dong
gildong@hero.com

단문독해 (p.240)

1. ▶▶해석
그녀의 음악적 재능이 그녀로 하여금 꽤 많은 예술가들과 교제를 유지하게 해 주었다. 그래서 나는 그녀가 연주하는 것을 듣고 그녀와 함께 극장, 음악회, 그리고 오페라에 가는 것을 좋아했다.
▶▶정답 ⑤
▶▶영작
Perseverance enabled him to attain his object.

2. ▶▶해석
지도를 한 번 보기만 해도, 그리스가 다른 유럽 국가들보다 먼저 개화한 이유를 알 수 있다. 그리스는 문명이 최초로 일어난 그런 나라들에 가장 가까이 있다. 그리스는 동양과 서양의 경계선이다.
▶▶정답 ②
▶▶영작
A glance at him told me that he was anything but satisfied.

3. ▶▶해석
운이니, 하나님의 은총이니 하는 것들이 인생의 여러 일에 관여하는 것처럼 보이지만, 그런 일들이 일어나는 원인을 좀 더 깊이 조사해 보면, 우리들 자신의 노력이 대부분의 사람들이 생각하는 것보다 훨씬 더 이런 일들의 원인이 되었다는 것을 알게 될 것이다.
▶▶정답 largely, destined
▶▶영작
Time will show us who is right or wrong.

4. ▶▶해석
오래 전에 나는 우연히 영국인 일행과 함께 한 적이 있었다. 그런데 그들은 모두 함께 있을 때 말 할 가치가 있는 것에 대해 말하는 법이 없었다. 젊은이들이 쉽게 결론을 내리듯이 나는, 이들은 사람은 이삼십명인데 고작 생각은 여섯가지도 안된다는 결론을 내렸다. 조금만 숙고해 보았더라면 나 자신의 이야기도 그들의 이야기와 다를 바 없다는 것을 생각할 수 있었을 텐데.
▶▶정답 ④
▶▶영작
When he returned home after five years' absence, he was no better than a beggar.

5. ▶▶해석
나의 인생 여정이 성공으로 향하는 평이한 길을 따라 있다면 나는 어떤 반대도 없다. 그러나, 비록 나의 인생 여정이 힘든 길을 따라 있다고 해도, 또 그것이 아무리 험할지라도, 나는 그 여정을 평탄하게 하고 역시 내 목적을 달성할 것이다.
▶▶정답 ④
▶▶영작
Be it ever so dangerous, they continued to enjoy mountain climbing.

6. ▶▶해석
자연이 옷을 입는 방식은 인간의 방법과 정반대다. 여름에 자연은 가장 두터운 옷을 입고, 겨울에는 벌거숭이로 지낸다.
▶▶정답 ④
▶▶영작
The ship arrived at Sydney on her maiden voyage.

7. ▶▶해석
전쟁이, 우리의 일반적인 생활 분위기를 부드럽게 해주는 저 일상적인 예절에 바람직하지 못한 영향을 끼쳤다는 것은 누구나 다 동의하는 사실이다. 우리가 생활을 서로서로 즐겁고 참을 수 있게 하려면 우리는 그것들을 회복해야 한다.
▶▶정답 ③
▶▶영작
If you are to succeed in business, you must work hard and think big.

8. ▶▶해석
석달 후, 인간에게 알려진 최악의 질병의 하나인 공수병이 드디어 정복되었다고 그는 자신 있게 공표할 수 있었다. 이 기쁜 소식은 온 세계에 퍼져 나갔으며, 이 젊은 과학자의 명성을 크게 높여 주었다.
▶▶정답 ③
▶▶영작
The increase in utility rates has added to our difficulties.

9. ▶▶해석
남의 이익에 해로운 그런 행동에 대해 개인은 책임이 있으며, 만약 사회를 보호하기 위해 사회적 혹은 법률상의 처벌이 필요하다는 의견을 사회가 가지게 되면 개인은 이런 처벌을 받아도 될 것이다.
▶▶정답 ③
▶▶영작
He is accountable for the delay of the work.

10. ▶▶해석
비록 그의 악한 행위나, 혹은 어리석은 행위에 의해서 직접적인 해를 다른 사람에게, 어떤 사람이 끼치지 않아도, 그럼에도 불구하고 그의 본보기에 의해서 (남에게) 해를 끼친다고 말할 수 있다. 그래서, 그의 행동을 보고 그것을 알게 됨으로써 타락하고 혹은 잘못 인도될지도 모를 사람들을 위해 그 자신을 자제해야만 한다.
▶▶정답 ②
▶▶영작
You must be ready to lay down your life for the sake of your country.

장문독해 (p.244)

1 ▶▶해석
모든 인간이 평등하다는 것은, 평상시에는 정상적인 사람이라면 누구도 동의한 적이 없는 명제(命題)이다. 위험한 수술을 받아야 하는 사람은 이 의사나 저 의사나 매한가지라는 가정(假定)에 따라 행동하지 않는다. 편집자는 기고되는 원고를 모두 싣지는 않는다. 그리고, 공무원을 채용 모집할 때, 가장 민주적인 정부라도, 이론상으로는 평등하다고 하는 국민들 사이에서 신중히 선택하는 것이다. 그러므로, 평상시에는 우리는 인간은 평등하지 않다는 것을 완전히 확신하고 있다. 그러나, 민주 국가에서 우리가 정치적으로 생각하고 행동할 때는, (인간이 평등하지 않다는 것을 우리가 확신하는 것에 못지 않게) 인간은 평등하다는 것을 확신한다. 어쨌든 간에 — 그것은 실제상으로 마찬가지지만 — 우리는 인간의 평등을 확신하는 것처럼 행동한다. 이와 비슷하게, 교회 안에서는 적을 용서하고 다른 쪽 빰도 내놓는 것을 믿는 독실한 중세의 귀족이, 교회 밖으로 다시 나오자마자 아주 사소한 일에도 쉽게 성을 내어 기꺼이 칼을 뽑아들었다. 인간의 마음은 거의 무한한 모순의 가능성을 갖고 있다.

▶▶정답

1. ① 위험한 수술을 할 의사를 고를 때
   ② 공무원을 선발할 때
   ③ 편집인이 기고가들의 원고를 선별적으로 활자화할 때

2. ② 3. ⑤ 4. ④

▶▶영작

(1) You must make a careful investigation of the accident.
(2) I am certain that you will pass the entrance examination.
(3) He flares up at the slightest provocation.

2 ▶▶해석

언론과 출판의 자유의 민주적 원리는, 우리가 그것을 타고날 때부터의 양도할 수 없는 권리로 간주하건 안하건 간에, 어떤 가정들 위에 토대를 두고 있다. 이런 가정들 중의 하나는, 인간은 진실을 알고 싶어하며 진리에 의해 인도되기를 원한다는 것이다. 또 다른 가정은, 결국 진실에 도달되는 유일한 방법은 공개 토론장에서 의견의 자유로운 경쟁에 의한 방법이라는 것이다. 또 다른 가정은, 사람들이란 어쩔 수 없이 의견이 다르게 마련이니까, 각자가 똑같은 권리를 남에게 주는 한, 자신의 의견을 자유롭게 심지어 열렬히 주장하는 것이 허용되어야 한다는 것이다. 그리고 마지막 가정은, 이와 같은 상호 아량과 다양한 의견의 비교로부터 가장 합리적으로 보이는 의견이 나타나서 일반적으로 인정된다는 사실이다.

▶▶정답

1. ③ 2. 자유로운 자기 의사 표현의 권리
3. ① 4. ④

▶▶영작

(1) One of the ways in which we can live in peace is to tolerate the opinions and desires of others.
(2) Everyone must be allowed to express his or her own opinion freely in a democratic country.
(3) However foolish an opinion may seem, we should not prevent it from being expressed.

실력체크 I (p.248)

1

(1) perceptible (*or* perceived)
(2) comprehensible (*or* comprehended)
(3) excellence (4) intellectual
(5) what (6) remain

2

(A) love without knowledge
(B) knowledge without love

3 ②

(지금 사는 아내가 하도 악처가 돼서 자기가 죽어도 슬퍼하지 않을 테니, 재혼하면 그 남자가 그 여자에게 시달려 전 남편의 입장을 이해하고 자기를 슬퍼해 줄 테니까.)

4 ②

5 Science cannot be divorced from ethics.

6 ①

숙어 Exercise (p.254)

1. I'm not in favor of any tax increases.
2. The law has been in force for six years.
3. A farewell meeting was held in honor of Mr. Smith.
4. The sun was shining in our faces.
5. If you are sick, I'll (have to) go in place of you.
6. Their advice to her just went in one ear and out the other.
7. A police officer ran down the street in pursuit of the thief.
8. Strawberries are now in [out of] season.
9. He stood upside down on his hands.
10. In terms of sales, the book has (not) been successful.

제11장 관사

문법 · 작문 (p.260)

A.

(1) a jacket, The jacket
(2) the bell, the door
(3) the capital, the Netherlands
(4) the Pacific, the Atlantic Ocean
(5) The Thames
(6) the Himalayas
(7) the pound
(8) the shoulder
(9) the British Museum
(10) the violin
(11) a lovely cat; so lovely a cat
(12) short a time
(13) an intelligent
(14) a week
(15) the church
(16) an SOS

B.

(1) the Economist
(2) Hyde Park
(3) to prison
(4) chairman
(5) The Portuguese
(6) of King
(7) a trade
(8) by e-mail
(9) an 18th
(10) A full moon, a crescent moon
(11) Man
(12) in the country
(13) Many a little
(14) the sword, the pen
(15) to man

C.

(1) the (2) the
(3) the (4) the, the, the
(5) a
(6) X
(7) X
(8) ㉠ an ㉡ the ㉢ a[the] (※막연한 '새로운 세계'를 의미할 때는 a new world, '신대륙(미대륙)'을 의미할 때는 the new world로도 쓰일 수 있다.)
㉣ the ㉤ the ㉥ the

D.

(1) I make it a rule to call on him two or three times a month.
(2) She is an earnest Christian, and never fails to go to church on Sundays.
(3) Mr. Anderson, mayor of our city, gave an opening address.
(4) He caught me by the arm and asked me to help him.
(5) He had the kindness to show me the way to the station.
(6) Owing to the heavy rain, the Han River has risen by four feet.
(7) He is such a reliable person that he will be able to finish the project in time.
(8) A black and white cow is grazing in the pasture.

Mon., March 10. Fine and windy.
Got up at six. Before breakfast studied English for half an hour. Started for school earlier than usual. During noon recess played baseball. After school, visited Gilsoo and had a chat till six. At the supper table talked about the upcoming exams. After supper watched television for half an hour. Finished the homework at nine. Went on to read Animal Farm; it's a very interesting novel. Fell asleep while reading.

단문독해 (p.262)

1. ▶▶해석

우리는 대학 시절에 만났다. 우리들은 서로 매우 좋아한다거나 또 매우 친근한 사이도 아니었지만 성질이 서로 거의 비슷했기 때문에, 수월하게 교제할 수가 있었다.

▶▶정답 ①

▶▶영작

They were all of the same opinion as to the settlement of the problem.

2. ▶▶해석

그가 문명사회로 돌아왔을 때 Livingstone의 옷은 누더기였고, 그야말로 피골이 상접한 해골 같은 사람이었다. 오직 놀라운 용기와 인내심만이 지금까지 그를 지탱하게 할 수 있었을 것이다. 아프리카에서 16년을 보내고 난 후, 그는 영국을 향해 배를 타고 떠났다.

▶▶정답 ⑤

▶▶영작

His strong constitution carried him through his long illness.

3. ▶▶해석

하루에도 몇 번씩, 나는 나의 외적·내적 생활이 지금 살고 있거나 죽은 동료 인간들의 노력에 의하여 얼마나 많이 이루어지고, 또 그럼으로써 나는 내가 받은 것만큼 그 대가로서 주기 위해 얼마나 열심히 노력해야 될 것인가를 느낀다. 내 마음은 다른 사람들로부터 내가 너무 많이 빌리기만 했다는 우울한 느낌 때문에 자주 괴롭다.

▶▶정답 ⑤

▶▶영작

Every man must exert himself for the general good.

4. ▶▶해석

어머니는 나의 손을 붙잡고 있었다. 우리는 죽어 누워있는 나보다 두 살 위인 나의 형 침대 옆에 무릎을 꿇고 앉아 있었다. 눈물이 어머니의 두 뺨 밑으로, 닦으려고도 하지 않고 그냥 줄줄 흘러내리고 있었다. 어머니는 신음하고 있었다. 그 소리를 내지 않고 괴로워하며 울던 모습이 아직도 어머니의 모습과 더불어 잊혀지지 않는 매우 강한 인상을 나에게 남겼다.

▶▶정답 ②

▶▶영작

She looked him in the face with her eyes filled with tears.

5. ▶▶해석

인간은 이성적 동물이다. 적어도 나는 그렇게 들어 왔다. 나의 긴 한 평생 이 진술을 뒷받침해 주는 증거를 나는 열심히 찾아 왔다. 그러나, 비록 내가 세 대륙에 걸쳐 있는 여러 나라에서 찾아 왔지만, 여태껏 그것을 불행히도 만나지 못했다. 그와 반대로, 나는 점점 이 세상이 미쳐 가고 있는 것을 보아 왔다.

▶▶정답 ⑤

▶▶영작

He had the misfortune to be captured by armed hijackers.

6. ▶▶해석

인간은 결국 죽게 마련이라는 사실을 알고 있지만 대부분의 사람에게 있어서 이것은 현재 자기가 살고 있다는 기쁨을 약화시키지 않는다. 시인에게는 시들 운명의 꽃, 너무도 빨리 끝나는 봄을 바라볼 때 오히려 더 세상이 아름답게 보인다.

▶▶정답 mortality, reduces

▶▶영작

This is too good a chance to miss.

7. ▶▶해석

나로서는 호주머니에 돈이 좀 있었으므로, 육로로 런던까지 여행했다. 그리고 거기서도, 도중에서와 마찬가지로 어떤 직업을 택할 것인가, 집으로 돌아갈까 혹은 선원이 될까 마음 속으로 여러 생각을 하며 괴로워했다.

▶▶정답 ②

▶▶영작

In theory as well as in practice, his idea is unreasonable.

8. ▶▶해석

오늘날 어떤 사람이 모든 것에 관해 약간씩 다 알려고 한다면, 시간 배당은 매 제목마다 1분밖에 돌아가지 않을 것이다. 그리하여, 그는 마치 나비가 이 꽃 저 꽃으로 날아다니듯이 이 제목 저 제목으로 날아다닐 것이다. 오늘날 상업의 성공이건, 문학의 성공이건, 발명의 성공이건, 모두가 정신 집중을 뜻한다.

▶▶정답 ②

▶▶영작

The poor old man begged from door to door, stick in hand.

장문독해 (p.266)

1 ▶▶해석

거의 전통이 되어 버린 미국 문화의 한 특징은 자수성가한 사람 — 대개 (육체적) 노동으로 시작하여 자신의 노력을 통하여 정상에 오른 사람 — 의 찬미이다. 사업 혹은 산업 분야의 지도자나 대학 교수가 자기 아버지는 농장 품팔이꾼으로 혹은 어떤 종류의 노동자로서 미국에서의 생활을 시작했다는 사실을 일부러 끄집어내기도 한다. 육체 노동에 대한 이 태도는 미국 생활의 여러 분야에서 볼 수 있다. 우리가 어떤 안락할 뿐만 아니라 심지어 사치스럽게 꾸며진 집으로 저녁에 초대를 받게 된다. 그러나, 그 집 안주인이 대개 자기가 직접 식사를 준비하고, 차리고, 나중에 직접 설거지를 한다. 그리고, 남편은 지적(知的) 직업인이지만, 세차하는 것, 꽃밭을 파는 것, 집 칠하는 것, 혹은 지하실의 휴게실 마루에 타일을 까는 것 등에 관해 이야기한다. 남편이 아내의 설거지를 흔히 돕듯이, 아내는 남편의 이런 일들을 돕기도 한다. 대학 공부를 하려고 멀리 나가 있는 아들은 식비를 벌기 위해 식탁 시중을 들고 또 그릇을 닦는다. 혹은 여름 방학이면 다음 해의 학비를 벌기 위해, 새로 나는 도로에서 막벌이 인부들과 끼어 일을 하기도 한다.

▶▶정답

1. manual labor
2. independent
3. ③
4. ④

▶▶영작

(1) Americans take pride in having succeeded in life, beginning by working with their hands.

(2) I'm going to try hard in order to get the contract.

(3) In most American families husbands help their wives wash the dishes after dinner.

2 ▶▶해석

교육 문제들이, 그 안에서 또 그것을 위해 행해지는 사회 조직과는 관계가 없는 것처럼 논의되는 적이 많다. 이것이 바로 교육 문제에 대한 해답이 흔히 불만족스러운 이유의 하나이다. 한 교육 조직이 어떤 의미를 갖는 것은 어떤 특정한 사회 조직 안에서 뿐이다.

오늘날 교육이 악화되고, 점점 무질서해지고, 의미를 잃는 것처럼 보인다면, 그것은 주로 우리가 확고한 만족스러운 사회 기구를 갖고 있지 않기 때문이며, 우리들이 어떤 종류의 사회를 원하는가에 대한 의견이 막연하고 구구하기 때문이다. 교육은 (다른 문제들을 떠난) 빈터에서 논할 수 없는 문제이다.

즉, 우리의 교육문제는 다른 사회적·경제적·재정적·정치적인 문제를 일으킨다. 그리고, 나아가 이런 것들보다 더 궁극적인 문제들과 관계가 있다. 교육에 있어서 우리들이 무엇을 원하는가를 알기 위해서는, 우리들이 일반적으로 무엇을 원하는가를 알고, 우리의 교육 이론을 우리의 인생관에서 끌어 내야 한다. 그 문제는 결국 종교적인 문제가 된다.

▶▶정답

1. 교육 문제가 사회제도와 무관한 것처럼 생각하는 것
2. ③
3. ④
4. ③

▶▶영작

(1) He entered the room looking as if nothing had happened.
(2) It was while in London last year that I got acquainted with him.
(3) I thought he was a sincere man but he turned out to be a cheat.

실력체크 I (p.270)

1 ③

2 (1) — ⑤
(2) — ①
(3) — ③
(4) — ④
(5) — ②

3 (1) natural resources
(2) social and political ability
(3) technical efficiency

4 if you do (혹은 marry)

숙어 Exercise (p.276)

1. I have a (high) fever and a runny nose in [into] the bargain.
2. In (the) light of your (recent) behavior, (I'm afraid) I must ask you to leave the company.
3. A lot of crimes are committed in the name of justice.
4. The candidates were interviewed in turn.
5. We tried in vain to make him change his mind.
6. Miniskirts are back in vogue.
7. He jotted her address down on his notebook.
8. Take your umbrella with you just in case.
9. The teacher kept an eye on the boys in the back row.
10. She kept after her children to clean (up) their rooms.

제 12 장 대명사 I

문법 · 작문 (p.284)

A.

(1) We (2) it
(3) It (4) it
(5) those (6) such
(7) it (8) himself
(9) hers (10) one
(11) one, the other (12) herself
(13) it (14) another

B.

(1) it ⇨ one
(2) it ⇨ one
(3) lemon one ⇨ lemon (tea)
(4) others ⇨ the others
(5) either ⇨ any
(6) another ⇨ the other
(7) she ⇨ her
(8) His all ⇨ All (of) his
(9) me ⇨ mine

C.

(1) that, those (2) ones
(3) such (4) mine, yours

D.

(1) I don't understand all of his speech.
(2) Nobody can be an Edison.
(3) All of his family are not happy. (혹은 Everyone of his family is not happy.)
(4) I invited neither of them.
(혹은 I did not invite either of them.)
(5) His parents are not both at home.

E.

(1) he (2) his
(3) that (4) those
(5) Nobody could (6) us

F.

(1) It is two miles from here to the school and it takes nearly thirty minutes to go there on foot.
(2) It was on a fine morning in autumn that I met her in the park.
(3) It is no use trying to persuade him.
(4) It is not yet certain whether he will come or not.
(5) I think it your duty to be diligent in your study.
(6) I'd like to excuse myself for not attending the meeting.
(7) The cold of this year is more severe than that of last year.
(8) Nobody will agree to such a plan.
(9) I could not answer all the questions.

'My Father'

My father is 50 years old and has been in the government service for about 25 years. He is interested in many things, including traveling and fishing, but he is no expert in any of them. Though his speciality is the study of law, he is not so cold-hearted as most lawyers. He loves his family and often takes us to places of interest.

단문독해 (p.286)

1. ▶▶해석

사람은 나이를 먹어감에 따라 점점 말이 적어진다. 젊었을 때는 자신을 세상 사람에게 기꺼이 토로하려고 한다. 그는 다른 사람들과 매우 강렬한 동료심을 느낀다. 자기를 남들의 품안에 던지고 싶고, 또 남들이 자기를 받아 주리라고 느낀다. 그는 남들에게 흉금을 털어놓고 싶어한다. 여러 개울물이 바다에 흘러 들어가 하나가 되듯이, 자기의 생활도 남들의 생활 속으로 넘쳐 흘러 들어가 하나가 되는 것처럼 보인다.

▶▶정답 ④

▶▶영작

Our staff is always ready to work overtime if necessary.

2. ▶▶해석

모든 것을 다 읽은 사람들은 역시 모든 것을 다 이해하겠거니 생각된다. 그러나, 반드시 그런 것은 아니다. 독서는 마음에 지식의 재료만을 제공해 준다. 우리가 읽는 것을 우리의 것으로 만들어 주는 것은 바로 사고력이다.

▶▶정답 ③

▶▶영작

He who has learned much does not always succeed in life.

3. ▶▶해석

문자는 그 자체로는 언어가 아니며, 단지 언어를 구성하는 소리를 나타내기 위해 사용되는 부호에 불과하다. 씌어진 부호(문자) 그것만으로는 아무런 생명도 없고, 뜻도 없다.

▶▶정답 ④

▶▶영작

The U.N. forces will be composed of multinational troops.

4. ▶▶해석

우리가 그곳에 갔을 때, 그들은 죄의식을 조금도 갖고 있지 않았다. 그들은 계율을 차례차례로 위반했으며, 그러면서도 그들이 나쁜 짓을 하고 있다는 것을 몰랐다. 원주민들에게 죄의식을 불어넣는 것, 그것이 나의 일의 가장 어려운 부분이었다고 나는 생각한다.

▶▶정답 ③

▶▶영작

We faced difficulties one after the other with bravery and dedication.

5. ▶▶해석

나는 사람의 가치를 그의 지력과 학식에 의해서 판단하곤 했다. 나는 논리가 없는 곳에서 선을 볼 수 없었고, 배움이 없는 곳에서 매력을 볼 수 없었다. 지금 나는 두 가지의 지성, 즉 두뇌의 지성과 마음의 지성 [감성]을 우리는 구별해야 한다고 생각한다. 그런데, 나는 후자가 훨씬 더 중요하다고 여기게끔 되었다.

▶▶정답 ③

▶▶영작

The traffic jams in Seoul are more serious than those in any other city in the world.

6. ▶▶해석

그의 의견은 이렇게 요약할 수 있다. 권력욕은 허영심처럼 정상적인 인간 본성에 있어서 강렬한 요소이다. 그래서, 그런 것으로서 받아들여야만 한다. 다만 그것이 지나칠 때에만 그것은 개탄스러운 것이 된다.

▶▶정답 ③

▶▶영작

Love of power is found in almost all of us, but those who are only in pursuit of power are to be despised.

7. ▶▶해석

공인(公人)은 거의 항상 과도한 비난과 과찬을 받고 있는데, 그들이 자신을 보다 잘 알면 알수록, 전자에 의해 공연히 부당하게 풀이 죽거나 후자에 의해 공연히 우쭐해할 것 같지는 않다.

▶▶정답

ⓐ 과도하게 비난받는 것

ⓑ 지나치게 칭찬받는 것

▶▶영작

The American has a good knowledge of Seoul.

8. ▶▶해석

아마 어떤 젊은이도 위대한 책의 내용을 즉시 간파할 수는 없다. 그런 책 속에 담겨 있는 모든 것을 찾아내는 데 있어서, 대부분의 경우, 인류에게 수 백년이 걸렸다는 것을 기억하라. 그러나, 책이 그에게 새로운 의미를 나타내느냐는 그의 지식과 인생의 경험에 달려있다.

▶▶정답 ④

▶▶영작

It took us three hours to climb up to the top of the mountain.

장문독해 (p.290)

1 ▶▶해석

선량한 농부는 항상 우리 사회에서 가장 총명하고 가장 교양 있는 사람들의 한 사람이다. 우리는 무모한 산업 발달로, 농업이 우리의 모든 경제의 바탕이며, 국가의 경제구조에 있어서 (그것이) 항상 초석(礎石)이라는 사실을 잊어버리는 경향이 있어 왔다. 농업은 모든 역사에 있어서 여태껏 그래 왔고, 이 지상에 사람이 존재할 때까지 계속 그러할 것이다. 땅을 소유하고 그것을 중히 여기고 그것을 잘 가꾸는 사람이 경제적인 의미에서뿐만 아니라 사회적 의미에 있어서도 국가로서의 우리의 안정의 근원이라는 것을 우리는 잊기 쉽다.

대도시의 빈민굴이나 혹은 심지어 대도시 근교에서 위대한 지도자들이 나온 예는 드물다. 어느 나라에서나 국가의 운명을 형성한 대부분의 사람들은 농촌이나 소도시 출신이다. 심지어 산업계나 금융계의 대부분의 지도자들도 거기 출신이다. 나는 여러 나라에서 여러 종류의 사람들을 사귀어 왔고, 그분들 중 많은 분들이 저명 인사들이지만, 교제를 하고, 좋은 대화를 주고받고, 지성에 있어서나 사람의 마음을 자극하는 힘에 있어서, 선량한 농부보다 내가 더 앞세우고 싶은 사람은 아무도 없다.

▶▶정답

1. ⓐ 농업, ⓒ 농촌이나 소도시
2. Agriculture, foundation
3. ③
4. ④

▶▶영작

(1) We are inclined to feel sleepy after heavy meals.

(2) Few people live to be ninety.

(3) I do this for my own benefit; there is no other reason at all.

(4) We are apt to forget that agriculture is the foundation of the nation.

2 ▶▶해석

사고(思考)는 자유이다라는 말은 흔히 하는 말이다. 자기가 생각하는 것을 그가 감추기만 하면 자기가 좋아하는 어떤 생각을 하건 방해받지 않는다. 인간의 정신 작용은 그의 경험의 범위와 상상력에 의해서만 한정된다. 그러나, 이러한 개인적인 사고의 본래의 자유도 별로 가치가 없다.

만약 어떤 사람이 자기의 사상을 남에게 전달하는 것이 허용되지 않는다면 그것을 생각하는 사람 자신에게는 만족스럽지 못하고, 심지어 고통스럽기조차 하다. 그리고, (그것은) 명백히 그의 이웃들에게 아무런 가치가 없는 것이다. 더구나, 다소라도 마음을 지배하는 생각을 감춘다는 것은 지극히 어렵다. 만약 어떤 사람의 생각이 자기 주변 사람들의 행위를 규제하는 사상이나 관습을 회의케 하고 또 그들이 갖고 있는 믿음을 배척케 하고 또 그들이 따르는 것보다 더 좋은 생활 방식을 보게끔 그를 이끌어 준다면 그는, 자기의 추리가 옳다고 확신할 경우, 침묵이나 우연한 말 혹은 일반적인 태도에 의해 자기는 그들과 다르며 그들의 의견에 동조하지 않는다는 것을 드러내지 않을 수가 거의 없다.

자기들의 생각을 감추기보다는 차라리 소크라테스처럼 죽음을 택해 온 사람들이 있어 왔고, 오늘날도 어떤 사람들은 그럴 것이다. 그러므로, 어떤 귀중한 의미에 있어서 사상의 자유는 언론의 자유를 내포하는 것이다.

▶▶정답

1. this natural liberty of private thinking
2. speech, thought
3. ④
4. ③

▶▶영작

(1) It is obvious that even such a good idea is of little value if it cannot be put into practice.
(2) Her smile led him to give her his word.
(3) He was convinced of the truth of his theory and preferred to face death rather than deny it.

실력체크 I (p.294)

1

(1) 우리가 생각하는 것처럼 남들이 생각하지 않는다고 해서 화를 내다.
(2) peace
(3) 평화롭게 살기 위해서, 우리는 남들의 의견과 소망이 우리의 것과 다르다고 할지라도 아량 있게 받아들어야 한다.

2

(1) 소설에서는 연애를 인생에서 가장 중요한 것처럼 강조하고 있는데 실생활에 있어서는 그렇지가 않다.
(2) love (3) men (4) (ㄷ)

3

(1) ⓐ the Greeks ⓑ this freedom of spirit ⓒ their assertion of the principle of liberty
(2) ⑤

4

(1) 부와 여가가 과도하게 넘쳐 사치가 극에 달할 때
(2) 여가(leisure)와 일(work)
(3) 근원적이며, 가장 지속적인, 가장 확실한 행복의 원천은 일이다.

숙어 Exercise (p.300)

1. Keep [Bear] in mind that a lot of people are interested in buying the land.
2. Never call Jim before noon; he keeps late hours and sleeps all morning.
3. I've done this before so I know the ropes; shall I show you how to do it?
4. Foods lacking in vitamins are not good for our health.
5. An opposition spokesman [party] lashed out against the government policy.
6. During the recession they laid us off for three months.
7. These days my son is trying to learn the multiplication table by heart.
8. You (have) left out her name on this list.
9. He asked me where she was, but I didn't let on.
10. (Please) let go of my arm.

제13장 대명사 II

문법 · 작문 (p.308)

A.

(1) I wanted to know how much this would cost.

(2) Do you remember when horse-drawn carriages disappeared?

(3) Do you know what is the matter with him?

(4) What time do you suppose he will be arriving?

B.

(1) You are clearly one of those men (whom) everything goes wrong with.
(혹은 You are clearly one of those men with whom everything goes wrong.)

(2) All this was done by the man (whom) we thought to be a mere dreamer.
(혹은 All this was done by the man who we thought was a mere dreamer.)

(3) She was a well-known singer whose voice delighted the whole world.

(4) This is the car the engine of which is of the latest type.

(5) I was unable to find out the name of the man who called on me yesterday.

(6) I bought many books, all of which I have not read.

(7) We went to the seashore, on which we found many shells.

C.

(1) the men who have (2) How ⇨ What

(3) That ⇨ What (4) where ⇨ which

(5) but을 뺌 (6) who ⇨ as

(7) whomever ⇨ whoever

(8) Do you know who was

(9) that을 뺌

(10) he told me about [of]

D.

(1) who (2) who

(3) what 혹은 whatever (4) which

(5) that (6) than (7) whom

(8) what (9) which (10) what

(11) who (12) whose

E.

(1) What do you think he did?

(2) Do what you believe to be right.
(혹은 Do what you believe is right.)

(3) This is Mr. Johnson who they say took the difficult task.

(4) I gave him what money I had with me.

(5) I bought a bicycle, which was stolen the next day.

(6) She is not the cheerful woman she used to be.

(7) She is kind, what is better still, very beautiful.

(8) He is the only man that can solve this problem.

(9) Whoever solves this question first will be awarded the prize.

'My Mother'

My mother is 45 years old and has two sons and one daughter. She likes to stay at home and seldom goes out to see movies or buy things at department stores. But she does not feel unhappy, for she enjoys cooking, sewing and washing. Whenever her friend comes to see her, she likes to talk with her as long as possible about various things. Of these, she is most interested in the problem of women, perhaps because she is always thinking of the future of her only daughter.

단문독해 (p.310)

1. ▶▶해석

나는 아폴로 15호에서나 이 우주 과학 시대에서 하느님에 대한 나의 신념을 약화시키는 어떤 것도 만난 적이 없다. 사실, 나는 달에 있을 때 어떤 영감을 느꼈다. 즉, 어떤 분이 나를 지켜보며, 나를 보호하며, 나와 같이 있다는 느낌이 들었다. 임무가 불가능해 보일 때도 몇 번 있었다……. 그러나, 그 때마다 모두가 잘 되어 나갔다.

▶▶정답 ④

▶▶영작

This is the very book that I have been looking for.

2. ▶▶해석

아테네 군대의 위대한 장군이었던 그의 아버지는 그가 매우 어렸을 때 죽었는데, 그의 아버지는 자기 돈을 어떤 나쁜 사람에게 맡겼으나, 그들은 그것을 써버렸다.

▶▶정답 ③

▶▶영작

We will leave our house in the care of our friend while we are away this summer.

3. ▶▶해석

내가 의사로서 그 병원에서 보낸 그 몇 년간이 나에게 인간 본성에 대한 완전한 지식을 주었다고는 일시라도 주장하고 싶지 않다. 나는 어떤 사람도 그것(인간 본성에 대한 완전한 지식)을 가지기를 바랄 수 있다고 생각하지 않는다. 나는 그것을 의식적으로 혹은 무의식적으로 40년 간 연구해 오고 있다. 그러나 아직도, 인간은 설명할 수 없다고 나는 생각한다. 내가 친근하게 아는 사람이, 도저히 그런 것을 할 수 없다고 내가 생각한 어떤 행동을 해서 나를 놀라게 할 수 있다.

▶▶정답 ⑤

▶▶영작

I think he is capable of any crime.

4. ▶▶해석

나는 새로운 생활을 시작했다. 지난날의 나와 당시의 나 사이에는 매우 현저한 차이가 있었다. 단 하루 사이에 나는 놀랄 만큼 성숙했다. 다시 말해서, 그것은 틀림없이 내가 지금까지 나도 모르게 발전해 오던 힘과 감각을 의식적으로 갑자기 즐기게 되었다는 것을 의미하는 것이다.

▶▶정답 ④

▶▶영작

Economists entered into a discussion about the cause of recession.

5. ▶▶해석

그렇게도 많은 사람들이 불평하는 그런 환경은, 우리가 가지고 일할 바로 그 도구이며, 우리가 발판으로 해서 오를 디딤돌로서 간주해야 한다. 그것들은 인생 항로의 바람이며 조수이다. 그런데, 노련한 선원은 대개 이것들을 이용하거나 극복한다.

▶▶정답 ④

▶▶영작

It is not desirable to take advantage of those who are in trouble.

6. ▶▶해석

봄의 미묘한 영향으로 거의 모든 종류의 식물이 눈을 뜨고, 땅 밑에서 겨울을 보내는 수백만의 숨은 식물이 두껍게 쌓인 낙엽을 뚫고 움틀 때, 한가한 몇 시간을 보내기에 숲보다 더 즐거운 곳은 없다.

▶▶정답 ②

▶▶영작

We looked for shade in which to take a rest in the sultry afternoon.

7. ▶▶해석

늘 입는 성직자의 옷을 입고 싶지 않아서, 이렇게 말한 어느 성직자의 이야기가 있다. "나는 다른 사람들과 나를 구별하는 그런 옷은 안 입겠다." 그런데, 그의 이 말이 신문에 보도되었을 때, 잘못하여 콤마가 그 문장 안에 들어가게 되었다. 그래서, 그 문장은 다음과 같이 읽히게 되었다. '나는 옷을 안 입겠다. 그러면, 그것이 나를 다른 사람들과 구별해 줄 것이다.'

▶▶정답 ⑤

▶▶영작

He was too young to distinguish right from wrong.

8. ▶▶해석

예술, 문학, 학문의 모든 세계는 국제적이다. 한 국가에서 이루어진 것은 그 나라만을 위해서 이루어진 것이 아니라 인류를 위해 이루어진 것이다. 인간을 다른 어떤 동물보다 더 가치 있게 만드는 것이 무엇이냐 하고 스스로 묻는다면, 그것은 온 세상 사람들이 모두 공유(共有)할 수 있는 것(예술, 문학, 학문)이라는 것을 발견할 것이다.

▶▶정답

모든 사람이 공유할 수 있는 예술, 문학, 학문

▶▶영작

He shared in my sorrows as well as in my joys.

9. ▶▶해석

한편으로는 더위와 또 한편으로는 갈증으로 해서 나는 너무나 뭍에 닿고 싶어서, 드디어 우리의 배가 뭍으로 향해 미끄러져 갈 때, 나는 뛰어내릴 준비를 하고 뱃전에 서 있었다.

▶▶정답 hot, thirsty

▶▶영작

He went there ready to die.

10. ▶▶해석

사회는 건물과 같다. 그것은 그 기초가 튼튼하고 모든 재목이 완전할 때 굳건히 선다. 신용할 수 없는 사람이 사회에 대한 관계는, 한 조각의 썩은 재목이 집에 대한 관계와 같다.

▶▶정답 ②

▶▶영작

Leaves are to the plant what lungs are to the animal.

11. ▶▶해석

이 세상이 점점 현대로 다가옴에 따라, 인간은 점점 싸움을 즐기게 되었다. 인간은 그들이 발견한 반짝이는 황금의 소유권을 갖고 예전보다 더 심하게 싸웠다. 그리고, 더욱 나쁜 것은, 그들은 철로써 날카로운 칼과 다른 무기를 만들어 서로 맹렬하게 싸웠다.

▶▶정답 violent

▶▶영작

We made many paper cranes out of paper.

12. ▶▶해석

이 짧은 인생에서 어떤 위대한 일을 하려고 하는 사람은, 단지 향락하기 위해서만 사는 게으른 방관자에게는 미친 것처럼 보이는 그런 힘의 집중을 갖고(그렇게 힘을 집중하여) 일에 전심 전력을 다해야 한다.

▶▶정답 concentrate, efforts

▶▶영작

As many men as are necessary have to be mustered.

13. ▶▶해석

그 여자의 얼굴에 있는 주름, 그 여자의 부드럽고 졸리는 듯한 음성에서 나오는 음조, 어느 것 하나 그 여자가 자기의 생활에 완전히 만족하고 있다는 것을 말하지 않는 것은 없었다. 이런 여자를 불행히 여겼다면, 그것은 정말 어리석은 교만이었을 것이다.

▶▶정답 ④

▶▶영작

Throughout his book he spoke of the abuse of the power of government.

14. ▶▶해석

나는 교과 과정의 첫 2년 동안이 매우 따

분한 것을 알고, 시험에 겨우 통과하는 데 필요한 것 이상은 공부에 주의를 기울이지 않았다. 따라서, 나는 성적이 좋지 못한 학생이었다.

▶▶정답 interest, best

▶▶영작

It seems that nowadays parents give their children more money than is necessary.

15. ▶▶해석

어느 날 대통령이 Bradley 장군과 나와 같이 차를 타고 갈 때, 우리의 전쟁 지도자들 중 몇 사람의 장래에 관해 토의하기 시작했다. 나는 조용한 고향에 돌아가, 거기서 전쟁이 이 세상에 가져온 몇 가지 커다란 변화를 우리 국민들이 이해하도록 돕기 위해, 내가 할 수 있는 미력이나마 다하고 싶은 욕망 외에는 아무런 야망도 없다고 대통령에게 말했다.

▶▶정답 ③

▶▶영작

I will do what little I can to help you.

16. ▶▶해석

그는 이제, 자기는 살인자와 다름없다는 것을 명백하게 알았다. 이 발견으로부터 오는 극단적인 고민이 살아가는 것을 견딜 수 없게 했고 그를 자결의 길로 몰았다.

▶▶정답 ②

▶▶영작

People treated him as though he was no better than a brute.

17. ▶▶해석

죄를 짓고서 자기 마음에 양심의 가책을 받지 않는 사람은 아무도 없다. 죄의식은 고발자가 필요 없으며, 반면 깨끗한 양심은 아무도 두렵지 않다.

▶▶정답 ⑤

▶▶영작

Is there anyone that we know who is as talented as he is?

18. ▶▶해석

나의 생각의 상당한 부분을 차지한 남자나 여자가 나의 정신적 혹은 육체적 행복에 기여하지 않은 경우를 나는 회상할 수 없다.

▶▶정답 whoever, contribution

▶▶영작

There is nothing worth having that can be had without labor.

19. ▶▶해석

어린애들을 다루는 사람은 누구나, 너무 지나친 동정은 잘못이라는 것을 안다. 물론, 동정을 너무 안 하면 그것은 더 나쁜 잘못이다. 그러나, 동정심에 있어서도 다른 모든 것에 있어서와 같이 어느 쪽이나 너무 지나친 극단은 (즉, 너무 동정하거나 너무 무정하면) 나쁘다.

▶▶정답

Too little sympathy, too much sympathy

▶▶영작

Whoever commits a crime will soon be captured and punished.

장문독해 (p.318)

1 ▶▶해석

우리에게 "Please"를 말하도록 강요하는 법이 없다는 것은 사실이지만, 우리에게 공손하라고 지시하는, 어떤 법보다 더 오래되고 더 신성한 사회적인 관습은 있다. 그리고, 공손함의 첫째 요건은 남의 수고를 인정해야 한다는 것이다. "Please"와 "Thank you"는, 우리가 사회적 존재로서 빚지지 않고 살아가게 해주는 잔돈이다. 그것들은, 인생이라는 기계에 윤활유를 치고 그것을 잘 돌아가게 하는 작은 예의이다. 그것들은 우리의 교제를, 윗사람이 아랫사람에게 지시하는 그런 바탕 위에서가 아니라 다정한 협조, 서로 주고받는 상호 양보의 토대 위에 놓는다. 부탁하기만 하면 도움을 받을 수 있고, 더구나 화를 내는 대신에 기꺼이 선의로써 도움을 받을 수 있는

데, 굳이 명령을 하고자 하는 사람은 그야말로 저속한 사람이다.

▶▶정답

1. "Please" and "Thank you"
2. the small change
3. ⑤ 4. ④

▶▶영작

(1) While what you suggest is theoretically possible, it is practically impossible.
(2) I heard my name called behind me.
(3) The door would not open, and we were forced to break it open.

2 ▶▶해석

그가 세상을 떠난 지 50년도 못되어 자연의 문은 열리고 우리는 선택이라는 두려운 중책을 맡게 되었습니다. 일찍이 하나님께 돌렸던 많은 권능을 우리 인간이 빼앗아 왔습니다. 두렵고 아무런 준비도 없이 우리는 모든 생물계의 사활을 지배하게 되었습니다. 위험, 영광, 그리고 선택은 드디어 인간에게 달려 있습니다. 인간이 과연 완전한가를 시험할 때가 가까이 다가왔습니다. 하나님과 같은 권능을 갖게 되었으니, 우리가 일찍이 신에게 빌었던 책임과 예지를 인간 자신 속에서 찾아야 합니다. 인간 자신이 우리의 가장 커다란 위험이 되었고 또한 우리의 단 하나의 희망이 되었습니다. 그래서 오늘날 사도 성 요한의 말씀을 이렇게 바꿔 써도 좋을 것입니다. 「마지막에 말씀이 있나니 그 말씀은 곧 인간이요, 그 말씀은 인간과 더불어 있나니라.」

▶▶정답

1. ④ 2. future
3. responsible, wise 4. ②

▶▶영작

(1) He ascribed his failure to fate.
(2) The prize is awarded for the best novel of the year.
(3) Her son has won the first prize; she may well be proud of her son.

실력체크 I (p.322)

1

(1) 자전거로 통근하는 사람들이 늘면, 도시의 중심가의 차량 혼잡이 완화되고, 배기 가스에 의한 대기 오염이 감소된다.
(2) ③

2

(1) 될 수 있으면 빈자리를 찾으려 하며, 빈자리가 없어 타인과 동석했을 때도 몇 마일을 가나 말없이 여행한다.
(2) 냉정하다고 생각된다.
(3) 사실은 따뜻한 마음을 가지고 있으며, 타인이 먼저 이 겸양의 장벽을 무너뜨려주면 마음으로부터 기뻐하는 사람들이다.

3 ②

숙어 Exercise (p.328)

1. He'll be dismissed because he always lies down on the job.
2. We'll live it up this summer vacation.
3. The new machine hasn't lived up to our expectations.
4. He likes to look back on his school days.
5. You shouldn't look down on a man because he is poor.
6. He is a celebrity everyone looks up to.
7. He lost no time in doing his homework.
8. He is very patient, so he never loses his temper.
9. She has made another mistake; she must be losing her touch.
10. He lost himself in writing his new novel.

제14장 형용사 I

문법 · 작문 (p.334)

A.
(1) much (2) few (3) a little
(4) strange (5) free (6) sweet
(7) a living (8) afraid (9) like
(10) content (11) worthy (12) sure of
(13) either (14) well, good

B.
(1) sick and wounded
⇨ the sick and the wounded
(2) Little ⇨ A little (3) high ⇨ tall
(4) cold something ⇨ something cold
(5) more ⇨ much
(6) An old kind ⇨ A kind old
(7) climbers ⇨ climber
(8) great ⇨ a great (9) a little ⇨ little
(10) little ⇨ few (11) is ⇨ are
(12) It is possible for him to ~ .
(13) two first ⇨ first two
(14) left money ⇨ money left
(15) more six ⇨ six more

C.
(1) March the tenth; March ten
(2) Queen Elizabeth the second
(3) Chapter five
(4) six five p.m.
(5) eighteen eighty; sixteen hundred
(6) two hundred and five; one thousand and twenty-eight; two hundred and sixty three thousand, nine hundred and seventy-five; seven million, five hundred and twenty four thousand, eight hundred and seventy-six
(※ 미국 구어에서는 hundred 다음의 and를 생략하는 것이 보통이다.)
(7) one fifth; seven and three eighths; three hundred and nineteen over [upon] four hundred and fifty-six
(8) four seven five, seven two seven two

D.
(1) many (2) Little [Never]
(3) possible (4) good (5) few

E.
(1) invisible (2) inaudible
(3) undeniable (4) unquestionable

F.
(1) Tens of thousands of people came to see the international soccer game.
(2) I got up so late that I missed the 6 a.m. train.
(3) Two-thirds of my classmates are going to look for jobs after graduation.
(4) He went red with anger.
(5) I like him not because he has few faults but because he has a few faults.
(6) The number of cars in that country is now thirty times that of the pre-war days. (혹은 At present there are in that country thirty times as many cars as there were before the war.)
(7) When his parents died in the 1930's, he was in his mid-teens.

'My Hometown'

My hometown is a small place in Gangwon-do. The town has a population of about nine hundred and most of the townspeople are farmers. Though they are not rich, they live a contented and cozy life. In a sense they are proud of being honest farmers in a quiet, beautiful town. I love my hometown so much that I am afraid I might feel homesick when I study in Seoul, so noisy and crowded a place.

단문독해 (p.336)

1. ▶▶해석

틀림없이 돈 때문에 망한 사람이 매우 많다. 대체적으로, 부자들이 아마 가난한 사람들보다 더 돈에 대해 근심한다. 부(富)는 현명한 사람들에게만 행복을 가져올 수 있다. 부자가 되려고 너무 갈망하는 사람은 항상 가난하다.

▶▶정답 ⑤

▶▶영작

Many people are anxious about what their future will be.

2. ▶▶해석

우리들이 경험할 수 있는 가장 아름답고 가장 심오한 감정은 신비감이다. 그것은 모든 참된 예술과 과학의 근원이다. 이 감정을 모르며, 잠시 걸음을 멈추고 경탄하며, 또 경외심으로 황홀해서 넋을 잃을 줄 모르는 사람은 죽은 것이나 다름없다. 그의 눈은 닫혀 있는 것이다.

▶▶정답 ④

▶▶영작

I am a stranger to music.

3. ▶▶해석

공공생활을 하는 사람에게, 20년간 자기와 더불어 꾸준히 우정을 지속해 나가는 한 친구를 사귀는 것이, 매년 20명의 추종자들을 발견하여 그 모두(20명)를 잃거나 혹은 20명의 10분의 1, 즉 2명이라도 잃어버리는 것보다 훨씬 중요하다.

▶▶정답 ④

▶▶영작

He made ten mistakes in as many lines in the exam.

4. ▶▶해석

우리의 모든 가로에는 나무가 줄지어 서 있다 [가로수가 있다]. 이 나무들의 잎과 가지 사이에서 가로등이 마치 별처럼 반짝인다. 우리들이 이 가로등 밑을 지날 때, 빛이 자기 가까이에 있는 나뭇잎을 초록 잿빛으로 어떻게 물들이는가를 볼 수 있다.

▶▶정답 ③

▶▶영작

Trees shed their leaves in autumn.

5. ▶▶해석

라 카치라는, 그렇게도 매력적인 젊은이는 틀림없이 여자들의 많은 미소를 즐기리라는 것을 알면서도, 그 소년에게 애인이 있느냐고 물었다. 그리고, 그 소년이 자기는 매일 저녁을 일하면서 보낸다고 맹세했을 때, 그가 거짓말을 한다는 것을 알았다.

▶▶정답 ②

▶▶영작

Are you aware that your car is illegally parked?

6. ▶▶해석

핵무기를 개발할 수 있는 국가의 수가 최근에 20개국 이상으로 증가했다. 만약 이 치명적인 무기를 소유하는 국가가 증가하면, 그 무기의 관리가 그만큼 더 어려워질 것이다. 그리하여, 결국 핵 무정부 상태의 출현을 초래하고 핵전쟁의 위험을 증가시킬 것이다.

▶▶정답 ②, ⑤

▶▶영작

His tiredness resulted from lack of sleep and it finally resulted in a car accident.

7. ▶▶해석

일반적으로 개는 영리하지만, 잊어서는 안 될 것은, 개에게는 한계가 있으며, 한 번에 일정한 양만 흡수할 [이해할] 수 있으므로, 개를 훈련할 때 무리를 해서는 안 된다는 것이다.

▶▶정답 ⑤

▶▶영작
While I agree with her, I do not believe that her plan is best.

8. ▶▶해석
우리는 하루에 몇 시간을 일한다. 그리고, 먹고 쇼핑하는 그런 일에 필요한 최소한의 시간을 할당하고는, 그 나머지는 레크리에이션으로 알려진 활동에 보낸다.
▶▶정답 ③
▶▶영작
His father allows him 100 dollars a month for pocket money.

9. ▶▶해석
지구 표면 위의 우리의 모든 힘은 전적으로, 지구가 태양으로부터 받는 에너지의 공급에 의존하기 때문에 우리는 필연적으로 태양에 의존하며, 만약 태양이 차가워진다면 우리의 어떤 소망도 실현할 수 없을 것이다.
▶▶정답 source, survive
▶▶영작
Your success is entirely dependent on your own efforts.

10. ▶▶해석
나는 그 당시 혼자 있는 것을 결코 두려워하지 않았다. 왜냐하면, 나는 너무도 외진 시골에서 자라서, 밤에 사람들을 보지 않는 것이 보는 것보다 두렵지가 않았기 때문이었다.
▶▶정답 ③
▶▶영작
As I was brought up in the country, I always long for a rural life.

11. ▶▶해석
프랑스 사람들은 모든 사람 중에서 가장 검소한 사람으로 항상 간주되어 왔는데, 그것은 당연하다. 그들의 수입을 모두 쓰며 사는 프랑스인은 거의 없다. 그들은 불행한 때를 대비하여 무엇인가 저축하려고 애쓴다. 그리고, 더욱 좋은 것은, 적으나마 가산을 일으키고 혹은 이에 보탬을 한다.
▶▶정답 ②
▶▶영작
We put some money aside for a rainy day every month.

12. ▶▶해석
지구보다 별로 크지 않은 별이 몇 개 알려져 있기는 하다. 그러나, 별의 대부분은 너무나 크기 때문에 수십만 개의 지구 덩어리를 그 별 하나하나에 꾸려 넣을 수도 있으며, 그리고도 여분의 공간이 남는다.
▶▶정답 vastness
▶▶영작
I am sorry there is no room for you in this car.

13. ▶▶해석
너 자신을 의지하는 것을 일찍이 배우는 것이 중요하다. 왜냐하면, 자기를 도와줄 사람을 항상 찾고 있는 사람들이 이 세상에서 한 일이란 별로 없기 때문이다.
▶▶정답 ④
▶▶영작
Those who always rely on others can hardly expect to succeed in life.

14. ▶▶해석
위대한 과학의 발견들 중에는 우연히 이루어진 것이 적지 않다. 어떤 목적에 도달하려고 출발하고 난 후, 연구가는 도중에서 처음 목적에는 들어 있지 않았던 법칙 혹은 요소를 만나게 된다. 이 발견은 그의 활동의 부산물이다.
▶▶정답 ④
▶▶영작
Occasionally we would meet by accident on the street.

15. ▶▶해석

적은 지식은, 네가 그것이 적다는 것을 알고 있는 한 그리 위험하지 않다. 위험은 네가 실제 아는 것보다 더 잘 알고 있다고 생각하는 데서 시작된다. 사람을 잘못 이끄는 것은, 많건 적건, 지식이 아니라 지식의 자부심이다.

▶▶정답 ④

▶▶영작

It was not his refusal but his rudeness that embarrassed her.

16. ▶▶해석

이 세상에서 가장 중요한 것은 우리의 현 위치가 아니라 우리가 어떤 방향으로 가고 있느냐이다. 항구에 도달하기 위해, 우리는 가끔 순풍을 타고 혹은 어떤 때는 역풍을 안고 항해하여야만 한다. 그러나, 어쨌든 우리는 표류할 수도 없고, 닻을 내리고 정박해 있을 수도 없으며, 항해를 계속해야 하는 것이다.

▶▶정답 ③

▶▶영작

He couldn't so much as hold the instrument correctly, let alone play it.

17. ▶▶해석

그는 그 여자의 얼굴을 똑바로 바라볼 수 없었다. 그 여자는 이것을 주시하고 그를 찬찬히 지켜보았다. 그리고, 매우 침착하게 이야기했다.

▶▶정답 ④

▶▶영작

The observant detective looked him straight in the face and discovered something important.

18. ▶▶해석

저명 인사들의 모임에서 주인 역할을 하는 데 익숙해 있었으므로, 그는 자기가 접근하는 모든 사람들을 매혹시키고 그들을 좌지우지했다. 그의 사람 접대에는 매력적이고 권위 있는 무엇이 있었다. 그리고, 그의 비범한 침착성은 이 사교계에서 그에게 또 다른 명성을 주었다.

▶▶정답 ④

▶▶영작

(1) Tired, I went to bed earlier than usual.

(2) He is at once stern and tender.

장문독해 (p.344)

1 ▶▶해석

'영국인의 가정은 그의 성이다.'라고 말해지곤 했다. 이 말이 영국인의 가정에는 방어적이고 무뚝뚝한 무엇이 있다는 인상을 주는 한, 이것은 큰 오해를 낳기 마련이다. 왜냐 하면, 영국만큼 가정 생활이 항상 친구들에게, 아니 심지어 낯선 사람들에게도 기꺼이 개방되어 있는 나라는 없기 때문이다. 그러나 이것은, 영국인은 방해받기를 싫어하며, 이웃 사람들과 너무 가까운 접촉 없이 살고 싶어한다는 의미에 있어서는 어느 정도의 진실을 나타낸다. 그는 그러고 싶으면[마음이 내키지 않으면], 혼자 있으며 남들과 어울리지 않아도 되기를 바란다. 그는 자기와 마음이 맞는 사람들과 기꺼이 교제한다. 그러나, 자기를 어중이떠중이들과 접촉하게 하는 그런 종류의 공동생활을 좋아하지 않는다. 그러므로, 그는 아파트에서 사느니보다 독채에서 살기를 더 좋아한다.

▶▶정답

1. 영국인은 외부인의 간섭을 싫어한다.
2. The Englishman's home is his castle.
3. aloof 4. ⑤ 5. ④

▶▶영작

(1) You may get a job if it doesn't interfere with your schoolwork.

(2) There is no country where the right to privacy is more respected than in England.

(3) She kept the secret to herself.

2 ▶▶해석

우리가 모든 길을 다 갈 수는 없다. 성공은 한 분야에서 얻어야 한다. 우리 직업을 오직 하나의 인생의 목표로 삼아야 하며, 다른 모든 것은 이것에 종속되어야 한다. 나는 일을 어중간하게 하는 것을 싫어한다. 그것이 옳으면 대담하게 하여라. 그것이 그르면 하지말고 내버려두어라. 이상(理想)을 가지고 산다는 것은 성공적인 삶이다. 사람을 강하게 만드는 것은, 사람이 하는 일이 아니라, 하고자 노력하는 것이다. "영원한 경계는 자유를 얻는 대가이다." 라고 말해 왔다. 똑같이 진실되게, "끊임없는 노력은 성공을 얻는 대가이다." 라고 말할 수 있다. 우리가 모든 힘을 다하여 일하지 않으면 남들이 그렇게 할 것이며, 그리하여 그들은 인생의 경주에서 우리를 패배시키고, 상품을 우리의 손아귀에서 빼앗아 갈 것이다. 성공은 운이나 기회에 점점 덜 좌우된다. 자기 불신은 대부분의 실패의 원인이다. 성공의 커다란 필수불가결의 도움은 인격이다. 인격은 훈련과 신념의 소산인, 결정화된 습관이다.

▶▶정답

1. an ideal 2. utmost
3. ④ 4. ③

▶▶영작

(1) Every athlete cannot become a popular idol.
(2) Don't do things by halves.
(3) You must work with all your might in order to succeed in life.
(4) Your success depends on your own efforts rather than on luck and chance.

실력체크 I (p.348)

1

(1) There never was a piece of writing that couldn't be improved by rewriting.
(2) When your mind is clear and rested

2

(1) 첫째 견해 — 인간이 우주 속으로 멀리 나가면 나갈수록, 무한한 우주에 비해 인간이 얼마나 보잘것 없는 존재인가를 깨닫게 된다.
둘째 견해 — 인간이 우주 속으로 멀리 나가면 나갈수록, 인간의 존재와 능력이 얼마나 위대하며 강력한 존재인가를 깨닫게 된다.
(2) 달나라에 세 우주 비행사와 더불어 모든 인간이 결국은 같이 갔다는 뜻. 즉, 인간의 위신이 그들과 더불어 높아졌다는 뜻이다.

3 (1) ④ (2) ①

4

(1) ②
(2) He advises us to do our fellow beings justice without reference to their external appearance.

숙어 Exercise (p.354)

1. Exercise can make a big difference to your state of health.
2. They made a fuss over the play, but it wasn't a success.
3. We must make allowance(s) for his lack of experience.
4. The burglars made off with all his money and jewelry.
5. He made believe not to hear me.
6. Due to the recession most people cannot make ends meet.
7. We had to make do with a little money.
8. I'm sure he'll make good in his new job.
9. I couldn't make head or tail of what she was saying.
10. He made much of the advice his father had given him.

제15장 형용사 II

문법 · 작문 (p.358)

A.

(1) drier, driest (2) bad, worst
(3) late, latest (4) late, latter
(5) thinner, thinnest
(6) more famous, most famous

B.

(1) like ⇨ like better (혹은 prefer)
(2) than ⇨ to (3) prettier ⇨ the prettier
(4) other를 뺌
(5) any woman ⇨ all (the) women
(6) of ⇨ in
(7) more it becomes difficult
⇨ more difficult it becomes
(8) most ⇨ more (9) more ⇨ less
(10) shier ⇨ more shy (11) than ⇨ to
(12) prefer staying at home to going
(혹은 than to go ⇨ rather than (to) go)
(13) later ⇨ latter (14) little ⇨ less
(15) farther ⇨ further (16) more를 뺌
(17) old ⇨ older (18) more ⇨ less
(19) very ⇨ much (20) the를 뺌
(21) as rich ⇨ as rich as
(22) something to ⇨ something else to
(23) no richer man ⇨ no man richer

C.

(1) More (2) coal, iron
(3) smaller [greater] (4) worse
(5) else, less (6) the (7) less
(8) later (9) more (10) few

D.

(1) most, of (2) more, other, playwright
(3) more, than (4) as

E.

(1) No period of life is as happy as one's school days.
(2) Perhaps Big Ben is larger than any other clock in the world.
(혹은 Perhaps no (other) clock is larger than Big Ben in the world.)
(3) No (other) seaport in Korea is as good as Busan.
(4) This is the most beautiful sight that I have ever seen.
(5) He was the bravest soldier that ever shouldered a gun.
(6) Nothing is more precious than health.
(혹은 Health is more precious than anything else.)
(7) It seems not as difficult as before.
(혹은 It does not seem as difficult as before.)
(8) She is quite as lovely as her sister.
(9) It is the most dangerous thing to try to appear what one is not.

F.

(1) 겨우 10명의 사람들만이 그 일자리에 지원했다. (no more than = only)
10명이나 되는 사람들이 그 일자리에 지원했다. (no less than = as many as)
(2) 그 정치 집회에는 기껏해야 100명의 사람들이 있었다. (not more than = at most)
그 정치 집회에는 적어도 100명의 사람들이 있었다. (not less than = at least)
(3) 고래가 물고기가 아닌 것은, 말이 물고기가 아닌 것과 같다.
(4) 그는 자기 동생들만큼 정력적이다. (as ~ as)
그는 자기 동생들 못지않게 정력적이다. (perhaps more ~ than)
(5) 그는 자기 반의 다른 학생들보다 더 총명하지 않다.
그는 자기 반의 다른 학생들처럼 총명하지 않다.
(6) 그는 거지나 다름없다. (as good as)
그는 그런 비위를 상하게 하는 일을 할 만큼 바보는 아니다. (= He is not so foolish

as to do such an offensive thing.)
(7) 누구나 자기의 자유를 향유할 권리가 있다. 하물며 자기의 생명은 더욱 그렇다.
나는 거의 걸을 수 없다. 하물며 뛰지는 더욱 못한다.
(8) 그의 선생님이 그를 칭찬했기 때문에, 그는 더욱 더 열심히 공부했다.
나는 그가 결점이 있음에도 불구하고 여전히 그를 사랑한다.
(9) 나는 그 소식에 매우 기뻤다.
(10) 내가 잔디 깎기를 시작하자마자 비가 오기 시작했다.
(11) 그것이 흥미만 있으면 어떤 것이나 괜찮다.
내가 살아있는 동안은 너에게 아무 부족함이 없게 해 주겠다.
(12) 그는 결코 자기 아내와 아이들을 버릴 사람이 아니다.
나는 그 콘서트 티켓을 사기 위해 줄을 선 마지막 사람이었다.
(13) 그녀는 애완동물로 두 마리의 개 뿐만 아니라 고양이도 한 마리 가지고 있다.
(A as well as B = not only B but also A)
(14) 그 영화는 교육적이기도 하고 재미있기도 하다.
(at once A and B = both A and B)
(15) 그 여자는 매우 거만하다.
(16) 나는 수원까지 너와 같이 가겠다.
(as far as = ~까지 [거리])
(17) 그는 이 나라에 복무한 어느 사관에 못지않게 훌륭한 사관이었다.
그는 학급의 어느 학생 못지않게 부지런했다.
(as ~ as ever 동사 ; as ~ as any 명사)
(18) 고객의 주문 마감시한이 다가옴에 따라 우리는 매우 바빴다.
(19) 가장 현명한 사람일지라도 이따금 실수를 한다.
(20) 녹이 쇠를 침식하듯이, 근심은 마음을 갉아 먹는다.
(21) 그 여자는 매우 친절하다.

G.
(1) Which do you prefer [like better], English or mathematics?
(2) Of Tom and Judy, Tom is the taller.
(3) He has three times as many books as I have.
(4) She is not as young as she looks.
(5) It is getting colder and the days are getting shorter.
(6) I like him all the better because he is modest.
(7) A strong healthy child can no more sit still than a puppy can.
(8) I have never seen a picture more beautiful than this.
(9) The more chances we have to meet foreigners, the more necessary it becomes to study foreign languages.
(10) He is as bright as any student in his class.
(11) She is more proud than vain.
(12) He can speak French, much [still] more English.
(13) He considers himself inferior to her.
(14) He is the last man to betray his friends.
(15) I am none the better for taking the medicine.
(16) There is nothing as pleasant as walking along the beach on a fine spring day.
(17) The youngest student in this class is two or three years older than your older brother.

'My Family'

My family is large. It consists of eight, of whom I am the youngest.
Grandfather is very proud that it has been an honorable and respectable family in Seoul for eleven generations. We are all very democratic and respect each other. We often discuss various problems and every member of the family is encouraged to express his or her opinion on them. My family is a really happy one.

단문독해 (p.362)

1. ▶▶해석

어머니가 돌아가셨을 때, 나는 불과 다섯 살이었다. 그러나, 20년이 지난 오늘에도 어머니의 모습은 돌아가실 때처럼 내 마음에 생생하다. 나는 어머니를 부드러운 미소와 상냥하고 즐거운 음성을 지닌, 창백한 안색의 품위 있는 사람으로 기억한다.

▶▶정답 vivid

▶▶영작

I was only a child when the incident happened.

2. ▶▶해석

대부분의 인간의 생활에 있어서 걱정은 희망보다 더 큰 역할을 한다. 그들은 자기들의 생활이나 그들이 접촉하는 다른 사람들의 생활에 있어서 자기들이 창조할 수도 있는 기쁨에 대한 생각보다는, 다른 사람들이 자기들로부터 소유물을 빼앗아 가지나 않을까 하는 생각으로 더 차 있다.

▶▶정답

자신의 재산을 다른 사람에게 빼앗기지 않을 까 하는 두려움

▶▶영작

Have you been in contact with your lawyer recently?

3. ▶▶해석

인간의 운명은 지상에 자기가 존재하는 것에만 한정되지 않는다. 그는 한평생 수행하는 행동에 의해서보다는 유성처럼 뒤에 남겨 놓는 자국에 의해 존재한다.

▶▶정답 eternal

▶▶영작

The new edition of Encyclopedia Britannica is less expensive than the old one.

4. ▶▶해석

사람들은 흔히 본능적으로 올바른 사람을 선택한다. 그러나, 불행하게도 이따금 그들의 선택이 후보자의 통치력과는 관계 없는 감정적인 척도에 의하여 결정된다. 그리고, 그들은 너무 늦게야 사람을 잘못 뽑았다는 것을 알게 된다. 그러나, 이제 그들이 그를 선택한 것처럼 그렇게 쉽게 그를 제거할 수는 없다.

▶▶정답 ④

▶▶영작

You must get rid of that bad habit of yours as soon as possible.

5. ▶▶해석

부모의 사랑만큼 그렇게 희생적인 사랑은 없다. 자식의 최대의 행복만큼 참된 부모가 마음에 두는 것은 아무것도 없다. 자식은 자기 자신의 최대의 이익을 위한 것을 하는 것 외에 더 부모를 즐겁게 해 주는 방법은 없다.

▶▶정답

자식이 자신의 최대의 이익이 되는 일을 하는 것

▶▶영작

Nothing in business is as important as credit.

6. ▶▶해석

세계의 어떤 지방에는 사막이라고 불리는 광대한 지역이 있다. 이런 사막들에서는, 시선이 닿는 한, 모래와 돌과 바위 외에는 아무것도 안 보인다.

▶▶정답 only, see

▶▶영작

The city was a sea of fire as far as the eye could see [reach].

7. ▶▶해석

언어는 인간 정신의 산물이며, 인간 정신의 작용을 반영한다. 그러므로, 인간 정신이 온 세계 어느 곳에서나 동일한 한, 인간의 언어가 어디에 존재하건, 그것은 어떤 공통된 특징을 나타내게 마련이다.

▶▶정답 ③

▶▶영작
If you have problems at home, it is bound to affect your work.

8. ▶▶해석
가끔 우리는 국가가 우리에게 개인적으로 피해를 주었다고 생각하지만, 그렇다고 그것이 국가를 사랑하지 않을 권리를 주지 않는 것은, 우리들의 부모로부터 해를 입었다고 해서 부모를 미워할 권리를 갖지 못하는 것과 마찬가지다.
▶▶정답 ⑤
▶▶영작
A home without love is no more a home than a body without a soul is a man.

9. ▶▶해석
우리 자신이 안전하다고 생각할 때보다 더 위험할 수 없으며, 사실 우리들이 위험해 보일 때보다 더 안전할 수는 없다.
▶▶정답 security
▶▶영작
The old man was never happier than when he was surrounded by children.

10. ▶▶해석
John은 그녀보다 8살 위였으며, 오랫동안 그녀에게 별로 관심 갖지 않았다. 비록 결국에 가서는 그들이 서로 결혼하게 될 것이라는 것을 당연하게 여겼지만. 그것은 약혼 증서가, 그가 아직 어렸고 Judith가 단지 젖먹이였을 때 서명되었기 때문이었다.
▶▶정답 ③
▶▶영작
I took it for granted that he would help us.

11. ▶▶해석
우리가 관찰력을 창조할 수 없는 것은 기억력을 창조할 수 없는 것과 마찬가지다. 그러나, 이 둘을 발전시키기 위해 우리는 많은 것을 할 수가 있다.
▶▶정답 inherent, developed

▶▶영작
You cannot always be unlucky any more than you can always be lucky.

12. ▶▶해석
바보가 배우는 오직 하나의 학교는 경험의 학교다(바보는 경험을 통해서만 배운다)라는 것은 누구나 다 아는 속담이다. 만약 경험의 교훈이 바보 학생에게도 유익하다면, 현명한 학생에게는 더욱 그럴 것임에 틀림없다.
▶▶정답 importance
▶▶영작
There is an old saying that time and tide wait(s) for no man.

13. ▶▶해석
교양은 언어를 꾸미기 위한 장식품이 아니며, 더구나 너의 지식을 자랑하기 위한 장식품은 아니다. 그것은 정신을 풍부하게 하기 위해 힘들여 얻은 수단이다.
▶▶정답 culture
▶▶영작
He enriched his experiences with foreign travels.

14. ▶▶해석
연령은 인생의 길이를 판단할 수 있는 합당한 척도가 아니다. 사람의 일생은 그 속에서 그가 하는 일, 그가 느끼는 것에 의해 측정되어야 한다. 그가 유용한 일을 많이 하면 할수록, 많이 생각하고 느끼면 느낄수록, 그는 정말로 더 많이 사는 셈이 된다. 그의 수명은 아무리 연장되건, 게으르고 쓸모 없는 사람은 단지 식물처럼 무위도식할 따름이다.
▶▶정답 ②
▶▶영작
The more I think of his proposal, the less I like it.

15. ▶▶해석
오늘날 우리가 향유하는 정치적 자유를 보존하기가 그렇게 쉬운 것은 아니다.

이것은 투쟁으로부터 왔으며, 아직도 보존하려면 투쟁이 필요한 것이다. 이것은 지혜와 인내로부터 나왔다. 우리 자신이 직접 위험한 시기에 살므로 독립 선언을 한 우리 조상들이 겪은 위험과 그들의 용기를 우리가 알기 때문에, 더욱 더 그 조상들을 존경하게 된다.

▶▶정답 투쟁, 지혜, 인내

▶▶영작

We can never be too old to learn.

16. ▶▶해석

"아무리 약한 사람이라도," 카알라일은 말한다, "단 하나의 목적에 자기의 온 힘을 다함으로써 무엇인가 성취할 수 있으나, 반면에 아무리 강한 자라도 그의 힘을 많은 목적에 분산하면 어떤 것이나 성취하지 못할 수가 있다."

▶▶정답 concentrated, dispersed

▶▶영작

(Even) The best swimmer can drown.

17. ▶▶해석

때가 일러서, 도서관에는 나 외에는 단 한 사람밖에 없었다. 그는 책에 몰두하여 큰 가죽 의자에 앉아 있었다. 나는 그 사람이 래리 씨인 것을 알고 놀랐다. 그는 내가 이런 장소에서 만나리라고는 기대하지도 않은 사람이었다.

▶▶정답 ④

▶▶영작

He was walking in the park absorbed in thought.

18. ▶▶해석

그러나, 체념도 역시 행복을 얻는데 있어서 자기의 몫을 한다. 체념은 노력에 의한 역할에 못지 않게 필수적인 역할을 한다. 현명한 사람은, 비록 피할 수 있는 불행 밑에서 가만히 앉아 있지는 않지만, 피할 수 없는 그런 불행 밑에서 시간과 감정을 헛되이 낭비하지는 않는다.

▶▶정답 ③

▶▶영작

He played an important part in the settlement of the dispute.

19. ▶▶해석

집은 신선한 공기뿐만 아니라 많은 빛을 받아들이도록 지어야 한다. 전자는 건강한 신체 조건에 후자 못지 않게 필요하다. 식물이 빛을 빼앗겼을 때 그 줄기와 잎이 하얗게 되듯이, 사람도 땅 밑에서 살 때 창백해지고 건강이 나빠진다.

▶▶정답 ③

▶▶영작

They sell books as well as newspapers.

20. ▶▶해석

그 가족들은 매우 가난했지만, 젊은 Sam은 영국의 어느 귀족 아들에 못지 않게 자존심이 있었다. 사실은 자기가 비범한 센스와 능력을 가지고 있다고 느꼈으며, 그의 의견으로는 그것 때문에 자기는 세상 사람들로부터 매우 존경을 받을 자격이 있다는 것이었다.

▶▶정답 ④

▶▶영작

Poor as he is, he is honest.

21. ▶▶해석

그는 자기가 잘못이라는 것을 인정했기 때문에, 사과문을 쓰는 수밖에 없었다. 그것을 쓰는 것은, 그가 겪은 것 중 어떤 것에도 못지 않은 가장 기분 나쁜 일이었다.

▶▶정답 ⑤

▶▶영작

There was nothing for it but to admit that I was wrong.

22. ▶▶해석

내가 태어났을 때 나의 집은 결코 부유하지는 않았다. 아버지가 이제 확고히 자립했다고 느끼기까지 수십 년이 지나야만 했다. 그것은 내가 기억하는 한, 부모님은 나의 온 청춘 시대를 그늘지게 했던 무거운 재정 문제와 싸워야 했기 때문이다.

▶▶정답 ③

▶▶영작

It is by no means easy to learn a foreign language.

23. ▶▶해석

짐승들은 건강과 충분한 먹을 것만 있으면 행복하다. 우리가 느끼기를 인간도 당연히 그러려니 하지만, 그러나 적어도 대부분의 경우에 있어서 인간은 그렇지 못하다.

▶▶정답 Unlike, desires

▶▶영작

You have nothing to fear so long as you are innocent.

24. ▶▶해석

시칠리아 섬은 지중해의 중심에 삼각형으로 놓여 있다. (이 섬보다) 더 자연의 혜택을 입은 섬은 거의 없었다. 이 섬의 기후는 온화하고, 경치는 아름답다. 그러나, 인간은 이 섬에 대해서 (자연만큼) 친절하지 않았다. 지리상으로 시칠리아 섬은 유럽 세력과 아프리카 세력 간의 불가피한 싸움터가 되었다.

▶▶정답 Sicily

▶▶영작

You couldn't have come at a more convenient time.

25. ▶▶해석

나쁜 예절이 전염성이 있는 것처럼 좋은 예절도 역시 그러하다. 만일 우리가 무례함에 마주치게 된다면 우리들 대부분이 무례하게 되기 쉽다. 그러나 쾌활한 사람들에게 불쾌해 할 사람은 없다. 이는 예절에 있어서도, 날씨에 관해서도 마찬가지다.

▶▶정답 fine

▶▶영작

Nowadays teenagers are apt to disobey if they are blamed too often.

26. ▶▶해석

다른 사람들도 우리들과 마찬가지로 살 권리가 있으며, 또한 거리에서 우리에게 방해가 되는 사람들이 고의나 혹은 악의로써 그러지 않는다는 사실을 우리가 받아들이자마자, 이 세상은 참으로 살기 좋은 곳이다.

▶▶정답 recognize, intentionally

▶▶영작

He is always getting in my way.

27. ▶▶해석

백인 의사가 도착했다는 소문이 퍼지자마자, 여러 가지 질병으로 고생하는 원주민들이 곧 그를 둘러쌌다.

▶▶정답 heard, treated

▶▶영작

No sooner had he seen me than he ran away.

장문독해 (p.372)

1 ▶▶해석

사람들로 하여금 만원 지하철에 대해 불평하게끔 하고, 될 수 있으면 다시는 지하철을 타지 않겠다고 맹세케 하는 것이 무엇일까? 대부분의 사람들은, 그것은 아마 흔히 겪는 불편 때문일 것이라고 상상하는 것 같다. 그러나, 나는 실은 (그것은) 모욕감 때문일 것이라고 생각한다. 결국 따지고 보면, 약 10분 가량 서 있어야 한다는 것은 우리들 대부분에게 그리 큰 고역은 아니다. 더구나, 우리가 놀라운 속도로 우리의 목적지로 향해 수송되고 있다는 것을 알 때는 그렇다. 그러나, 이런 러시아워에 당하는 모욕은 틀림없이 불쾌하다. 인간들이 — 당신도 포함하여 — 갑자기 짐꾸러미로 변한다. 꼬리표(승차표)가 승객들의 손에 떠맡겨지고, 기차는 당장 승객들로 가득히 짐처럼 실려진다. 승객들을 태우기 위해 문이 열리고 닫힌다. 손님들을 떠밀다시피 밖으로 내민다(하차시킨다). 엘리베이터로 손님들을 쏘아 올린다. 이 때가 되어서야, 향긋하고 차가운 참 바람이 (지하 철도 안의 바람은 참된 바람이 아니니까) 그들에게 불어올 때에야 (즉 지하철도를 벗어 나와 밖으로 나왔을 때에야) 그들은 다시 정상적인 남녀로 돌아갈 수 있다.

▶▶정답

1. 사람들이 복잡한 지하철에 대해 불평하

고 될 수 있으면 다시는 지하철을 타지 않겠다고 하는 이유

2. tickets 3. ③ 4. ④

▶▶영작

(1) I don't want to go out in such a heavy rain if I can help it.

(2) He said he would not attend the meeting, but he did after all.

(3) He will stay with us for a week or so.

(4) We turn back into ordinary men and women only when we get back home from our daily work.

2 ▶▶해석

나는 평화 옹호가들은, 오늘의 정책이 필연적으로 가져올 말할 수 없이 비참한 재난뿐만 아니라, 우리가 싸움을 (잊어) 버리면 우리에게 열리는 유례 없는 행복의 새로운 세계도 똑같은 정도로 강조해야 한다고 생각한다. 인간은 힘에 있어서 자기보다 월등한 사나운 짐승들에 의해 끊임없이 위협을 받으며, 정기적으로 비참한 기근에 의해 인구가 격감이 되며, 겉보기에 적대적인 자연계를 바라봄으로써 생기는 공포감에 사로잡힌채, 희귀한 쫓기는 종족으로부터 서서히 성장해 왔다. 인간은 외부 위험을 정복하게까지 되었지만 그는 증오, 시기, 자만이라는 자신의 격정에 의해 생기는 내부 위험을 정복하는데까지는 이르지 못했다. 인간은 이런 내부의 위험을 정복해야 하며, 그렇지 않으면 자기가 사자나 호랑이보다 더 위험한 사나운 짐승이라는 사실을 인정해야 할 때가 왔다. 우리가 우리 자신의 격정(증오심, 시기심, 자만심 등)을 정복하는 정복의 마지막 단계를 획득할 수 없기 때문에, 원시 시대 이래 이룩해 온 그 모든 엄청난 진보를 버려야 할지도 모른다고 생각하니 참을 수 없다.

▶▶정답

1. ③

2. 야생동물의 끊임없는 공격, 비참한 기근, 겉보기에 적대적인 자연계를 대하고 생기는 공포감

3. ⑤ 4. ④

▶▶영작

(1) He came back satisfied with the result and hopeful of success.

(2) They prepared for the coming war, determined to make any sacrifices necessary to defend their fatherland.

(3) It is unbearable to think that he should have failed after all his efforts.

실력체크 I (p.376)

1

(1) things

(2) 현대 기계 문명화 과정

(3) 물질문명은 발달하였는데, 그 결과로서 인명경시 풍조가 생겼다. 각자 개인의 몸단장은 깨끗이 하면서도 공해문제는 외면한다. 인간은 자신의 재주로 기발한 물건을 만들어 내지만 그 결과는 생각하지 않는다.

2 ④

3 이 세상에는 할 일이 너무도 많은데, 한가롭게 옷맵시나 외모에 신경을 쓰는 사람을 보면 이해가 가지 않는다.

4

(1) If such an event should occur,

(2) 싸우고 있는 양쪽

(3) 영국인은 무례함이라도 낮은 목소리로 나타내는 것

(4) 미국

숙어 Exercise (p.382)

1. I can't make out what he is trying to say.
2. The basement will be made over into my office.
3. We must make the best of what we have.
4. She (has) made the grade as a lawyer.
5. The class quickly made the most of the teacher's absence.
6. The story is made up to deceive us.
7. Her new job didn't measure up to her expectations.
8. In math, she is second to none in her class.
9. The mystery guest was none other than Mr. Smith.
10. My injuries are nothing to speak of; they are just a few scratches.

제16장 부 사

문법 · 작문 (p.390)

A.

(1) late
(2) even
(3) yet, already
(4) very
(5) Yes
(6) pretty
(7) little, less
(8) least

B.

(1) quickly ⇨ soon
(2) much ⇨ (much) better
(3) hadn't scarcely ⇨ scarcely had
(4) how ⇨ what
(5) When ⇨ As
(6) near ⇨ nearly
(7) highly ⇨ high
(8) freely ⇨ free
(9) much ⇨ very
(10) get hardly ⇨ hardly get

C.

(1) where
(2) why
(3) Where
(4) how
(5) how

D.

(1) She is a good dancer.
(2) She is a good cook.
(3) Mary is a good violinist.
(4) He is an earnest teacher.
(5) He is a late riser.
(6) She made a polite answer.

E.

(1) seldom leaves
(2) often takes
(3) warm enough
(4) was deeply moved
(5) there quietly all day
(6) beautifully in the concert at the Town Hall last night
(7) to the concert with Tom last night
(8) Perhaps the most
(9) is quite

F.

(1) 양보의 부사절
(2) 장소의 부사절
(3) 명사절
(4) 형용사절

G.

(1) He visited the village where he was born after ten years' absence.
(2) This is how he managed to do it.
혹은 This is the way (that) he managed to do it.
(3) Do you know the reason why he was praised?

H.

(1) The reason why he left his native place is not known to anybody.
(2) This is the house where the poet passed his boyhood.
(3) Recently prices have gone up considerably.
(4) He always rises early and goes to bed late.
(5) The milkman always passes here early in the morning.
(6) He worked the harder because he had been praised.
(7) The day will surely come when you will be sorry for your foolishness.
(8) Wherever you go, you will never find a better place than your home.
(9) Why do you think he got angry with her?

'Love'

I cannot forget my mother's love. My father died when I was five years old, and so my mother had to work very hard to support her family. One day when I was a little schoolboy, I saw a friend of mine riding a brand-new shiny bicycle. I had no bicycle, so I teased my mother for one, and at last I began to cry. I think then she was very pressed for money; she was looking at me sorrowfully with her eyes filled with tears. Suddenly she hugged me to her breast without any words. On the evening of that day she bought me a new bicycle, but I do not know how she got the money …… It has been three years since my dear mother died.

단문독해 (p.392)

1. ▶▶해석
오늘날 자연이 인간보다 위대하다는 사실을 너무도 쉽사리 잊어버리기 쉬운 대도시에서 그렇게도 많은 사람들이 어쩔 수 없이 살고 있으므로, 자연을 사랑하는 마음은 예전보다 더욱 더 필요하다.

▶▶정답 ②

▶▶영작
I was compelled to comply with his request.

2. ▶▶해석
천재는 태어나는 것이지 만들어지는 것이 아님은 틀림없는 사실이다. 그러나, 어떤 사람이 천재인 이유를 찾으려고 애쓰는 것은 잘못인 반면, 그의 천재성이 자신의 환경의 결과로 어떻게 어떤 모습을 띠고 어떤 방향을 택했는가를 주목하는 것은 옳고 매우 흥미 있는 일이다.

▶▶정답 ⑤

▶▶영작
Come and see me this evening.

3. ▶▶해석
많은 사람들에게, 영화는 따분한 현실로부터 비현실적인 낭만의 세계, 거기에서는 악이 항상 벌을 받고, 선은 항상 보답을 받고, 또 거기에서는 모든 여자들이 아름답고 남자는 멋있고, 부는 행복을 가져오고 가난은 만족을 가져오고, 모든 이야기는 행복한 결말을 가져오는 세계에로의 도피구를 제공해 주었다.

▶▶정답 ④

▶▶영작
Wait till Tuesday, when I will tell you everything.

4. ▶▶해석
담배를 거의 혹은 전혀 볼 수 없었던 영국에 미국으로부터 담배를 가져온 Walter Raleigh경에 대해 재미있는 이야기가 있다. 그는 담배 피우기를 좋아했는데, 그의 하인이 주인의 입에서 연기가 나오는 것을 처음 보았을 때, 그는 주인이 지금 불에 타고 있다고 생각하고, 그 불을 끄기 위해 그에게 물을 한 양동이 부었다는 것이다.

▶▶정답 ④

▶▶영작
The house is on fire; fire engines are coming to put it out.

5. ▶▶해석
자본이 사업에서 가장 필요(중요)하다는 것은 두 말할 필요가 없다. 그러나 당신의 자본이 아무리 많아도, 만약 당신이 그것을 잘못 사용한다면, 당신은 성공하기를 바랄 수 없다. 게다가 사업을 함에 있어 신용은 거의 자본만큼이나 중요하다는 것을 당신은 알아야 한다.

▶▶정답 trust, use

▶▶영작
It goes without saying that someone with lung problems should not smoke.

6. ▶▶해석
당신이 소유하고 있는 책을 모두 다 읽

을 수는 없으므로, 당신은 읽을 수 있을 만큼의 책을 소유하면 족하다. 항상 권위 있는 작가의 책을 읽어야 한다. 그리고, 기분 전환을 바랄 때도, 전에 읽은 작가의 작품을 읽어라(의지하라).

▶▶정답 ③

▶▶영작

In an emergency we can fall back on our savings.

7. ▶▶해석

생존하는 적자가 어떤 절대적인 기준에서 볼 때 반드시 가장 좋고 가장 고귀한 것은 아니며, 단지 어떤 주어진 조건(상태)에 대해 가장 적합할 뿐이라는 사실을 명백히 이해해야 한다.

▶▶정답 superior, surroundings

▶▶영작

Do you know about the survival of the fittest and natural selection?

8. ▶▶해석

책은 당신의 이웃사람의 생활에 비유될 수 있다. 그것이 좋으면 아무리 오래 계속되어도 지나치지 않고, 나쁘면 그것을 아무리 빨리 제거해도 지나치지 않다.

▶▶정답 sooner, better

▶▶영작

I simply cannot get rid of this cold.

9. ▶▶해석

세계 역사상 새로운 상황이 발생했다. 그것의 본질은 처음으로 세계의 6대 대륙이 서로 중요한 관계를 갖게 되었다는 사실이다. 적어도 앞으로 오랜 동안, 어느 한 대륙에서 흉년이 들거나 경제적 불경기가 오면 나머지 다른 대륙에 영향을 미칠 것이고, 어디에서 전쟁이 일어나건 이것은 곧 세계 도처에서 일어나는 전쟁으로 번질 수 있다.

▶▶정답 global

▶▶영작

You will be sorry for this thoughtless act of yours for a good time to come.

10. ▶▶해석

사상간에도 생존 경쟁이 있으며, 인류의 상황 변화에 부합하는 사상들이 이기는(살아남는) 경향이 있다는 믿음을 많은 것이 뒷받침해 주고 있다. 그러나 반드시 이긴 사상들이 (경쟁에서) 패한 사상들보다 도덕적으로 더 훌륭하다거나 자연의 법칙에 훨씬 더 충실하다는 결론이 되는 것은 아니다.

▶▶정답 meet, greater

▶▶영작

Money does not necessarily bring happiness to us.

장문독해 (p.396)

1 ▶▶해석

우리가 인생과 행복의 불안정함을 항상 의식한다면, 우리는 쉽게 병적이게 되고 일과 즐거움에 대한 열망을 곧 잃어버릴 것이다. 그러나, 만약 우리가 그것을 결코 의식하지 않는다면, 우리는 아무 가치가 없는 것에 거짓 가치를 부여하기 쉽고, 추구할 가치가 없는 것을 추구하며 세월을 보내기 쉽다. 그러므로, 우리는 언젠가는 무너져내려 우리 자신, 우리 재산, 그리고 우리 야망에 끝장을 가져올 나약한 땅껍질을 타고 허공을 여행하고 있다고 가끔 느끼는 것이 우리의 정신에 좋은 약이 된다. 많은 철학자들이 적어도 그렇게 생각해 왔고, 또 우리는 죽음의 그늘 밑에서 사업을 세우고 꿈을 추구하고 있다고 우리를 깨우쳐 주는 것을 그들의 일(직무)로 삼아 왔다. 우리는 모두 사형 선고를 받고 있는데, 그러나 무기한 집행유예의 선고를 받고 있다고 말해 왔다. 그러므로, 우리는 인생에 있어서, 이 사실을 고려하지 않는 표준에 의해 무엇이나 그 가치를 측정해서는 안된다.

▶▶정답

1. come
2. 우린 모두 사형선고를 받고 살아가는 존재라는 것
3. ③ 4. ②

▶▶영작

(1) She sets a high value on his pictures.
(2) We are all in pursuit of happiness; and therefore, the opportunity to attain it should be equally open to all of us.
(3) A fruitless end came to the attempt because of lack of funds.
(4) I remind all of you again that smoking is not allowed here.

2 ▶▶해석

그림을 그리는 것은 하나의 오락(기분전환)으로서 완벽하다. 그림을 그리는 것보다 더 우리의 신체에 피로를 주지 않고 정신을 몰두케 하는 일을 나는 전혀 알지 못한다. 현재의 근심이 무엇이든, 앞으로 올 위협이 무엇이든, 일단 그림이 흐르기 시작하면 우리의 마음에 그러한 근심, 위협을 생각할 여유가 없어진다. 그런 것들은 그림자 속으로, 어둠 속으로 사라진다. 비록 변변치는 못하지만, 우리의 정신적인 빛이 그 일에(그림 그리기에) 집중된다. 시간은 점잖게 저만큼 물러선다(시간 가는 줄도 모른다). 여러 번 망설이고 나서야 점심이 무뚝뚝하게 문을 노크한다(식사하는 것도 잊어버리게 한다). 한 번에 반 시간 동안 분열식 혹은 심지어 — 섭섭한 이야기지만 — 예배보려고 서 있어야 할 때도 나는 꼿꼿이 서 있는 기립 자세는 인간에게 자연스럽지 못한 자세이며, 단지 힘들여서 얻을 수 있으며, 그것을 유지하려면 피곤하고 어려운 자세라는 것을 항상 느껴 왔다. 그러나, 그림 그리기를 좋아하는 사람은 휴식 없이 한 번에 세 시간, 혹은 네 시간 그림을 그리며 서 있을 때도 흥미가 지속되는 동안은 조금도 불편을 느끼지 않는다.

▶▶정답

1. forgets	2. painting
3. track	4. ④
5. interest	6. ④

▶▶영작

(1) Once you have crossed the river, you will be safe.
(2) Whatever the result is, I am determined to carry out my plan.
(3) As long as your interest holds, you are sure to make progress in your study.
(4) It was only after much hesitation that I knocked at his door.

실력체크 I (p.400)

1 ②

2 ③

3 (1) ⑤ (2) ①
(3) ③ (4) ④
(5) ⑦

4 현대인은 물품의 질보다는 새로운 것을 추구한다.

숙어 Exercise (p.406)

1. There were a lot of odds and ends in the attic.
2. He told me his comments were off the record.
3. I can't think of the answer off the top of my head.
4. He joined the army of his own accord.
5. The washing machine is on the blink again.
6. You can trust Susan; she's on the level.
7. The agreement will pave the way for a lasting peace.
8. He was put in prison for paying the cop off.
9. She couldn't pick up on what he meant.
10. The minister tried to play down the serious disaster.

제17장 일치와 화법

문법 · 작문 (p.416)

A.

(1) is (2) is
(3) are (4) has
(5) makes (6) were
(7) believe (8) are
(9) was (10) are
(11) had come (12) could
(13) is (14) were
(15) was (16) seems
(17) is (18) is
(19) has (20) is
(21) is (22) were
(23) are (24) is
(25) is (26) is
(27) has (28) is
(29) order (30) is
(31) is (32) was
(33) is (34) makes
(35) will (36) speaks
(37) lives (38) does

B.

(1) He said that he would pay me double if I got the work finished by the next day.
(2) She said that she would keep her promise.
(3) He told me that he had been reading that book since the night before.
(4) Last night she told me that her mother wanted to see me today.
(5) He answered in the affirmative. He said yes. He agreed.
He answered in the negative. He said no. He denied.
(6) He said that he wished he were rich enough to buy a private plane.
(7) He said, "I will not attend the meeting."
(8) He said that he would be back as soon as he could.
(9) She asked me what she could do for me.
(10) I asked the clerk if [whether] I could use that telephone.
(11) She said to a girl at the post office, "How many days does it take a parcel to reach Chicago by air mail?"
(12) He said to me, "How about having lunch with me tomorrow?"
(13) He said that the flu is an infectious disease, but that cancer isn't.
(14) He wondered if he should ever forget her.
(15) She said that she would come if she could get permission.
(16) He said to me, "If I were [was] you, I would not worry about it."
(17) He said (that) it was a holiday that day, and that they had no school.
He said (that) it was a holiday that day, also that they had no school.
혹은 He said that as it was a holiday that day they had no school.
(18) He proposed that we (should) go for a swim.
(19) He told her to help him or she would be sorry.
He told her that unless she helped him she would be sorry.
(20) His wife told me that he had gone to the barber's an hour before and that she thought he would be back very soon, and asked me to step in and wait.
(21) He told me to go and see who it was.

(22) Father told me not to forget to leave a space.

(23) He told [advised] me to disinfect the wound before I bandaged it.

(24) He suggested (to us) that we (should) have a cup of coffee.

(25) He said to me, "Don't speak until you are spoken to."

(26) I said to her, "Let's eat out at a posh restaurant next Sunday."

(27) The boys exclaimed with joy that they had won the race.

(28) He cried (out) in sorrow that he had failed again.

(29) He exclaimed how pretty my picture was.

혹은 He told me that my picture was very pretty.

(30) He cried (out) what a disaster it was.

혹은 He said that it was a terrible disaster.

(31) He prayed God to help the poor.

혹은 He prayed that God might help the poor.

(32) She said, "Hurrah! I've beaten him!"

(33) He said that it was a very glorious day and suggested to me that we should go out for a drive.

(34) Mother asked the boys to be quiet and said that the baby had just gone to sleep.

혹은 Mother asked the boys to be quiet, saying that the baby had just gone to sleep.

* saying that 대신에 as를 써도 된다.

(35) She said that she had been very busy some days before, but that she was presently quite free.

(36) He asked me which of the two I liked better.

(37) The clerk said, "I have never refused to help the obnoxious customer."

C.

(1) In those days nobody believed that the earth is round like a ball.

(2) I thought that he would come back in an hour or two, and waited for three hours, but he did not come back after all.

(3) I asked him what time the bus usually arrives here.

(4) He asked me if I had ever been to America.

(5) He said to me, "You may return the money when it is convenient for you."

(6) He told me that he had been to the airport to see her off.

(7) He said, "Oh, how foolish I have been!"

(8) He said to me, "I have not read today's newspaper yet. Is there anything interesting in it?"

(9) My father told me to study hard to pass the entrance examination.

'Winter'

I was born in the southern part of Korea where we seldom have snow. I don't know how enjoyable skiing and skating are. Nor do I know how beautiful a landscape of snow is. Last January my cousin in Chunchon wrote to me, saying that his house was covered with deep snow, but I could hardly imagine the sight. I long to experience a few winters with much snow. Silly as it may sound, that's one of the reasons why I have chosen to enter a college in Seoul

단문독해 (p.419)

1. ▶▶해석

내가 파리에 도착하니 택시 운전사가, 모든 호텔은 만원이며 교외로 나가지 않으면 방을 얻는 데 무척 힘들 것이라고 나에게 말했다.

▶▶정답 downtown, outskirts

▶▶영작

(1) I had no difficulty in finding his house.

(2) He phoned me that he would leave without me unless I came immediately.

2. ▶▶해석

나는 어떤 내과의사에게, 소금은 불필요하고 심지어 해롭다고까지 주장하는 동료 의사들의 의견에 동의하느냐고 물었다. 그는 그렇지 않다고 힘주어 부인했다. 그는, 우리들이 먹는 음식물이 우리 인체가 요구하는 염분을 포함하고 있다는 것을 인정하려 하지 않았다.

▶▶정답 necessary, additional

▶▶영작

He told me that the trains start every half an hour.

3. ▶▶해석

나는 그 편지에서, 지금 백달러가 필요하며, 그 돈을 내가 갚을 수 있을 때까지 빌려 주면 매우 고맙겠으며, 그리고 그 돈이 왜 필요한지는 후에 말씀드리겠다고 그녀에게 썼다.

▶▶정답 ③

▶▶영작

(1) What do you want it for?

(2) I am much obliged to you for your kind help.

4. ▶▶해석

아버지께서는 시골 생활의 가장 수치스러운 특징 중 한 가지는 작은 마을의 장사꾼들의 일반적인 비능률성과 느슨함이라고 종종 단언하셨다. 그는 다음과 같이 말씀하셨다: 자신은 처음에는 그러한 사람들이 장사에 관심이 있다고, 그리고 그 이유로 가게를 열고 그 가게에 자본을 투자했을 것이라고 생각했지만 아니었다. 그들은 가게를 잡담을 하고 자는 곳으로 밖에 사용하지 않았다. 그들은 개화된 방식에는 관심이 없었다. 아마 그들은 그런 것이 있다는 것을 들어보지도 못했을 것이다.

▶▶정답 ②

▶▶영작

I will do anything but that.

5. ▶▶해석

최근에 나는 나이보다 적어도 20년은 젊어 보이는 여든 살 노신사 한 분을 알게 되었다. 그는 일생 동안 단 하루도 아픈 적이 없었기 때문에 만약 의사들이 환자로서 자기와 같은 사람들을 의존해야 한다면, 그들은 모두 폐업을 해야 할 것이라고 내게 말했다.

▶▶정답 age, practicing

▶▶영작

As he is an orphan, he has no one to depend on for help.

6. ▶▶해석

뉴턴은, 지구를 포함하여 혹성은 그의 이른바 인력의 법칙에 의해 태양 주위를 돈다는 것을 발견했으나 우주에 관한 그의 위대한 발견으로 그가 받은 보답은 무신론자라는 비난이었다.

▶▶정답 disagreed

▶▶영작

The teacher told the students that the earth goes [moves] around the sun once a year.

7. ▶▶해석

Sam으로 부터의 편지는 그녀에게 이렇게 알려 주고 있었다. 즉, 그는 뜻밖에도 운 좋게 상점을 하나 구했고, 지금 그것을 소유하고 있으며, 그것은 과일과 야채를 파는 거리에서 가장 큰 상점이며, 자기 생각에는 이 상점이 언젠가는 그녀의 체면에 손상됨이 없는 훌륭한 가정을 이룰 수 있을 테니, 지금 당장 상경하여 그녀를 만나 봐도 되겠느냐는 것이었다.

▶▶정답 financial, proposal

▶▶해석

I informed my boss that I was going to take a day off next week.

장문독해 (p.422)

1 ▶▶해석

나의 경험은 빛깔도 없고 소리도 없는 세계에 사는 사람의 한정된 경험이었다. 그러나, 학생 시절부터 나는, 신체적인 장애는 어떤 점에 있어서도 나의 정신의 일부분이 아니니까 나의 존재의 본질적인 부분은 아니라는 즐거운 확신을 품어왔다. 이 신념은, 데카르트의 「나는 사고한다. 고로, 나는 존재한다.」라는 금언에 접했을 때 확고히 (뇌리에) 박혔다. 이 다섯의 힘있는 말은 그 이후로 결코 잠잔적이 없는 무언가를 내 마음 속에 일깨워주었다. 나는 그 때 나의 정신은, 어둡고 소리 없는 공간을 활기에 넘치는 빛으로 가득 찬 행복의 개념으로 다리 놓을 수(연결할 수) 있는 적극적인 도구가 될 수 있다는 것을 알았다. 밖에서 어떤 재난이 우리에게 닥쳐올지라도, 우리의 내부에서 빛과 음 그리고 질서를 창조할 수 있다는 것을 나는 알았다.

▶▶정답

1. ⑤

2. mind, obstacles

3. ①

4. ③

▶▶영작

(1) It has been ten years since I came here.

(2) Since she spoke in French, I could not understand her.

(3) There is a possibility that I may not be with you on your birthday.

(4) Though Franklin Roosevelt was physically handicapped, he became one of the greatest presidents of America.

2 ▶▶해석

달은 너무 황량하고, 너무 마음이 끌리지 않으며(매력 없고), 생명체가 전혀 없으며, 혹은 도대체 생명체가 있었다는 것을 나타내 줄 아무 것도 없었다.달에서 본 지구의 경치는 나를 매혹시켰다. 그것은 24만 마일이나 떨어져 있는 작은 원반(圓盤)이었다. 저렇게 작은 물체가 그렇게도 많은 문제들, 그렇게도 많은 좌절들을 담고 있다는 것은 생각하기가 힘들었다. 맹렬한 국가 이익, 기근, 전쟁, 질병은 그렇게 먼 곳에서는 보이지 않는다.나는, 우주선을 탄 어떤 정처 없이 떠도는 낯선 외계인이 우주의 어떤 다른 부분으로부터 와서, 지구를 바라볼 수는 있으나 거기에 사람이 살고 있다고는 결코 생각지 않을 것이라고 확신한다. 그러나, 그 정처 없이 떠도는 외계인은, 만약에 지구에 사람이 살고 있다고 하면 거기에 살고 있는 모든 사람들의 운명은 어쩔 수 없이 서로 얽혀 있고 결합되어 있다는 것을 본능적으로 틀림없이 알 것이다. 우리들은 우주에 떠 있는 흙, 물, 공기, 구름의 한 덩어리이다. 우주 공간에서 보면 지구는 진실로 "하나의 세계"이다.

▶▶정답

1. a small disk / that little thing / one hunk of ground, water, air, clouds
2. ④ 3. ② 4. ④

▶▶영작

(1) The sun has shown itself above the horizon.
(2) I am convinced that he is innocent of the crime.
(3) Our earth is a mere speck in the boundless universe.
(4) He must be crazy to act like that.

실력체크 I (p.426)

1

(1) 내가 연설을 잘하건 못하건, 그것이 그리 중요한 게 아니라고 여기게 되자 신경과민도 사라지고 오히려 연설을 더 잘하게 되었다.
(2) 연설을 잘하는 경우나 못하는 경우나 어느 쪽 경우에도

2

인용부호: "How ~ can." "Well ~ way." "Go ~ me." "Oh ~ Renvil." "Patricia ~ be." "Oh ~ account."

* (1) 목사 (2) Dodd
 (3) 4 (4) Renvil
 (5) Patricia (6) Dodd

3

(1) what (2) with (3) no
(4) in (5) by (6) for
(7) help (8) as (9) with
(10) on

4

(1) 팔(완력)을 사용할 필요가 있을 때에는
(2) ⓐ Charley에게
 ⓑ 먼저 올라가서 Smith 양에게 손님이 왔다고 알리지 못함을 용서해 달라고
 ⓒ 발이 아파서
(3) 11시 이후는 남자 손님은 출입 금지

숙어 Exercise (p.432)

1. I don't know anything about it, so I'll play it by ear.
2. He always plays up to his boss to get a raise in salary.
3. The kids poked fun at him for his ridiculous clothes.
4. I prevailed on him to drive me to the airport.
5. I'll pull in to the shop on the way to the party.
6. The trick seemed impossible, but he pulled it off.
7. I'm sure your mother will pull through the illness.
8. Can you put me through to this number?
9. You'd better not read any criticism into what I'm saying to you.
10. The guard referred me to the information desk.

Do all the good you can,
By all the means you can,
In all the ways you can,
In all the places you can,
At all the times you can,
To all the people you can,
As long as you can.

— *John Wesley* —

할 수 있는 모든 선을 행하라,
할 수 있는 모든 수단을 다해,
할 수 있는 모든 방법으로,
할 수 있는 모든 장소에서,
할 수 있는 모든 시간에,
할 수 있는 모든 사람에게,
네 생명이 다할 때까지

— 죤 웨슬리 —

제18장 전치사

문법 · 작문 (p.440)

F.

(1) of (2) in (3) at (4) by
(5) by (6) in (7) of (8) in
(9) between (10) as (11) without (12) for

G.

(1) I waited for him till eight, but he did not come after all.
(2) This morning I met a teacher of my primary school days on my way to school.
(3) Nowadays many women are in their late twenties or early thirties when they have their first child.
(4) Those who flatter you to your face are apt to speak ill of you behind your back.
(5) His success is entirely due to the assistance of his wife.
(6) If you get riches and power at the cost of your conscience, it is rather a great failure in life.
(7) A monument was erected in memory of the event.
(8) A man will succeed in proportion to his perseverance.
(9) You must not cross the street against the red light.
(10) While others are idling away their time, this student goes on steadily with his studies.
(11) If your friend kindly reminds you of your faults, take what he says thankfully.

'Which country would you like to visit, and why?'

England is the country which I would like to visit most. The first reason is that I am so much interested in English literature that I wish to see places associated with the famous English men of literature and their works. The next reason is that I wish to see with my own eyes how English democracy is going on. I don't think book knowledge about democracy is sufficient.

단문독해 (p.447)

1. ▶▶해석

인생에서 내가 보아온 최고로 성공한 사람들은 항상 명랑하고 희망에 찬 사람들이었으며, 그들은 얼굴에 웃음을 띠고 자신의 일을 열심히 하였고, 성공과 실패를 오는 그대로 직면하며, 이 인생의 변화와 기회를 남자답게 받아들였다.

▶▶정답 ups, downs

▶▶영작

You will have a rise and a fall in your life; such is life.

2. ▶▶해석

그는 두 어깨 위로, 그리고 등과 다리 위로 담요를 끌어당겼다. 그는 두 팔을 뻗고 손바닥을 위로 하고 신문지 위에 엎드려 잠을 잤다.

▶▶정답 stomach

▶▶영작

Don't sleep with the window open.

3. ▶▶해석

학교에 가서 1주일도 되지 않아 그는 향수병이 났다. 그의 선생님과 친구들이 할 수 있는 모든 일을 다했으나, 그의 슬픔이 너무 깊어, (말로) 타일러서 (슬픔을) 없앨 수가 없었다.

▶▶정답 ⑤

▶▶영작

I slept off the tiredness of the journey.

4. ▶▶해석

틀림없이 내가 그 짐승(고양이)을 더 미워하게 된 것은 그것을 집으로 가져온 다음날 아침, 그것이 눈이 하나 없는 것을 발견했기 때문이었다. 그러나, 이러한 사정은 고양이가 내 아내의 사랑을 더 받을 수 있게 해줄 뿐이었다.

▶▶정답 ③

▶▶영작

Her kindness of heart endears her to all.

5. ▶▶해석

어떤 종류의 독단적 태도를 벗어나는 좋은 방법은 자기 자신이 속하는 사회[집단]과는 다른 사회[집단]의 의견을 아는 것이다. 만약 의견이 다른 쪽과 교제가 없다면, 당신과 의견이 다른 사람들을 찾아내든지 당신이 속하지 않은 단체의 신문을 읽어라.

▶▶정답 dogmatic, different

▶▶영작

He hates anyone who does not agree to his opinion.

6. ▶▶해석

새해 결심을 하는 관습은 오늘날은 인기가 없는 것 같다. 그러나, 여러 나라에서 사람들이 보다 나은 새해를 갖기 위하여 혹은 그들의 나쁜 습관을 정복하기 위하여 새해 맹세를 하곤 했다.

▶▶정답 ④

▶▶영작

He bought the land for the purpose of building his office on it.

7. ▶▶해석

유럽 문화가 위대한 진보를 했다고 해서, 아프리카 흑인이나 에스키모인이 보다 온화한 지역의 주민보다 덜 총명하다고 생각할 이유는 전혀 없다. 에스키모인은 도구를 만드는 원료가 부족하기 때문에 미개의 상태로 남아있는 것이다. 그것은 도구가 없으면 문명생활은 불가능하기 때문이다.

▶▶정답 resources, intelligence

▶▶영작

He has every reason for being displeased.

8. ▶▶해석

소설을 읽는 최선의 방법은 옛날과 요즘의 소설을 섞어서 읽는 것이지, 과거의 작품은 읽지 않고 현대 작품만 좋아하거나, 또는 현대 작품을 읽지 않고 과거의 작품만을 좋아하는 것은 아니다. 그리고 만일 이런 방법이 추구된다면, 현대 작품은 과거의 위대한 작품과 비교하여 빈약하고 하찮게 보일 것이라고는 생각하지 말아라. 반드시 그런 것만은 아니다.

▶▶정답 ⑤

▶▶영작

The fox escaped from the trap at the expense of one of its legs.

9. ▶▶해석

16살 때 그는 말을 타고 황소와 투우할 허가를 간신히 받았다. 그런데, 그는 구경꾼들이 감탄하게도, 그의 창으로 단 한 번에 소를 찔러 죽여 버렸다.

▶▶정답 a bullfighter

▶▶영작

To my disappointment he failed the examination.

장문독해 (p.450)

1 ▶▶해석

나는 교육을 너무도 많은 분리된 여러 과목의 훈련이라고 생각할 수는 없다. 교육은 통합적이다. 교육은 전인(全人), 즉 완전한 인간의 성장을 격려하는 것이다. 그러므로, 교육은 전적으로 아니 주로 책공부일 수만은 없다는 결론이 된다. 왜냐 하면, 그것은 우리 본성의 한 부분, 즉 개념이나 추상적 내용을 다루는 정신의 그 부분의 교육에 불과하기 때문이다. 이런 지름길의 방법[추상적인 책공부]에 의하여 사고할 수 있을 만큼 성숙하지 못한 어린이에게 있어서, 교육은 주로 감각, 즉 시각, 촉각, 청각의 교육이 되어야 한다. 한마디로 말해서, 감각 교육이 되어야 한다. 이런 견지에서 볼 때, 예술과 과학에는 뚜렷한 구별이 없다. 단지 다양한 흥미와 능력을 갖는 전인만이 있으며, 교육의 목표는 이런 흥미와 능력을 조화롭게 완전하게 발전시키는 것이어야 한다.

▶▶정답

1. 책으로 공부하는 것
2. 예술과 과학교육은 모두 먼저 감각 교육을 통해 이루어질 수 있으므로
3. ⑤ 4. ③

▶▶영작

(1) Just because she is rich, it doesn't necessarily follow that she's happy.
(2) The usage of computer software is dealt with in more detail in Chapter Four.
(3) There is almost no distinction in the appearance of identical twins.

2 ▶▶해석

국가 정상들은 우선, 무엇 때문에 정상 회담이 필요한가를 생각해 보는 것이 유용할 것 같다. 만일 국제 연합의 기구가 예정된(의도된) 일을 수행할 수 있었다면, 정상회담 같은 것은 필요하지 않을 것이다. 만일 국제 연합이 존속하려면, 필요한 것은 각국이 여러 문제들을 유엔에 넘기는 자발성보다, 관련 국가들이 원하든 원하지 않든 행동할 수 있는 유엔의 절대적 권위이다. 현재 유엔은 관련 국가들의 동의를 받아 행동한다. 이와 같이, 유엔은 입법이나 법률 집행 기관 대신 중재 기관이 되어버렸다. 어떤 경찰이 자기 직무를 수행하기에 앞서 법 위반자의 동의를 얻어야 한다면, 그는 경찰이 아니라 탄원자의 신세가 되고 만다. 국가를 영도하는 인사들은 유엔을 무한정 선택의 자유가 있는 장소[결정이 좋으면 따르고 싫으면 거부하는 그런 구실만 하는 장소]로부터 구속력 있는 기구로 바꾸기 위한 유엔 기구 개편 회의에 찬동할 의무를 가지고 있다.

▶▶정답

1. 입법 기능, 법집행 기능
2. a supplicant 3. ② 4. ④

▶▶영작

(1) This tax is intended for the development of the tourist industry.
(2) If you are to see her again, you should apologize sincerely to her.
(3) The criminal refused to name another suspect involved in the murder.
(4) The mayor will call an emergency committee for the purpose of coping with the strike by public transportation workers.

실력체크 I (p.454)

1

1. the sunset
2. 나이가 들어 체력이 약해졌으므로 : the best point of view = the summit
3. many walks
4. I wish ~ rambling.

2 PAROLE

3 (a) — ③ (b) — ④ (c) — ⑦ (d) — ② (e) — ⑩

숙어 Exercise (p.460)

1. I had to resign myself to waiting a bit longer.
2. You can rest assured that I'll never break a promise.
3. It's a very difficult task, but I'm sure you'll rise to the occasion.
4. Her rude behavior rubbed her mother the wrong way.
5. The truck suddenly skidded and ran into a streetlight.
6. My car ran out of gas three miles from town.
7. I saw fit to stay late and help him with his work.
8. I could see through all his lies from the start.
9. I saw to it that the electric bill was paid.
10. Winter sets in early in the north.

제19장 접속사

문법 · 작문 (p.466)

A.
(1) and (2) as
(3) hardly [scarcely, barely]
(4) Now (5) because
(6) Whether (7) when [before]
(8) as (9) whether [if]
(10) until (11) nor
(12) if (13) if
(14) lest (15) as
(16) that (17) than
(18) than (19) and
(20) otherwise (21) the, time
(22) as [like] ※미국 구어에서는 as 대신에 like를 더 많이 쓰는 경향이 있다.

B.
(1) neither had ⇨ had neither
(2) until ⇨ before (3) except ⇨ unless
(4) that ⇨ whether [if] (5) till ⇨ before
(6) when ⇨ before (7) tea ⇨ to tea

C.
(1) 명사절 (2) 부사절
(3) 부사절 (4) 명사절
(5) 명사절 (6) 부사절
(7) 명사절

D.
(1) Wise men seek after truth, while fools despise it.
(2) She did not answer but put the book on the table and went away.
(3) He hurried on lest he (should) be late.
(4) I cannot understand you unless you speak more slowly.
(5) Though Mr. Kim has never been either to England or to America, he is a good speaker of English.
(6) ① As soon as we sat down, we knew [realized] it was time to go.
② No sooner had we sat down than we knew [realized] it was time to go.
③ We had no sooner sat down than we knew [realized] it was time to go.
④ Hardly [Scarcely, Barely] had we sat down when [before] we knew [realized] it was time to go.
⑤ We had hardly [scarcely, barely] sat down when [before] we knew [realized] it was time to go.
(7) A man ought to be sound in body as well as in mind.
(8) They had not been married a month before they began to quarrel.
(9) People do not know the importance of health until they lose it.
(10) Do not read books simply because others are reading them.
(11) As time passed, things seemed to get worse.

'My hobby'

My hobby is collecting postage stamps. My collection amounts to some 600 stamps, among which there are some quite rare ones. My hobby has enabled me to make many friends all over the world. They send me their beautiful and interesting stamps, and I send ours to them. Through our common hobby our friendship is deepening and our appreciation of each other's culture is growing. Whenever I see my collection, I feel as if I were reading a human history and enjoying a pleasant chat in a human family.

단문독해 (p.468)

1. ▶▶해석
학생이 비록 머리가 둔할지라도, 학과(과목)가 첫눈에는 어려워 보일지라도, 그가 인내할 수 있고 공부를 게을리 하지 않으면, 공부가 (전보다) 더 수월해지거나 적어도 덜 어려워진다는 것을 알게 될 것이다.
▶▶정답 perseverance
▶▶영작
He fell in love with her at first sight.

2. ▶▶해석
한때 Thoreau(소로우)를 매우 좋아했지만, 나는 돈을 결코 노예화의 원인으로 간주한 적이 없다는 것을 고백한다. 나는 호주머니에 단 25세트밖에 없을 때보다 1달러를 가지고 있을 때 항상 마음이 더 자유로웠다. 버스 대신에 택시를 탈 수 있는 것이 나에게는 바람직한 자유인 것이다.
▶▶정답 ②
▶▶영작
Do not look (up)on your work as a dull duty but try to interest yourself in it.

3. ▶▶해석
우리의 과학이 완전하다면, 그것은 인간 정신의 본질을 설명할 것이다. 그러나 (사실은) 불완전하기 때문에, 인간의 육체에 관해서는 더 많이 알려주면서도 인간 정신의 본질에 대해서 알려 주는 것은 불과 얼마 되지 않는다.
▶▶정답 less, spirit, body
▶▶영작
I got a glimpse of the house through the window of the train.

4. ▶▶해석
그는 비록 위대한 물리학자이지만, 인간으로서(인간적인 면에서) 더욱 위대하다. 그 사람만큼 명성에 무관심하고 또 남에게 널리 알려지는 것을 불편하게 여기는 사람도 없지만, 그는 다른 어떤 과학자의 명성보다 더 큰 명성을 얻었다. 명성과 외부적 환경은 그를 거의 변화시킬 수 없다.
▶▶정답 ②
▶▶영작
She is very interested in politics while he is indifferent to them.

5. ▶▶해석
대학 교육 과정을 통과한 젊은이는 절대로 단순 재미를 위해 책을 읽지 않도록 일찍이 자신을 훈련시켜야 한다. 그리고 일단 이 훈련의 습관이 형성되면 단순 재미를 위한 독서는 불가능하다는 것까지 알게 될 것이다.
▶▶정답
오락 위주의 독서를 하지 않는다는 원칙
▶▶영작
Once you get to the island, you'll understand why I like it so much.

6. ▶▶해석
이 세상 사람은 누구나 다른 어떤 사람보다 낫다. 나의 학생 중 하나가 부자이건 가난하건, 백인이건 흑인이건 황인종이건, 머리가 총명하건 둔하건, 그에게 인간미가 있고—열의가 있고—진실과 명예를 사랑하면, 그런 것들은 나에게 중요한 것이 아니다.
▶▶정답 financial, intelligence
▶▶영작
It doesn't matter whether you turn left or right. Both roads lead to the park.

7. ▶▶해석
사람들은 가끔 고전작품의 연구가 드디어 좀더 현대적이고 실용적인 공부에 자리를 내줄 것처럼 이야기한다. 그러나, 모험을 좋아하는 학생들은 고전이 어떤 언어로 쓰여졌건, 그리고 아무리 오랜 된 것이어도 고전을 항상 연구할 것이다. 왜냐 하면, 고전이라는 것은 가장 고상한 기록된 인간의 사상 바로 그것이기 때문이다(고전이란 인간의 가장 고상한 기록된 사상 외에 무엇이겠는가?).

▶▶정답
가장 고상한 인간 사상을 기록한 것이 고전이므로

▶▶영작
I will make way for a younger man.

8. ▶▶해석
책이 없는 집은, 아무리 비싼 페르시아산(産) 양탄자가 깔리고 가구가 아무리 우아해도, 속없고 인격이 없는 집이다. 페르시아산 양탄자는 단지 그 집 주인이 돈을 가지고 있다는 것만 말해 주지만, 책은 그가 역시 정신도 가지고 있다는 것을 말해준다.

▶▶정답 ④

▶▶영작
No matter how talented you are, you cannot expect to succeed without making efforts.

9. ▶▶해석
천지 창조의 이슬이 맺힌 아침, 아직 지구가 젊고 신선하고, 짓밟는 수백만의 인간 발자국이 풀을 밟아 먼지로 만들지 않았던 그 때는, 지구가 좀 더 좋았음에 틀림없다는 것을 부인할 수 없다.

▶▶정답 man

▶▶영작
There is no knowing what may happen in the future.

10. ▶▶해석
신문은 거의 모든 사람이 읽는 유일한 읽을 거리이다. 자기 일에 아무리 바쁜 사람이라도, 신문 읽을 시간이 없는 사람은 없다(신문 읽을 시간은 낼 수 있다).

▶▶정답 tied

▶▶영작
The reporter is still occupied with writing an article on the World Cup.

11. ▶▶해석
과연 과학은 좋은 것이지만, 과학 그 자체가 목적은 아니다. 그것은 어떤 목적에 이르는 수단이고 그 목적이란 인간의 진보이다. 과학자들이 계속 주장하고 있듯이, 과학적 발견에는 선도 없고 악도 없다. 그것을 유익하게 또는 위험하게 만드는 것은 그것이 사용되는 용도이다. 그리고 그러한 결정은 과학자들의 몫이 아니라 사회의 몫이다.

▶▶정답 ③

▶▶영작
It lies with us to decide what actions to take.

12. ▶▶해석
지금까지, 그는 그 학교의 대수롭지 않은 학생, 즉 운동에도 공부에도 뛰어나지 못한, 아무것도 기대할 수 없는, 좀처럼 말썽도 일으키지 않는 그런 학생 중 하나였다.

▶▶정답 ⑤

▶▶영작
He seldom, if ever, makes mistakes.

13. ▶▶해석
매스미디어(대중매체)가 원자탄과 훨씬 더 강력한 수소폭탄이 사용될 가능성에 대해 너무 많이 언급해 왔기 때문에, 우리는 원자력의 올바른 사용을 통해 그것이 우리의 복지와 건강을 위해 할 수 있는 일들을 잊기 쉽다.

▶▶정답 ④

▶▶영작
This machine has lately come into common use.

14. ▶▶해석

사진술은 이미 카메라가 도달할 수 없는 사물이 자연계에 거의 없을 정도의 완벽한 단계에 이르렀다.

▶▶정답 developed, picture

▶▶영작

It is beyond the comprehension of the ordinary man.

15. ▶▶해석

세상은, 자기를 사랑하는 사람을 지금 가지고 있지 않거나 가져본 적이 없는 사람이 사는 일은 결코 발생하지 않도록 만들어져 있다. (세상에는) 부모님의 사랑, 형제 자매의 사랑, 그리고 친척과 동료들의 사랑이 있다.

▶▶정답 no, not

▶▶영작

The bridge is so made that it opens in the middle.

16. ▶▶해석

많은 사람들이 가지고 있기는 하지만 충분히 사용하는 사람이 거의 없는 재능 중의 하나는 표현의 재능이다. 학창 시절에 편지나 논문밖에는 아무것도 써 보려고 하지 않았다고 해서, 너에게 문학적 재능이 없다고 믿을 아무 이유도 없다.

▶▶정답 ②

▶▶영작

A man does not always deserve respect because he is learned.

17. ▶▶해석

나는 아이들이 이렇게 교육받는 것을 보고 싶다. 즉, 단지 어떤 다른 사람들이 그것을 좋아한다고 말하기 때문에 자기가 좋아하지도 않는 것을 좋아한다고 말해서는 안 된다고. 그리고, 자기들이 그것에 대하여 아무것도 이해하지 못하면서 이것을 믿느니 저것을 믿느니 하는 것이 얼마나 어리석은가를.

▶▶정답 ④

▶▶영작

I don't like to see you disappointed.

18. ▶▶해석

저런 천재들은 어떤 특별한 직업이 가장 좋다고 생각하거나, 혹은 그것이 가장 많은 영광, 돈, 또는 행복을 약속해 주기 때문이 아니라, 어쩔 수 없는 이유로 그 직업을 선택하며, 또 바로 그 이유로 생명이 계속되는 한 그것(직업)에 집착하는 것이다.

▶▶정답 ④

▶▶영작

He sticks to any task until he finishes it.

19. ▶▶해석

새들은 본래 이 세상에서 가장 즐거운 생물이다. 그것은 당신이 새를 보거나 새소리를 들을 때 그들(새들)이 항상 당신에게 기쁨을 주기 때문이 아니라, 새들이 어떤 다른 동물보다 더 많은 기쁨을 느끼기 때문이다. 다른 동물들은 대개 심각하고 엄숙해 보이며, 또 심지어 우울해 보이는 동물도 많다. 그러나, 새들은 대부분 그들의 여러 동작과 모습으로 자신을 매우 즐겁게 나타낸다(매우 즐거워하는 모습을 보여준다).

▶▶정답 ③

▶▶영작

We spent the day for the most part looking around the museum.

20. ▶▶해석

우리 시대에 있어서, 과학은 지상의 모든 생물을 말살할 수 있는 힘을 인간의 손에 쥐어 주었다. 세계의 여러 사람들이 그들의 손에 이런 치명적인 무기를 가지고 서로 대결하게 되었기 때문에, 신중, 관용, 지혜와 — 이것들보다 훨씬 더 — 사랑의 미덕들이 문자 그대로 생활의 필수품이 되고 말았다.

▶▶정답 ④

▶▶영작

Their marriage life was in every sense a happy one.

21.▶ ▶해석

인간 행위의 가장 중요한 법칙이 하나 있다. 만약 우리가 그 법칙을 따르면, 우리는 거의 아무런 말썽도 일으키지 않을 것이다. 사실, 그 법칙을 따르면, 수많은 친구들과 변함 없는 행복을 우리에게 가져다 줄 것이다. 그러나, 우리가 이 법칙을 어기자마자 우리는 끝없는 곤경에 처할 것이다. 그 법칙은 이것이다: 항상 상대방으로 하여금 잘났다고 느끼게 하라.

▶▶정답 ②

▶▶영작

The moment you violate [break] the rule, you'll get into trouble.

장문독해 (p.476)

1 ▶▶해석

만약 지성적 도덕적 가치의 직관적 혹은 이성적 지각에 의해 지배되지 않으면 지성만으로는 위험하다. 그것은 물질주의뿐만 아니라, 여러 괴물도 낳고 말았다. 갑자기 일반 대중들은, 놀라운 과학의 승리가 잔인하게 인간의 안전에 도전하고 있다는 것을 깨닫게 되었다. 그리고 즉시, 소위 문명 제국들은 도덕적 결합만이 그들을 이 위협에서 보호해 줄 수 있다는 것을 이해하게 되었다. 시간이 너무 촉박하여 유일한 가능한 보호를 문서 협정에서 찾지 않을 수 없었다. 그러나, 문서 협정은 그 협정의 서명자와 같은 정도의 효력과 믿음밖에 없으며, 또이 사람이 정직하고 성실하지 않으면, 그가 진정으로 그의 명예를 건 약속을 지지해 줄 국민을 대표할 수 있는 존재가 아니라면, 그런 협정들은 전혀 무의미한 것이라는 것을 누구나 다 안다. 인간 역사상 처음으로, 순수 지성과 도덕 가치의 충돌이 죽느냐 사느냐의 문제가 되었다. 이제 우리가 할 수 있는 일은, 우리가 이 교훈에 의해 이익을 얻어 주었으면 하고 바랄 뿐이다. 그러나 슬프게도, 우리는 이것을 의심한다.

▶▶정답

1. 놀라운 과학의 승리가 잔인하게 인간 생존을 위협하는 것

2. ② 3. ③ 4. ③

▶▶영작

(1) The failure of the agreement would bring a great disaster not only to both countries, but to the whole world.

(2) We are all subject to the law of our country, and a mere ignorance of the law does not justify a law-breaker.

(3) Do you have anything particular in mind for this coming Sunday? If not, how about going on a picnic with us?

2 ▶▶해석

생계 수단에 대해 끊임없이 근심해야 하는 것처럼 창피한 것은 없다. 나는 돈을 멸시하는 사람들을 경멸할 따름이다. 그들은 위선자이거나 바보다. 돈은 여섯 번째의 감각과 같아서, 그것이 없으면 다른 오감(五感)을 완전히 사용할 수 없다. 적당한 수입이 없으면 인생의 가능성이 절반 사라진다. 우리가 꼭 유의해야 할 것은, 우리가 버는 1달러에 대해 1달러 이상은 우리가 지불하지 않는다는 사실이다(돈과 노력은 에누리가 없다). 가난이 예술가에게 가장 좋은 자극제가 된다고 사람들이 말하는 것을 우리는 듣는다. 그런 사람들은 가난의 쓰라림을 직접 느껴 보지 못한 사람들이다. 그들은 가난이 우리를 얼마나 비열하게 만드는가를 모른다. 가난은 우리를 끝없는 수모를 받게 하고, 가난은 너의 날개를 잘라 버리고(너의 자유를 빼앗고), 가난은 마치 암처럼 너희 영혼을 갉아먹는다. 우리가 원하는 것은 (엄청난) 재산이

아니라, 우리의 위신(품위)을 지킬 수 있고, 방해받지 않고 일할 수 있고, 관대할 수 있고, 솔직할 수 있고, 독립할 수 있는 만큼의 양뿐이다. 나는 그가 글을 쓰건 그림을 그리건, 자기의 생계를 전적으로 자기의 예술에 의존하는 예술가를 진정으로 불쌍히 여긴다.

▶▶정답

1. 수입이 1 달라면 1달러만큼의 결과밖에 안 나온다(가난은 가난한 결과(작품)만 낳는다.)
2. devote, financial
3. ② 4. ③

▶▶영작

(1) You are hunting for a bargain, but you will soon find that you get what you pay for.

(2) Her e-mail saying that he died was nothing but a lie.

(3) The commander's careless order exposed many soldiers to radiation.

(4) Water pollution killed millions of fish on which many fishermen are dependent for their livelihood.

실력체크 I (p.480)

1

(1) * 제1요소: 인물과 시대를 배경으로 그린 "역사"라는 점.
* 제2요소: 성격 발전을 단계적으로 다룬 "개인"의 묘사라는 점.
* 제3요소: 정확한 영어와 문체로 쓴 "문학의 한 부분"이라는 점.

(2) * pure한 것: 3요소를 고루 갖추고, 인물의 정확한 묘사 이외의 목적을 갖지 않는 것.
* impure한 것: 3요소의 균형을 잃고, 전기의 목적에서 이탈하여 기술의 정확성을 잃는 것.

2

(1) * 둘째 paragraph의 시작:
The great cities have been …
* 첫째 paragraph의 요지:
In the organization of industrial life the influence of the factory upon the physiological and mental state of the workers has been completely neglected.
* 둘째 paragraph의 요지:
The great cities have been built with no regard for us.

(2) 최저의 비용으로 최대의 생산을 하여, 될 수 있는 한 돈을 많이 벌겠다는 생각.

(3) 토지 평방 피트당의 수익을 최대로 올리며, 세든 사람들에게 마음에 드는 사무실과 아파트를 제공할 필요성.

3 you would be done by

숙어 Exercise (p.486)

1. The family settled down in the Midwest and began farming.
2. We shopped around to buy a good but inexpensive car.
3. I slept on it, and I've decided to accept your offer.
4. If you don't like your job, it stands to reason that you should find another one.
5. He stormed out of the office, shouting "I quit!"
6. I can't tell you what to do, so suit yourself.
7. He always takes advantage of every opportunity (that comes his way).
8. Don't eat so fast! Take your time and enjoy your meal.
9. He often takes his anger out on me.
10. I took the liberty of borrowing your car while you were away.

제20장 도치·강조·생략·공통관계·삽입·동격

문법 · 작문 (p.492)

A.

(1) rich and poor (2) gate, way (3) nobody
(4) week (5) smoke (6) she
(7) they (8) lamp, box

B.

(1) Little did I dream ~. (2) I do wish ~.
(3) Down came the rain in torrents.
(4) He arrived at that very moment.
(5) Why is it that you are so mad?
(6) No sooner had the runner finished the marathon~.

C.

(1) is, is (2) having been
(3) it is (4) which was
(5) he would look (6) come
(7) for
(8) 두 번째 the weather's, good

D.

(1) I hope (it will) not (rain).
(2) and (you will) spoil
(3) until (you are) spoken
(4) how (we live) (5) If (it is) wisely
(6) (Keep your) Hands off.

E.

(1) himself (2) development
(3) anyone to love him

F.

(1) 그는 크기와 힘에서 자기가 부족한 것을 민첩성과 기술로 보충한다.
(2) 인생은 어떤 사람들에게는 쾌락이고, 다른 사람들에게는 가장 소중한 모든 것이다. 그러나 인생이 쾌락이건 혹은 다른 무엇이건, 사람의 일이 그의 인생이며 그의 인생이 그의 일이어야 한다.
(3) 그리스의 대중유희는 대체로 종교적인 축제와 관련이 되고 또 그 일부를 이루고 있는 여러 종류의 운동경기에 (놓여) 있었다.

G.

(1) He rarely speaks at a meeting, but when he does speak, he always speaks to the point.
(2) There is no knowing when a misfortune will come, but when it does come, you must be prepared to meet it with composure.
(3) Some say that they cannot find time to do what they wish to, but in most cases it is not really the time but the will that is lacking.
(4) It goes without saying that nothing is as necessary for the economic independence of our country as to promote foreign trade.
(5) There arose the question whether we should do it or not.
(6) When I left my hometown twenty years ago, little did I dream that I would never see it again.
(7) We must be careful in small matters as well as in great ones.

'Write a Story'

One day a hare met a tortoise, and laughed at his slow way of walking. The tortoise said to the hare, "Then let's run a race."
"Very well, we will try," replied the hare. Both of them started. But the hare took a nap on the way, while the patient tortoise walked on without resting, and reached the goal before the hare.
This story teaches us that slow and steady wins the race.

단문독해 (p.494)

1. ▶▶해석

진리를 존중하는 인간의 마음의 쇠퇴는 자선심의 퇴보와 밀접한 관련이 있다. 세계 역사상 금세기의 정치적, 경제적 독재자들에 의해서처럼 파렴치하게 조직적인 허위를 감행한 적은 어떤 시기에도 없었다.

▶▶정답 organized lying

▶▶영작

He was so angry that he could hardly speak.

2. ▶▶해석

다른 사람의 나쁜 점은 우리 눈앞에 내세우지만, 자신의 나쁜 점은 등 뒤에 숨긴다. 그러므로, 자기 자신의 결점이 더 많은 사람들이 타인의 결점을 용서하지 않는 일이 자주 있다.

▶▶정답 ④

▶▶영작

I firmly believe that he has done it.

3. ▶▶해석

하도 자주 나는 이사를 해 왔고, 이사할 때마다 많지도 않은 나의 장서를 그렇게도 난폭하게 다루어 왔고, 그리고 사실을 말하면, 평상시에도 장서 보존에 그리도 주위를 해 오지 않았기 때문에, 나의 책들 중에서 (외관이) 가장 매력적인 것조차도 부당한 취급을 받은 결과를 나타내고 있다.

▶▶정답 rough treatment

▶▶영작

Little did I think that I would win the prize.

4. ▶▶해석

비록 그는 나의 형님이었지만, 그는 자신을 나의 주인으로 생각하고, 나를 자기의 견습공으로만 여겼다. 따라서, 그는 다른 견습공으로부터 자기가 바라는 것과 똑같은 노역을 나로부터 기대했다. 반면에, 나는 그가 나에게서 너무 많은 것을 요구한다고 생각했는데, 나는 형님으로부터 좀더 관대함을 기대했던 것이다.

▶▶정답 ④

▶▶영작

When left alone, she was at a loss what to do.

5. ▶▶해석

돈이 끝장나고 나서야 돈의 가치를 생각하는 사람들이 있다. 그리고, 시간에 대해서도 그와 마찬가지로 생각하는 사람들이 많다. 잃어버린 재산은 근면과 절약에 의해 다시 얻을 수 있고, 잃어버린 지식은 공부에 의해 다시 얻을 수 있으며, 잃어버린 건강은 절제와 약으로써 다시 얻을 수 있지만, 잃어버린 시간은 영원히 가 버리고 만다.

▶▶정답 regained, recover

▶▶영작

Some people go to the mountain and others to the seaside for the summer vacation.

6. ▶▶해석

해가 저무는 것 (1년이 끝나는 것)은, 우리에게 정신적인 휴식과 반성의 자연스러운 기회를 제공한다. 우리는 과거를 돌이켜보고, 만약 우리가 진지하다면 새해의 기회를 잘 선용할 결심을 하고, 또 용기를 가지고 새해의 시련과 훈련에 직면하겠다 결심하고 앞을 내다본다.

▶▶정답 ③

▶▶영작

He came back, resolved to make a new start.

7. ▶▶해석

예술은 항상 사물의 현상에 관계가 있는 것과 마찬가지로, 사람들이 사물에 대해 느끼는 방법에도 매우 관계가 있다. 대개 지식과 감정이 합쳐서 그림을 이루게 된다. 그래서 회화는, 그 화가가 보았거나 안 것에 더 흥미를 가졌느냐 혹은 자기가 느낀 것에 더 흥미를 가졌느냐, 그리고 또한 어느 만큼 그가 보았느냐, 알았느냐, 느꼈느냐에 따라서 서로 다르다.

▶▶정답 ④

▶▶영작

Man is not the creature, but the creator, of circumstances.

8. ▶▶해석

저의 어머니가 아버지와 결혼한 것은 주로, 아버지가 어미 없는 다섯 어린애들을 키워 나가는 것을 돕기 위해서였던 것 같다. 저의 어머니가 자신의 어린애를 갖는다는 것은 부차적인 생각이었다. 그러나, 어머니는 딸을 낳았다. 그 다음에도 또 딸을 낳았다. 물론 두 딸을 갖는 것은 매우 좋은 일이었으나, 좀 실망스러웠다. 그것은 저의 어머니가, 아들을 낳는 것을 정말로 중요한 사건으로 여기던 그런 세대와 전통 속에 있었기 때문이었다. 그런 다음에 내가 아주 건강한 아기로 태어났다.

▶▶정답 ④

▶▶영작

I helped him through his work.

9. ▶▶해석

인간과 하등 동물 간에는 이런 차이가 있다. 즉, 인간은 자기가 하는 것에 대해 그 하는 방법을 배워야 하는데, 한편 동물은 자기들이 수행하는 대부분을 소위 본능에 의해서 할 수 있다. 즉, 그 방법을 배울 필요가 없다.

▶▶정답 learn, instinctively

▶▶영작

Democracy is based on the idea that all men are created equal.

장문독해 (p.498)

1 ▶▶해석

어떤 사람은 자기가 실패자라고 생각하기 때문에 술에 빠지게 된다. 그리고, 음주 때문에 더욱 완전히 실패하고 만다. 지금 영어에 일어나는 것도 어느 정도 이와 비슷하다. 우리의 사고가 어리석기 때문에 영어는 추해지고 정확해지지 못한다. 그러나, 한편 우리 언어가 단정하지 못하기 때문에 우리들이 어리석은 생각을 보다 쉽게 가지게 된다. 문제는 이 과정이 뒤바뀔 수 있다는 사실이다. 현대 영어 특히 문어는, 모방에 의해 퍼져 나가는, 그러나 우리가 필요한 수고를 아끼지 않으면 피할 수 있는 나쁜 습관들로 가득 차 있다. 이런 습관들을 제거하면, 보다 명료하게 사고할 수 있다. 그리고, 명료하게 사고하는 것은 정치 쇄신의 첫 필수 조건이다. 그러므로, 나쁜 영어와 우선 싸워야 하는 것은 하찮은 일이 아니며, 또 전문 저술가들의 독점적인 관심사는 아니다.

▶▶정답

1. ③
2. 어리석은 사고 때문에 언어는 추해지고, 추한 언어 때문에 사고는 어리석어 진다.
3. ④ 4. ④

▶▶영작

(1) You must not feel yourself a failure because you did not achieve your objective.

(2) He has a few faults, but I love him none the less.

(3) That bad habit of yours must be gotten rid of immediately.

(4) He is always willing to help a friend in need.

2 ▶▶해석

왜 로마제국이 성장했으며, 또 왜 그것이 그렇게 완전히 몰락했을까? 처음에 로마 국민이라는 국민 의식이 로마를 한데 묶었기 때문에 로마는 성장했다. 팽창하는 공화국 시기를 통하여, 그리고 초기 제국 시기까지도 로마의 국민임을 의식하고, 그것을 특권과 의무로 느끼고, 로마의 법 밑에서 그들의 권리를 확신하고 로마의 이름으로 기꺼이 희생을 감수하려는 많은 시민들이 남아 있었다. 그러나, 로마 국민이라는 의식이 부와 노예 제도의 성장으로 점점 약화되고 있었다. 국민의 숫자는 늘었지만 국민 의식은 그렇지 못했다. 로마 제국은 증가하는 많은 국민들을 교육시키지 않았고, 자기를 설명치 않았고, 또 국가의 시책을 결정할 때 국민의 협조를 구하지 않았다. 권력 투쟁을 하던 모험 자들은 국사에 대해 국민의 여론을 형성하여 불러들일 생각은 아예 안했다. 궁극적으로 모든 제국, 모든 국가, 인간 사회의 모든 조직체는 이해와 소망의 소산인 것이다. 로마 제국을 바라는 소망이 이미 사라졌고, 그리하여 로마 제국은 끝이 난 것이다.

▶▶정답

1. ②
2. 로마 국민(시민) 의식의 강화와 약화
3. ⑤　　4. ④

▶▶영작

(1) The country called in the aid of her neighbor.
(2) I am quite willing to do anything for you.
(3) At last the first term came to an end and there started the long-awaited summer vacation.
(4) We must know that we have obligations to fulfill as well as our rights to demand.

실력체크 I (p.502)

1

(1) 보다 나은 생활에로의 일보 일보의 진보는 거의 예외 없이 환경을 희생하여 이루어져 왔다.
(2) 급격한 성장의 포기, 세금이 올라가는 것, 물가가 올라가는 것
(3) 그것들[오염물질]을 흡수하면 반드시 해로운 결과를 낳는다.

2 ④

3

(1) ⓐ It is a bit of luck for me that I'm placed next to you.
(2) ⓑ 누가 운이 좋은지는 두고 봐야죠.
ⓔ 굳이 말씀하시겠다면 하셔야죠.
(3) ⓒ When I heard this remark,
(4) ⓓ tell me the story
(5) ⓕ tell you the story

4 ⓓ

숙어 Exercise (p.508)

1. Can't we talk it over without arguing?
2. The boss told him off for not finishing his work on time.
3. She thinks nothing of walking 3 miles to work every day.
4. It's a good offer but I'll have to think it over.
5. It's the weekend, so I can sleep to my heart's content.
6. He decided to turn over a new leaf and study harder.
7. The project (to build a new factory) is still up in the air.
8. The soldiers used up all their ammunition.
9. Workers are threatening to walk out (unless their demands are met).
10. Don't waste your breath by complaining to the supervisor; it won't help.
11. My son wears out a pair of running shoes every three months.
12. The whole village was wiped out in the air raid.

> The submission to passion is human bondage, but the exercise of reason is human liberty.
>
> 격정에 굴복하면 속박을 당하고, 이성을 행사하면 자유를 얻는다.
> (격정에의 굴복은 인간속박이요, 이성의 행사는 곧 인간자유이다.)

성문 종합영어

2004년 1월 15일 개정판 인쇄
2004년 1월 20일 중판발행

저 자 宋 成 文
발행인 宋 哲
발행처 성문출판사

137-130 서울시 서초구 양재동 209-3
등록 2000. 8. 18 제 22-1799호
Tel (02)554-2636, 567-5188
Fax (02)553-6330

인 쇄 보광문화사
인터넷 http://www.sungmoonbook.co.kr
파본은 구입서점 및 본사에서 교환해드립니다.

ISBN 89 - 86451 - 00 - X 53370